Rover 2000 & 2200 Owners Workshop Manual

by J H Haynes
Member of the Guild of Motoring Writers

and B L Chalmers - Hunt
T Eng(CEI), AMIMI, AMIRTE, AMVBRA

Models covered
Rover 2000 SC and TC models (1978 cc)
Rover 2200 SC and TC models (2204 cc)
Covers manual and automatic transmission models.
Does not cover 6 cyl. or V8 models.

ISBN 0 85696 496 4

Printed in England *(034-11 E3)*

HAYNES PUBLISHING GROUP
SPARKFORD YEOVIL SOMERSET ENGLAND
distributed in the USA by
HAYNES PUBLICATIONS INC
861 LAWRENCE DRIVE
NEWBURY PARK
CALIFORNIA 91320
USA

Acknowledgements

Thanks are due to the Jaguar, Rover, Triumph subsidiary of B. L. Limited for the assistance given in the supply of technical material and illustrations. The Champion Sparking Plug Company supplied the illustrations showing the various spark plug conditions. The bodywork repair photographs used in this manual were provided by Lloyds Industries Limited who supply 'Turtle Wax', 'Dupli-color Holts', and other Holts range products.

The supply of illustrations and material by the Jaguar, Rover, Triumph subsidiary of B. L. Limited does not imply that Rover have approved the contents of this book or is in any way responsible for the accuracy of any information printed. The copyright in illustrations and other technical material provided by Rover remains vested in the Jaguar, Rover, Triumph subsidiary of B. L. Limited.

Lastly, thanks are due to all those people at Sparkford who helped in the production of this manual, particularly Rod Grainger, Stanley Randolph, Ian Coomber, and David Neilson.

About this manual

Its aims

The aim of this manual is to help you to get the best value from your car. It can do so in several ways. It can help you decide what work must be done (even should you choose to get it done by a garage), provide information on routine maintenance and servicing, and give a logical course of action and diagnosis when random faults occur. However, it is hoped that you will use the manual by tackling the work yourself. On simpler jobs it may even be quicker than booking the car into a garage, and going there twice to leave and collect it. Perhaps most important, a lot of money can be saved by avoiding the costs the garage must charge to cover its labour and overheads.

The manual has drawings and descriptions to show the function of the various components so that their layout can be understood. Then the tasks are described and photographed in a step-by-step sequence so that even a novice can do the work.

Its arrangement

The manual is divided into thirteen Chapters, each covering a logical sub-division of the vehicle. The Chapters are each divided into Sections, numbered with single figures, eg 5, and the Sections into paragraphs (or sub-sections), with decimal numbers following on from the Section they are in, eg 5.1, 5.2, 5.3 etc.

It is freely illustrated, especially in those parts where there is a detailed sequence of operations to be carried out. There are two forms of illustrations; figures and photographs. The figures are numbered in sequence with decimal numbers, according to their position in the Chapter: eg Fig. 6.4 is the 4th drawing/illustration in Chapter 6. Photographs are numbered (either individually or in related groups) the same as the Section or sub-section of the text where the operation they show is described.

There is an alphabetical index at the back of the manual as well as a contents list at the front.

References to the 'left' or 'right' of the vehicle are in the sense of a person in the driver's seat facing forwards. Unless otherwise stated, nuts and bolts are removed by turning anticlockwise, and tightening by turning clockwise.

Whilst every care is taken to ensure that the information in this manual is correct no liability can be accepted by the authors or publishers for loss, damage, or injury caused by any errors in, or omissions from, the information given.

Contents

Rover 2000 TC

Rover 2200TC

Buying spare parts and vehicle identification

Buying spare parts

Spare parts are available from many sources. BL Cars have many dealers throughout the UK, and other dealers, accessory stores and motor factors will also stock Rover spare parts. Our advice regarding spare part sources is as follows:

Officially appointed vehicle main dealers — This is the best source of parts which are peculiar to your vehicle and are otherwise not generally available (eg complete cylinder heads, internal transmission components, badges, interior trim etc). It is also the only place at which you should buy parts if your vehicle is still under warranty. To be sure of obtaining the correct parts it will always be necessary to give the storeman your vehicle's engine and chassis number, and if possible, to take the 'old' part along for positive identification. Remember that many parts are available on a factory exchange scheme — any parts returned should always be clean! It obviously makes good sense to go straight to the specialists on your vehicle for this type of part, for they are best equipped to supply you.

Other dealers and auto accessory shops — These are often very good places to buy materials and components needed for the maintenance of your vehicle (eg oil filters, spark plugs, bulbs, fan belts, oils and greases, touch-up paint, filler paste etc). They also sell general accessories, usually have convenient opening hours, charge lower prices and can often be found not far from home.

Motor factors — Good factors will stock all of the more important components which wear out relatively quickly (eg clutch components, piston, valves, exhaust systems, brake cylinders/pipes/hoses/seals/shoes and pads etc). Motor factors will often provide new or reconditioned components on a part exchange basis — this can save a considerable amount of money.

Vehicle identification numbers

If you want to re-touch the paintwork you can obtain an exact match (providing the original paint has not faded) by quoting the paint code number in conjunction with the model number.

The chassis serial number or commission number as it is sometimes called, on early models will be found on a plate attached to the left-hand front door hinge post. It will be visible when the door is opened. On later produced models the chassis serial number will be found on the top of the right-hand wing valance and is visible when the bonnet is opened.

The engine serial number is stamped on the right-hand side of the cylinder block at the rear. On later produced cars this will be found stamped on an extension in front of the timing chain case.

The four speed gearbox serial number is stamped on the underside of the gearbox housing. The serial number for automatic transmission units will be found on a white plate attached to the left-hand side of the transmission unit.

The final drive serial number is stamped on the underside of the drive-housing.

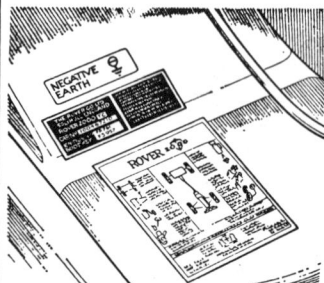

Location of chassis serial number, late models

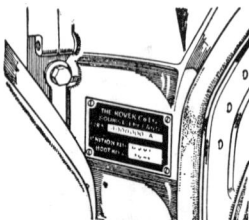

Location of chassis serial number, early models

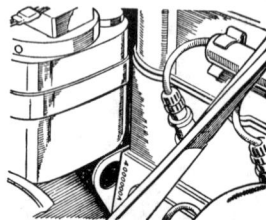

Location of engine serial number, early models

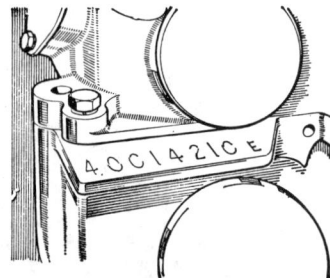

Location of engine serial number, late models

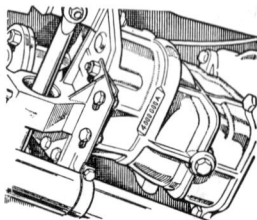

Location of four-speed gearbox serial number

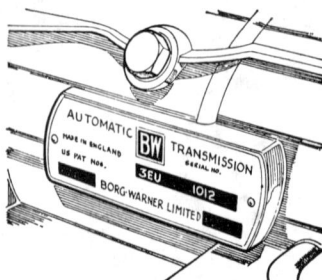

Location of automatic transmission serial number

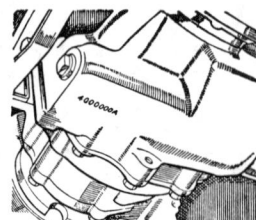

Location of final drive serial number

Tools and working facilities

Introduction

A selection of good tools is a fundamental requirement for anyone contemplating the maintenance and repair of a motor vehicle. For the owner who does not possess any, their purchase will prove a considerable expense, offsetting some of the savings made by doing-it-yourself. However, provided that the tools purchased are of good quality, they will last for many years and prove an extremely worthwhile investment.

To help the average owner to decide which tools are needed to carry out the various tasks detailed in this manual, we have compiled three lists of tools under the following headings: *Maintenance and minor repair, Repair and overhaul,* and *Special.* The newcomer to practical mechanics should start off with the *Maintenance and minor repair* tool kit and confine himself to the simpler jobs around the vehicle. Then, as his confidence and experience grows, he can undertake more difficult tasks, buying extra tools as, and when, they are needed. In this way, a *Maintenance and minor repair* tool kit can be built-up into a *Repair and overhaul* tool kit over a considerable period of time without any major cash outlays. The experienced do-it-yourselfer will have a tool kit good enough for most repair and overhaul procedures and will add tools from the *Special* category when he feels the expense is justified by the amount of use to which these tools will be put.

It is obviously not possible to cover the subject of tools fully here. For those who wish to learn more about tools and their use there is a book entitled *How to Choose and Use Car Tools* available from the publishers of this manual.

Maintenance and minor repair tool kit

The tools given in this list should be considered as a minimum requirement if routine maintenance, servicing and minor repair operations are to be undertaken. We recommend the purchase of combination spanners (ring one end, open-ended the other); although more expensive than open-ended ones, they do give the advantages of both types of spanner.

Combination spanners — 7/16 to 15/16 in AF
Adjustable spanner   9 inch
Engine sump/gearbox/rear axle drain plug key (where applicable)
Spark plug spanner (with rubber insert)
Spark plug gap adjustment tool
Set of feeler gauges
Brake adjuster spanner (where applicable)
Brake bleed nipple spanner
Screwdriver — 4 in long x ¼ in dia (flat blade)
Screwdriver — 4 in long x ¼ in dia (cross blade)
Combination pliers — 6 inch
Hacksaw, junior
Tyre pump
Tyre pressure gauge
Grease gun (where applicable)
Oil can
Fine emery cloth (1 sheet)
Wire brush (small)

Funnel (medium size)

Repair and overhaul tool kit

These tools are virtually essential for anyone undertaking any major repairs to a motor vehicle, and are additional to those given in the *Maintenance and minor repair* list. Included in this list is a comprehensive set of sockets. Although these are expensive they will be found invaluable as they are so versatile — particularly if various drives are included in the set. We recommended the ½ in square-drive type, as this can be used with most proprietary torque wrenches. If you cannot afford a socket set, even bought piecemeal, then inexpensive tubular box spanners are a useful alternative.

The tools in this list will occasionally need to be supplemented by tools from the *Special* list.

Sockets (or box spanners) to cover range in previous list
Reversible ratchet drive (for use with sockets)
Extension piece, 10 inch (for use with sockets)
Universal joint (for use with sockets)
Torque wrench (for use with sockets)
'Mole' wrench — 8 inch
Ball pein hammer
Soft-faced hammer, plastic or rubber
Screwdriver — 6 in long x 5/16 in dia (flat blade)
Screwdriver — 2 in long x 5/16 in square (flat blade)
Screwdriver — 1½ in long x ¼ in dia (cross blade)
Screwdriver — 3 in long x 1/8 in dia (electricians)
Pliers — electricians side cutters
Pliers — needle nosed
Pliers — circlip (internal and external)
Cold chisel — ½ inch
Scriber
Scraper
Centre punch
Pin punch
Hacksaw
Valve grinding tool
Steel rule/straight edge
Allen keys
Selection of files
Wire brush (large)
Axle-stands
Jack (strong scissor or hydraulic type)

Special tools

The tools in this list are those which are not used regularly, are expensive to buy, or which need to be used in accordance with their manufacturers' instructions. Unless relatively difficult mechanical jobs are undertaken frequently, it will not be economic to buy many of these tools. Where this is the case, you could consider clubbing together with friends (or a motorists' club) to make a joint purchase, or borrowing the tools against a deposit from a local garage or tool hire specialist.

The following list contains only those tools and instruments freely available to the public, and not those special tools produced by the vehicle manufacturer specifically for its dealer network. You will find occasional references to these manufacturers' special tools in the text of this manual. Generally, an alternative method of doing the job without the vehicle manufacturer's special tool is given. However, sometimes, there is no alternative to using them. Where this is the case and the relevant tool cannot be bought or borrowed you will have to entrust the work to a franchised garage.

Valve spring compressor
Piston ring compressor
Balljoint separator
Universal hub/bearing puller
Impact screwdriver
Micrometer and/or vernier gauge
Carburettor flow balancing device (where applicable)
Dial gauge
Stroboscopic timing light
Dwell angle meter/tachometer
Universal electrical multi-meter
Cylinder compression gauge
Lifting tackle (photo)
Trolley jack
Light with extension lead

Buying tools

For practically all tools, a tool factor is the best source since he will have a very comprehensive range compared with the average garage or accessory shop. Having said that, accessory shops often offer excellent quality tools at discount prices, so it pays to shop around.

Remember, you don't have to buy the most expensive items on the shelf, but it is always advisable to steer clear of the very cheap tools. There are plenty of good tools around at reasonable prices, so ask the proprietor or manager of the shop for advice before making a purchase.

Care and maintenance of tools

Having purchased a reasonable tool kit, it is necessary to keep the tools in a clean serviceable condition. After use, always wipe off any dirt, grease, and metal particles using a clean, dry cloth, before putting the tools away. Never leave them lying around after they have been used. A simple tool rack on the garage or workshop wall, for items such as screwdrivers and pliers is a good idea. Store all normal spanners and sockets in a metal box. Any measuring instruments, gauges, meters, etc. must be carefully stored where they cannot be damaged or become rusty.

Take a little care when tools are used. Hammer heads inevitably become marked and screwdrivers lose the keen edge on their blades from time to time. A little timely attention with emery cloth or a file will soon restore items like this to a good serviceable finish.

Working facilities

Not to be forgotten when discussing tools, is the workshop itself. If anything more than routine maintenance is to be carried out, some form of suitable working area becomes essential.

It is appreciated that many an owner mechanic is forced by circumstances to remove an engine or similar item, without the benefit of a garage or workshop. Having done this, any repairs should always be done under the cover of a roof.

Wherever possible, any dismantling should be done on a clean flat workbench or table at a suitable working height.

Any workbench needs a vice; one with a jaw opening of 4 in (100 mm) is suitable for most jobs. As mentioned previously, some clean dry storage space is also required for tools, as well as the lubricants, cleaning fluids, touch-up paints and so on which become necessary.

Another item which may be required, and which has a much more general usage, is an electric drill with a chuck capacity

of at least 5/16 in (8 mm). This, together with a good range of twist drills, is virtually essential for fitting accessories such as wing mirrors and reversing lights.

Last, bot not least, always keep a supply of old newspapers and clean, lint-free rags available, and try to keep any working area as clean as possible.

Spanner jaw gap comparison table

Jaw gap (in)	Spanner size
0.250	¼ in AF
0.275	7 mm
0.312	5/16 in AF
0.315	8 mm
0.340	11/32 in AF; 1/8 in Whitworth
0.354	9 mm
0.375	3/8 in AF
0.393	10 mm
0.433	11 mm
0.437	7/16 in AF
0.445	3/16 in Whitworth; ¼ in BSF
0.472	12 mm
0.500	½ in AF
0.512	13 mm
0.525	¼ in Whitworth; 5/16 in BSF
0.551	14 mm
0.562	9/16 in AF
0.590	15 mm
0.600	5/16 in Whitworth; 3/8 in BSF
0.625	5/8 in AF
0.629	16 mm
0.669	17 mm
0.687	11/16 in AF
0.708	18 mm
0.710	3/8 in Whitworth; 7/16 in BSF
0.748	19 mm
0.750	¾ in AF
0.812	13/16 in AF
0.820	7/16 in Whitworth; ½ in BSF
0.866	22 mm
0.875	7/8 in AF
0.920	½ in Whitworth; 9/16 in BSF
0.937	15/16 in AF
0.944	24 mm
1.000	1 in AF
1.010	9/16 in Whitworth; 5/8 in BSF
1.023	26 mm
1.062	1 1/16 in AF; 27 mm
1.100	5/8 in Whitworth; 11/16 in BSF
1.125	1 1/8 in AF

A Haltrac hoist and gantry in use during a typical engine removal sequence

Routine maintenance

The maintenance instructions listed below are basically those recommended by the manufacturer. They are supplemented by additional maintenance tasks which, through practical experience, the author recommends should be carried out at the interval suggested.

The additional tasks are indicated by an asterisk and are primarily of a preventative nature in that they will assist in eliminating the unexpected failure of a component due to fair wear and tear.

The levels of the engine oil, radiator cooling water, windscreen washer water and battery electrolyte, also the tyre pressures, should be checked weekly, or more frequently if experience dictates this to be necessary. Similarly it is wise to check the level of the fluid in the clutch and brake master cylinder reservoirs at monthly intervals. If not checked at home it is advantageous to use regularly the same garage for this work as they will soon get to know your preferences for particular oils and the pressures at which you like to run your tyres.

5,000 miles

1 Run the engine until it is hot and place a container of at least 10 pints capacity under the drain plug on the right-hand side of the sump and allow the oil to drain for at least 10 minutes. Clean the plug and surrounding area around the plug hole in the sump and replace the plug, tightening it firmly. Refill the sump with 8 pints (SC models), 9 pints (TC models) plus 1 pint for the filter of a recommended grade of oil and clean off any oil which may have been spilt over the engine or its components. The interval between oil changes should be reduced in very hot or dusty conditions or during cold weather with much slow stop/start driving.

2 Place an absorbant cloth under the oil filter and unscrew the filter. Wipe the area around the filter mounting and screw on a new filter together with a new sealing washer.

3 With the car standing on level ground, remove the oil level plug on the left-hand side of the gearbox. Top up if necessary (with a can or dispenser having a flexible nozzle) until the oil starts to run out of the filler/level hole. Allow the surplus oil to drain away before cleaning the oil filler plug and surrounding area. Refit the plug tightening it firmly.

4 If the car is fitted with automatic transmission refer to Chapter 6, Section 15, and check the fluid level. Top up if necessary.

5 With the car standing on level ground, remove the oil level

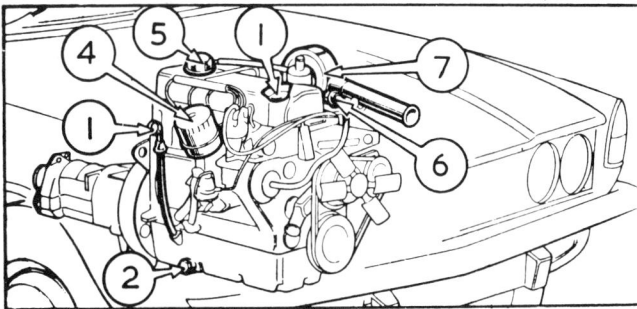

SC models only

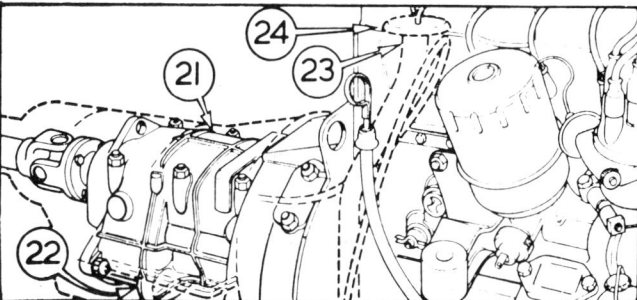

SC and TC models

1 Oil filler cap and oil level dipstick
2 Engine sump drain plug
3 Oil cooler drain plug
4 Oil filter for engine
5 Engine breather filter
6 Crankcase emission control, flame trap
7 Air cleaner
8 Air cleaner removal
9 Elements for air cleaner
10 Carburetter slow-running adjustment
11 Lift pin for carburetter
12 Carburetter slow-running adjustment
13 Hydraulic damper for carburetter
14 Fuel sediment bowl
15 Sparking plug and cover
16 Cleaning sparking plug
17 Contact points for distributor
18 Distributor maintenance
19 Ignition timing
20 Dynamo lubrication
21 Oil filler/level plug for 4 speed gearbox
22 Drain plug for 4 speed gearbox
23 Fluid level dipstick tube, automatic transmission
24 Fluid level dipstick, automatic transmission
25 Oil level/filler plug & drain plug for final drive
26 De Dion tube
27 Steering box lubrication and adjuster
28 Ball joints, repeated on opposite side
29 Fan belt adjustment
30 Water level, windscreen washer
31 Radiator filler cap
32 Drain plug for radiator
33 Drain tap for cylinder block
34 Front hub lubrication
35 Rear hub lubrication
36 Adjuster for front wheel alignment
37 Propeller shaft lubrication
38 Brake fluid reservoir
39 Front brake pads
40 Rear brake pads
41 Bleed nipple for front brake
42 Bleed nipple for rear brake
43 Clutch master cylinder and fluid reservoir
44 Bleed nipple for clutch slave cylinder
45 Battery)
46   )

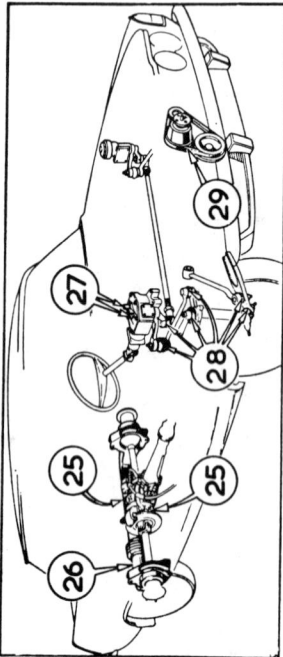

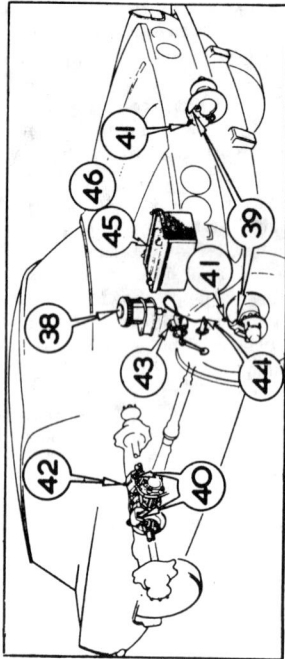

SC and TC models

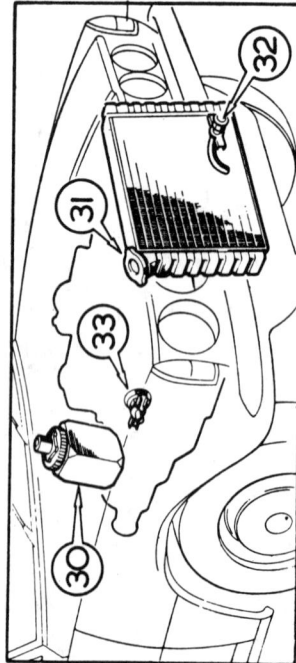

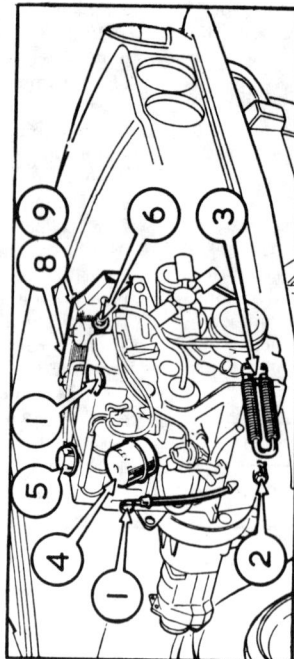

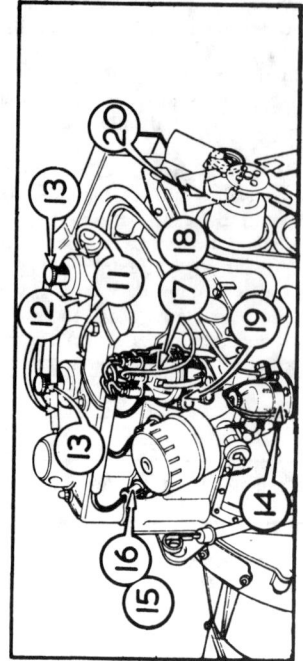

TC models only

SC and TC models

plug on the rear of the final drive casing. This is the upper of the two plugs and access is gained through the rear mounting bracket. If necessary, top up the final drive with recommended grade oil (with a can or dispenser having a flexible nozzle) until the oil starts to run out of the filler hole. Allow surplus oil to drain away before cleaning the oil filler plug and surrounding area. Refit the plug, tightening it firmly.

6 Wipe the tops of the brake and clutch fluid reservoirs and unscrew the caps. Check the hydraulic fluid level and top up as necessary with the recommended grade hydraulic fluid. The correct level for the brake fluid in the reservoir is to the rib on the master cylinder body and the correct level for the clutch reservoir is to the top of the filler neck. Check for correct operation of the brake fluid level safety switch and warning light as detailed in Chapter 10, Section 51.

7 Unscrew the carburettor damper dashpot cap/s and top up the level to within half an inch of the top of the piston rod with engine oil.

8 On TC models, fit new air cleaner elements as detailed in Chapter 3, Section 2.

9 Lubricate the generator rear bearing with a few drops of engine grade oil.

10 Lubricate the propeller shaft sliding joint at the grease nipple with the grease gun. If the car is operating in sandy or dusty conditions, lubricate more frequently.

11 Check and reset the carburettor slow running adjustment. See Chapter 3 for further details.

12 Remove the spark plugs for cleaning and adjust the gaps to 0.025 inch (0.64 mm). Clean the ceramic insulators and examine them for cracks or other damage likely to cause 'tracking'.

13 Clean and adjust the contact breaker points. See Chapter 4, Section 3, for further details.

14 Remove the distributor rotor arm and apply a few drops of oil in the centre of the cam spindle and on the moving contact breaker pivot. Grease the cam surface very slightly. Apply a few drops of engine oil through the hole in the contact breaker base plate to lubricate the automatic timing control. Remove any excess oil or grease with a clean rag.

15 Check the free movement at the rim of the steering wheel and adjust if necessary as detailed in Chapter 11, Section 24.

16 Inspect the front and rear brake pads for wear as detailed in Chapter 9, and fit new pads if necessary.

*17 Examine and renew any defective hoses in the braking system. Ensure that there is adequate clearance between them and any chassis or other components to eliminate chafing.

*18 Examine tyres and, should wear be apparent, take the appropriate action to correct the cause, eg misalignment, or wheel balancing, over or under inflation. If there is any doubt a Rover garage should be consulted especially where alignment is suspect because complicated and expensive equipment is required to carry out the necessary check. Remove any flints or other road matter from the treads. Check the wheel nuts for tightness.

*19 Inspect the exhaust system for leaks or blow holes.

*20 Lubricate all hinges, locks, catches and controls to allow them to work freely, and to prevent unnecessary wear.

*21 Check the operation of all electrical equipment, particularly stop/tail lamps, number plate illumination and side lights.

*22 Remove the carpets or mats and thoroughly clean the interior of the car. Beat out or vacuum clean the carpets. If the upholstery is soiled apply an upholstery cleaner with a damp sponge and wipe off with a clean dry cloth.

10,000 miles

1 Carry out the maintenance tasks listed for the 5,000 miles service.

2 With the car standing on level ground, check the level of oil in the De Dion tube and top up as necessary using engine grade oil. The filler/level plug hole is situated at the top and in the centre. Also check that the rubber boots are not damaged and have not become dislodged.

3 Check the level of oil in the steering box and top up with SAE 90 EP gear oil until the oil is level with the bottom of the filler/lever plug hole which is located in the cover plate next to the adjuster screw.

4 Remove the crankcase breather filter and wash in petrol. When dry re-oil using engine grade oil and refit. If the car is operating in dusty conditions clean the element more frequently.

5 Remove the air cleaners, discard the filter elements, wipe out the air cleaner body and refit with new filter element/s.

6 Check for signs of lubricant leakage from the front and rear wheel hubs which, if evident, rectify accordingly as detailed in Chapter 11.

7 Lubricate all carburettor controls.

8 Fit new spark plugs. Set the gaps to 0.025 inch (0.64 mm).

9 Check and adjust the fan belt tension.

10 Check all rubber boots on the steering joint, ball swivels, radius rods and De Dion tube.

11 Check all steering joints for signs of wear.

12 Clear the top of the battery and battery terminal. Check tightness of the terminals and coat with a little vaseline to prevent corrosion.

13 Check headlamp beam settings. Further information on this subject will be found in Chapter 10, Section 45.

14 Change around the road wheels, side to side only and not diagonally.

*15 Fit new wiper blades.

*16 It is a sound scheme to visit your local main agent and have the underside of the body steam cleaned. This will take about 1½ hours. All traces of dirt and oil will be removed and the underside can then be inspected carefully for rust, damaged hydraulic pipes, frayed electrical wiring and similar maladies. The car should be greased on completion of this job where necessary.

*17 At the same time the engine compartment should be cleaned. If steam cleaning facilities are not available, then brush on 'Gunk' or a similar cleaner over the whole engine and engine compartment with a stiff paint brush working it well in where there is accumulation of oil and dirt. Do not paint the ignition system but protect it with oily rags when the 'Gunk' is washed off; as the 'Gunk' is washed away it will take with it all traces of oil and dirt, leaving the engine looking clean and bright.

20,000 miles

1 Carry out the maintenance tasks listed for the 5,000 and 10,000 miles service.

2 Clean the petrol pump sediment bowl and filter in the pump.

3 Manual gearbox. With the oil in the gearbox warm, place a container of at least 2 pints capacity under the gearbox drain plug and allow the oil to drain for at least 10 minutes. Clean the plug and surrounding area around the plug hole and replace the plug. Refill the gearbox with 1¾ pints of recommended grade oil.

4 With the oil in the final drive warm, place a container of at least 3 pints under the drain plug to be found at the rear of the casing, and allow the oil to drain out for at least 10 minutes. Clean the plug and surrounding area around the plug hole and replace the plug. Refill the final drive with 2½ pints of recommended grade oil.

5 Take the car to the local Rover garage and have the front wheel alignment checked and reset as necessary.

40,000 miles

Every 40,00 miles or three years.

1 Carry out the maintenance tasks listed for the 20,000 miles service.

2 All seals and flexible hoses throughout the braking system should be removed and renewed, the brake cylinders and pistons should be examined and replaced if wear is found, and brake pipes replaced if any rust or damage is present.

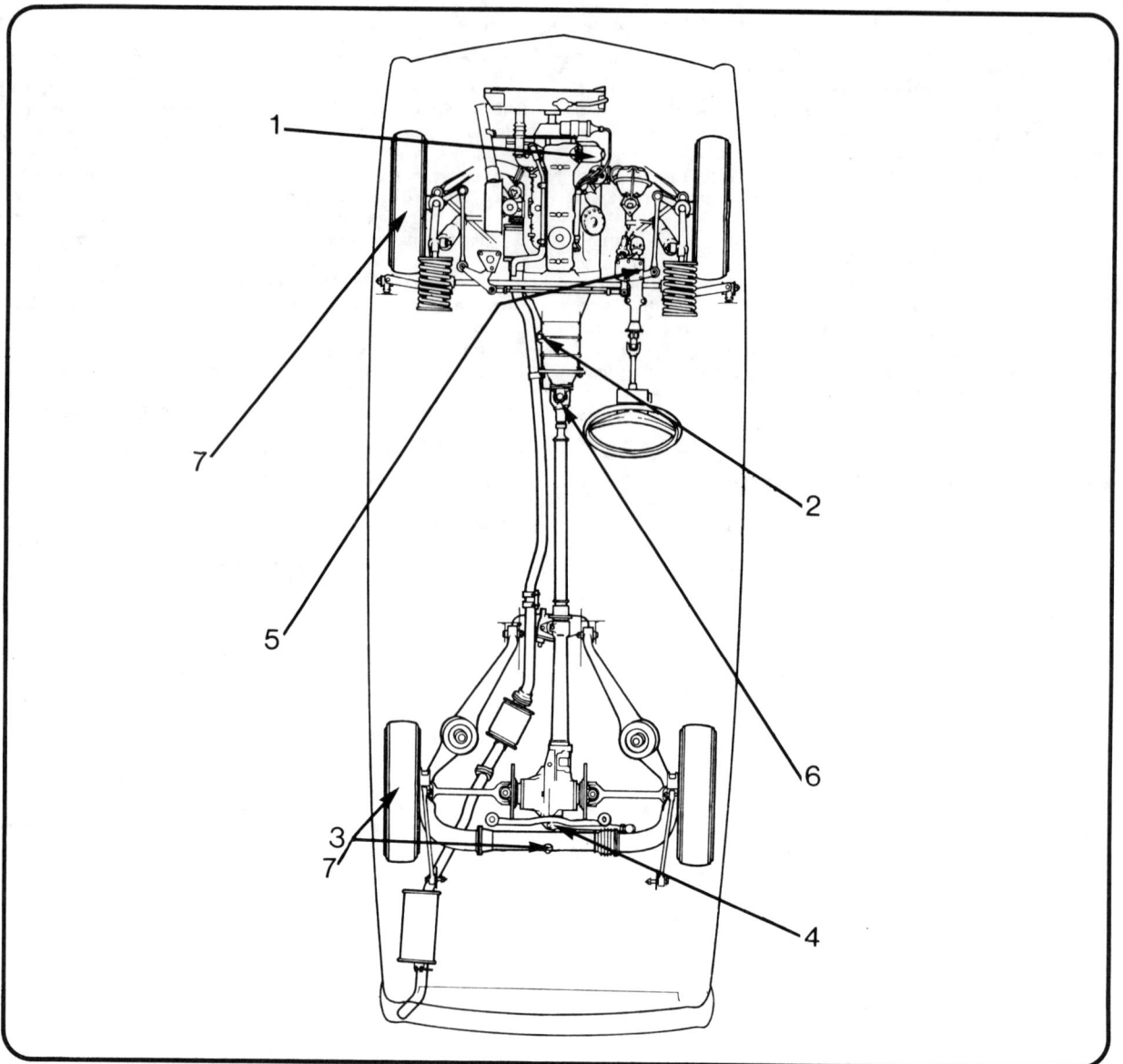

Recommended Lubricants and Fluids

COMPONENT	TYPE OF LUBRICANT OR FLUID	CASTROL PRODUCT
ENGINE (1)	Multi-grade engine oil	Castrol GTX
MANUAL GEARBOX (2)	SAE 20W	Castrol GTX
DE DION TUBE (3)	SAE 20W	Castrol GTX
AUTOMATIC TRANSMISSION	... ...	Castrol TQF
FINAL DRIVE UNIT (4)	SAE 90 EP	Castrol Hypoy
STEERING BOX (5)	SAE 90 EP	Castrol Hypoy
PROPELLER SHAFT SLIDING SPLINE (6)	... ...	Castrol LM grease
FRONT & REAR HUBS (7)	... ...	Castrol LM grease
BRAKE & CLUTCH FLUID	Hydraulic fluid	Castrol Girling Brake & Clutch Fluid

Additionally Castrol 'Everyman' oil can be used to lubricate
door, boot and bonnet hinges, locks & pivots etc.

Chapter 1 Engine

Contents

Specifications

Engine - general

Engine type	Water-cooled, overhead camshaft
Number of cylinders	Four
Capacity	120.8 cu. in. (1978 c.c.)
Bore	3.375 in. (8.57 cm)
Stroke	3.375 in. (8.57 cm)
Firing order	1, 3, 4, 2

Compression ratio

Standard	9 : 1 (SC), 10 : 1 (TC)
For certain export territories	7.5 : 1 (SC), 9 : 1 (TC)

Brake horsepower - SC

	9 : 1 compression ratio	7.5 : 1 compression ratio
Gross	99 at 5,000 rpm	87.5 at 5,000 rpm
Installed	90 at 5,000 rpm	80 at 5,000 rpm

Maximum torque - SC

	9 : 1 compression ratio	7.5 : 1 compression ratio
Gross	121 lb/ft. (16.6 mkg) at 3,600 rpm	113 lb/ft. (15 mkg) at 3,350 rpm
Installed	113.5 lb/ft. (15.5 mkg) at 2,750 rpm	106 lb/ft. (14.8 mkg) at 2,500 rpm

Brake horsepower - TC

	10 : 1 compression ratio	9 : 1 compression ratio
Gross	124 at 5,500 rpm	117 at 5,500 rpm
Installed	114 at 5,500 rpm	107 at 5,500 rpm

Maximum torque - TC

	10 : 1 compression ratio	9 : 1 compression ratio
Gross	132 lb/ft. (18.2 mkg) at 4,000 rpm	125 lb/ft. (17.2 mkg) at 3,750 rpm
Installed	126 lb/ft. (17.3 mkg) at 3,500 rpm	120 lb/ft. (16.5 mkg) at 3,250 rpm

Auxiliary drive unit

Auxiliary drive unit	Oil pump, distributor and fuel pump
Type of drive	Duplex chain
End-float of drive shaft	.002 to .006 in. (0.05 to 0.15 mm)

Camshaft

Drive	Two duplex endless chains
Diameter of journals	1.125 in. (28.5 mm)
Thrust taken	No. 1 bearing cap

Camshaft bearings

Type	Steel shell lined with white metal
Number of bearings	6
Bearing clearance	.0008 to .0028 in. (0.020 to 0.070 mm)
Bearing nip	.0015 to .0025 in. (0.014 to 0.060 mm)

Chains and chain wheels

Chain type	Duplex endless
Number of pitches:	
Bottom crankshaft to intermediate	74
Upper intermediate to camshaft	78
Chain tensioners	Two, Reynolds hydraulic
Vibration dampers	Two

Connecting rod

Length between centres...	5.781 in. (197.5 mm)
Big-end bearings	Detachable, lead-bronze steel shell positioned by tab
Bearing clearance	.0008 to .0023 in. (0.020 to 0.058 mm)
End-float connecting rod on crankpin	.004 to .010 in. (0.10 to 0.25 mm)
Bore diameter of little end bush	1,000 in. (25.40 mm)
Connecting rod bearing nip	.002 to .004 in. (0.05 to 0.10 mm)

Crankshaft and bearings

Number of main journals	5
Width of main journals	1.375 in. (40 mm)
Nominal diameter of crank journals	2.5 in. (63.50 mm) main bearings; 2.0 in. (50.80 mm) big ends
Width of crankpin	0.969 in. (24.5 mm)
Thrust taken	Thrust washers on No. 4 main bearing
End-float	.002 to .006 in. (0.050 to 0.15 mm)
Bearing type	Lead-bronze steel shell positioned by tab
Bearing clearance	.001 to .0025 in. (0.025 to 0.063 mm)
Bearing nip	.004 to .006 in. (0.10 to 0.15 mm)
Crankshaft damper	'Holset' Harmonic

Cylinder block

Type	Monobloc, integral with crankcase. Stamped Z, A, B, C or D to denote standard piston grade
Cylinder reboring limit	.040 in. (1.0 mm)

Flywheel

Run-out permissible	.002 in. (0.05 mm)
Number of teeth on starter ring	93

Pistons and rings

Type	Bricromatic with combustion chamber in piston crown
Standard size	Graded 'Z' to 'D'
Oversize	.010 to .040 in. (0.25 to 1.00 mm) - not graded
Clearance in bore measured at bottom of skirt at right angles to gudgeon pin	.0015 to .0020 in. (0.038 to 0.050 mm)
Compression rings	2
Scraper ring	1
Clearance in groove:	
Compression	.001 to .003 in. (0.02 to 0.07 mm)
Scraper	.001 to .003 in. (0.02 to 0.07 mm)
Gap when fitted:	
Compression ring, chrome	.019 to .024 in. (0.45 to 0.60 mm)
Scraper ring	.014 to .019 in. (0.35 to 0.48 mm)
Taper ring	.017 to .022 in. (0.43 to 0.55 mm)
Gudgeon pin outer diameter	1.000 in. (25.4 mm)
Fit in little-end bush	Light push fit
Location in piston	By circlips

Valves

	Inlet	Exhaust
Valve face angle	30°	45°
Stem diameter	.3145 in. (7.98 mm)	.3415 in. (8.67 mm)
Stem clearance in guide	.001 to .003 in. (0.02 to 0.07 mm)	.002 to .004 in. (0.05 to 0.10 mm)
Valve stem oil seals	Rubber 'O' ring in valve guides	
Head diameter	1.654 to 1.650 in. (42.01 to 41.9 mm)	1.341 to 1.337 in. (34.0 to 33.95 mm)

Valve guides

	Inlet	Exhaust
Bore diameter	.315 in. (8.00 mm)	.3438 in. (8.73 mm)
Bore length	2.525 to 2.531 in. (64.13 to 64.28 mm)	2.525 to 2.531 in. (64.13 to 64.28 mm)

Valve seats

	Inlet	Exhaust
Material	Bricromium	Brimo-chrome
Angle	30°	46°
Seat width	.035 to .055 in. (0.88 to 1.39 mm)	.045 to .065 in. (1.14 to 1.65 mm)

Valve springs

	SC engines	TC engines
Single carburettor engines		
Free length, inner	1.960 in. (49.78 mm)	1.921 in. (48.79 mm)
Free length, outer	2.190 in. (55.60 mm)	2.27 in. (57.66 mm)
Fitted length and load, inner	1.443 in. at 32.39 lb. ± 1.62 lb. (36.65 mm at 14.84 kg ± 0.78 kg)	1.443 in. at 32.8 lb. ± 1.69 lb. (36.65 mm. at 14.88 kg ± 0.76 kg)
Fitted length and load, outer	1.827 in. at 59.53 lb. ± 3 lb. (46.4 mm. at 27.0 kg ± 1.36 kg)	1.827 in. at 73.0 lb. ± 3.65 lb. (46.4 mm. at 33.1 kg ± 1.66 kg)

Tappets

Operation	Camshaft operated direct on to valve tappets
Exhaust tappet clearance	.013 to .015 in. (0.33 to 0.38 mm) cold
Inlet tappet clearance	.008 to .010 in. (0.20 to 0.25 mm) cold
Clearance adjustment	Selective shims, 0.074 to 0.352 in. (1.87 to 8.94 mm) in 26 sizes

Lubrication System

Type	Full pressure
Nominal pressure	50 to 60 lb/sq.in. (3.5 to 4.2 kg/cm^2) at 30 mph (50 kph)
Sump capacity:	
Single carburetter engines	8 Imperial pints (9.5 US pints, 4.5 litres) plus 1 Imperial pint (1.2 US pints, 0.5 litres) after fitting new filter
Twin carburetter engines	9 Imperial pints (10.5 US pints, 5 litres) plus 1 Imperial pint (1.2 US pints, 0.5 litres) after fitting new filter
Oil pump position...	External on right-hand side of cylinder block
End-float, outer rotor..	.005 in. (0.12 mm)
End-float, inner rotor..	.005 in. (0.12 mm)
Rotor diametrical clearance...	.010 in. (0.25 mm)
Clearance between lobes of inner and outer rotors...	.006 in. (0.15 mm)
Oil pressure release spring:	
Free length...	2.673 in. (67.8 mm)
Load, fitted	22 lb. (10 kg)
Number of working coils..	14

Oil Cooler

On twin carburetter engines this is situated as a separate compartment in the base of the main coolant radiator. The cooler is in series with the oil pump delivery side and the main oil gallery in the cylinder block.

Oil Filter

Full-flow internal	Gauze pump intake filter
Full-flow external	AC Delco No.7965022, type SC

Dipstick position	Right-hand side of engine	
Oil pressure light	On early models the green light on instrument panel operates when pressure drops below 10 lb/sq.in. (0.70 kg/cm^2); on late models the critical pressure is 18 to 28 lb/sq.in. (1.2 to 1.9 kg/cm^2)	

Torque Wrench Settings	lb/ft.	kgm
Bellhousing to engine sump...	25	3.5
Bellhousing to cylinder block	30	4.0
Connecting rod	30	4.0
Crankshaft pulley...	150	20.5
Cylinder head at camshaft bearing block assembly:—		
All steel gasket...	55	7.6
Steel asbestos gasket	70	9.6
Cylinder at front of timing case..	10	1.4
Flywheel to crankshaft	120	16.5
Automatic transmission drive plate to crankshaft	120	16.5
Intermediate chainwheel..	80	11.0
Main bearing caps...	65	9.0
Driving chain dampers	10	1.4
Dynamo pulley	25	3.5
Fuel pump retaining bolts	15	2.0
Spark plugs...	18 – 22	2.5 to 3.0
Camshaft chainwheel to hub	10	1.4
Clutch assembly to flywheel	12	1.65

1. General Description

The engines fitted to the Rover 2000 SC and TC models are basically similar in construction and design so that throughout this chapter any deviations will be dealt with in the respective sections, whilst full specifications and data for both engines are given at the beginning of this chapter.

The engine is a four cylinder, overhead valve type, operating on the 4 'Otto' cycle. It is supported in the front of the car by means of three flexible mountings in the interests of silence and lack of vibration.

The engine is water cooled and incorporates an impeller type water pump which is driven by a 'V' belt from the combined crankshaft pulley and torsional vibration damper assembly. The generator pulley is also driven by the same 'V' belt. Mounted on the water pump hub is a four blade fan to assist air flow through the radiator matrix at low car speeds.

A thermostat located at the front end of the cylinder head controls the operating temperature of the engine by regulating the water flow. When cold the thermostat is closed and prevents the coolant flowing through the radiator until a pre-determined temperature is reached when the thermostat begins to open so allowing the water to flow around the complete cooling systems circuit.

Incorporated in the radiator filler cap is a pressure relief valve which opens when the pressure within the cooling system exceeds 7 lb/per sq.in.

There are basically four versions of the Rover 2000 engine with the variations being in the form of carburetter installation and compression ratio. The compression ratio is altered by changing the volume in the hemispherical combustion chambers within the piston crown. The carburetter installation takes the form of a single SU type HS6 carburetter mounted on the side of the cylinder head (SC models) or two SU type HD8 carburetters mounted on adaptors on the side of the cylinder head (TC models). The cylinder heads are different between the two models.

The SC engine is available in two forms, either a 7.5:1 or 9.5:1 compression ratio and the TC engine which can have a compression ratio of either 9.1:1 or 10.1:1. Engines with a compression ratio other than 9.1:1 are identified by a label appropriately marked and fitted on the right-hand side cylinder block water jacket covers.

The engine's design is such that the valves are operated by a single overhead camshaft which operates directly on the top of the valve assemblies. The camshaft is driven by a 3/8 inch pitch duplex roller chain system from the crankshaft with an intermediate sprocket cluster. There are two chains, one from the crankshaft to the intermediate sprocket cluster and the second from the intermediate sprocket cluster to the camshaft. The intermediate sprocket cluster is keyed to the shaft which drives the fuel pump, distributor and oil pump, all mounted together on the right-hand side of the engine.

The cylinder head is made of cast aluminium and is designed to incorporate the induction manifold with a detachable aluminium top cover plate. As the underside of the cylinder head is machined flat the combustion chambers are with the hemispherical shaped piston. It is secured to the cylinder block by means of long bolts (8 bolts early models, 10 bolts later models).

The camshaft runs in six replaceable shell bearing inserts and is mounted in a detachable carrier on the top of the cylinder head. It is secured by the bearing caps using the cylinder head bolts with the exception of the first bearing cap. The first camshaft bearing is positioned directly in front of the second one and the gap should be used to determine the camshaft end float as the camshaft is designed with a thrust flange positioned in the gap between the first and second bearing caps. The front camshaft bearing is secured to the camshaft carrier by two cap screws which are not to be mistaken as cylinder head bolts. Machined in the camshaft carrier are vertical bores in which the inverted bucket type tappets are able to move vertically so transferring the action of the passing of the camshaft cam lobe over the bucket to the valve assembly. Adjustment is achieved by steel shims or discs placed between the end of the valve stem and the underside of the inverted bucket. These steel discs are available in a wide range of sizes so as to allow accurate setting of the valve clearances.

The inlet and exhaust ports in the cylinder head are on one side of the cylinder head with a separate cast iron exhaust manifold and is attached to the cylinder head under the carburetter installation by bolts, studs and nuts.

To act as a seal between the cylinder head and cylinder block is a gasket of either thin steel or a composite steel and asbestos gasket. The latter is to be found on engines having a letter G incorporated in the engine number. Mounted on the top of the cylinder head is a cast aluminium valve cover and is secured by nuts and special sealing washers. A laminated cork gasket is fitted on the cylinder head mating flange.

Mounted on the front of the cylinder block and head is the timing chest in which are the timing chains and two spring loaded Reynolds hydraulic type chain tensioners, one for each chain. On the slack

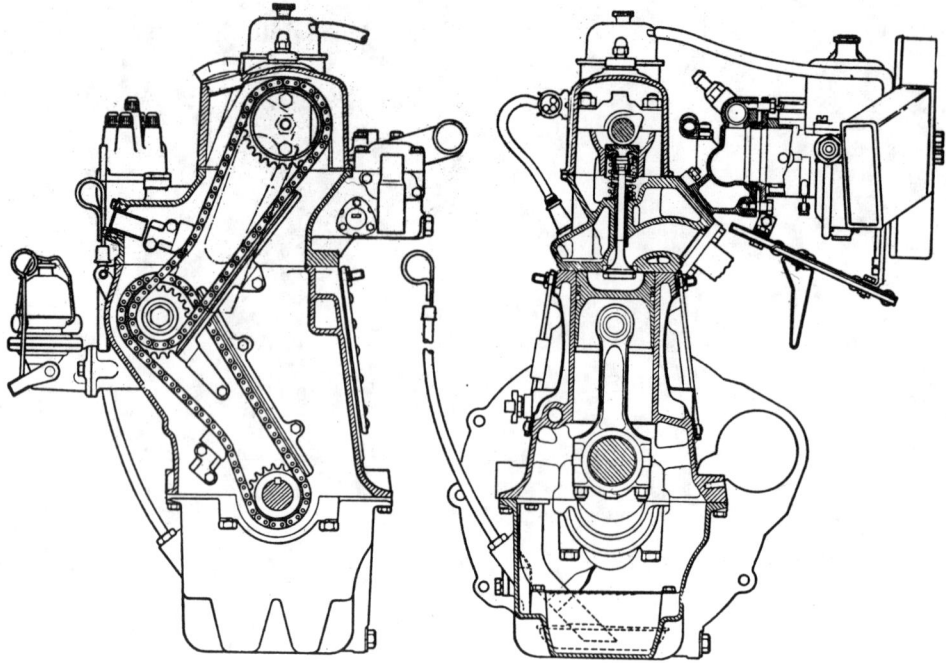

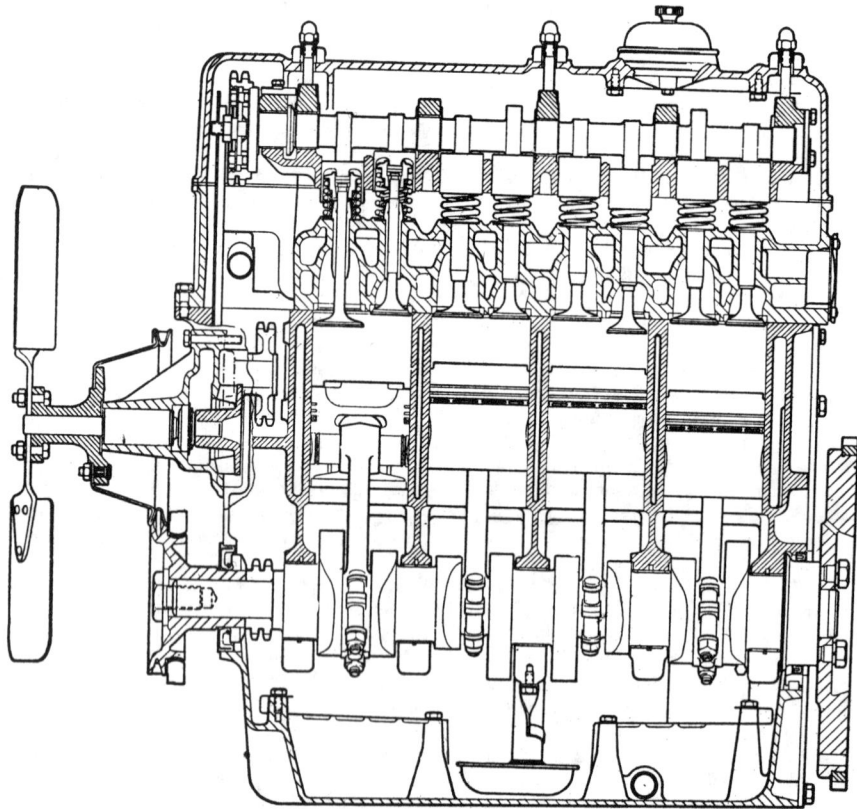

Fig.1.1. Longitudinal and cross section of SC engine.

side of each chain is a neoprene thrust pad to stop chain noise.

The cylinder block, unlike the cylinder head, is made of cast iron with large open sides to reduce the weight of the unit. The sides are covered with pressed steel plate with a compressed asbestos fibre gasket placed between the plate and the block. To ensure a watertight joint 22 screws are used to hold each cover plate in position and in addition 2 large diameter studs which screw into the cylinder block just below the top flange of the cover plate. These studs are used as locations for the engine mounting.

As the cylinder bores are machined in the cylinder block there is no need for separate dry or wet type liners.

The cast aluminium alloy oil sump is mounted to the underside of the cylinder block and is level with the centres of the crankshaft main bearing.

The fuel pump, oil pump and ignition distributor are mounted on an aluminium casing on the rear face of the timing chest where it projects from the right-hand side of the cylinder block. The auxiliary drive shaft carrying the camshaft drive chain intermediate sprockets runs in two plain bearing bushes in the casting. A machined worm near to the end of the auxiliary drive shaft is in mesh with the distributor drive gear which is connected to the distributor via a dog type connection. Located at the lower end of the distributor drive gear is a machined eccentric which operates the AC type mechanical fuel pump via a small plunger which slides in a drilling in the side of the casting.

The oil pump drive shaft has external serrations on its end which engage with internal serrations in the end of the auxilary drive shaft. Full details of the engine lubrication system may be found in Section 22 of this Chapter.

The crankshaft is of forged steel and runs in five main steel backed shell bearing inserts which are lined with lead bronze, lead plated indium flashed bearing material. As will be seen from the specifications bearing shells are available in standard and four undersizes. Crankshaft end float is controlled by semi-circular steel backed thrust washers which are lined with lead-bronze and fitted to both sides of No. 4 main bearing journal. Matching main bearing thrust washers are available in standard and four oversizes.

The connecting rods are 'I' beam section steel forgings and they run on the crankpins in steel backed shell bearing inserts lined with the same soft bearing metal as used for the main bearings. These bearings are available in standard and four undersizes. The little end bearings are replaceable bronze bushes.

The pistons are made of aluminium alloy but are of a rather unusual design with deep hemispherical bowls in the piston crowns and these are the combustion chambers. Also the piston crowns are recessed to accommodate inlet and exhaust valve protrusion. Each piston is fitted with two compression rings, the second ring being tapered, and one oil control ring, all being fitted above the fully floating piston pins which are kept in position with circlips.

Attached to the rear of the crankshaft by 8 bolts is the flywheel to which is bolted the 8.5 inch Borg and Beck diaphragm spring clutch. Attached to the engine backplate is the gearbox bellhousing.

Important

Where cars are fitted with air conditioning equipment, the removal of certain engine components and auxiliary items may necessitate the disconnection and possible removal of part of the air conditioning system. If this is the case at any time then the air conditioning system must first be depressurised. This task can only be undertaken by a British Leyland dealer having the necessary equipment for this operation. Should you have any problems with the air conditioning circuit consult your Leyland dealer for advice and if necessary repair. The system circuit is shown in Chapter 13 and those operations that you can undertake are given in that chapter.

2. Routine Maintenance

1. Once a week, or more frequently if necessary, remove the dipstick and check the engine oil level which should be at 'MAX' mark. Top up the oil in the sump with the recommended grade oil (see page 10). On no account allow the oil to fall below the 'MIN' mark on the dipstick.

2. Every 5,000 miles, run the engine until it is hot, place a container with a capacity of at least 10 pints under the drain plug in the sump, undo and remove the drain plug and allow the oil to drain for at least 10 minutes. While the oil is draining, wash the oil filler cap and breather filter in petrol. Shake the breather filter dry and re-oil using clean engine grade oil.

3. Clean the drain plug, ensure the washer is in place and refit the plug to the sump, tighten the plug firmly. Refill the sump with 8 pints (SC), 9 pints (TC) of the recommended grade of oil (see page 10 for details). With filter change allow 1 additional pint of oil.

4. Every 5,000 miles the oil filter element should be renewed as described in the routine maintenance section.

5. In very hot or dusty conditions in cold weather with much slow/stop driving and much use of the choke, or when the engine has covered a very high mileage, it is beneficial to change the engine oil and filter more frequently.

3. Major Operations with Engine in Place

The following operations can be carried out with the engine in place in the bodyframe.
1. Removal and replacement of the cylinder head.
2. Removal and replacement of the sump.
3. Removal and replacement of the internal oil filter.
4. Removal and replacement of the big end bearings.
5. Removal and replacement of the pistons and connecting rods.
6. Removal and replacement of the crankshaft front oil seal.
7. Removal and replacement of the timing chains.
8. Removal and replacement of the camshaft.
9. Removal and replacement of the dynamo.
10 Removal and replacement of the starter.
11 Removal and replacement of the water pump.
12 Removal and replacement of the fan.
13 Removal and replacement of the choke warning light switch.
14 Removal and replacement of the air cleaner.
15 Removal and replacement of the carburetter installation.
16 Removal and replacement of the manifolds.
17 Removal and replacement of the fuel pump.
18 Removal and replacement of the distributor and drive shaft.
19 Removal and refitting of the oil pump.
20 Removal and refitting of the auxilary drive housing.

4. Major Operations with the Engine Removed

The following major operations can be carried out with the engine away from the car and on the bench or floor:—
1. Removal and replacement of the main bearings.
2. Removal and replacement of the crankshaft.
3. Removal and replacement of the flywheel.

5. Methods of Engine Removal

There are two methods of removing the engine, but in both cases it must be removed through the top of the engine compartment. The first method is to remove the complete engine and gearbox assembly whilst the second method is to remove the engine once it has been disconnected from the gearbox. Although the manufacturer recommends that the engine should be removed using the first method, the author does, however, consider that the best procedure for a person having limited workshop facilities is to separate the engine from the gearbox and then removing by pulling the engine forwards and lifting away through the engine compartment.

In both cases substantial lifting equipment in the form of an

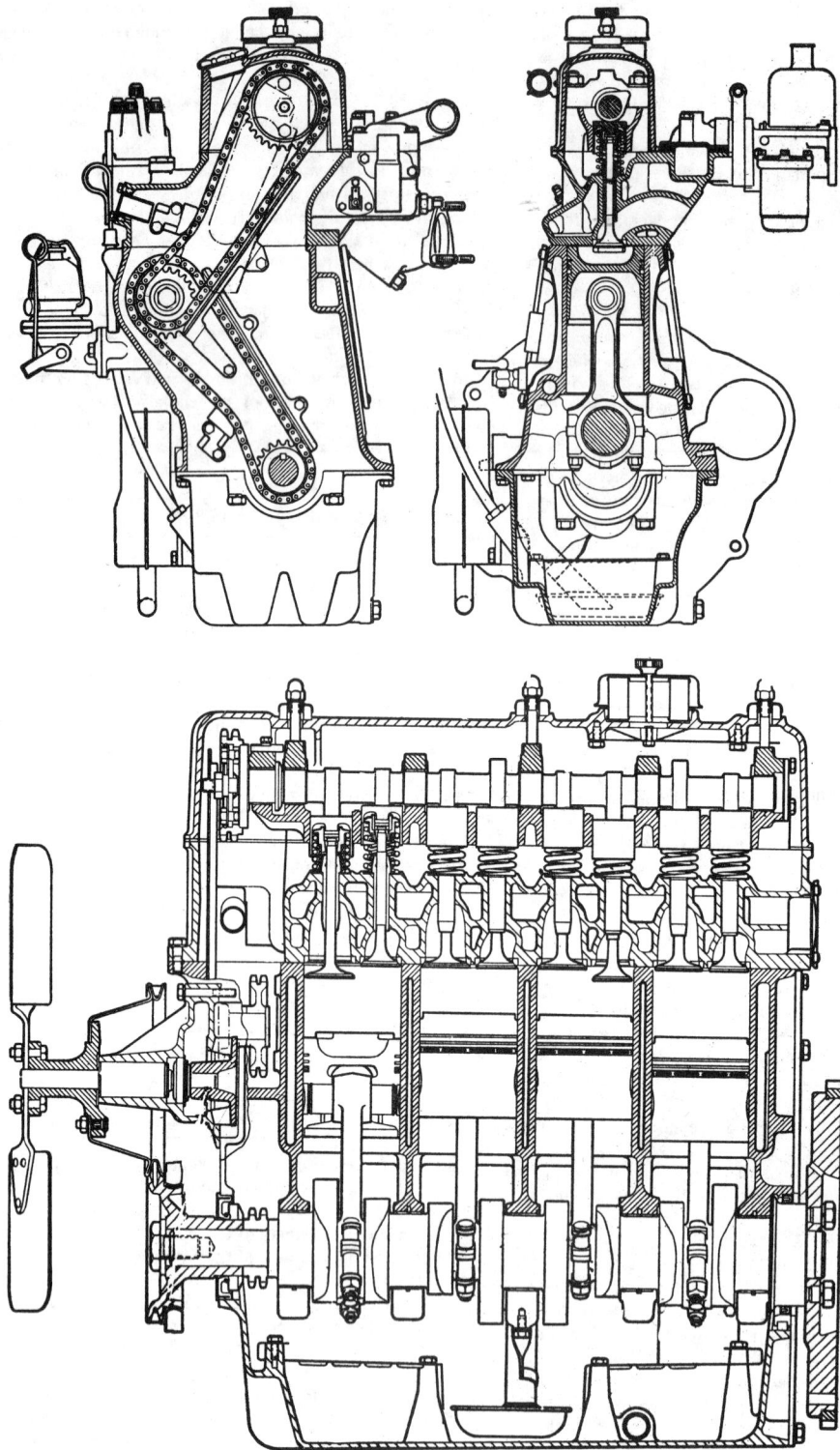

Fig.1.2. Longitudinal and cross section of TC engine.

overhead hoist or a beam crane as illustrated in photo 6.68A, page 25. Also a small garage hydraulic jack will be of considerable assistance during disconnection of the engine from the gearbox.

6. Engine Removal — Manual Gearbox

1. Practical experience has proved that the engine can be removed by one person in about 8 hours but this time will depend a considerable amount on the workshop facilities and also if assistance is available during the latter stages of removal.

2. Open the bonnet and secure in the open position.

3. Place some old blankets over the wings and the body below the windscreen so that the paintwork is not damaged.

4. Undo the screws in the centre of the battery terminal caps (photo) and take the terminal caps off the terminal post. Undo the battery carrier clamp bar wing nuts and lift away the clamp bar and the battery. Disconnect the two long clamp bar threaded rods and lift away the battery tray.

5. Remove the radiator filler cap and put in a safe place. Move the heater temperature control to the 'HOT' position and open the drain tap to be found on the right-hand side of the cylinder block side plate. Also undo and remove the radiator drain plug (Fig.1.3).
NB. Do not drain the water in your garage or place where you will remove the engine unless receptacles are at hand to catch the water. The capacity of the cooling system is 17 pints.

6. Place a container able to hold at least 10 pints under the engine drain plug on the sump and undo the drain plug. Allow the oil to drain out for at least 10 minutes and then replace the plug.

7. The bonnet should next be removed. Disconnect the screen washer jet hose end. With the assistance of a second person take the weight of the bonnet (it is made of aluminium so it is not very heavy, but take care because it is easily scratched or damaged). Undo the two retaining bolts to each hinge and lift away the bolts, spring and plain washers.

8. This photo shows the forward hinge securing bolt being removed and it should be noted that it also secures the front wing upper rear mounting bracket which is 'pop' riveted to the wing panel.

9. With the bolts free, carefully slide the bonnet rearwards about 2 inches for the hinges to clear the wing upper mounting brackets. Lift the rear of the bonnet up and then lift away the complete bonnet from the front of the car (photo). Put in a safe place where it will not be damaged.

10 Slacken the top radiator hose front clip (photo).

11 Slacken the top radiator hose rear clip and ease the hose from the thermostat cover and water outlet pipe (photo). Then remove the top hose from the radiator top tank.

12 Slacken the lower radiator hose clips at the water pump elbow and radiator bottom tank. Ease the hose from the water hose elbow and then the radiator and lift away the hose (photo).

SC Models

13 Soak the lower radiator mounting bolt in penetrating oil and very carefully remove the bolt, spring and plain washer that secures the radiator to the bracket. There is a captive nut on the inside of the radiator bottom tank into which screws the bolt and should this nut come free due to either seizure of the bolt or over zealous removal of the bolt the only course of action is to cut through the bracket about ½ inch behind the second hole (not counting the bolt hole) and then make up two plates so as to sandwich the bracket and secure with two bolts, nuts and spring washers upon refitting of the radiator to the car. Seal the area around the bolt and bracket in the bottom of the radiator with Cataloy. This photo shows the bolt in position.

14 Undo and remove the two radiator upper mounting bolts, one each side of the radiator top tank and lift away the bolt and spring washer (photo).

15 The radiator may now be lifted away from the engine compartment. (photo).

TC Models

16 Disconnect the expansion tank from the radiator filler cap neck.

17 Before removing the radiator it will be necessary to drain the oil from the oil cooler. Place a container under the hexagonal plug located at the bottom of the oil return pipe from the oil cooler to the engine as shown in Fig.1.4.

18 Slacken the clips that secure the oil cooler pipes to the car body.

19 Undo and remove the two nuts and spring washers at each flange of the supply and return oil pipes at the oil cooler. Carefully pull the two flanges away from the oil cooler and recover the two 'O' ring oil seals located in the recess in the oil cooler.

20 Remove the radiator and oil cooler retaining nuts and bolts. There are two nuts and bolts at the top securing the radiator to the brackets and one nut and bolt securing the radiator lower bracket to the body.

21 The radiator and oil cooler may now be lifted away from the engine compartment.

All Models

22 Make a note of the electrical cable connections to the electric screen washer pump. The green cable is connected to the right-hand (-ve) terminal. Disconnect the two cables (photo).

23 The screen washer bottle may now be lifted from its bracket and rubber retaining strap (photo).

24 Turn the fuel reservoir switch to the midway position so as to prevent petrol syphoning from the main fuel feed pipe from the fuel tank.

25 Undo the union securing the main feed pipe to the fuel pump. Take care not to twist the pipe. Plug the end of the pipe with a screw to stop dirt ingress.

26 Undo the union securing the fuel pipe to the carburetter installation from the side of the fuel pump (photo). Wrap the end of the union in some clean non-fluffy rag to stop dirt ingress.

27 Undo and remove the two nuts and spring washers that secure the fuel pipe to the side of the auxilary housing. Lift away the fuel pump (photo). The fuel pump is operated by a small pushrod to be found in a little drilling in the side of the auxilary housing, and it is recommended that this be left in position until it is required to remove it as oil will otherwise drain out. Put a piece of tape over the end to stop the pushrod falling out.

SC Models

28 Undo and remove the wing nuts securing the air cleaner cover to the body (photo).

29 With a screwdriver tap the side of the air cleaner cover to release it from the backplate (photo). By careful manipulation the air cleaner cover can be removed over the stirrup on the backplate. Lift away the element.

30 Undo the bolt that secures the air cleaner intake pipe and HT cable bracket to its support arm. Remove the bolt and spring washer (photo).

31 Disconnect the small bore rubber pipe fitted between the air cleaner backplate and the top of the carburetter float chamber from the rear of the backplate (photo).

32 Undo and remove the two nuts and spring washers that secure the air cleaner backplate studs to the mounting flange of the carburetter (photo). Lift away the air cleaner backplate.

33 Using two spanners as shown in the photograph, undo the fuel feed pipe union at the carburetter float chamber. Take care not to twist the pipe.

34 Disconnect the choke inner cable from the cam lever on the side of the carburetter using a screwdriver and small open-ended spanner or pliers (photo).

35 The outer cable may simply be pulled upwards out of its location on the side of the carburetter body.

36 Spring back the accelerator link control rod securing clip with a screwdriver and separate the cup from the ball by pulling sharply away from the coupling shaft lever.

TC Models

37 Undo and remove the two brass tube nuts and fibre washers that

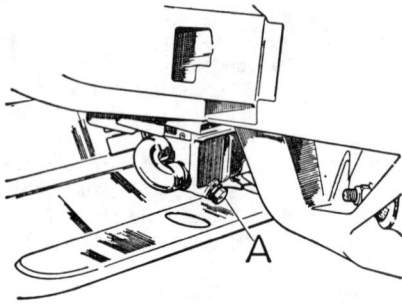

Fig.1.3. RADIATOR DRAIN PLUG (TC MODELS)
A Drain plug

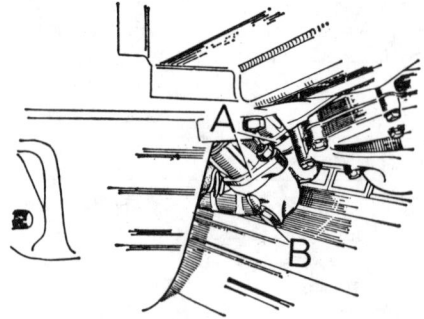

Fig.1.4. OIL COOLER DRAIN PLUG (TC MODELS)
A Flanges, oil pipes to oil   B Drain plug on oil return
cooler   pipe

6.4

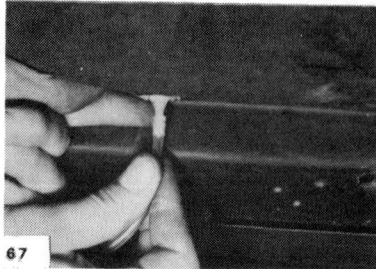

6.7

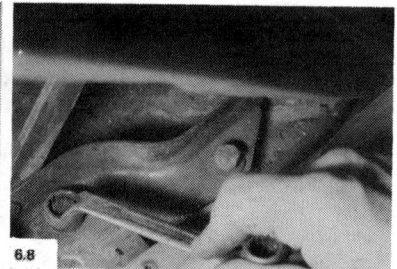

6.8

6.9

6.10

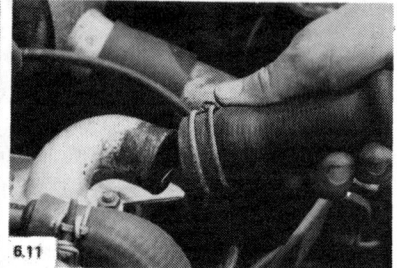

6.11

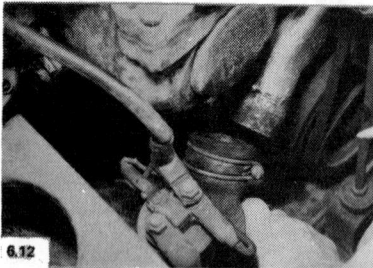

6.12

6.13

6.14

6.15

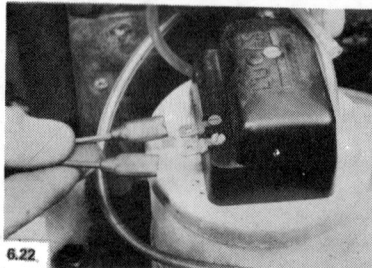

6.22

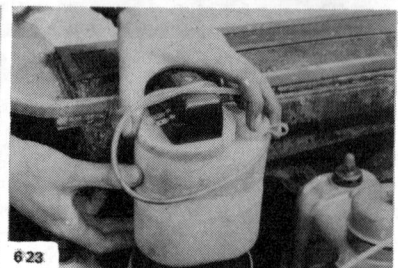

6.23

secure the air cleaner installation to the carburetter adaptors and lift away the complete assembly.

38 Recover the two rubber rings from the faces of the carburetter adaptors.

39 Using two spanners undo the fuel feed pipe union from the pipe at the front carburetter float chamber. Take care not to twist the pipe.

40 Disconnect the choke inner cable from the front carburetter jet lever. Release the clip that secures the outer cable.

41 Spring back the accelerator link control rod securing clip with a screwdriver and separate the cup from bore by pulling sharply away from the coupling shaft lever.

All Models

42 Slacken the heater hose clip at the heater unit located as shown in the photo and disconnect the hose.

43 Slacken the heater hose clip from its location at the rear of the side face of the cylinder head and disconnect the hose. This photo shows the cylinder head fitted to SC engines, but the hose location is the same for both SC and TC engines.

44 Slacken the vacuum hose clip located at the hose to metal pipe joint at the top of the valve cover and disconnect the vacuum hose from the metal pipe (photo).

45 Disconnect the electrical cable terminal from the water temperature transmitter located at the side of the thermostat housing (photo).

46 Disconnect the electrical cable terminal from the choke warning light switch located at the front of the thermostat housings. Note that this cable is coloured white with a blue tracer.

47 This photo shows the position of the choke warning light switch.

48 Disconnect the low tension cable from the side of the distributor body (photo).

49 Disconnect the electrical cable terminal from the oil pressure warning light switch located at the back of the oil filter.

50 Disconnect the two electrical cable terminals from the rear of the dynamo. Note that one cable is larger in diameter and has a bigger terminal connector than the other, so it is not possible to inter-change the two cables.

51 Working at the front of the engine release the locknut from the top of the engine tie-rod and undo the two nuts. It is not necessary to completely remove them (photo).

52 Undo the bolt at the bottom of the engine tie-rod with an open-ended spanner. Lift away the bolt, spring and plain washer (photo).

53 The tie-rod, complete with rubber mountings, may be lifted upwards and disengaged from the tie-rod upper mounting bracket on the front of the cylinder head.

54 Working underneath the car, unclip the clutch hydraulic pipe from the clip on the side of the engine in line with the sump joint (photo).

55 Disconnect the heavy duty cable from the rear of the starter motor by undoing the large brass nut and slipping off the cable terminal.

56 Soak the three nuts and bolts at the exhaust system front pipe to centre pipe connection in penetrating oil. Undo and remove the three nuts, bolts and spring washers and tap back the moveable flange (photo).

57 Disconnect the HT cable from the centre of the ignition coil located at the front of the left-hand inner wing panel.

58 Extract the circlip (or spring clip on automatic transmission models) between the throttle linkage coupling shaft and the fork. Detach the control rod from the fork by lifting away the plain washer and spring. This can be clearly seen in photo 6.43.

59 Undo and remove the nut and spring washer securing the battery earth strap to the rear upper engine mounting bracket stud (photo).

60 Undo the large union nut to be found at the base of the engine oil level dipstick housing. Lift away the dipstick and housing. Also undo and remove the two long bolts and spring washers that secure the suction and pressure oil pipe unions to the right-hand side of the engine.

61 Undo and remove the nut, large plain washer, long bolt, rubber pad and plain washer securing each of the engine mounting brackets to the body mounting bracket.

62 Release the exhaust centre pipe from the mounting located at the engine to bellhousing joint by undoing and removing the nut, spring washer and bolt.

63 Undo and remove the two nuts and bolts that secure the starter motor to the gearbox bellhousing and engine backplates. Lift away the starter motor making sure that its weight is not allowed to hang on the armature shaft which can be easily bent.

64 Using the garage hydraulic jack, support the weight of the gearbox and then undo and remove the remaining nuts and bolts securing the gearbox bellhousing flange to the engine backplate (photo).

65 Place chains or a strong rope in the two engine lifting point locations. One is to be found on the front left-hand bracket which acts as a mounting for the air cleaner intake (SC model), and the other at the rear right-hand side of the engine. Support the weight of the engine with the mountings about ½ inch off the engine body mounting bracket. Carefully check that no cables, pipes or other connections have been left connected to the engine.

66 Chock the front and rear wheels to stop the car moving forwards and with the assistance of a second person pull the engine forwards until the gearbox primary pinion is clear of the clutch pressure plate assembly.

67 Raise the engine by about 6 inches, manipulating the auxiliary drive housing around the brake servo unit mounted on the right-hand wing inner panel (photo 6.67A and 6.67B).

68 Now continue lifting the engine until the engine sump is level with the top of the front grille. Then move the front of the engine towards the front left-hand corner of the engine compartment (Photo 6.68A and 6.68B).

69 With the engine straight again, lift it until it is clear of the front grille and, depending on the method of lifting, either move the car rearwards or pull the engine forwards away from the engine compartment. If the former method has been used make sure that the garage hydraulic jack wheels are parallel with those of the car wheels so that the jack will also travel back with the car.

70 Carefully lower the engine to the ground, bearing in mind that it has an aluminium sump which is easily damaged.

71 Using cord or wire support the gearbox and exhaust pipe so that the car can be easily moved.

72 With the engine away from the car, thoroughly wash the exterior with paraffin or grease solvent such as 'Gunk'. Wash off with a strong water jet, dry thoroughly. The unit is now ready for dismantling.

7. Engine Removal — Automatic Transmission

The procedure for removing the engine on models fitted with automatic transmission is basically identical to that for cars fitted with a manual gearbox and will present no problems provided that care is taken. Details of separating the automatic transmission unit from the rear of the engine will be found in Chapter 6, Section 17.

Refitting can present a problem in re-connecting the engine to the automatic transmission and the author recommends the best approach is that once the engine is removed the automatic transmission unit is then removed. The engine can be inserted into the engine compartment at a steep angle and the automatic transmission unit reconnected to the engine. Both units can then be refitted into their correct positions in the car. However, if substantial lifting tackle is available the engine can be removed with the automatic transmission still attached and refitted in the reverse manner to removal. This is because of the weight considerations and such equipment will not usually be found outside a commercial repair workshop.

8. Dismantling The Engine — General

1. It is best to mount the engine on a dismantling stand, but if one is not available, then stand the engine on a strong bench so as to be at a comfortable working height. Failing this, the engine can be

6.25

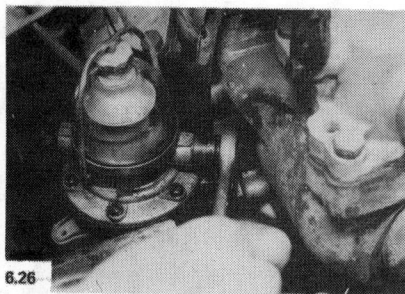
6.26

6.27

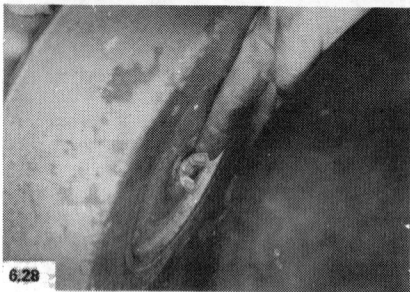
6.28

6.29

6.30

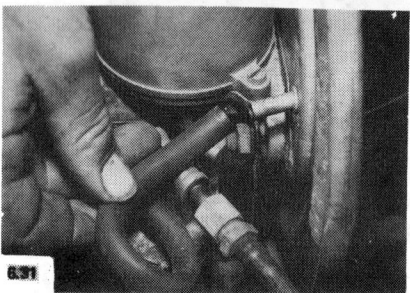
6.31

6.32

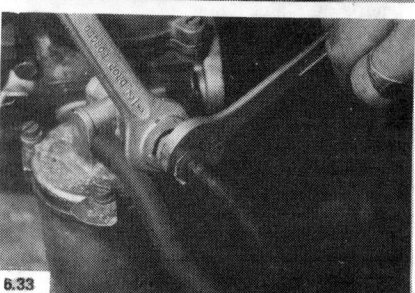
6.33

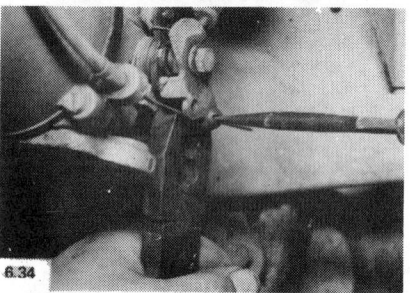
6.34

6.36

6.42

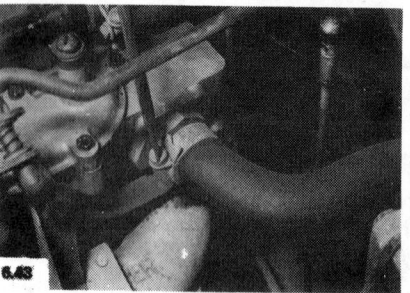
6.43

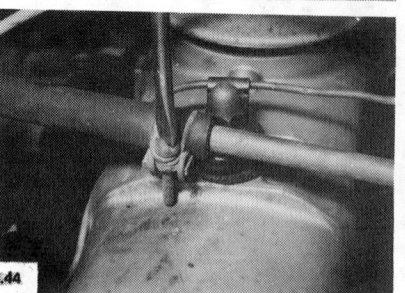
8.44

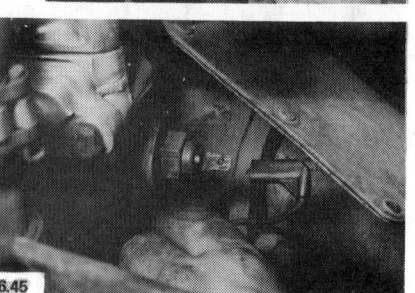
6.45

6.47

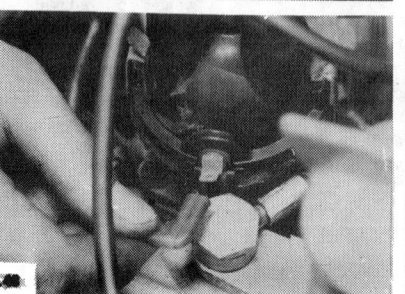
6.48

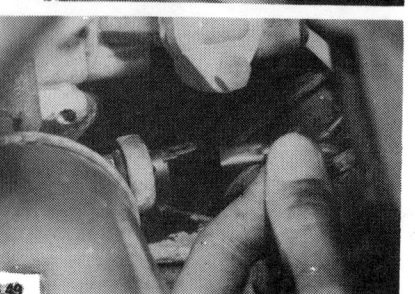
6.49

stripped down on the floor.

2. During the dismantling process the greatest care should be taken to keep the exposed parts free from dirt. As an aid to achieving this, it is a sound scheme to thoroughly clean down the outside of the engine, removing all traces of oil and congealed dirt.

3. Use paraffin or a good grease solvent such as 'Gunk'. The latter compound will make the job much easier, as, after the solvent has been applied and allowed to stand for a time, a vigorous jet of water will wash off all the solvent and the grease and filth. If the dirt is thick and deeply embedded, work the solvent into it with a stiff brush.

4. Finally wipe down the exterior of the engine with a rag and only then, when it is quite clean should the dismantling process begin. As the engine is stripped clean each part in a bath of paraffin or petrol.

5. Never immerse parts with oilways in paraffin, i.e. the crankshaft, but to clean, wipe down carefully with a petrol dampened rag. Oilways can be cleaned out with pipe cleaners. If an air line is present all parts can be blown dry and the oilways blown through as an added precaution.

6. Re-use of old engine gaskets is a false economy and can give rise to oil and water leaks, if nothing worse. To avoid the possibility of trouble after the engine has been reassembled always use new gaskets throughout.

7. Do not throw the old gaskets away as it sometimes happens that an immediate replacement cannot be found and the old gasket is then very useful as a template. Hang up the old gaskets, as they are removed, on a suitable hook or nail.

8. To strip the engine it is best to work from the top down. The sump provides a firm base on which the engine can be supported in an upright position. When the stage where the sump must be removed is reached, the engine can be turned on its side and all other work carried out with it in this position.

9. Wherever possible, replace nuts, bolts and washers finger tight from where they were removed. This helps avoid later loss and muddle. If they cannot be replaced then lay them out in such a fashion that it is clear from where they came.

9. Removing Ancillary Engine Components

1. Before basic engine dismantling begins the engine should be stripped of all its ancillary components. These items should also be removed if a factory exchange reconditioned unit is being purchased, the items comprise:—

Dynamo and dynamo bracket OR
Alternator and alternator bracket;
Water pump, heater pipes and thermostat housing;
Starter motor:
Distributor, sparking plugs and ignition coil;
Inlet manifold adaptors and carburetter/s;
Exhaust manifold and heat shield;
Fuel pump and operating rod;
Fuel pipes;
Oil filter and dipstick tube;
Oil filler cap;
Clutch assembly;
Crankcase breather (if fitted).

2. Without exception all these items can be removed with the engine in the car if it is merely an individual item which requires attention. (It is necessary to remove the gearbox if the clutch is to be renewed with the engine in-situ).

3. Starting work on the left-hand side of the engine slacken off the dynamo or alternator retaining bolts, and remove the unit, followed by the shaped mounting bracket on the side of the crankcase. This is shown in Fig.1.5.

4. Take off the distributor vacuum advance pipe from the vacuum unit on the side of the distributor.

5. Remove the two distributor body clamp bolts which hold the distributor clamp plate to the engine and remove the distributor. NOTE: If it is not wished to disturb the ignition timing setting, then under no circumstances, should the clamp pinch bolt, which secures the distributor in its relative position in the clamp be loosened. Providing the distributor is removed without the clamp being loosened from the distributor body and the engine is not turned, the timing will not be lost.

6. The fuel pump is removed once the two pipes have been disconnected. Undo and remove the two retaining nuts and spring washers and lift the pump away. As the pump is actuated by a small pushrod located in the side of the distributor drive housing this pushrod should be withdrawn and kept in a safe place (Fig.1.6).

7. Undo and remove the low oil pressure warning switch on the oil filter housing. Next unscrew the filter from the housing being prepared to catch a little oil with an absorbant cloth.

8. Undo and remove the three nuts and spring washers that secure the thermostat top housing to the top of the cylinder head, located as shown in Fig.1.7. Lift the thermostat top housing and gasket from the studs, if necessary carefully tapping the side of the housing if it should be a tight fit on the studs due to corrosion. The thermostat may now be removed from its location in the top of the cylinder head.

9. Remove the carburetter installation as detailed in Chapter 3, Section 4 (SC models) or Section 9 (TC models).

10 Undo and remove the two bolts with spring washers securing the heat shield to the manifold casting. (Photo SC model).

11 Undo and remove the bolts and nuts that secure the exhaust manifold to the side of the cylinder head and lift away the bolts, nuts, spring washers and lock washers, followed by the exhaust manifold itself.

12 Remove all heater pipes from the engine.

13 Undo and remove the four nuts and spring washers that secure the fan blade to the fan and pulley hub. Lift away the fan blades, fan pulley and distance shims.

14 Undo and remove the six bolts and spring washers that hold the water pump to the front face of the cylinder block. Lift away the water pump.

15 Where a crankcase breather is fitted undo and remove the two securing bolts and copper washers and lift away the breather and its gasket.

16 Undo a quarter of a turn at a time the six bolts which hold the clutch pressure plate assembly to the flywheel. Lift away the pressure plate together with the loose friction plate.

17 Check that all the items listed in paragraph 1 of this section have been removed. The engine is now stripped and ready for major dismantling to begin.

10. Camshaft — Removal

1. Open the bonnet and disconnect the two battery terminals, release the battery clamp and lift away the battery.

2. Undo and remove the three shaped nuts securing the engine top cover in place. Lift away the sealing washers noting the location of the various parts followed by the top cover.

3. Remove the timing cover from the bellhousing and then rotate the engine using a large spanner on the crankshaft pulley securing bolt until the EP marking on the flywheel is visible, as shown in Fig.1.8.

4. Insert the timing locking pin into the flywheel. Check that the number 1 cylinder exhaust (A) valve is fully open. Release the camshaft hub locking key securing bolts (B) Fig.1.9, and insert the key into the camshaft hub.

5. Remove the two upper chain tensioner cover plate bolts and spring washers located at the right-hand side of the chain chest and lift away the cover plate and its gasket.

6. Make sure that the tube is correctly inserted so that the tensioner plug and washer are not accidentally dropped into the sump and remove the plug and washer. Using an 1/8 inch Allen key turn the tensioner in a clockwise direction until it is inoperative.

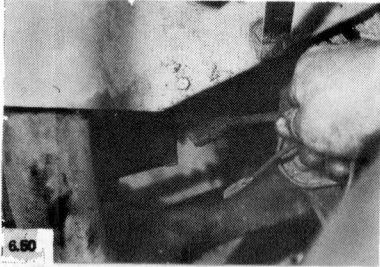
6.50

6.51

6.53

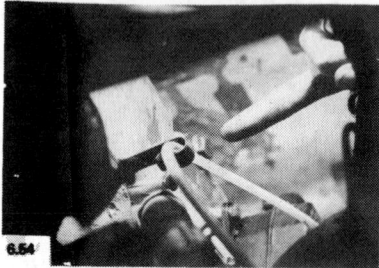
6.54

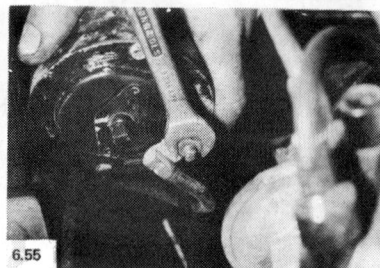
6.55

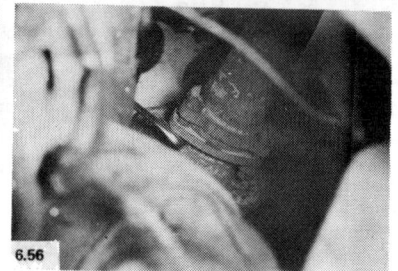
6.56

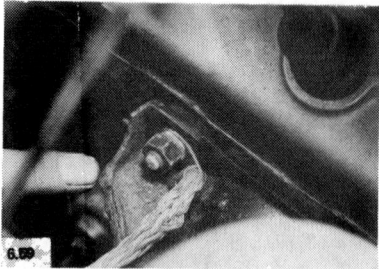
6.59

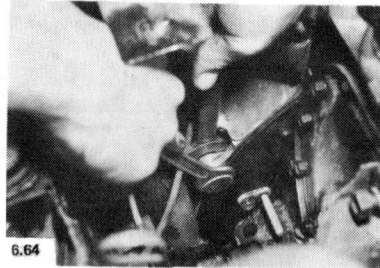
6.64

6.67A

6.67B

6.68A

6.68B

6.71

9.10

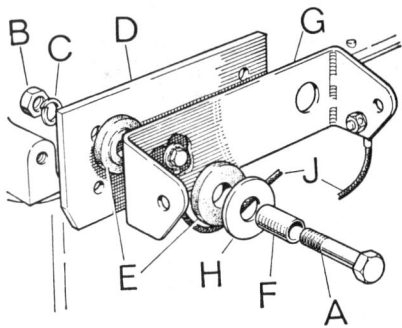

Fig.1.5. DYNAMO SUPPORT BRACKET (FLEXIBLE MOUNTED
TYPE)

A   Bolt   )
B   Nut   ) Fixing support bracket
C   Spring washer)
D   Adjusting support bracket for dynamo
E   Rubber bush for support bracket
F   Sleeve for rubber bush
G   Support bracket for dynamo
H   Plain washer for rubber bush
J   Earth lead

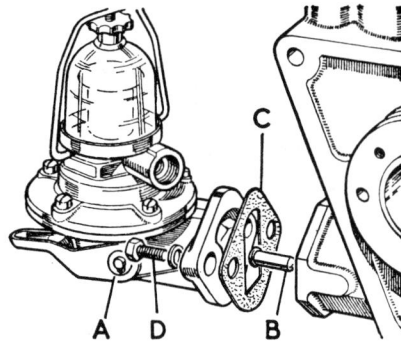

Fig.1.6. FUEL PUMP MOUNTING & PUSHROD LOCATION

A   Fuel pump   C   Gasket
B   Pushrod   D   Bolt

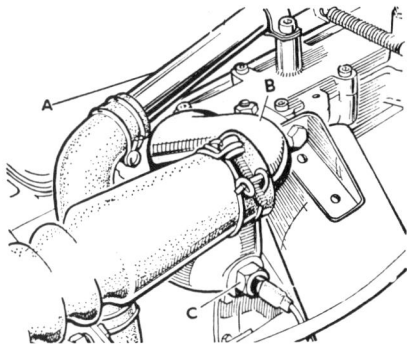

Fig.1.7. THERMOSTAT HOUSING & HEATER PIPE LOCATION

A   Heater pipe
B   Thermostat housing
C   Water temperature transmitter

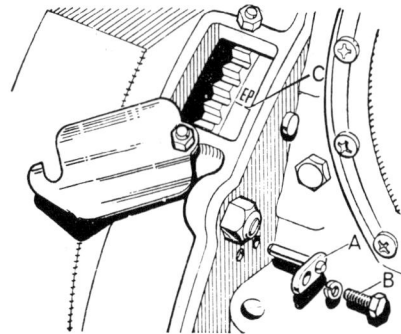

Fig.1.8. FLYWHEEL TIMING LOCK PIN

A   Timing lock pin   washer
B   Securing bolt and spring   C   EP mark in line with pointer

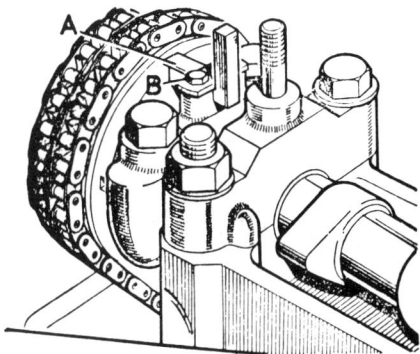

Fig.1.9. CAMSHAFT LOCKING KEY

A   Locking key located in slot   B   Set bolts

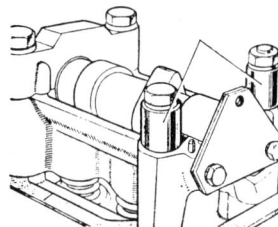

Fig.1.10. CYLINDER HEAD BOLT DISTANCE PIECES

11.11

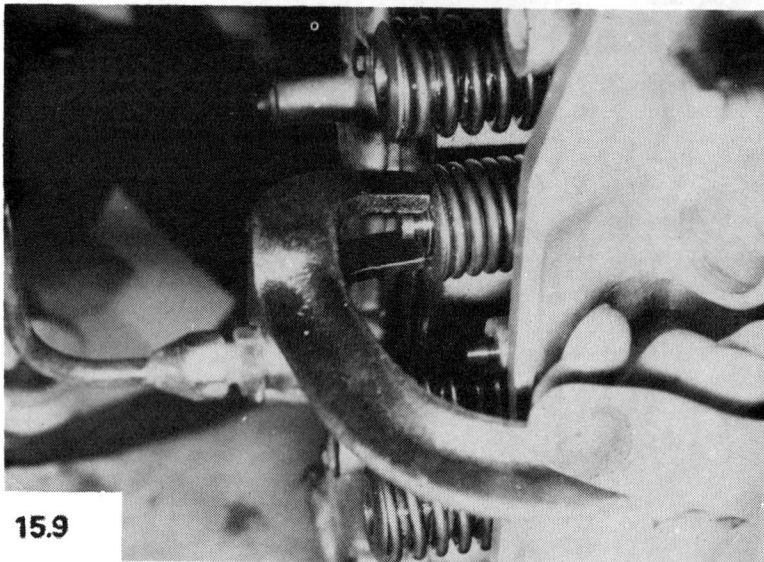

15.9

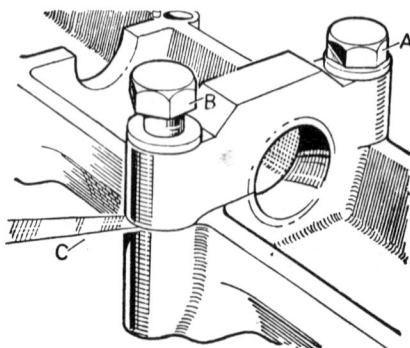

Fig.1.11. CAMSHAFT BEARING NIP CHECK USING A FEELER GAUGE

A Set bolt tightened down
B Set bolt slackened
C Feeler gauge

7. Undo and remove the two bolts and lock plate from the chain-wheel and secure the chainwheel to the mounting bracket using a 3/8 inch UNF nut and plain washer.

8. Remove the end plate from the camshaft rear bearing and discard the gasket.

9. Make up 10 distance pieces A as shown in Fig.1.10, out of some metal tube of suitable diameter.

10 Remove the number 2 camshaft bearing end cap and fit two distance pieces to the cylinder head bolts. Tighten the bolts to a torque wrench setting of 55 lb/ft. (All steel cylinder head gasket) or 70 lb/ft. (Steel asbestos cylinder head gasket).

It is recommended that as each bolt is removed the case hardened plain washers are inspected for chafing which, if evident, new ones obtained under part number 564214 ready for final refitting.

11 Proceed to replace the clearing caps with distance pieces in the order of 6, 5, 4, and at each stage tightening the bolts to the correct torque wrench setting.

12 Remove the camshaft locking key followed by Number 1 bearing cap. The two set bolts fixing the Number 1 camshaft bearing cap to the cylinder block are identified by the letter 'T' or the letter 'V' stamped on the head. Those with a letter 'T' should be tightened to a torque wrench setting of 55 lb/ft. and those with a letter 'V' should be tightened to 70 lb/ft.

13 The last end cap, number 3, should be removed. It is important that the above prescribed sequence is adhered to as Number 1 exhaust and Number 2 inlet valves will be open and will cause internal stress to the camshaft if not adhered to.

14 The camshaft may now be removed followed by the shell bearings. Keep the bearings in their correct pairs and also in their correct fitting order if they are to be re-used.

15 If new bearings are to be fitted, lift the camshaft away from the cylinder head and fit new bearings to Number 1 end cap and bearing block. Replace the cap bolts and tighten to the recommended torque figure. Slacken one of the two bolts.

16 With a feeler gauge check that there is a clearance of between 0.0015 and 0.0025 inch at the base of the cap as shown in Fig.1.11. Select new bearings if the clearance is not correct.

17 Repeat the procedure above for all the end caps.

18 Number 1 bearing end cap takes the camshaft end thrust. To check this place the camshaft into position and fit the end cap into the location dowels. Check that there is end float.

19 Refitting is the reverse sequence to removal but it will be necessary to re-check the valve clearances as detailed in Section 55 of this Chapter.

11. Cylinder Head Removal — Engine Away From Car (SC Models)

1. Follow paragraphs 2 to 14 inclusive in Section 10 to remove the camshaft.

2. If the carburetter installation is still attached to the cylinder head refer to Chapter 3, Section 4, and remove the core, the carburetter and adaptor.

3. Disconnect the front exhaust pipe from the exhaust manifold and slacken the lower mounting nuts and bolts. It will not be necessary to completely remove them.

4. On early produced engines with two cylinder head studs remove the distributor as detailed in Chapter 4, Section 6.

5. Disconnect the brake servo pipe connection from the union on the cylinder head.

6. On models fitted with crankcase emission control remove the top breather hose as well as the control valve and connecting hoses if they are still in position.

7. Remove the chain tensioner oil feed pipe at the union on the cylinder head. With a piece of slightly bent wire extract the nylon filter from the chain housing.

8. Undo and remove the bolts that secure the front lifting bracket and tie-rod to the cylinder head and the fan set bolts and spring washers from around the front of the timing chain casing.

9. Disconnect the water temperature connection at thermostat housing.

10 Using a magnet remove the tappets and shims from the valve springs and keep in their original order to ensure correct refitting.

11 Remove the cylinder head bolts and distance pieces in the reverse order to that shown in Fig. 1.38. Lift off the cylinder head from the top of the cylinder block (photo). If the joint is difficult to break lightly tap the side with a soft faced hammer to break the seal. Do not use a chisel as otherwise the cylinder head could be irreparably damaged.

12 Remove the top chain tensioner piston and pad so that they are not accidentally misplaced.

12. Cylinder Head Removal — Engine Away From Car (TC Models)

The procedure is basically the same as for SC models with the exception that the exhaust manifold will have to be completely removed. The manifold is shown in Fig.1.15. Information of the removal of the twin carburetter installation will be found in Chapter 3, Section 8.

13. Cylinder Head Removal — Engine in Car (SC Models)

1. Open the bonnet, disconnect the two battery terminals, release the battery clamp and lift the battery.

2. Drain the engine coolant as detailed in Chapter 2, Section 2.

3. Remove the air cleaner and carburetter installation as detailed in Chapter 3, Section 4.

4. The procedure for removal of the cylinder head is now the same as that described in Section 11.

14. Cylinder Head Removal — Engine in Car (TC Models)

1. Open the bonnet, disconnect the two battery terminals, release the battery clamp and lift away the battery.

2. Drain the engine coolant as detailed in Chapter 2, Section 2.

3. Remove the air cleaner and carburetter installation as detailed in Chapter 3, Section 8.

4. The procedure for removal of the cylinder head is now the same as that described in Section 12.

15. Valve Removal

1. The valve assemblies fitted to SC and TC models differ slightly as will be seen in Fig.1.16 and Fig.1.17.

2. The inner and outer valve springs of SC engines are an interference fit and should this fit be lost due to wear or loss of tension new springs in pairs must be fitted.

3. The inner and outer valve springs of TC engines are of the non-interference type.

4. The exhaust valve on SC engines is fitted with a sleeve and special spring cap to enable the valve to rotate.

5. The exhaust valve on TC engines is not fitted with this sleeve and the inlet and exhaust valve spring caps are identical.

6. It is important that the exhaust valves are correctly matched to the engine as the valve material used on SC engine applications is different from that used on the TC engine and must not be interchanged.

7. To remove the valves first remove the wire circlip that retains the tappet shims in position on early produced engines. This will be found on the top of each valve assembly.

8. Remove the shims with a magnet and keep in their order of removal so that they may be fitted in their original position. If a magnet is not available a small amount of grease on a bolt lead will serve the same purpose.

9. Using a valve spring compressor correctly located as shown compress the springs sufficiently to be able to remove the collets (photo).

10 If when the valve spring compressor is screwed down the valve spring cap refuses to free and expose the split collet, do not continue

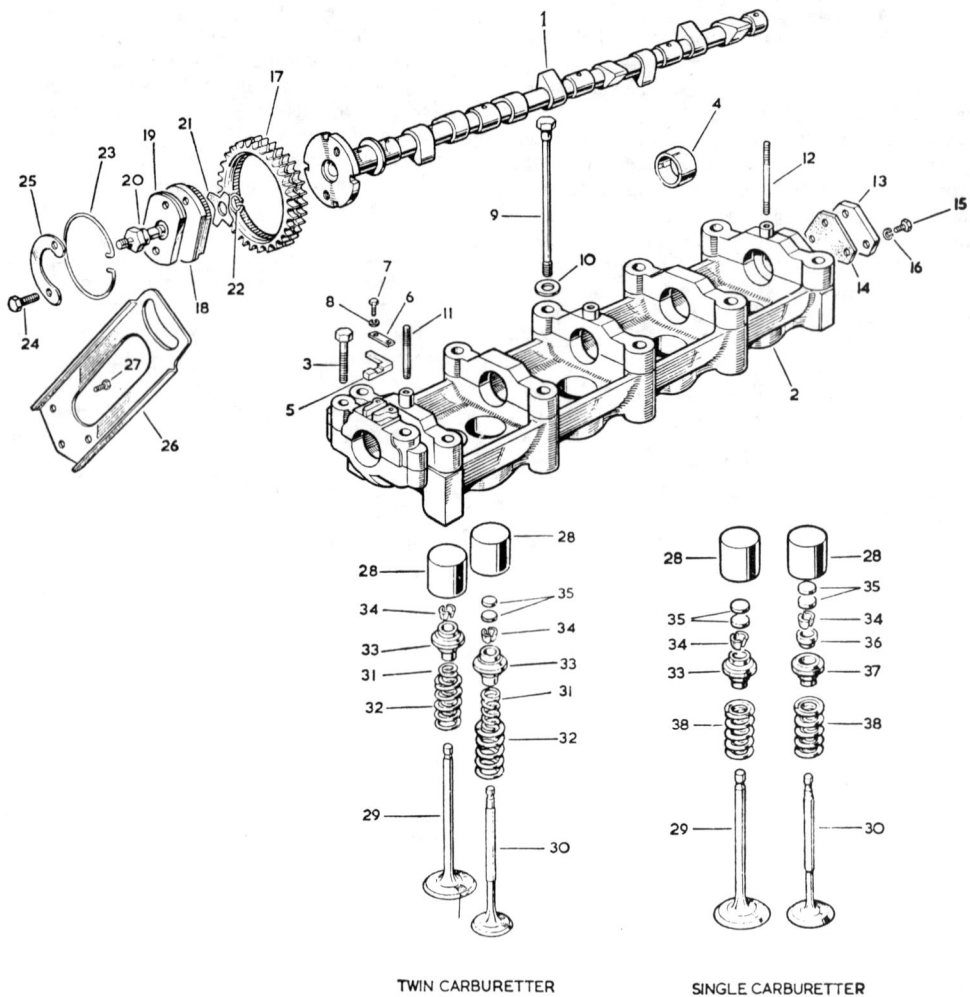

TWIN CARBURETTER

SINGLE CARBURETTER

Fig.1.12. CAMSHAFT & VALVE COMPONENTS

1 Camshaft
2 Bearing block assembly for camshaft
3 Set bolt
4 Bearing for camshaft, pairs
5 Locking key for camshaft
6 Securing plate for locking key
7 Set bolt
8 Spring washer
9 Special set bolt
10 Plain washer

11 Stud, front
12 Stud, centre and rear
13 Rear cover plate for camshaft
14 Joint washer for rear cover plate
15 Set bolt
16 Spring washer
17 Chainwheel for camshaft
18 Splined ring for chainwheel
19 Clamping plate for splined ring
20 Retaining stud for splined ring
21 Retaining washer

22 Circlip
23 Spring ring retaining splined ring in chainwheel
24 Set bolt
25 Lockwasher
26 Support plate for cam-shaft chainwheel
27 Self-locking set bolt
28 Valve tappet
29 Inlet valve
30 Exhaust valve

31 Valve spring, inner,TC
32 Valve spring, outer,TC
33 Cap for valve spring,TC
34 Split cone for valve, halves
35 Shim for tappet adjustment
36 Sleeve for exhaust cap, SC
37 Cap for exhaust valve spring, SC
38 Valve springs, inner and outer, SC

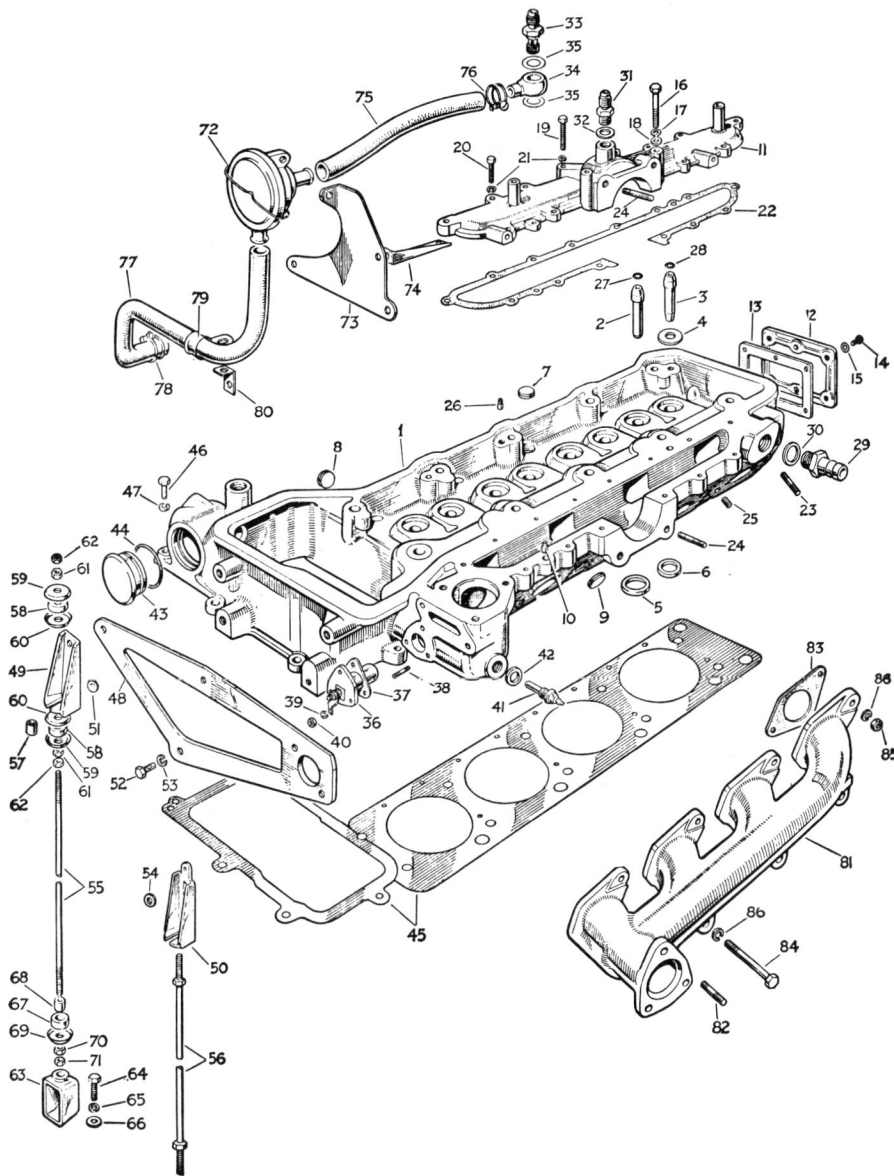

Fig.1.13. CYLINDER HEAD COMPONENTS — SC MODELS

1 Cylinder head assembly
2 Valve guide, inlet
3 Valve guide, exhaust
4 Washer for valve spring
5 Insert for inlet valve seat
6 Insert for exhaust valve seat
7 Core plug, top
8 Core plug, right-hand side
9 Core plug, left-hand side
10 Dowel for inlet manifold cover
11 Inlet manifold cover
12 Rear cover plate
13 Joint washer for rear cover plate
14 Set bolt
15 Plain washer
16 Set bolt
17 Spring washer
18 Plain washer
19 Set bolt
20 Set bolt
21 Spring washer
22 Joint washer for inlet manifold cover
23 Stud for exhaust manifold
24 Stud for carburetter
25 Helicoil insert for exhaust manifold bolts
26 Dowel for camshaft bearing block
27 Rubber ring for inlet valve guide
28 Rubber ring for exhaust valve guide
29 Adaptor for heater outlet
30 Joint washer for heater outlet adaptor
31 Adaptor for brake servo
32 Joint washer for brake servo adaptor
33 Adaptor for brake servo
34 Banjo
35 Joint washer for banjo and adaptor
36 Thermostat switch for choke warning light
37 Joint washer for thermostat switch
38 Stud
39 Spring washer
40 Nut
41 Water temperature unit
42 Joint washer for water temperature unit
43 Sealing plug for cylinder head
44 'O' ring for sealing plug
45 Cylinder head gasket
46 Set bolt
47 Spring washer
48 Front lifting bracket
49 Stabiliser mounting bracket. Up to engines numbered suffix 'C'
50 Stabiliser mounting bracket. From engines numbered suffix 'D' onwards
51 Distance piece for stabiliser mounting bracket
52 Set bolt
53 Spring washer
54 Plain washer. From engines numered suffix 'D'
55 Engine tie rod. Up to cars numbered suffix 'A'
56 Engine tie rod. From cars numbered suffix 'B' onwards
57 Distance tube
58 Rubber mounting
59 Guide washer, small
60 Guide washer, large
61 Nut
62 Locknut
63 Bracket for tie rod
64 Set bolt
65 Spring washer
66 Plain washer
67 Rubber mounting
68 Distance tube
69 Guide washer, large
70 Nut
71 Locknut, bottom
72 Crankcase emission control valve
73 Support bracket for control valve
74 Brace for control valve support bracket
75 Hose control valve to servo adaptor banjo
76 Clip for hose, banjo end
77 Hose cylinder block to control valve
78 Clip for hose, cylinder block end
79 Support clip for clip
80 Bracket for support clip
81 Exhaust manifold
82 Stud for exhaust pipe
83 Joint washer, manifold to cylinder head
84 Set bolt
85 Nut for manifold studs
86 Lockwasher

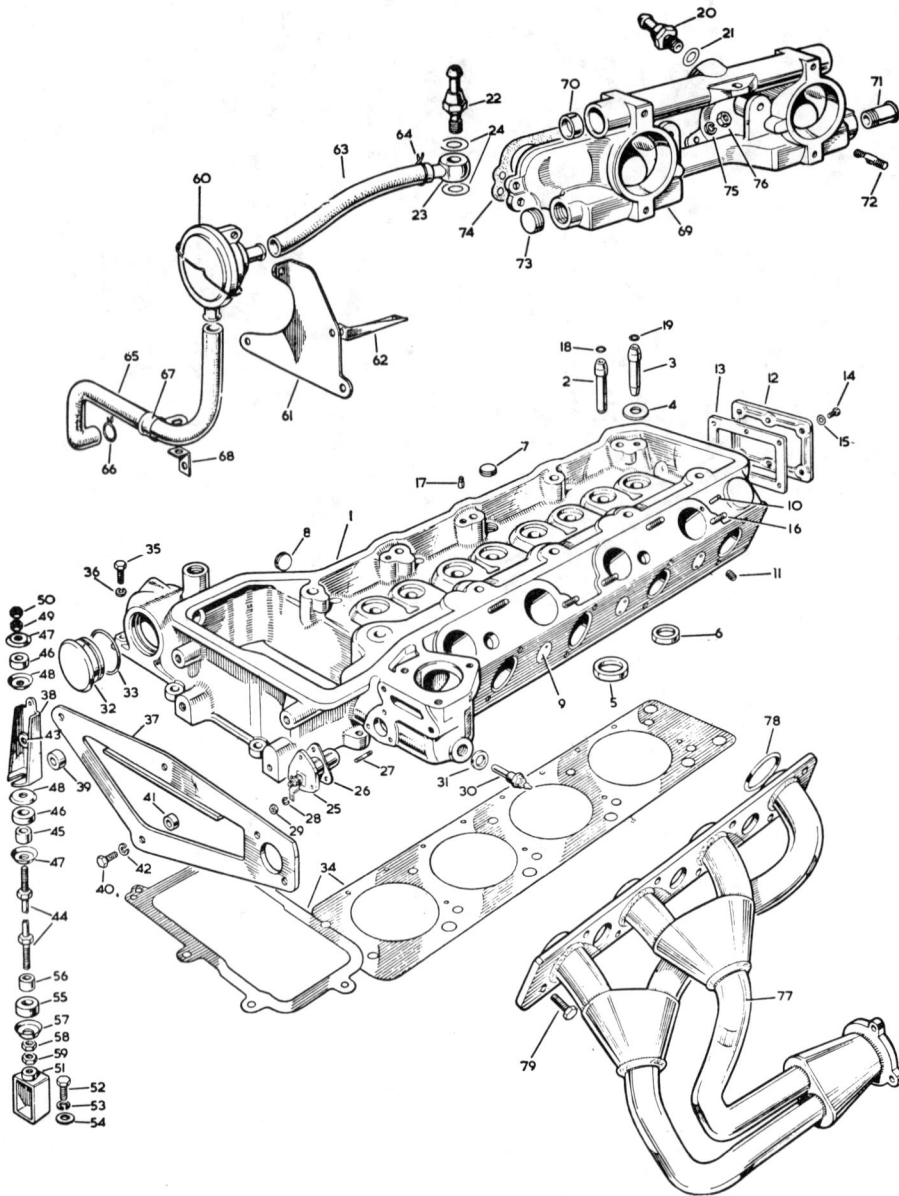

Fig.1.14. CYLINDER HEAD COMPONENTS — TC MODELS

1 Cylinder head assembly	23 Banjo	46 Distance tube	65 Hose
2 Valve guide, inlet	24 Joint washer	46 Rubber mounting	66 Clip for hose
3 Valve guide, exhaust	25 Thermostat switch	47 Guide washer, small	67 Support clip for hose
4 Washer for valve spring	26 Joint washer	48 Guide washer, large	68 Bracket for support
5 Insert for inlet valve seat	27 Stud	49 Nut (5/16 in.UNF)	clip
6 Insert for exhaust valve seat	28 Spring washer	50 Locknut(5/16 in.UNF thin)	69 Inlet manifold
7 Core plug, top	29 Nut (10 UNF)	51 Bracket for tie rod	assembly
8 Core plug, RH side	30 Water temperature unit	52 Set bolt	70 Cup plug
9 Core plug, LH side	31 Joint washer	53 Spring washer	71 Adaptor for heater
10 Dowel for inlet manifold	32 Sealing plug for cylinder head	54 Plain washer	water pipe
11 Helicoil insert	33 'O' ring for sealing plug	55 Rubber mounting	72 Stud for carburetter
12 Rear cover plate	34 Cylinder head gasket	56 Distance tube	tie bar
13 Joint washer	35 Set bolt	57 Guide washer, large	73 Core plug for water
14 Set bolt	36 Spring washer	58 Nut (5/16 in.UNF)	jacket
15 Plain washer	37 Front lifting bracket	59 Locknut, bottom	74 Joint washer
16 Stud for inlet manifold	38 Stabiliser mounting bracket	60 Crankcase emission	75 Spring washer
17 Dowel	39 Distance piece	control valve	76 Nut (5/16 in.UNF)
18 Rubber ring	40 Set bolt	61 Support bracket	77 Exhaust manifold
19 Rubber ring	41 Distance piece	62 Brace	78 Joint washer
20 Non-return valve for servo	42 Spring washer	63 Hose	79 Set bolt
21 Joint washer	43 Plain washer	64 Clip for hose, banjo end	
22 Non-return valve for servo	44 Engine tie rod	Cleat, hose to heater pipe	

to screw down on the compressor as there is a likelihood of damaging it. Gently tap the top of the tool directly over the cap with a light hammer. This will free the cap. To avoid the compressor jumping off the spring retaining cap when it is tapped, hold the compressor firmly in position with one hand.

11 It is essential that the valves are kept in their correct sequence unless they are so badly worn that they are to be renewed. If they are going to be kept and used again place them in a sheet of card numbered 1 to 8 corresponding with the relative position the valves were in when fitted. Also keep the valve springs, caps and collets etc, in the correct order.

12 When the springs are suitably compressed lift out the two collets (photo).

13 Lift out the spring cap and rotating sleeve (SC model only) followed by the springs (photo).

16. Camshaft Chains — Removal

1. Should it be necessary to remove the camshaft drive chains this operation can be done with the engine in the car. There will be a certain amount of preliminary work involved, and particulars of this will be found in the relevant sections detailed as necessary. If the engine is away from the car, start at the point which has been reached in the removal of the necessary ancillary equipment as listed.

2. Disconnect the battery terminals, release the battery clamp and lift away the battery.

3. Remove the radiator as detailed in Chapter 2, Section 5.

4. Slacken the dynamo or alternator mounting bolts and remove the fan belt (Chapter 2, Section 10).

5. Remove the fan blades and water pump as detailed in Chapter 2, Section 8.

6. On early produced models up to engine number 40036435F and 40000002F remove the external oil filter and the right-hand mounting bracket.

a) Unscrew the external oil filter by hand or if tight using a strap wrench or chisel and place an absorbent cloth under the oil filter to catch any oil draining out. Lift away the rubber sealing ring.

b) Remove the set bolt locating the engine tie-rod bottom bracket to the engine compartment front crossmember and also the two bolts at the stabiliser mounting bracket. Lift away the tie-rod.

c) Undo the engine mounting bolt and self locking nut and withdraw the bolt. Using a garage jack suitably placed or lifting tackle take the weight of the engine from the mounting. The mounting should be completely removed having first undone and removed the two nuts and spring washers from the top of the mounting and the bolt and spring washer from the lower part of the mounting.

d) Note that the engine earth strap and fan drive washer is fitted to the top rear stud.

7. Remove both chain tensioners as detailed in Section 26 of this Chapter.

8. With a wide bladed screwdriver remove the plastic plug from the left-hand side of the engine backplate. Rotate the engine by means of the driving pulley set bolt until the EP locating hole in the flywheel is visible and then lock the flywheel using a piece of suitable diameter metal rod. This will enable the crankshaft pulley bolt to be removed. DO NOT use the timing locking pin as it will probably sheer.

9. With the crankshaft suitably locked remove the fan driving pulley and damper assembly bolt and plain washer. Carefully withdraw the pulley and damper.

10 Remove the front crankshaft oil seal.

11 Remove the distributor cap from the distributor body (engine in car) and tie back to one side away from the working area.

12 Disconnect the vacuum advance pipe from the vacuum unit on the distributor. Also disconnect the low tension lead from the side of the distributor body.

13 Slacken the pinch bolt on the clamp plate and also slacken the bolts that secure the clamp plate to the auxiliary drive housing so as to relieve tension of the clamp on the distributor body.

14 Lift away the distributor from the auxiliary drive housing.

15 Remove the fuel pump - first turn the reserve fuel tap to the central position to stop petrol syphoning from the fuel tank.

16 Disconnect the two fuel hoses from the fuel pump.

17 Undo and remove the two retaining nuts and spring washers and lift the pump away.

18 Remove the two set bolts with spring and plain washers that secure the distributor clamp plate to the auxiliary drive housing.

19 Carefully lift out the distributor housing assembly and drive dog.

20 Insert a long 5/16 inch UNF bolt into the distributor drive dog driving gear and withdraw the distributor driving gear. This is shown in Fig.1.19.

21 Using a wide blade screwdriver or tyre lever remove the remaining sealing plugs and 'O' rings from the front of the drive chain chamber.

22 It should now be noted that an intermediate chainwheel cluster has been introduced on engines as detailed below and this replaces the separate intermediate chainwheels for the oil pump drive and camshaft that were previously used. This modification was required because the load on the chainwheel drive key previously used was higher and combining the chainwheels reduces the load and the possibility of key failure.

a) To accommodate this modification the crankshaft chainwheel has been reduced in length and the fan driving pulley and damper have also been modified so as to suit the new length of chainwheel.

b) This modification occurred on SC and Automatic Transmission models from engine numbers incorporating a suffix letter 'H' and onwards. On TC models the effective engine number incorporated a suffix letter 'B'.

c) The crankshaft chainwheel and fan driving pulley and damper can be used on earlier models but must be fitted in pairs.

d) The modified intermediate chainwheel cluster and associated parts can be used on earlier models but must be fitted in sets comprising the following:—

Intermediate chainwheel cluster.
Driving shaft for oil pump and distributor.
Oil thrower for oil pump driving shaft.
Key fixing chainwheel to oil pump driving shaft.

23 Engines fitted with early separate intermediate chainwheels: Undo and remove the bolt that secures the two chainwheels onto the auxiliary drive shaft.

24 To remove the oil pump and auxiliary drive housing with the necessary pipes detached, use a soft metal drift and drive the shaft out of the intermediate chainwheels.

25 Remove the engine top cover by undoing and lifting away the shaped nuts and sealing washers followed by the cover itself. Note the order of the washers to ensure correct refitting.

16 Release the locking tabs and unscrew the two securing set bolts from the camshaft chainwheel. Lift away the chainwheel.

27 Carefully lift the top chain from the chain chamber with the two chainwheels still in mesh in the chain.

28 Remove the two timing chain vibration damper pads by undoing the two bolts, plain and spring washers securing each damper pad in position.

29 Disengage the lower chain from the crankshaft and remove downwards.

30 Engines fitted with the later combined intermediate chainwheels: Undo and remove the bolt that secures the chainwheel onto the auxiliary drive shaft.

31 To remove the oil pump and auxiliary drive housing with the necessary pipes detached, use a soft metal drift and drive the shaft out of the intermediate chainwheel cluster.

32 Remove the upper and lower timing chain vibration damper pad securing bolts, plain and spring washers and withdraw the lower damper. It will not be possible to remove the upper one yet until the lower chain is removed.

33 Remove the engine top cover by undoing and lifting away the shaped nuts and sealing washers followed by the cover itself. Note the order of the washers to ensure correct refitting.

34 Release the locking tabs and unscrew the two securing set bolts

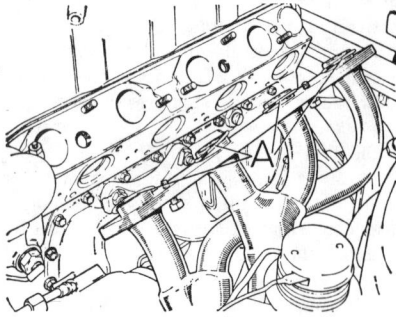

Fig.1.15. EXHAUST MANIFOLD & GASKET REMOVAL
(TC MODELS)
A Exhaust manifold gaskets

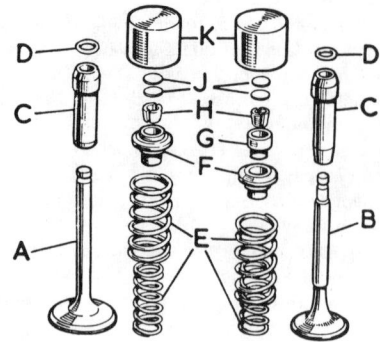

Fig.1.16. VALVE ASSEMBLY COMPONENT PARTS (SC
(SC MODELS)

A	Inlet valve	F	Spring caps
B	Exhaust valve	G	Rotating sleeve
C	Valve guide	H	Split cones
D	Rubber ring for valve guide	J	Shims
E	Valve spring, interference fit	K	Tappet

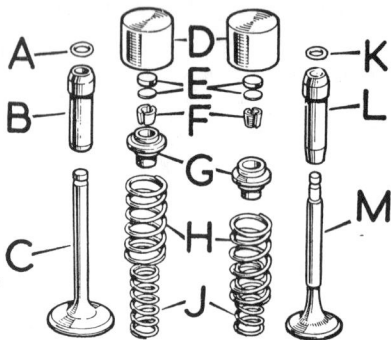

Fig.1.17. VALVE ASSEMBLY COMPONENT PARTS
(TC MODELS)

A	Rubber ring for inlet valve guide	H	Valve spring, outer, non-interference type
B	Valve guide inlet	J	Valve spring, inner, non-interference type
C	Inlet valve		
D	Tappet	K	Rubber ring for exhaust valve guide
E	Shims		
F	Split cones	L	Valve guide exhaust
G	Valve cap	M	Exhaust valve

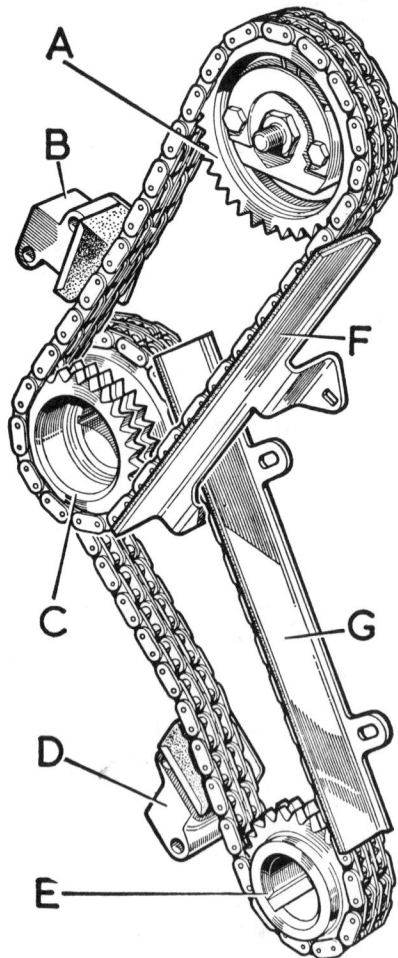

Fig.1.18. CAMSHAFT DRIVE CHAINS & CHAINWHEELS

A	Camshaft chainwheel	E	Crankshaft chainwheel
B	Top chain tensioner	F	Chain vibration damper pad, top chain
C	Auxiliary drive chainwheels		
D	Bottom chain tensioner	G	Chain vibration damper pad, bottom chain

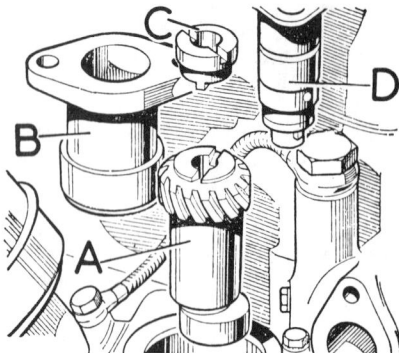

Fig.1.19. DETAILS OF THE DISTRIBUTOR DRIVE

A	Distributor driving gear, showing the offset dog in the correct timing position.	B	Distributor housing assembly
		C	Driving dog for distributor
		D	Distributor shaft

from the camshaft chainwheel. Detach the chainwheel from the camshaft and the upper chain and lift away.

35 Hold the intermediate chainwheel cluster towards the rear of the engine, and then detach the top chain from the front sprocket. Lift the upper chain upwards away from the chain chamber.

36 Continue holding the lower chain and intermediate chainwheel cluster towards the rear of the engine, carefully manipulate the chainwheel out of the links of the lower chain.

37 Allow the chain to drop and then withdraw the intermediate chainwheel cluster up through the timing chain aperture. During this operation it is necessary to move the vibration damper into the most convenient position so as to allow the chainwheel to be removed. This is a process of trail and error but can be done.

38 Withdraw the lower chain from below and then lift away the top damper upwards through the timing chain aperture.

17. Sump, Piston, Connecting Rod & Big End Bearing Removal

1. This job can be done with the engine either in the car or on the bench. There will be a certain amount of preliminary work and details of this will be found in the relevant sections, detailed as necessary. If the engine is away from the car start at the part which has been reached in the removal of the necessary ancillary equipment as listed.

2. Disconnect the battery terminals, release the battery clamp and lift away the battery.

3. Drain the engine oil into a container of suitable size.

4. Lift out the oil level dipstick and unscrew the tube nut. The tube may now be lifted away from the side of the sump.

5. If a crankcase breather is fitted it should be removed next. Undo and remove the two securing bolts and copper washers and lift away the breather and joint washer.

6. Undo and remove the two lower bellhousing securing bolts and spring washers if the engine is still in the car.

7. Remove the clutch slave cylinder from the bellhousing and clip locating the flexible pipe to the sump. Support the slave cylinder using a piece of string or wire.

8. There are twenty six bolts and spring washers that secure the sump to the underside of the crankcase and these should next be removed. Leave one bolt on each side loose to support the sump and then when all other bolts are free, remove the last two bolts and lift away the sump. If a jointing compound has been previously used it may be necessary to break the seal by using a soft faced hammer on the mating flange.

9. Cars fitted with automatic transmission. Make sure that the oil cooler pipes are adequately supported before finally removing the sump.

10 Refer to the respective Section 11 and remove the camshaft and cylinder head. Take care not to rotate the crankshaft or camshaft with drive chains removed as otherwise there is a possibility of the piston crown touching an open valve causing serious damage.

11 If the flywheel has been locked either with the timing pin or a rod this should be removed next. Also remove the internal oil filter having first undone the three securing bolts and spring washers located as shown in Fig.1.23.

12 Remove the big end caps one at a time taking care to keep them in the right order although they are marked on the left-hand side of the engine face. Each end cap is secured in position with two self-locking nuts which must always be renewed. Ensure that the shell bearings are kept with their correct connecting rods and caps unless they are to be renewed.

13 If the big end caps are difficult to remove they should be gently tapped with a soft hammer.

14 To remove the shell bearings, press the bearing opposite the groove in both the connecting rod and connecting rod caps and the bearings will slide out easily.

15 Withdraw the pistons and connecting rods upwards and ensure they are kept in the correct order for replacement in the bore. Refit the connecting rod caps and bearings to the rods if the bearings do not require renewal to minimise the risk of getting the caps and rods muddled.

18. Gudgeon Pin — Removal

1. To remove the gudgeon pin to free the piston from the connecting rod, remove one of the circlips from either end of the pin with a pair of circlip pliers.

2. Press out the pin from the rod and piston with your finger.

3. If the pin shows reluctance to move, then on no account force it out, as this could damage the piston. Immerse the piston in a pan of boiling water for three minutes. On removal the expansion of the aluminium should allow the gudgeon pin to slide out easily.

4. Make sure the pins are kept with the same piston for ease of refitting.

19. Piston Ring — Removal

1. To remove the piston rings, slide them carefully over the top of the piston taking care not to scratch the aluminium alloy. Never slide them off the bottom of the piston skirt. It is very easy to break the iron piston rings if they are pulled off roughly so this operation should be done with extreme caution. It is helpful to make use of an old hacksaw blade with the tooth offset ground down or better still an old 0.020 inch feeler gauge.

2. Lift one end of the piston ring to be removed out of its groove and insert the end of the feeler gauge under it.

3. Turn the feeler gauge slowly round the piston and as the ring comes out of its groove apply slight upward pressure so that it rests on the land above. It can then be eased off the piston with the feeler gauge stopping it from slipping into an empty groove, if it is any but the top piston ring that is being removed.

20. Flywheel & Engine End Plate — Removal

Having removed the clutch (see Chapter 5) the flywheel and engine backplate can be removed. It is possible for this operation to be carried out with the engine in the car.

1. Lock the flywheel by first removing the plastic plug from the left-hand side of the engine end plate and rotate the flywheel by means of a large spanner on the crankshaft driving pulley set bolt until the EP locating hole in the flywheel is visible. Lock the flywheel using a piece of metal rod, as shown in Fig.1.24. DO NOT use the timing locking pin because the flywheel retaining bolts are very tight and it would be easy to sheer the pin.

2. Remove the eight bolts that secure the flywheel and reinforcing plate.

3. Using a soft faced hammer tap the flywheel from its locating dowel in the end of the crankshaft.

4. If the car is fitted with an automatic transmission the unit should be disconnected from the drive plate and the bellhousing removed as well as the unit.

5. To remove the drive plate it must be locked and to do this use a 3/8 inch UNF bolt $1^{7}/8$ inch long and substitute this for one of the 3/8 inch set bolts securing the end plate to the cylinder block.

6. Undo and remove the eight securing bolts reinforcing plate, drive plate and spacer ring from the end of the crankshaft. These parts are shown in Fig.1.25.

7. To remove the end plate undo and remove the bolts and spring washers that secure it to the rear of the cylinder block. Mind the timing pointer as it is sharp and can cause a nasty scratch on the hand (photo).

8. With a soft faced hammer tap the end plate from off its two locating dowels.

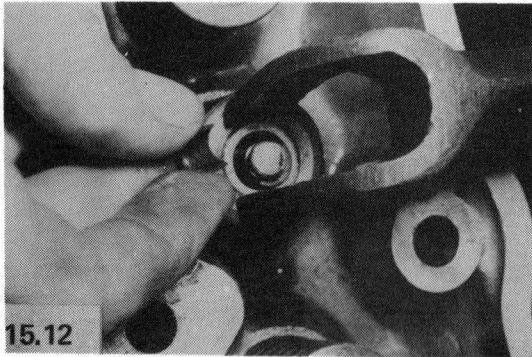

15.12

15.13

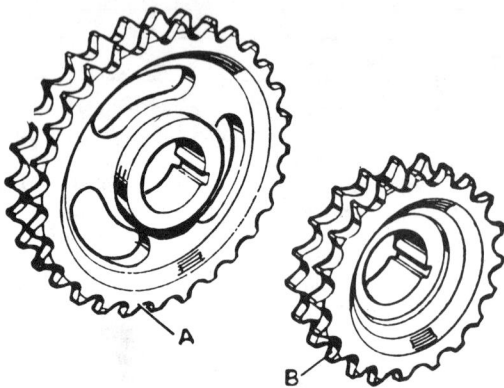

Fig.1.20. THE CORRECT ASSEMBLY ORDER OF THE IN-
TERMEDIATE CHAINWHEELS (EARLY TYPE)

A Large chainwheel with boss   B   Small chainwheel with boss
   outwards   inwards

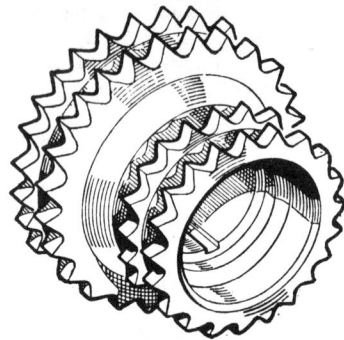

Fig.1.21. THE LATER TYPE INTERMEDIATE CHAINWHEEL

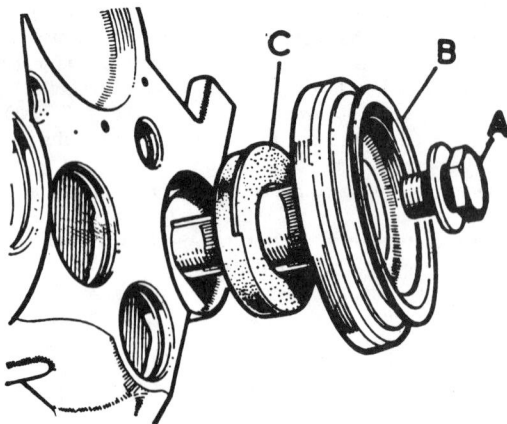

Fig.1.22. FRONT OIL SEAL & FAN DRIVING PULLEY

A   Special set bolt
B   Pulley
C   Oil seal

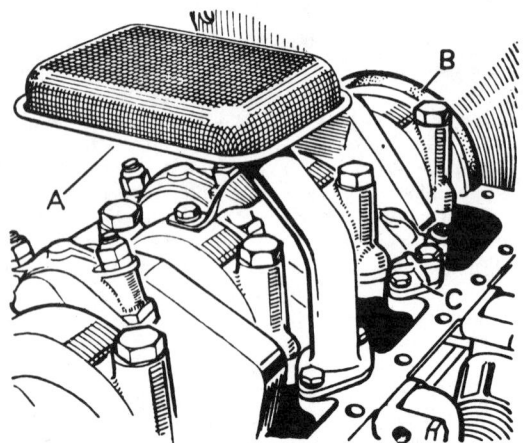

Fig.1.23. INTERNAL OIL FILTER & SUPPORT BRACKET

A   Internal oil filter   C   Sealing plate for pressure
B   Rear sump oil seal in position   drilling

21. Crankshaft & Main Bearing — Removal

With the engine out of the car, remove the camshaft drive chains and crankshaft chainwheel, big ends, pistons and connecting rods, flywheel and end plate.

1. The crankshaft front oil seal should be removed having first noted which way round it is fitted. This may be done by easing it forwards with a wide bladed screwdriver behind the lip.

2. Undo and remove the two bolts that secure the rear main bearing. This is located by two dowels so to release the cap tap the end cap lightly with a soft faced hammer. Note that the sump rear seal is also located on the rear end cap.

3. Remove all the main bearing cap securing bolts and put in a safe place in their order of removal so that they may be fitted in their original positions. There are two bolts for each cap and the total number of end caps is five. Each cap is identified by a number on its left-hand side.

4. When removing the Number 4 end cap note that the crankshaft thrust washers are fitted in this location. Note which way round the thrust washers are fitted.

5. Keep the bearing shells and thrust washers in matched order ready for inspection as detailed in Section 28 of this Chapter.

6. Remove the crankshaft by lifting it away from the crankcase.

7. If the cylinder block is being completely dismantled the remainder of the attachments such as the camshaft chainwheel support plate should be removed.

8. It will be observed that these are bolted on side covers and during periods of major overhaul it is recommended by the author that these be removed for cleaning out of the water jacket to ensure that there is no localised overheating at a later time.

9. Note the position of the special studs for the engine mounting brackets and remove them completely first. Next undo the 22 securing set bolts and plain washers and also the special set screw on the left-hand side cover. Lift away the side covers. It may be necessary to ease them from the side of the cylinder block if a jointing compound has been previously used but do this with a wide bladed screwdriver taking extreme care not to distort the side cover or score the mating faces.

10 With the cylinder block completely stuffed it should be thoroughly cleaned and dried. Use a pipe cleaner to clear the oilways and a screwdriver to remove any rust desposits in the water jacket passages.

22. Lubrication & Crankcase Ventilation Systems — Removal

Description

A forced feed system of lubrication is shown in diagrammatic form in Fig.1.26, and it will be seen that oil is drawn from the sump via a flexible steel pipe to a Hobourn Eaton eccentric rotor type pump which is driven by a shaft in an extension in the auxiliary drive housing. The oil pump itself is housed in the aluminium casting which is secured to the rear of the auxilary shaft casting. It also accommodates the oil pressure relief valve and forms the mounting for an AC type SC full flow oil filter. This comprises an impregnated paper element of the disposable type which is retained by a threaded hollow stud. An unusual feature of the pump is in its mounting position which is higher than usual and because of this the inlet part is connected to a small aluminium casting which contains a weir, this being full of oil at all times. The weir is interconnected to a dulling in the base of the cylinder block by means of the flexible pipe and serves to prime the oil pump whilst the engine is being started.

A second flexible pipe conveys the oil from the oil pump outlet to a transverse drilling in the cylinder block and from there into a longitudinally drilled main oil gallery. A small bore flexible pipe passes oil from an outlet above the pump housing situated on the top of the timing chest. It is from here that the upper automatic chain tensioner is supplied with oil under pressure.

Oil drawn from the sump passes through a wire gauze strainer to the pump where it is pressurised and passed to the auxiliary shaft bearings, top chain tensioner and to the oil filter. Inside the filter housing is a non-return valve which prevents oil inside the filter housing from draining back into the sump when the engine is stationary. Also inside the filter housing is the pressure relief valve which comes into operation and opens if the filter element becomes choked causing a restriction in the circulation of oil through the filter.

The main system oil pressure relief valve is fitted to the underside of the oil pump body and ensures that the pressure in the system does not exceed a maximum of between 50 to 60 lb/sq.in. Oil is fed from the main oil gallery through cross drillings in the crankcase main bearings. The crankshaft main bearing journals are drilled so that each main bearing supplies its neighbouring big end bearing with oil.

The camshaft is longitudinally drilled and is fed with oil from the main oil gallery by means of an externally fitted oil pipe. Each bearing journal is cross drilled. To provide lubrication the bearing shells are chamfered at their inner longitudinal edges so that oil sprayed from the gaps is splashed over the cams, the valve tappets and the valve stems.

The small end bushes and cylinder bores are splash lubricated by the movement of the crankshaft.

Details of the crankcase emission control are given in Section 60 of this Chapter.

Removal of Crankcase Breather

The crankcase breather is fitted to the side of the crankcase and is secured in position with two setscrews and copper washers. To remove the breather undo and remove the two setscrews and copper washers and lift away the breather and its gasket.

It may be easily cleared by washing in petrol or paraffin and wiped dry with a non-fluffy rag.

When refitting always use a new gasket to safeguard against oil leaks.

23. Oil Filter — Removal & Replacement

External Oil Filter

1. The external oil filter is screwed into the rear oil pump housing and is removed by unscrewing the complete unit. Place an absorbant cloth underneath the filter to catch any oil drained out.

2. If it is difficult to remove use either a chisel hammered through the complete cannister and rotate or alternatively use a strap wrench.

3. It is important that the correct new oil filter is used and should be ordered under Part Number AC796502 type SC. This filter is easily identified by the large rectangular section oil sealing ring which is attached to the base with special adhesive.

4. Wipe the sealing ring seating on the housing free of any dust and refit the oiler filter only tightening it hand tight.

5. Start the engine and run for a couple of minutes and then stop it. Check the oil level and top up as necessary.

Internal oil filter

The internal oil filter is of the wire gauze mesh type and is bolted to the bottom face of the crankcase inside the sump. Normally it is not necessary to remove the sump and clean this filter except during major engine overhauls.

Nylon mesh oil filter

Located in the top of the chain chamber is a nylon mesh oil filter (Fig.1.27). To gain access undo and remove the banjo bolt that secures the oil supply pipe to the top of the chain chamber. Lift away the two joint washers.

To extract the filter insert a suitable length of stiff wire slightly hooked at the lower end and carefully withdraw the filter.

Wash in petrol and if necessary scrub with an old toothbrush to remove ingrained particles of sediment. Insert the filter and

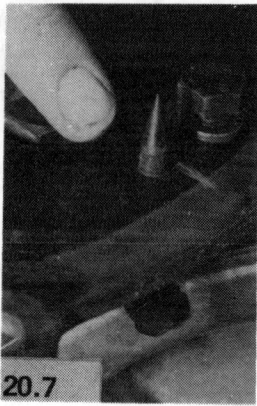

20.7

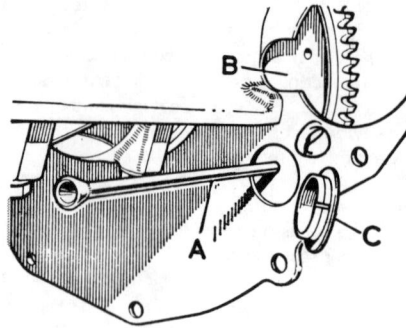

Fig.1.24. Correct method of locking flywheel

A Suitable diameter rod
B Flywheel
C Plastic blanking plug

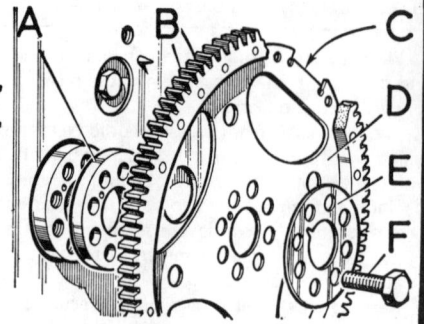

Fig.1.25. Starter ring and drive plate as fitted to cars with automatic transmission

A Spacer ring
B Starter ring
C Timing marks
D Flexible drive plate
E Reinforcing plate
F Special set bolt

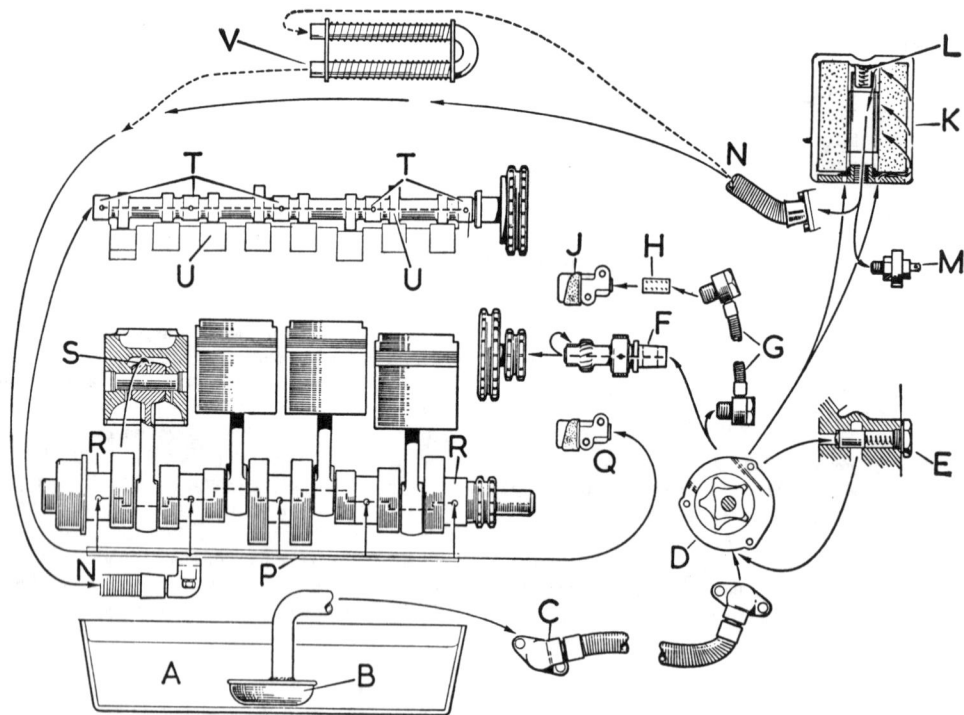

Fig.1.26. DIAGRAMMATIC LAYOUT OF LUBRICATION SYSTEM (SC MODELS)

A Engine oil sump
B Internal oil filter
C External pipe, suction
D Rotor-type oil pump
E Oil pressure release valve
F Oil pump and auxiliary drive shaft bearings
G Flexible feed pipe, top tensioner
H Nylon mesh filter
J Top chain tensioner
K External oil filter
L Safety valve
M Oil pressure switch
N External pipe, pressure
P Main oil gallery
Q Bottom chain tensioner
R Crankshaft main bearings, and big ends
S Little end and gudgeon pin, splash feed
T Camshaft bearings
U Oil bath, cams and tappets lubrication
V Oil cooler, where fitted

replace the banjo bolt with new fibre washer. Tighten the bolt securely and with the engine running check for oil leaks.

24. Oil Pressure Relief Valve — Removal & Replacement

During production of Rover 2000 models three types of oil pressure relief valves have been fitted. The original assembly comprising a separate ball, plunger, spring, washer and plug was fitted as shown in Fig.1.28. The intermediate assembly comprised a ball and captive plunger as a complete assembly, spring, washer and plug. The latest valve assembly had a sleeved oil release valve comprising a liner, plunger, spring, washer and plug as shown in Fig.1.29. The last design overcame the possibility of the plunger sticking in the guide.

It should be noted that the latest design of oil pump and auxiliary drive assembly, pump housing and filter head assembly can be used on earlier produced engines. Also the latest type liner, plunger, spring, washer and plug for the oil pressure release valve can also be used as a set in the earlier type oil pump housing.

1. It is possible to remove the oil pressure release valve assembly for inspection or renewal purposes without removing the oil pump from the engine but if it is necessary to inspect or check the valve seating it will be necessary to remove the pump first.

2. Undo and remove the plug and washer located at the base of the pump and withdraw the components noting the order in which they were fitted.

3. Wash all the parts in petrol and inspect for signs of wear.

4. Always renew the spring at a major overhaul. Reassemble the release valve components to the oil pump body and fit the retaining plug with a new washer.

25. Oil Pump Removal & Replacement

To remove the oil pump on early produced engines up to numbers 40036435F and 40000002F it is necessary to support the engine and remove the fabricated right-hand engine mounting in order to remove the oil pump. On later produced models using a cast alloy mounting bracket it will not be necessary to remove the bracket. In this case do not carry out paragraphs 7, 9 and 10 of this Section.

1. Undo and remove the banjo bolt securing oil feed pipe to the top drive chain tensioner ((Fig.1.27)), and lift away the nylon mesh oil filter using a piece of stiff wire slightly bent at one end.

2. SC models. Undo and remove the two bolts and spring washers that secure the oil suction and pressure pipe flanges at the side of the cylinder block. Lift away the two 'O' ring seals.

3. TC models. Undo and remove the two bolts and spring washers that secure the oil suction pipe flange to the cylinder block. Undo and remove the two socket lead screws and spring washers that secure the pressure oil pipe to the oil pump. Lift away the two 'O' ring seals. On early produced models the operation is easier once the engine mounting has been removed.

4. Unscrew the external oil filter by hand or if tight using a strap wrench or chisel and place an absorbant cloth under the oil filter to catch any oil draining out. Lift away the rubber sealing ring.

5. Release the oil pressure light switch Lucar connector from its terminal on the switch, (Fig.1.32).

6. On later produced models fitted with alloy casting mounting brackets remove the two set bolts that secure the weir housing to the oil pump. Also remove the oil pressure switch using a suitable open-ended spanner.

7. Early produced engines with fabricated engine mountings: Slacken the set bolt locating the engine tie-rod bottom bracket to the engine compartment front crossmember and also the two bolts at the stabiliser mounting bracket.

8. On later produced engines where there are slotted holes in the stabiliser mounting bracket it is only necessary to slacken off the two locating set bolts.

9. Undo the engine mounting bolt and self locking nut and with-

draw the bolt. Using a garage jack suitably placed or lifting tackle take the weight of the engine from the mounting. The mounting should be completely removed having first undone and removed the two nuts and spring washers from the top of the mounting and the bolt and spring washer from the lower part of the mounting.

10 Note that the engine earth strap and fan disc washer is fitted to the top rear stud.

11 Undo and remove the three nuts and spring washers which retain the oil pump to the rear auxiliary drive housing.

12 If the mounting bracket is left in position it will be necessary to retain the shaft and rotors in the auxiliary drive housing and not to attempt to remove them with the oil pump. The rotors will be extracted after the removal of the pump housing.

13 Ease the pump and rotor rearwards so as to disengage the drive splines and then lift away from the side of the engine.

14 If considered desirable remove the oil pipe/s from the pump.

15 It is recommended that whilst the pump is being inspected or overhauled the oil pressure relief valve be checked to see if the latest type has been fitted to the pump. The reason for this is that the plunger or ball type previously used were liable to stick in operation. Further details may be found in Section 24 of this Chapter.

16 To refit the oil pump first replace the oil pipe/s if previously removed using new 'O' ring oil seals.

17 Place the inner rotor splined shaft into the auxiliary drive housing and outer rotor in the oil pump casing.

18 On the later produced engines with the engine mounting in position the splined shaft and rotors must next be inserted into the auxiliary drive housing prior to offering up the pump housing.

19 Fit the pump assembly using a new 'O' ring oil seal to the auxiliary drive housing, engaging the outer rotor with the inner rotor or pump housing with the outer rotor where applicable and positioning the pump on to the securing studs.

20 Replace the three nuts and spring washers onto the studs and tighten securely.

21 Refit the oil feed pipe from the oil pump to the camshaft chain drive chamber placing a new joint washer on the union. Make sure that the nylon filter is fitted at the chain drive chamber end.

22 TC models. Fit the flexible oil pressure pipe to the pump with a new 'O' ring oil seal and the two special bolts.

23 If the weir housing was removed from the pump refit this next using a new 'O' ring oil seal and secure in position with the two bolts and spring washers.

24 Refit the oil pressure switch and tighten using an open ended spanner.

25 Early models. Refit the right-hand engine mounting bracket and secure in position with the bolt and spring washer at the lower end and the two nuts, spring washer, earth lead and fan disc washer. The earth lead is fitted to the rearmost mounting, and the assembly order for this is as follows:— The eyelet of the earth lead positioned next to the engine mounting followed by the fan disc washer and then the sherardized nut. Note there is no spring washer fitted to this stud. Next lower the engine mounting onto the flexible mounting, insert the mounting bolt and secure with a plain washer and self locking nut.

26 Tighten the engine tie-rod and bracket mounting bolts making sure that the engine is correctly aligned within the engine compartment.

27 Refit a new external oil filter and rubber sealing ring. Details of the type are given in Section 23, paragraph 3.

28 Reconnect the oil pressure switch cable connector to the terminal.

29 SC models. Refit the oil pump suction and delivery pipes to the cylinder block with new 'O' ring oil seals. It will be observed that one of the securing bolts is shorter than the rest and must be placed at the rear of the pressure pipe flange. Replace all four bolts and spring washers and tighten securely.

30 TC models. Refit the oil pump suction pipe to the cylinder block using a new 'O' ring oil seal.

31 Start the engine and check for signs of oil leaks. Finally it will be necessary to top up the engine oil.

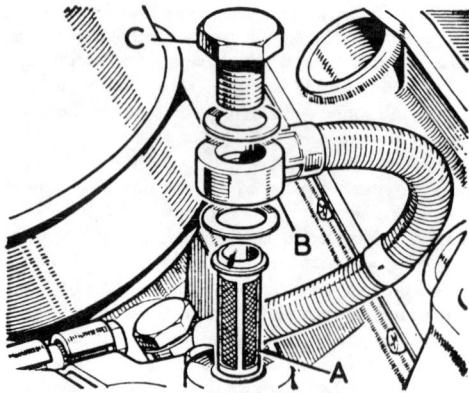

Fig.1.27. COMPONENT PARTS OF NYLON MESH OIL
STRAINER

A Oil strainer
B Banjo
C Bolt

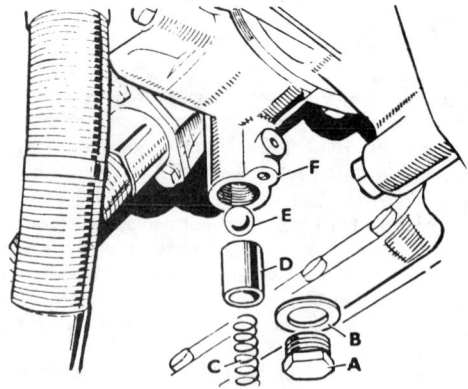

Fig.1.28. OIL PRESSURE RELIEF VALVE — EARLY MODELS

A Retaining plug   D Plunger
B Washer   E Ball valve
C Spring   F Oil pump body

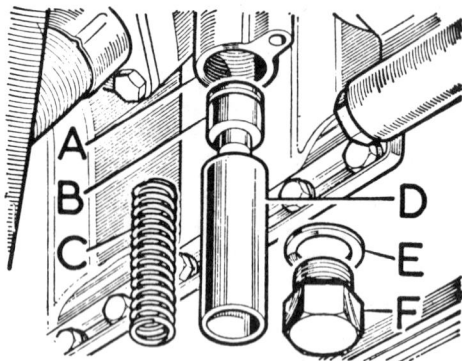

Fig.1.29. OIL PRESSURE RELIEF VALVE — LATER MODELS

A Oil pump body   D Sleeve
B Plunger   E Washer for plug
C Spring   F Plug

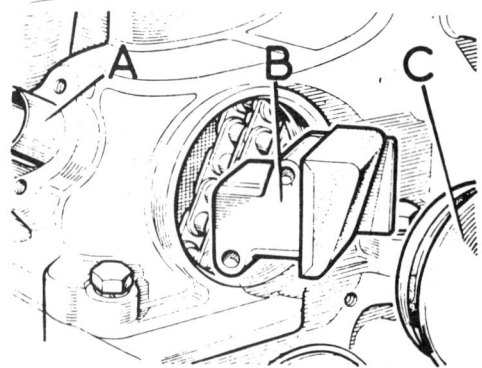

Fig.1.30. REMOVAL OF TOP CHAIN TENSIONER

A Tube   C Cylinder head sealing
B Chain tensioner   plug

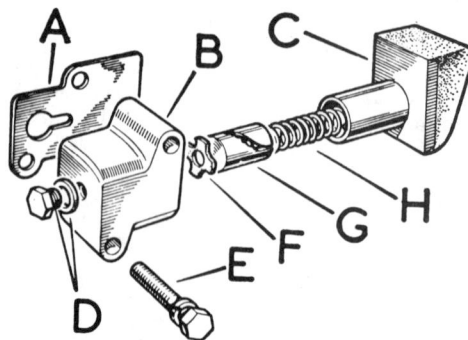

Fig.1.31. CHAIN TENSIONER COMPONENTS

A Backplate   E Securing bolts and washers
B Body   F Rubber washer
C Tensioner pad   G Restraint cylinder
D Plug and washer   H Retaining spring

26. Camshaft Chain Tensioners — Removal

Top Tensioner

1. To gain access to the top tensioner it will be necessary to remove the battery. Disconnect the two electrical cables from the terminal posts and release the battery clamp. Lift away the battery.

2. Using a wide blade screwdriver or a tyre lever very carefully prise the sealing plug and 'O' ring from the cylinder head. This will expose the top chain tensioner.

3. Undo and remove the two set bolts and spring washers that secure the top chain tensioner cover plate to the side of the cylinder head. Lift away the cover plate and joint washer.

4. Make sure that the tube is positioned against the tensioner to prevent the plug or washer entering the sump (Fig.1.30) and with a socket undo and remove the plug and copper washer from the tensioner.

5. Insert a 1/8 inch Allen key into the tensioner and rotate in a clockwise direction until the restraint cylinder is fully retracted into the body.

6. Withdraw the tube from the access hole.

7. Undo and remove the two set bolts and spring washers that retain the top tensioner and back plate in position and carefully lift the tensioner away through the sealing plug hole.

8. Inspect the tensioner as detailed in Section 35 of this Chapter. See paragraph 12 of Bottom Tensioner removal and refitting details about tensioner rattle.

9. To refit the top tensioner it must first be assembled and the restraint cylinder backed off so that the tensioner head is not under the influence of the spring. Insert the 1/8 inch Allen key into the restraint cylinder and turn in a clockwise direction until the cylinder is fully retracted. The tensioner head should now be free. The component parts of the chain tensioner are shown in Fig.1.31.

10 Replace the tensioner and backplate and secure in position with the two set bolts and spring washers.

11 Refit the tube into the access hole and apply tension to the top chain by inserting the Allen key and turning in a clockwise direction until the tensioner head moves forwards under the action of the spring against the chain. DO NOT use any force or turn the Allen key in an anti-clockwise direction.

12 Replace the plug and copper washer to the top tensioner.

13 Place the top tensioner cover plate and joint washer onto its location on the side of the cylinder head and secure with two set bolts and spring washer.

14 Fit a new 'O' ring seal to the sealing plug and apply a little grease to assist seating of the 'O' ring. With a wooden or soft faced hammer tap the plug into position until the 'O' ring is seating in its groove.

15 Refit the oil strainer to the cylinder head (if removed for cleaning. See Section 23 for further information) followed by the pipe union not forgetting to use new sealing washers.

16 Replace the battery and clamp in place. Reconnect the terminals, start the engine and allow to turn for a few minutes. Check for oil leaks.

Bottom Tensioner

1. Before the bottom chain tensioner can be removed it will be necessary to jack up the front of the car and remove the sump. This is a straightforward operation and will present no problems.

2. Drain the engine oil into a container of suitable size.

3. Lift out the oil level dipstick and unscrew the tube nut. The tube may now be lifted away from the side of the sump.

4. If a crankcase breather is fitted it should be removed next. Undo and remove the two securing bolts and copper washers and lift away the breather and joint washer.

5. Undo and remove the two lower bellhousing securing bolts and spring washers.

6. Remove the clutch slave cylinder from the bellhousing and clip locating the flexible pipe to the sump. Support the slave cylinder using a piece of string or wire.

7. There are twenty-six bolts and spring washers that secure the

sump to the underside of the crankcase and these should next be removed. Leave one bolt on each side loose to support the sump and then when all other bolts are free remove the last two bolts and lift away the sump. If a jointing compound has been previously used it may be necessary to break the seal by using a soft faced hammer on the mating flange.

8. Cars fitted with automatic transmission. Make sure that the oil cooler pipes are adequately supported before finally removing the sump.

9. Remove the plug from the bottom chain tensioner and relieve the tension on the bottom chain by inserting an 1/8 inch Allen key and turning in a clockwise direction until the restraint cylinder is fully retracted into the body.

10 Remove the sealing plug and 'O' ring from in front of the bottom tensioner using a wide blade screwdriver or tyre lever.

11 Undo and remove the two securing bolts and spring washer and lift away the bottom tensioner and backplate.

12 If chain tensioner rattle has been experienced on the early produced engines a little rubber pad (F) may be fitted as shown in Fig.1.31.

13 Inspect the tensioner as detailed in Section 35 of this Chapter.

14 To refit the bottom tensioner it must first be assembled and the restraint cylinder backed off so that the tensioner head is not under the influence of the spring. Insert the 1/8 inch Allen key into the restraint cylinder and turn in a clockwise direction until the cylinder is fully retracted. The tensioner lead should now be free

15 Replace the tensioner and backplate and secure in position with the two set bolts and spring washers.

16 Apply tension to the bottom chain by inserting the Allen key and turning in a clockwise direction until the tensioner head moves forwards under the action of the spring against the chain. DO NOT use any force or turn the Allen key in an anti-clockwise direction.

17 Replace the plug and copper washer to the bottom tensioner.

18 Refitting the sump, dipstick tube and crankcase breather is the reverse sequence to removal.

19 Fit a new 'O' ring seal to the sealing plug and apply a little grease to assist seating of the 'O' ring. With a wooden or soft faced hammer tap the plug into position until the 'O' ring is seating in its groove.

20 Lower the car to the ground and refill the sump with oil. Run the engine and check for oil leaks.

27. Examination & Renovation — General

With the engine stripped down and all parts thoroughly cleaned, it is now time to examine everything for wear. The following items should be checked and where necessary renewed or renovated as described in the following sections:

28. Crankshaft — Examination & Renovation

1. Examine the crankpin and main journal surfaces for signs of scoring or scratches. Check the ovality of the crankpins at different positions with a micrometer. If more than 0.001 inch out of round, the crankpin will have to be reground. It will also have to be reground if there are any scores or scratches present. Also check the journals in the same fashion.

2. On highly tuned engines the centre main bearings have been known to break up. It is not always immediately apparent, but slight vibration in an otherwise normally smooth engine and a very slight drop in oil pressure under normal conditions are clues. If the centre main bearings are suspected of failure it should be immediately investigated by dropping the sump and removing the centre main bearing cap. Failure to do this will result in badly scored centre main journals. If it is necessary to regrind the crankshaft and fit new bearings, your local Rover agent or engineering works will be able to decide how much metal to grind off and the correct undersize bearings to be fitted.

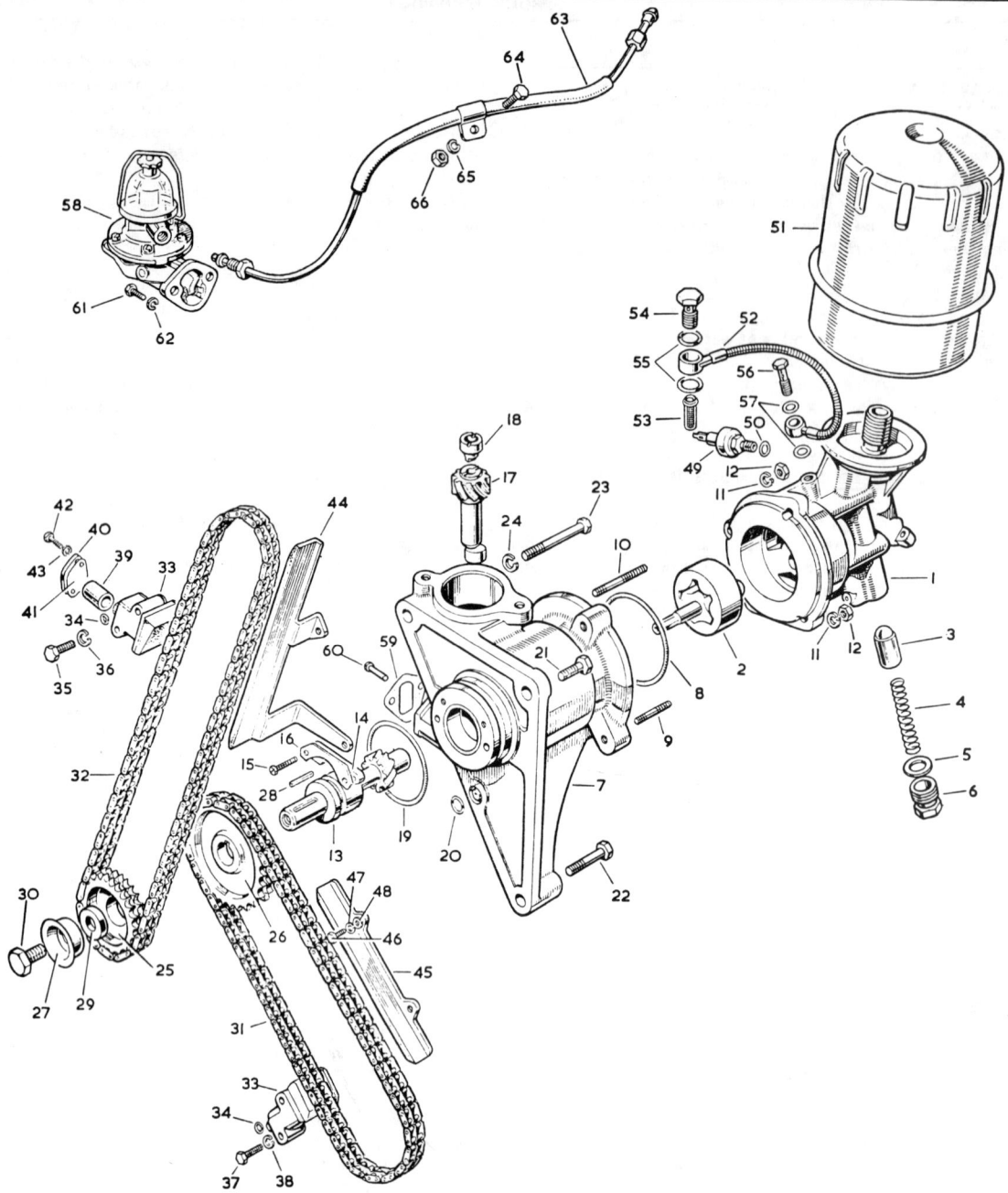

Fig.1.32 CAMSHAFT DRIVE CHAINS & OIL PUMP ASSEMBLIES

1 Oil pump housing and filter head
2 Shaft and rotors complete, for oil pump
3 Plunger and ball
4 Spring
5 Washer
6 Plug
7 Auxiliary drive housing
8 'O' ring, auxiliary drive housing to oil pump
9 Stud, short
10 Stud, long
11 Spring washer
12 Nut
13 Driving shaft for oil pump and distributor
14 Thrust and locking plate for driving shaft
15 Set bolt
16 Locker
17 Driving gear for distributor
18 Driving dog for distributor
19 'O' ring, large
20 'O' ring, small
21 Set bolt
22 Set bolt
23 Set bolt
24 Spring washer
25 Intermediate chainwheel, small, outer
26 Intermediate chainwheel, large, inner
27 Oil thrower for oil pump driving shaft
28 Key
29 Retaining washer
30 Set bolt
31 Driving chain, lower, crankshaft to intermediate wheel
32 Driving chain, upper, intermediate wheel to camshaft
33 Tensioner for driving chains
and fuel pump
34 Sealing washer for chain tensioners
35 Set bolt
36 Spring washer
37 Set bolt
38 Spring washer
39 Tube for chain tensioner, upper
40 Cover plate for chain tensioner, upper
41 Joint washer for cover plate
42 Set bolt
43 Spring washer
44 Vibration damper for driving chain, upper
45 Vibration damper for driving chain, lower
46 Set bolt
47 Spring washer
48 Plain washer
49 Oil pressure switch
50 Joint washer for oil pressure
switch
51 Oil filter
52 Oil feed pipe for upper chain tensioner
53 Oil strainer, in cylinder head, for oil feed pipe
54 Banjo bolt
55 Joint washer
56 Banjo bolt
57 Joint washer
58 Mechanical fuel pump, AC Delco
59 Joint washer for fuel pump
60 Pushrod for fuel pump
61 Set bolt
62 Spring washer
63 Fuel pipe, pump to carburetter
64 Bolt
65 Spring washer
66 Nut

29. Big End & Main Bearings — Examination & Renovation

1. Big end failure is accompanied by a noisy knocking from the crankcase, and a slight drop in oil pressure. Main bearing failure is accompanied by vibration which can be quite severe as the engine speed rises or falls and a drop in oil pressure.

2. Bearings which have not broken up, but are badly worn will give rise to low oil pressure and some vibration. Inspect the big ends, main bearings and thrust washers for signs of general wear, scoring pitting and scratches. The bearings should be matt grey in colour. With lead/indium bearings, should a trace of copper colour be noticed, the bearings are badly worn as the lead bearing metal has worn away to expose the indium underlay. Renew the bearings if they are in this condition or if there is any sign of scoring or pitting.

3. The undersizes available are designed to correspond with the regrind sizes, i.e. 0.010 inch bearings are correct for a crankshaft reground, minus 0.001 inch undersize. The bearings are, in fact, slightly more than the stated undersize as running clearances have been allowed for during their manufacture.

4. Very long engine life can be achieved by changing big end bearings at intervals of 30,000 miles, and main bearings at intervals of 50,000 miles, irrespective of bearing wear. Normally, crankshaft wear is infinitesimal and a change of bearings will ensure mileages of between 100,000 and 120,000 miles before crankshaft regrinding becomes necessary. Crankshafts normally have to be reground because of scoring due to bearing failure.

30. Cylinder Bores — Examination & Renovation

1. The cylinder bores must be examined for taper, ovality, scoring and scratches. Start by carefully examining the top of the cylinder bores. If they are at all worn a very slight ridge will be found on the thrust side. This marks the top of the piston ring travel. The owner will have a good indication of the bore wear prior to dismantling the engine, or removing the cylinder head. Excessive oil consumption accompanied by blue smoke from the exhaust is a sure sign of worn cylinder bores and piston rings.

2. Measure the bore diameter just under the ridge with a micrometer and compare it with the diameter at the bottom of the bore, which is not subject to wear. If the difference between the two measurements is more than 0.006 inch then it will be necessary to fit special piston and rings or to have the cylinders rebored and fit oversize pistons. If no micrometer is available remove the rings from the piston and place the piston in each bore in turn about ¾ inch below the top of the bore. If an 0.010 inch feeler gauge can be slid between the piston and the cylinder wall on the thrust side of the bore then remedial action must be taken.

3. If the bores are slightly worn, but not so badly worn as to justify reboring them, then special oil control rings and pistons can be fitted which will restore compression and stop engine burning oil. Several different types are available and the manufacturers instructions concerning their fitting must be followed closely.

4. If new pistons are being fitted and the bores have not been reground, it is essential to slightly roughen the hard glaze on the sides of the bores with fine glass paper so the new piston rings will have a chance to bed in properly.

31. Pistons & Piston Rings   Examination & Renovation

1. If the old pistons are to be refitted carefully remove the piston rings and then thoroughly clean them. Take particular care to clean out the piston ring grooves. At the same time do not scratch the aluminium in any way. If new rings are to be fitted to the old pistons then the top ring should be stepped so as to clear the ridge left in the bore above the previous top ring. If a normal but oversize new ring is fitted, it will hit the ridge and break, because the new ring will not have worn in the same way as the old one, which will have

worn in unison with the ridge.

2. Before fitting the rings on the pistons each should be inserted approximately 3 inches down the cylinder bore and the gap measured with the feeler gauge. This should be between the limits given in the engine specifications at the beginning of this Chapter. It is essential that the gap should be measured at the bottom of the ring travel, as if it is measured at the top of a worn bore and gives a perfect fit, it could easily seize at the bottom. If the ring gap is too small rub the ends of the ring with a very fine file until the gap, when fitted, is correct. To keep the rings square in the bore for measurement, line each up in turn by inserting an old piston in the bore upside down about 3 inches. Remove the piston and measure the piston ring gap.

3. When fitting new pistons and rings to a rebored engine the piston ring gap can be measured at the top of the bore as the bore will not now taper. It is unnecessary to measure the side clearance in the piston ring grooves with the rings fitted as the groove dimensions are accurately machined during manufacture. When fitting new oil control rings to old pistons it may be necessary to have the grooves widened by machining to accept the new wider rings. In this instance the manufactuer's representative will make this quite clear and will supply the address to which the pistons must be sent for machining.

32. Camshaft & Camshaft Bearings — Examination & Renovation

1. On all engines the camshaft bearings are of similar material to that used for the crankshaft bearings and therefore by referring to section 28 full information will be found.

2. The camshaft itself should show no signs of wear, but, if very slight scoring on the cams is noticed, the score marks can be removed by very gently rubbing with a very fine emery cloth. The greatest care should be taken to keep the cam profile smooth.

33. Valves & Valve Seats — Examination & Renovation

1. Examine the heads of the valves for pitting and burning, especially the heads of the exhaust valves. The valve seating should be examined at the same time. If the pitting on valve and seat is very slight, the marks can be removed by grinding the seats and valves together with coarse, and then fine, valve grinding paste. Where bad pitting has occured to the valve seats it will be necessary to re-cut them and fit new valves. If the valve seats are so worn that they cannot be re-cut, then it will be necessary to fit new valve seat inserts. These latter two jobs should be entrusted to the local Rover agent or engineering works. In practice it is very seldom that the seats are so badly worn that they require renewal. Normally, it is the exhaust valve that is too badly worn for replacement, and the owner can easily purchase a new set of valves and match them to the seats by valve grinding.

2. Valve grinding is carried out as follows:—
    Smear a trace of coarse carborundum paste on the seat face and apply a suction grinder tool to the valve head. With a semi-rotary motion, grind the valve head to its seat, lifting the valve occasionally to redistribute the grinding paste (photo). When a dull matt even surface finish is produced on both the valve seat and the valve, wipe off the paste and repeat the process with fine carborundum paste, lifting and turning the valve to redistribute the paste as before. A light spring placed under the valve head will greatly ease this operation. When a smooth, unbroken ring of light grey matt finish is produced, on both valve and valve seat faces, the grinding operation is completed.

3. Scrape away all carbon from the valve head and valve stems. Carefully clean away every trace of grinding compound, taking great care to leave none in the ports or in the valve guides. Clean the valves and valve seats with a paraffin soaked rag, then a clean rag, and finally, if an air line is available, blow the valves, valve guides and valve ports clean.

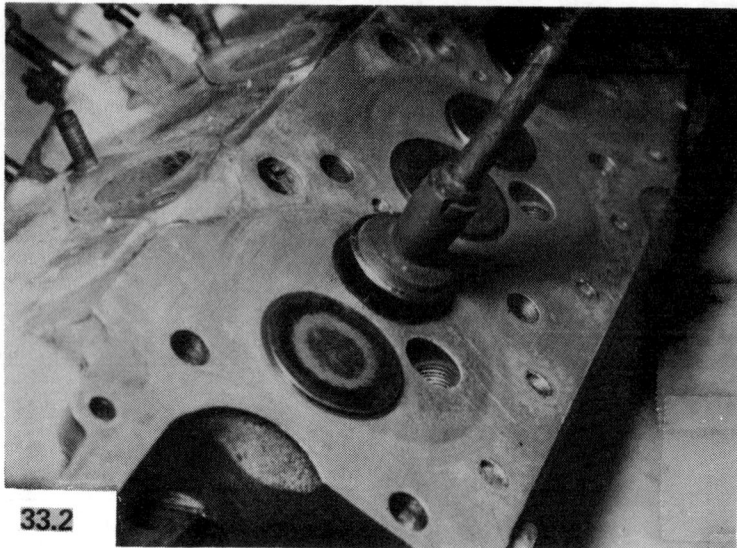

33.2

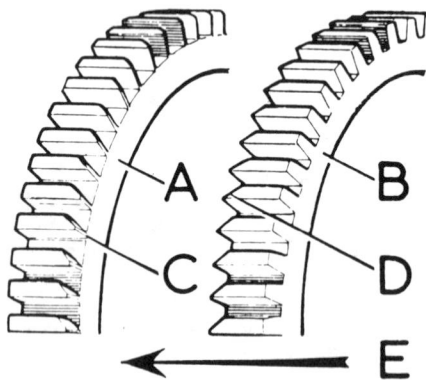

Fig.1.33. CORRECT FITTING OF STARTER RING GEAR ONTO DRIVE PLATE (AUTOMATIC TRANSMISSION MODELS)

A Starter ring assembly. All RHD models, LHD modesl up to engine serial number 40501161G.
B Starter ring assembly. LHD models only from engine serial number 40501162G onwards.
C Lead at rear of teeth
D Lead at front of teeth
E To engine

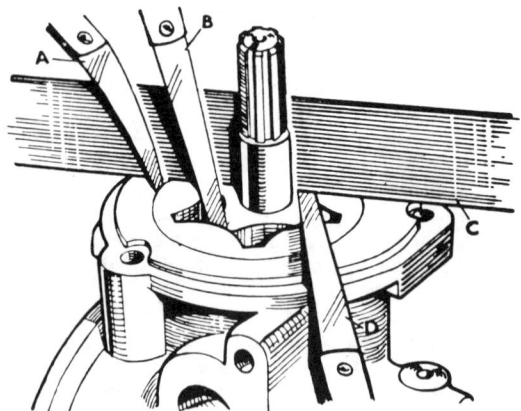

Fig.1.34. CORRECT METHOD OF CHECKING OIL PUMP

A 0.010 in. C Straight edge
B 0.006 in. D 0.005 in.

34. Camshaft Drive Gears & Chain — Examination

1. Examine the teeth in the crankshaft, camshaft and auxiliary drive gearwheels for wear. Each tooth forms an inverted 'V' with the gearwheel periphery, and if worn, the side of each tooth under tension will be slightly concave in shape, when compared with the other side of the tooth, i.e. one side of the inverted 'V' will be concave when compared with the other. If any sign of wear is present the gearwheel must be renewed.
2. Examine the links of the chains for side slackness and renew the chain if any slackness is noticeable when compared with a new chain. It is a sensible precaution to renew the chain about 30,000 miles and at a lesser mileage if the engine is stripped down for a major overhaul. The actual rollers on a very badly worn chain may be slightly grooved.

35. Camshaft Chain Tensioners — Examination & Renovation

1. If the timing chains are badly worn it is more than likely that the tensioner will be too.
2. Examine the side of the tensioner that bears against the chain and renew it if it is grooved or ridged. See also Section 34 for further details.

36. Camshaft Chain Vibration Dampers — Examination

1. The rate of wear of a vibration damper is usually less than that for a chain tensioner but is well worthwhile fitting a new vibration damper if new tensioners are being fitted.
2. Inspect the pad face that is in contact with the chain and if it shows signs of grooving then it should be renewed.
3. Do not forget that there are two dampers, one for each of the two chains.

37. Flywheel Starter Ring — Examination & Renovation

1. If the teeth of the starter ring gear fitted to the flywheel of a manual gearbox engine installation are badly worn or if some are missing, then it will be necessary to remove the starter ring. This is achieved by splitting the ring with a cold chisel. The greatest care should be taken not to damage the flywheel during this process. Note which way round the teeth face.
2. To fit a new ring heat it gently and evenly with an oxyacetylene flame until a temperature of approximately 350° is reached. This is indicated by a light metallic blue surface colour. With the ring at this temperature, fit it to the flywheel with the teeth facing the correct way round. The ring should be tapped gently down onto its register and left to cool naturally when the shrinkage of the metal on cooling will ensure that it is a secure and permanent fit. Great care must be taken not to overheat the ring, as if this happens the temper of the ring will be lost.
3. If it is necessary to remove the starter ring gear from the drive plate as fitted to cars with automatic transmission undo and remove the ¼ inch UNF set bolts, locking tabs and reinforcing plates.
4. To refit a new ring gear make sure that the bolts and threads are clean by washing in methylated spirits and apply a little 'Loctite' Grade AVV to the threads. Fit new tab washers and tighten the bolts in a diagonal manner to a torque wrench setting of 10 lb/ft. The ring gear should be fitted the correct way round as shown in Fig.1.33.
5. It should be noted that on later models the drive gear is fitted with reinforcing plates and special thin washers. The new plates are retained by four bolts fixing the drive plate to the starter ring at the balancing holes.
6. Reinforcement plates are not fitted to cars destined for the export market.

38. Oil Pump — Examination & Renovation

1. Thoroughly clean all the component parts in petrol and then check the rotor endfloat and lobe clearance in the following manner:
2. Position the outer rotor in the pump and place a straight edge of a ruler 'C', Fig.1.34, across the joint face of the pump. Measure the gap between the bottom of the straight edge and the top of the rotors with a feeler gauge (D). If the measurement exceeds 0.005 inch a new rotor assembly or housing should be fitted
3. Fit the inner rotor to the above assembly and check the clearance between the lobes of the inner and outer rotors using a feeler gauge (B). This clearance should not exceed 0.006 inch, which if exceeded, a new rotor assembly should be fitted.
4. Next assemble the outer rotor in the pump body and check the clearance between the rotor periphery and the body using feeler gauges (A). This clearance should not exceed 0.010 inch.
5. If any of the clearances mentioned above are exceeded new rotors should be fitted as a pair and a new body fitted as applicable otherwise the performance of the lubrication system will be affected.

39. Cylinder Head — Decarbonisation

1. This can be carried out with the engine either in or out of the car. With the cylinder head off, carefully remove, with a wire brush and blunt scraper, all traces of carbon deposits from the combustion area and the ports. The valve head, stems and valve guides should also be freed from any carbon deposits. Wash the combustion spaces and ports down with petrol and scrape the cylinder head surface free of any foreign matter with the side of a steel rule or a similar article.
2. Clean the pistons and top of the cylinder bores. If the pistons are still in the block it is essential that great care is taken to ensure that no carbon gets into the cylinder bores as this could scratch the cylinder walls or cause damage to the piston and rings. To ensure that this does not happen, first turn the crankshaft so that two of the pistons are at the top of their bores. Stuff rag into the other two bores or seal them off with paper and masking tape. The waterways should also be covered with small pieces of masking tape to prevent particles of carbon entering the cooling system and damaging the water pump.
3. There are two schools of thought as to how much carbon should be removed from the piston crown. One school recommends that a ring of carbon should be left round the edge of the piston and on the cylinder bore as an aid to reduce low oil consumption. Although this is probably true for early engines with worn bores, on later engines the thought of the second school can be applied, which is that for effective decarbonisation all traces of carbon should be removed.
4. If all traces of carbon are to be removed, press a little grease into the gap between the cylinder walls and the two pistons which are to be worked upon. With a blunt scraper carefully scrape away the carbon from the piston crown, taking great care not to scratch the aluminium. Also scrape the carbon away from the surrounding lip of the cylinder wall. When all the carbon has been removed, scrape away the grease which will now be contaminated with carbon particles, taking care not to press any into the bores. To assist prevention of carbon build up the piston crown can be polished with a metal polish such as Brasso. Remove the rags or masking tape from the other two cylinders and turn the crankshaft so that the two pistons which were at the bottom are now at the top. Place rag or masking tape in the cylinders which have been decarbonised and proceed as before.
5. If a ring of carbon is going to be left round the piston this can be helped by inserting an old piston ring into the top of the bore to rest on the piston and ensure that carbon is not accidentally removed. Check that there are no particles in the cylinder bores. Decarbonising is now complete.

43.2

43.3

43.5

43.8

43.9

43.10

43.11

43.12

43.15

43.16

43.17

43.20

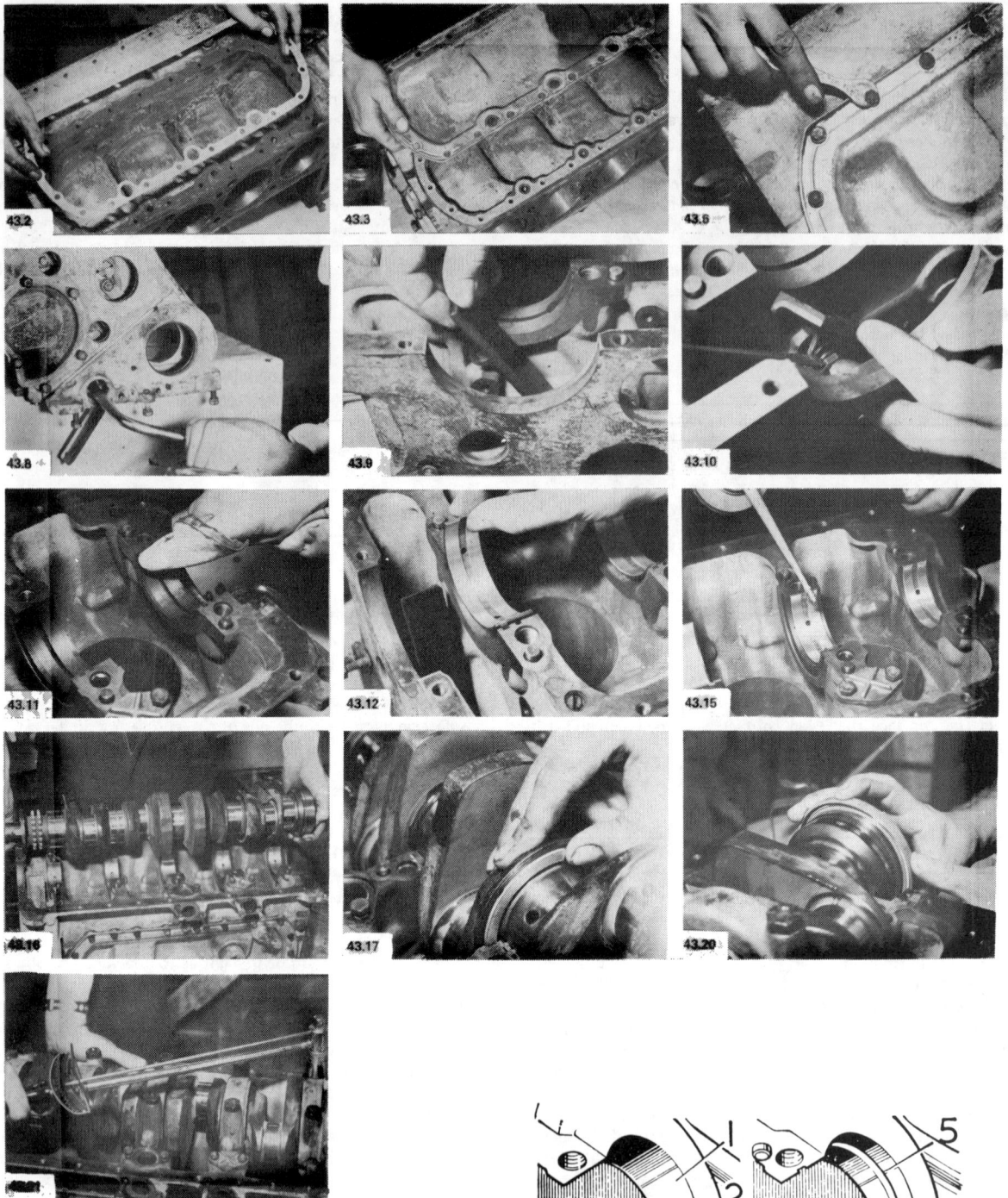

Fig.1.35. IDENTIFICATION OF CENTRE BEARING CAP &
MAIN BEARING

A—Early-type centre bearing cap and main bearing
1 No oil groove in cylinder block
2 One large oil hole, no groove in top main bearing
3 No oil holes, no groove in bottom main bearing
4 No oil groove in main bearing cap

B—Later-type centre bearing cap and main bearing
5 Oil groove in cylinder block
6 Oil groove and holes in top and bottom main bearings
7 Oil groove in main bearing cap

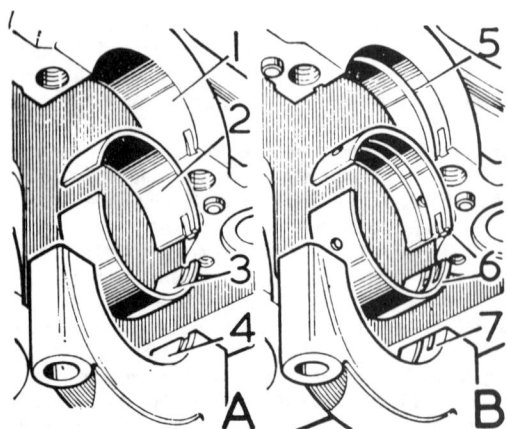

40. Valve Guides — Examination & Renovation

Examine the valve guides internally for wear. If the valves are a very loose fit in the guides and there is the slightest suspicion of lateral rocking using a new valve, then new guides will have to be fitted.

The author recommends that if new valve guides are necessary then this be left to the local Rover agent who will have the facilities to extract the old ones and for inserting the new ones.

41. Sump — Examination & Renovation

It will be seen that the sump has two shaped internal baffle plates which should be removed. Undo the small bolts and remove together with the spring washers. Lift out the two baffles.

Thoroughly wash out the sump and also the baffle plates and wipe dry using a clean non-fluffy rag.

Inspect the casing for signs of cracking which could be caused by incorrect positioning of a jack or hitting a high object on the road surface. If a crack is evident, it may be repaired by welding using the services of a firm of specialists, otherwise obtain a new sump casting.

Check that none of the threads have been stripped and the washer faces are free of deep scoring which, if evident, should be filed flat.

42. Engine Reassembly — General

1. To ensure maximum life with minimum trouble from a rebuilt engine, not only must everything be correctly assembled but all parts must be spotlessly clean; the oilways must be clear, locking washers and spring washers must always be fitted where indicated and all bearing and other working surfaces must be thoroughly lubricated during assembly. Before assembly begins renew any bolts or studs the threads of which are in any way damaged, and wherever possible use a new spring washer.
2. Make sure that the water jackets are completely free of rust and sediment as otherwise any build up especially in the corners can cause localised overheating.
3. Apart from your normal tools, a supply of clean rag, an oil can filled with engine oil (an empty plastic detergent bottle thoroughly cleaned and washed out, will invariably do just as well), a new supply of assorted spring washers, a set of new gaskets, and preferably a torque spanner, should be collected together.

43. Cylinder Block Side Covers & Crankshaft Refitting

1. Make sure that the mating faces of the side covers and the cylinder block are really clean and free of old gasket or jointing compound by scraping with a sharp knife and coat both faces with a smear of 'Wellseal'.
2. Select the correct side cover gasket and carefully place in position on the side of the cylinder block (photo).
3. Place one side cover in position on the gasket. Note that the right-hand side cover has the drain tap in the side whilst the left-hand one does not (photo).
4. Screw in the 22 special head screws but do not tighten fully yet.
5. Note that there are three large holes in each of the side covers. These accommodate the special shaped studs for the engine mounting brackets. On the left-hand side plate the two forward holes are used for the studs and the third accommodates the blanking stud, whereas on the right-hand side plate the two rear holes are used. Using two nuts tighten the studs making sure that the larger diameter seats inside the hole in the side plate. It may be necessary to tap the side plate slightly to locate the holes correctly. When both studs are in position tighten the blanking plug and then tighten the locknuts securely.

6. Working in a diagonal manner tighten the 22 securing bolts.
7. Repeat the foregoing procedure for the second engine side cover.
8. Move the cylinder block to one side of the back and with the camshaft chain chest overhanging and locate the upper chain vibration damper pad inside the chest. Secure with bolts and spring washers but do not tighten fully (photo).
9. Place the lower chain vibration damper in position (photo).
10 The lowermost bolt is a little difficult to start so use the fingers and a screwdriver first before screwing in with a socket.
11 Using a clean rag wipe all the crankshaft main bearing locations in the crankcase and also the end caps. Remember that the end caps are matched and must not be mixed up although they are marked during manufacture to assist correct matching (photo).
12 Place the new bearing half shells in position in the crankcase making sure that the tab on the back of each shell correctly engages in the locating groove; the plain shell correctly engages in the locating groove; the plain shell bearing with no oil drillings or oilway fits in the centre main bearing position (photo).
13 If the old main bearing shells are to be re-used they should be refitted if they are virtually new. Make quite sure that there are no signs of wear or scoring. It should be noted that from engines having a serial number with a suffix G and onwards have a modified centre main bearing cap so that a common bearing can be used in all positions. The two types may be seen in Fig.1.35.
14 With the five upper bearing shells securely in place, fit the five lower shell bearings to their caps ensuring that the right shell goes into the right cap if the old bearings are being refitted.
15 Generously lubricate the crankshaft journals and the upper and lower main bearing shells (photo).
16 Carefully lower the crankshaft into position and rotate several times to ensure that it is free to rotate (photo).
17 Wipe the crankshaft thrust washers and slide the two upper half washers, milled sides (oil grooves) outwards into their locations on the second to rear main bearing. This is easily done by rotating the crankshaft in the direction towards the main bearing tab (so that the main bearing shells do not slide out). At the same time feed the thrust washers into thin locations with their oil grooves outwards away from the bearing (photo).
18 Fit all but the rearmost main bearing caps in position making sure that they locate properly. The mating surfaces must be spotlessly clean or the caps will not seat correctly. As the bearing caps are assembled to the cylinder block and then line bored during manufacture, it is essential that they are returned to the same positions from which they were removed.
19 Refit the main bearing cap bolts.
20 Well lubricate the rear oil seal and very carefully slide in position on the rear of the crankshaft and crankcase. The lip should face inwards (photo).
21 Fit the rear main bearing cap and bolts and tighten all the main bearing cap bolts to a torque wrench setting of 65 lb/ft. (photo).
22 Test the crankshaft for freedom of rotation. Should it be very stiff to turn or possess high spots a most careful inspection must be made, preferably by a qualified mechanic with a micrometer to get to the cause of the trouble. It is very seldom that any trouble of this nature will be experienced when fitting the crankshaft.
23 Check the crankshaft end float with a feeler gauge measuring the longitudinal movement between the crankshaft and a thrust washer. End float should be between 0.002 and 0.006 inch. If end float is excessive, oversize thrust washers can be fitted.

44. Piston & Connecting Rod - Reassembly

1. If the same pistons are being used, then they must be mated to the same connecting rod with the same gudgeon pin. If new pistons are being fitted it does not matter which connecting rod they are used with. The gudgeon pins are supplied fitted to the pistons and should not be interchanged.
2. All engines use fully floating gudgeon pins which in theory are a push fit at 68° but this is not always as simple as it seems.

44.3

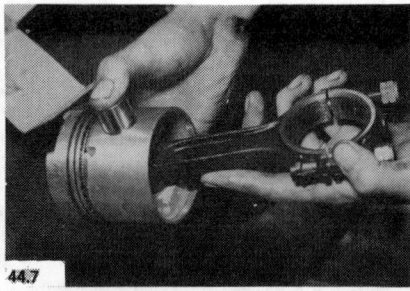

44.7

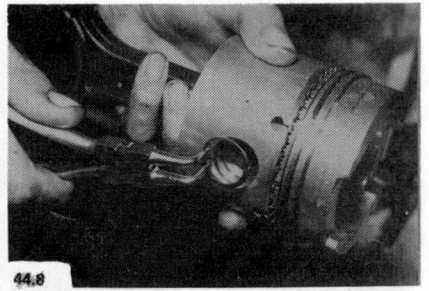

44.8

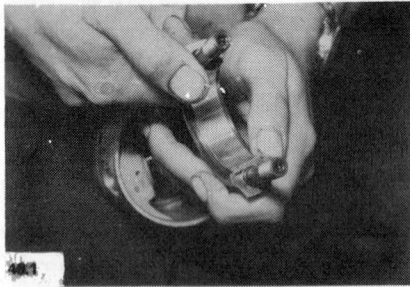

46.1

46.5

46.7

46.8

46.9

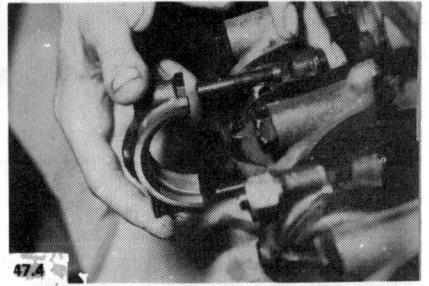

47.4

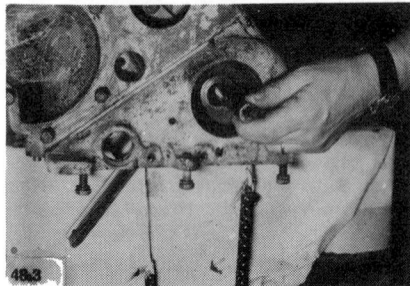

48.3

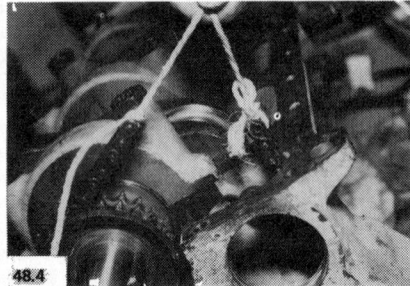

48.4

48.5

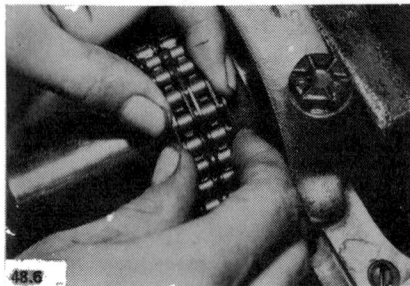

48.6

49.1

49.2

49.3

49.4

3. Because aluminium alloy, when hot expands more than steel, the gudgeon pin may be a very tight fit in the piston when they are cold. To avoid any damage to the piston it is best to heat it in boiling water when the pin will slide in easily (photo).
4. Lay the correct piston adjacent to each connecting rod and remember that the same rod and piston must go back into the same bore. If new pistons are being used it is necessary to ensure only that the right connecting rod is placed in each bore.
5. Fit a gudgeon pin circlip in position at one end of the gudgeon pin hole in the piston using a pair of circlip pliers.
6. Locate the connecting rod in the piston with the arrows and number stamped on the piston crown towards the front and the big end numbers to the left-hand side of the engine as shown in Fig.1.36.
7. Slide the gudgeon pin through the hole in the piston and through the connecting rod little end until it rests against the previously fitted circlip (photo). NOTE: The pin should be a push fit.
8. Fit the second circlip in position (photo). Repeat this procedure for all four pistons and connecting rods.
9. Where special oil control rings are being fitted, should the position of the top ring be the same as the position of the top ring on the old piston, ensure that a groove has been machined on the top of the new ring so no fouling occurs between the unworn portion at the top of the bore and the piston ring when the latter is at the top of its stroke.

45. Piston Ring — Replacement

1. Check that the piston ring grooves and oilways are thoroughly clean and unblocked. Piston rings must always be fitted over the head of the piston and never from the bottom.
2. The easiest method to use when fitting rings is to wrap a 0.020 inch feeler gauge round the top of the piston and place the rings one at a time, starting with the bottom oil control ring, over the feeler gauge.
3. The feeler gauge, complete with ring, can then be slid down the piston over the other piston ring grooves until the correct groove is reached. The piston ring is then slid gently off the feeler gauge into the groove.
4. An alternative method is to fit the rings by holding them slightly open with the thumbs and both of the index fingers. This method requires a steady hand and great care as it is easy to open the ring too much and break it.
5. Rings marked with a 'T' must have this side fitted to the top.

46. Piston & Connecting Rod Replacement

1. Remove the connecting rod big end caps and place in order so that they are not interchanged. Wipe the connecting rod half of the big end bearing cap and the underside of the shell bearing, and fit the shell bearing in position with its locating tongue engaged with the corresponding cut-out in the rod (photo).
2. If the old bearings are nearly new and are being refitted then ensure that they are replaced in their correct locations on the connecting rods.
3. The pistons complete with connecting rods are now ready for refitting to the cylinder bores.
4. With a wad of clean rag wipe the cylinder bores clean and then well lubricate with engine grade oil.
5. The pistons, complete with connecting rods, are fitted to their bores from the top of the block (photo).
6. As each piston is inserted into its bore ensure that it is the correct piston/connecting rod assembly for that particular bore; that the connecting rod is the right way round; and that the front of the piston as marked by arrows on the crown is towards the front of the bore, i.e. towards the front of the engine.
7. The piston will slide down the bore only as far as the oil control ring (photo).
8. Lubricate the piston rings and compress the piston rings in a

special clamp (photo). If a proper piston ring clamp is not available then a suitable jubilee clip does the job very well.
9. Gently tap the crown of the piston with a wooden or plastic hammer, preferably with one firm movement, until the piston rings are all in the bore (photo). If movement suddenly stops and the piston feels firm withdraw the piston from the bore and refit the piston ring clamp as this means that one of the rings has not been sufficiently compressed.

47. Connecting Rod to Crankshaft Reassembly

1. Wipe clean the connecting rod bearing cap and back of the shell bearing and fit the shell bearing in position ensuring that the locating tongue at the back of the bearing engages with the locating groove in the connecting rod cap.
2. Generously lubricate the crankpin journals with engine oil, and turn the crankshaft so that the crankpin is in the most advantageous position for the connecting rods to be drawn onto it.
3. Push the piston further down the bore and guide the connecting rod half bearing into position on the crankpin.
4. Make sure the big end bearing cap is the correct way round relative to the connecting rod and slide on over the two bolts (photo). They are in fact numbered on the left-hand side.
5. Fit new connecting rod self-locking nuts and tighten to a torque wrench setting of 30 lb/ft.
6. Using feeler gauges, check that the connecting rod end float is between 0.004 and 0.010 inch.

48. Camshaft Lower Drive Chain — Refitting

1. Fit the crankshaft front oil thrower with the flange facing outwards. This may be seen in photo 48:4.
2. Feed the two ends of a piece of string over the crankshaft sprocket and down through the drive chain chest until the ends appear below the cylinder head mating face. Select the lower chain and tie the ends onto the two ends of the string.
3. Obtain a piece of metal rod about 7/8 inch diameter and 6 inches long. Insert the intermediate chainwheel cluster with the larger diameter towards number 1 cylinder and allow to remain in its approximate position with the metal rod. Make sure that the string is on the outer circumference of the chainwheel (photo). It should be noted that on early produced engines two separate chainwheels were fitted but on later engines a single two track chainwheel was fitted.
4. Pull on the string so drawing the chain upwards until the ends appear by the crankshaft sprocket (photo).
5. Remove the string and allow the ends of the chain to engage on the crankshaft sprocket. Insert the joining link from the front (photo).
6. Refit the joining link side member and finally secure with the shaped spring clip with the open ends trailing in the normal direction of rotation of the chain (photo).

49. Engine Backplate, Flywheel — Refitting

1. Make sure that the mating faces of the rear of the cylinder block and the engine backplate are clean and place the backplate in position. Secure with four setscrews and spring washers tightening in a diagonal manner (photo).
2. Wipe the mating faces of the crankshaft and flywheel and place the flywheel in position. It will only fit one way because of a dowel in the end of the crankshaft (photo).
3. This photo shows the dowel hole in the flywheel.
4. Replace the special plate aligning the notch with the dowel hole and lightly secure with the eight bolts (photo).
5. Tighten the flywheel securing bolts to a torque wrench setting of 120 lb/ft.

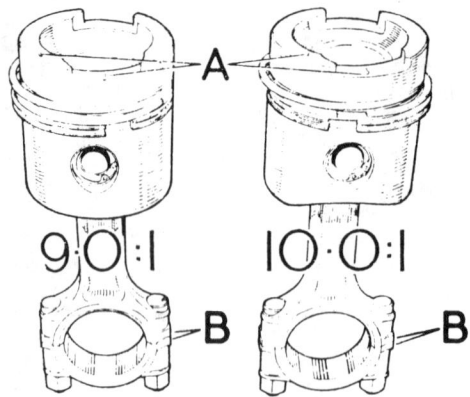

Fig.1.36. PISTON IDENTIFICATION & MATCHING TO CONNECTING ROD
A Arrows and number to front
B Big end numbers to left-hand side

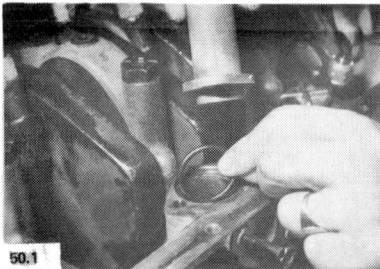

50.1

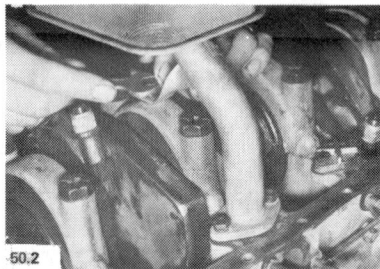

50.2

50.3

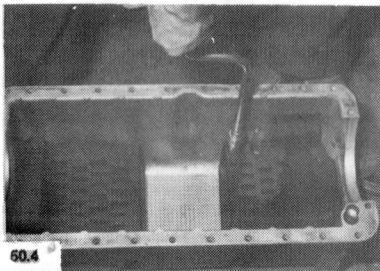

50.4

50.5

50.6

50.7

50.8

51.2

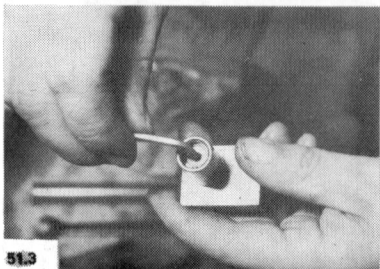

51.3

51.4

51.5

6. Note that on cars fitted with automatic transmission a starter ring gear and drive plate are used instead of a flywheel. In this case there is an additional spacer to be used, its location being shown in Fig.1.25. Make sure that the drive plate is fitted the correct way round.

50. Engine Sump -- Refitting

1. Wipe the mating faces of the crankcase and the oil strainer and fit a new 'O' ring oil seal to its location in the crankcase (photo).
2. Lower the oil strainer into position and secure with two setscrews and spring washers. There is a little bracket which is secured to the main bearing end cap with a further setscrew and spring washer (photo).
3. The baffle plates should have been previously removed from inside the sump for cleaning purposes so now they should be refitted. This photo shows their locations relative to the sump.
4. Secure the baffle plates to the sump using setscrews and spring washers. Carefully tighten in a diagonal manner (photo). Do not forget the little setscrew that secures an extension of the right-hand baffle to the side of the sump.
5. Carefully fit the oil seal to rear main bearing end cap (photo).
6. Place the front oil seal over the nose of the crankshaft and push into position on the front of the camshaft drive chain chest (photo).
7. Wipe the mating faces of the sump and crankcase and apply a little 'Wellseal' to the two faces. Carefully lower the sump into position on the crankcase (photo).
8. Replace the 26 setscrews and spring washers. Note that four longer bolts are used at the locations nearest to the crankshaft. There is a little clip which is retained by the setscrew to the right of the socket seen in the photo. Do not forget to refit it. Tighten the setscrews in a diagonal manner taking care not to overtighten as the threads are easily stripped.

51. Camshaft Upper Drive Chain, Auxiliary Drive & Tensioners – Refitting

1. With the help of an assistant invert the engine and allow it to rest on a flat surface on the underside of the sump.
2. Replace the upper drive chain tensioner body and secure with the two setscrews and spring washers (photo).
3. Using a small Allen key wind in the tensioner pad spring and automatic adjuster until the spring is fully tensioned (photo). Refit the tensioner pad and automatic adjuster assembly to the chain tensioner body.
4. Refit the upper chainwheel support plate and secure with three setscrews and spring washers (photo).
5. Tighten the upper chain vibration pad mounting setscrews and spring washers (photo). In this photo it will be seen that the intermediate chainwheel has now been secured in place with string in place of the previously used metal rod.
6. Mount the camshaft drive chainwheel onto the chainwheel support and temporarily secure with a nut and plain washer.
7. Fit the smaller diameter intermediate chainwheel into the upper chain and place the chain onto the camshaft drive chainwheel (photo).
8. Refer to Fig.1.18, and rotate the crankshaft until the keyway is in the position indicated. The pointer mounted on the engine back-plate should line up with the EP mark on the flywheel (photo).
9. Rotate the intermediate gear cluster until the keyways are in line as shown in Fig.1.18. For this it is just possible to disengage the lower chain and rotate the intermediate gear until the keyway is correctly positioned (photo).
10 Make sure that the driving shaft for the oil pump and distributor is correctly positioned in the auxiliary drive housing. Wipe the mating faces of the rear of the camshaft drive chain chest and auxiliary drive housing clean.
11 Place the key in its location on the drive shaft and carefully insert the drive shaft into the intermediate chainwheel cluster.
12 Secure the auxiliary drive housing in position with five setscrews and spring washers. Note that setscrews of different lengths are used. Tighten the setscrews fully.
13 On early engines assemble the retaining washer (29), Fig.1.30, oil thrower (27) and set bolt (30) to the front face of the intermediate chainwheel cluster. Later engines used the plain retaining washer and set bolt (photo). Tighten the set bolt to a torque wrench setting of 80 lb/ft.
14 The next item to refit is the lower drive chain tensioner. Refer to paragraph 51.3 and tension the spring in the adjuster. Insert the pad and adjuster assembly into the body of the chain tensioner (photo).
15 Remove the adjuster access hole blanking plug (photo).
16 Tie some strong string around the chain tensioner assembly as shown in this photo, insert the small Allen key into the adjuster and release the spring tension. The string will stop the adjuster assembly flying apart (photo). Refit the blanking plug and locking tab washer. Tie a further piece of string onto the adjuster so that if dropped into the sump it can be easily recovered.
17 Insert the adjuster into the access hole in the front of the camshaft drive chain chest and secure with two setscrews and spring washers. It is recommended that the lower setscrew is fitted first and then the upper one can be positioned using a screwdriver to move the adjuster body as necessary until the holes are in line. Do not tighten the setscrews yet (photo).
18 Cut the string and pull it away from the adjuster The setscrews may now be fully tightened.
19 Adjust the lower chain vibration damper position using a long feeler gauge to give a clearance of between 0.002 and 0.010 inch between the pad and timing chain. Tighten the securing bolts to a torque wrench setting of 10 lb/ft.
20 Fit new 'O' rings to all the timing chest sealing plugs, apply a little grease and using a hammer and block of wood tap the plugs into position. Insert the plugs only far enough for the 'O' ring to locate in the internal groove (photo).

52. Water Pump & Crankshaft Pulley – Refitting

1. Make sure that the mating faces of the water pump and cylinder block are clean and free of old gasket or jointing compound. Apply a little 'Wellseal' to both surfaces.
2. Fit a new gasket onto the water pump (photo).
3. Position the water pump onto the front face of the cylinder block and secure in position with the setscrews and spring washers. Note that setscrews of different lengths are used.
4. Lubricate the outer face of the crankshaft pulley which runs in the front oil seal and carefully refit the crankshaft pulley making sure that it fits well onto the key in the crankshaft (photo).
5. Replace the retaining bolt and washer and tighten to a torque wrench setting of 150 lb/ft. This is very tight but necessary so if it is not possible to borrow a torque wrench apply a little Loctite to the threads and tighten as much as possible

53. Engine Mountings, Dynamo, Oil Pump & Pipes – Refitting

1. Provided that the engine mounting studs were correctly positioned as detailed in Section 43 the engine mounting refitting will present no problems.
2. Make sure that the locknut on the rear blanking plug is very tight otherwise water leaks can occur at this point (photo).
3. Refit the left-hand mounting first and secure in the two studs with nuts and spring washers. Do not forget to replace the bolt and spring washer on the lower end of the mounting.
4. Repeat the previous paragraph for the right-hand mounting.
5. Replace the dynamo mounting bracket and secure with two bolts and plain spring washers.
6. Refit the dynamo to the mounting bracket but do not tighten yet.
7. If the heat shield was removed from the dynamo this should be

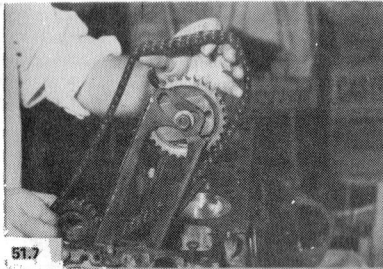
51.7

51.8

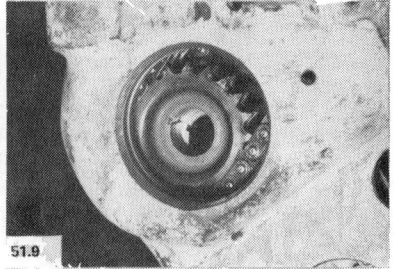
51.9

51.13

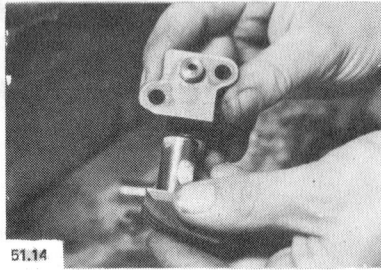
51.14

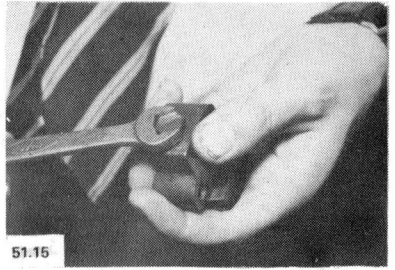
51.15

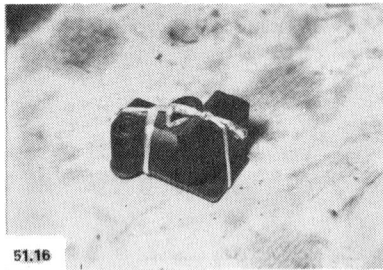
51.16

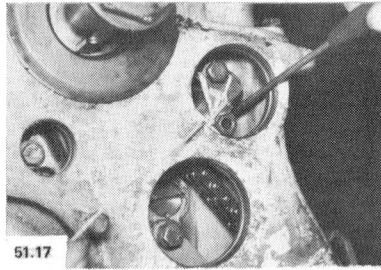
51.17

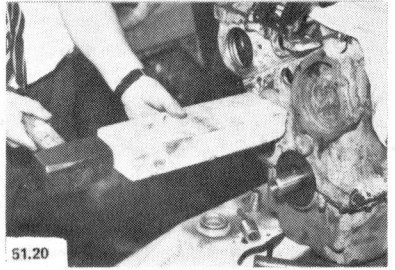
51.20

52.2

52.3

52.4

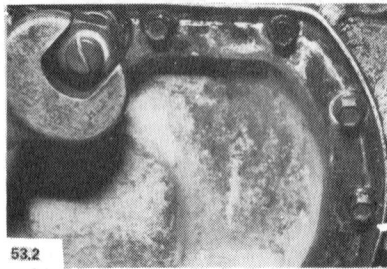
53.2

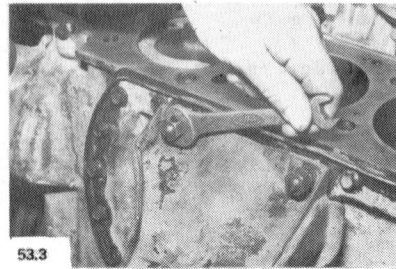
53.3

replaced next.

8. Reconnect the dynamo upper mounting to the adjustment link (photo).

9. Wipe the oil pump outer rotor and the inner rotor and shaft to make sure that there is no dirt at all on any of the precision machined faces. Also wipe the faces of the auxiliary drive housing and oil pump body.

10 Carefully ease the oil pump inner and outer rotors into mesh with the auxiliary drive shaft (photo). Lubricate the inner and outer rotors with clean engine oil.

11 Refit the oil pump body over the outer rotor and studs and secure in position with nuts and spring washers (photo).

12 Wipe the mating faces of the feed and pressure pipe unions and thin locations on the side of the crankcase. Fit new 'O' ring seals and secure the unions in place with two bolts and spring washers. Tighten the bolts securely (photo).

13 Refit the dipstick tube to the side of the sump and secure with the union nut. Take great care when starting the thread as it is easy to cross the threads (photo).

14 Wipe the mating faces of the sump and the breather. Fit a new gasket and secure in position with two set bolts and spring washers (photo).

54. Cylinder Head -- Refitting

1. Thoroughly clean the top of the cylinder block and the underside of the cylinder head.

2. Place a new 'O' ring oil seal in the little well at the rear right-hand corner of the cylinder block (photo).

3. Lubricate the cylinder bores and pistons to ensure adequate lubrication upon initial starting of the engine (photo).

4. Position a new cylinder head gasket on the top face of the cylinder block (photo). It is important to note that engines with a serial number having a suffix G and onwards that the height of the cylinder block has been reduced by 0.013 inch to suit a new steel and asbestos cylinder head gasket. The cylinder blocks can be identified by the cast boss situated on the cylinder block adjacent to the auxiliary drive sealing plug as shown in Fig.1.37.

The correct types of gasket to be used are given below:—

a) Early type. Cylinder block without identification boss casting -- use the all steel 'Corgasyl' type cylinder head gasket.

b) Later type. Cylinder block with identification boss casting -- use the steel and asbestos type cylinder head gasket.

5. When using the all steel 'Corgasyl' type cylinder head gasket it must be separated into two parts by cutting the linking tabs between the main part of the gasket and timing case section. Lightly smear both sides of each gasket with 'Wellseal' and place the two gaskets into position with the corrugations facing towards the block.

6. If the steel and asbestos gasket is being fitted ensure that the wrapover side of the gasket faces the cylinder block. It is not necessary to use any sealing compounds with this type of gasket.

7. Before actually refitting the cylinder head make sure that the small angled hose is fitted to the water pump and is in the vertical position as shown in photo 54:9.

8. Lift up the cylinder head and ease the front over the camshaft chainwheel (photo).

9. Carefully lower the cylinder head into position. If an assistant is available he should lead the thermostat housing elbow into the angled hose fitted to the water pump (photo).

10 Finally make sure that the head is located correctly on the dowels on the top face of the camshaft drive chain chamber.

11 Check that the EP mark on the flywheel is still in line with the pointer (see photo 51.8). Then check that the distributor drive dog is in position with the wide segment towards the distributor clamp pinch bolt to obtain correct timing. Should this not be in the correct position turn the crankshaft a full revolution and then lock the crankshaft with the timing lock pin.

12 If it was not found necessary to grind the valve, clearances will

not require to be reset. Should, however, it be necessary to reset the valve clearances, further information will be found in Section 55.

13 Place the shims previously removed from on top of the valves back in their original positions (photo).

14 The thick shim should be placed on top and the thinner shim underneath (photo).

15 Place the tappets in their original positions over the valve springs (photo).

16 Refit the camshaft and bearing block assembly onto the cylinder head whilst at the same time entering the tappets into their respective bores (photo).

17 The camshaft bearing caps are numbered on the right-hand side next to the bolt hole so that they are not interchanged accidentally.

18 Inspect the plain washers that fit under the head of the cylinder lead bolts and if they show signs of scoring or deformation they must be renewed by a set of new case hardened washers. Ordinary plain washers will not do.

19 Screw in all the cylinder head securing bolts with plain washers. This should be done a turn at a time once the bolts are in tension so that no undue strain is placed on the camshaft or cylinder head.

20 Refer to Fig.1.38 and tighten the bolts in the order shown until they are all tightened to a torque wrench setting of 55 lb/ft.

21 If a steel and asbestos gasket is being used tighten the bolts to a torque wrench setting of 70 lb/ft. in the order shown in Fig.1.38.

22 Note that the two set bolts that secure the No.1 camshaft bearing cap to the bearing block are identified by a letter 'T' or 'V' on the bolt head. These two bolts should be tightened to a torque wrench of 55 lb/ft. (T) or 70 lb/ft. (V).

23 The four bolts securing the front portion of the cylinder head should be tightened to a torque wrench setting of 10 lb/ft. These are marked with an 'X' in Fig.1.38.

24 Replace the plate at the rear of the camshaft bracket using a new joint washer and tighten the securing bolts.

25 Using a 'C' spanner or large adjustable wrench rotate the camshaft for at least two complete turns (photo). This is to make sure that all the moving parts are free.

26 Replace the camshaft locking key and make sure that it is engaged in the hub of the camshaft with one key vertical. Secure the locking key in this position (photo).

27 Remove the camshaft chainwheel from its retaining bracket and place on the driving flange register. Remove the spring ring and splined ring from the centre.

Note that a re-designed splined ring and clamping plate for the camshaft chainwheel was introduced from engines having a suffix 'D' in the engine number. These two parts must be renewed in pairs as shown in Fig.1.39.

28 Hold the upper camshaft drive chain tight on the driving side and insert the splined ring into the centre of the chainwheel at the same time lining up the fixing holes in the ring and camshaft flange.

29 Should this not be possible withdraw the splined ring and rotate in the appropriate direction by an amount equivalent to one vernier spline. If this does not give alignment then the splined ring should be removed and rotated through 180° in which position assembly should be possible.

30 When alignment is correct secure the clamping plate with the two bolts and tab washers and tighten to a torque wrench setting of 10 lb/ft. Do not bend over the tabs yet (photo).

31 Refit the retaining spring ring.

32 Remove the camshaft lock (photo).

33 Apply tension to the chain by inserting the Allen key and turning in a clockwise direction until the head moves forward under spring pressure against the chain (photo).

34 Refit the chain tensioner plug and washer (photo). Remove the flywheel locking pin.

35 For safety reasons check the timing by rotating the crankshaft in the direction of engine rotation until Number 1 exhaust valve is again fully open and the EP mark on the flywheel is in line with the pointer. The keyway in the front cap and the camshaft hub should be in line. Make sure that the timing chain is very tight on the

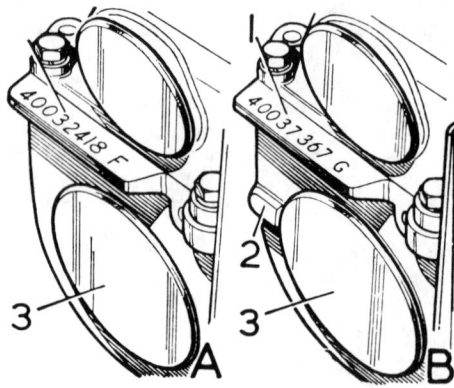

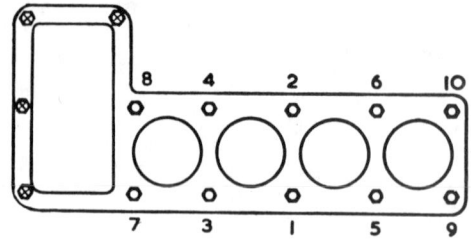

Fig.1.37. CYLINDER BLOCK IDENTIFICATION

A Early-type cylinder block
B Late type cylinder block
1 Machined casting for engine serial number
2 Cast boss on late-type cylinder block
3 Sealing plug, auxiliary drive

Fig.1.38. Tightening sequence for cylinder head bolts.

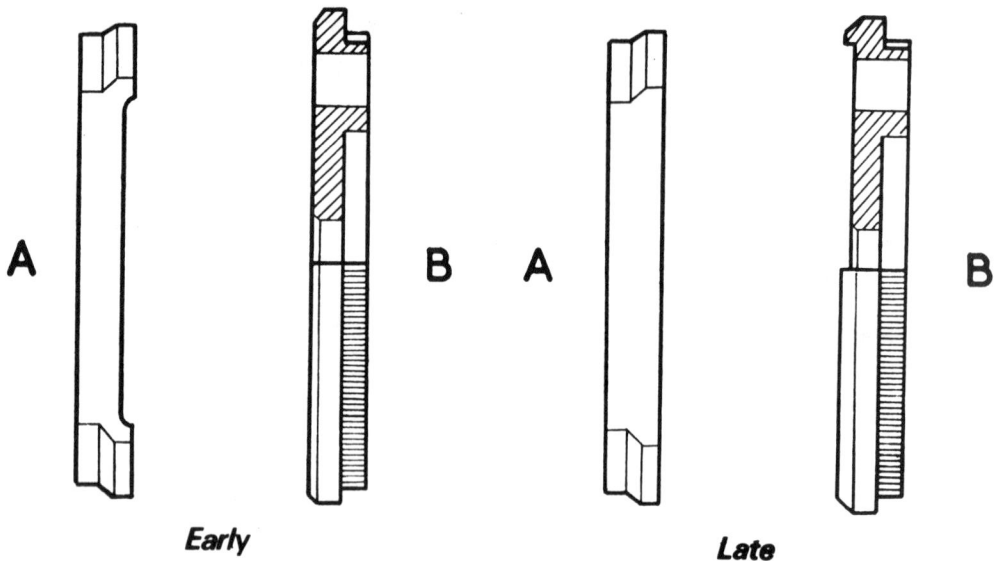

Early

Late

Fig.1.39. EARLY & LATE TYPE SPLINED RING & CLAMPING PLATE
A Splined ring
B Clamping plate

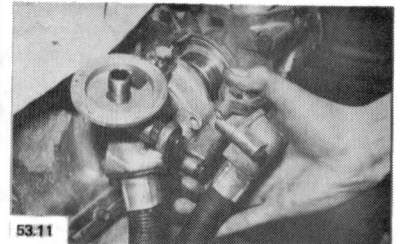

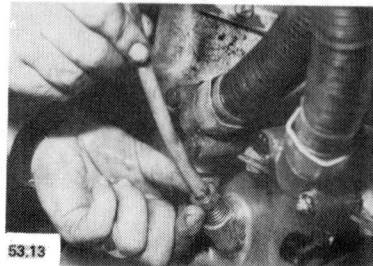

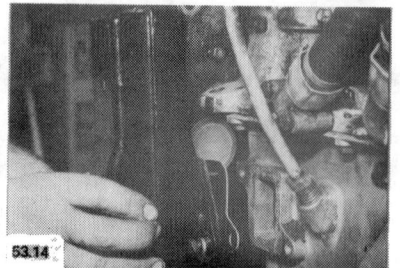

driving side.

36 If the check is satisfactory secure the camshaft lock in the normal inoperative position. This is shown in photo 5:32.

37 Bend over the two tab washers (photo).

38 Replace the top chain tensioner cover plate using a new joint washer (photo).

39 Refit the tensioner filter and reconnect the banjo bolt.

40 Make sure that the mating faces of the top cover and cylinder head are clean and free of old jointing compound or gasket and fit a new gasket to the cylinder head.

41 Carefully lower the top cover into place ensuring that the gasket is correctly seating and secure in place with the three domed fixing nuts, rubber washers and caps. There are two copper washers and distance pieces on the centre and rear studs and one copper washer on the front stud.

55. Valve Tappet Adjustment

If it has been necessary to fit new valves, grind in the original ones or if the tappet clearances are suspect after the engine has been run for a considerable period of time, it will be necessary to check the adjustment and fit new shims where applicable.

This operation may be done either with the engine on the bench or in the car and for this the engine top cover and spark plugs will have to be removed.

Should it be necessary to check the clearance during the rebuilding of the engine, the original shims must be refitted so as to give a datum for calculation of the thickness of the new shims.

1. Rotate the engine until the valve to be checked is fully open. Then continue rotating a further 180° until the back of the cam lobe is on the tappet.

2. Using a feeler gauge as shown in Fig.1.41, determine the clearance between the back of the cam lobe and the tappet. Make a note of the clearance.

3. Repeat the previous paragraph for all the valves.

4. The correct clearance for the inlet valves is between 0.008 and 0.010 inch and the exhaust valve clearance between 0.013 and 0.015 inch when the engine is cold.

5. Determine which valve clearances are incorrect and then it will be necessary to remove the camshaft.

6. Remove the timing cover from the bellhousing and turn the crankshaft until the flywheel EP marking is in line with the pointer. Check that Number 1 cylinder exhaust valve is fully open and insert the timing locking pin.

7. Insert the locking key into the camshaft hub.

8. Remove the two bolts and lockwashers securing the cover plate to the right-hand side of the chain housing. Lift away the cover plate.

9. Unscrew the plug in the body of the automatic chain tensioner and lift away the plug and copper washer. Use a socket with thick grease in the end to prevent the plug and copper washer dropping into the chain chamber.

10 Using an Allen key turn the tensioner in a clockwise direction until it is inoperative.

11 Undo and remove the two bolts and lock plate from the chainwheel and secure the chainwheel to the mounting bracket using a 3/8 inch UNF nut and plain washer.

12 Remove the end plate from the rear camshaft bearing and discard the old gasket. A new one will have to be refitted upon reassembly.

13 Obtain a piece of tube and cut off ten pieces the length being the depth of the camshaft bearing caps. These are shown in Fig.1.10.

14 Remove Number 2 camshaft bearing cap and fit two distance pieces to the cylinder head bolts and tighten to the correct torque wrench setting as follows:—

| Steel asbestos gasket | 70 lb/ft. |
| All steel gasket | 55 lb/ft. |

15 The two set bolts that fix No.1 camshaft bearing cap to the bearing block are identified by the letter 'T' or the letter 'V' on the head. Those with the letter 'T' should be tightened to a torque

wrench setting of 55 lb/ft, and those with the letter 'V' 70 lb/ft.

16 Continue substituting the distance pieces for the camshaft bearing caps in the order of Number 6, 5 and 4.

17 Remove the camshaft locking key and Number 1 bearing cap.

18 Remove Number 3 bearing cap. Do not deviate from the recommended order otherwise undue stress will be placed on the camshaft by Number 1 exhaust and Number 2 inlet valves which are fully open.

19 Lift away the camshaft taking care that the bearing half shells remain in position.

20 Using a magnet remove the necessary valve tappets and place them in order so that they will not be accidentally interchanged.

21 Using the magnet remove the adjusting shims from on top of the valves. On early engines there will be two shims, one thin and one thick.

22 Using a micrometer (photo) determine the thickness of the existing shim/s and then by calculation using the required clearance and the existing clearance determine the new thickness of shim required. These are available in the following sizes:—

Shim (in.)	Shim (mm)	Shim (in.)	Shim (mm)	Shim (in.)	Shim (mm)
0.074	1.88	0.083	2.10	0.282	7.16
0.075	1.90	0.092	2.33	0.292	7.41
0.076	1.93	0.102	2.59	0.302	7.67
0.077	1.95	0.112	2.84	0.312	7.92
0.078	1.98	0.122	3.09	0.322	8.17
0.079	2.00	0.132	3.35	0.332	8.43
0.080	2.03	0.142	3.60	0.342	8.68
0.081	2.05	0.262	6.65	0.352	8.94
0.082	2.08	0.272	6.90		

23 When all the shims have been obtained replace them in their correct positions.

24 Replace the valve tappets in their correct bores. Should they have been accidentally interchanged the location numbers are etched on the inside wall of the valve tappet.

25 If it was found that one of the tappets was worn requiring renewal they must be replaced as a complete set and not individually.

26 Replace the camshaft and bearing caps in the reverse order commencing with Number 3 bearing making sure that only one cap is fitted at a time. Tighten the cap bolts to the correct torque wrench setting as quoted in paragraph 14 of this Section.

27 Re-check the tappet clearances to make sure that the clearances are correct before proceeding further.

28 Make sure that the camshaft is still locked in the EP position and the timing locking pin is still inserted into the flywheel.

29 Offer the chainwheel to the camshaft hub and check that the bolt holes are in line while holding the chain tight on the drive side.

30 Secure the chainwheel to the hub with the securing bolts and new lock plate.

31 Release the camshaft drive chain tensioner using the Allen key and then refit the plug using a new copper washer.

32 Refit the chain tensioner cover plate using a new gasket and secure with the two bolts and spring washers.

33 Refit the cover plate onto the rear camshaft bearing using a new gasket.

34 Remove the locking device from the camshaft and also from the flywheel and refit them in their original places.

35 Replace the timing cover over the flywheel and finally the engine top cover.

56. Distributor Refitting

It is important to set the distributor drive correctly as otherwise the ignition timing will be totally incorrect. It is easy to set the distributor drive in apparently the right position but in fact exactly 180° out, by omitting to select the correct cylinder which must not

54.2

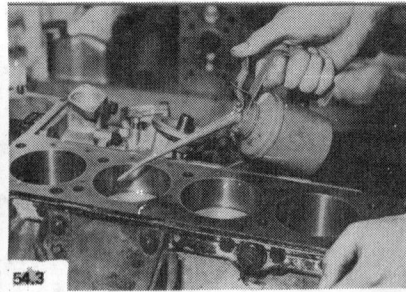
54.3

54.4

54.8

54.9

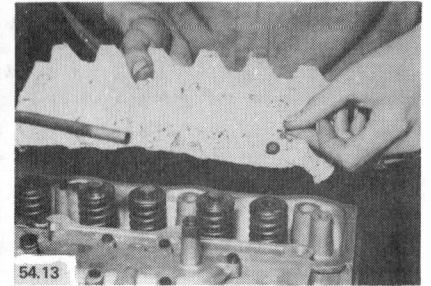
54.13

54.14

54.15

54.18

54.25

54.26

54.30

54.32

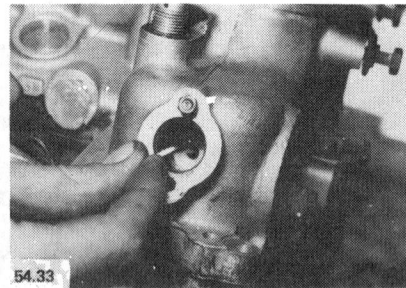
54.33

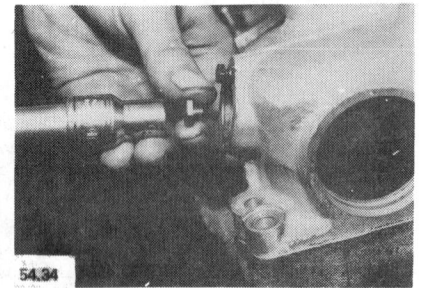
54.34

54.37

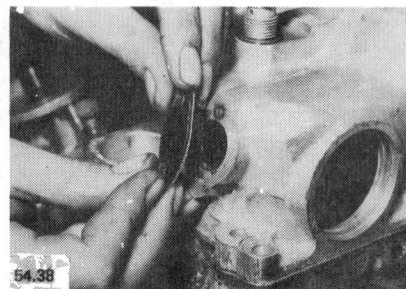
54.38

54.41

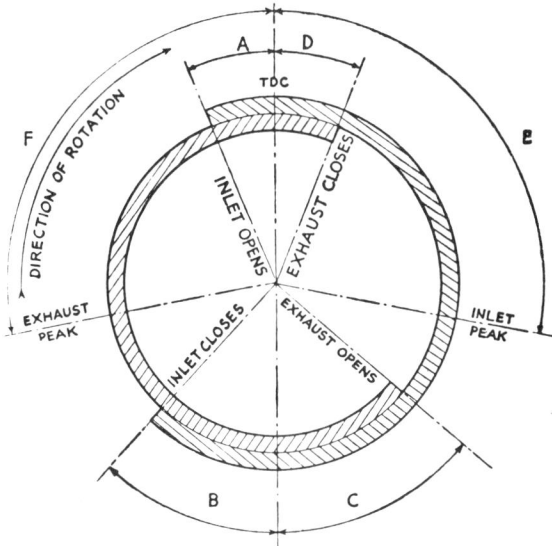

Fig.1.40. VALVE TIMING DIAGRAM

Single carburetter models

A 18° BTDC   D 12° ATDC
B 42° ABDC   E 102° ATDC
C 48° BBDC   F 108° BTDC. EP position

Twin carburetter models

A 14° BTDC   D 16° ATDC
B 46° ABDC   E 106° ATDC
C 44° BBDC   F 104° BTDC. EP position

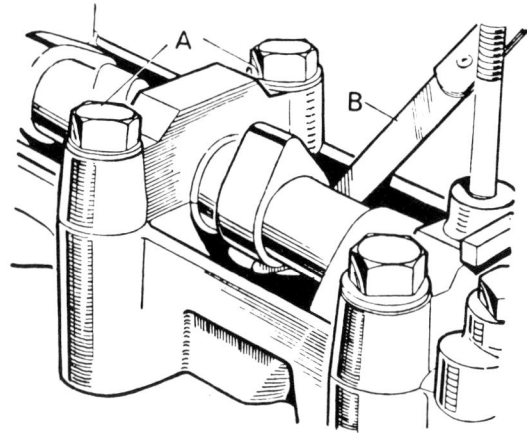

Fig.1.41. CHECKING TAPPET CLEARANCES USING FEELER GAUGES

A Slave bolts and nuts securing camshaft assembly and the cylinder head to the cylinder block
B Feeler gauge

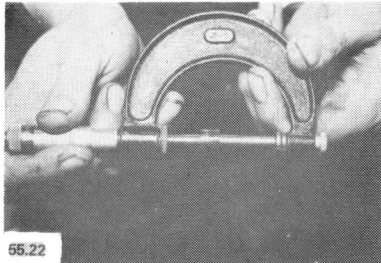
55.22

56.5

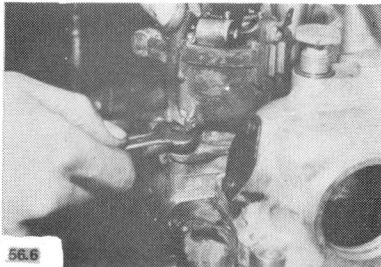
56.6

57.1

57.3

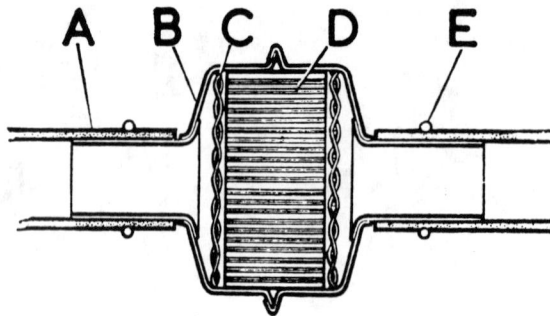

Fig.1.42. CROSS SECTIONAL VIEW THROUGH FLAME TRAP

A Rubber hose   C Wire mesh   D Filter   E Hose clip
B Housing

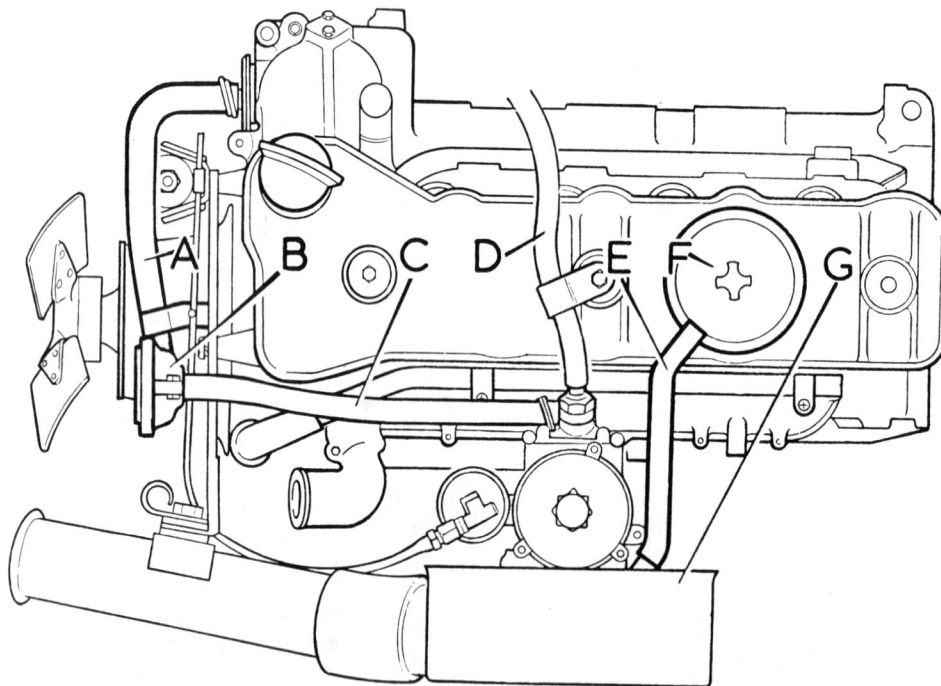

Fig.1.43. DIAPHRAGM—TYPE CRANKCASE EMISSION CONTROL , SC MODEL

A Hose, crankcase adaptor   valve   D Hose to brake servo   F Top cover breather
   to valve   C Hose, control valve to E Hose, air cleaner to top   G Air cleaner
B Diaphragm—type control   servo adaptor banjo   cover breather

be at TDC but must also be on its firing stroke with both valves closed The distributor drive should, therefore, not be fitted until the cylinder head is in position and the valves can be observed.

If the distributor drive has not been disturbed in its housing proceed direct to paragraph 5 from paragraph 1, otherwise proceed as follows:—

1. Align the 4 degree BTDC (SC engines), or 6 degree BTDC (TC engines) mark on the flywheel with the pointer when both valves of Number 4 cylinder are fully closed. This means the engine is just commencing on the firing stroke.
2. Using a bolt of suitable thread mesh the distributor drive gear with the auxiliary drive shaft so that the driving slot is as nearly as is possible in line with the distributor housing bolt holes. The narrower side of the slot must be towards the timing case.
3. Coat the underside of the distributor housing assembly, 'B', Fig.1.19, with a jointing compound and place in position.
4. Refit the driving dog (C).
5. Place the distributor in position with the rotor arm pointing to No.4 plug lead (photo).
6. Adjust the position of the distributor until the contact breaker points are just opening and then tighten the clamp and housing bolts (photo).

57. Oil Filter, Exhaust Manifold & Carburetter — Refitting

1. Before refitting the oil filter wipe the face of the filter mounting to ensure there is no dirt on the face which could inhibit the seal.
2. Make sure the rubber 'O' ring seal is in place on the new filter cannister and screw it into position hand tight only (photo).
3. Ensure that the mating faces of the exhaust manifold and cylinder head are clean and free of old gasket or jointing compound.
4. Fit new gaskets to the securing studs. Take particular care to ensure that the gaskets are fitted correctly with the steel face fitted on the exhaust manifold side.
5. Place the front two bolts and lock washers in position in the manifold and position against the cylinder head. Start the two bolts but do not tighten fully yet.
6. Replace the four nuts and rear two bolts using new spring washers as the original ones will have lost their flexibility.
7. Tighten the nuts and bolts fully. The manufacturers recommend that the bolts and nuts be re-tightened and the lock tab washers bent over when the engine is hot so make a note of this for work to be done once the engine has been run (photo).
8. The carburetter installation heat shield and carburetters should next be refitted as follows:
9. SC Models. Refer to Chapter 3, Section 4, Paragraph 10.
10 TC Models. Refer to Chapter 3, Section 8, Paragraph 53.

58. Engine Refitting

The method of engine removal will to a certain extent govern the method of engine refitting. If the engine was removed still connected to the gearbox then, obviously as the facilities available made this possible, the easiest way to refit the unit will be a direct reversal of the removal sequence.

Engine refitting with the gearbox still in-situ in the car is easily achieved provided that the clutch disc has been centralised when the clutch has been refitted to the flywheel. This again is the direct reversal of the removal sequence.

Cars fitted with an automatic transmission unit require a slightly different reassembly procedure due to difficulties that could be experienced in reconnecting the transmission unit to the engine and also because of the additional weight involved. The authors' recommendations are to be found in Section 7 of this Chapter.

The following additional items should be noted which will assist in making sure that no problems arise.
1. Always fit a new fan belt and new cooling system hoses and jubilee clips as this will help eliminate the possibility of failure while on the road.
2. Two pairs of hands are better than one when refitting the bonnet. Do not tighten the bonnet securing bolts fully until it is ascertained that the bonnet is on straight.
3. Clean the battery terminals and terminal posts before reconnecting. Do not forget to refit the fuel lines before opening the main supply/ reserve tap.
4. Check that the drain taps are closed and refill the cooling system with water and the engine with Castrol GTX oil.

59. Engine — Initial Start Up After Overhaul or Major Repair

1. Make sure that the battery is fully charged and that all lubricants, coolants and fuel are replenished.
2. If the fuel system has been dismantled it will require several revolutions of the engine on the starter motor to get the petrol up to the carburetter installation. An initial 'prime' of about 1/3 of a cupful of petrol poured down the intake of the carburetter/s will help the engine to fire quickly thus relieving the load on the battery. Do not overdo this, however, as flooding may result.
3. As soon as the engine fires and runs keep it going at a fast tickover only (no faster) and bring it up to normal working temperature.
4. As the engine warms up there will be odd smells and some smoke from parts getting hot and burning off oil deposits. The signs to look for are leaks of oil or water which will be obvious if serious. Check also the exhaust manifold to front pipe connections. When the engine is hot tighten the exhaust manifold nuts and bolts and bend over the lockwasher tabs.
5. When normal operating temperature has been reached adjust the idling speed as described in Chapter 3.
6. Stop the engine and wait a few minutes to see if any lubricant or coolant is dripping out when the engine is at rest.
7. Road test the car to check that the ignition timing is correct and giving the necessary smoothness and power. Do not race the engine - if new bearings and/or pistons and rings have been fitted it should be treated as a new engine and run in at reduced revolutions for 500 miles.

60. Crankcase Emission Control

Depending on local anti-pollution regulations one of two types of crankcase emission control may be fitted during the manufacturing stage of the car. These are the diaphragm type and the flame trap type.

In both cases the engine fumes from within the engine are re-routed through pipe connections to the carburetter intake and are subsequently burned within the combustion chambers with the normal petrol/air charge instead of breathing direct to the atmosphere.

Servicing is simple and confined to making sure that all the hoses are in good condition and have not perished. The top cover breather is sealed and usually requires no attention except removal every 20,000 miles for cleaning. To do this remove the rubber pipe and unscrew the nut on the top. Remove the sealing washer and lift off the breather. Wash in petrol or paraffin and allow to dry before refitting. Make sure that the sealing washer is sound and fitted correctly.

At 20,000 miles the flame trap valve should be removed and washed in petrol. This valve is shown in cross sectional form in Fig.1.42. Release the two hose clips 'E' and pull off the rubber hoses 'A'. Lift away the flame trap.

By referring to Fig.1.43, Fig.1.44 and Fig.1.45, the layout of each system and its application may be seen.

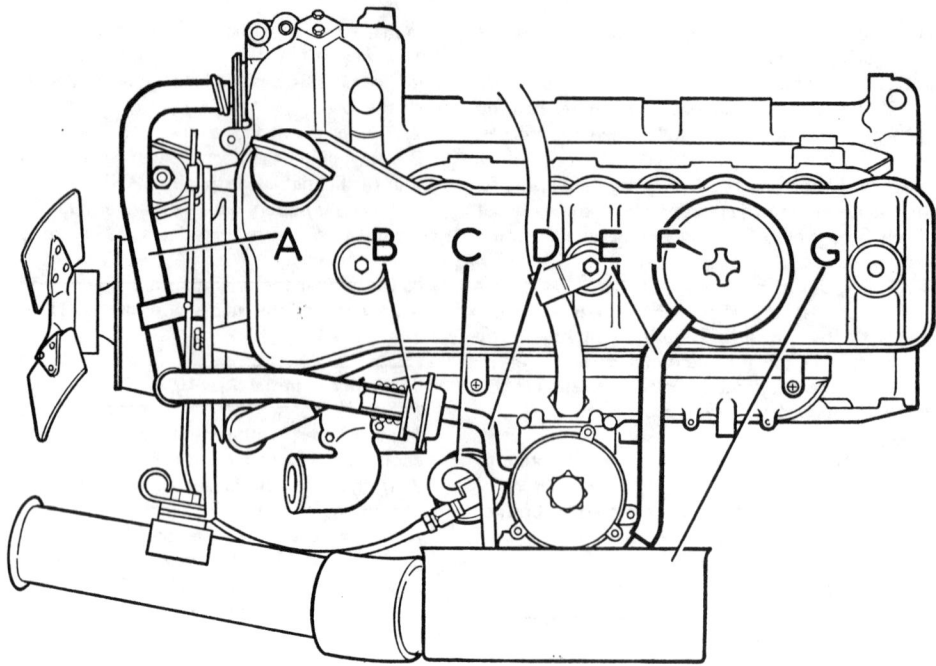

Fig.144. FLAME TRAP TYPE CRANKCASE EMISSION CONTROL

A Hose, crankcase adaptor to flame trap
B Flame trap
C Hose, carburetter to air cleaner
D Hose, flame trap to carburetter
E Hose, air cleaner to engine breather
F Engine breather
G Air cleaner

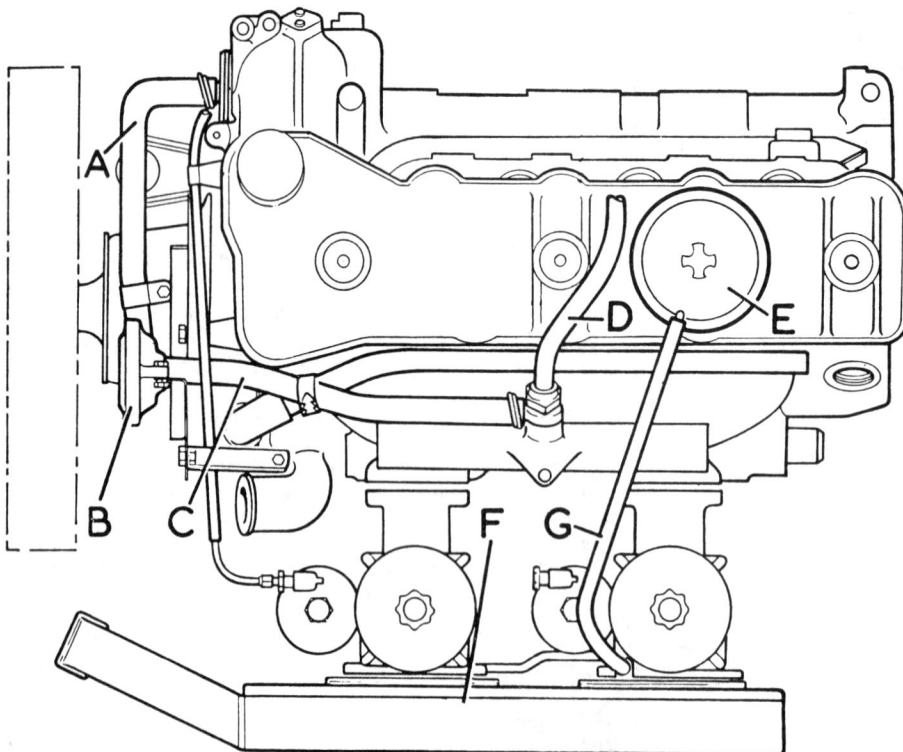

Fig.1.45. DIAPHRAGM—TYPE CRANKCASE EMISSION CONTROL, TC MODEL

A Hose, crankcase adaptor to diaphragm valve
B Diaphragm-type control valve
C Hose, control valve to servo adaptor banjo
D Hose to brake servo
E Top cover breather
F Air cleaner
G Hose, air cleaner to top cover breather

Fault Finding Chart - Engine

Symptom	Reason/s	Remedy
No current at starter motor	Discharged or defective battery.	Charge or replace battery, Push-start car.
	Loose battery leads.	Tighten both terminals and earth ends of earth lead.
	Defective starter solenoid or switch or broken wiring.	Run a wire direct from the battery to the starter motor or by-pass the solenoid.
	Engine earth strap disconnected.	Check and retighten strap.
Current at starter motor	Jammed starter motor drive pinion.	Place car in gear and rock from side to side. Alternatively, free exposed square end of shaft with spanner.
	Defective starter motor.	Remove and recondition.
No spark at spark plug	Ignition damp or wet.	Wipe dry the distributor cap and ignition leads.
	Ignition leads to spark plugs loose.	Check and tighten at both spark plug and distributor cap ends.
	Shorted or disconnected low tension leads.	Check the wiring on the CB and SW terminals of the coil and to the distributor.
	Dirty, incorrectly set, or pitted contact breaker points.	Clean, file smooth, and adjust.
	Faulty condenser.	Check contact breaker points for arcing remove and fit new.
	Defective ignition switch.	By-pass switch with wire.
	Ignition leads connected wrong way round.	Remove and replace leads to spark plugs in correct order.
	Faulty coil.	Remove and fit new coil.
	Contact breaker point spring earthed or broken.	Check spring is not touching metal part of distributor. Check insulator washers are correctly placed. Renew points if the spring is broken.
No fuel at carburetter float chamber or at jets	No petrol in petrol tank.	Refill tank!
	Vapour lock in fuel line. (In hot conditions or at high altitude.)	Blow into petrol tank, allow engine to cool, or apply a cold wet rag to the fuel line.
	Blocked float chamber needle valve.	Remove, clean, and replace.
	Fuel pump filter blocked.	Remove, clean, and replace.
	Choked or blocked carburetter jets.	Dismantle and clean.
	Faulty fuel pump.	Remove, overhaul, and replace. Check CB points on SU pump.
Excess of petrol in cylinder or carburetter flooding	Too much choke allowing too rich a mixture to wet plugs.	Remove and dry spark plugs or with wide open throttle, push-start the car.
	Float damaged or leading or needle not seating.	Remove, examine, clean and replace float and needle valve as necessary.
	Float lever incorrectly adjusted.	Remove and adjust correctly.
No spark at spark plug	Ignition failure - sudden.	Check over low and high tension circuits for breaks in wiring.
	Ignition failure - misfiring precedes total stoppage.	Check contact breaker points, clean and adjust. Renew condenser if faulty.
	Ignition failure - in severe rain or after traversing water splash.	Dry out ignition leads and distributor cap.
No fuel at jets	No petrol in petrol tank.	Refill tank.
	Petrol tank breather choked.	Remove petrol cap and clean out breather hole or pipe.
	Sudden obstruction in carburetter/s.	Check jets, filter, and needle valve in float chamber for blockage.
	Water in fuel system.	Drain tank and blow out fuel lines.
Intermittent sparking at spark plug	Ignition leads loose.	Check and tighten as necessary at spark plug and distributor cap ends.

Symptom	Reason/s	Remedy
Intermittent sparking at spark plug	Battery leads loose on terminals.	Check and tighten terminal leads.
	Battery earth strap loose on body attachment point.	Check and tighten earth lead to body attachment point.
	Engine earth lead loose.	Tighten lead.
	Low tension leads to SW and CB terminals on coil loose.	Check and tighten leads if found loose.
	Low tension lead from CB terminal side to distributor loose.	Check and tighten if found loose.
	Dirty, or incorrectly gapped plugs.	Remove, clean, and regap.
	Dirty, incorrectly set, or pitted contact breaker points.	Clean, file smooth, and adjust.
	Tracking across inside of distributor cover.	Remove and fit new cover.
	Ignition too retarded.	Check and adjust ignition timing.
	Faulty coil.	Remove and fit new coil.
Fuel shortage at engine	Mixture too weak.	Check jets, float chamber needle valve, and filters for obstruction. Clean as necessary. Carburetter/s incorrectly adjusted.
	Air leak in carburetter/s.	Remove and overhaul carburetter.
	Air leak at inlet manifold to cylinder head, or inlet manifold to carburetter.	Test by pouring oil along joints. Bubbles indicate leak. Renew manifold gasket as appropriate.
Mechanical wear	Incorrect valve clearances.	Check and reset clearances using shims.
	Burnt out exhaust valves.	Remove cylinder head and renew defective valves.
	Sticking or leaking valves.	Remove cylinder head, clean, check and renew valves as necessary.
	Weak or broken valve springs.	Check and renew as necessary.
	Worn valve guides or stems.	Renew valve guides and valves.
	Worn pistons and piston rings.	Dismantle engine, renew pistons and rings.
Fuel/air mixture leaking from cylinder	Burnt out exhaust valves.	Remove cylinder head, renew defective valves.
	Sticking or leaking valves.	Remove cylinder head, clean, **check**, and renew valves as necessary.
	Worn valve guides and stems.	Remove cylinder head and renew **valves** and valve guies.
	Weak or broken valve springs.	Remove cylinder head, renew **defective** springs.
	Blown cylinder head gasket. (Accompanied by increase in noise).	Remove cylinder head and fit new gasket.
	Worn pistons and piston rings.	Dismantle engine, renew pistons and rings.
	Worn or scored cylinder bores.	Dismantle engine, rebore, renew pistons and rings.
Incorrect adjustments	Ignition timing wrongly set. Too advanced or retarded.	Check and reset ignition timing.
	Contact breaker points incorrectly gapped.	Check and reset contact breaker points.
	Incorrect valve clearances.	Check and reset clearances using shims.
	Incorrect set spark plugs.	Remove, clean, and regap.
	Carburation too rich or too weak.	Tune carburetter/s for optimum performance.
Carburation and ignition faults	Dirty contact breaker points.	Remove, clean, and replace.
	Fuel filters blocked causing top end fuel starvation.	Dismantle, inspect, clean, and replace all fuel filters.
	Distributor automatic balance weights or vacuum advance and retard mechanisms not functioning correctly.	Overhaul distributor.
	Faulty fuel pump giving top end fuel starvation.	Remove, overhaul, or fit exchange reconditioned fuel pump.
Oil being burnt by engine	Badly worn, perished or missing valve stem oil seals.	Remove, fit new oil seals to valve stems.

Fault Finding Chart - Engine

Symptom	Reason/s	Remedy
Oil being burnt by engine	Excessively worn valve stems and valve guides.	Remove cylinder head and fit new valves and valve guides.
	Worn piston rings.	Fit oil control rings to existing pistons or purchase new pistons.
	Worn pistons and cylinder bores.	Fit new pistons and rings, rebore cylinders.
	Excessive piston ring gap allowing blow-by.	Fit new piston rings and set gap correctly.
	Piston oil return holes choked.	Decarbonise engine and pistons.
Oil being lost due to leaks	Leaking oil filter gasket.	Inspect and fit new gasket as necessary.
	Leaking top cover gasket.	Inspect and fit new gasket as necessary.
	Leaking timing case gasket.	Inspect and fit new gasket as necessary.
	Leaking sump gasket.	Inspect and fit new gasket as necessary.
	Loose sump plug.	Tighten, fit new gasket if necessary.
Unusual noises from engine	Worn valve gear. Noisy tapping from top cover.	Check valve clearances. Check camshaft bearings.
	Worn big end bearing. Regular heavy knocking .	Drop sump, if bearings broken up clean out oil pump and oilways, fit new bearings. If bearings not broken but worn fit bearing shells.
	Worn timing chains and gears (rattling from front of engine.)	Fit new timing wheels and timing chains.
	Worn main bearings. (Rumbling and vibration).	Drop sump, remove crankshaft, if bearings worn but not broken up, renew. If broken up strip oil pump and clean out.
	Worn crankshaft. (Knocking, rumbling and vibration).	Regrind crankshaft, fit new main and big end bearings.

Chapter 2 Cooling system

Contents

Specifications

Type	Pressurised radiator, thermo-syphon pump assisted and fan cooled. Separate expansion tank (TC models only)
Water Capacity	17 pints
Temperature Control	Thermostat
Thermostat Setting	Opens at 77°C (170°F)
Pressure Cap	5 lb/per sq.in. (early model) 7 lb/per sq.in. (later model)

Water Pump

Type	Centrifugal
Drive	'V' belt

Fan

	Number of Blades
Home market	4 blades
Export market	6 blades
Overall diameter	15 7/16 inch
Fan belt tension	5/16 inch between fan and crankshaft pulleys

1. General Description

The engine cooling water is circulated by a thermo-syphon, water pump assisted system, and the coolant is pressurised. This is primarily to prevent premature boiling in adverse conditions and also to allow the engine to operate at its most efficient running temperature, this being just under the boiling point of water. On TC models an overflow pipe from the radiator is connected to an expansion chamber which makes topping up unnecessary. The coolant expands when hot, and instead of being forced down the overflow pipe and lost, it flows into the expansion chamber. As the engine cools, the coolant contracts and because of the pressure differential flows back into the top tank of the radiator. Instead of the radiator pressure cap being fitted to the neck on the top of the radiator top tank it is fitted to the neck of the expansion chamber. A plain radiator sealing cap is fitted to the radiator.

The radiator cap is set to a pressure of 5 lb/per sq.in. (early models) or 7 lb/per sq.in. (later model) which increases the boiling point of the coolant. If the coolant temperature exceeds this figure and the water boils, the pressure in the system forces the internal valve of the cap off its seat, thus exposing the overflow pipe down which the steam from the boiling water escapes and so relieves the pressure. It is, therefore, important that the radiator cap and seating are in good order. Most garages have a special tool which enables a radiator cap to be pressure tested.

The cooling system comprises the radiator, top and bottom hoses, heater hoses (if a heater/demister is fitted), the impeller water pump (mounted on the front of the engine, it carried the fan blade and is driven by the 'V' belt), the thermostat and the drain plug and tap.

The system functions in the following manner:-

Cold water from the bottom of the radiator circulates up the lower radiator hose to the water pump where it is pushed round the water passages in the cylinder block, helping to keep the cylinder bores and pistons cool.

The water then travels up into the cylinder head and circulates round the combustion spaces and valve seats, absorbing more heat. Then, when the engine is at its correct operating temperature the water travels out of the cylinder head, past the open thermostat into the upper radiator hose, and so into the radiator header tank. The water travels down the radiator where it is rapidly cooled by the rush of cold air through the radiator core. The water, now cool, reaches the bottom of the radiator, when the cycle is repeated.

The fan is designed to increase the flow of cool air through the radiator core when the car is stationary or travelling slowly.

When the engine is cold, the thermostat (a valve able to open and close according to the temperature) maintains the circulation of the water in the engine, by returning it to the cylinder block. Only when the correct minimum operating temperature has been reached as shown in the specification, does the thermostat begin to open, so allowing water to return to the radiator.

2. Cooling System — Draining

1. If the engine is cold, remove the pressure cap from the radiator (SC models) or expansion chamber (TC models) by turning it in an anti-clockwise direction. If the engine is hot, having just been run, then turn the cap very slightly until the pressure in the system has had time to disperse. Use a rag over the cap to protect your hand from the escaping steam. If, with the engine very hot, the cap is released suddenly, the drop in pressure can result in the water boiling. With the pressure released, the cap can now be removed. On TC models remove the radiator filler cap.
2. Turn the heater control to the 'HOT' position so as to avoid an air lock or water being retained in the heater radiator and hoses.
3. If anti-freeze is used in the cooling system, drain it into a clean bowl or tub of at least 17 pints capacity, for re-use.
4. Open the tap located at the rear right-hand side of the cylinder block and remove the drain plug at the base of the radiator bottom tank.
5. When the coolant has finished running, probe the drain plug and tap orifices with a short piece of wire to dislodge any particles of rust or sediment which may be causing a blockage and preventing all the water running out.

3. Cooling System — Flushing

With time, the cooling system will gradually lose its efficiency as the radiator becomes choked with rust, scale deposits from the water and other sediment. To clean the system out, remove the radiator cap and drain plug and leave a hose running in the radiator cap neck for 10 to 15 minutes.

In very bad cases the radiator should be reverse flushed. This can be done with the radiator in position. The cylinder block tap is closed and a hose with a suitably tapered adaptor placed in the radiator drain plug hole. Water under pressure is then forced through the radiator and out the header tank neck.

The hose is then removed and placed in the radiator cap neck and the radiator washed out in the usual manner.

4. Cooling System — Filling

1. Close the engine drain tap and refit the radiator drain plug.
2. Fill the system slowly to ensure that no air locks develop. If a heater unit is fitted, check that the valve in the heater unit is open, otherwise an air lock may form in the heater. The best type of water to use in the cooling system is rainwater, so use this whenever possible
3. Completely fill the radiator and replace the cap.
4. If an anti-freeze mixture is to be used in the cooling system, always use an anti-freeze with an ethylene glycol or glycerine base.
5. Run the engine at a fast idle speed for approximately half a minute and remove the radiator cap slowly. Top up, if necessary, to the top of the filler neck and replace the cap.
6. Top up the level of water in the expansion tank until it is at least

half full (TC models only).

5. Radiator — Removal, Inspection & Cleaning

Removal SC models
1. Refer to Section 2 of this chapter and drain the cooling system.
2. Undo the top and bottom hose clips from the radiator top and bottom tank connections and disconnect the two hoses.
3. Undo the two nuts and bolts 'A' (Fig.2.1.) that attach the top radiator fixing brackets to the radiator.
4. Undo the lower radiator to mounting bracket nut and bolt 'A', (Fig.2.2.).
5. The radiator may now be lifted upwards through the front of the engine compartment. Take care not to damage the fragile radiator core with the fan blades.

Removal TC models
1. Refer to Section 2 of this chapter and completely drain the cooling system.
2. It will be necessary to drain the oil from the oil cooler. Place a container under the hexagonal plug located at the bottom of the oil return pipe from the oil cooler to the engine (Fig.2.3.).
3. Undo the top and bottom hose clips from the radiator top and bottom tank connections and disconnect the two hoses.
4. Disconnect the positive and negative terminals from the battery, by undoing the two self-tapping screws. Lift away the cables.
5. Undo and remove the two wing nuts and battery clamping plate. Lift away the battery followed by the battery mounting tray.
6. Slacken the clips that secure the oil coolant pipes to the base unit.
7. Undo and remove the two nuts and spring washers at each flange of the supply and return oil pipes at the oil cooler. Carefully pull the two flanges away from the oil cooler and recover the two 'O' ring oil seals located in the recess in the oil cooler.
8. Remove the radiator and oil cooler retaining nuts and bolts. There are two nuts and bolts at the top securing the radiator to the brackets and one nut and bolt securing the radiator lower bracket to the base unit.
9. The radiator and oil cooler assembly may now be lifted upwards through the front of the engine compartment. Take care not to touch the fragile radiator core with the fan blades.

With the radiator away from the car, any leaks can be soldered or repaired with a suitable substance such as 'Cataloy'. Clean out the inside of the radiator by flushing as detailed in Section 3 of this chapter. When the radiator is out of the car, it is advantageous to turn it upside down and reverse flush. Clean the exterior of the radiator by carefully using a compressed air jet or strong water jet to clear away road dirt, flies, etc.

Inspect the radiator hoses for cracks, internal or external perishing, and damage by overtightening of the securing clips. Replace the hoses if suspect. Examine the radiator hose securing clips and renew them if they are rusted or distorted. The drain plug should be renewed if leaking or the threads are worn.

6. Radiator — Replacement

SC models
1. Carefully lower the radiator into position in the engine compartment.
2. Refit the two upper mounting nuts and bolts ('A', Fig.2.1.), but do not tighten fully at this stage.
3. Refit the lower mounting nut and bolt (Fig.2.2) and then tighten all three mountings.
4. Reconnect the top and bottom hoses and tighten the two hose clips. If new hoses have been fitted and are a little difficult to refit, smear a trace of soap on the inside of the end of the hoses to act as a lubricant.
5. Refill the cooling system as detailed in Section 4 of this chapter.

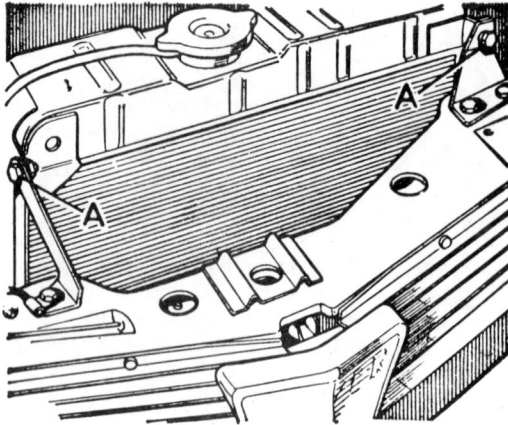

Fig.2.1. RADIATOR UPPER MOUNTING
A Fixing point

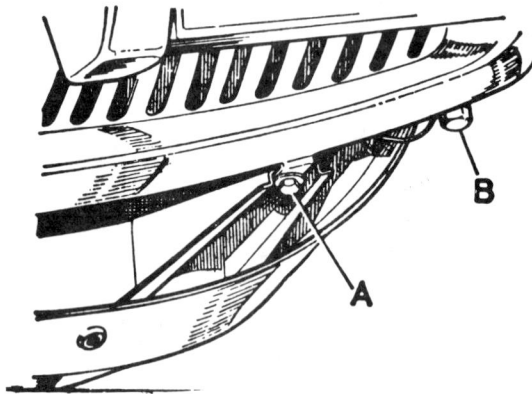

Fig.2.2. RADIATOR LOWER MOUNTING
A Fixing
B Drain plug

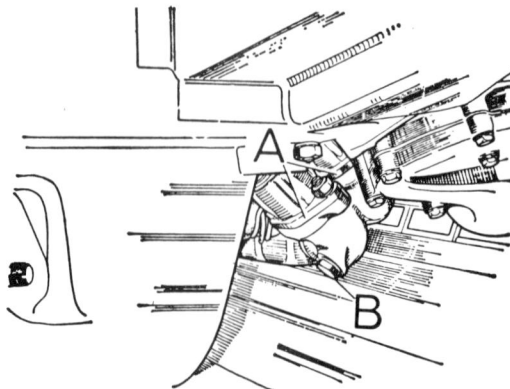

Fig.2.3. OIL COOLER DRAIN PLUG LOCATION (TC MODELS)
A Flanges, oil pipes to oil cooler
B Drain plug on oil return pipe, oil cooler

TC Models

1. Carefully lower the radiator and oil cooler assembly into position in the engine compartment.
2. Refit the upper mounting nuts and bolts securing the radiator assembly to the mounting, but do not tighten fully yet.
3. Refit the lower mounting nut and bolt to the base unit and then tighten all three mountings.
4. Fit new 'O' ring oil seals into the recesses in the oil cooler and locate the two oil pipe flanges. Secure the flanges in place with the two nuts and spring washers to each flange.
5. Tighten the clips that secure the oil cooler pipes to the base unit.
6. Refit the battery tray and replace the battery in its original position. Reconnect the two battery cables and secure with the self-tapping screws. Secure the battery in position with the clamping plate and two wing nuts.
7. Replace the oil cooler hexagonal drain plug and top up the engine oil level by the amount of oil drained from the oil cooler during dismantling.
8. Refill the cooling system as described in Section 4 of this chapter.

7. Thermostat — Removal, Testing & Replacement

1. Partially drain the cooling system by removing the radiator drain plug and allowing about six pints of coolant to drain out. Refit the drain plug.
2. Slacken the hose clip (35) (Fig.2.4) on the hose (34) at the front end of the heater pipe (37) and disconnect the hose.
3. If the engine is fitted with a diaphragm type crankcase emission control at the front of the engine, it will be necessary to remove the brace for the control valve support brackets.
4. If the engine is fitted with a flame trap type emission control next to the carburetter, disconnect the flame trap hose at the carburetter. Next disconnect the support for the flame trap at the thermostat. Using string or wire, tie back the flame trap clear from the thermostat housing.
5. Undo and remove the two Phillips head screws and spring washers which secure the heater pipe to the induction manifold. Move the pipe out of the way of the thermostat housing (23) and, if necessary, tie back with string or wire.
6. Slacken the hose clip on the top hose to thermostat top housing (23) connection and disconnect the top hose.
7. Undo and remove the three nuts (27) and spring washers (26) that secure the thermostat top housing (23) to the top of the cylinder head. Lift the thermostat top housing and gasket (24) from the studs (25), if necessary, carefully tapping the side of the housing should it be a tight fit on the studs due to corrosion.
8. The thermostat (22) may now be removed from its location in the top of the cylinder head.

Test the thermostat for correct functioning by suspending it on a string in a saucepan of cold water, together with a thermometer which must be similarly suspended. Heat the water and note the temperature at which the thermostat begins to open. This should be 77°C (170°F). Discard the thermostat if it opens too early. Continue heating the water until the thermostat is fully open. Then let it cool down naturally. If the thermostat does not fully open in the boiling water, or does not close down as the water cools, then it must be discarded and a new one fitted. If the thermostat is stuck open when cold, this will be apparent when removing it from the housing.

On earlier models, a methyl-alcohol bellows thermostat was fitted, but was replaced by a wax type thermostat on later models. Both are interchangeable.

Refitting the thermostat is the reverse procedure to removal. Always ensure that the cylinder head and thermostat top housing faces are clean and flat. If the top housing is badly corroded and eaten away, fit a new top housing. A new paper joint must always be used.

Thermostats should last for at least two to three years.

8. Water Pump — Removal

1. Refer to Section 5 and remove the radiator.
2. Slacken, but do not remove the generator mounting bolts. NOTE: On models fitted with air conditioning an alternator is fitted instead of a dynamo, but is mounted in the same manner.
3. Push the generator towards the engine and lift away the fan belt (21), (Fig.2.4).
4. Undo and remove the four nuts (20) and spring washers (19) that secure the fan blade (17) to the fan and pulley hub (7). Lift away the fan blades (17), fan pulley (12), and distance shims (13).
5. Slacken the two water pump hose clips and disconnect the two hoses.
6. Undo and remove the six bolts (9) and spring washers (11) that hold the water pump (1) to the front face of the cylinder block.
7. Push the generator away from the engine as far as possible, and lift away the water pump (1).
8. Remove the gasket (8) placed between the face of the water pump and the cylinder block, and also any traces of jointing compound that may have been used previously.

9. Water Pump — Dismantling, Reassembly & Replacement

If the water pump starts to leak; show signs of excessive movement of the spindle; or is noisy during operation, the pump can be dismantled and overhauled. A special overhaul kit comprising a new spindle with bearings, impeller, carbon ring seal unit and joint gasket may be obtained from Rover agents. Alternatively, a service exchange re-conditioned pump may be obtained. To dismantle the pump proceed as follows:—

1. Refer to Fig.2.4, and using a three-legged puller or a universal ball joint separator, draw the fan and pulley hub (7) from the spindle and bearing assembly (2).

2. Undo and remove the bolt (3) that locks the bearing to the housing (1).

3. Place the water pump cylinder block mating face in the jaws of a vice and with a soft faced hammer drift the spindle and bearing assembly, complete with the impeller, through the rear of the water pump body.

4. Apply a few drops of thick oil into the location hole of the bearing. Very carefully align the locating tapped hole in the bearing with the hole in the water pump body, and drift the spindle and bearing into the body from the front so that the longer end of the spindle relative to the bearing is towards the front.

5. Fit the bearing locking bolt (3) and tighten securely.

6. Using suitable packing pieces support the rear end of the shaft with the pump vertical, and carefully drift the fan and pulley hub onto the spindle until the front face of the rear hub flange is correctly positioned as determined by dimension 'A', Fig.2.5.

7. Invert the water pump and refit the water seal onto the spindle with the carbon ring facing forwards

8. Suitably support the front end of the spindle but not resting on the fan and pulley hub. Drift on the impeller (6), until dimension 'B', Fig.2.5 is achieved.

9. As a safety precaution recheck dimension 'A' and adjust accordingly with the three-legged puller or universal ball joint separator.
10 Before refitting the water pump, clean the mating faces of the water pump body and cylinder block and, to ensure a good water-tight joint, always fit a new paper joint gasket.
11 As the bearings are pre-packed, they do not require maintenance attention.
12 Check the alignment of the dynamo and fan pulleys using a straight edge. Adjust the position of the fan pulley, by inserting or removing shims (13), Fig.2.4, located behind the fan pulley (12).

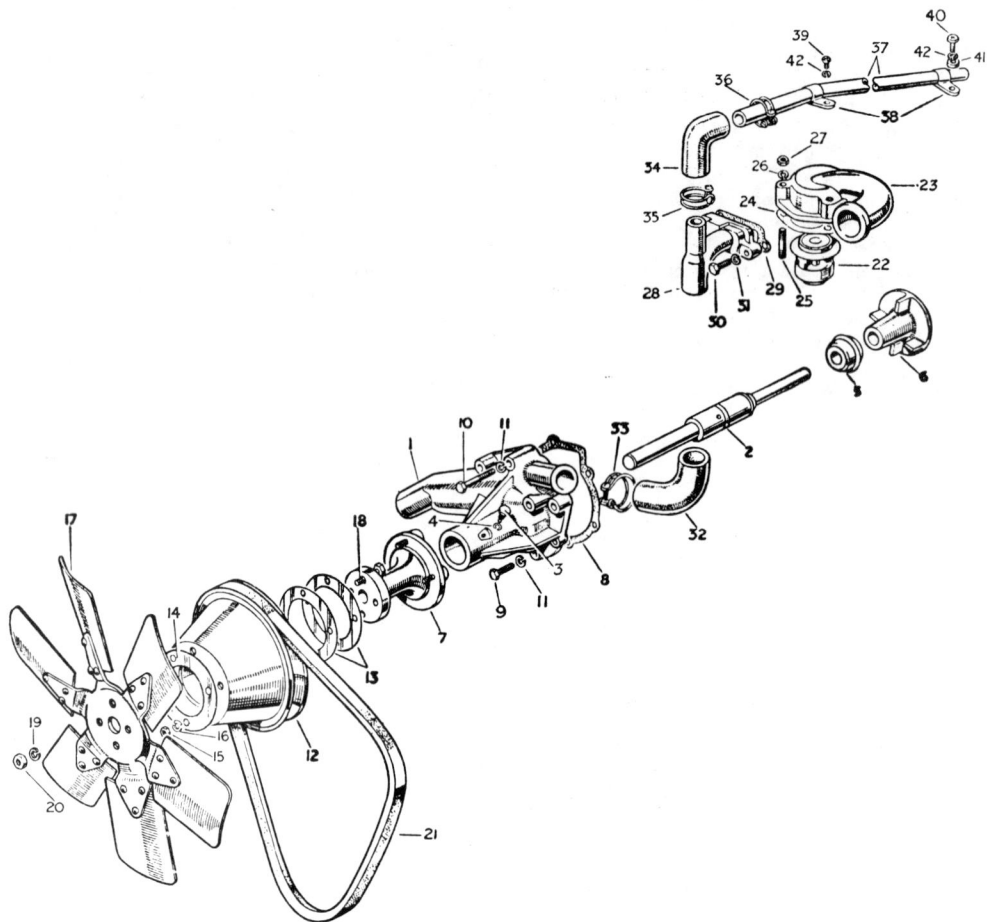

Fig.2.4. WATER PUMP, FAN & THERMOSTAT

1 Casing for water pump	12 Fan pulley	outlet pipe to radiator
2 Spine & bearing complete	13 Shim for fan pulley	24 Joint washer
3 Special set bolt	14 Reinforcing plate	25 Stud
4 Spring washer	15 Nut (¼ in.UNF)	26 Spring washer
5 Carbon ring & seal	16 Spring washer	27 Nut (¼ in.UNF)
6 Impellor for pump	17 Fan blade, balanced	28 Adaptor
7 Hub for fan & pulley	18 Bolt	29 Joint washer
8 Joint washer for water	19 Spring washer	30 Set bolt
pump	20 Nut (5/16 in.UNF)	31 Spring washer
9 Set bolt	21 Fan belt	32 Hose
10 Set bolt	22 Thermostat	33 Clip for hose
11 Spring washer	23 Thermostat cover & water	34 Hose

35 Clip, 1.1/8 in. diameter
36 Clip, 1 in. diameter
37 Outlet pipe
38 Support clip
39 Set screw
40 Set screw
41 Distance piece
42 Spring washer

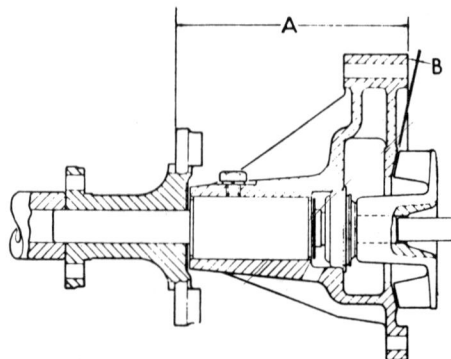

Fig.2.5. WATER PUMP REASSEMBLY DIMENSIONS
A = 4.522 + .008 inch
B = 0.020 + .004 inch

10. Fan Belt - Removal & Replacement

If the fan belt is worn or has stretched unduly, it should be renewed. The most usual reason for replacement is that the belt has broken in service. It is therefore recommended that a spare belt is carried in the car. Replacement is a reversal of the removal sequence, but as replacement due to breakage is the most usual operation, it is described below.

1. Loosen the two generator pivot bolts and the bolt on the adjusting link, and push the generator in towards the engine.
2. Slip the belt over the crankshaft, generator and water pump pulleys.
3. Adjust the belt as described in the following section, and tighten the generator mounting bolts. NOTE: After fitting a new belt it will require adjustment 250 miles later.

11. Fan Belt - Adjustment

It is important to keep the fan belt correctly adjusted and although manufacturers recommend that its tension should be checked every 10,000 miles, it is advisable to check it every 5,000 miles, as a precautionary measure.

If the belt is loose it will slip, wear rapidly and cause the generator and water pump to malfunction. If the belt is too tight, the generator and water pump bearings will wear rapidly causing premature failure of these components.

The fan belt tension is correct when there is a 5/16 inch of lateral movement at the midpoint position between the generator pulley and the crankshaft pulley.

To adjust the fan belt, slacken the generator securing bolts and move the generator in or out until the correct tension is obtained. It is easier if the generator bolts are slackened only a little so it requires some force to move the generator. In this way the tension of the belt can be arrived at more quickly than by making frequent adjustments. If difficulty is experienced in moving the generator away from the engine, a tyre lever placed behind the generator and resting against the block gives good control, so that the generator can be held in position whilst the securing bolts are tightened.

12. Choke Warning Light Switch - Removal & Refitting

The switch is located at the front of the thermostat housing in the cylinder head.
1. To remove this switch it will be necessary to drain part of the cooling system. Remove the radiator drain plug and allow about 6 pints of coolant to drain out. Refit the drain plug.
2. Disconnect the feed cable to the switch at the Lucar connector.
3. Undo the three nuts with spring washers and withdraw the switch and its cork gasket.
4. To test the operation of the switch, insert in a saucepan of cold water and connect this switch to a test light and battery.
5. Heat the water gradually and note if the switch will operate. If it fails to work the switch will require renewal.
6. Refitting the switch is the reverse sequence to removal. Always clean the two mating faces free of old cork gasket and jointing compound, if previously used, and use a new cork gasket.

13. Temperature Gauge & Thermal Transmitter

The thermal transmitter is placed in the cylinder head thermostat housing just below the thermostat. It is connected to the gauge located on the instrument panel by a cable in the main ignition feed circuit and a special bi-metal voltage stabiliser.

If unsatisfactory gauge readings are being obtained, the thermal transmitter may be tested by removing the cable connection on the transmitter and placing the cable metal end on a good earthing point, for example, a paint-free part of the cylinder head. Switch on the ignition and note the movement of the gauge needle. If the needle moves into the hot sector a new thermal transmitter should be fitted. If the needle fails to move, then a break in the wiring or a fault in the gauge (which is tested by substitution) will be the cause of the trouble.

To remove the thermal transmitter, partially drain the cooling system (usually 6 pints is enough) and unscrew the transmitter from the side of the cylinder head. Refitting is the reverse procedure to removal. Always fit a new joint washer.

Fault Finding Chart - Cooling System

Symptom	Reason/s	Remedy
Heat generated in cylinder not being successfully disposed of by radiator	Insufficient water in cooling system. Fan belt slipping. (Accompanied by a shrieking noise on rapid engine acceleration).	Top up radiator. Tighten fan belt to recommended tension or replace if worn.
	Radiator core blocked or radiator grille restricted.	Reverse flush radiator, remove obstructions.
	Bottom water hose collapsed, impeding flow.	Remove and fit new hose.
	Thermostat not opening properly.	Remove and fit new thermostat.
	Ignition advance and retard incorrectly set. (Accompanied by loss of power, and perhaps, misfiring).	Check and reset ignition timing.
	Carburetter/s incorrectly adjusted (mixture too weak.	Tune carburetter/s.
	Exhaust system partially blocked.	Check exhaust pipe for constrictive dents and blockages.
	Oil level in sump too low.	Top up sump to full mark on dipstick.
	Blwon cylinder head gasket. (Water/steam being forced down the radiator overflow pipe under pressure).	Remove cylinder head, fit new gasket.
	Engine not yet run-in	Run-in slowly and carefully.
	Brakes binding.	Check and adjust brakes if necessary.
Too much heat being dispersed by radiator	Thermostat jammed open.	Remove and renew thermostat.
	Incorrect specification thermostat fitted allowing premature opening of valve.	Remove and replace with new thermostat which opens at a higher temperature.
	Thermostat missing.	Check and fit correct thermostat.
Leaks in system	Loose clips on water hoses.	Check and tighten clips if necessary.
	Top, bottom, or by-pass water hoses perished and leaking.	Check and replace any faulty hoses.
	Radiator core leaking.	Remove radiator and repair.
	Thermostat gasket leaking.	Inspect and renew gasket.
	Radiator pressure cap spring worn or seal ineffective.	Renew radiator pressure cap.
	Blown cylinder head gasket. (Pressure in system forcing water/steam down overflow pipe).	Remove cylinder head and fit new gasket.
	Cylinder wall or head cracked.	Dismantle engine, dispatch to engineering works for repair.

Chapter 3 Fuel system and carburation

Contents

Specifications

Carburetter

Type:—
SC models	SU HS6
TC models	SU HD8

Needle:—
SC models (home)	RN
SC models (export)	RR
TC model	UI

Piston Spring:—
SC model	Green
TC model	Blue and black

Jet Size:—
SC model	0.1 inch diameter
TC model	Number 125

Float Level:—
SC model	1/8 to 3/16 inch. in closed position
TC model	7/16 inch. in closed position
Damper Oil	SAE 20
Choke setting	1/16 inch out - idle
	½ inch out - fast idle
	1¼ inch out - full choke
Engine idle speed	625 to 675 rpm

Fuel Pump
Type	AC mechanical
Delivery pressure	2—3 lb/sq.in.

EXHAUST EMISSION CONTROL MODIFICATIONS

Carburetter

2000 TC models from engine number 415 and 416 (suffix 'C' on):-
Type	SU — HS8 (air damped piston)
Bore	2.00 in
Needle	AAA
Jet size (diameter)	0.90 in
Float level	5/16 in
Damper oil	SAE 20

2000 TC models from engine number 436 and 445 on:-
(Specifications are as per the above SU HS8 carburettor but with the following difference):
Needle	AAB

2000 SC models from engine number 436 and 445 on:-
Type	SU — HS6 (single)
Bore	1.75 in
Needle	BAF
Jet size	0.100 in
Float level	1/8 to 3/16 in
Damper oil	SAE 20
Engine idle speed	625 to 675 rpm
Fast idle speed	1100 to 1200 rpm
CO — maximum permissible emission	4%

Fuel Pump

Type	AC mechanical
Delivery pressure	2¾ — 4½ lb/sq.in.
Fuel spill back line restrictor	0.030 inch diameter

Fuel Tank Capacity

Total capacity (including reserve)	12 Imperial gallons
Reserve	1¼ Imperial gallons

1. General Description

The fuel system on models covered by this manual comprises a 12 gallon fuel tank, located in the boot of the car, an AC mechanical fuel pump and a single SU carburetter type HS6 (SC models) or twin SU carburetter type HD8 (TC models).

Fitted to the underside of the fuel tank is the gauge unit and two outlet pipes, one being the main feed pipe and the other the reserve pipe. A vent pipe is fitted to the top of the tank and passes up the inside of the rear left-hand quarter panel. The reserve fuel system is brought into operation from the driver's seat by a cable operated mechanical two-way tap located on the right-hand side of the engine compartment.

The mechanical fuel pump is fitted to the right-hand side of the engine and is operated by a small pushrod, one end of which rests on the side of the offset cam at the base of the distributor drive shafts.

Both types of carburetter installation have an air cleaner with a renewable paper element type filter which removes dust and dirt from the air before it reaches the carburetter/s.

2. Air Cleaners — Removal, Replacement & Servicing

It is recommended that the air cleaner element/s be renewed every 5,000 miles (TC models) or 10,000 miles (SC models), or at 12 monthly intervals or earlier when the car is being used in dusty conditions.

SC models

To remove the air cleaner (Fig.3.1), first detach the rubber balance pipe from the carburetter float chamber. Undo and remove the two nuts and spring washers that secure the air cleaner backplate 'A' to the carburetter flange. The cleaner may now be lifted away and at the same time disconnected from the rubber connection at the air intake tube.

The elements 'B' may now be removed by undoing and removing the wing nut in the centre of the cover 'D' and lifting away the cover. Remove the old filter elements 'B' and wipe the interior of the air cleaner to remove any accumulated dust.

It is important that the correct specification element is fitted and that the new gaskets are used.

Reassembly is the reverse sequence to removal.

TC models

Undo and remove the two brass tube nuts ('B', Fig.3.2) and fibre washers that secure the air cleaner installation 'A' and lift away the complete assembly.

The two halves of the casing may be separated by inserting a screwdriver into the centre slot and twisting. Lift out the old elements and wipe the interior of the air cleaner to remove any accumulated dust.

To reassemble, place the new elements into the casing half, and engage the lip of the cover with the recess at the bottom of the body. Carefully press the two halves together until the top lips engage with their recess.

Inspect the two rubber rings for signs of perishing or cracking and obtain new ones if their condition has deteriorated. Make sure that they are correctly fitted and replace the air cleaners as one unit. Secure in position with the two brass tube nuts and fibre washers.

3. Carburetter — Description

1. Although slightly different in design, the SU HS6 carburetter operates basically in the same manner as the HD8 carburetter. This type of carburetter differs from most other carburetters in that instead of having a number of various sized fixed jets for different conditions, only one variable jet is fitted to deal with all possible requirements.

2. Air passing rapidly through the carburetter draws petrol from the jet so forming the petrol/air mixture. The amount of petrol drawn from the jet depends on the position of the tapered carburetter needle, which moves up and down the jet orifice according to the engine load and throttle opening, thus effectively altering the size of jet so that exactly the right amount of fuel is metered for the prevailing road conditions.

3. The position of the tapered needle in the jet is determined by engine vacuum. The shank of the needle is held at its top end in a piston which slides up and down the dashpot in response to the degree of manifold vacuum.

4. With the throttle fully open, the full effect of inlet manifold vacuum is felt by the piston which has an air bleed into the choke tube on the outside of the throttle. This causes the piston to rise fully, bringing the needle with it. With the accelerator partially closed, only slight inlet manifold vacuum is felt by the piston (although, of course, on the engine side of the throttle the vacuum is greater), and the piston only rises a little, blocking most of the jet orifice with the metering needle.

5. To prevent the piston fluttering, and giving a richer mixture when the accelerator is suddenly depressed, an oil damper and light spring are fitted into the dashpot.

6. The only portion of the piston assembly to come into contact with the piston chamber or dashpot is the actual central piston rod. All the other parts of the piston assembly, including the lower choke portion, have sufficient clearance to prevent any direct metal to

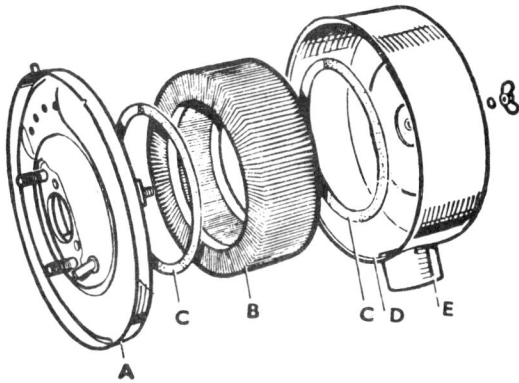

Fig.3.1. AIR CLEANER ASSEMBLY (SC MODELS)

A Backplate for air cleaner
B Element
C Gaskets
D Cover for air cleaner
E Air cleaner intake

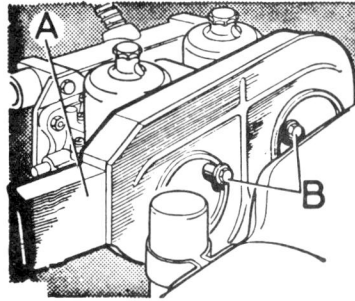

Fig.3.2. AIR CLEANER MOUNTING BOLT LOCATION (TC MODELS)

A Air cleaner body
B Brass tube nuts, air cleaner body to adaptors

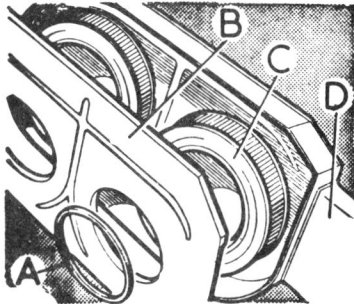

Fig.3.3. AIR CLEANER COMPONENT PARTS (TC MODELS)

A Rubber rings, carburetter adaptors
B Air cleaner cover
C Elements
D Air cleaner body

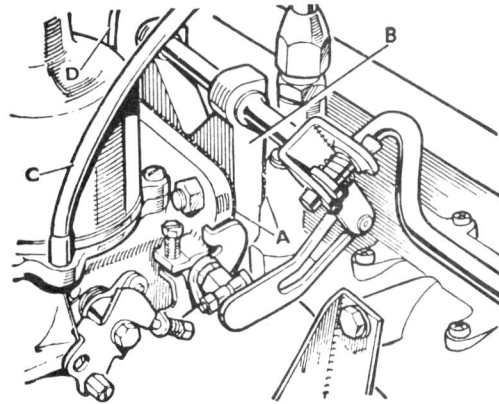

Fig.3.4. CARBURETTER LINKAGE (SC MODELS)

A Position of gaskets
B Throttle counter-shaft adaptor
C Cold-start control cable
D Vacuum pipe

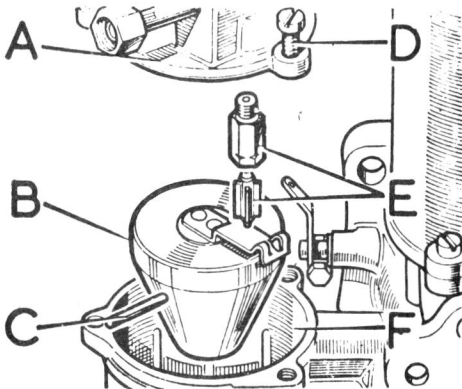

Fig.3.5. FLOAT CHAMBER PARTS

A Float chamber lid
B Float and lever complete
C Mills pin
D Screws retaining float chamber lid
E Needle valve and seat
F Float chamber

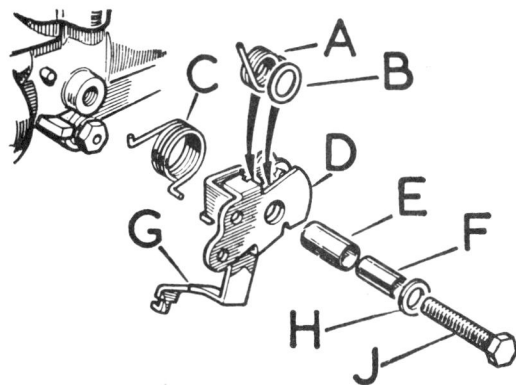

Fig.3.6. CARBURETTER PICK UP LINK ASSEMBLY

A Return spring for cam lever
B Washer for return spring
C Spring for pick-up lever
D Cam lever
E Tube, outer
F Tube, inner
G Pick-up lever and link assembly
H Washer
J Bolt securing assembly to carburetter body

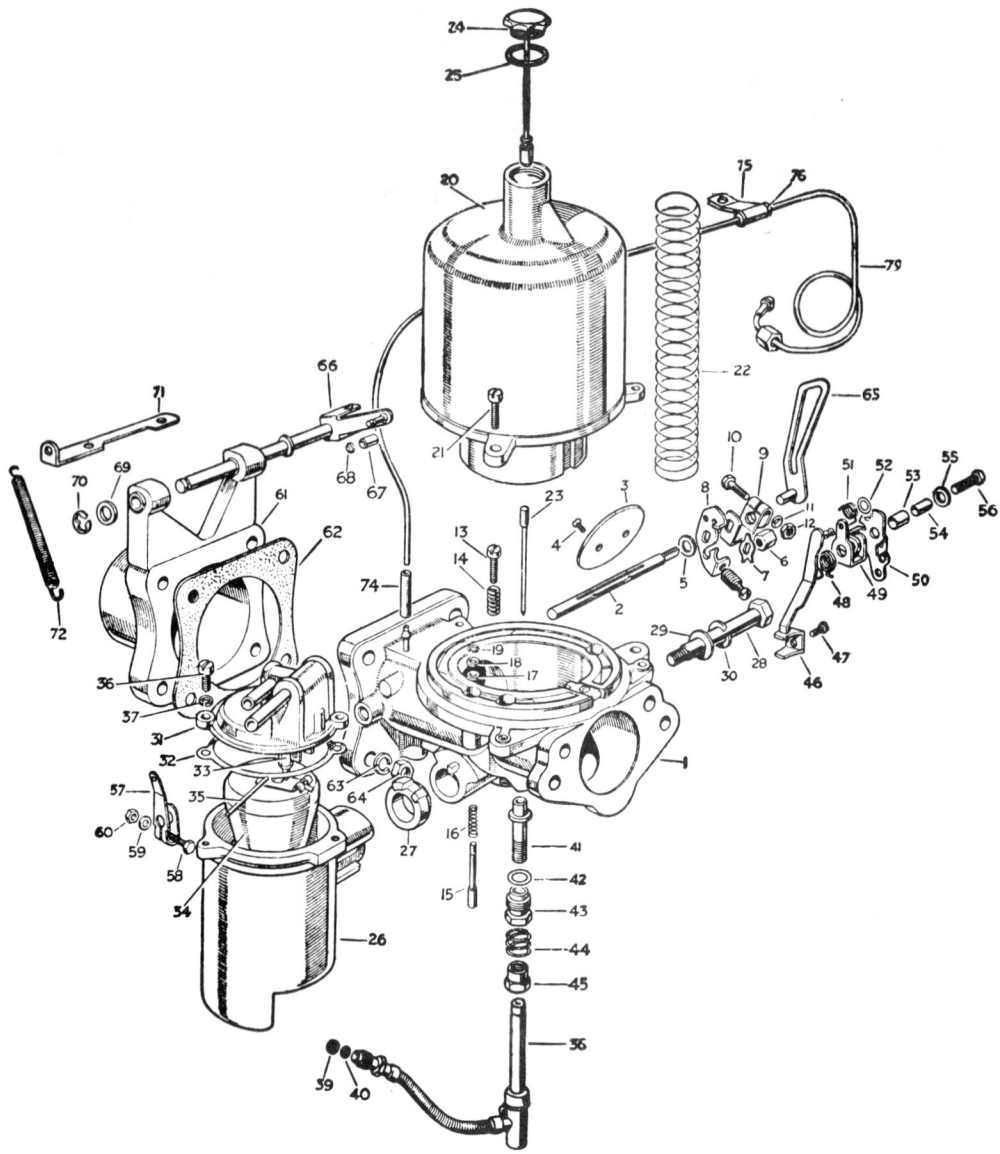

Fig.3.7. CARBURETTER COMPONENT PARTS (SC MODELS)

1 Carburetter body	21 Special screw	41 Jet bearing	59 Plain washer
2 Throttle spindle	22 Spring for piston (green)	42 Brass washer for jet	60 Special nut
3 Throttle butterfly	23 Needle, RN	bearing	61 Adaptor for carburetter
4 Screw for throttle butterfly	24 Oil cap & damper complete	43 Special nut fixing jet	62 Joint washer
5 Washer for throttle spindle	25 Washer for oil cap	bearing	63 Spring washer
6 Special nut for spindle	26 Float chamber	44 Lock spring	64 Nut (5/16 in. UNF)
7 Tab washer for nut	27 Adaptor for float chamber	45 Adjusting nut	65 Lever
8 Lever for throttle spindle	28 Special bolt	46 Pick-up lever and link	66 Countershaft and lever
9 Coupling clip for spindle	29 Plain washer	47 Self-tapping screw	67 Roller
10 Special bolt	30 Spring washer	48 Spring for pick-up lever	68 Circlip securing roller
11 Plain washer	31 Lid for float chamber	49 Bracket for jet link	69 Plain washer
12 Special nut	32 Joint washer	50 Cam lever	70 Circlip
13 Throttle adjustment screw	33 Needle valve & seat	51 Spring for cam lever	71 Anchor
14 Spring for adjustment screw	34 Float & lever complete	52 Shim washer	72 Throttle return spring
15 Piston lift pin	35 Pin for float lever	53 Tube, outer	73 Suction pipe complete
16 Spring	36 Special screw	54 Tube, inner	74 Tube
17 Neoprene washer	37 Spring washer	55 Skid washer	75 Clip for suction pipe
18 Brass washer	38 Jet & pipe complete	56 Pivot bolt	76 Rubber grommet for
19 Circlip	39 Gland washer	57 Lever	clip
20 Suction chamber & piston	40 Brass washer	58 Special bolt	

metal contact, which is essential if the carburetter is to function correctly.

7. The correct level of the petrol in the carburetter is determined by the level of the petrol in the float chamber. When the level is correct, the float rises and by means of a lever resting on the top of it, closes the needle valve in the cover of the float chamber. This closes off the supply of fuel from the pump. When the level of the float chamber drops as the fuel is used in the carburetter, so the float drops. As it does, the float needle is unseated, so allowing more fuel to enter the float chamber and restore the correct level.

4. Carburetter (SC) – Removal & Replacement

1. Refer to Section 2 of this chapter and remove the air cleaner assembly.

2. Disconnect the fuel supply pipe to the carburetter by using two open ended spanners; one to hold the hexagon on the pipe and the other to turn the hexagon nearest to the carburetter. Using this method ensures that the pipe is not twisted.

3. Release the throttle return spring from the anchor plate and then from the throttle lever.

4. Disconnect the rubber sleeve connection ('D', Fig.3.4) from the distributor advance/retard vacuum pipe on the carburetter body.

5. Undo and remove the two bolts and plain washers that secure the heat shield to the cylinder head. Lift away the heat shield.

6. Remove the circlip, anti-rattle spring and washers, that secure the accelerator coupling shaft to the carburetter countershaft (B). Separate the coupling shaft from the countershaft. NOTE: On cars fitted with automatic transmission, a hairpin spring clip is used instead of the circlip.

7. If the car is fitted with automatic transmission and also crankcase emission control, it will be necessary to disconnect the hose and flame trap at the carburetter.

8. Disconnect the choke control cable (C) from the carburetter.

9. Undo and remove the four nuts and spring washers that secure the carburetter to the inlet manifold and carefully lift away the carburetter complete with throttle countershaft, adaptor and gaskets (A), (photos).

10 Refitting the carburetter is the reverse sequence to removal, but the following additional points should be noted:—

a) Always fit new gaskets (A) to the manifold and adaptor plate flanges in the following order:— Place a new gasket onto the inlet manifold, then fit the adaptor and then follow by a second new gasket.

b) It will assist refitting if the throttle linkage is engaged at the same time as the carburetter is being placed in position on the studs.

5. Carburetter SC – Dismantling & Reassembly

1. All reference numbers refer to Fig.3.7, unless stated otherwise. Unscrew the piston damper (24) and lift away from the chamber and piston assembly (20).

2. Using a screwdriver or small file, scratch identification marks on the suction chamber and carburetter body (1) so that they may be fitted together in their original position. Remove the three suction chamber retaining screws (21) and lift the suction chamber from the carburetter body, leaving the piston in position. Lift away the piston spring (22) from the piston, noting which way round it is fitted.

3. Very carefully lift the piston from the body (1). Invert it and allow the oil in the damper bore to drain out. Place the piston in a safe place, so that the needle will not be touched or the piston roll onto the floor. It is recommended that the piston be placed on the neck of a narrow jam jar with the needle inside so acting as a stand.

4. Mark the position of the float chamber lid (31) relative to the body and unscrew the three screws (36) holding the float chamber lid to the float chamber body (26). Lift away the screws (36), spring washers (37), float chamber lid (31) and joint washer (32).

5. Withdraw the Mills pin ('C', Fig.3.5), thereby releasing the float and float lever 'B'. Recover the needle valve from the needle valve assembly in the lid. Using a box spanner, remove the needle valve assembly body from the float chamber lid.

6. Using the fingers, apply pressure to the cam lever ('D', Fig.3.6), and remove the Phillips head screw from the base of the jet assembly. Release the pick-up link 'G'.

7. Remove the bolt ('J', Fig.3.6) and plain washer 'H' that secures the pick-up assembly and at the same time, release the spring 'A'.

8. Refer to Fig.3.6, and compare the parts with those on the carburetter, making particular note of the order of fitting, and then withdraw the pick-up link assembly which will be seen to comprise pick-up lever and pick-up assembly 'G', spring 'A', inner and outer distance tube 'F', 'E', cam lever 'D', spring 'A' and spring washer 'B'.

9. Undo and remove the bolt ('B', Fig.3.8), spring washer and plain washer that secures the float chamber 'C' to the carburetter body.

10 Carefully remove the float chamber ('C', Fig.3.8) and adaptor 'A' from the carburetter body, at the same time withdrawing the jet 'F' and the jet bearing 'J' at the base of the carburetter body.

11 Using an open ended spanner, undo the gland nut at the end of the jet assembly flexible pipe and securing it to the float chamber, and lift away the jet assembly ('F', Fig.3.8) complete with gland washer 'D' and brass washer 'E'.

12 Undo and remove the jet adjusting nut ('H', Fig.3.8) together with the spring 'G'. Also undo and remove the jet bearing securing nut 'L', brass washer 'K' and jet bearing 'J'.

13 Undo and remove the clamp bolt, nut and plain washer that secures the throttle return spring lever ('A', Fig.3.9) to the throttle spindle 'G'. Lift away the lever 'A'.

14 Undo and remove the bolt, nut and plain washer ('E', Fig.3.9) from the coupling clip 'F' and remove the throttle lever 'L'.

15 Bend back the tab washer tabs ('J', Fig.3.9) from the spindle nut 'K' and remove the nut 'K', coupling 'F' and tab washer 'J'. Also remove the throttle stop lever 'H' and brass washer 'D'.

16 Using a pair of pliers close the splayed out ends of the two screws ('B', Fig.3.9) that secure the throttle butterfly 'C' into the throttle spindle. Undo and remove the two screws 'B'. Note the position of the butterfly to ensure it is fitted in its original position and slide the butterfly from the spindle 'G'.

17 Withdraw the throttle spindle 'G' from the carburetter body.

18 Reassembly is an exact reversal of the dismantling procedure and no trouble will be encountered providing that care was taken during dismantling to ensure every part was placed in order on the bench. Fig.3.5 shows an exploded view of the complete carburetter and supplementary illustrations, Fig.3.6 3.8, and 3.9 show in more detail some of the assembly details.

6. Carburetter (SC) – Examination & Repair

The SU carburetter generally speaking is most reliable, but even so it may develop one of several faults which may not be readily apparent unless a careful inspection is carried out. The common faults the carburetter is prone to are:—

1. Piston sticking.
2. Float needle sticking.
3. Float chamber flooding.
4. Water and dirt in the carburetter.

In addition the following parts are susceptible to wear, after long mileage, and as they vitally affect the economy of the engine, they should be checked and renewed where necessary, every 24,000 miles:—

a) The carburetter needle. If this has been incorrectly fitted at some time, so that it is not centrally located in the jet orifice, then the metering needle will have a tiny ridge worn on it. If a ridge can be seen, then the needle must be renewed. SU carburetter needles are made to very fine tolerances and should a ridge be apparent no attempt must be made to rub the needle down with fine emery paper. If it is wished to clean the needle it can be polished lightly

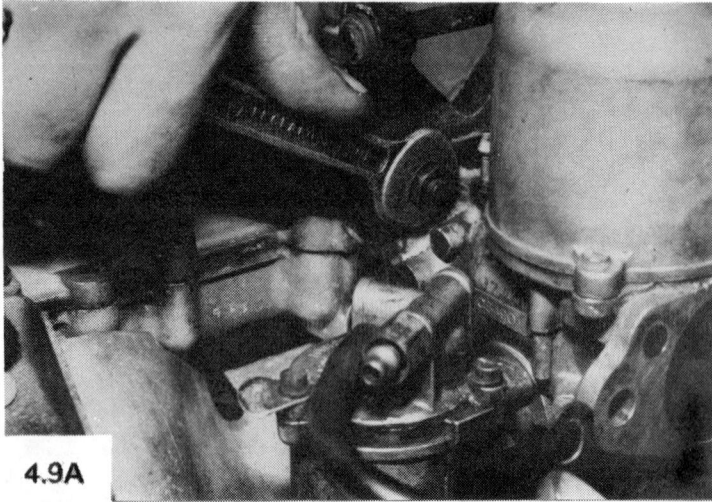

4.9A

4.9B

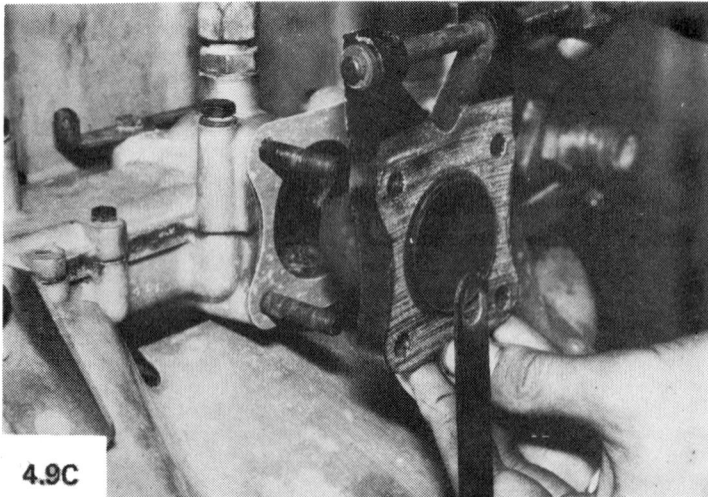

4.9C

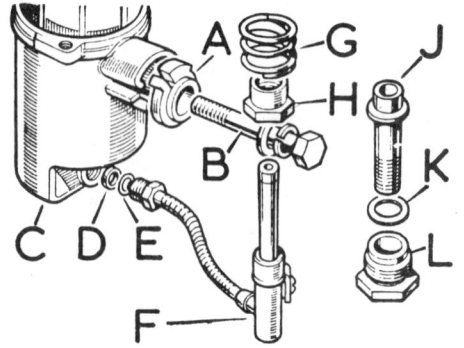

Fig.3.8. FLOAT CHAMBER AND
JET ASSEMBLY
A Adaptor for ffoat chamber
B Bolt fixing float chamber
C Float chamber
D Gland washer
E Brass washer
F Jet assembly
G Lock spring
H Adjusting nut
J Jet bearing
K Brass washer
L Special nut fixing jet bearing

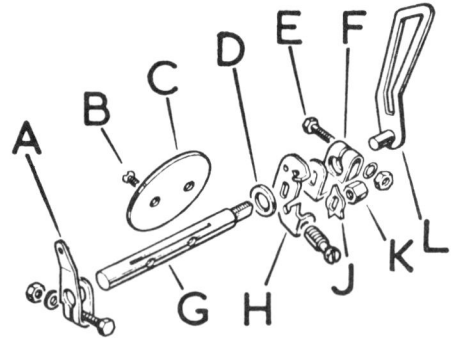

Fig.3.9. THROTTLE SPINDLE
LEVER & STOP LEVER
A Return spring lever
B Screws for butterfly
C Butterfly
D Brass washer
E Bolt, nut and plain washer
   securing throttle lever
F Coupling clip
G Throttle spindle
H Throttle stop lever
J Tab washer
K Spindle nut
L Lever, countersunk

with metal polish.

b) The carburetter jet. If the needle is worn it is likely that the rim of the jet will be damaged, where the needle has been striking it. It should be renewed as otherwise fuel consumption will suffer. The jet can also be badly worn or ridged on the outside from where it has been sliding up and down between the jet bearing every time the choke has been pulled out. Removal and renewal is the only answer as well.

c) Check the edges of the throttle and the choke tube for wear. Renew if worn.

d) The washers fitted to the base of the jet and under the float chamber lid may leak after a time and can cause a great deal of fuel wastage. It is wisest to renew them automatically when the carburetter is stripped down.

e) After high mileages, the float chamber needle and seat are bound to be ridged. They are not an expensive item to replace and must be renewed as a set. They should never be renewed separately.

Piston Sticking

1. The hardened piston rod which slides in the centre guide tube in the middle of the dashpot is the only part of the piston assembly (which comprises the jet needle, suction disc, and piston choke) which should make contact with the dashpot. The piston rim and the choke periphery are machined to very fine tolerances so that they will not touch the dashpot or the choke tube walls.

2. After high mileages, wear in the centre guide tube may allow the piston to touch the dashpot walls. This condition is known as sticking.

3. If piston sticking is suspected or it is wished to test for this condition, rotate the piston about the centre guide tube at the same time as sliding it up and down inside the dashpot. If any portion of the piston makes contact with the dashpot wall, then that portion of the wall must be polished with a metal polish until clearance exists. In extreme cases, very fine emery cloth can be used.

The greatest care should be taken to remove only the minimum amount of metal to provide the clearance as too large a gap will cause air leakage and will upset the functioning of the carburetter. Clean down the walls of the dashpot and the piston rim and ensure that there is no oil on them. A trace of oil may be judiciously applied to the piston rod.

5. If the piston is sticking, under no circumstances try to clean it by trying to alter the tension of the light return spring.

Float Needle Sticking

1. If the float needle sticks, the carburetter will soon run dry and the engine will stop despite there being fuel in the tank. The easiest way to check a suspected sticking float needle is to remove the inlet pipe at the carburetter and, where a mechanical fuel pump is fitted, turn the engine over on the starter motor by pressing the solenoid rubber button. Where an electric fuel pump is fitted, turn on the ignition but do not start the engine. If fuel spurts from the end of the pipe (direct it towards the ground or onto a wad of cloth or jar) then the fault is almost certain to be a sticking float needle.

2. Remove the float chamber, dismantle the valve and clean the housing and float chamber out thoroughly.

Float Chamber Flooding

1. If fuel emerges from the breather hole in the cover of the float chamber, this is known as flooding. It is caused by the float chamber needle not seating properly in its housing; normally this is because a piece of dirt or foreign matter is jammed between the needle and needle housing. Alternatively, the float may have developed a leak or be maladjusted so that it is holding open the float chamber needle valve even though the chamber is full of petrol. Remove the float chamber cover, clean the needle assembly, check the setting of the float as detailed in the next column, and shake the float to verify if any has leaked into it.

Water or Dirt in the Carburetter

1. Because of the size of the jet orifice, water or dirt in the carburetter

is normally easily cleared. If dirt in the carburetter is suspected, lift the piston assembly and flood the float chamber. The normal level of the fuel should be approximately 1/16 inch below the top of the jet, so that on flooding the carburetter the fuel should flow out of the jet hole.

2. If little or no petrol appears, start the engine (the jet is never completely blocked) and with the throttle fully open, blank off the air intake. This will cause a partial vacuum in the choke tube and help suck out any foreign matter from the jet tube. Release the throttle as soon as the engine speed alters considerably. Repeat this procedure several times, stop the engine and then check the carburetter as detailed in the first paragraph of the Section.

3. If this fails to do the trick, then there is no alternative but to remove and blow out the jet.

Jet Centring

1. This operation is always necessary if the carburetter has been dismantled; but to check this, if necessary, on a carburetter in service, first screw up the jet adjusting nut as far as it will go without forcing it, and lift the piston and let it fall under its own weight. It should fall onto the bridge making a soft metallic click. Now repeat the above procedure but this time with the adjusting nuts screwed right down. If the soft metallic click is not audible in either of the two tests, proceed as follows:

2. Disconnect the jet link, see Fig.3.7, from the bottom of the jet, and the nylon flexible tube from the underside of the float chamber. Gently slide the jet and the nylon tube from the underside of the carburetter body. Next unscrew the jet adjusting nut and lift away the nut and the locking spring. Refit the adjusting nut without the locking spring and screw it up as far as possible without forcing. Replace the jet and tube, but there is no need to reconnect the tube.

3. Slacken the jet locking nut so that it may be rotated with the fingers only. Unscrew the piston damper and lift away the damper. Gently press the piston down onto the bridge and tighten the locknut. Lift the piston using the lifting pin, and check that it is able to freely fall under its own weight. Now lower the adjusting nut and check once again and if this time there is a difference in the two metallic clicks repeat the centring procedure until the sound is the same for both tests.

4. Gently remove the jet and unscrew the adjusting nut. Refit the locking spring and jet adjusting nuts. Top up the damper with oil if necessary and replace the damper. Connect the nylon flexible tube to the underside of the float chamber and finally reconnect the jet link.

Float Chamber Fuel Level Adjustment

1. It is essential that the fuel level in the float chamber is always correct as otherwise excessive fuel consumption may occur. On reassembly of the float chamber, check the fuel level before replacing the float chamber cover in the following manner.

2. Invert the float chamber cover so that the needle valve is closed. It should be just possible to place a 3/16 inch bar parallel to the float chamber cover without fouling the float or if the float stands proud of the bar then it is necessary to bend the float lever slightly until the clearance is correct. This is shown in Fig.3.10.

Needle Replacement

1. Should it be necessary to fit a new needle, first remove the piston and suction chamber assembly, marking the chamber for correct reassembly in its original position.

2. Slacken the needle clamping screw and withdraw the needle from the piston.

3. Upon refitting a new needle it is important that the shoulder on the shank is flushed with the underside of the piston. Use a straight edge such as a metal rule for the adjustment. Refit the piston and suction chamber and check for freedom of piston movement.

7. Carburetter (SC) — Adjustment & Tuning

1. To adjust and tune the SU carburetter proceed in the following

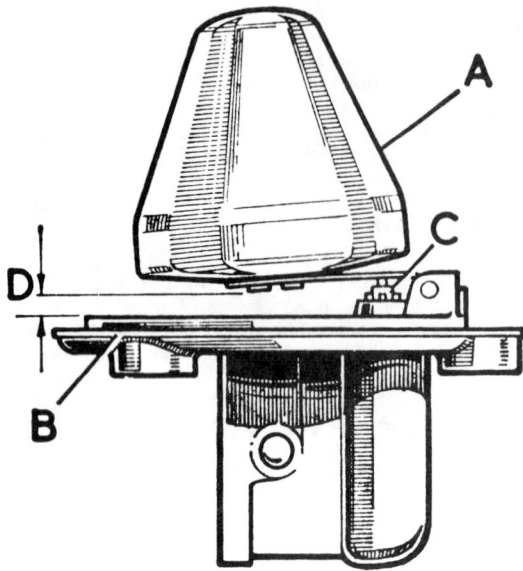

Fig.3.10. FLOAT CHAMBER FUEL LEVEL SETTING
A Nylon float   C Needle valve
B Gasket   D 3/16 inch clearance

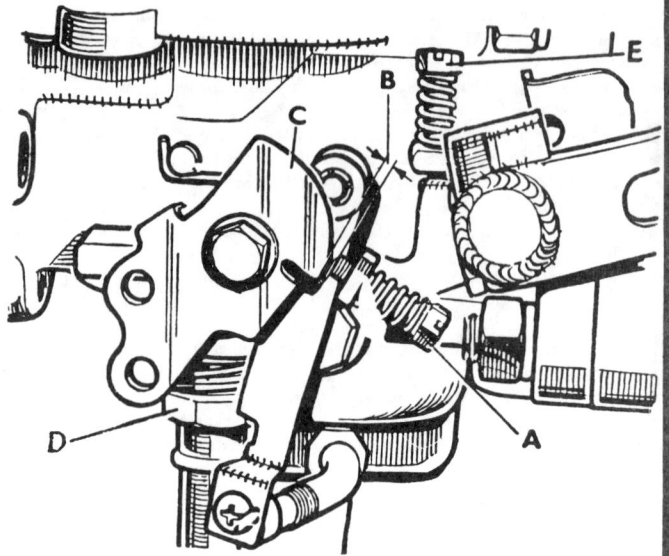

Fig.3.11. CARBURETTER ADJUSTMENT SCREWS
A Fast idle adjustment   C Cam
   screw   D Jet adjusting nut
B Clearance   E Throttle adjusting screw

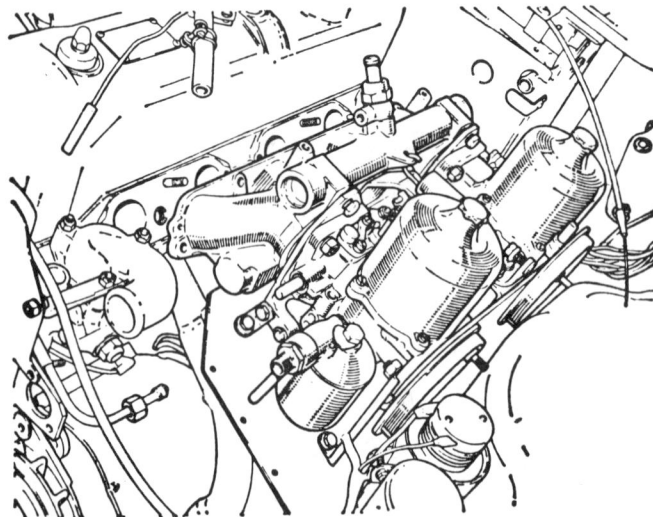

Fig.3.12. Carburetter and inlet manifold removal (TC models)

manner:— Check the colour of the exhaust at idling speed with the choke fully in. If the exhaust tends to be black and the tail pipe interior is also black it is a fair indication that the mixture is too rich. If the exhaust is colourless and the deposit in the exhaust pipe is very light grey it is likely that the mixture is too weak. This condition may also be accompanied by intermittent misfiring, while too rich a mixture will be associated with 'hunting'. Ideally, the exhaust should be colourless with a medium grey pipe deposit.

2. The exhaust pipe deposit should only be checked after a good run of at least 20 miles. Idling in city traffic and stop/start motoring is bound to produce excessive dark exhaust pipe deposit.

3. Once the engine has reached its normal operating temperature, refer to Section 2 of this chapter and remove the air cleaner.

4. Top up the carburetter dashpot with SAE 20 grade oil.

5. Disconnect the choke control cable wire from the carburetter.

6. Refer to Fig.3.11, and unscrew the throttle adjusting screw 'E' until the face of the screw clears the stop.

7. Check the carburetter spindle lever position so that when engaged with the countershaft the butterfly is in the closed position. Should adjustment be necessary, slacken the lever clamp bolt, reset the lever and tighten the clamp bolt.

8. Screw the throttle adjusting screw down one and a half turns only.

9. Screw up the jet adjusting nut ('H', Fig.3.8) until the jet is flushed with the bridge of the carburetter. DO NOT OVERTIGHTEN. Next screw back the jet adjusting nut two complete turns only.

10 Again run the engine for a few minutes so that it is at normal running temperature and adjust the throttle adjusting screw ('E', Fig.3.11), until the engine idles at a speed of approximately 550 — 600 r.p.m.

11 Slowly turn the jet adjusting nut until the fastest idling speed is obtained with no signs of engine misfiring. Screwing the nut up weakens the mixture and screwing it down enriches the mixture. It will be observed that as the mixture is adjusted, the engine will most likely run faster and therefore the speed will have to be adjusted back to the desired idling speed.

12 Check the mixture strength by lifting the carburetter piston 1/32 inch using the little lift pin located on the side of the carburetter and check for one of the following conditions:—

a) If the engine speed increases and continues to increase, it is an indication that the mixture is too rich.

b) If the engine speed decreases immediately it is an indication that the mixture is too weak.

c) If the engine speed momentarily increases very slightly the mixture is correct.

When the mixture is correct the exhaust notes should be regular and even, whereas if it gives a splashy sound with a colourless exhaust it is an indication that it is too weak. Alternatively, if there is a regular and rhythmical type of misfire accompanied by a dark exhaust it is an indication that the mixture is too rich. Once the mixture adjustment is correct proceed to the next stage.

13 Switch off the ignition and slacken the clamp bolt that retains the throttle spindle to the countershaft lever. Then restart the engine and pull out the choke control knob until the point where the warning light just comes on.

14 Refer to Fig.3.7, and slowly turn the fast idle cam lever in a clockwise direction until it just makes contact with the jet bracket and whilst in this position, retighten the choke cable clamp.

15 Adjust the fast idle screw ('A', Fig.3.11), until a fast idle speed of between 1,000 and 1,200 r.p.m. is obtained.

16 Push the choke control fully home and switch off the engine. Next pull down the throttle lever until the countershaft roller is at the end of the slot, making sure that the roller DOES NOT touch the sides of the slot at any point. Tighten the clamp bolt.

17 Pull out the choke control slowly and check that the roller does not make contact with the sides of the throttle lever slot at any time.

18 The carburetter may now be considered to be correctly adjusted providing that the foregoing instructions have been rigidly adhered to.

8. Carburetters (TC) — Removal & Refitting

1. To remove the twin carburetter installation, it is recommended that the carburetters be left attached to the inlet manifold and removed as one unit from the engine.

2. Refer to Section 2 of this chapter and remove the air cleaner assembly.

3. Refer to Chapter 2, Section 2, and drain the cooling system.

4. Undo the fuel pipe union to the front carburetter and disconnect the fuel pipe.

5. Ease back the spring clip and disconnect the throttle pedal linkage at the upper ball joint of the vertical rod. Then disconnect the coupling shaft support bracket.

6. Release the choke control cable at the front carburetter jet lever. Also release the clip that secures the choke control outer cable. Remove the rubber cleat securing the choke control cable to the heater outlet hose.

7. Ease back the rubber connecting tube from the front carburetter body for the distributor automatic advance retard vacuum system.

8. If a hose is fitted between the top cover and the rear of the air cleaner adaptor, this should be next be disconnected.

9. If a hose is fitted between the crankcase emission control valve to the banjo union on the inlet manifold, this should be disconnected. Also remove the cleat that secures this hose to the heater outlet pipe.

10 Slacken the hose clips for the heater outlet pipe and disconnect the hose. Remove the two Phillips head screws that secure the pipe to the manifold and lift away the heater outlet pipe, clips and spacer.

11 Slacken the hose clip for the heater inlet hose at the inlet manifold and disconnect this hose from the manifold.

12 Slacken the hose clip for the brake servo unit hose at the inlet manifold union and disconnect the hose from the union. Release the clip that secures the brake servo unit hose and vacuum pipe to the top cover.

13 Undo and remove the six nuts and spring washers that secure the inlet manifold to the cylinder head studs.

14 Carefully lift away the inlet manifold complete with carburetters and heat shields. Remove the joints from the cylinder head and blank off the inlet ports to stop any dirt ingress.

15 Remove the circlip and plain washer that retains the throttle countershaft as shown in Fig.3.13, and disconnect the throttle countershaft.

16 Disconnect the throttle return spring.

17 Undo and remove the two-way banjo from the front carburetter float chamber and then the banjo to the rear carburetter float chamber and lift away the fuel pipe interconnecting the front and rear carburetter float chambers. NOTE: The locations of the fibre washers and spring loaded filter at the float chamber inlet are clearly shown in Fig.3.18.

18 Undo and remove the heat shield, two retaining set bolts and a further two nuts, bolts and spring washers that secure the heat shield to the brackets. Lift away the heat shield.

19 Undo and remove the self-locking nut that secures the support spring to the tie-bar. Unhook the spring from the manifolds. (Fig. 3.14).

20 Remove the two nuts and spring washers that secure the tie-bar to the link plate. Also undo and remove the four nuts and spring washers that secure the link plate, air cleaner adaptors, and heat shield brackets to the carburetter bodies

21 Disconnect and remove the jet connecting rods.

22 Slacken the two nuts of the folded coupling on the throttle spindle and connecting rod. Gently slide the coupling towards the rear carburetter and remove it together with the connecting rod.

23 Undo and remove the four nuts and spring washers from each carburetter flange and then lift away the carburetters and gaskets from the studs on the adaptor.

24 Undo and remove the two retaining bolts from each carburetter adaptor and very carefully ease the adaptors from the inlet manifold.

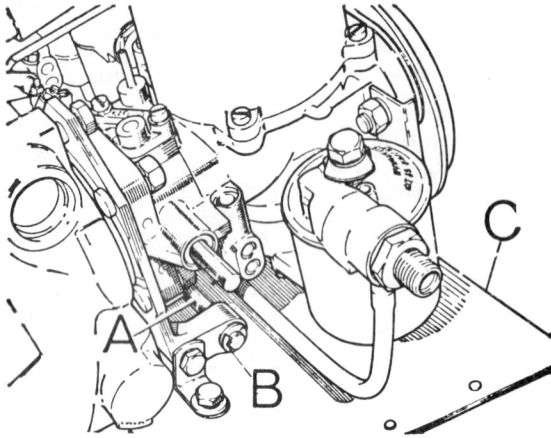

Fig.3.13. THROTTLE COUNTERSHAFT REMOVAL

A Throttle countershaft   C Heat shield
B Circlip for countershaft

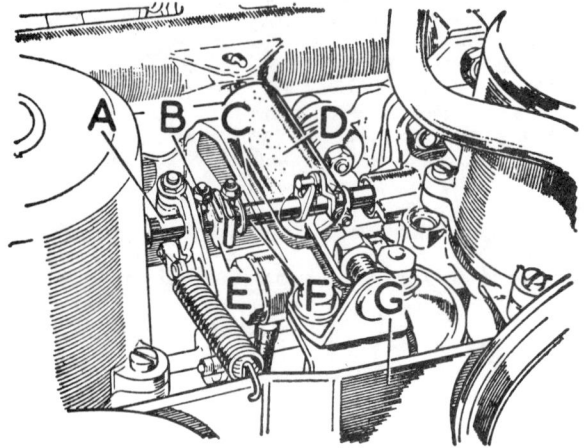

Fig.3.14. CARBURETTER THROTTLE LINKAGE

A Front throttle shaft   E Folded coupling
B Clamp nut   F Connecting rod
C Tie bar   G Link plate
D Support spring and sleeve

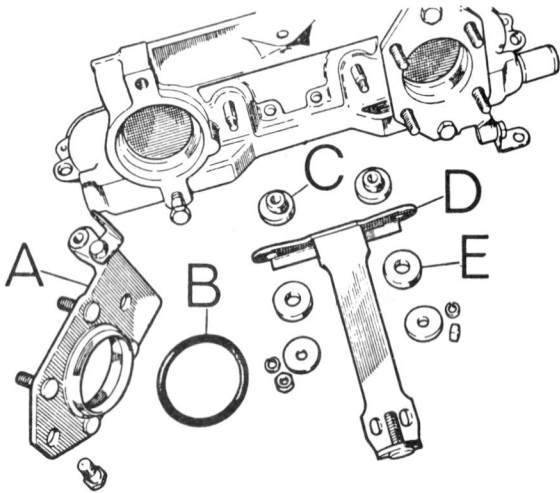

Fig.3.15. CARBURETTER ADAPTOR & TIE BAR
ATTACHMENTS

A Carburetter adaptor   D Tie bar
B 'O' ring   E Rubber washer
C Rubber bush

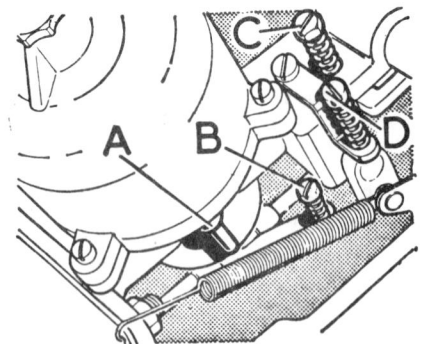

Fig.3.16. CARBURETTER ADJUSTMENT SCREWS

A Carburetter piston lift pin   C Throttle adjustment screw
B Mixture adjustment screw   D . Fast idle adjustment screw

Lift away the 'O' rings to be found in the manifold recess.

25 Remove the two nuts, spring washers, plain washers and rubber washers, that secure the tie-bar to the inlet manifold. Lift away the tie-bar and rubber bushes. The carburetter and inlet manifold assembly are now completely dismantled.

26 Before reassembly, obtain a block of wood, slightly larger and wider than the mounting face of the inlet manifold and place between the jaws of a vice. Using two wood screws and plain washers, secure the inlet manifold to the wood. This will act as a holding jig to facilitate refitting and alignment of the carburetters.

27 Smear a little Silicone Compound MS4 onto the two 'O' rings ('B', Fig.3.15), and then fit them into the manifold recess, making sure that they are not twisted or kinked.

28 Smear the leading edge of the front carburetter adaptor with a little Silicone Compound MS4 and press the adaptor into the 'O' ring until the recess engages with the 'O' ring.

29 Apply a little 'Loctite' sealant, Grade AVV to the threads of the special adaptor bolts and refit the adaptors to the inlet manifold.

30 Repeat the procedures in paragraphs 28 and 29 for the rear adaptor.

31 Refer to Fig.3.15, and fit the rubber bushes (C) of the tie-bar (D) over the two mounting studs. Smear the surfaces of the rubber bushes (C, E) and washers that contact the tie-bar with Silicone Compound MS4. Loosely assemble the rubber washers, plain washers, spring washers, and nuts.

32 Undo the throttle adjusting screw ('C', Fig.3.16), and the fast idling screw (D), on each carburetter, until they are just clear of the pads when the throttle butterflies are fully closed.

33 Fit a new gasket to the front carburetter adaptor mounting and refit the front carburetter. Screw on the four flange nuts but do not tighten fully yet.

34 Refit the folded coupling to the throttle connecting rod and fit to the rear carburetter, making sure that the lost motion fork is engaged with the pin.

35 Fit a new gasket to the rear carburetter adaptor mounting and screw on the four flange nuts. Again do not tighten these nuts fully.

36 Carefully slide the folded coupling into position on the front throttle spindle so that the centre fold is equidistant from the ends of the front throttle spindle and connecting rods.

37 Refit the link plate ('G', Fig.3.14), and air cleaner adaptors to the two carburetter bodies with new gaskets each side of the link plate. It will be noted that the adaptors are marked FRONT and REAR.

38 Fit the heat shield brackets onto the forward studs of each adaptor. Replace the four spring washers and nuts to the adaptors but leave them loose.

39 Refit the two plain washers, spring washers and nuts that secure the tie-bar to the link plate and leave them loose.

40 By careful manipulation adjust the carburetters on the adaptors until the two throttle spindles are in alignment with each other, both horizontally and vertically. Gently tighten the nuts that secure the link plate and air cleaner adaptors whilst keeping the throttle spindle alignment correct. Once the nuts are tight, check that the throttle spindles are free to move throughout their complete travel.

41 Adjust the carburetter flange adaptors until there is equal clearance at each side of the retainer bolts. Gently tighten the four nuts securing each carburetter flange.

42 Refit the carburetter support spring so that the end of the loop in the inlet manifold is facing uppermost. Screw the self-locking nut onto its stud but do not tighten yet.

43 Support the weight of the carburetter assembly by hand, so that the flange adaptors are parallel with the face of the inlet manifold whilst at the same time pushing the assembly towards the manifold.

44 Tighten the two nuts that secure the tie-bar to the inlet manifold and also the two nuts that secure the tie-bar to the link plate.

45 The tension of the support spring should next be adjusted until it maintains the carburetter assembly at 90° to the inlet manifold, as viewed at the adaptor to manifold flanges as shown in Fig.3.17. NOTE: It may be necessary to reset the spring tension once the assembly is back on the engine to compensate for the weight of the air cleaners.

46 Check the throttle spindle movement again to ensure that it is still free throughout its travel. If any sign of sticking is evident it is important that the procedures in paragraphs 39 to 45 are repeated.

47 Refer to Fig.3.17a, and set the jet levers (A) until they are just touching the enrichment lever pads (B). Insert the jet connecting rod into the UPPER hole of the front lever and adjust the fork end until the clevis pin can just be inserted through the fork and the upper hole of the rear lever.

48 Tighten the locknut at the fork end. Refit the plain washers onto the clevis pin and insert the split pin but DO NOT open the split pin legs yet.

49 Refit the throttle countershaft with the flat washer and the circlip.

50 Refit the fuel filters to the carburetter fuel inlet unions and refit the fuel pipe connecting the front and rear carburetters.

51 Refit the throttle return springs with the end of the loop at the air cleaner end uppermost to ensure correct action of the spring.

52 The heat shield should next be refitted. Should it be necessary to slacken the link plate nuts to obtain correct alignment of the mounting brackets, the freedom of the throttle linkage must now be re-checked.

53 Remove the inlet manifold and carburetter assembly from the wooden jig. If the inlet ports have been sealed with rag to prevent dirt ingress remove the rag. Fit new inlet manifold gaskets to the cylinder head, making sure that all traces of old gasket or jointing compound have been previously removed.

54 Refit the six nuts and spring washers that secure the inlet manifold to the cylinder head. Tighten in a diagonal manner.

55 Reconnect the brake servo unit hose to the inlet manifold union and also refit the clip that secures the servo unit hose and distributor vacuum pipe to the top cover.

56 Reconnect the heater inlet hose to the inlet manifold. Also refit the heater outlet hose together with the clips and spacer. Refit the two Phillips head screws that secure the pipe to the inlet manifold.

57 Reconnect the distributor vacuum pipe to the front carburetter body. Also, if there is a pipe from the rear carburetter air cleaner adaptor to the top cover, this should next be refitted. If there is a pipe from the crankcase emission control valve to the banjo union on the inlet manifold, this should next be refitted. Refit the cleat that secures the latter hose to the heater outlet pipe.

58 Refit the choke control outer cable clip and reconnect the inner cable to the front jet lever of the front carburetter. Refit the rubber cleat that secures the choke cable to the heater outlet hose.

59 Reconnect the throttle pedal linkage at the upper ball joint of the vertical rod and also the coupling shaft support bracket.

60 Reconnect the main fuel feed pipe to the front carburetter float chamber union.

61 Refer to Chapter 2, Section 4, and refill the cooling system.

62 Refer to Section 2 of this chapter and refit the air cleaner assembly.

63 It will now be necessary to tune the carburetters, details of which are given in Section 11 of this chapter.

9. Carburetters (TC) — Dismantling & Reassembly

1. All reference numbers refer to Fig.3.22, unless stated otherwise. Unscrew the piston damper (27) and lift away from the chamber and piston assembly (23).

2. Using a screwdriver or small file, scratch identification marks on the suction chamber and carburetter body (1), so that they may be fitted together in their original positions. Remove the four screws (24), securing the suction chamber and lift away the suction chamber from the carburetter body leaving the piston in position. Lift away the piston spring (25) from the piston noting which way round it is fitted.

3. Very carefully lift the piston from the body (1). Invert it and allow the oil in the damper bore to drain out. Place the piston in a safe place so that the needle (26) will not be touched or the piston roll onto the floor. It is recommended that the piston be placed on the neck of a narrow jam jar with the needle inside, so acting as a

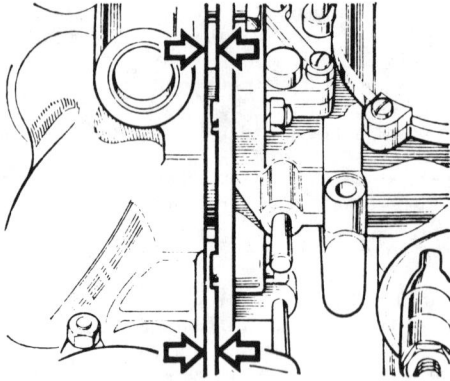

Fig.3.17. Alignment of carburetter adaptor to inlet manifold

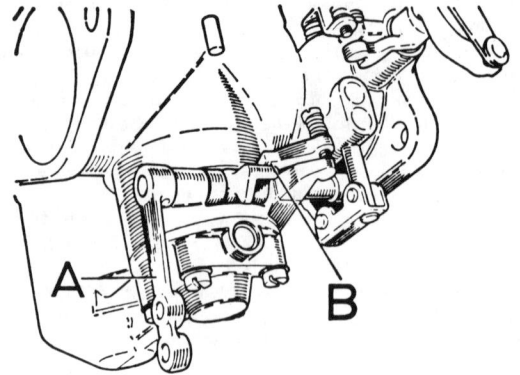

Fig.3.17a. JET LEVER SETTING

A Jet lever   B Enrichment lever pad

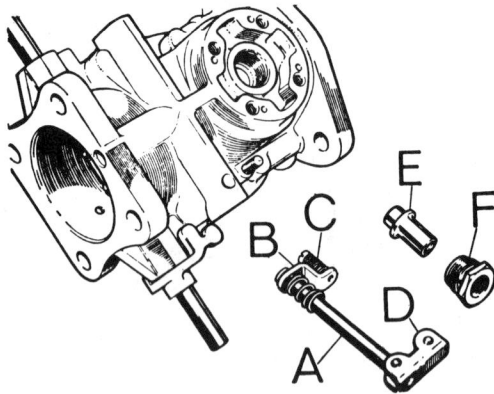

Fig.3.18. CARBURETTER JET BEARING & SLIDING ROD
A Sliding rod   D Cam shoe
B Top plate   E Jet bearing
C Fast idle screw   F Jet screw

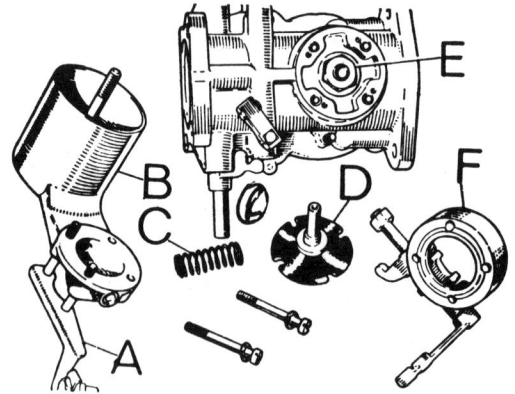

Fig.3.19. FLOAT CHAMBER & JET ASSEMBLY
A Choke cable bracket (front   D Jet with diaphragm
   carburetter only)   E Jet screw and jet bear-
B Float chamber   ing
C Jet return spring   F Jet body

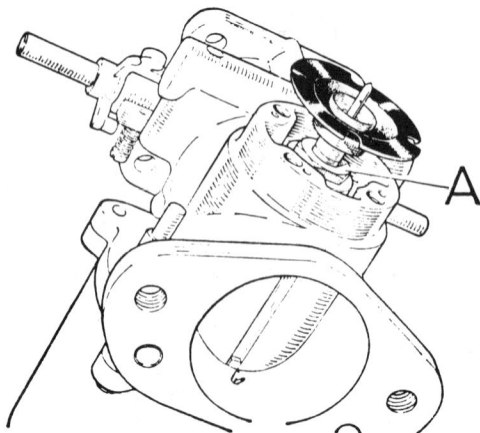

Fig.3.20. CARBURETTER JET CENTRING
A Jet screw

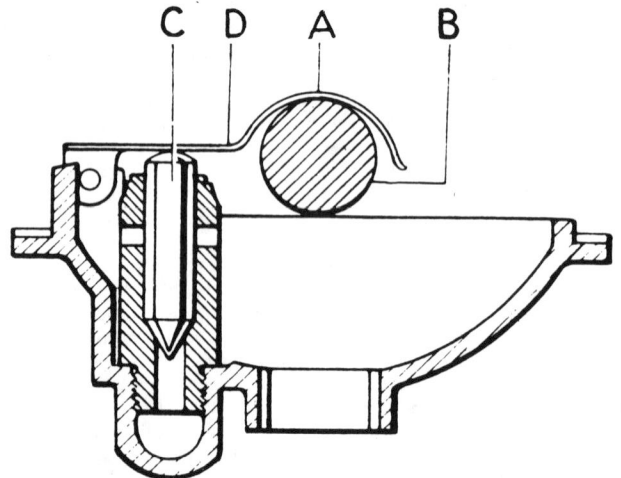

Fig.3.21. FLOAT CHAMBER FUEL LEVEL ADJUSTMENT
A Fork   C Needle valve
B 7/16 inch diameter bar   D Fork setting adjustment point

stand.

4. Undo and remove the petrol pipe union (58), followed by the fibre washer (60), gauze filter and spring (61).

5. Mark the position of the float chamber lid (42), relative to the body and unscrew the centre bolt (50). Lift away the bolt (50), plain washer (49) and cover cap (48). Lift away the float chamber lid (42) and gasket (43). The float (45) may now be lifted out.

6. If necessary, remove the float lever pivot pin (47) and lift away the float lever (46) and needle valve. The needle valve seat (44) may be unscrewed from the inside of the float chamber lid using a box spanner.

7. Undo and remove the screw (37) and shakeproof washer (38) that secures the top plate (35) to the sliding rod. This can be seen in Fig.3.19. Remove the top plate with the fast idle screw, then the second shakeproof washer and the spring. Carefully withdraw the sliding rod and cam shoe from the carburetter body.

8. Undo and remove the four long screws (51) and shakeproof washers that secure the float chamber (41) and jet housing (33) to the underside of the carburetter. NOTE: On the front carburetter two of the four screws also secure the choke cable bracket (53).

9. Carefully lift away the float chamber (41) and the small jet return spring (32).

10 Remove the diaphragm. and jet assembly (29). Next lift away the complete jet housing (33).

11 Undo and remove the hexagonal headed jet screw (31) from the underside of the carburetter body and withdraw the jet bearing (30).

12 Slacken the bolts (63) that secure the throttle lever (62) to the throttle spindle and slide the lever from the spindle.

13 If considered necessary to remove the throttle butterfly (4) from the spindle (3) close the ends of the two special screws and undo the screws. Note the position of the butterfly relative to the spindle and slide the butterfly from the spindle. The spindle may now be withdrawn from the carburetter body.

14 Carefully lever out both end caps (13) and lift away the spring (12), gland washer (11) and gland (10), from the carburetter body.

15 The piston lift pin may be removed by first extracting the little circlip and lifting away the brass washer and neoprene washer. Withdraw the lift pin and spring.

16 The piston guide may be removed from the carburetter body by first closing the end of the special guide retaining screw and removing the screw. Lift away the shaped piston guide.

17 Fitted to the front carburetter is a distributor vacuum pipe adaptor (14) which may be removed by undoing the two screws (16) and removing together with the shakeproof washers (17). Lift away the adaptor (14) and its gasket (15).

18 Reassembly is the exact reversal of the dismantling procedure and no troubles will be encountered providing that care was taken during dismantling to ensure that every part was placed in order on the bench. Fig.3.22 shows an exploded view of the complete carburetter installation and supplementary figures 3.18 and 3.19 show in detail some of the more complicated parts. It will be necessary to centre the jet assembly before the jet housing and piston and suction chamber are refitted. Details of this operation are given in Section 10 of this chapter.

10. Carburetter (TC) – Examination & Repair

The basic procedures for the examination and repair of the carburetter as fitted to the TC models covered by this manual are similar to that for the single carburetter installation and full details will be found in Section 6 of this chapter. However, as the jet assembly is of a slightly different design and the procedure for adjusting the float chamber fuel level different, full details are given below:—

Jet Centring (during overhaul)

1. This operation is always necessary if the carburetter has been dismantled. Remove the piston from the suction chamber and fit the piston and needle assembly to the carburetter.

2. Lubricate the piston rod using a few drops of light oil and fit the piston spring and suction chambers. Make sure that the suction chamber fits squarely over the spigot.

3. Fit the four securing screws and tighten them in a diagonal manner. Now hold the carburetter upright and check that the piston is able to fall freely. The damper of the piston will always restrict its free fall, but a definite metallic click should be clearly heard as the piston strikes the jet bridge.

4. Now invert the carburetter and refit the jet whilst the piston is kept in position with the needle protruding into the jet to its fullest extent. Rotate the jet to centre the bearing and tighten the jet screw ('A', Fig.3.20). Again check that the jet is quite free to rotate when the screw is tight.

5. Next remove the jet and fit the jet housing to the carburetter body so that the jet lever is facing towards the air cleaner flange.

6. Insert the jet and carefully align the holes in the diaphragm with the corresponding holes in the jet housing. Refit the jet return spring and float chamber so that the float chamber is facing towards the front of the carburetter. Replace the four screws and shakeproof washers, but do not tighten fully yet. If the front carburetter is being worked upon do not forget that the choke cable bracket is retained in position with the two bolts at the front of the carburetter.

7. Operate the jet lever and move the jet up and down several times. Then tighten the four screws whilst the jet is up as far as it will go.

8. Hold the carburetter upright and raise the piston fully. Allow it to drop and again it should fall freely and a definite metallic click be heard as it strikes the jet bridge. If there are any signs of the needle sticking, the jet must, once again, be re-centred.

Float Chamber Fuel Level Adjustment

1. It is essential that the fuel level in the float chamber is always correct otherwise excessive fuel consumption could occur. On re-assembly of the float chamber check the fuel level before replacing the float chamber lid in the following manner:

2. Invert the float chamber lid so that the needle valve is closed. It should just be possible to place a 7/16 inch bar ('B', Fig.3.21), parallel to the float chamber cover without fouling the float, or if the float stands proud of the bar, then it is necessary to bend the float lever fork (A) at the point (D) until the clearance is correct.

11. Carburetters (TC) – Adjustment & Tuning

To adjust twin carburetters it is important that if a satisfactory result is to be obtained, an electric tachometer and a Crypton 'Synchro Check' carburetter throttle calibration tool be used. Also a piece of rubber hose 2 inch external diameter by $1^1/8$ inch long will be required to act as an extension to clear the air cleaner stud.

If the owner feels that he would like to attempt this adjustment using the equipment mentioned in the previous paragraph full details are given below. To conclude this Section notes are given on how to tune the carburetters without using the specialist equipment but it must be stressed that the results may not be exact.

Before carburetter tuning is commenced it is important that the tappet clearances as well as the distributor contact breaker gap and the sparking plug type and gaps are correct. Then proceed as follows:-

1. Allow the engine to run until it reaches its normal operating temperature.

2. Refer to Section 2 and remove the air cleaners.

3. Extract the split pin and remove the clevis pin from the choke link rod located at the rear carburetter. Also release the choke inner cable at the front jet lever.

4. Undo both the mixture adjustment screws and then slowly screw in both screws until they are just touching the cast metal pad. Then turn in the two screws a further 3½ turns only.

5. Slacken, but do not remove, the bolt that locks the lost motion link to the rear carburetter and also slacken the bolt locking the folded coupling to the lost motion shaft.

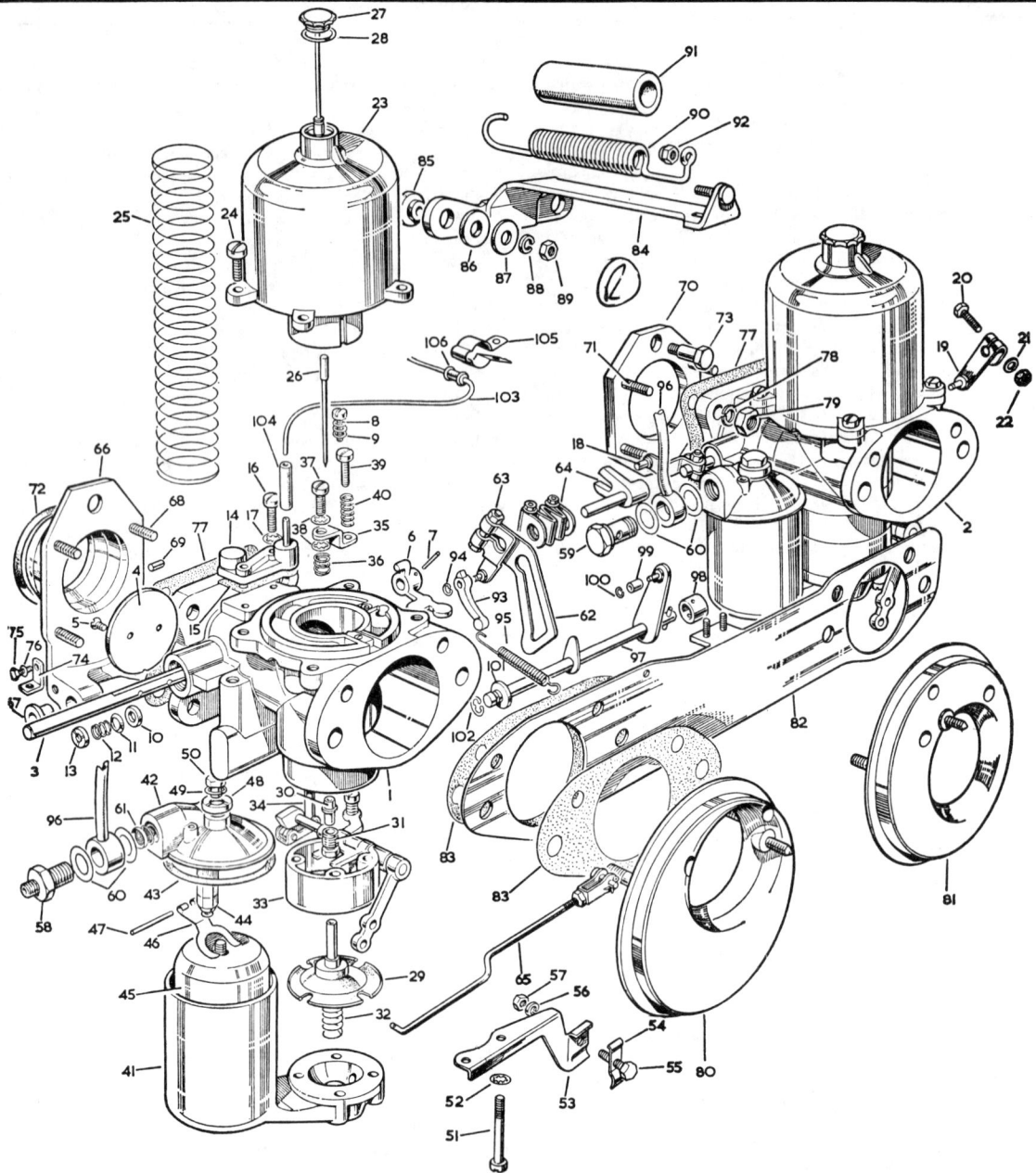

Fig.3.22. CARBURETTER & INSTALLATION MOUNTING PARTS (TC MODELS)

1 Carburetter body, front	27 Damper complete	54 Clip for cable bracket	80 Adaptor for air cleaner front
2 Carburetter body, rear	28 Washer for damper	55 Special bolt	81 Adaptor for air cleaner rear
3 Throttle spindle	29 Jet complete	56 Spring washer	82 Link plate for carburetters
4 Throttle butterfly	30 Jet bearing	57 Special nut	83 Joint washer
5 Screw for throttle butterfly	31 Lock screw	58 Banjo bolt, two-way	84 Tie bar for carburetters
6 Throttle stop lever	32 Spring for jet	59 Banjo bolt	85 Rubber bush
7 Taper pin for stop lever	33 Jet housing complete	60 Joint washer for banjo	86 Rubber washer
8 Throttle adjustment screw	34 Cam shoe and rod	bolts	87 Plain washer
9 Spring	35 Top plate	61 Filter and spring	88 Spring washer
10 Gland for throttle spindle	36 Spring for sliding rod	62 Throttle lever	89 Nut
11 Gland washer	37 Screw for sliding rod	63 Nut (10 UNF)	90 Support spring
12 Spring	38 Shakeproof washer	64 Connecting rod	91 Sleeve for support spring
13 End cap	39 Stop screw	65 Connecting rod for jet lever	92 Self-locking nut
14 Adaptor for suction pipe	40 Spring for stop screw	66 Adaptor assembly	93 Link for throttle return spring
15 Joint washer for adaptor	41 Float chamber	67 Bush for adaptor	94 Circlip retaining link
16 Special screw	42 Lid for float chamber	68 Serrated bolt	95 Throttle return spring
17 Shakeproof washer	43 Joint washer	69 Dowel	96 Fuel pipe
18 Lost motion lever	44 Needle valve and seat	70 Adaptor assembly	97 Countershaft and lever
19 Spring anchor lever	45 Float	71 Serrated bolt	98 Coupling
20 Special bolt	46 Float lever	72 'O' ring	99 Roller
21 Plain washer	47 Pin for float lever	73 Special bolt	100 Circlip
22 Special nut	48 Cover cap	74 Bracket	101 Plain washer
23 Suction chamber and	49 Plain washer for cap nut	75 Bolt	102 Circlip
piston complete	50 Cap nut	76 Spring washer	103 Suction pipe complete
24 Special screw	51 Special screw	77 Joint washer	104 Tube
25 Spring	52 Shakeproof washer	78 Spring washer	105 Clip for suction pipe
26 Needle, 'U1'	53 Cable bracket	79 Nut	106 Rubber grommet

6. Unscrew the two throttle adjusting screws and the two fast idle screws until they are clear of the pads with the throttles in the closed position.

7. Rotate the lost motion link until near to a vertical position is reached and yet it is still just possible to tighten the 2 BA locking screw. When in this position, tighten the 4 BA folded coupling screw.

8. A clearance of between 0.008 and 0.010 inch should be set between the pin and the edge of the slot at the cylinder head side as shown in Fig.3.25. Tighten the locking screw and re-check the clearance.

9. Make sure that the countershaft roller is at the end of the slot on the first carburetter throttle lever and also that it is approximately central. Also make sure that the roller is not touching the sides of the slot. If this condition is not existent, slacken the clamp bolt and move the lever as necessary until the required position is obtained, and then tighten the clamp bolt.

10 It should be noted that when the throttle lever is correctly adjusted, the nylon spring arm should touch the throttle spindle before full throttle conditions are reached. The linkage is specially designed to do this so that spring tension is reduced at the higher throttle openings and must not be considered as maladjustment.

11 Align the rear carburetter throttle lever and spring arm with that of the front carburetter. If adjustment is necessary slacken the clamp bolt and move the rear lever to obtain this condition. Tighten the clamp bolt.

12 Refer to paragraph 10 above and ensure that the condition is also evident on the rear carburetter linkage.

13 Fit the tachometer to the engine according to the manufacturer's recommendation. If the special Rover tachometer, Part No.601284 is being used the red lead should be connected to the battery positive and the black lead to the battery negative terminal. The green lead should be connected to the low tension terminal situated on the side of the distributor body.

14 Run the engine until it has reached normal operating temperature again and then by adjusting the throttle adjusting screw, set the engine speed to between 700 and 750 r.p.m.

15 Place the rubber hose previously prepared on the intake of the front carburetter and place the carburetter balancing device on the end of the rubber hose as shown in Fig.3.23. Slowly turn the throttle adjusting screws until identical readings on the scale are obtained for each of the carburetters. The engine idle speed should not be altered from the original settings.

16 By adjusting the mixture adjusting screws in or out as necessary, obtain the fastest idling speed without any trace of engine hesitation or misfiring. It will be noted that as the mixture is adjusted it will be found necessary to re-adjust the setting of the throttle adjusting screws by turning them an equal amount in order to maintain synchronisation. As each adjustment is made, sharply depress and release the throttle pedal to enable the carburetter piston needle to settle to its newly adjusted position.

17 Using the lift pin situated on the right-hand side of the carburetter body, lift the front carburetter piston by approximately 1/32 inch. Note that there is approximately 3/16 inch free movement before the pin touches the underside of the piston. If the engine speed increases and remains at a higher speed, it is an indication that the mixture is too rich and the mixture adjustment screw should be turned in an anti-clockwise direction. Conversely, if the engine speed decreases it is an indication that the mixture is too weak, and the mixture adjustment screw should be turned in a clockwise direction. The mixture is considered correct when the engine speed increases momentarily and then settles down to its original speed.

18 When the front carburetter adjustment is correct the procedures in paragraphs 16 and 17 should be repeated for the rear carburetter.

19 When the correct rear carburetter setting has been obtained, re-check the front carburetter setting.

20 Using the tachometer and carburetter balancing device re-check the engine idle speed and the throttle balance for the two carburetters. The two carburetters may now be considered correctly balanced.

21 Adjust the length of the choke link rod until the clevis pin can

just be inserted through the yoke and upper hole of the rear jet lever when both jet levers are touching the enrichment lever pads.

22 Tighten the yoke locknut and fit a new split pin but do not bend the split pin legs over yet.

23 Push the choke control fully home and tighten the screw that secures the inner cable to the front jet lever. Then pull out the choke control fully whereupon the warning light should be on when the ignition switch is on. Slowly push the choke control cable in until the warning light just goes out.

24 Screw in the fast idle screws until they just touch the pad.

25 Watching the tachometer, slowly turn each fast idle screw until a fast idle speed of between 1,100 and 1,200 r.p.m. is obtained. (On new cars or after complete engine overhaul, 1,400 and 1,500 r.p.m. whereupon it should be reset after the first 1,500 miles has been covered). After each adjustment has been made blip the throttle pedal to ensure that the fast idle screws seat on the pads.

26 Repeat the procedure in paragraph 23 and re-check the engine fast idle speed.

27 Remove the electric tachometer cable connections and refit the air cleaners as detailed in Section 2 of the chapter.

28 Top up each carburetter dashpot using an SAE 20 grade oil to within ½ inch of the top of the piston rod.

Twin Carburetter Adjustment Without Specialist Equipment

1. The basic procedure is identical to that given above with the exception that the engine idle speed will have to be judged as an even idle speed with no signs of hesitation and with the ignition warning light just glowing.

2. As the aim is to adjust the throttle butterfly so that an equal amount of the air enters each carburetter, instead of using the carburetter balancing device use a piece of rubber tubing inserted into the air intake of each carburetter in turn and listen to the hiss from each carburetter. If a difference in intensity is noticed between them, then unscrew the throttle adjusting screw until the hiss for both carburetters is the same.

12. Fuel Pump -- General Description

All figures refer to Fig.3.28. The fuel pump is mechanically operated by a rocker arm (20) via a pushrod, one end of which rests on the side of the offset cam at the base of the distributor drive shaft. The rocker arm (20) is in turn, in contact with the operating link (15) which is hooked onto the pull rod of the diaphragm (9).

When the centre of the diaphragm is pulled down by the pull rod, sufficient vacuum is created to draw fuel through the inlet port of the upper pump body (6), through the bowl (2) and filter (3) and the inlet valve (8, left) into the chamber above the diaphragm. When the rocker arm is released on the cam, the diaphragm spring (10) pushes the diaphragm (9) upwards. The one-way inlet valve closes under pressure and the fuel is forced out of the outlet valve (8, right) to the carburetter.

The rocker arm and link are split in effect at the pivot pin (16) so that the return action of the diaphragm is governed by the spring only. Any obstruction to the outlet flow would stop the diaphragm and the rocker arm (20) would move independently. This is, in effect, what happens as the delivery capacity of the pump is always in excess of the carburetter requirements.

13. Fuel Pump -- Testing, Cleaning, Removal & Refitting

1. If the fuel pump is suspected of not working it can be checked easily. Disconnect the fuel lead pipe from the carburetter float chamber. Also remove the HT lead from the centre of the coil.

2. Place a container under the disconnected pipe and with the assistance of a second person operate the starter motor by turning the ignition switch. A good spurt of petrol should come from the fuel pump every second revolution of the engine.

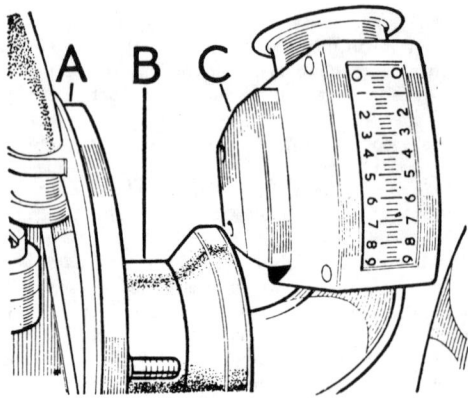

Fig.3.23. USE OF CRYPTON 'SYNCHRO CHECK' TO TUNE
CARBURETTER

A Air cleaner adaptor   C Crypton 'synchro check'
B Rubber hose

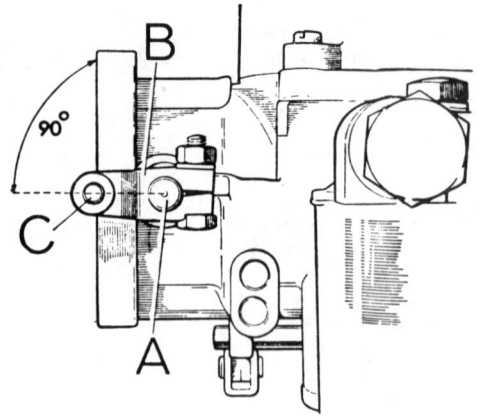

Fig.3.24. LOST MOTION LEVER SETTING —REAR CAR-
BURETTER

A Throttle spindle   C Pin horizontal with throttle
B Lost motion lever   closed

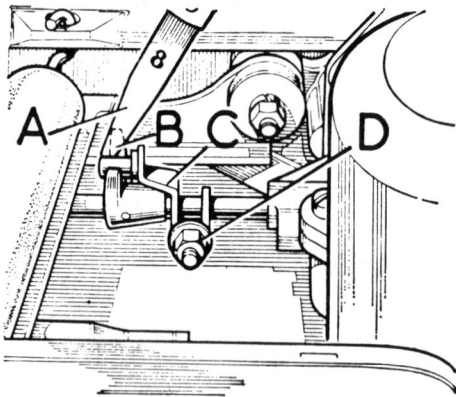

Fig.3.25. LOST MOTION LINK SETTING

A Feeler gauge   C Lost motion pin
B Edge of slot   D Nut securing lost motion link

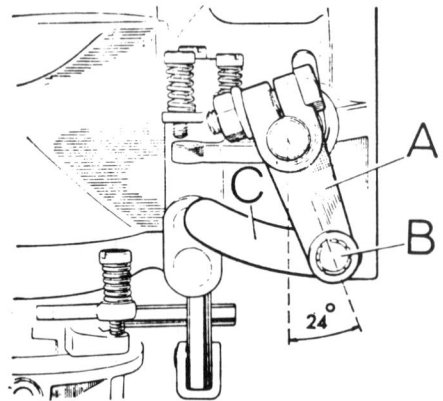

Fig.3.26. REAR CARBURETTER THROTTLE LEVER SET-
TING

A Rear throttle lever   vertical with throttle closed
B Lever 24° forward of   C Spring arm

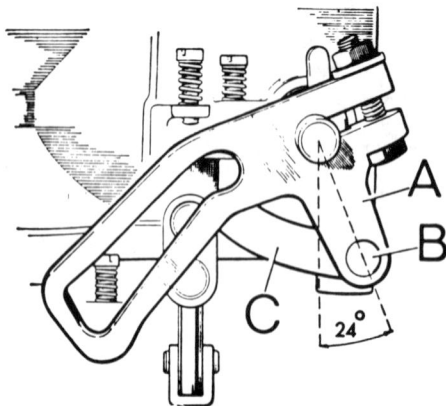

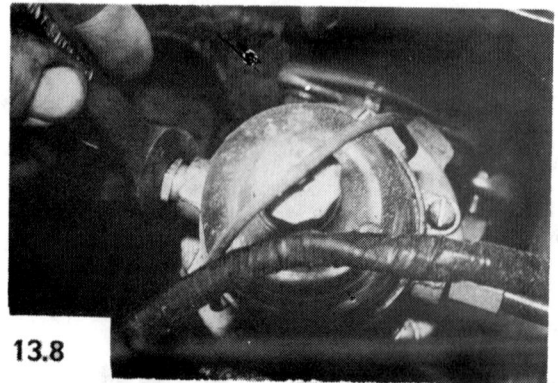

Fig.3.27. FRONT CARBURETTER THROTTLE LEVER SET-
TING

A Front throttle lever   vertical with throttle closed
B Lever 24° forward of   C Spring arm

13.8

3. If the pump is away from the engine, it may be tested by holding a finger over the inlet nozzle and operating the rocker arm through three complete strokes. When the finger is released a suction noise should be heard. Next hold a finger over the outlet nozzle and press the rocker arm fully. The pressure generated should hold for a minimum of 15 seconds.

4. To clean the sediment bowl, first unscrew the knurled nut over the glass bowl until the retainer can be moved aside and the bowl lifted off. Lift out the gauze filter which may be cleaned in petrol if necessary, and with a small brush remove any sediment that may be lying under the filter in the body of the pump.

5. Check that the sealing ring is in good order and shows no sign of cracking, distortion or heavy grooving, caused by the sediment bowl being too tightly fitted previously. Fit a new sealing ring if suspect.

6. Replace the glass bowl and retainer, turning the knurled nut no more than finger tight. Check that the sealing ring under the bowl is not leaking by running the engine for a few minutes.

7. To remove the fuel pump first turn the reserve fuel tap to the central position to stop petrol syphoning from the fuel tank.

8. Disconnect the two fuel hoses from the fuel pump (photo).

9. Undo and remove the two retaining nuts and spring washers and lift the pump away.

10 The pump is actuated by a small pushrod located in the side of the distributor drive housing. It is recommended that this pushrod be left in position as otherwise oil will flow out of the pushrod bore.

11 Replacement is a simple reversal of removal. Always fit a new gasket as a safeguard against oil leaks.

14. Fuel Pump — Dismantling, Examination & Reassembly

1. All figures in the text refer to Fig.3.28. Remove the pump from the engine as described in Section 13. Slacken the knurled clamping nut, push the bowl retainer (1) to one side and lift off the glass bowl (2). Remove the sealing washer (4) from the upper body (6). Also lift away the gauze filter (3).

2. Mark the upper and lower pump bodies (6,13) so that they can be put together again the same way and then remove the six screws (5) holding the two halves together.

3. Mark the position of the tag on one side of the diaphragm, so that it may be fitted in its original position.

4. To remove the diaphragm (9) from the lower pump body (13), turn the body upside down and press the centre of the diaphragm in with the thumbs and then turn it through 90°. This will disengage the diaphragm rod from the slotted end of the operating link (15). Carefully release the diaphragm (9) and spring (10) and lift away.

5. Examine the diaphragm for signs of perishing, cracking, stiffness or puncturing and renew if suspect.

6. The lower oil seal retainer (11) and sealing washer (12) may be hooked out of the base of the lower body if it is considered necessary to renew them.

7. The two valves (8) and gaskets (11) are fixed in the upper pump body by a retaining plate and two screws. Undo and remove the two screws and retaining plate ('D', Fig.3.29). Note which way round the two valves are fitted and then lift away the valves (B,C) and the gaskets (A). On early models of the pump a single gasket was used, but on later models two small circular gaskets were fitted.

8. There is no need to dismantle the operating link (15) and rocker arm (20) from the lower pump body unless either one is badly worn or bent, or if there is a lot of play in the pivot pin.

9. To dismantle the lower half operating mechanism, remove the pivot pin (16), two washers (17), rocker arm pin retainers (18), return spring (19) and the rocker arm (20).

10 Thoroughly wash all components in petrol and dry using a clean rag or an air jet. Inspect the valves (8) for evidence of damage and the valve springs inside the valve assemblies for weakness or distortion. Check to see that the diaphragm spring (10) and operating link return spring (19) are not distorted or unserviceable. Generally inspect all parts for cracks, distortion or stripped threads. Also the operating link (15) and pin (16) for wear.

11 When reassembling, first assemble the operating link (15) to the rocker arm (20), insert the pin (16) and refit the washers (17) and rocker arm pin retainers (18). Place the return spring (19) onto the rocker arm peg and insert the complete assembly into the lower body (13).

12 If the oil seal washers (12) and retainer (11) have been removed, they should next be inserted into the lower body.

13 Place the diaphragm spring (10) onto its recess in the lower body and carefully push the dipahragm rod through the sealing washers (12). Line up the diaphragm tab so that when turned through 90° the tab corresponds with the previously made mark. See also Fig.3.30. Press the diaphragm down with the thumbs, inverting the body to facilitate connecting the pushrod to the operating link.

14 Refit the gasket (7) and valves (8) to the upper body with the valves in their original position and secure in place with the retainer and two screws.

15 Line up the screw holes in the diaphragm and the two halves of the body, ensuring that the marks previously made line up. Replace the screws (5) and tighten in a diagonal manner.

16 Fit a new sealing ring (4) into the upper body groove, replace the filter (3) and the glass sediment bowl (2) and secure in place by tightening the bowl retainer knurled nut (1).

17 Before replacing the pump, place a finger over the inlet nozzle and operate the rocker arm through three complete strokes. When the finger is released a suction noise should be heard. Next hold a finger over the outlet nozzle and press the rocker arm fully. The pressure generated should hold for a minimum of 15 seconds. If both these tests are satisfactory, the pump is now ready for refitting back to the engine.

15. Accelerator Pedal & Linkage — Removal, Refitting & Adjustment

Upon reference to Fig.3.31, Fig.3.32 and Fig.3.33, it will be seen that the accelerator pedal and linkage systems vary between the SC and TC models as well as for cars fitted with automatic transmission. To remove the accelerator pedal and linkage proceed as follows:—

1. Disconnect the two ball joints that secure the vertical rod and remove the vertical rod.

2. On cars fitted with automatic transmission release the spring clip and clevis pin that secures the downshift cable. (Fig.3.33).

3. Remove the special retainer from the coupling rod between the bulkhead and the carburetter. Note the location of the spring and the three plain washers and lift away the coupling rod.

4. Disconnect the accelerator return spring from the lever.

5. Locate the two nuts under the right-hand front wing that secure the accelerator pedal bracket fixing to the bulkhead and undo the two nuts. Lift away the two nuts and bolts followed by the accelerator pedal bracket fixing.

6. Undo and remove the clamping bolt and nut that secures the lever to the cross shaft and withdraw the lever. It is not normally considered necessary to remove the cross shaft bracket from the cross shaft.

7. Disconnect the clutch and brake pedal return springs and carefully withdraw the accelerator cross shaft and pedal assembly through the bulkhead into the inside of the car. Take care not to damage the interior trim.

8. To refit the accelerator pedal and linkage is the reversal of the removal procedure. It will, however, be necessary to adjust the linkage.

9. Hold the accelerator pedal firmly against the carpeting in the wide open throttle position. If an assistant is not available to do this a few bricks will overcome the problem.

10 Tighten the lower ball joint locknut and then hold the accelerator coupling shaft in the fully open throttle position.

11 Adjust the upper ball joint by turning it on the control rod until it just slips over the ball and onto the coupling shaft. Reassemble the ball joint and secure the locknut.

12 Release the accelerator pedal and check that the pedal operation

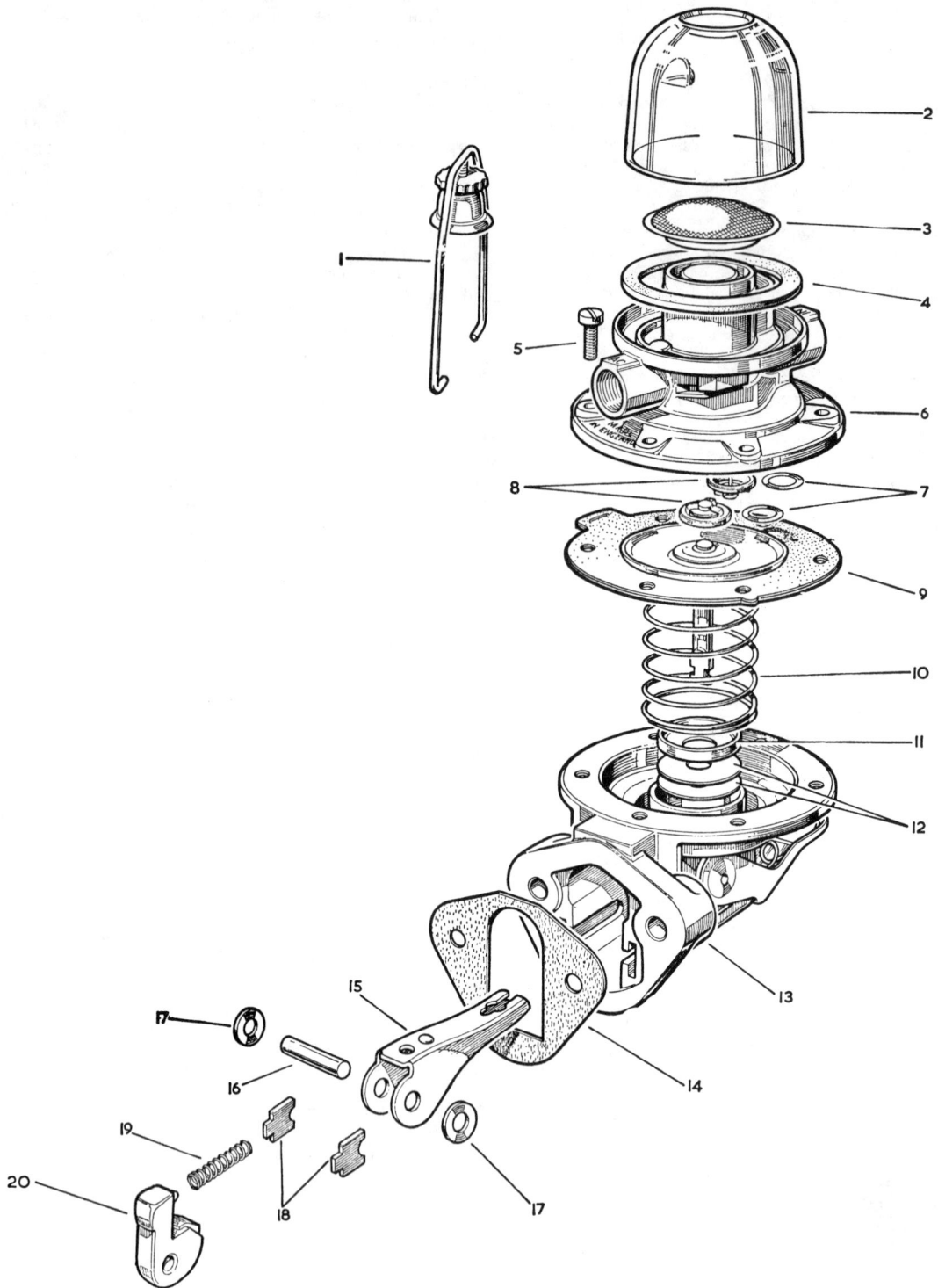

Fig.3.28. EXPLODED VIEW OF A.C. MECHANICAL FUEL PUMP

1 Bowl retainer	6 Upper casing	11 Oil seal retainer	16 Rocker arm pin
2 Sediment bowl	7 Valve gaskets	12 Sealing washers	17 Washer
3 Gauze filter	8 Valves	13 Lower casing	18 Rocker arm pin retainer
4 Sealing ring	9 Diaphragm assembly	14 Gasket	19 Return spring
5 Cover screw	10 Diaphragm spring	15 Operating link	20 Rocker arm

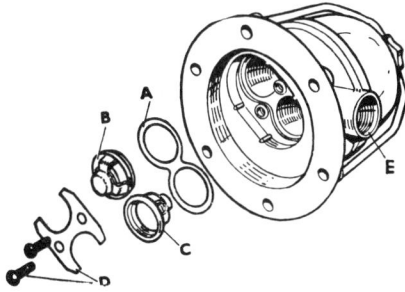

Fig.3.29. FUEL PUMP VALVE ASSEMBLY

A Gasket
B Fuel inlet valve
C Fuel outlet valve

D Retaining plate and
   screws
E Fuel outlet connection

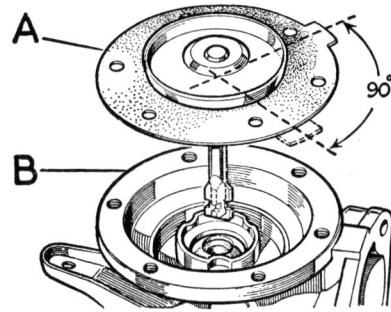

Fig.3.30 CORRECT POSITIONING OF DIAPHRAGM

A Diaphragm   B Fuel pump body

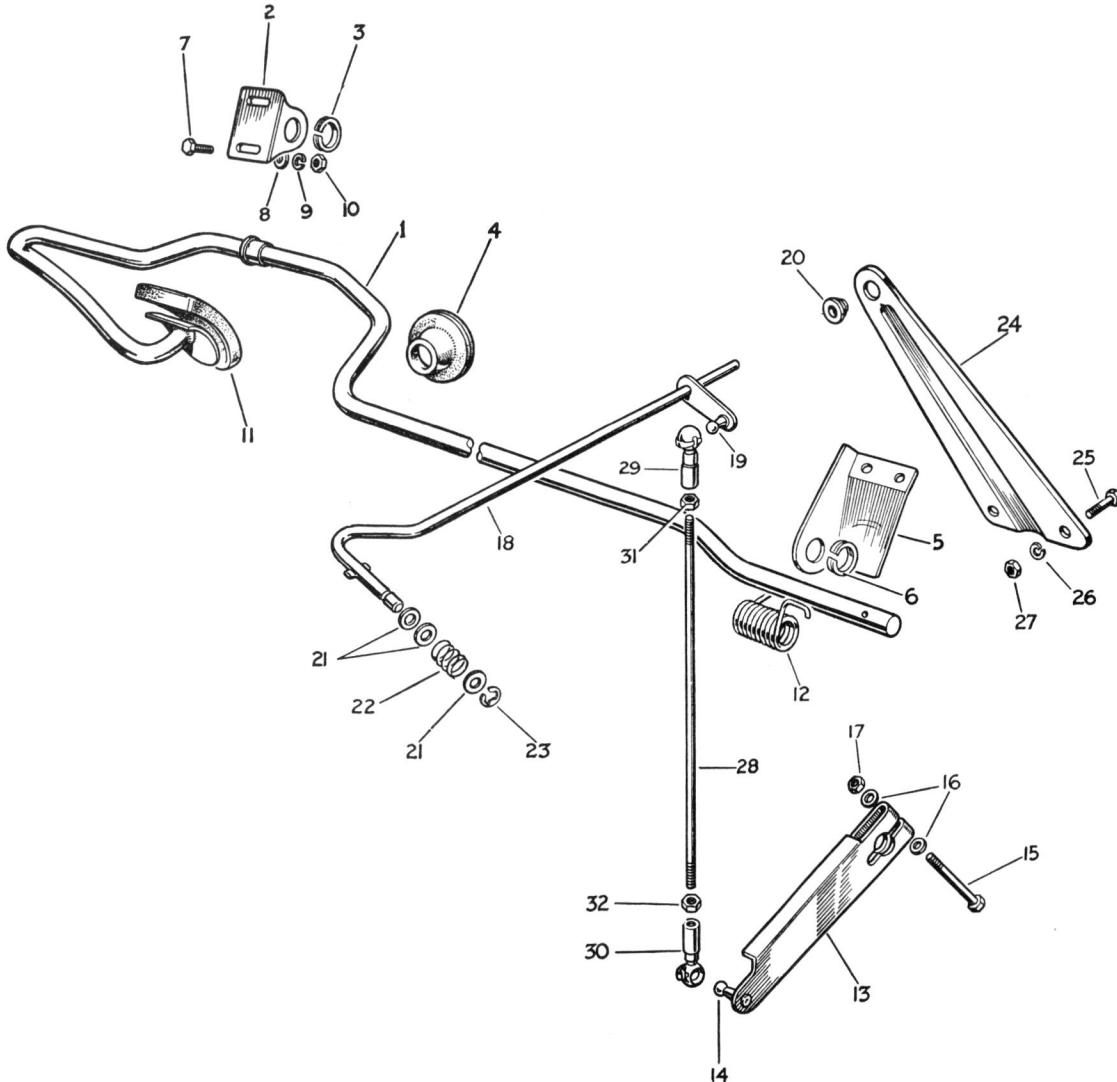

Fig.3.31. ACCELERATOR PEDAL & LINKAGE (SC MODELS)

1 Accelerator cross-shaft and pedal	shaft mounting bracket, LH	15 Bolt
2. Mounting bracket for cross-shaft, RH	7 Bolt	16 Plain washer
	8 Plain washer	17 Self-locking nut
3 Nylon bearing for cross-shaft mounting bracket, RH	9 Spring washer	18 Accelerator coupling shaft assembly
	10 Nut	
4 Grommet for cross-shaft in bulkhead	11 Rubber pad for accelerator pedal	19 Ball end for lever on coupling shaft
5 Mounting bracket for cross-shaft, LH	12 Accelerator return spring	20 Nylon bearing for coupling shaft
	13 Lever assembly for accelerator cross-shaft	21 Plain washer
6 Nylon bearing for cross-	14 Ball end for lever	22 Anti-rattle spring
		23 Circlip

24 Bracket for accelerator coupling shaft
25 Bolt
26 Spring washer
27 Nut
28 Control rod, accelerator shaft to coupling shaft
29 Ball joint, RH thread
30 Ball joint, LH thread
31 Locknut, RH thread
32 Locknut, LH thread

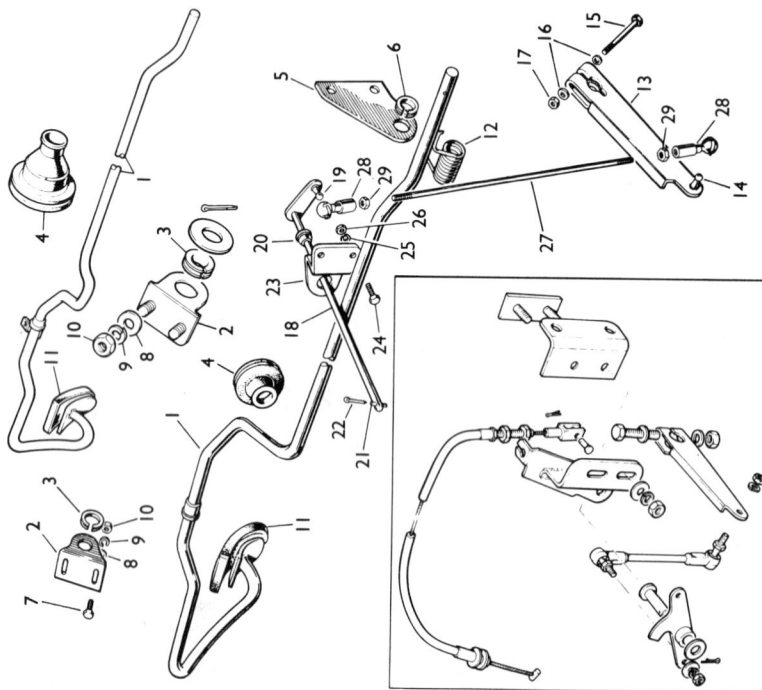

Fig. 3.32. ACCELERATOR PEDAL & LINKAGE (TC MODELS)

1 Accelerator cross shaft and pedal
2 Mounting bracket for cross shaft, RH
3 Nylon bearing for cross shaft mounting
   bracket, RH
4 Grommet for cross shaft in bulkhead
5 Mounting bracket for cross shaft, LH
6 Nylon bearing for cross shaft mounting
   bracket, LH
7 Bolt, RH side
8 Plain washer
9 Spring washer
10 Nut
11 Rubber pad for accelerator pedal
12 Accelerator return spring
13 Lever assembly for accelerator cross shaft
14 Ball end for lever
15 Bolt
16 Plain washer
17 Self-locking nut
18 Accelerator coupling shaft assembly
19 Ball end for lever on coupling shaft
20 Bearing for coupling shaft
21 Tubular pin
22 Split pin
23 Bracket for coupling shaft
24 Bolt
25 Spring washer
26 Nut
27 Control rod, accelerator shaft to
   coupling shaft
28 Ball joint, RH thread
29 Locknut, RH thread

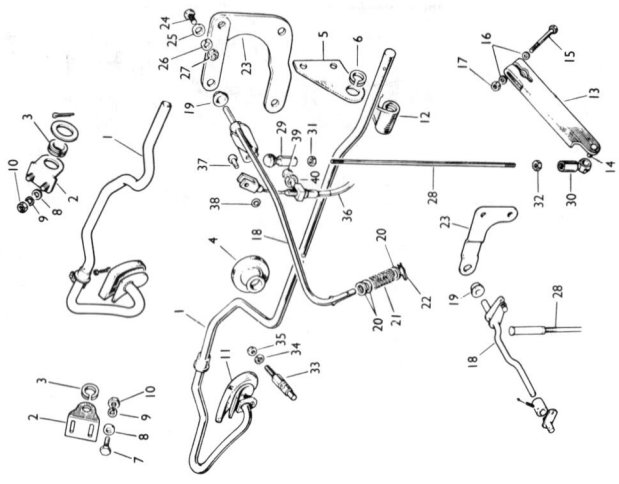

Fig.3.33. ACCELERATOR PEDAL & LINKAGE (AUTOMATIC TRANSMISSION MODELS)

1 Accelerator cross shaft and pedal
2 Mounting bracket for cross shaft, RH
3 Nylon bearing for cross shaft bracket, RH
4 Grommet for cross shaft in bulkhead
5 Mounting bracket for cross shaft, LH
6 Nylon bearing for cross shaft bracket, LH
7 Bolt
8 Plain washer
9 Spring washer
10 Nut
11 Rubber pad for accelerator pedal
12 Accelerator return spring
13 Lever assembly for accelerator cross shaft
14 Ball end for lever
15 Bolt
16 Plain washer
17 Self-locking nut
18 Accelerator coupling shaft assembly
19 Nylon bearing for coupling shaft
20 Plain washer
21 Anti-rattle spring
22 Spring clip
23 Bracket for accelerator coupling shaft
24 Bolt
25 Plain washer
26 Spring washer
27 Nut
28 Control rod
29 Ball joint, RH thread
30 Ball joint, LH thread
31 Locknut, RH thread
32 Locknut, LH thread
33 Accelerator pedal detent stop
34 Spring washer
35 Nut
36 Downshift cable
37 Clevis
38 Plain washer
39 Nut
40 Plain washer

is free throughout its complete travel and also that the carburetter throttle butterflies open and close fully. To be really sure about this, remove the air cleaner, raise the piston with a small screwdriver and with a mirror look down the air intake. The reason for this is to ensure that the linkage is not strained and that the full throttle position is determined by the pedal touching the carpet and not by the lever on the carburetter spindle reaching the cast stop on the carburetter body.

13 On cars fitted with automatic transmission, the downshift cable should be reconnected to the accelerator coupling shaft and secured with the clevis pin and spring clip. Refer to Chapter 6, Section 20. and check the downshift cable adjustment.

16. Fuel Tank — Removal & Refitting

1. If it is previously known that the fuel tank is to be removed, allow the level of petrol to fall, preferably to the reserve supply level which will facilitate storage of petrol when the tank is drained.
2. For safety reasons disconnect the battery earth terminal.
3. Note the two electrical cable connections ('C', Fig.3.35), to the tank unit located on the underside of the tank and disconnect the two terminals. The green and black cable should be connected to the vertical connector and the plain black cable to the offset connector.
4. Obtain a clean container of suitable capacity to collect the petrol drained from the tank, and disconnect the two fuel pipes (A,B) from the tank unit. Take care not to twist the pipes whilst the unions are being unscrewed.
5. Remove the spare wheel from its location within the luggage compartment.
6. Undo and remove the four screws that secure the rear luggage compartment panel covering the fuel tank. Lift away the panel.
7. Slacken the hose clips that secure the upper hose to the tank and separate the hose from the tank. It may be necessary to cut the hose, in which case a new hose will be required, but with patience it should be possible to disconnect this hose.
8. Undo and remove the four screws that secure the fuel filler assembly to the body and withdraw the filler assembly.
9. Disconnect the fuel tank breather union from the top of the tank next to the filler pipe.
10 Slacken the hose clip that secures the lower filler hose to the tank filler pipe and disconnect the hose from the filler pipe.
11 Unscrew the two tank clamping strap bolts and withdraw the clamps. The fuel tank may now be lifted out.
12 If a fuel tank is damaged or leaks then it must be specially prepared if any heat is to be used to rectify the trouble. Most small repairs can be carried out using resin based filler pastes, such as 'Cataloy'. Ensure they are fully hardened before the tank is replaced or filled for testing. If heat is used for repair work it is important that the tank is completely emptied and thoroughly steamed out and ventilated for at least 24 hours.
13 Flush out the tank with clean petrol to remove any sediment and/or water.
14 Refitting the fuel tank is the reverse procedure to removal. It is recommended that the filler hoses are sealed with a suitable sealant such as Bostik 1753.

17. Fuel Tank Sender Unit — Removal & Refitting

1. If it is previously known that the fuel tank sender unit is to be removed, allow the level of petrol in the tank to fall, preferably to the reserve supply level, which will facilitate storage of the petrol when the tank is drained.
2. For safety reasons disconnect the battery earth terminal.
3. Note the two electrical cable connections ('C', Fig.3.35), to the fuel tank sender unit located on the underside of the tank and disconnect the two terminals. The green and black cable should be connected to the vertical connector and the plain black cable to the

offset connector.
4. Obtain a clean container of suitable capacity to collect the petrol drained from the tank and disconnect the two fuel pipes (A,B) from the tank unit. Take care not to twist the pipes whilst the unions are being unscrewed.
5. Using two screwdrivers placed on the sender unit lock rings in a crossed manner, unscrew the locking ring in an anti-clockwise direction.
6. The tank sender unit may now be lifted away from the underside of the tank taking extreme care not to bend the float arm. Lift away the seating ring from the recess in the tank.
7. Release the filter retaining spring and lift away the nylon filter.
8. Using a small stiff brush clean the nylon filter.
9. Refitting the fuel tank sender unit is the reverse sequence to removal. Make sure that the electrical connections are correctly re-made and test the unit for correct operation by inspection of the fuel gauge when the tank is being refilled.

18. Cold Start Cable — Removal & Refitting

1. Undo and remove the two self-tapping screws that secure the radio speaker panel in place. Lift away the speaker panel.
2. Note the two wires to the cold start warning light switch situated behind the panel and disconnect the two terminals.
3. Undo the cable clamping bolt and remove the switch.
4. Using an open ended spanner undo the nut that secures the outer cable to the console unit panel.
5. Release the clip that secures the cable to the bottom bolt of the clutch bellhousing timing inspection cover and separate the cable from the clip.
6. The cold start cable may now be disconnected from the carburetter installation and then withdrawn through the panel of the console unit.
7. Refitting the cable is the reverse sequence to removal, but the following additional points should be noted:—
a) Before feeding the cable through the bulkhead panel grommet do not forget to fit the spring washer and nut to the cable.
b) If the outer cable is difficult to pass through the bulkhead grommet lubricate with a little MS4S Silicone grease.
c) When reconnecting the cable to the carburetter installation there must be approximately 1/16 inch free movement before it starts to pull the cam off the cold start system.

19. Fuel Reserve Tap Cable — Removal & Refitting

1. Undo and remove the two self-tapping screws that secure the radio speaker panel in place. Lift away the speaker panel.
2. Using an open ended spanner undo the nuts securing the outer cable through the console panel.
3. Disconnect the outer cable from the fuel reserve tap bracket and the inner cable from the connection on the tap lever. The tap is located below the right-hand front engine mounting.
4. The cable may now be withdrawn from the console panel.
5. Refitting is the reverse sequence to removal, but the following additional points should be noted.
a) Before feeding the cable through the bulkhead panel grommets, dot not forget to fit the spring washer and nut to the cable.
b) If the outer cable is difficult to thread through the bulkhead grommet, lubricate with a little MS4 Silicone grease.

20. Fuel Reserve Tap — Removal & Refitting

1. If it is previously known that the fuel reserve tap is to be removed, allow the level of petrol to fall, preferably to the reserve supply level which will facilitate storage of petrol when the tank is drained.
2. For safety reasons, disconnect the battery earth terminal.

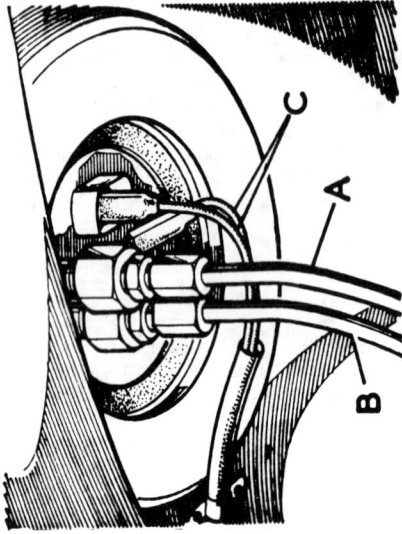

Fig.3.35. FUEL TANK GAUGE UNIT PIPE & ELECTRICAL CONNECTIONS

A Main pipe
B Reserve pipe
C Tank unit to indicator wires

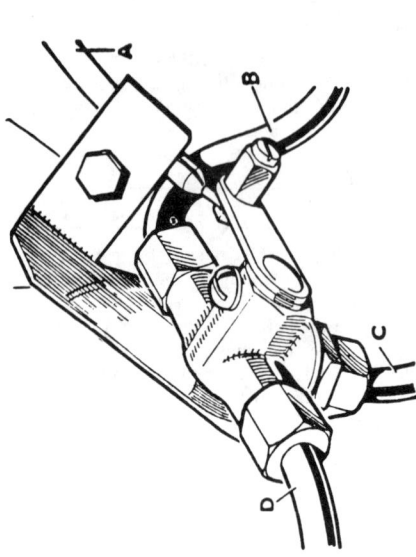

Fig.3.36. FUEL RESERVE TAP PIPE CONNECTIONS

A Operating cable
B Main supply
C Reserve supply
D Outlet to fuel pump

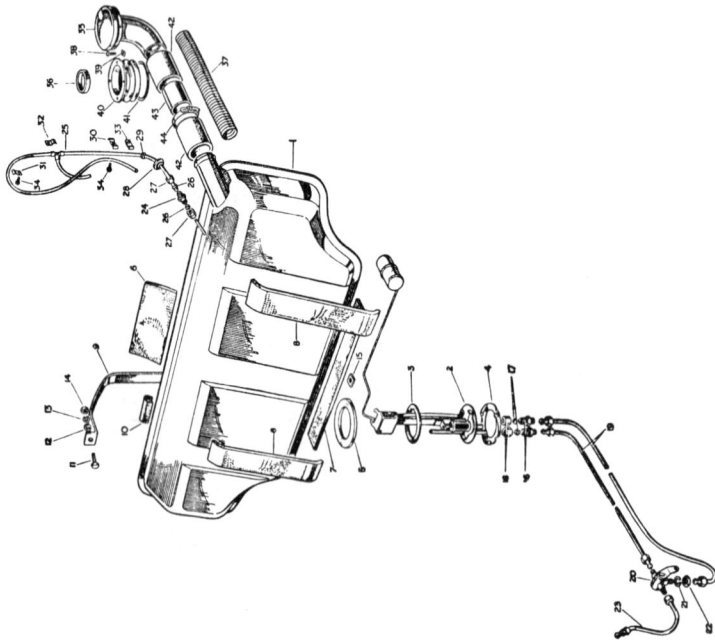

Fig.3.34. FUEL TANK & ANCILLARY PARTS

1 Fuel tank
2 Gauge unit and fuel outlet pipes
3 Sealing ring for gauge unit
4 Locking ring for gauge unit
5 Sealing washer, tank to base unit
6 Insulation felt for fuel tank,lower,thick
7 Insulation felt for fuel tank,lower,thin
8 Insulation felt for fuel tank,front,thin
9 Retaining strap for tank
10 Rubber pad for retaining straps
11 Bolt
12 Plain washer
13 Spring washer
14 Nut
15 Nut plate for strap adjustment
16 Adaptor for fuel pipes
17 Olive
18 Union nut
19 Fuel pipe complete,tank to reserve tap
20 Reserve tap
21 Spring washer
22 Special nut
23 Fuel pipe complete, reserve tap to petrol pump
24 Connector for breather pipe
25 Breather & drain pipe for fuel tank
26 Olive
27 Union nut
28 Grommet, large
29 Grommet, small
30 Spire nut clip, double
31 Spire nut clip, single
32 Clip
33 Clip
34 Drive screw fixing clips
35 Filler pipe and cap complete
36 Sealing ring for filler cap
37 Filler pipe, inner, flexible
38 Drive screw
39 Clinch nut
40 Grommet for fuel filler
41 Wire ring for fuel filler grommet
42 Hose for fuel filler
43 Connecting pipe for hose
44 Clip for filler hoses

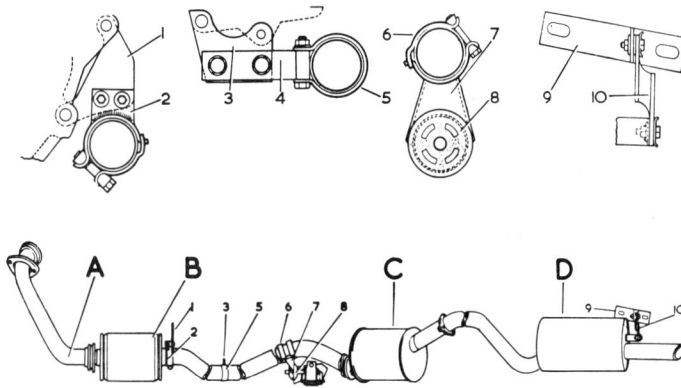

Fig. 3.37. LAYOUT OF 'THREE CAN' EXHAUST SYSTEM (1st TYPE) SC MODELS

Main Components
A Front exhaust pipe
B Centre pipe and expansion chamber
C Intermediate silencer
D Silencer and tailpipe

Exhaust Mountings
1 Support for mounting bracket
2 Exhaust mounting bracket
3 Exhaust hanger bracket
4 Exhaust mounting bracket

5 Clip for exhaust pipe
6 Clamp plate for exhaust pipe
7 Exhaust mounting bracket
8 Mounting rubber for bracket

9 Support bracket for rear silencer
10 Mounting rubber for rear silencer

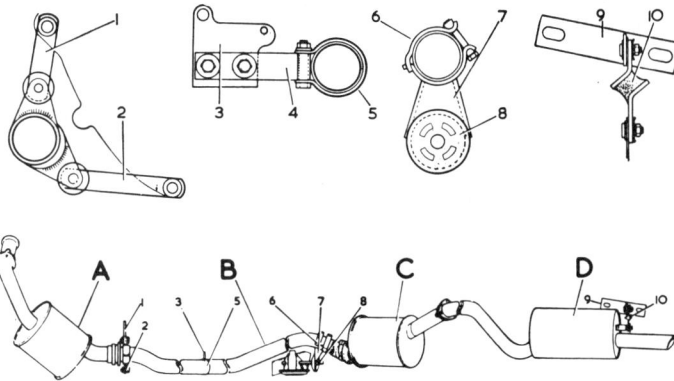

Fig. 3.38. LAYOUT OF 'THREE CAN' EXHAUST SYSTEM (2nd TYPE) SC MODELS

Main Components
A Front exhaust pipe and expansion chamber
B Centre exhaust pipe
C Intermediate silencer
D Silencer and tailpipe

Exhaust Mountings
1 Support strap, top
2 Support strap, bottom
3 Exhaust hanger bracket

4 Exhaust mounting bracket
5 Clip for exhaust pipe
6 Clamp plate for exhaust pipe
7 Exhaust mounting bracket

8 Mounting rubber for bracket
9 Support bracket for rear silencer
10 Mounting rubber for rear silencer

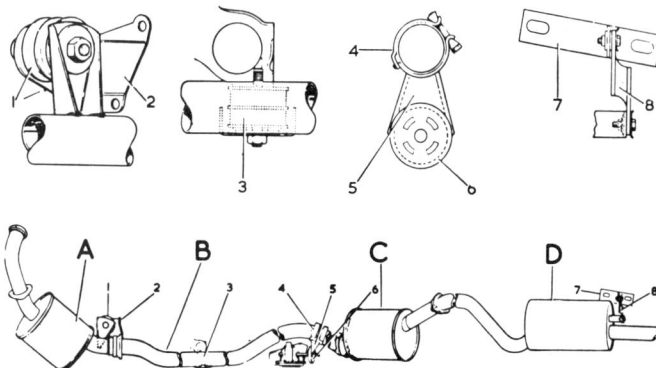

Fig. 3.39. LAYOUT OF 'THREE CAN' EXHAUST SYSTEM (3rd TYPE) SC MODELS

Main Components
A Front exhaust pipe and expansion chamber
B Centre exhaust pipe
C Intermediate silencer
D Tailpipe silencer

Exhaust Mountings
1 Rubber mounting for exhaust pipe
2 Exhaust hanger bracket

3 Rubber mounting for exhaust pipe at gearbox
4 Clamp plate for exhaust pipe
5 Exhaust mounting bracket

6 Mounting rubber for bracket
7 Support bracket for rear silencer
8 Mounting rubber for rear silencer

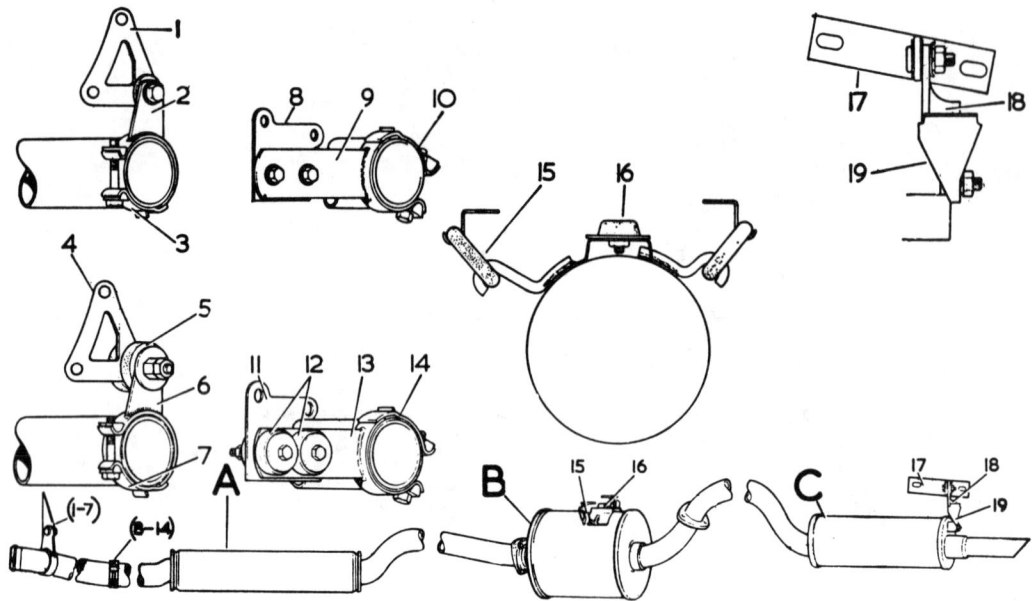

Fig. 3.40. LAYOUT OF 'THREE CAN' EXHAUST SYSTEM (4th TYPE) TC MODELS

Main Components
A Centre exhaust pipe and expansion chamber
B Intermediate silencer
C Silencer and tailpipe

Exhaust Mountings
1 Support bracket
2 Clamp bracket
3 Clamp plate
4 Support bracket
5 Mounting rubber
6 Clamp bracket
7 Clamp plate
8 Exhaust hanger bracket
9 Clamp bracket
10 Clamp plate
11 Exhaust hanger bracket
12 Mounting rubber
13 Clamp bracket
14 Clamp plate
15 Rubber ring
16 Bump stop rubber
17 Support bracket for rear silencer
18 Mounting rubber for rear silencer
19 Later control bracket

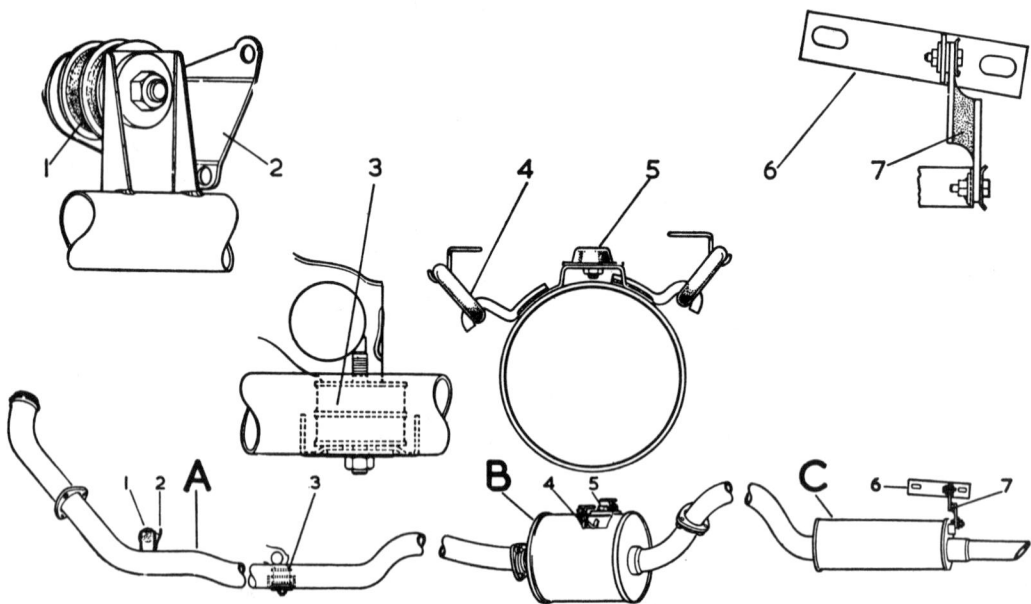

Fig. 3.41. LAYOUT OF 'TWO CAN' EXHAUST SYSTEM (5th TYPE) SC, TC & AUTOMATIC MODELS

Main Components
A Front exhaust pipe
B Intermediate silencer
C Silencer and tailpipe

Exhaust Mountings
1 Mounting rubber
2 Support bracket
3 Mounting rubber at gearbox
4 Rubber ring
5 Bump stop rubber
6 Support bracket for silencer and tailpipe
7 Mounting rubber for silencer and tailpipe

3. Obtain a clean container of suitable capacity to collect the petrol drained from the tank, and disconnect the two fuel pipes (A,B, Fig.3.36), from the tank unit. Take care not to twist the pipes whilst the unions are being unscrewed.

4. Carefully disconnect the three pipe connections from the reserve tap, which is located below the right-hand front engine mounting.

5. Disconnect the outer cable from the fuel reserve tap bracket and the inner cable from the connection on the tap lever.

6. Undo and remove the nut that secures the tap to the bracket. The tap may now be lifted away from the bracket.

7. Refitting is the reverse sequence to removal.

21. Exhaust System

1. Examination of the exhaust pipe and silencer at regular intervals is worthwhile as small defects may be repairable whereas, if they are left, almost certainly renewal of one of the sections of the system will be required. Also, any leaks, apart from the noise factor, can cause poisonous exhaust gases to find their way into the car, which can be unpleasant, to say the least, even in mild concentration. Prolonged inhalation can cause sickness and giddiness.

2. As the sleeve connections and clamps are usually very difficult to separate, it is quicker and easier in the long run to remove the complete system from the car, when renewing a section. It can be expensive if another section is damaged when trying to separate a bad section from it.

3. Removal of the exhaust system is a straightforward operation and by referring to the illustration showing the exhaust system of the model applicable, the various mountings and layout are clearly illustrated. Removal is simply a matter of systematically releasing the exhaust system from the mounting.

22. Modifications to the Fuel System – Exhaust Emission, USA Requirement

Due to the increasing concern of atmospheric pollution in various countries and the appearance of new regulations appertaining to motor cars, certain modifications have to be made to either the engines, the exhaust system or the fuel tank breathing system. In some cases a combination of two or three modifications has to be incorporated, depending entirely on the local regulations relative to the country in which the car is being operated.

Rover 2,000 SC and TC models require certain modifications which have to be carried out in order to comply with the US Federal requirements and a summary of these are given below.

Normally a car produced specifically for this market is modified at the production stage.

1. Fuel Spill Back System

When a car is operating in relatively high temperatures, or is being used for long runs at high speeds the engine compartment temperature can be relatively high causing fuel vapour locks in the main feed line. To counteract this, the fuel feed lines are modified so that fuel is able to flow at a reasonably constant rate between the fuel tank, pump, carburetter/s and then back to the fuel tank again. As fuel is required by the carburetter/s, so it is drawn off from the constant flow of cool fuel.

A fuel pump having a higher capacity is fitted and the flow is increased to give a pressure of between 2¾ and 4¼ lbs/per sq.in. Instead of having the conventional glass sediment bowl, a metal bowl is fitted. Also the carburetter float chamber lid is modified to incorporate a take-off pipe to return the fuel to the fuel tank. These items are shown in Fig.3.42.

2. Distributor Modification

A modified distributor is fitted and a retarded static ignition timing of 4° ATDC (6° ATDC early produced cars) is necessary.

The automatic advance of the ignition timing now commences at 900 r.p.m. but the overall characteristics of the advance degrees/ crankshaft r.p.m. remains the same, but all occur slightly earlier than with the unmodified distributor.

When a modified distributor is fitted two other modifications are required as detailed in paragraphs 3 and 4 of this section, so as to produce an acceptable level of exhaust emission. Also to counteract the very high hydro-carbon emission produced by the engine during normal manual transmission gearchanges, a throttle damper is required as detailed in paragraph 5 of this section.

3. Fuel & Air Deflector

This is a little device in the form of a pressed metal sheet with a hole whose profile has a specially formed toothed edge to give better turbulence to the fuel/air charge after initial mixing in the carburetter body. Because of the extra turbulence, the fuel vapour is able to mix better with the air, so stopping the formulation of fuel droplets accumulating on the inlet manifold walls.

It is fitted between the carburetter and inlet manifold on SC engines and between the carburetters and adaptors on TC engines. The principle is shown in Fig.3.43.

4. Throttle Butterfly Poppet Valve

A small spring loaded poppet valve is fixed onto the throttle butterfly as shown in Fig.3.44. It functions when there is a high inlet manifold depression as when the engine is in the over-run condition with the throttle butterfly closed, the little valve will be drawn open and will allow extra air to bleed through the throttle butterfly giving a weaker fuel/air charge. When accompanied with the retarded ignition timing as described in paragraph 2 of this section, correct combustion will be maintained, so decreasing exhaust emission.

5. Throttle Damper

On TC models, a little pneumatic damper acts on the throttle spindle as shown in Fig.3.45, so that the throttle butterflies are prevented from suddenly closing when the accelerator pedal is released, as occurs during normal manual gearbox gearchanges. As the gear changing system is controlled and slower with cars fitted with automatic transmission, the throttle damper is not required to be fitted on these models.

6. Jet Adjustment Restriction

The carburetter/s are specially and accurately set at the factory to give the maximum richness which is allowed by the US Federal regulations. A special locking device is fitted as shown in Fig.3.46 (SC models) or Fig.3.47 (TC models), so that any adjustment is restricted and should any attempt be made it will only weaken the setting.

7. Jet Compensators

Little bi-metal discs are fitted between each jet assembly and carburetter body as shown in Fig.3.48, and these discs act against the jets to compensate for any fluctuations in temperature of the carburetter body.

8. Carburetter Tuning

Any car which is specially modified for exhaust emission control has a special label warning the owner about the US Federal standards and against any unauthorised adjustments to the carburetter and inlet manifold installation.

If any serious repair work has been carried out it is important that an exhaust gas analysis be made by the local Rover agent to ensure that the Federal requirements are completely complied with.

Normally, as the equipment is specially checked for correct operation, only mechanical adjustments will be required and jet sizes etc, may be considered as satisfactory. Before any adjustments are made to the carburetters, it is important that the ignition timing is checked first. Then the adjustments may be made providing that

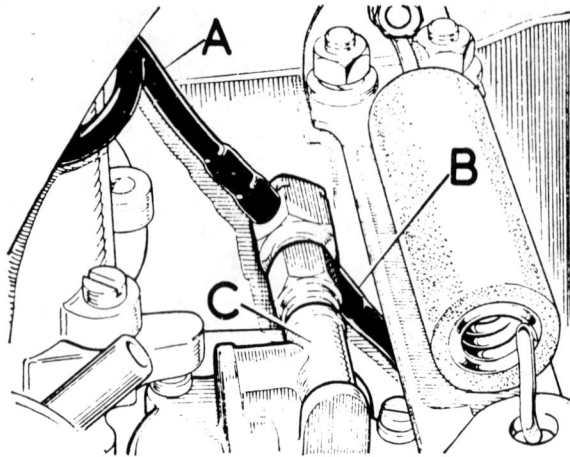

Fig.3.42. FUEL SPILL—BACK CONNECTION AT CARBURET-
TER FLOAT CHAMBER

A Fuel spill-back pipe   C Float chamber top (rear
B Fuel feed pipe   carburetter)

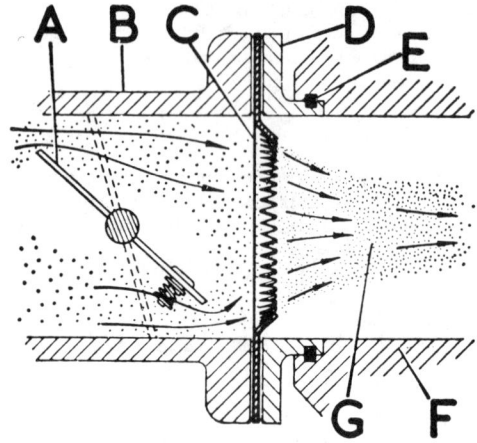

Fig.3.43. FUEL DEFLECTOR

A Butterfly   E Adaptor seal
B Carburetter body   F Inlet manifold
C Deflector plate   G Mixture flow
D Adaptor

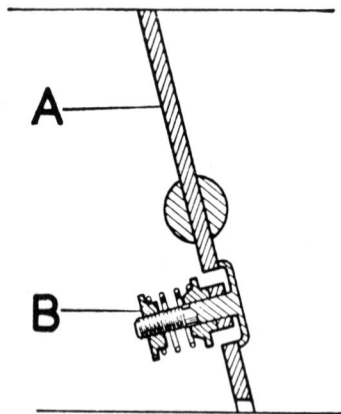

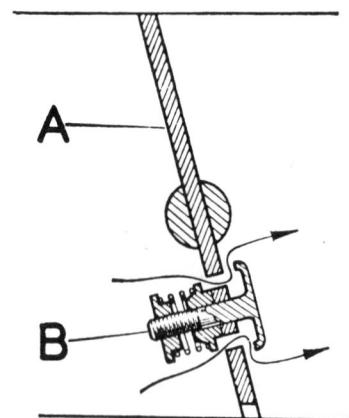

Fig.3.44. BUTTERFLY POPPET VALVE

A	B
A Butterfly	A Butterfly
B Poppet valve closed	B Poppet valve open
C Low manifold depression	C High manifold depression

Fig. 3.47. JET RESTRICTOR (TC MODELS)
A Jet adjusting screw
B Locknut
C Restrictor device

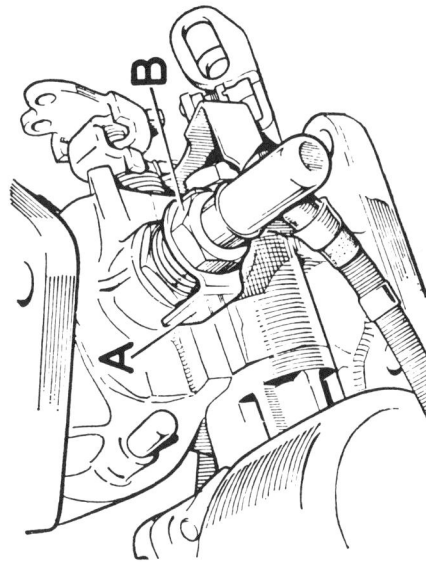

Fig. 3.48. JET COMPENSATOR
A Carburetter body
B Jet bearing
C Needle
D Belleville washers
E Jet
F Compensator tag for operating fork
G Copper washer for jet
H Jet compensator

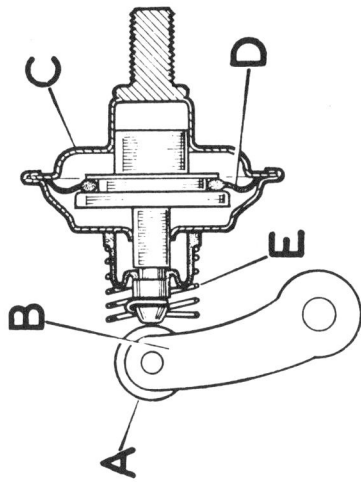

Fig. 3.45. THROTTLE DAMPER (TC MODELS ONLY)
A Nylon roller
B Lever on throttle spindle
C Damper housing
D Diaphragm
E Return spring

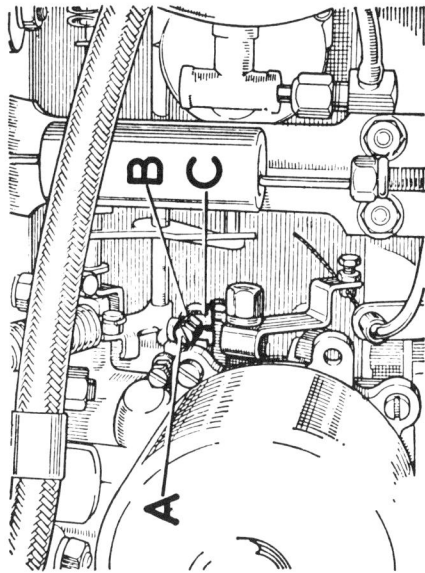

Fig. 3.46. JET RESTRICTOR (SC MODELS)
A Restrictor device
B Jet adjusting nut

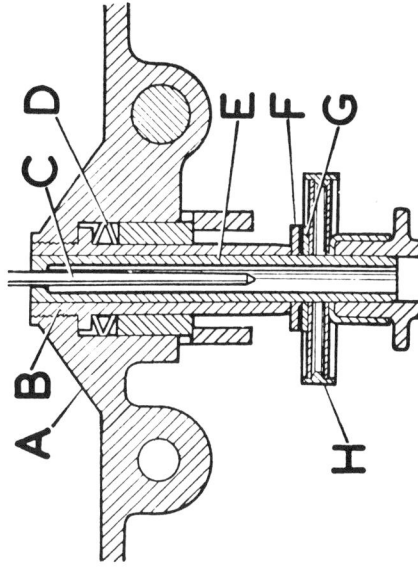

the ambient temperature is between 60°F and 80°F. Any adjustment made outside this temperature range could give inaccurate results.

Special locknuts are fitted to the carburetter idling speed and fast idle speed adjustment screws to prevent loss of adjustment caused by vibration or accidental movement.

9. Carburetters 2,000 TC Models

Two HS8 carburetters are fitted to TC models converted for exhaust emission control. Their design is basically the same as that for the HD8 type of carburetter.

Some models have carburetters with a spring loaded needle in the piston and it is very important that it is correctly fitted with the line on the upper face of the bias face, or shoulder, pointing towards and central to the air passage in the piston.

It is important that the level of fuel in the carburetter float chamber is correctly set. A 0.312 inch diameter metal rod should be able to be inserted between the fork in the float lever and the top of the float chamber. Also there must be a gap of between 0.125 and 0.1875 inch between the hinged type float and the rim of the float chamber lid when the needle valve is closed.

The throttle damper should be correctly set so that when the throttle butterflies are closed, the lever on the throttle spindle must also be adjusted to allow the nylon roller to be in contact with the damper plunger. When the damper plunger is pressed fully home, check that there is a gap of between 0.150 and 0.160 inch between the roller and the plunger. Any adjustment may be made by re-setting the damper lever.

Check the time that it takes from the damper to start to operate to the time the throttle butterflies are completely closed. It should take one second and if the dampers fitted give an appreciably different result, new ones must be fitted.

10. Carburetter Spare Parts

Due to the need of special parts for anti-pollution carburetters, it is important that any parts obtained have the following identification numbers on the packaging:— SU,AUD 267, AUD 254, AUD 311 or AUD 329.

Although some parts may look similar to those fitted to standard carburetters they are, in fact, not the same as they are produced to much finer degrees of accuracy.

Fault Finding Chart - Fuel System & Carburation

Symptom	Reason/s	Remedy
Carburation and ignition faults	Air cleaner choked and dirty giving rich mixture.	Remove, clean and replace air cleaner.
	Fuel leaking from carburetter/s, fuel pumps, or fuel lines.	Check for and eliminate all fuel leaks. Tighten fuel line union nuts.
	Float chamber flooding.	Check and adjust float level.
	Generally worn carburetter/s.	Remove, overhaul and replace.
	Distributor condenser faulty.	Remove, and fit new unit.
	Balance weights or vacuum advance mechanism in distributor faulty.	Remove, and overhaul distributor.
Incorrect adjustment	Carburetter/s incorrectly adjusted mixture too rich.	Tune and adjust carburetter/s.
	Idling speed too high.	Adjust idling speed.
	Contact breaker gap incorrect.	Check and reset gap.
	Valve clearances incorrect.	Check rocker arm to valve stem clearances and adjust as necessary.
	Incorrectly set spark plugs.	Remove, clean and regap.
	Tyres under-inflated.	Check tyre pressures and inflate if necessary.
	Wrong spark plugs fitted.	Remove and replace with correct units.
	Brakes dragging.	Check and adjust brakes.
Dirt in system	Petrol tank air vent restricted.	Remove petrol cap and clean out air vent.
	Partially clogged filters in pump and carburetter/s.	Remove and clean filters.
	Dirt lodged in float chamber needle housing.	Remove and clean out float chamber and needle valve assembly.
	Incorrectly seating valves in fuel pump.	Remove, dismantle, and clean out fuel pump.
Fuel pump faults	Fuel pump diaphragm leaking or damaged.	Remove, and overhaul fuel pump.
	Gasket in fuel pump damaged.	Remove, and overhaul fuel pump.
	Fuel pump valves sticking due to petrol gumming.	Remove, and thoroughly clean fuel pump.
Air leaks	Too little fuel in fuel tank (prevalent when climbing steep hills).	Refill fuel tank.
	Union joints on pipe connections loose.	Tighten joints and check for air leaks.
	Split in fuel pipe on suction side of fuel pump.	Examine, locate, and repair.
	Inlet manifold to block or inlet manifold to carburetter/s gasket leaking.	Test by pouring oil along joints — bubbles indicate leak. Renew gasket as appropriate.

Chapter 4 Ignition system

Contents

Specifications

Sparking Plugs

Type	Champion 14 mm
2000 SC	9 : 1 compression N9Y
	7.5:1 compression N5
2000 TC	9:1 and 10:1 compression N6Y
2200 SC and automatic	N9Y
2200 TC	N7Y
Plug gap	0.025 inch
Firing order..	1, 3, 4, 2

Coil ... ...   Lucas HA 12 (positive or negative)

Resistance at 20°C (68°F) in primary winding...	3.1 to 3.5 ohms.
Consumption - ignition switched on	3.9 amp
Coil 7V	Lucas BA 7

Distributor - Standard

Type

Single carburetter...	9:1 compression	Lucas 25D4—41119
	7.5:1 compression	Lucas 25D4—41036
Twin carburetter	10:1 compression	Lucas 25D4—41085
	9:1 compression	Lucas 24D4—41141

Contact point gap setting	0.014 to 0.016
Direction of rotation...	Anti-clockwise
Dwell angle	57° — 63°
Condenser capacity	0.18 — 0.24 mF
Automatic advance	Vacuum and centrifugal

Maximum vacuum advance:—

Single carburetter	16° crankshaft angle
Twin carburetter...	12° crankshaft angle

Maximum centrifugal advance:—

Single carburetter	24 - 28° crankshaft angle
Twin carburetter...	18 - 22° crankshaft angle

Advancement begins at:—

Single carburetter	1 to 5° at 1,100 rpm.
Twin carburetter :—	
9:1 compression	11 to 15° at 1,120 rpm.
10:1 compression	6 to 10° at 1,000 rpm.

Advancement finishes at:—

Single carburetter	5,200 rpm.
Twin carburetter...	3,250 rpm.

Total advancement:—

Single carburetter	40 to 44°
Twin carburetter...	30 to 34°

Distributor micrometer adjustment ... ...   1 division equals approximately 4°

Distributor — Emission Control

2000 SC automatic transmission	Lucas 25D4—41200	
Vacuum advance unit	4 – 14 – 8	
2000 TC automatic transmission	Lucas 25D4– 41199	
Vacuum advance unit	4 – 7 – 6	

Timing - Static - Full Retard

Single carburetter...	9:1 compression	4° BTDC
Single carburetter...	7.5:1 compression	6° BTDC
Twin carburetter	10:1 compression	6° BTDC
Twin carburetter	9:1 compression	6° BTDC
All 2200 models	9:1 compression	8° BTDC

Timing - Exhaust Emission Control

Static	4° ATDC (6° on early models)
Dynamic	4° ATDC at 700--800 rpm. (6° on early models)

1. General Description

In order that the engine may run correctly, it is necessary for an electrical spark to ignite the fuel/air charge in the combustion chamber at exactly the right moment in relation to engine speed and load. The ignition system is based on supplying low tension voltage from the battery to the ignition coil, where it is converted to high tension voltage. The high tension voltage is powerful enough to jump the sparking plug gap in the cylinders many times a second providing that the ignition system is in good working order and that all adjustments are correct.

The ignition comprises two individual circuits known as the low tension circuit and the high tension circuit.

The low tension circuit (sometimes known as the primary circuit) comprises the battery, lead to the control box, lead to the ignition switch, and then to the low tension or primary coil windings, and the lead from the low tension coil windings to the contact breaker points and condenser in the distributor.

The high tension circuit (sometimes known as the secondary circuit) comprises the high tension or secondary coil winding, the heavily insulated ignition lead from the centre of the coil to the centre of the distributor cap, the rotor arm, the sparking plug leads and the sparking plugs.

The complete ignition system operation is as follows:—

Low tension voltage from the car battery is changed within the ignition coil to high tension voltage by the opening and closing of the contact breaker points in the low tension circuits. High tension voltage is then fed via the carbon brush in the centre of the distributor cap to the rotor arm in the distributor. The rotor arm revolves inside the distributor cap. Each time it comes in line with one of the four metal segments in the cap, these being connected to the sparking plug leads, the opening and closing of the contact breaker points causes the high tension voltage to build up, jump the gap from the rotor arm to the appropriate metal segment and so via the sparking plug lead to the sparking plug, where it finally jumps the gap between the two sparking plug electrodes, one being connected to earth.

The ignition timing is advanced and retarded automatically to ensure the spark occurs at just the right instant for the particular load at the prevailing engine speed.

The engine advance is controlled both mechanically and by a vacuum operated system. The mechanical governor mechanism comprises two weights, which move out under centrifugal force from the central distributor shaft as the engine speed rises. As they move outwards they rotate the cams relative to the distributor shaft, and so advance the spark. The weights are held in position by two light springs and it is the tension of the springs which is largely responsible for correct spark advancement.

The vacuum control comprises a diaphragm, one end of which is connected via a small bore tube to the carburetter installation, and the other side to the contact breaker plate. Depression in the induction manifold and carburetter, which varies with the engine speed and

throttle opening, causes the diaphragm to move, so moving the contact breaker plate and advancing or retarding the spark. A fine degree of control is achieved by a spring in the vacuum assembly.

On the very latest produced Rover 2000 TC models, a speed limiting rotor arm is fitted to the distributor in place of the conventional rotor arm. This is a device which contains a centrifugal switch which operates at about 6,500 r.p.m. and Rovers suggest that it is fitted to the earlier produced TC models. It may be obtained under part number 587687. Any replacement distributor will now incorporate the new type rotor arm.

The reason for fitting the speed limiting device is to act as an over-riding safety control as it operates above the recommended maximum engine rpm speed. It does not release the driver from the obligation to stay out of the red zone on the revolution counter.

2. Contact Breaker — Adjustment

1. To adjust the contact breaker points so that the correct gap is obtained, first release the two clips securing the distributor cap to the distributor body, and lift away the cap. Clean the inside and outside of the cap with a dry cloth. It is unlikely that the four segments will be badly burned or scored, but if they are the cap must be renewed. If only a small deposit is on the segments it may be scraped away using a small screwdriver.

2. Push in the carbon brush located in the top of the cap several times to ensure that it moves freely. The brush should protrude by at least ¼ inch.

3. Gently prise the contact breaker points (7), Fig.4.1, open to examine the condition of their faces. If they are rough, pitted or dirty, it will be necessary to remove them for refacing or for replacement points to be fitted.

4. Presuming the points are satisfactory, or that they have been cleaned or replaced, measure the gap between the points by turning the engine over until the contact breaker arm is on the peak of one of the four cam lobes. A 0.015 inch feeler gauge should now just fit between the points.

5. If the gap varies from this amount, slacken the contact plate securing screw and adjust the contact gap by inserting a screwdriver into the notched hole at the end of the plate, turning clockwise to decrease and anti-clockwise to increase the gap. Tighten the securing screw and re-check the gap.

6. Replace the rotor arm and distributor cap and clip the spring blade retainers into position.

3. Contact Breaker Points - Removal & Replacement

1. If the contact breaker points are burned, pitted or badly worn, they must be removed and either replaced, or their faces filed smooth.

2. To remove the points, unscrew the terminal nut (B) Fig.4.2.,

and remove it together with the washer under its head. Remove the flanged nylon bush and then the condenser lead and the low tension lead from the terminal pin. Lift off the contact breaker arm and then remove the large fibre washer from the terminal pin.

3. The adjustable contact breaker plate is removed by unscrewing one holding down screw (A) and removing it, complete with spring and flat washer.

4. To re-face the points, rub the faces on a fine carborundum stone, or on fine emery paper. It is important that the faces are rubbed flat and parallel to each other, so that there will be complete face to face contact when the points are closed. One of the points will be pitted and the other will have deposits on it.

5. It is necessary to remove completely the built-up deposits, but not necessary to rub the pitted point right to the stage where all the pitting has disappeared, though obviously if this is done it will prolong the time before which the operation of re-facing the points has to be repeated.

6. To replace the points, first position the adjustable contact breaker plate, and secure it with its screw, spring and flat washer. Fit the fibre washer to the terminal pin, and fit the contact breaker arm over it. Insert the flanged nylon bush with the condenser lead immediately under its head, and the low tension lead under that, over the terminal pin. Fit the steel flat washer and screw on the securing nut.

7. The points are now reassembled and the gap should be set as described in the previous section.

4. Condenser — Removal, Testing & Replacement

1. The purpose of the condenser, (sometimes known as a capacitor), is to ensure that when the contact breaker points are open there is no sparking across them which would waste voltage and cause wear.

2. The condenser is fitted in parallel with the contact breaker points. If it develops a short circuit, it will cause ignition failure as the points will be prevented from interrupting the low tension circuit and serious arcing will occur.

3. If the engine becomes very difficult to start or begins to miss after several miles running, and the contact breaker point shows signs of excessive burning or overheating, then the condition of the condenser must be suspect. A further test can be made by separating the points by hand with the ignition switched on. If this is accompanied by a flash it is indicative that the condenser has failed.

4. Without special test equipment the only sure way to diagnose condenser trouble is to replace a suspected unit with a new one and note if there is any improvement.

5. To remove the condenser from the distributor, remove the distributor cap and the rotor arm. Unscrew the contact breaker arm terminal nut, and remove the nut, washer and flanged nylon bush and release the condenser. Replacement of the condenser is simply a reversal of the removal process. Take particular care that the condenser lead does not short circuit against any portion of the contact breaker plate.

5. Distributor — Lubrication

1. It is important that the distributor cam is lubricated with petroleum jelly at the specified mileages, and that the breaker arm, governor weights, and cam spindle are lubricated with engine oil every 10,000 miles. In practice it will be found that lubrication every 5,000 miles is preferable, although this is not recommended by the makers.

2. Great care should be taken not to use too much lubricant, as any excess that might find its way onto the contact breaker points could cause burning and misfiring.

3. To gain access to the cam spindle, lift away the rotor arm. Drop no more than two drops of engine oil onto the screw head. This will run down the spindle when the engine is hot and lubricate the bearings. No more than ONE drop of oil should be applied to the

pivot post.

6. Distributor — Removal & Replacement

1. To remove the distributor from the engine start by unclipping the distributor cap and moving the cap to one side.

2. If the distributor and cap are to be renewed, mark the HT leads at the distributor cap end and remove all the leads from the distributor cap.

3. Unscrew the distributor vacuum advance pipe union from the vacuum unit on the side of the distributor and release the pipe.

4. Disconnect the LT lead from the terminal connector on the side of the distributor.

5. Remove the distributor body clamp bolts (two) which hold the distributor clamp plate to the engine and remove the distributor. NOTE: If it is not wished to disturb the ignition timing setting, then under no circumstances should the clamp pinch bolt, which secures the distributor in its relative position in the clamp, be loosened. Providing the distributor is removed without the clamp being loosened from the distributor body and the engine is not turned, the timing will not be lost.

6. Replacement is a reversal of the above procedure. If the engine has been turned it will be necessary to re-time the ignition. This will also be necessary if the clamp pinch bolt has been loosened.

7. Distributor — Dismantling

1. With the distributor removed from the car and on the bench, remove the distributor cap (2) Fig.4.1, and lift off the rotor arm (5). If very tight, lever it off gently with a screwdriver.

2. Remove the contact breaker points from the distributor as detailed in Section 3.

3. Remove the condenser (6) from the contact breaker base plate (9) by releasing its securing screw.

4. Unlock the vacuum unit spring from its mounting pin on the moving contact breaker plate.

5. Unscrew the two screws and lockwashers which hold the contact breaker base plate in position and remove the earth lead from the relevant screw. Remember to replace this lead on reassembly.

6. Lift out the contact breaker base plate.

7. NOTE the position of the slot in the rotor arm drive in relation to the offset drive dog at the opposite end of the distributor. It is essential that this is reassembled correctly as otherwise the timing may be 180° out.

8. Unscrew the cam spindle retaining screw which is located in the centre of the rotor arm drive shaft (10), and remove the cam spindle.

9. Lift out the centrifugal weights (12), together with their springs (11).

10 To remove the vacuum unit, spring off the small circlips securing the advance adjustment knurled nut, which should then be unscrewed. With the micrometer adjusting nut removed, release the spring and the micrometer adjusting nut lock spring clip. This is the clip that is responsible for the 'clicks' when the micrometer adjuster is turned, it is small and easily lost, as also is the circlip, so put them in a safe place. Do not forget to replace the lock spring clip on reassembly.

11 It is necessary to remove the distributor drive shaft or spindle only if it is thought to be excessively worn. With a thin punch drive out the retaining pin from the driving tongue collar on the bottom end of the distributor drive shaft. The shaft can then be removed. The distributor is now completely dismantled.

8. Distributor — Inspection & Repair

1. Check the contact breaker points as described in Section 3. Also check the distributor cap for signs of tracking, indicated by a thin

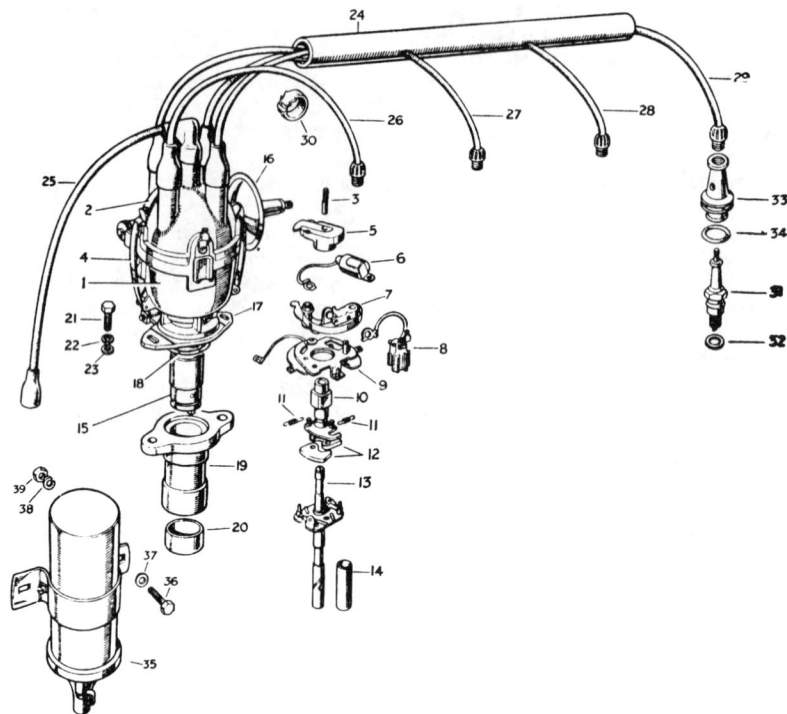

Fig.4.1. EXPLODED VIEW OF DISTRIBUTOR

1	Distributor complete	11	Auto advance spring, set	21	Set bolt	31	Sparking plug
2	Distributor cap	12	Auto advance weight	22	Spring washer	32	Washer for plug
3	Brush and spring for cap	13	Shaft and action plate	23	Plain washer	33	Cover for sparking plug
4	Clip for distributor cap	14	Bush for shaft	24	Ignition wire carrier	34	Sealing ring for plug
5	Rotor arm	15	Driving dog for distributor	25	Coil lead complete		cover
6	Condenser	16	Vacuum unit	26	Plug lead No.1	35	Ignition coil
7	Contact points	17	Clamp plate for distributor	27	Plug lead No.2	36	Bolt
8	Nylon bridge piece	18	'O' ring for distributor	28	Plug lead No.3	37	Plain washer
	and lead	19	Distributor housing assbly.	29	Plug lead No.4	38	Spring washer
9	Base plate	20	Bush in distributor housing	30	Cable cleat for HT leads	39	Nut
10	Cam		for drive shaft		at distributor		

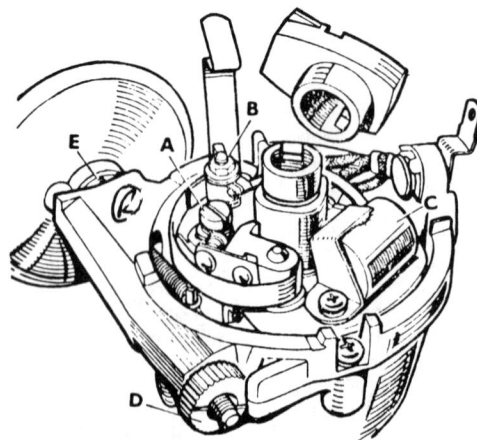

Fig.4.2. ADJUSTMENT POINTS FOR THE DISTRIBUTOR

A Contact breaker adjustment screw Terminal nut Capacitor   D Micrometer adjusting nut   E Micrometer scale

black line between the segments. Replace the cap if any signs of tracking are found.

2. If the metal portion of the rotor arm is badly burned or loose, renew the arm. If slightly burnt clean the arm with a fine file. Check that the carbon brush moves freely in the centre of the distributor cap.

3. Examine the fit of the contact breaker plate on the bearing plate, and also check the breaker arm pivot for looseness or wear, and renew as necessary.

4. Examine the balance weights and pivot pins for wear, and renew the weights or cam assembly if a degree of wear is found.

5. Examine the shaft and the fit of the cam assembly onto the shaft. If the clearance is excessive compare the items with new units, and renew either, or both, if they show excessive wear.

6. If the shaft is a loose fit in the distributor bushes and can be seen to be worn, it will be necessary to fit a new shaft and bushes. The older bushes in the early distributor, or the single bush in the later ones, are simply pressed out. NOTE: Before inserting new bushes they should be stood in the engine oil for at least 24 hours.

7. Examine the length of the balance weight springs and compare them with new springs. If they have stretched they should be renewed.

8. IMPORTANT: It is essential that when a distributor, having an exhaust emission control specification is being serviced that replacement parts are obtained applicable to the modified distributor. These parts include the cam, auto-advance springs and vacuum unit. If incorrect parts are fitted the exhaust emission control system will not operate satisfactorily.

9. Distributor — Reassembly

1. Reassembly is a straightforward reversal of the dismantling process, but there are several points which should be noted in addition to those already given in Section 7.

2. Lubricate the balance weights and other parts of the mechanical advance mechanism, the distributor shaft and the portion of the shaft on which the cam bears, with SAE 20 engine oil, during reassembly. Do not oil excessively but ensure that these parts are adequately lubricated.

3. On reassembling the cam driving pins to the centrifugal weights, check that the cam is in its correct position so that when viewed from above, the rotor arm should be at the 6 o'clock position, and the small offset on the driving dog must be on the right.

4. Check the action of the weights in the fully advanced and retarded positions and ensure that they are not binding by holding the shaft and action plate (13) and rotating the cam (10).

5. Tighten the micrometer adjusting nut to the middle position on the timing scale.

6. Finally, set the contact breaker gap to the correct clearance of 0.015 inch.

10. Ignition Timing

1. If the clamp plate pinch bolt has been loosened on the distributor and the static timing has been lost, or if for any other reason it is wished to set the ignition timing, proceed as follows:—

2. The static advance is checked at the exact moment of opening of the contact breaker point relative to the alignment of the timing marks on the flywheel and the pointer. Access is obtained by slackening the cover plate nuts and rotating the plate in an anti-clockwise direction.

3. Rotate the crankshaft so that No.4 piston is coming up to TDC on the compression stroke. This can be checked by removing No.4 sparking plug and feeling the pressure being developed in the cylinder, or by removing the distributor cap and noting the position of the rotor arm relative to No.4 sparking plug lead. If this check is not made it is all too easy to set the timing 180° out.

4. Continue turning the engine until the timing mark on the flywheel or crankshaft pulley is in line with the little pointer. The

correct setting for the different models is given in the Specification Section.

5. Remove the distributor cover and slacken off the distributor body clamp bolt, and with the rotor warm towards No.4 distributor cap segment (check this position with the distributor cap and lead to No.4 sparking plug), insert the distributor into the distributor housing. The dog on the drive shaft should match up with the slot in the distributor drive spindles.

6. Insert the two bolts holding the distributor in position.

7. With the engine set in the correct position, and the rotor arm opposite the correct segment for No.4 cylinder, turn the advance/retard knurled adjuster nut on the distributor until the contact points are just beginning to open. One complete division on the vernier scale is equal to approximately 4°.

8. If the range of adjustment provided by this adjuster is not sufficient, then, if the clamp bolt is not already slackened, it will be necessary to slacken it, and turn the distributor body half a graduation as marked on the adjusting spindle barrel. Sufficient adjustment will normally be found available using the distributor micrometer adjuster. When this has been achieved, the engine is statically timed.

9. Difficulty is sometimes experienced in determining when the contact breaker points actually open. This can be ascertained most accurately by connecting a 12 volt bulb in parallel with the contact breaker points (one lead to earth and the other to the distributor low tension terminal). Switch on the ignition and turn the advance and retard adjuster until the bulb lights up, indicating that the points have just opened.

10 If a stroboscopic timing light is being used, attach one lead to No.4 sparking plug, and attach the other end to the free end of No.4 plug HT cable leading from the distributor. Start the engine and shine the light on the flywheel and timing pointer. If the engine idles at more than between 700 and 800 r.p.m. then the correct static timing will not be obtained as the centrifugal weights will have started to advance.

11 If the light shows the mark in the flywheel to be the right of the pointer, then the ignition is too far advanced. If the mark appears to the left of the pointer, then the ignition is too far retarded. Turn the distributor body or micrometer adjuster until the timing marks and pointer are just in the right position.

12 Tighten the clamp bolt and re-check that the timing is still correct, making any small correction necessary with the micrometer adjuster.

13 A better result can sometimes be obtained by making slight re-adjustments under running conditions.

14 First start the engine and allow to warm up to normal operating temperature, and then accelerate in top gear from between 30 to 50 m.p.h. listening for heaving pinking of the engine. If this occurs, the ignition needs to be retarded slightly until just the faintest trace of pinking can be heard under these operating conditions.

15 Since the ignition advance adjustment enables the firing point to be related correctly in relation to the grade of fuel used, the fullest advantage of any change of fuel will only be attained by re-adjustment of the ignition settings.

16 This is done by varying the setting of the index scale on the vacuum advance mechanism one or two divisions, checking to make sure that the best all round result is attained.

17 IMPORTANT: If the engine is fitted with emission control equipment, the ignition timing must only be set using the stroboscopic timing method as detailed in Section 11.

11. Stroboscopic Timing - Emission Control

1 Where applicable slacken the two access cover plate securing nuts and rotate the plate in an anti-clockwise direction.

2 Connect the strobe light according to the manufacturers instructions but with the HT connection to No.4 sparking plug.

3 Unscrew the union holding the vacuum pipe to the distributor vacuum hosuing and tape up the end of the pipe.

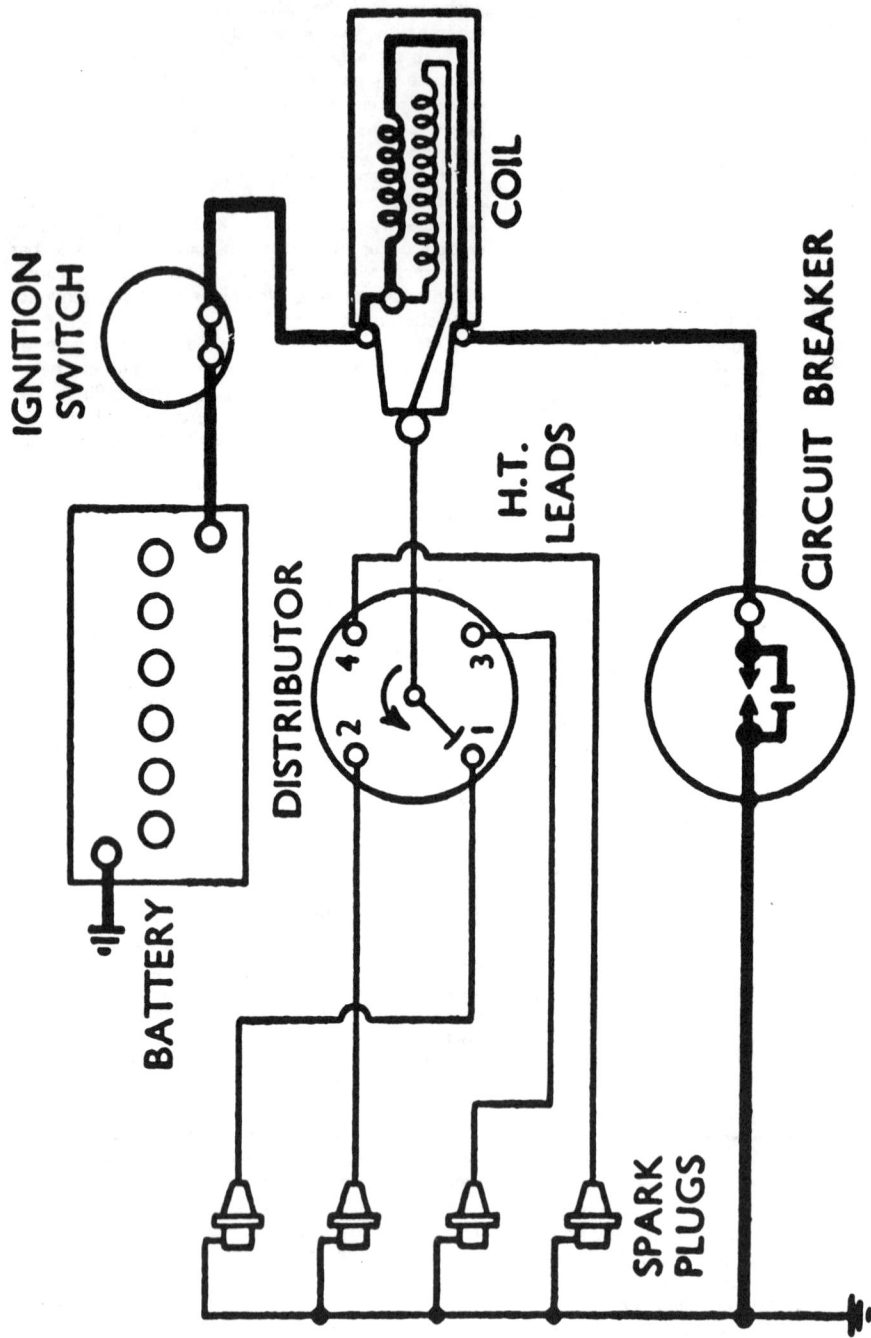

IGNITION SWITCH

COIL

BATTERY

DISTRIBUTOR

H.T. LEADS

SPARK PLUGS

CIRCUIT BREAKER

Fig.4.3. DIAGRAM OF THE IGNITION CIRCUIT
Primary circuit (low tension) is indicated by the heavier lines.

Measuring plug gap. A feeler gauge of the correct size (see ignition system specifications) should have a slight 'drag' when slid between the electrodes. Adjust gap if necessary

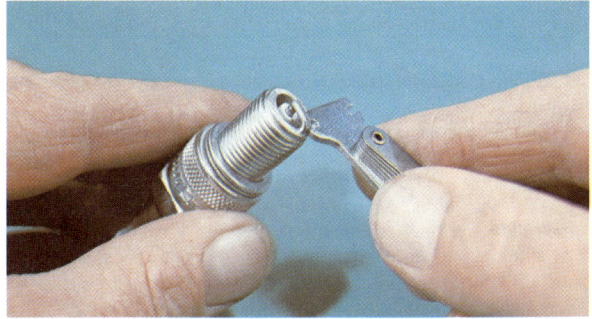

Adjusting plug gap. The plug gap is adjusted by bending the earth electrode inwards, or outwards, as necessary until the correct clearance is obtained. Note the use of the correct tool

Normal. Grey-brown deposits, lightly coated core nose. Gap increasing by around 0.001 in (0.025 mm) per 1000 miles (1600 km). Plugs ideally suited to engine, and engine in good condition

Carbon fouling. Dry, black, sooty deposits. Will cause weak spark and eventually misfire. Fault: over-rich fuel mixture. Check: carburettor mixture settings, float level and jet sizes; choke operation and cleanliness of air filter. Plugs can be re-used after cleaning

Oil fouling. Wet, oily deposits. Will cause weak spark and eventually misfire. Fault: worn bores/piston rings or valve guides; sometimes occurs (temporarily) during running-in period. Plugs can be re-used after thorough cleaning

Overheating. Electrodes have glazed appearance, core nose very white – few deposits. Fault: plug overheating. Check: plug value, ignition timing, fuel octane rating (too low) and fuel mixture (too weak). Discard plugs and cure fault immediately

Electrode damage. Electrodes burned away; core nose has burned, glazed appearance. Fault: pre-ignition. Check: as for 'Overheating' but may be more severe. Discard plugs and remedy fault before piston or valve damage occurs

Split core nose (may appear initially as a crack). Damage is self-evident, but cracks will only show after cleaning. Fault: pre-ignition or wrong gap-setting technique. Check: ignition timing, cooling system, fuel octane rating (too low) and fuel mixture (too weak). Discard plugs, rectify fault immediately

4. Connect an accurate electric tachometer to the engine according to the manufacturers instructions.

5. Start the engine and allow to run at a fast idle until normal operating temperature is reached. Then reset the engine idle speed to between 700 and 800 r.p.m.

6. Turn the vernier adjustment nut on the side of the distributor to the fully advanced position and slacken the distributor clamp bolt.

7. With the engine running at the correct idle speed, slowly rotate the distributor until the stroboscopic light synchronises with the timing pointer and appropriate timing mark.

8. Retighten the distributor clamp bolt and re-check the stroboscopic timing.

9. Disconnect the electric tachometer and timing light. Reconnect the vacuum advance pipe to the vacuum unit on the side of the distributor.

12. Sparking Plugs & Leads

1. The correct functioning of the sparking plugs is vital for the correct running and efficiency of the engine.

2. At intervals of 5,000 miles the plugs should be removed, examined, cleaned and if worn, excessively, replaced. The sparking plugs should be changed every 10,000 miles.

3. The condition of the sparking plugs will also tell much about the overall condition of the engine.

4. If the insulator nose of the sparking plug is clean and white, with no deposits, this is indicative of a weak mixture, or too hot a plug (a hot plug transfers heat away from the electrode slowly - a cold plug transfers heat away quickly).

5. The sparking plugs fitted as standard are Champion N9Y, (single carburetter 9:1 compression), Champion N5 (single carburetter 7.5:1 compression) or Champion N6Y (twin carburetter 9:1 and 10:1 compression). If the top and insulator nose is covered with hard black-looking deposits, then this is indicative that the mixture is too rich. Should the plug be black and oily, then it is likely that the engine is fairly worn, as well as the mixture being too rich.

6. If the insulator nose is covered with light tan to greyish brown deposits, then the mixture is correct and it is likely that the engine is in good condition.

7. If there are any traces of long brown tapering stains on the outside of the white portion of the plug, then the plug will have to be renewed, as this shows that there is a faulty joint between the plug body and the insulator and compression is being allowed to leak away.

8. Plugs should be cleaned by a sand blasting machine, which will free them from carbon better than cleaning by hand. The machine will also test the condition of the plugs under compression. Any plug that fails to spark at the recommended pressure should be renewed.

9. The sparking plug gap is of considerable importance, as, if it is too large or too small, the size of the spark and its efficiency will be seriously impaired. The sparking plug gap should be set to 0.025 inch for the best results.

10 To set it, measure the gap with a feeler gauge, and then bend open, or close, the outer plug electrode until the correct gap is achieved. The centre electrode should never be bent as this may crack the insulation and cause plug failure, if nothing worse.

11 When replacing the plugs, remember to use new washers, and replace the leads in the distributor in the correct firing order, which is 1, 3, 4, 2, No.1. cylinder being the one nearest the radiator.

12 The plug leads require no routine maintenance other than being kept clean and wiped over regularly. At intervals of 5,000 miles, however, pull each lead off the plug in turn and remove them from the distributor by slackening the screws located inside the cap. Moisture can seep down into these joints, giving rise to a white corrosive deposit which must be carefully removed from the end of each cable.

13. Ignition System — Fault Finding

By far the majority of breakdown running troubles are caused by faults in the ignition system, either in the low tension or high tension circuits shown diagrammatically in Fig.4.3.

14. Ignition System — Fault Symptoms

There are two main symptoms indicating ignition faults. Either the engine will not start or fire, or the engine is difficult to start and misfires. If it is a regular misfire, i.e. the engine is only running on two or three cylinders, the fault is almost sure to be in the secondary, or high tension circuit. If the misfiring is intermittent, the fault could be in either the high or low tension circuits. If the engine stops suddenly, or will not start at all, it is likely that the fault is in the low tension circuit. Loss of power and overheating, apart from faulty carburation settings, are normally due to faults in the distributor or incorrect ignition timing.

15. Fault Diagnosis — Engine Fails to Start

1. If the engine fails to start and it was running normally when it was last used, first check there is fuel in the petrol tank. If the engine turns over normally on the starter motor and the battery is evidently well charged, then the fault may be either in the high or low tension circuits. First check the HT circuit. NOTE: If the battery is known to be fully charged, the ignition comes on, and the starter motor fails to turn the engine, CHECK THE TIGHTNESS OF THE LEADS ON THE BATTERY TERMINALS and also the secureness of the earth lead to its CONNECTION TO THE BODY. It is quite common for the leads to have worked loose, even if they look and feel secure If one of the battery terminal posts gets very hot while trying to work the starter motor, this is a sure indication of a faulty connection to that terminal.

2. One of the commonest reasons for bad starting is wet or damp sparking plug leads and distributor. Remove the distributor cap. If condensation is visible internally, dry the cap with a rag and also wipe over the leads. Replace the cap.

3. If the engine still fails to start, check that current is reaching the plugs, by disconnecting each plug lead in turn at the sparking plug end, and holding the end of the cable about 3/16 inch away from the cylinder block. Spin the engine on the starter motor, by pressing the rubber button on the starter solenoid switch (under the bonnet). NOTE: On cars fitted with automatic transmission the starter solenoid switch is specially blanked off so that the engine may not be started from under the bonnet.

4. Sparking between the end of the cable and the block should be fairly strong with a regular blue spark (hold the lead with rubber to avoid electric shocks). If current is reaching the plugs, then remove them and clean and re-gap them to 0.025 inch. The engine should now start.

5. If there are no sparks at the plugs disconnect the cable from the centre of the distributor and hold about 3/16 inch from the block. Spin the engine as before, a rapid succession of loose sparks between the end of the lead and the block indicate that the coil is in order, and that either the distributor cap is cracked; the carbon brush is stuck or worn; the rotor arm is faulty; or the contact points are burnt, pitted or dirty. If the points are in bad shape, clean and reset them as described in Section 3.

6. If there are no sparks from the end of the lead from the coil, then check the connections to the lead to the coil and distributor head and if they are in order, check out the low tension circuit starting with the battery.

8. Switch on the ignition and turn the crankshaft so that the contact breaker points have fully opened. Then, with either a 20 volt voltmeter or bulb and length of wire, check that current from the battery is reaching the starter solenoid switch. No reading indicates

that there is a fault in the cable to the switch, or in the connections at the switch or at the battery terminals. Alternatively, the battery earth lead may not be properly earthed to the body.

9. If in order, check that current is reaching the terminal B (the correct terminal B is the one next to terminal E) in the control box by connecting the voltmeter across B and earth. If there is no reading, this indicates a faulty cable or loose connections between the solenoid switch and the B terminal. Remedy and the car will start.

10 Check with the voltmeter between the control box terminal B (this terminal B is next to terminal W) and earth. No reading means a fault in the control box. Fit a new control box and start the car.

11 If in order then check that current is reaching the ignition switch by connecting the voltmeter to the ignition switch input terminal (the one connected to the brown cable leading to terminal No.1 at the rear of the switch) and earth. No reading indicates a break in the wire or a faulty connection at the switch or the second B terminal.

12 If the correct reading (approximately 12 volts) is obtained check the output terminal on the ignition switch (the terminal connected to the white lead which is connected to terminal No.2 at the back of the switch). No reading means that the ignition switch is broken. Replace with a new unit and start the car.

13 If current is reaching the ignition switch output terminal, then check the terminal at the right-hand top end of the fuse unit, to which the white coloured cable is attached. No reading indicates a break in the wire or loose connections between the ignition switch and the terminal of the fuse box.

14 Check the switch terminal of the coil and the lead to the upper right-hand terminal of the fuse box. This cable is coloured white. NOTE: Even if the right-hand fuse is broken the current should still reach the coil as it does not pass through the fuse itself.

15 Check the contact breaker terminal on the coil and if no reading is recorded on the voltmeter then the coil is at fault and must be renewed. The car should start when a new coil has been fitted.

16 If a reading is obtained at the contact breaker terminal then check the wire from the coil to the side of the distributor for loose connections etc. This cable is coloured white with a black tracer. If a reading is obtained, then the final check on the low tension circuit is across the contact breaker point. No reading means a broken

condenser which, when replaced, will enable the car to finally start.

16. Fault Diagnosis — Engine Misfires

1. If the engine misfires regularly, run it at a fast idling speed, and short out each plug in turn by placing a short screwdriver across from the plug terminal to the cylinder block. Ensure that the screwdriver has a WOODEN OR PLASTIC INSULATED HANDLE.
2. No difference in engine running will be noticed when the plug in the defective cylinder is short circuited. Short circuiting the working plugs will accentuate the misfire.
3. Remove the plug lead from the end of the defective plug and hold it about 3/16 inch away from the blocks. Restart the engine. If the sparking is fairly strong and regular the fault must lie in the sparking plug.
4. The plug may be loose, the insulation may be cracked, or the points may have burnt away giving too wide a gap for the spark to jump. Worse still, one of the points may have broken off. Either renew the plug, or clean it, reset the gap, and then test it.
5. If there is no spark at the end of the plug lead, or if it is weak and intermittent, check the ignition lead from the distributor to the plug. If the insulation is cracked or perished, renew the lead. Check the connections at the distributor cap.
6. If there is still no spark, examine the distributor cap carefully for tracking. This can be recognised by a very thin black line running between two or more electrodes, or between an electrode and some other part of the distributor. These lines are paths which now conduct electricity across the cap, thus letting it run to earth. The only answer is new distributor cap.
7. Apart from the ignition timing being incorrect, other causes of misfiring have already been dealt with under the section dealing with the failure of the engine to start.
8. If the ignition timing is too far retarded, it should be noted that the engine will tend to overheat, and there will be quite a noticeable drop in power. If the engine is overheating and the power is down, and the ignition timing is correct, then the carburetter should be checked as it is likely that this is where the fault lies. See Chapter 3 for details on this.

Chapter 5 Clutch and actuating mechanism

Contents

Specifications

Type	Borg & Beck diaphragm
Operation	Lockheed hydraulic
Plate diameter	8.5 in. (216 mm)
Plate thickness (early)	0.285 in. (7.20 mm) at 950 lb.
Plate thickness (late)...	0.280 in. (7.11 mm) at 1,250 lb.
Withdrawal race thrust bearing...	Ball bearing
Clutch pedal free movement	¼ in. (6.0 mm)
Clutch pedal height	6½ in. (165 mm) minimum plus ¼ in. (6.0 mm) tolerance
Clutch plate identification	White and light green (2000)
	Red and violet (2200)
Clutch fluid	Castrol Girling Brake and Clutch Fluid (Specification SAE 70 R3)

Torque Wrench Settings

Clutch lever bolt	15 lb/ft. (2.0 kg.m)
Clutch assembly to flywheel	12 lb/ft. (1.6 kg.m)
Clutch withdrawal housing to bellhousing	15 lb/ft. (2.0 kg.m)
Flywheel to crankshaft	120 lb/ft. (16.5 kg.m)
Slave cylinder to bellhousing	30 lb/ft. (4 kg.m)

1. General Description

The object of the clutch unit being fitted between the engine and gearbox is so that the engine may be run without being connected to the transmission. Also it enables the engine torque to be progressively applied to the gearbox, so enabling the car to move off gradually from rest and then for the gear to be changed easily as the speed increases or decreases.

The main parts of the clutch assembly are the clutch driven plate assembly, the cover assembly and the release bearing assembly. Fig.5.1. shows the early assembly fitted to cars up to engines with a suffix 'D' in the engine number, whereas Fig.5.2. shows the later clutch assembly with the three tangential supporting straps.

When the clutch is in use, the driven plate assembly being splined to the gearbox primary drive pinion shaft is sandwiched between the flywheel and pressure plate by the diaphragm springs. Engine torque is therefore transferred from the flywheel to the clutch driven plate assembly and then to the gearbox primary drive shaft.

By depressing the clutch pedal, the piston in the master cylinder moves forwards so forcing hydraulic fluid through the clutch hydraulic pipe to the slave cylinder. The piston in the slave cylinder moves forward on the entry of the fluid and actuates the clutch withdrawal lever by a short pushrod. The release bearing assembly is pushed against the diaphragm spring thrust pad which releases its pressure on the driven plate assembly and so breaks the drive between engine and gearbox.

When the clutch pedal is released, the pressure plate diaphragm spring forces the pressure plate into contact with the high friction linings on the clutch driven plate, at the same time forcing the clutch driven plate assembly against the flywheel and so taking the drive up.

As the friction lining on the clutch driven plate wears, the pressure plate automatically moves closer to the driven plate, to compensate. This makes the centre of the diaphragm spring move nearer to the release bearing, so decreasing the release bearing movement but not the clutch free pedal travel, as unless the master cylinder has been disturbed, this is compensated for automatically.

2. Maintenance

1. Routine maintenance consists of checking the level of hydraulic fluid in the master cylinder reservoir every 3,000 miles and topping up with Castrol Girling Brake and Clutch Fluid (specification SAE 70 R3) if the level has fallen.

2. If it is noted that the level of fluid has fallen considerably, then

an immediate check should be made to determine the source of the leak.

3. Before checking the level of the fluid in the master cylinder reservoir, carefully clean the cap and body of the reservoir unit with clean rag, so as to ensure that no dirt enters the system when the cap is removed. On no account should paraffin or any other cleaning solvent be used, in case the hydraulic fluid becomes contaminated.

4. Check that the level of the hydraulic fluid is up to within ¼ inch of the filler neck and that the vent hole in the cap is clear.

3. Clutch Hydraulic System — Bleeding

Whenever the clutch hydraulic system has been overhauled, a part renewed, or the level in the reservoir is too low, air will have entered the system, necessitating the system to be bled. During this operation the level of hydraulic fluid in the reservoir should not be allowed to fall below half full, otherwise air will be drawn in again.

2. Obtain a clean and dry glass jam jar; plastic tubing at least 12 inches long and able to fit tightly over the bleed nipple of the slave cylinder; a supply of Castrol Girling Brake and Clutch Fluid; and someone to help.

3. Check that the master cylinder reservoir is full, and if it is not, fill it, and cover the bottom inch of the jar with hydraulic fluid.

4. Wipe the bleed nipple on the slave cylinder free of dust and dirt and open the bleed nipple one turn, preferably using a ring spanner, which should be kept in place on the bleed nipple.

5. Place one end of the tube squarely over the nipple and insert the other end in the jam jar so that the tube orifice is below the level of the fluid.

6. Insert a screwdriver into the slave cylinder pushrod fork end as shown in Fig.5.2a and lever the pushrod forwards so that it is in its fully retracted position. Hold the screwdriver in position until the bleed operation is complete.

7. The assistant should now pump the clutch pedal up and down in a succession of long and short strokes as indicated in Fig.5.3. with the pedal at the top of the stroke. The pedal should be pushed down through its full stroke to the stop and at this point the bleed nipple tightened. Allow the pedal to return to the clutch engaged position and slacken the bleed screw again. Depress the clutch pedal three rapid short strokes followed by a full downward stroke. Retighten the bleed screw. Continue this sequence until all air is eliminated from the system, this being indicated by the flow of air bubbles into the glass jar ceasing.

8. Should any difficulty be experienced in removing all air from the hydraulic system, it is recommended that the slave cylinder be removed and held in the vertical position with the bleed nipple at the top.

9. Remove the screwdriver and depress the clutch pedal three times, so as to allow the clutch slave cylinder to take up its correct operating condition.

10 NEVER use the fluid bled from the hydraulic system immediately for topping up the master cylinder, but allow to stand for at least 24 hours in a sealed airtight container, so allowing the minute air bubbles held in suspension to escape.

4. Clutch Slave Cylinder — Removal & Refitting

1. It is not necessary to drain the clutch master cylinder when removing the slave cylinder. If fluid is to be left in the master cylinder, however, it is essential to seal the vent hole in the reservoir cap, by screwing the cap down hard over a piece of polythene sheeting, so preventing loss of fluid.

2. Wipe the hydraulic pipe union at its connection on the slave cylinder with a clean rag. Detach the flexible pipe by undoing the union and wrap the end in a piece of clean non-fluffy rag to prevent dirt ingress.

3. On early models, undo and remove the two self-locking nuts that

secure the slave cylinder to the gearbox housing. On later models of gearboxes, having a serial number incorporating suffix E onwards, two long bolts with spring washers were used instead of studs.

4. Extract the split pin from the pushrod to clutch lever clevis pin, lift away the plain washer, and withdraw the clevis pin.

5. Lift the slave cylinder from the gearbox housing.

6. To refit the clutch slave cylinder, replace on the gearbox and tighten the securing nuts or bolts to a torque wrench setting of 30 lb/ft.

7. Reconnect the operating pushrod to clutch operating lever. At this stage it will be necessary to adjust the linkage, details of which are given in Section 11 of this Chapter.

8. Reconnect the flexible pipe to the slave cylinder and securely tighten the union.

9. Refer to Section 3 of this Chapter and bleed the hydraulic system.

5. Clutch Slave Cylinder — Dismantling, Examination & Reassembly

1. Clean the exterior of the slave cylinder using a clean dry rag.

2. Carefully ease back the rubber dust cover (B), Fig.5.4, from the cylinder body and lift away the dust cover.

3. Using a pair of circlip pliers, release the circlip (C) from the inside of the slave cylinder body.

4. The piston (D), piston cup seal (F), piston cup seal filler (G) and return spring (H) may now be removed from the cylinder body. Unscrew the bleed screw (J).

5. Thoroughly wash all parts in clean hydraulic fluid. Inspect the inside of the cylinder for score marks caused by impurities in the hydraulic fluid. If there are any found, the cylinder and piston will require renewal.

6. The old rubber seal will probably be swollen and visibly worn, so always fit a new seal after dismantling.

7. To reassemble, first smear the piston cup seal, piston and cylinder bore with clean hydraulic fluid.

8. Fit the return spring (H) to the piston cup seal filler (G) and place the piston cup seal (F) onto the filler. Insert the assembly into the cylinder bore, followed by the piston (D) and secure in the bore with the circlip (C).

9. Smear the inside of a new dust cover with a little special Girling grease and fit onto the cylinder. Insert the pushrod and operate the piston several times to ensure correct movement. Replace the bleed nipple.

6. Clutch Master Cylinder — Removal & Refitting

1. Drain the hydraulic fluid from the clutch hydraulic system by attaching a length of suitable size plastic tubing to the bleed screw on the slave cylinder. Place the other end in a clean jam jar. Open the bleed screw one turn and depress the clutch pedal. Tighten the bleed screw and allow the pedal to return. Repeat this procedure until the system has been drained.

2. Wipe the master cylinder flexible hydraulic pipe connection with a clean non-fluffy rag and disconnect the union. Wrap the end in a piece of clean rag to stop dirt ingress or fluid dripping onto the paintwork. Plug the master cylinder union connection to stop accidental dirt entry into the master cylinder.

3. Note that on LHD models it will be necessary to remove the air cleaner from the carburetter installation. Release the two clips that support the steel clutch hydraulic system pipe and disconnect the union from the master cylinder.

4. Undo and remove the two nuts and spring washers that secure the master cylinder to the mounting bracket on the body.

5. Undo and remove the locknut on the end of the master cylinder pushrod and screw the rod forwards through the adjuster trunnion. The master cylinder may now be lifted away taking extreme care not to allow any hydraulic fluid to drip onto the paintwork.

6. To refit the master cylinder, first approximately position the

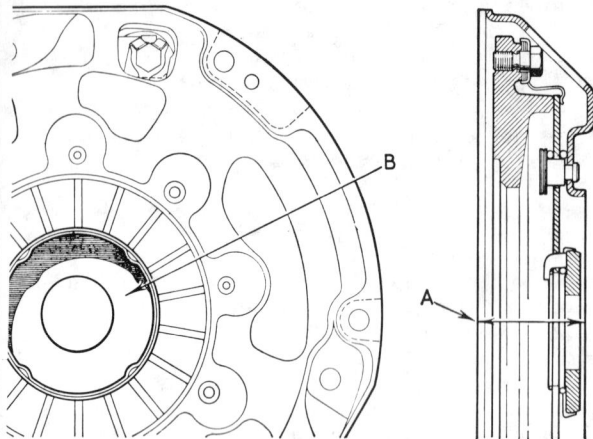

Fig.5.1. CLUTCH ASSEMBLY (EARLY TYPE)
A 1.860 inch   B Plain thrust pad

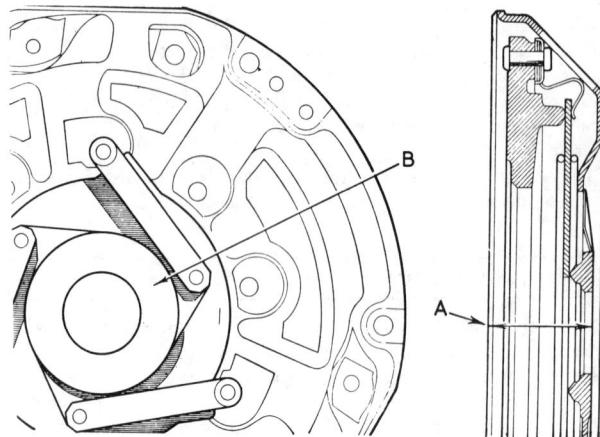

Fig.5.2. CLUTCH ASSEMBLY (LATER TYPE)
A 2.0 inch   B Strap supported thrust pad

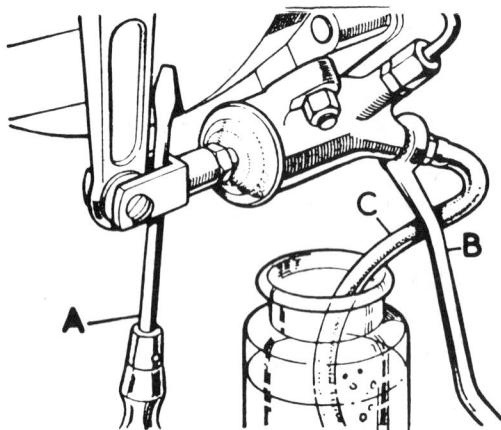

Fig.5.2a. BLEEDING THE CLUTCH HYDRAULIC SYSTEM
A Screwdriver   C Bleed tube
B Spanner for bleed screw

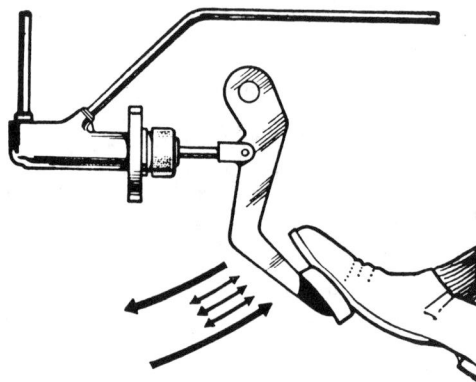

Fig 5.3. Operation of clutch pedal to bleed the hydraulic system

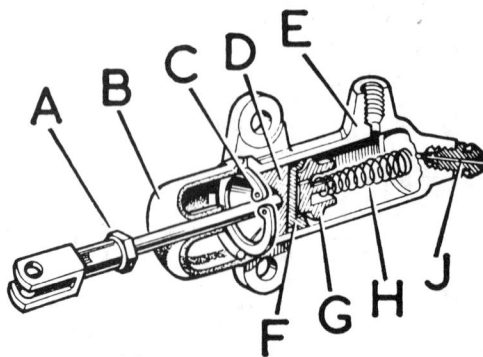

Fig.5.4. CLUTCH SLAVE CYLINDER ASSEMBLY

A Pushrod   D Piston   G Filler for piston   J Bleed screw
B Dust cover   E Body   seal
C Circlip   F Piston seal   H Return spring

master cylinder, and using a screwdriver carefully insert the pushrod into the pedal trunnion. Screw the pushrod through the trunnion about one inch.

7. Replace the two nuts and spring washers onto the master cylinder mounting studs and tighten securely.

8. Reconnect the hydraulic pipe union to the master cylinder, taking care not to cross-thread during the initial stages of reconnection.

9. Refer to Section 3, and bleed the clutch hydraulic system.

10 It may be necessary to adjust the clutch pedal height and clutch travel, and details for this operation may be found in Section 11 of this Chapter.

11 Once refitting has been completed and the necessary adjustments made, the car should be road tested to ensure correct operation of the system.

7. Clutch Master Cylinder — Dismantling, Examination & Reassembly

1. The letters in the text refer to Fig.5.5. Pull off the rubber dust cover (L) which exposes the circlip (J) which must be removed from the pushrod (K) complete with the metal retaining washer (H).

2. Pull the piston (F) and seal assembly as one unit from the master cylinder. Lift away the return spring (B).

3. Separate the piston seal (G) from the piston (F) and also the spring cap (C), cup seal (D) and piston washer (E).

4. Clean and carefully examine all parts, especially the rubber piston seal and cap seal, for signs of distortion, swelling, splitting or other wear and check the piston and cylinder for wear and scoring. Renew any parts that are suspect. It is recommended that whenever a master cylinder is dismantled new rubber seals are always fitted.

5. To reassemble, first refit the spring cap (C) to the spring (B) and insert into the master cylinders. Lubricate the cap seal (D) with clean hydraulic fluid and insert the correct way round into the cylinder bore.

6. Replace the piston washer (E) and insert the piston (F) into the bore.

7. Lubricate the piston seal (G) with clean hydraulic fluid and insert the correct way round into the bore.

8. Reassemble the piston stop washer (H), circlip (J) and dust cover (L) onto the pushrod (K) and insert into the end of the master cylinder.

9. Refit the circlip into its groove in the master cylinder bore, taking care not to scratch the bore.

10 Smear the inside of the rubber dust cover (L) with a little Girling grease and place in position. The master cylinder is now ready for refitting to the car.

8. Clutch — Removal, Inspection & Replacement

1. Remove the engine and gearbox as described in Chapter 1, Section 6, and separate the two units or as an alternative, remove the gearbox with the engine still in the car. Details of this are given in Chapter 6, Section 3.

2. Before removing the pressure plate assembly, it should be noted that it is located on the face of the flywheel by dowels. Look for marks on the pressure plate assembly coinciding with marks on the flywheel to ensure correct reassembly. If no marks are evident, make identification lines on these two parts so that upon reassembly the pressure plate is reassembled in its original position.

3. Bend back the locking tabs (photo) and slacken each of the six pressure plates to flywheel mounting bolts, a turn at a time, so releasing them evenly and progressively. As they are being released, check that the pressure plate flange is not binding on the dowels, otherwise it could fly off causing an accident.

4. Lift away the six bolts and spring washers, followed by the pressure plate assembly and driven plate.

5. Using a stiff brush or clean rag, dust the face of the flywheel, the pressure plate assembly and the driven plate. Note that the dust is harmful to the lungs as it contains asbestos.

6. It is important that neither oil nor grease comes into contact with the clutch facings and that absolute cleanliness is observed at all times.

7. Inspect the friction surfaces of the driven plate and, if worn, a complete new assembly must be fitted. The linings are completely worn out when the faces of the rivets are flush with the lining face. Check that the friction lining shows no sign of having glazing or oil impregnation which, if evident, means that a new assembly must be fitted. If a small quantity of lubricant has found its way onto the facing, due to heat generated by the resultant slipping, it will be burnt off. This will be indicated by darkening of the faces. This is not too serious provided that the grain of the facing material can still be clearly identified. Fit a new assembly if there is any doubt at all. It is important that if oil impregnation is present, the cause of the oil leak is found and rectified to prevent recurrence.

8. Carefully inspect the driven plate contact face of the flywheel for signs of overheating, distortion, cracking and scoring, and if any are evident fit a new flywheel.

9. Mount the driven plate on the gearbox primary pinion and check for looseness or wear on the hub splines. Also check the driven plate cushion springs for damage and looseness.

10 Inspect the clutch withdrawal lever assembly pivot cross shaft or race housing bores for wear and fit new parts as necessary.

11 Check that the clutch withdrawal race assembly is not badly worn or showing signs of overheating. It is normally recommended that if a new pressure plate assembly and driven plate assembly are being fitted then a new withdrawal race bearing be fitted as well.

12 Refitting the clutch components is the reverse sequence to removal, but the following points should be noted:—

a) Smear a light coating of high melting point grease onto the clutch cross shaft bore.

b) Refit the pressure and driven plate assemblies making sure that the alignment marks previously noted or made are correctly matched and that the longer side of the clutch disc hub face is away from the engine (photo).

c) The clutch disc must now be centralised by using either an old gearbox primary pinion or round wooden rod with one end shaped to the diameter of the crankshaft spigot and the other end to the diameter of the driven plate splined hub (photo).

d) Tighten the clutch cover assembly securing bolts in a diagonal manner (photo) to the specified torque.

NOTE: A modified clutch assembly was fitted from engines with numbers having a suffix letter E and onwards and also gearboxes with numbers having a suffix letter D onwards. It is possible to fit the later type clutch assembly, as shown in Fig.5.2. compared with the earlier clutch, Fig.5.1, but as the later assembly is deeper overall than the earlier type it will be necessary to reduce the length of the clutch withdrawal housing by 11/32 inch. Details of this modification are shown in Fig.5.6.

e) Bend back the bolt locking tabs (photo).

9. Clutch Withdrawal Race Housing Assembly

1. Remove the engine and gearbox as described in Chapter 1, Section 6, and separate the two units, or as an alternative remove the gearbox with the engine still in the car as detailed in Chapter 6, Section 3.

2. If the oil is still in the gearbox it should now be drained by undoing and removing the drain plug and fibre washer.

3. Undo and remove the pinch bolt and nut that secures the clutch withdrawal lever. Mark the relative position of the lever and splined shaft, and slide the lever from the shaft.

4. Undo and remove the six self-locking nuts that secure the clutch withdrawal housing to the bellhousing. Carefully remove the withdrawal race housing and joint washer from the studs on the front face of the bellhousing.

5. If a jointing compound has been used or the gaskets are stuck to the mating faces, thoroughly clean using a knife or wide bladed screwdriver.

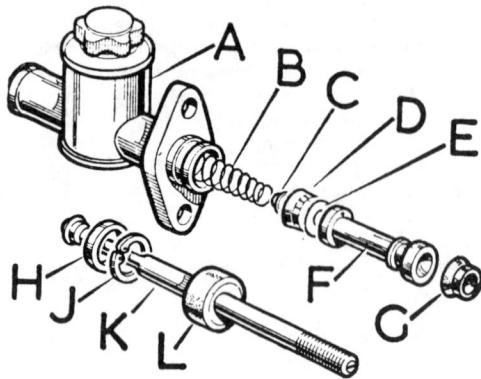

Fig.5.5. CLUTCH MASTER CYLINDER ASSEMBLY

A Barrel and reservoir
B Return spring
C Cap for spring
D Cap seal
E Piston washer
F Piston
G Piston seal
H Piston stop washer
J Circlip
K Pushrod
L Dust cover

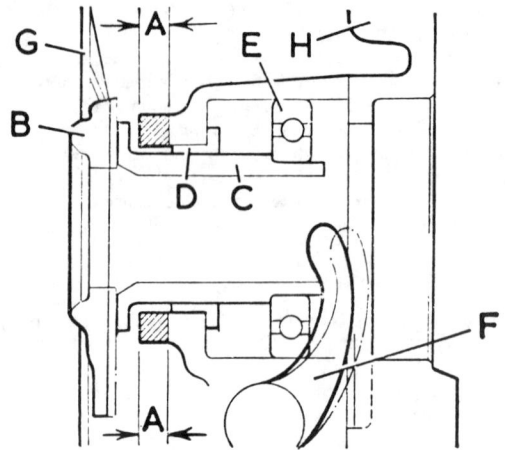

Fig.5.6. MODIFICATION TO CLUTCH WITHDRAWAL RACE HOUSING

A Reduce thickness of clutch withdrawal housing by approximately 11/32 in.
B Thrust pad
C Clutch withdrawal sleeve
D Bush for clutch with drawal sleeve
E Thrust bearing for clutch release sleeve
F Clutch operating fork
G Clutch assembly
H Bellhousing

8.3

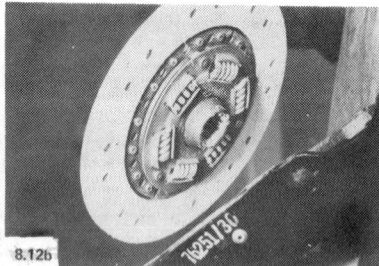

8.12b

8.12c

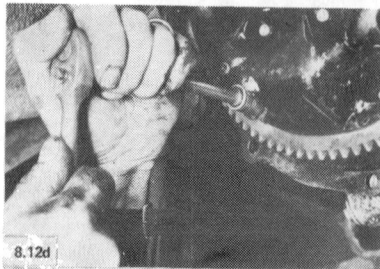

8.12d

8.12e

6. Remove the two set bolts and spring washers that secure the cross shaft end cover (A), Fig.5.7. Lift away the cover and joint washer.

7. Using a pair of circlip pliers, remove the circlip from the cross shaft (C). The thrust washer may now be lifted away from the end of the cross shaft.

8. Gently slide the cross shaft from the housing, if necessary tapping the end with a suitable diameter soft metal drift, as the splines could be a little tight in the operating fork.

9. Lift away the operating fork and thrust washer (E) from the housing, followed by the spring (D).

10 Carefully lift out the oil seal (F) from the housing.

11 Using a soft metal drift, very carefully tap out the sleeve (H) from the withdrawal race (G).

12 If necessary the withdrawal sleeve bush (J) may be pushed out of the withdrawal sleeve (G) using a vice and suitable packing pieces.

13 Thoroughly wash all parts and examine the withdrawal sleeve bush for wear. Refit the operating fork to the splines on the cross shaft and check that it is a good fit without signs of movement. Also fit the withdrawal lever to the cross shaft and check the splines for wear.

14 Inspect the withdrawal race for wear by holding the inner track and checking for movement on the outer track by rocking. Rotate the outer track and check for roughness in movement. If the race is suspect it should be renewed.

15 To reassemble is the reverse procedure to dismantling. However, there are certain points that should be noted:

a) Refer to the end of Section 8 where details of a modification are given. This may be necessary if a new type clutch assembly is to be fitted to an early model.

b) When the withdrawal race thrust bearing is being refitted, make sure that it is pressed fully home against the shoulder on the sleeve.

c) Pack the withdrawal bearing with a high melting point grease by carefully working it into the cage. Wipe away any excess grease.

d) When refitting the withdrawal lever, align the previously made identification marks or, if new parts have been fitted, refer to Fig.5.8, which shows the correct angle to which the lever should be set.

10. Clutch Pedal Assembly — Removal & Refitting

The clutch and brake pedals are mounted on a common fulcrum point attached to a bracket on the toe board. To remove the pedal assembly proceed as follows:—

1. Undo and remove the two bolts, nuts and spring washers that secure the accelerator cross shaft mounting bracket to the base unit. These bolts are accessible from beneath the front wing. NOTE: On LHD models, these two bolts are accessible from within the engine compartment and in fact also secure the pedal bolt.

2. Unhook the two pedal return springs from the pedals.

3. Working inside the car undo and remove the two bolts, nuts, plain and spring washers that secure the clutch pedal stop and bracket — these being shown in Fig.5.10. Lift away the bracket.

4. Undo and remove the four bolts with plain and spring washers that secure the pedal box (C), Fig.5.9 to the body bulkhead panel.

5. Release and undo the two locknuts from the clutch and brake pushrods and with a screwdriver screw the rods forwards through the pedal trunnions, whilst the pedal box assembly is being withdrawn. The two master cylinder pushrods may be left in position in the master cylinders. NOTE: On LHD models the accelerator mounting bracket will have to be held clear during this operation.

6. Undo and remove the bolt and spring washer that retains the pedal shaft to the pedal box and withdraw the shaft from the two pedals.

7. Lift away the two pedals from the pedal box and recover the two shim washers and double coil spring washers.

8. To reassemble first apply a little molybdenum disulphide grease to the pedal bushes and shaft, and assemble the two pedals, shim washers, and double spring washer to the pedal box, and insert the

pedal shaft. Secure the shaft in position with the lock bolt and spring washers.

9. Apply a little Bostik 692, or equivalent non-setting sealer to the pedal box flange and offer in position whilst at the same time locating the two pushrods in the trunnions using a small thin screwdriver. Screw the pushrods in an anti-clockwise direction until approximately one inch of thread is protruding from the trunnion.

10 Replace the pedal box and clutch stop bracket bolts with spring and plain washers. Do not tighten the bolts until all are in position.

11 Attach the accelerator cross shaft mounting bracket to the base unit and secure in position with the two bolts, nuts and spring washers. NOTE: On LHD models, this bracket is located by two of the bolts that secure the pedal box.

12 Reconnect the two pedal return springs.

13 Adjust the brake pedal height by screwing the master cylinder pushrod in or out. The correct setting is when a vertical distance of between 6½ to 6¾ inches exists between the underside of the pedal rubber and the floor panel. with the carpets removed. This dimension (F) is shown in Fig.10. Tighten the locknut.

14 Refer to Section 11 and adjust the clutch pedal and linkage.

11. Clutch Pedal & Linkage Adjustment

1. It is important that the clutch pedal and linkage is correctly adjusted so that the correct pedal load is obtained and also full engagement and release of the driven plate is achieved.

2. To carry out these adjustments jack up the car and place on firmly based stands.

3. Wipe the top of the clutch hydraulic fluid reservoir and remove the caps. Top up to the correct level.

4. Refer to Fig.5.8, and check that the external clutch withdrawal lever is correctly fitted to the clutch cross shaft. This is particularly important if the clutch withdrawal bearing housing has been dismantled. Hold the lever to the rear until the withdrawal sleeve is felt to contact the clutch pad. This lever should be 5° forwards to the vertical.

5. Remove the slave cylinder rubber dust cover from the slave cylinder and slacken the pushrod locknut.

6. Adjust the length of the pushrod so as to obtain a dimension of less than ½ inch between the piston and circlip whilst the external withdrawal lever is held in the fully rearwards position, and also whilst an assistant is exerting a slight pressure on the clutch pedal. This is to ensure that the slave cylinder piston is in contact with the pushrod. Lock the pushrod locknut. It is important that the piston stroke does not exceed .520 inch.

7. Measure the brake pedal height which should be between 6½ to 6¾ inches between the underside of the pedal rubber and the floor panel. This dimension (F) is shown in Fig.5.10, and may be adjusted by slackening the pushrod locknut and screwing the master cylinder pushrod in or out. Tighten the locknut.

8. The clutch pedal should next be checked for alignment with the brake pedal by using the same method of adjustment as in paragraph 7 above.

9. Slacken the clutch pedal stop bolt locknut and screw the stop bolt in so as to allow full pedal movement. Depress the pedal fully and screw out the pedal stop bolt until it just contacts the rear of the pedal. Then release the pedal and screw out the bolt one further complete turn. Tighten the stop bolt locknut.

10 Next depress the clutch pedal again until it is in contact with the stop bolt and check that the slave cylinder piston clears the circlip by a minimum of between 0.010 to 0.020 inch.

11 Refit the clutch slave cylinder rubber dust cover and finally recheck the level of fluid in the master cylinder reservoir.

12. Clutch Faults

There are four main faults to which the clutch and release mechanism are prone. They may occur by themselves or in conjunction

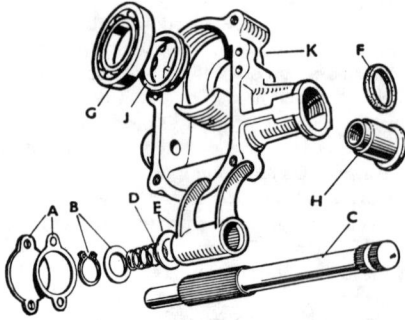

Fig.5.7. CLUTCH WITHDRAWAL RACE HOUSING

A End-cover & joint washer
B Circlip & thrust washer
C Cross-shaft
D Spring
E Operating fork and thrust
    washer
F Oil seal
G Withdrawal race
H Sleeve
J Bush for withdrawal
    sleeve
K Housing

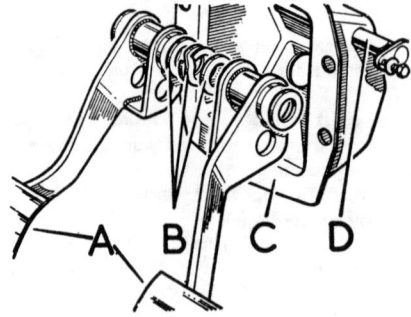

Fig.5.9. COMPONENT PARTS OF PEDAL BOX & SHAFT
ASSEMBLY

A Pedal
B Shim washers and double
    spring washer
C Clutch and brake pedal box
D Shaft

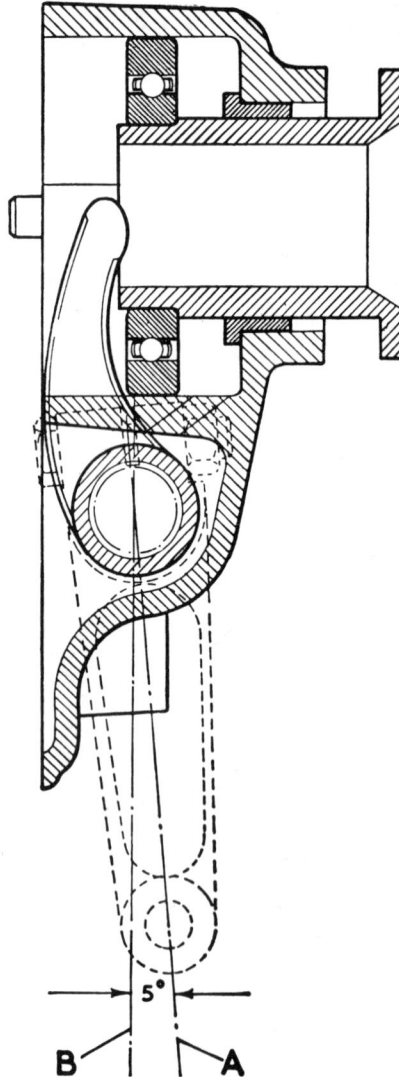

Fig.5.8. CROSS SECTION VIEW OF WITHDRAWAL RACE HOUSING
A = Lever 5° forwards of vertical
B = Vertical

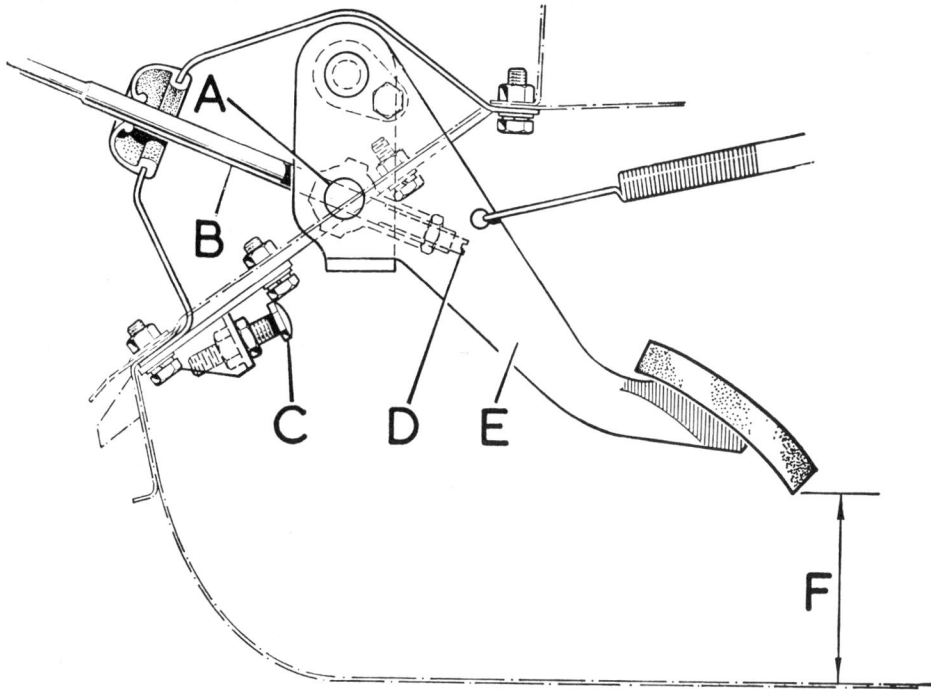

Fig.5.10. CLUTCH PEDAL ASSEMBLY

A Trunnion for adjuster
B Pushrod

C Pedal stop
D Adjustment screw for

    pedal height
E Pedal

F Pedal height 6½ to
    6¾ inch.

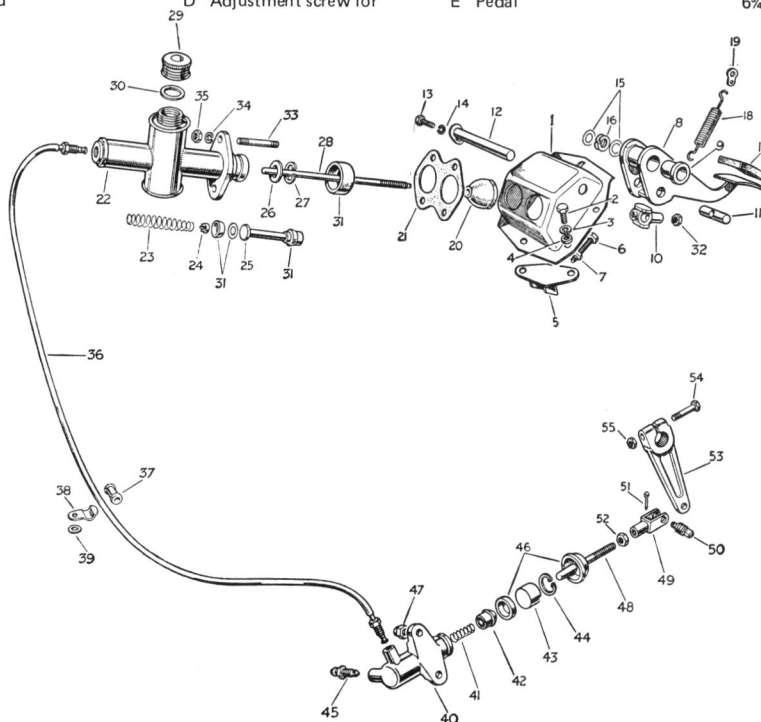

Fig.5.11. CLUTCH PEDAL & HYDRAULIC SYSTEM

1	Clutch & brake pedal box	15	Shim washer	29	Filler cap
2	Set bolt	16	Spring washer double coil	30	Joint washer, early models
3	Spring washer	17	Rubber pad for clutch pedal	31	Repair kit for master
4	Plain washer	18	Return spring		cylinder
5	Stop bracket	19	Anchor plate	32	Nut
6	Stop bolt	20	Grommet	33	Stud
7	Locknut	21	Packing plate	34	Spring washer
8	Clutch pedal assembly	22	Barrel and tank only	35	Nut
9	Bush for clutch pedal	23	Return spring	36	Flexible pipe complete
10	Adjuster for clutch pedal	24	Cap for spring	37	Grommet
11	Trunnion for adjuster	25	Piston	38	Clip
12	Shaft	26	Piston stop washer	39	Plain washer
13	Set bolt	27	Circlip	40	Body only
14	Spring washer	28	Push rod	41	Spring for filler

42	Filler for piston cup
43	Piston
44	Circlip
45	Bleeder screw
46	Repair kit for slave cylinder
47	Self-locking nut, early models
48	Push rod for slave cylinder
49	Clevis jaw
50	Clevis pin and spring
51	Split pin
52	Locknut
53	External declutching lever
54	Bolt
55	Nut

with any of the other faults. They are clutch squeal, slip, spin and judder.

13. Clutch squeal — Diagnosis & Cure

1. If on taking up the drive or when changing gear, the clutch squeals this is sure indication of a badly worn clutch release bearing. As well as regular wear due to normal use, wear of the clutch release bearing is much accentuated if the clutch is ridden or held down for long periods in gear, with the engine running. To minimise wear of this component the car should always be taken out of gear at traffic lights or for similar hold ups.
2. It may be found that if the clutch release bearing is very badly worn due to lack of lubrication or overheating a different type of noise, being of a more harsh or grinding nature, may be experienced.
3. The clutch release bearing is not an expensive item and it is recommended that it always be renewed during a major clutch overhaul.

14. Clutch slip — Diagnosis & Cure

1. Clutch slip is a self-evident condition which occurs when the clutch friction plate is badly worn, the release arm free travel is insufficient; oil or grease have got onto the flywheel or pressure plate faces; or the pressure plate itself is faulty.
2. The reason for clutch slip is that, due to one of the faults listed above, there is either insufficient pressure from the pressure plate, or insufficient friction from the friction plate to ensure solid drive.
3. If small amounts of oil get onto the clutch, they will be burnt off under the heat of clutch engagement, in the process gradually darkening the linings. Excessive oil on the clutch will burn off leaving a carbon deposit which can cause bad slip, or fierceness, spin and judder.
4. If clutch slip is suspected, and confirmation of the condition is required, there are several tests which can be made:-
a) With the engine in 2nd or 3rd gear and pulling lightly up a moderate incline, sudden depression of the accelerator pedal may cause the engine to increase its speed without any increase in road speed. Easing off on the accelerator will then give a definite drop in engine speed without the car slowing.
b) Drive the car at a steady speed in top gear and braking with the left leg, try to maintain the same speed by depressing down on the accelerator. Providing the same speed is maintained a change in the speed of the engine confirms that slip is taking place.
c) In extreme cases of clutch slip the engine will race under normal

acceleration conditions. If slip is due to oil or grease on the linings, a temporary cure can sometimes be effected in squirting carbon tetrachloride into the clutch housing. The permanent cure, of course, is to renew the clutch driven plate, and trace and rectify the oil leak.

15. Clutch Spin — Diagnosis & Cure

1. Clutch spin is a condition which occurs when there is a leak in the clutch hydraulic actuating mechanism; the release arm free travel is excessive; there is an obstruction in the clutch, either on the primary gear splines or in the operating lever itself; or oil may have partially burnt off the clutch linings and left a resinous deposit, which is causing the clutch disc to stick to the pressure plate or flywheel.
2. The reason for clutch spin is that due to any, or a combination of the faults just listed, the clutch pressure plate is not completely freeing from the centre plate, even when the clutch pedal is fully depressed.
3. If clutch spin is suspected, the condition can be confirmed by extreme difficulty in engaging first gear from rest, difficulty in changing gear, and very sudden take-up of the clutch drive at the fully depressed end of the clutch pedal travel as the clutch is released.
4. Check the operating lever free travel. If this is correct, examine the clutch master cylinder and slave cylinders and the interconnecting hydraulic pipe for leaks. Fluid in one of the rubber boots fitted over the end of either the master or slave cylinder is a sure sign of a leaking piston seal.
5. If these points are checked and found to be in order, then the fault lies internally in the clutch, and it will be necessary to remove the clutch for examination.

16. Clutch Judder — Diagnosis & Cure

1. Clutch judder is a self-evident condition which occurs when the gearbox or engine mountings are loose or too flexible; when there is oil on the faces of the clutch friction plate; or when the clutch pressure plate has been incorrectly adjusted.
2. The reason for clutch judder is that due to one of the faults just listed, the clutch pressure plate is not freeing smoothly from the friction disc, and is snatching.
3. Clutch judder normally occurs when the clutch pedal is released in 1st or reverse gears, and the whole car shudders as it moves backwards or forwards.

Chapter 6 Gearbox & Automatic Transmission

Contents

Specifications

Manual Gearbox

Type	Gearbox single helical constant mesh on all forward gears, synchro mesh on top, third, second and first

Gear Ratios

Fourth	1.000 : 1
Third	1.391 : 1
Second	2.133 : 1
First	3.625 : 1
Reverse	3.430 : 1

Overall Ratios

Fourth	3.54 : 1
Third	4.92 : 1
Second	7.55 : 1
First	12.83 : 1
Reverse	12.14 : 1
Speedometer drive ratio	2 : 1

Oil Grade

Capacity..	1¾ Imperial pints

Mainshaft distance sleeve end tolerance	0.001 in. maximum

Mainshaft gears end tolerance:

First	0.004 to 0.009 inch
Second	0.007 to 0.011 inch
Third	0.004 to 0.007 inch

Selector shaft over-travel:

Second speed...	0.045 to 0.050 inch
Third speed	0.025 to 0.030 inch
Reverse..	0.032 to 0.037 inch
Fourth speed selector shaft stop	0.010 to 0.020 inch
Reverse selector shaft stop	0.010 to 0.020 inch

Automatic Transmission

Type	Hydraulic torque converter, providing torque multiplication between the ratios 2:1 and 1:1. Planetary gear set comprising two sun gears, two sets of pinions, a pinion carrier and a ring gear. The various mechanical ratios are obtained by the engagement of hydraulically operated multi-disc clutches and brake bands.

Gear Ratios

		Torque converter stall ratio
Direct (top)	1:1) Torque...	2.16
Intermediate (second)	1.45:1) Converter ratio	2.16
Low (first)	2.39:1)	2.16
Reverse	2.09:1)	

Rear axle gear ratio ... ...   3.54 : 1

Engine torque ... ...   160 lb/ft. at 2,650 r.p.m.

Transmission fluid capacity from dry... ... ...

Torque converter	7 pints
Gearbox	4¼ pints
Cooler and pipes	¾ pints
	12 pints

Fluid temperature .. ..   Normal operating range 80º to 100ºC approximately

Identification ... ...   The Rover automatic transmission model 35 has a white name plate attached to the side of the transmission main casing with the commencing serial number EU1001

Torque Wrench Settings

Manual gearbox:—	lb.ft.	kg.m.
Clutch withdrawal race housing	25	3.5
Rear drive flange assembly locknut	75	10.5
Layshaft slotted nut	50	7
Gearbox top cover..	15	2.0
Gearbox to bellhousing	50	7
Selector shaft detent balls retaining plate..	8	1.0
Selector shafts sealing plate	8	1.0
Forward gear selector fork to shaft	20	2.8
Reverse gear shaft location	8	1.0
Reverse gear selector arm to shaft	12	1.6
Selector lever clamp bolt	17	2.3
Speedometer drive housing bolts:—		
¼ inch UNF..	8	1.0
3/8 inch UNF	25	3.6
Filler plug	20	2.8
Drain plug	20	2.8

Automatic transmission:		
Torque converter to drive plate	25 to 30	3.5 to 4.0
Drive plate to crankshaft	120	16.5
Transmission case to bellhousing	8 to 10	1.0 to 1.4
Oil pan to transmission case	8 to 10	1.0 to 1.4
Centre support to transmission case	10 to 13	1.4 to 1.8
Outer lever to manual valve shaft ... .:.	10 to 15	1.4 to 2.0
Oil pan drain plug...	10 to 14	1.4 to 1.9
Starter inhibitor switch locknut	4 to 6 (48 to 72 lb/in.)	0.55 to 0.8
Filler tube connector adaptor to transmission case...	20 to 30	2.8 to 4.0
Filler tube to connector sleeve nut	17 to 18	2.3 to 2.4
Stone guards to converter housing...	1.4 to 1.6 (17 to 19 lb/in.)	0.19 to 0.22
Coupling flange to driven shaft...	20 to 25	2.8 to 3.5
Oil cooler to transmission case connector..	6 to 10 (72 to 120 lb/in.)	0.8 to 1.4
Extension housing to mounting bracket on sub-frame...	25	3.5
Torque converter housing to support plate	30	4.0

1. General Description

The four forward speed gearbox has synchromesh action on all forward speeds and is controlled by a short remote gearchange lever which is fitted with a lift-up catch to prevent accidental engagement of reverse gear.

The gearbox is mounted at the rear of the engine in the conventional manner and the casing is made of a light alloy casting. The constant mesh gears are of helical cut profile to ensure quiet operation and the synchromesh is of the baulk-ring design. The remote gearchange lever operates three selector shafts, two of which are for the forward speeds and the remaining one for the reverse gear.

The primary shaft and mainshaft run in single track ball races, whilst the layshaft gear cluster has the rather unusual feature of being supported by a single track ball race at the front and a single track roller race at the rear.

Modifications to this gearbox are very few indeed and the only one which could catch the unwary is from gearbox No.40132489D onwards, whereby the shifter fork shafts have a 90º detent groove instead of the earlier groove angle of 120º.

Although the manufacturers recommend that the gearbox be removed, together with the engine, and then overhauled, the author did find it possible to remove the gearbox separately with the engine still in position in the car. As this is a more practical method of gearbox removal for the enthusiast having limited garage facilities and equipment, this method of gearbox removal is described in detail.

2 Routine Maintenance — Manual Gearbox

1 Once every 5,000 miles, check the level of oil in the gearbox, and top up as necessary using engine grade oil. The oil filler/level plug is located on the left-hand side of the gearbox and is accessible through the inspection hole in the side of the gearbox cover. Clean the area that surrounds the filler/level plug to prevent dirt entering the gearbox. Top up the oil until it is level with the bottom of the filler plug hole. DO NOT overfill, otherwise oil leaks will occur at the primary shaft and mainshaft oil seals. DO NOT use any anti-friction additives to the gearbox oil as it could effect the synchromesh action.

2 Although the manufacturers do not recommend oil changing as a routine maintenance task, the author has found from practical experience that it is better to change the oil every three years, or 35,000 miles, rather than to leave it in place for the life of the car. The reason for this is that although there may be no deterioration in the quality of the oil, it could become contaminated with minute particles of metal dust.

3 Gearbox - Removal and Replacement

1 There is no easy method. It is usually possible to remove the gearbox seperately from the engine from beneath the car but it means raising the car quite high off the ground, and delicately easing it out. This method is described here but is not always successful on the Rover 2000/2200. We advise that if you have the choice, the engine and gearbox be removed as described in Chapter 1. The assistance of a second person is essential.

2 Disconnect the battery earth terminal, raise the car and put on axle stands if a ramp is not available. The axle stand should be positioned as shown in Fig.6.1, the weight of the car being taken at the jacking points, with pieces of suitable diameter metal rod inserted into the jack location. The higher the car is off the ground, the easier it will be to work underneath.

3 Undo and remove the gearbox oil drain plug and allow the oil to drain out into the container having a capacity of at least 2 pints. Replace the drain plug.

4 Refer to Chapter 3, Section 21 and remove the exhaust system.

5 Undo and remove the two nuts that secure the exhaust system top support strap from the gearbox bellhousing (photo). Lift away the support straps.

6 Mark the mating flanges of the propeller shaft and the final drive extension shaft coupling to ensure correct refitting in their original position.

7 Apply the handbrake and undo the four nyloc nuts securing the propeller shaft flange to the final drive extension shaft coupling (photo). Push the four bolts from the coupling and lower the rear of the propeller shaft to the ground.

8 Mark the mating flanges of the front of the propeller shaft and the gearbox mainshaft to ensure correct refitting in their original position. Undo and remove the four nyloc nuts. Lift the propeller shaft away from the rear of the gearbox mainshaft coupling flange and remove the propeller shaft from underneath the car (photo).

9 If the gearbox is to be dismantled, it is recommended that the large nut at the rear of the gearbox transmission flange be undone as it is very tight. To do this select top gear and lock the engine using a rod through the flywheel and backplate. Using a socket slacken the nut.

10 Undo and remove the two nuts and bolts that secure the engine rear supports to the little brackets on the underside of the body (photo).

11 Very carefully lower the mounting, making a note of the location of the spring and rubber pads through which the two bolts passed (photo).

12 Temporarily reassemble the bolts, rubber pads and nuts to the engine rear support so that they are not lost.

13 The gear lever needs to be removed. Basically both the early and late type changes are removed in the same way. Remove the console, the rubber boot and then from underneath remove the gear lever remove change shaft bush retainer cap, disengage from the support plate and pull the lever downwards. Remove the cover from above (photo).

14 Drain the engine cooling system and release the top hose. See Chapter 2.

15 Release the upper engine stabiliser mounting adjacent to the radiatior. Then disconnect the accelerator pedal linkage from the body to the rear carburettor (TC models), or the one carburettor (SC models), remove cam box cover and air cleaners.

16 Place a jack (or supports) under the rear of the engine itself, jack up until the weight is just off the rear engine mounting shaft, remove the shaft. Lower the engine/gearbox about 1½ inches and remove the spindle drive reverse light switch wires (photo).

17 It will now be possible to slide the mounting shaft from the rubber insert located in the eye of the speedometer drive housing (photo).

18 This photo shows the mounting shaft.

19 By careful use of a spanner or socket with a universal coupling, undo the speedometer spindle housing retaining plate locknut and plain washer. Lift away the nut, plain washer and retaining plate. The speedometer drive may now be separated from the side of the gearbox (photo).

20 Undo and remove the two nyloc nuts that secure the clutch slave cylinder to the nuts on the side of the clutch bellhousing (photo). Lift away the clutch slave cylinder by drawing it forward so disengaging it from the pushrod. Tie back the slave cylinder using string or wire.

21 Note that on gearboxes having a gearbox number with a suffix 'E', the two studs have been replaced by two bolts. Undo the two bolts and lift away the clutch slave cylinder as detailed in paragraph 20.

22 Undo and remove the two bolts and spring washers located at the clutch bellhousing top mating flange (photo).

23 To undo the nuts and bolts at the side of the clutch bellhousing flange, a socket and universal coupling will be necessary due to the limited working space (photo).

24 Undo the retaining nuts and bolts that secure the clutch bellhousing to the engine backplate (photo). Two of the nuts and bolts secure the starter motor and this should be suspended with wire as far forwards as possible.

25 This photo shows the underside of the gearbox and engine with all the nuts and bolts removed ready for the separating of the gearbox from the engine. Note the position of the clutch slave cylinder mounting for future reference.

26 When the bellhousing bolts are free, rotate the gearbox in a clockwise direction so that the starter motor bulge is uppermost (photo).

27 Slide the gearbox back 1½ inches (to clear the primary shaft) then lower the rear of the gearbox down about 45° (photo).

28 Pull downwards - watch the reverse light switch and the primary shaft.

29 Refitting the gearbox is the reverse procedure to removal. Do not forget to tighten the large nut at the rear of the gearbox transmission coupling flange. Refill the gearbox with 1¾ pints of Castrol GTX oil.

4 Gearbox — Dismantling

1 For reference Fig.6.2 shows the external components of the gearbox and Fig.6.3 shows the internal moving parts, whilst Fig.6.4 shows the selector and gearchange system.

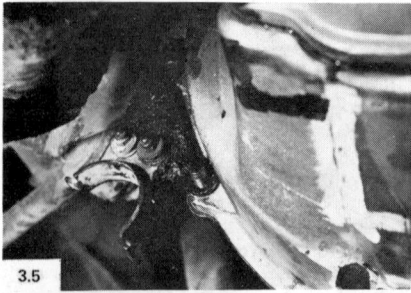

3.5

3.7

3.8

3.10

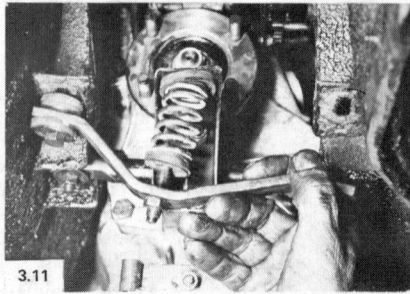

3.11

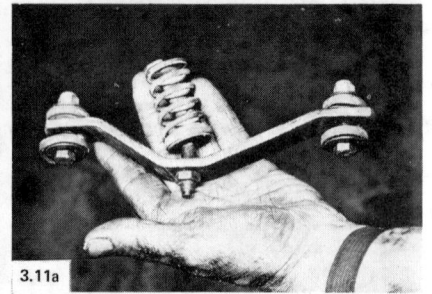

3.11a

3.13a

3.13b

3.13c

3.16

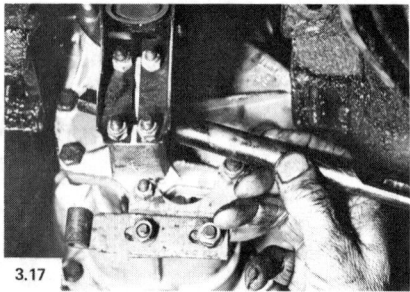

3.17

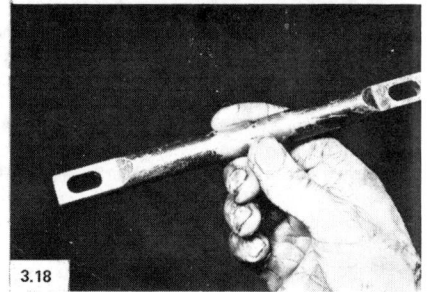

3.18

3.19

3.20

3.22

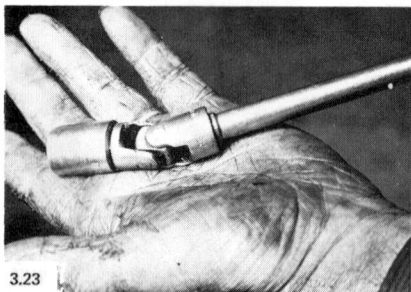

3.23

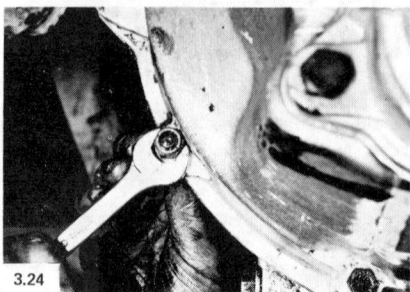

3.24

3.25

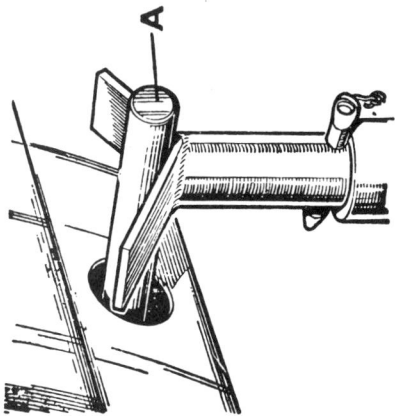

3.26

3.28

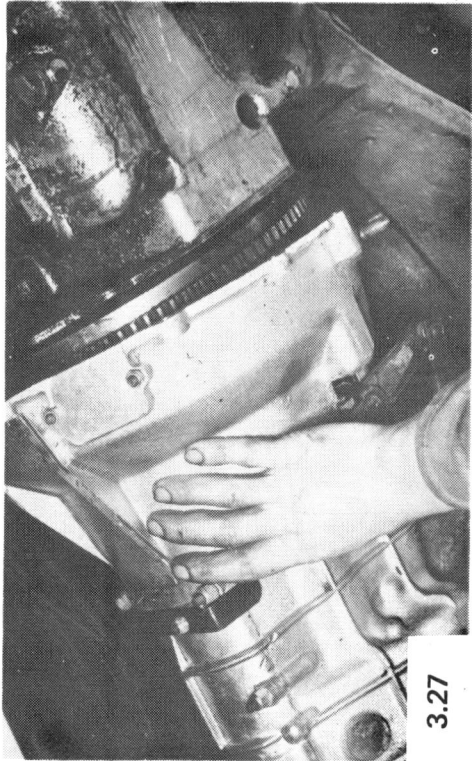

3.27

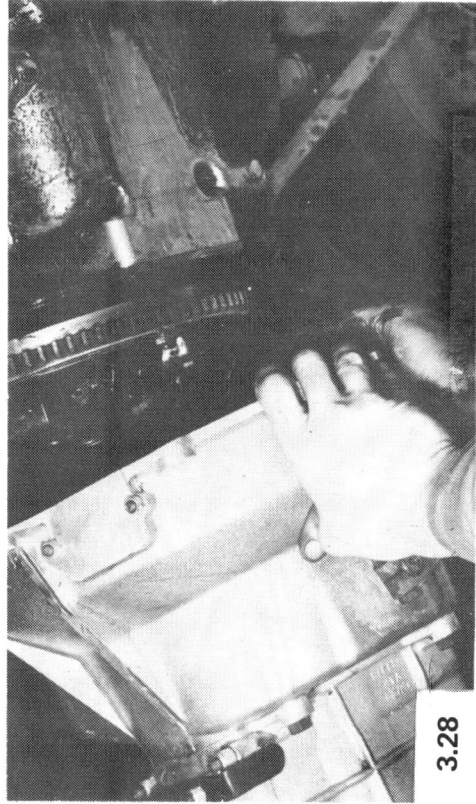

Fig.6.1. CORRECT METHOD OF SUPPORTING CAR ON STANDS

A Insert a suitable length of 7/8 inch diameter steel rod into **jacking tube.**

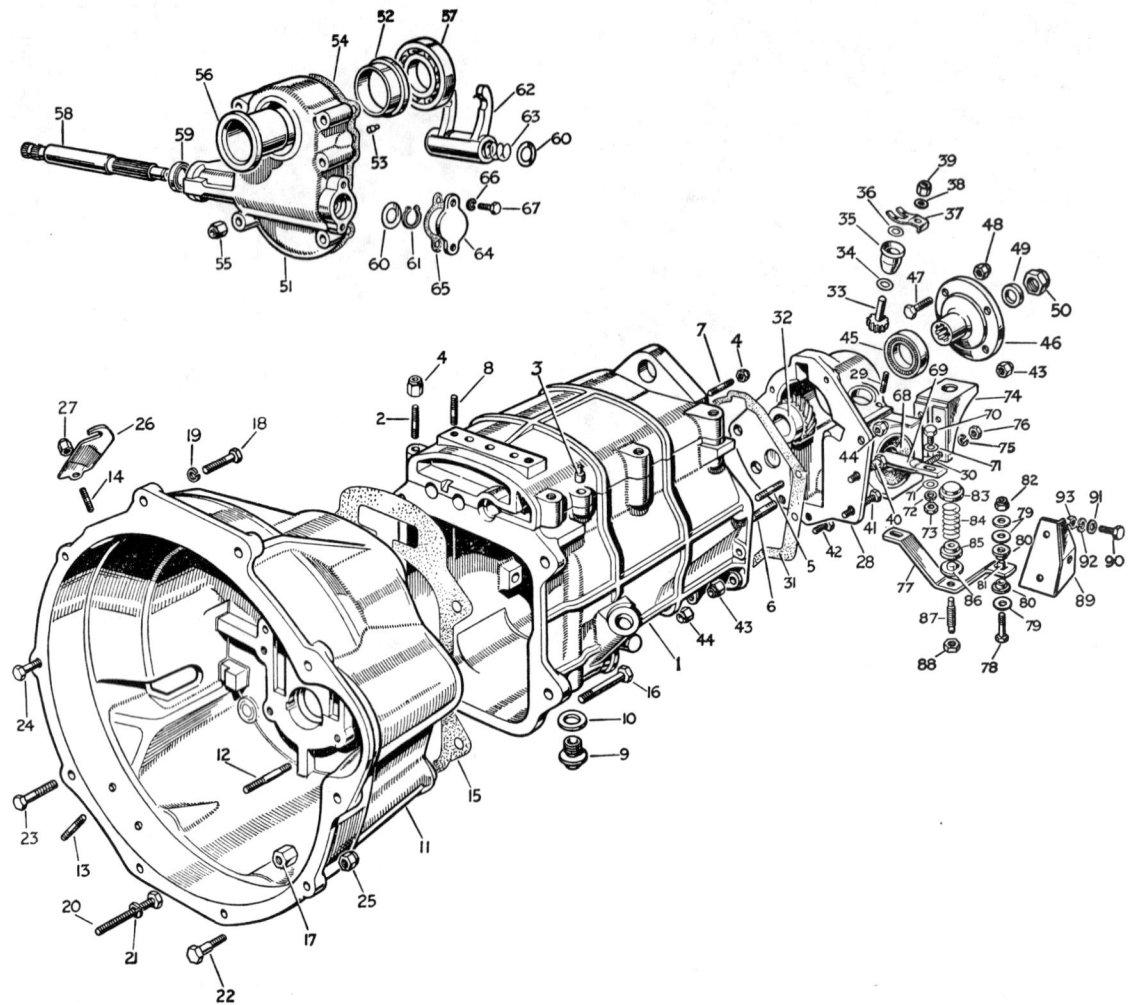

Fig.6.2. GEARBOX EXTERNAL COMPONENTS

1	Gearbox casing assembly	25	Self-locking nut	49	Special washer	70	Bolt
2	Stud	26	Timing cover	50	Self-locking nut	71	Plain washer
3	Dowel	27	Self-locking nut	51	Clutch withdrawal race	72	Spring washer
4	Self-locking nut	28	Housing		housing assembly	73	Nut
5	Stud	29	Stud, long	52	Bush	74	Extension bracket
6	Stud	30	Stud, short	53	Dowel locating housing	75	Spring washer
7	Stud	31	Joint washer	54	Joint washer	76	Nut
8	Stud	32	Speedometer worm	55	Self-locking nut	77	Support crossmember
9	Drain and filler plug	33	Spindle and gear	56	Sleeve	78	Bolt
10	Joint washer	34	Thrust washer for spindle	57	Withdrawal race thrust	79	Plain washer
11	Bellhousing assembly	35	Housing, nylon		bearing	80	Rubber bush
12	Stud	36	Oil seal for spindle	58	Cross-shaft	81	Spacing tube
13	Stud cylinder	37	Retaining plate	59	Oil seal for cross-shaft	82	Self-locking nut
14	Stud for timing cover	38	Plain washer	60	Thrust washer	83	Rubber retainer pad
15	Joint washer	39	Self-locking nut	61	Circlip for cross-shaft	84	Spring
16	Fitting bolt	40	Fitted bolt	62	Operating fork for clutch	85	Rubber cushion
17	Self-locking nut	41	Bolt	63	Anti-rattle spring for fork	86	Spring seat
18	Set bolt	42	Bolt	64	End cover for cross-shaft	87	Adjusting screw
19	Spring washer	43	Self-locking nut	65	Joint washer for end	88	Locknut
20	Set bolt	44	Self-locking nut		cover	89	Bracket, LH
21	Spring washer	45	Oil seal for mainshaft, rear	66	Spring washer	90	Bolt
22	Fitting bolt	46	Flange assembly	67	Set bolt	91	Plain washer
23	Bolt	47	Fitted bolt	68	Snub rubber	92	Spring washer
24	Bolt	48	Self-locking nut	69	Shaft	93	Nut

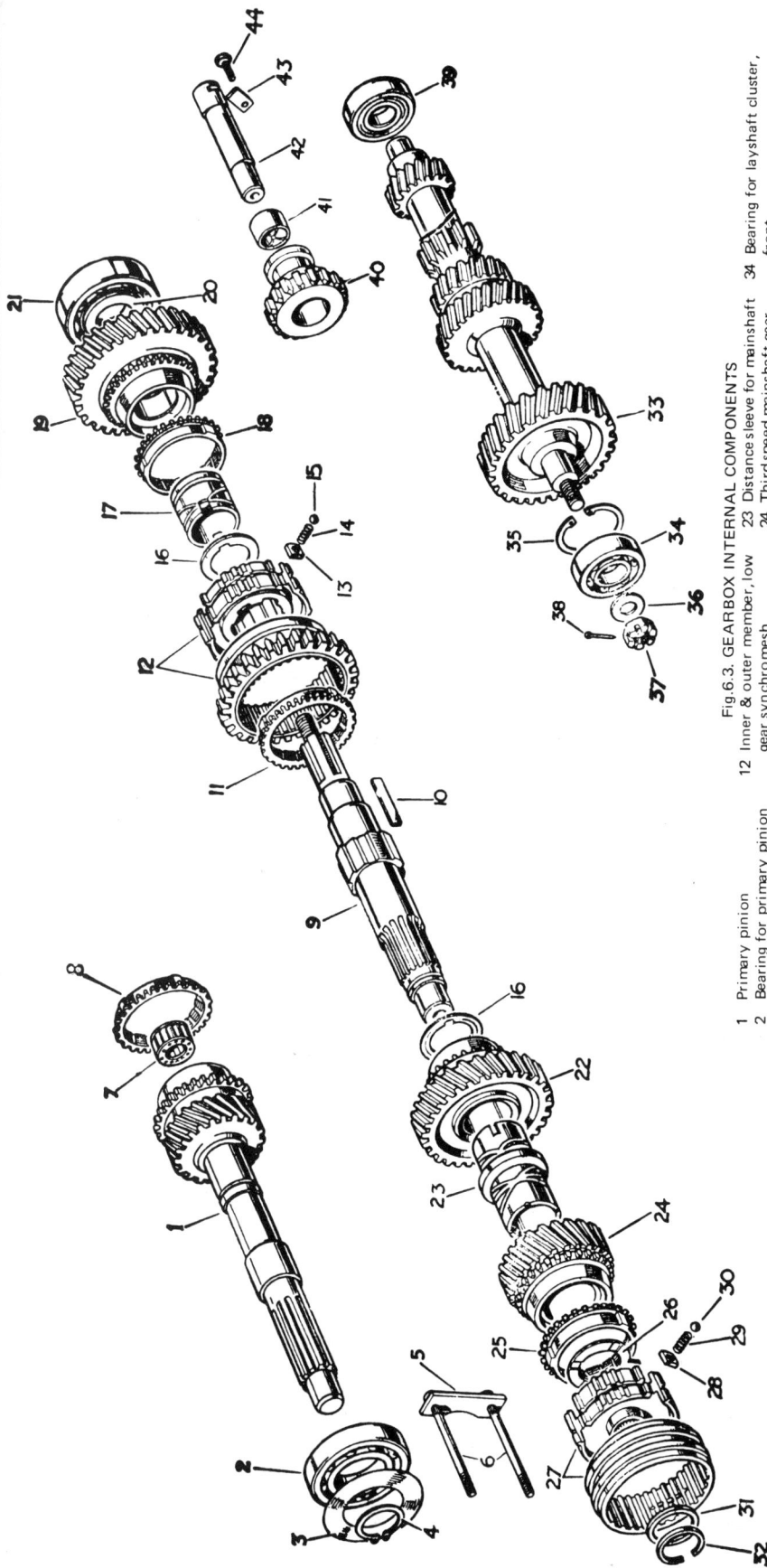

Fig.6.3. GEARBOX INTERNAL COMPONENTS

1   Primary pinion
2   Bearing for primary pinion
3   Baffle plate for primary pinion
4   Circlip, bearing to pinion
5   Retaining plate for primary pinion bearing
6   Serrated bolt fixing retaining plate to bellhousing
7   Needle roller race for primary pinion
8   Synchromesh cone, female, for primary pinion
9   Mainshaft
10 Key for thrust washers
11 Synchromesh cone, female, for second gear

12 Inner & outer member, low gear synchromesh
13 Sliding block for synchromesh ball
14 Spring for synchromesh ball
15 Synchromesh ball
16 Thrust washer, first and second mainshaft gear
17 Bush, first mainshaft gear
18 Synchromesh cone, female, for first gear
19 First speed mainshaft gear
20 Thrust washer for first mainshaft gear, rear
21 Bearing for mainshaft, rear
22 Second speed mainshaft gear

23 Distance sleeve for mainshaft
24 Third speed mainshaft gear
25 Synchromesh cone, female, for third gear
26 Thrust washer for third mainshaft gear, front
27 Inner and outer member, high gear synchromesh
28 Sliding block for synchromesh ball
29 Spring for synchromesh ball
30 Synchromesh ball
31 Spacing washer for inner member
32 Spring ring retaining high-speed inner member
33 Layshaft gear cluster

34 Bearing for layshaft cluster, front
35 Circlip fixing bearing to bellhousing
36 Plain washer
37 Slotted nut (7/16 in. UNF)
38 Split pin
39 Bearing for layshaft cluster, rear
40 Reverse gear assembly
41 Bush for reverse gear
42 Shaft for reverse gear
43 Retaining plate for reverse gear shaft
44 Set screw (¼ in.UNC x 5/8 in. long) fixing retaining plate

Fig. 6.4. GEARBOX SELECTOR & LEVER SYSTEM

1 Selector shaft assembly, first and second speed
2 Interlock pin
3 Peg fixing interlock pin
4 Selector fork, first & second speed
5 Selector shaft, third & fourth speed
6 Selector fork, third & fourth speed
7 Pad
8 Selector shaft, reverse
9 Selector arm, reverse
10 Set bolt
11 Set bolt
12 'O' ring sealing selector shafts
13 Steel ball
14 Spring
15 Interlock plunger
16 Rubber plug for interlock hole
17 Retaining plate
18 Joint washer for retaining plate
19 Set bolt
20 Spring washer
21 Set bolt
22 Adjusting bolt for reverse stop
23 Locknut
24 Distance piece
25 Striker for reverse light switch
26 Sealing plate, upper
27 Sealing plate, lower
28 Set bolt
29 Spring washer
30 Bracket for reverse light switch
31 Plain washer
32 Switch for reverse light
33 Self-locking nut
34 Self-aligning bush
35 Gear change shaft
36 Selector lever
37 Clamp bolt
38 Retainer cap and bush
39 Retaining plate for bush
40 Special bolt
41 Plain washer
42 Rubber bush
43 Self-locking nut
44 Gear lever complete
45 Spherical seat
46 Locating pin
47 Retaining cap
48 Cap, reverse stop and retaining finger
49 Set bolt
50 Spring washer
51 Plain washer
52 Sleeve
53 Spring for reverse stop
54 Retaining sleeve for spring
55 Knob for gear lever
56 Support plate for gear change
57 Tie bracket
58 Bolt
59 Top plate
60 Rubber mounting pad
61 Rubber sleeve
62 Distance tube
63 Rubber sealing pad
64 Plain washer
65 Self-locking nut
66 Rubber bush, rear
67 Rubber bush, front
68 Distance tube
69 Plain washer
70 Self-locking nut

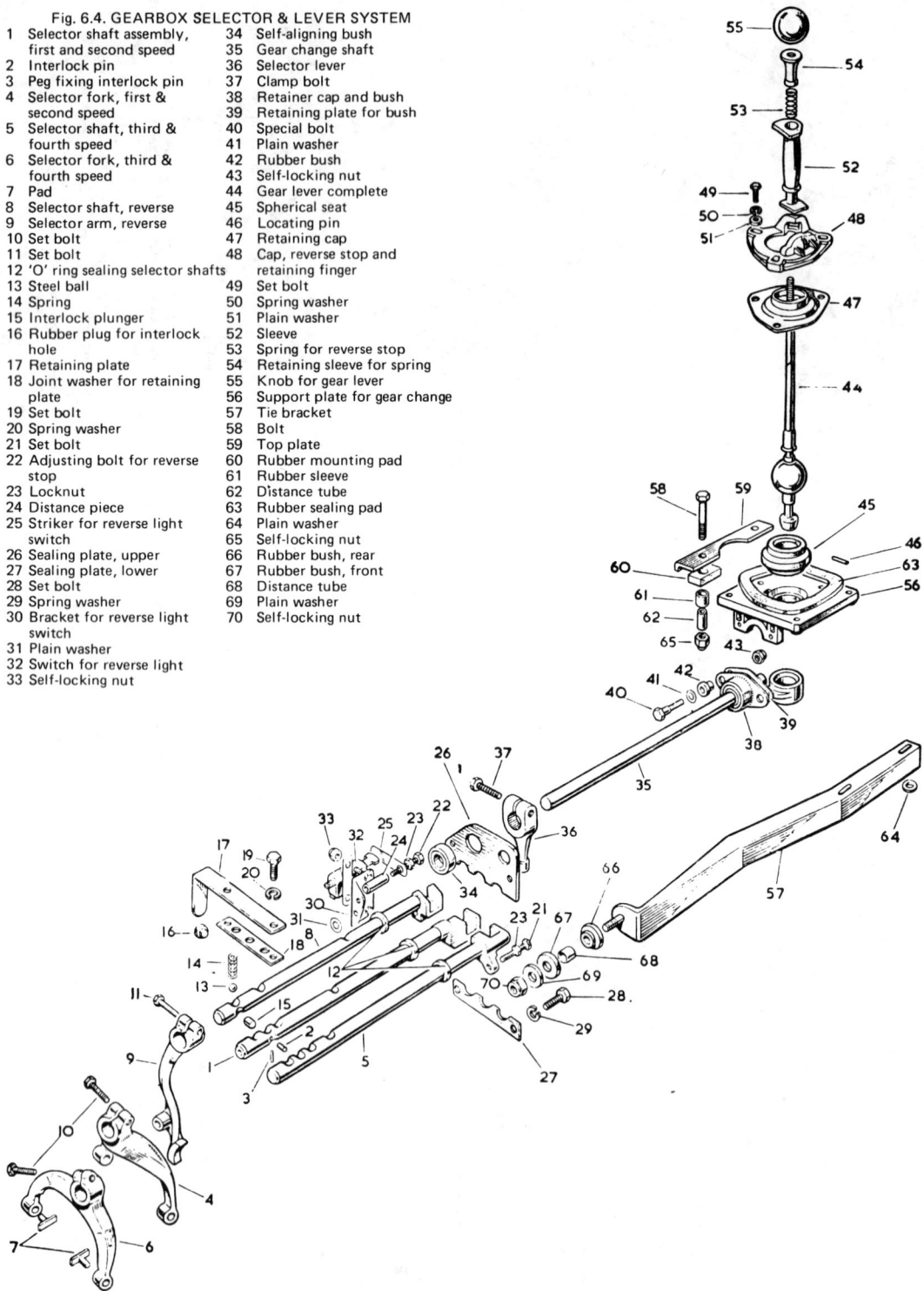

2. If the oil was not drained out prior to removal of the gearbox from the car, it should now be done. Undo the drain plug on the underside of the main casing and allow the oil to drain into a container, having a capacity of two pints. Replace the drain plug.

3. Place the gearbox on end with the clutch bellhousing facing upwards.

4. Undo and remove the pinch bolt and nut that secures the clutch withdrawal lever to the withdrawal shaft. Mark the relative position of the lever and splined shaft and slide the lever from the shaft.

5. Undo and remove the six self locking nuts that secure the clutch withdrawal housing to the inner face of the bellhousing. Carefully remove the withdrawal race housing and joint washer from the studs on the inner face of the bellhousing.

6. If a jointing compound has been used or the gasket stuck to the mating faces, thoroughly clean using a sharp knife or wide bladed screwdriver.

7. Invert the gearbox and stand on end on the bellhousing flange.

8. During removal of the gearbox, the large nut on the end of the transmission flange should have been slackened. It may now be removed, together with the special plain washer.

9. The transmission flange may now be removed by using either a soft metal drift and tapping rearwards, or a universal two or three-leg puller and suitable thrust pad so as not to damage the threads on the ends of the mainshaft.

10 Select first gear by drawing the left-hand selector rod rearwards at the same time turning the primary pinion to allow full engagement of the gear.

11 Undo and remove the eight nuts and bolts that secure the speedometer drive housing to the main casing. NOTE: Bolts of different threads and lengths are used, so make a careful note of their locations as they are removed so that they are refitted in their original positions.

12 Carefully withdraw the speedometer drive housing and gasket from the rear of the main casing.

13 Note which way round the speedometer drive worm gear fits onto the rear of the mainshaft and remove this gear.

14 The reverse light switch complete with mounting brackets should next be removed. Undo the two self locking nuts that secure the bracket in position and lift away the bracket with switch still attached, taking care to recover the plain washer situated at the front of the bracket.

15 Undo and remove the one remaining nut that secures the top half of the selector sealing plate and lift away the plate.

16 Undo the two bolts that secure the 'L' shaped bracket, one turn at a time, to release the selector shaft springs tension and when free lift away the two bolts, spring washers, 'L' shaped bracket and joint washer. NOTE: On some models two nuts and studs were used instead of two bolts.

17 Three springs may now be lifted out of the drillings and should be put in a safe place so that they are not lost. The detent ball bearings may either be removed using a magnet to draw them out of their drillings and put with the springs previously removed, or alternatively retained in position using a thick grease.

18 Slacken but do not yet remove the four self-locking nuts that secure the bellhousing to the main casing.

19 Undo and remove the six self locking nuts that secure the gearbox cover to the main casing. On later produced gearboxes, bolts and spring washers were used instead of self-locking nuts. Those are shown in Fig.6.5.

20 Very carefully lift away the gearbox cover from the casing, and, if the ball bearings in paragraph 17 above were not removed, this should now be done and the thick grease cleaned out of the holes.

21 Recover the two interlock plungers located between the three selector rods at the front face of the main casing. Lift away the rubber plug located on the side of the front face of the main casing.

22 Screw a 10 UNF size bolt into the reverse selector guide rod and withdraw the rod as shown in Fig.6.6.

23 Lift out the reverse gear selector fork and rod.

24 The two remaining selector rods with forks still attached may now be lifted out of the gearbox. This should be done with care so

that the little phosphor bronze shoes fitted into each fork do not fall into the gearbox.

25 Using a screwdriver or soft metal drift move the outer members of the synchronisers so as to engage two gears

26 With a pair of pliers, close the legs of the split pin on the front end of the layshaft, extract the split pin and undo the castellated nut. Do not remove it yet.

27 Reverse the sequence in paragraph 25 above and disengage the two gears previously selected.

28 Undo and remove the setscrew and retaining plate from the reverse gear idler shaft and pull out the shaft rearwards.

29 In paragraph 18 the four nuts which secure the bellhousing to the main casing were slackened. These should now be completely removed, together with their bolts.

30 With the gearbox still standing on the bellhousing flange carefully push the reverse gear assembly to one side so that it clears the first gear on the mainshaft.

31 Hold the main gear casing and lift it straight up and away from the gears. The mainshaft and layshaft assemblies will be left on the face of the bellhousing.

32 Lift out the reverse gear from the casing making a note which way round it is fitted.

33 Refer to Fig.6.7, and fit a jubilee clip onto the end of the mainshaft shown, so preventing the gear assemblies from falling off the mainshaft during subsequent operations.

34 Ease the upper end of the layshaft gear cluster away from the mainshaft and by gentle manipulation separate the complete mainshaft assembly from the primary pinion as shown in Fig.6.8. Lift away the mainshaft and place on one side making sure that it will not roll onto the floor.

35 Lift away the synchromesh cone and needle roller bearing from the end of the primary pinion.

36 Turn the gearbox bellhousing on one side and remove the nut and plain washer from the front of the layshaft. This nut was previously slackened in paragraph 26.

37 Using a soft faced hammer gently tap the layshaft and primary pinion rearwards. This must be done so that the two shafts move together. Take care that the oil baffle plate for the primary pinion bearing is not damaged.

38 The two half moon shaped retaining plates and four bolts will be drawn back with the primary pinion.

5. Gearbox — Examination & Renovation

1. Carefully clean and then examine all component parts for general wear, distortion, slackness of fit and damage to machined faces and threads.

2. Examine the gearwheels for excessive wear and chipping of teeth. Renew them as necessary. If a gear on the mainshaft needs replacement, check that the corresponding layshaft gear is not equally damaged. If it is, the whole laygear cluster may need replacing also.

3. All gears should be a running fit on the mainshaft, with no signs of rocking. The hubs should not be a sloppy fit on the splines.

4. As one of the main causes of most gearbox ailments is the failure of ball or roller bearings on the primary drive gear, mainshaft or laygear cluster, carefully inspect the bearings for wear or roughness, as wear may not readily be apparent. If there is any doubt always obtain and fit new bearings.

5. Inspect the four synchroniser rings, although for renewal of these the mainshaft has to be completely dismantled.

6. Selector forks and shafts should be examined for signs of wear or ridging on the faces which run in the hub grooves. Also inspect the two phosphor bronze shoes on the selector forks.

7. Before finally deciding to dismantle the mainshaft and replace parts, it is advisable to make enquiries regarding parts availability and cost and also to consider the acquisition of a new or used complete gearbox. There is a lot to be said for getting a unit from a breaker in the first place and fitting it to the car. The gearbox removed from the car can then be overhauled at leisure if necessary.

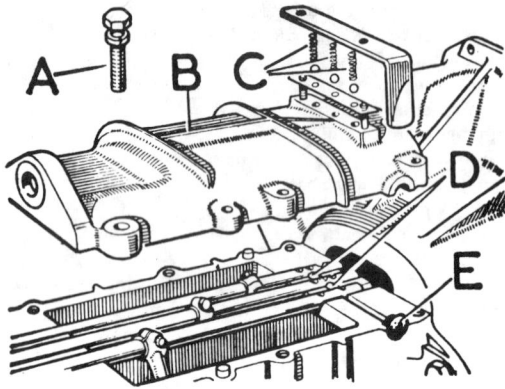

Fig.6.5. REMOVAL OF GEARBOX COVER

A Set bolt for gearbox
   cover
B Gearbox cover

C Springs for selector shafts
D Interlock plungers
E Rubber plug

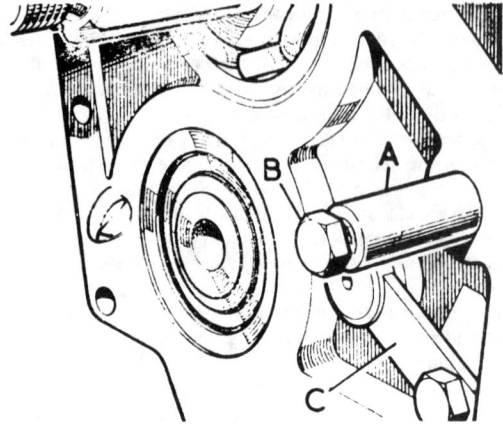

Fig.6.6. REMOVAL OF THE REVERSE SELECTOR GUIDE
ROD

A Reverse selector guide rod
B 10 UNF slave bolt

C Location plate for reverse
   gear idler shaft

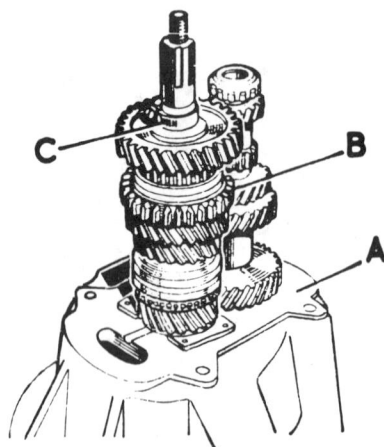

Fig.6.7. METHOD OF RETAINING GEAR ASSEMBLIES ON
MAINSHAFT

A Bellhousing
B Gear assemblies

C Jubilee clip

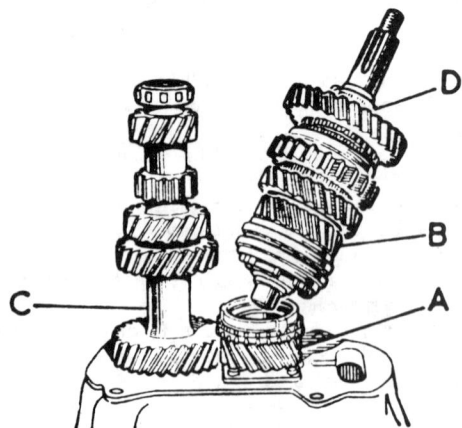

Fig.6.8. METHOD OF LIFTING MAINSHAFT CLEAR OF
PRIMARY PINION

A Primary pinion
B Mainshaft assembly

C Layshaft gear cluster
D Jubilee clip

8. If the gearbox is to be completely reconditioned, a matched set of gears is required comprising first speed mainshaft gear, second speed mainshaft gear, third speed mainshaft gear, primary pinion, reverse gear, inner and outer members for low gear and layshaft gear cluster.

9. To carry out a detailed check of gear tolerances, the mainshaft will have to be dismantled, details of which are given in Section 7.

10 There was a modification to improve mainshaft lubrication commencing from gearboxes numbered 40150567E (SC) and 40145850E (TC) models. This took the form of oil grooves being added to the mainshaft gears. The modified gears are fully interchangeable, either as a complete set or individually. Before fitting the modified gears make quite sure that all oil grooves are completely free of any dirt or preservative.

11 Gearboxes having the suffix 'E' incorporated in the number use bolts and spring washers instead of studs and self-locking nuts. If a new gear case or bellhousing is to be fitted it will be necessary to transfer the studs or alternatively, obtain new bolts. Your Rover dealer will be able to advise quantities and thread sizes as these are all clearly shown in the Official Parts Manual.

12 The selector shafts were modified from gear No.40132489D onwards, whereby the detent groove angle was decreased to 90° from 120°.

13 On later produced models the reverse gear selector arm is located with a 5/16 inch UNF set bolt.

14 Details of the modification to the clutch withdrawal race housing necessitated by the change in design of the thrust plate are given in Chapter 5, Section 8, paragraph 12 (d).

6. Primary Pinion — Dismantling & Reassembly

1. The primary pinion may be dismantled by first removing the circlip from its groove in the shaft.

2. Slide off the primary pinion baffle plate from the front of the bearing and then place the primary pinion horizontally between soft faces of a vice and, with a soft metal drift, gently tap the outer track of the bearing so drifting it forwards off its seating. Lift off the bearing noting which way round it is fitted.

3. As an alternative method of removing the bearing, use a long leg universal puller with a suitable thrust block.

4. To reassemble the primary pinion, first make sure that there are no burrs on the bearing seating or lead in. Refit the bearing the same way round as was noted upon removal and carefully drift into place using a soft metal drift on the inner track face. Alternatively, place on top of soft plywood pads on the top of the jaws of a vice and drift the primary pinion into the bearing using a soft metal drift located in the bore of the mainshaft needle roller bearing.

5. Replace the baffle plate and finally secure in place with a new circlip. Make sure that the circlip seats correctly in its groove.

7. Mainshaft — Dismantling, Inspection & Reassembly

The component parts of the mainshaft may be seen in Fig.6.3.

1. To dismantle the mainshaft, first undo and remove the jubilee clip previously fitted to the rear of the mainshaft.

2. The following parts may be removed from the rear of the mainshaft (make a note of the location, and which way round each part is fitted to ensure correct reassembly): Steel thrust washer; first speed gear; phospher-bronze bush; steel thrust washer; first/second synchromesh unit with reverse gear; and two synchromesh cones.

3. Turning to the front end of the mainshaft remove the following, (again noting the location and which way round each part is fitted): Spring steel clip; distance washer; and the third/fourth speed synchroniser unit and its core.

4. Remove the phospher bronze thrust washer; third speed gear; mainshaft distance sleeve; second speed gear; steel thrust washer; and locating steel key.

5. Thoroughly wash all parts and inspect for wear, as detailed in the relevant items of Section 5. A modified bush for the first mainshaft gear, distance sleeve for mainshaft second and third gears and rectangular rotating key have been introduced as well as different profile oil groups. These modifications were introduced from gearboxes having a suffix 'F' incorporated in the gearbox number. All parts are interchangeable in sets.

6. Details of other modifications are given in Section 5, paragraphs 8 and 10.

7. Should it be necessary to dismantle the synchromesh units, cover with a cloth to prevent loss of the little balls, springs and sliding blocks and then with a screwdriver, push the sliding blocks downwards so as to disengage the balls from the slots in the outer member.

8. Make sure that the cloth is in place and push the inner member right through the outer member. Carefully lift away the cloth and recover the balls, springs and slide blocks.

9. For reassembly of the mainshaft, it is important that various checks are made as detailed in the following paragraph.

10 To check the end tolerance of the second speed gear, refer to Fig.6.9, and assemble the second speed gear 'A' onto the mainshaft distance sleeve 'B'. Place a steel thrust washer in position and fit to the front end of the mainshaft. Using the fingers lightly press at the two points 'D' so that the distance sleeve is in contact with the thrust washer and mainshaft shoulder. With feeler gauges 'C' measure the clearance between the thrust face of the distance sleeve and the gearwheel. This should be between 0.007 — 0.011 inch.

11 Refer to Fig.6.10 and refit the third speed gear to the above assembly. Replace the phospher bronze thrust washer. Using the fingers lightly press at points 'D' and with feeler gauges measure the end tolerance of the gear wheel. This should be between 0.004—0.007 inch.

12 Should it be necessary to adjust the clearance in paragraphs 10 or 11 either obtain and fit a new bush or alternatively place some fine emery cloth on a surface plate and rub the appropriate end of the bush until the correct clearances have been obtained.

13 It is important that the mainshaft distance sleeve has a maximum end clearance of 0.001 inch. This is determined by the spacing washer fitted behind the spring clip at the front of the mainshaft and is available in four different thicknesses, 0.095, 0.098, 0.101 and 0.104 inch. The clearance is checked as shown in Fig.6.11 by fitting the steel thrust washer, distance sleeve, phospher bronze tab washer and the third/fourth synchroniser unit inner member to the mainshaft. Check the previously fitted parts are correctly located on the mainshaft and then select the correct spacing washer to take up all the clearance between the synchromesh unit and the spring ring. When the correct thickness spacing washer has been selected, remove the parts again from the mainshaft.

14 To check the end clearance between the first speed gear and the thrust washer, fit to the rear end of the mainshaft, the steel thrust washer 'A', Fig.6.12, first speed gear and bush, and the second steel thrust washer with the flat machined face towards the bush and gear. With the fingers apply light pressure 'E', against the thrust washer so as to keep the assembly in contact with the shoulder on the mainshaft and with feeler gauges check the end clearance between the gear and thrust washer. This should be between 0.004 and 0.009 inch.

15 Should it be necessary to adjust the clearance either obtain and fit a new bush or alternatively place some fine emery cloth on a surface plate and rub the end of the bush until the correct clearance has been obtained. Remove all parts from the mainshaft.

16 Before reassembly of the synchromesh units refer to Fig.6.3, and it will be seen that each unit comprises two synchromesh hubs, inner and outer sliding members, three springs, three balls and three sliding blocks. The outer member of the first/second synchromesh unit also carries spur gear teeth and forms part of the reverse gear train.

17 To reassemble the third/fourth synchromesh unit, first note the three machined cut-outs in the internal splines of the outer member. The three balls must be aligned to the centre of the cut outs when fitting the inner member to the splines. Insert the inner member to the outer member without the balls, springs and sliding blocks in

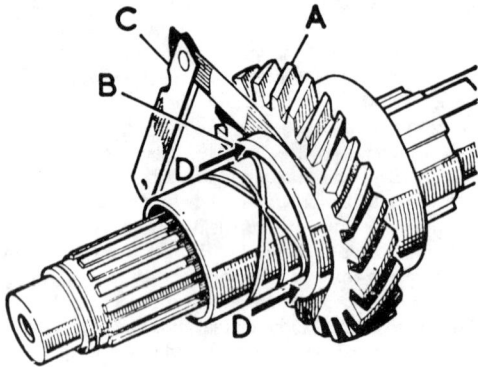

Fig.6.9. SECOND SPEED GEAR END TOLERANCE CHECK
A Second speed gear
B Flange of distance
   sleeve
C Feeler gauge
D Maintain pressure whilst
   checking tolerance

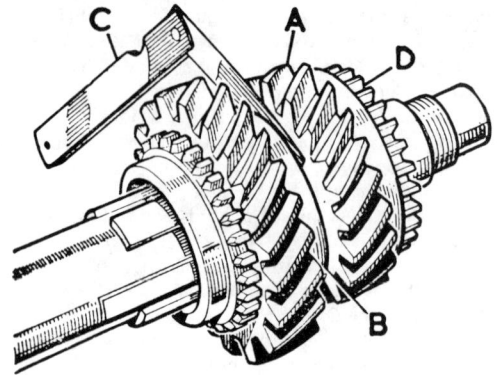

Fig.6.10. THIRD SPEED GEAR END TOLERANCE CHECK
A Third speed gear
B Flange of distance
   Sleeve
C Feeler gauge
D Maintain pressure whilst
   checking tolerance

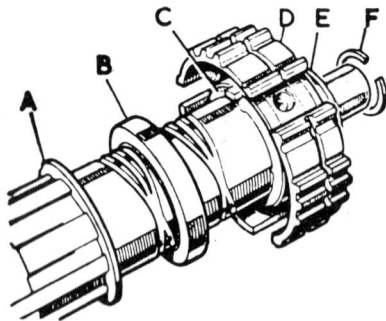

Fig.6.11. CHECKING THE MAINSHAFT DISTANCE SLEEVE
A Steel thrust washer
B Mainshaft distance sleeve
C Phospher – Bronze thrust
   washer
D Synchromesh unit inner
   member
E Spacing washer
F Spring ring

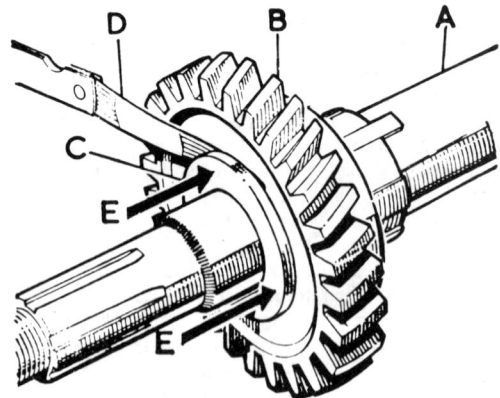

Fig.6.12. FIRST SPEED GEAR END TOLERANCE CHECK
A Mainshaft
B First speed gear
C Thrust washer
D Feeler gauge
E Maintain pressure whilst
   checking tolerance

one of the three possible positions and check for freedom of sliding movement. Repeat this procedure on the other two possible fitting positions and with a pencil mark the best of the three positions for freedom of movement.

18 Fit the inner and outer member in the position selected in paragraph 17. Inspect the sliding blocks and locate the radius of the sliding blocks which should coincide with the contour of the outer member.

19 Refer to Fig.6.13, and fit one of the springs and sliding blocks over a short length of 1/8 inch diameter wire and then with the inner and outer members aligned as shown, fit the sliding block spring to the inner member. The wire will hold the inner member in place.

20 Repeat the previous paragraph for the other two springs and sliding block assemblies.

21 Very gently withdraw one wire and insert a steel ball whilst at the same time holding the remaining wires in a downward position press the ball inwards and downwards, so that the sliding block and ball moves behind the outer member. Repeat this procedure for the other two balls and then firmly press the inner member down until the balls click into place in the cut outs of the outer member.

22 To reassemble the first/second synchromesh unit assemble the outer and inner members so that the longer splines of the inner member are on the same side as the gear wheel teeth of the outer member.

23 Repeat the procedure detailed in paragraph 17.

24 Fit the inner and outer member in the position selected in paragraph 23.

25 Support the inner member and assemble the synchromesh unit as detailed in paragraphs 19 – 21 inclusive.

26 Place both assembled synchromesh units in a safe place until required.

27 The mainshaft is now ready for reassembly. As each part is assembled, lubricate with clean oil so as to provide lubrication to all parts before the oil has had time to circulate for the first time.

28 Refer to Fig.6.3, and fit the second speed gear to its location on the keyway end of the distance sleeve.

29 Refit the steel thrust washer onto the rear of the mainshaft with the oil grooves facing towards the rear of the mainshaft.

30 Position the key into its seating on the mainshaft and retain in position with a little thick grease.

31 Slide the distance sleeve and gear assembly onto the mainshaft, making sure that the thrust washer and distance sleeve are correctly located on the key. Then fit the third speed gear to the distance sleeve.

32 Position the phosphor bronze thrust washer against its location on the inner member of the third/fourth speed synchromesh unit and retain in position with a dab of thick grease.

33 Place the synchromesh cone onto the synchromesh unit and carefully tap the assembly home on the splines of the mainshaft making sure that the thrust washer tab is not dislodged.

34 Fit the previously selected spacing washer, together with a new spring ring, onto the mainshaft. DO NOT use the old spring ring.

35 Fit the two synchromesh cones to the first/second synchromesh unit and place this on the mainshaft spline. The lead on the gear teeth must face towards the rear of the mainshaft.

36 Place the second steel thrust washer onto the key together with the bush for the first speed mainshaft gear. The thrust washer oil grooves must be placed next to the bush.

37 Refit the first speed gear onto the bush and finally fit the large steel thrust washer with the flat machine side facing towards the bush and gear.

38 Using the jubilee clip again, retain the assembled parts onto the mainshaft.

39 Place the second synchromesh cone onto the fourth synchromesh unit.

8. Gearbox Bearings — Removal & Refitting

1. If, after a preliminary inspection, it is decided that one or more of the bearings must be renewed, the following procedure should be adopted. In all cases, make a note of which way round the original bearing is fitted.

2. Details of the bearing removal from the primary pinion are given in Section 6 of this Chapter.

3. To remove the bearing from the front of the mainshaft, remove the circlip that retains it in the bellhousing, using a pair of circlip pliers.

4. Place the bellhousing in a container of very hot water and allow to stand for a few minutes. This is to cause the aluminium to expand making removal easier as the rate of expansion of the aluminium compared with the steel of the bearing track is higher. DO NOT just pour boiling water onto the bearing and immediate area around it as this will cause internal stresses in the aluminium with the possibility of it cracking across the thinner sections.

5. Using a soft metal drift, carefully tap out the bearing.

6. Refitting this bearing is the reverse sequence to removal.

7. To remove and refit the outer track of the layshaft gear cluster rear roller bearing, repeat the procedure outlined in paragraphs 4 and 5 of this Section. Make sure that the outer track is drifted fully home, using a piece of suitable diameter tube. It must be fitted flush with the rear face of the casing and with the shoulder towards the outside of the casing. The inner track and race of the layshaft gear cluster rear bearing may be removed using a universal two or three-leg puller. Use a piece of tube having an internal diameter just a little larger than the internal diameter of the bearing location on the layshaft gear cluster and drift the rear bearing into position.

8. Removal of the mainshaft rear bearing is effected by drifting out the old bearing rearwards, using a soft metal drift placed on the outer track.

9. To refit the mainshaft rear bearing, carefully drift it into position using a piece of tube located on the outer track of the bearing.

10 The needle roller bearing located in the rear of the primary pinion may be lifted out from its bore in the rear of the pinion and the new one inserted into place.

9. Gearbox Reassembly

1. With the gearbox casing clean and all traces of old gasket and jointing compound removed, and the new parts obtained and fitted as necessary, the gearbox can now be reassembled.

2. Place the bellhousing in a container of very hot water and allow to stand for a few minutes. This will allow the primary pinion bearing bore to expand, so making fitting of the bearing easier.

3. Place the gearbox bellhousing flange downwards on the bench and fit the primary pinion together with the oil baffle plate and the layshaft gear cluster.

4. Using a soft metal drift, located in the needle roller bearing bore, gently tap the primary pinion and bearing into position. Take care that the bearing is fitted squarely into its bore before drifting into place.

5. Place the two retaining plates for the primary pinion bearing in position and insert the four bolts.

6. Refit the castellated nut and plain washer to the front of the layshaft gear cluster, but do not tighten fully yet.

7. If the needle roller bearing has not been previously fitted into its bore in the rear of the primary pinion, it should now be inserted. Lubricate it well with clean oil.

8. Check that the mainshaft has been correctly assembled and then fit the mainshaft to the rear of the primary pinion. It will require a little patience and care in manipulating the third/fourth synchromesh unit, keeping the layshaft gear cluster slightly pushed to one side.

9. Undo and remove the jubilee clip that was placed on the rear of the mainshaft.

10 The reverse gear may now be put in place in the gearbox main casing. The lead on the gear teeth must face towards the front of the gearbox.

11 Make sure that the mating faces of the bellhousing and main casing are very clean and place a new gasket on the bellhousing case.

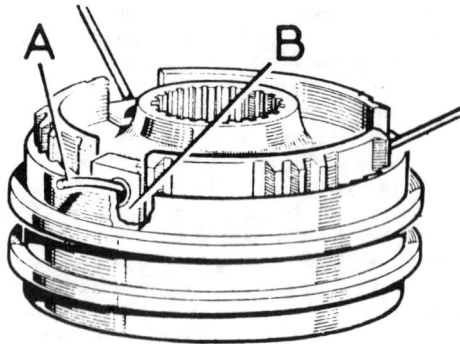

Fig.6.13. METHOD OF FITTING BLOCK & SPRING
A 1/8 inch diameter wire   B Sliding block

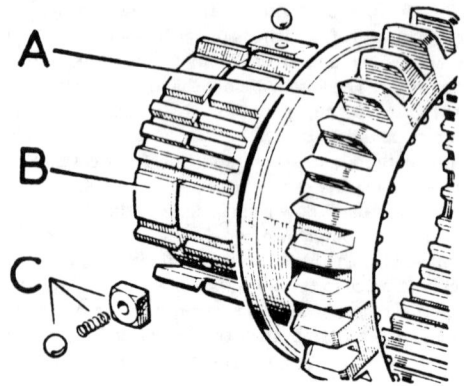

Fig.6.14. FIRST/SECOND SPEED SYNCHROMESH UNIT AS
SEMBLY
A Selector fork guide channel   C Locating ball, spring and
B Offset groove in inner member   sliding block

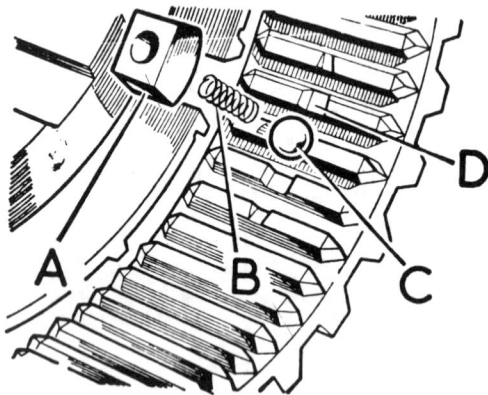

Fig.6.15. FIRST/SECOND SPEED SYNCHROMESH UNIT BALL
LOCATION
A Sliding block   C Ball
B Spring   D Locating grooves

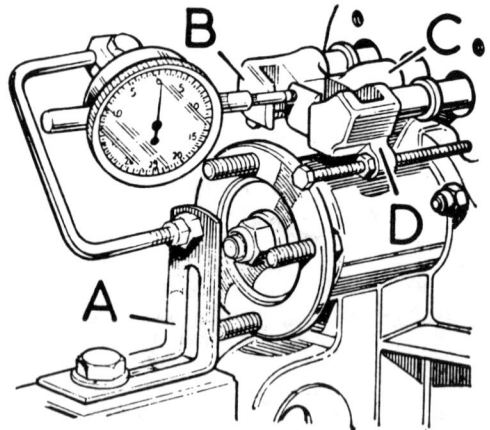

Fig.6.16. METHOD OF SETTING UP DIAL TEST INDICATOR
A Dial gauge mounting bracket   C First/Second speed selector
B Third/Fourth speed selector   shaft
   shaft   D Reverse selector shaft

12 Hold the reverse idler to one side and gently lower the main casing over the mainshaft and layshaft gear cluster until it is resting on the bellhousing.

13 Refit the four nuts and bolts but only tighten two of the four nuts. These two nuts should be diagonally opposed, i.e. top right and bottom left.

14 At this stage hold the layshaft gear cluster and check fore and aft movement. There should be definite signs of movement. If this is not evident, re-check that all the bearings have been fitted correctly during overhaul.

15 Using a screwdriver or soft metal drift, move the synchromesh units outer members so as to engage two gears and then tighten the layshaft gear cluster castellated nut to a torque wrench setting of 50 lb/ft. Lock the nut with a new split pin and bend over the legs.

16 Return the synchromesh units outer members to the neutral position.

17 Slacken the two nuts previously tightened that secure the bellhousing to the main casing.

18 The reverse idler gearshaft is next to be refitted. Note the slot for the retaining plate in the large diameter end. This must be aligned with the retainer plate location upon insertion. Insert the idler gear shaft and lock in position with the bolt and retaining plate. NOTE: If a new lock plate is to be fitted, it may be necessary to file a little of the flat end to make it a better fit in its recess in the reverse gear idler shaft. DO NOT use any washers as otherwise the head will foul the speedometer drive housing. Tighten the bolt to a torque wrench setting of 8 lb/ft.

19 If the selector forks have been removed from the selector shafts, they should next be refitted. By referring to Fig.6.4, the forks and shafts may be easily identified. Fit each selector fork to its shaft not forgetting the oil seal which must have its smallest diameter facing towards the fork. Screw in the pinch bolt but do not tighten yet.

20 Place the first/second and third/fourth forks and shaft assemblies into the gearbox, making sure that the little phospher bronze bushes engage correctly in their respective synchromesh unit outer members. The oil seals should be slid along the shaft so as to clear their grooves.

21 Replace the reverse fork and shaft assembly and make sure that it is correctly engaged with the reverse gear pinion. The oil seal, as with the previous selector rod oil seal, should be slid along the shaft to clear the groove.

22 It is now necessary to adjust the selector shafts. If the selector forks were not removed from the selector shafts, slacken the pinch bolt.

23 Select 2nd gear by pushing the first/second synchromesh outer member forwards with a soft metal drift or screwdriver and rotating the primary pinion to assist engagement.

24 Place the top cover with a new joint washer in position on the gearbox casing and referring to Fig.6.16, attach a dial indicator gauge and support to the gearbox, so that the probe is on the end of the second/first speed selector shaft.

25 Drop one of the three detent balls and springs into its applicable bore in the top cover and with the thumb compress the spring so as to hold the shaft in the second gear detent position. With the selector shaft in this correct position, zero the dial indicator gauge needle so as to act as a datum for future reference.

26 Very carefully lift away the top cover, joint washer, ball bearing and spring. Gently slide the selector shaft forwards towards the bellhousing a distance of between 0.045 and 0.050 inch, using the dial indicator gauge to show when this point has been reached.

27 Hold the selector shaft in the new position and ease the selector fork fully forwards until contact is made between the front face of the synchromesh unit outer member and the face of the second speed mainshaft gear (Fig.6.7). Tighten the selector fork pinch bolt.

28 Re-check the setting to ensure that the required movement of zero to 0.045 − 0.050 inch is achieved.

29 The reverse selector fork and shaft should next be reset. Place the top cover and joint washer in position and insert a ball and spring into its respective bore and compress the bore with the thumb.

30 Refit the reverse stop bolt minus the distance piece and reverse switch striker arm. Screw the bolt in until there is a clearance of between 0.032 and 0.037 inch between the end of the bolt and the abutment pad on the gearbox casing. This measurement may be obtained using feeler gauges. Remove the top cover, spring and bore.

31 Next move the first/second synchromesh unit outer member rearwards and select first gear. Locate the primary pinion to assist selection. Hold the gear in the fully rearwards position and then move the reverse selector shaft forwards until the stop bolt contacts the gearbox casing. In this condition all clearance will be taken up.

32 Holding the two selector shafts in this position, carefully slide the fork and gear forwards, whilst at the same time rotating the mainshaft and noting the idler gear through the top cover aperture. When the idler just makes contact with the gearteeth on the outer member of the first and second speed synchroniser but is NOT rotated by it, this is the condition at which the fork pinch bolt should be tightened. Fig.6.18 shows this point of contact.

33 Double check the setting in the previous paragraph making quite sure that the reverse stop bolt is held in contact with the casing and that the first gear selector shaft is held fully rearwards.

34 Undo and remove the stop bolt and refit complete with switch, striker arm and distance piece. Do not tighten the bolt fully yet.

35 Move the third/fourth synchromesh unit outer member rearwards and select third gear. Rotate the primary pinion to assist selection.

36 Place the top cover with a new joint washer in position on the gearbox casing and attach a dial indicator gauge and support to the gearbox, so that the probe is on the end of the third/fourth speed selector shaft.

37 Drop one of the three detent balls and springs into the applicable bore and compress the spring with the thumb, so as to hold the shaft in the second gear detent position.

38 With the selector shaft in this correct position, zero the dial indicator gauge needle so that it acts as a datum for future reference.

39 Very carefully lift away the top cover, joint washer, ball bearing and spring. Gently slide the selector shaft rearwards the distance of between 0.025 and 0.030 inch using a dial indicator gauge to show when the point has been reached.

40 Hold the selector shaft in this new position and ease the selector fork fully rearwards until contact is made between the rear face of the synchromesh outer member and the face of the third speed mainshaft gear (Fig.6.19). Tighten the selector fork pinch bolt.

41 Re-check the setting to ensure that the required clearance of 0.025 − 0.030 inch is achieved.

42 Tighten the forward speed selector fork pinch bolts to a torque wrench setting of 20 lb/ft. and the reverse gear selector pinch bolt to a torque wrench setting of 12 lb/ft.

43 The final adjustments are the stop bolts for the top and reverse gears. With the cover removed and the gearbox bellhousing nuts and bolts still loose, place the two interlock plungers in the groove in the casing.

44. Refit the top cover with the new joint washer and position the three selector shaft sealing rings in their grooves, taking extreme caution not to damage the paper gasket between the bellhousing and gearbox main casing. Secure with six self-locking nuts or bolts (as applicable) to a torque wrench setting of 15 lb/ft. Then tighten the four bellhousing fixing bolts to a torque wrench setting of 50 lb/ft

45 Insert the three detent balls and springs and replace the retaining plate and rubber plug.

46 Replace the oil seal retaining plates and reverse light switch.

47 Move the reverse selector so to engage reverse gear. Rotate the primary pinion to assist gear engagement.

48 Screw the stop bolt in or out to give a clearance between the end of the bolt and the abutment pad on the gearbox casing of between 0.010 and 0.020 inch (Fig.6.20). When the clearance has been obtained, tighten the locknut.

49 Next move the reverse selector backwards into the neutral position and then select fourth gear by moving the third/fourth gear selector rod forwards, rotating the primary pinion to assist gear engagement.

50 Adjust the stop bolt so as to give a clearance between the end of

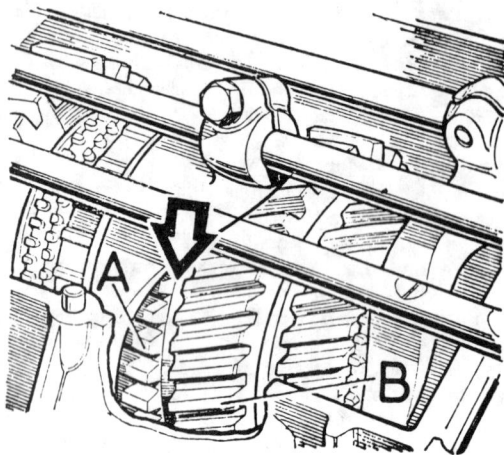

Fig.6.17. OUTER MEMBER OF SYNCHROMESH UNIT IN
CONTACT WITH SECOND SPEED MAINSHAFT GEAR
A Synchromesh outer member   B Second speed mainshaft gear

Arrow indicates point of contact

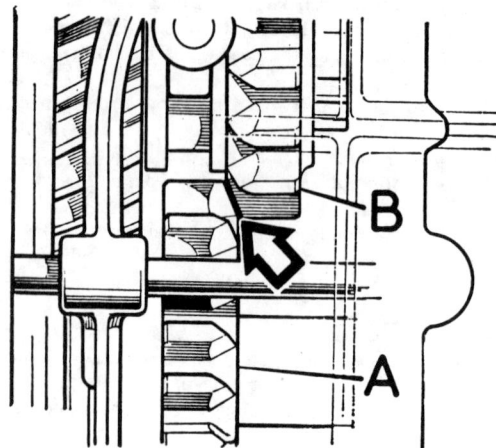

Fig.6.18. THE REVERSE IDLER GEAR JUST IN CONTACT
WITH THE TEETH OF THE REVERSE MAINSHAFT GEAR
A Reverse idler   B Mainshaft gear teeth

Arrow shows point of contact

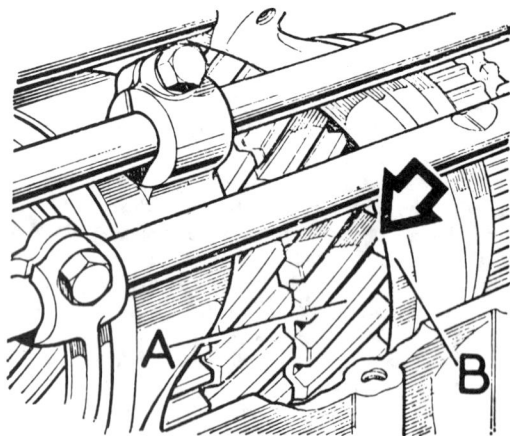

Fig.6.19. OUTER MEMBER OF SYNCHROMESH UNIT IN
CONTACT WITH THIRD SPEED MAINSHAFT GEAR
A Third speed mainshaft gear   B Synchromesh outer member

Arrow shows point of contact

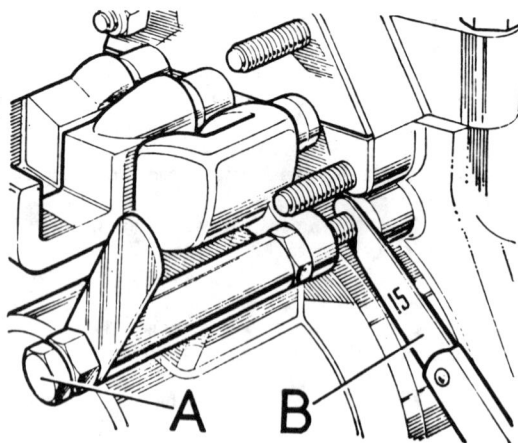

Fig.6.20. REVERSE GEAR STOP BOLT ADJUSTMENT
A Stop bolt   B 0.015 inch feeler gauge

the bolt and the abutment pad on the gearbox casing of between 0.010 and 0.020 inch (Fig.6.21). When the clearance has been obtained tighten the locknut.

51 Refit the steel shim washer, speedometer spindle and gear and the nylon bushing to the speedometer gear housing. Make sure that the spindle rotates easily.

52 Refit the speedometer worm gear, boss end first, onto the mainshaft.

53 Lightly coat the gearbox face of a new speedometer housing joint washer with 'Wellseal' and position it on the rear of the gearbox housing face. Then lightly coat the speedometer gear housing face with 'Wellseal' and fit to the gearbox. Select first gear and fit the securing nuts and bolts noting that the bolt heads 'A', Fig.6.22 are facing rearwards.

54 Tighten the 9/16 inch nuts to a torque wrench setting of 25 lb/ft. and the 7/16 inch nuts to a torque wrench setting of 8 lb/ft.

55 Make sure that the mainshaft splines are free from grease, and then lightly coat with Loctite sealant Grade AVV. Fit the coupling flange, special plain washer and nut onto the end of the mainshaft. Tighten the nut to a torque wrench setting of 75 lb/ft.

56 If difficulty is experienced in holding the gearbox when tightening the nut, leave it until the gearbox is back in the car. Tie a label on the flange to act as a reminder before the propeller shaft is finally refitted.

57 Make sure that the mating faces of the clutch withdrawal race housing and the gearbox main casing are clean. Gearboxes numbered 40158712F onwards had a joint washer 0.006 inch thick compared with the earlier joint washer of 0.015 inch thick. Normally the modified joint washer will be supplied but should one not be available it is permissible to use two thin joints in its place. Do not use any jointing compounds when fitting the clutch withdrawal race housing.

58 Refit the six nuts that secure the clutch withdrawal race housing to the gearbox casing and tighten to a torque wrench setting of 15 lb/ft.

59 The external declutching lever should be fitted with the lower end 5° forwards of the vertical when the cross shaft is being held in a clockwise direction and the withdrawal sleeve is in contact with the clutch thrust pad.

60 The gearbox is now ready for refitting to the car.

10. Gearchange Lever — Removal & Refitting

The gearchange lever may be removed from the car whilst the gearbox is still in position. Gearboxes produced from No.40139331E had an improved gearchange lever mounting, whereby a rubber mounted tie bracket was fitted between the gearchange mechanism mountings and the gearbox, so as to allow for a little movement between the gearbox and the body. To remove the gearchange lever, proceed as follows:—

1. Refer to Fig.6.4, and slacken the gearchange lever knob locknut, Unscrew the gearchange lever knob (55).

2. Unscrew and remove the knob locknut and spring retaining sleeve (54). Lift away the spring (53).

3. Remove the front and rear ashtrays from the gearbox tunnel moulded cover.

4. Locate and remove the two nuts to be found under the rear ashtray location and the single nut under the front ashtray location.

5. Undo and remove the two Phillips head screws at the front of the moulded cover.

6. Lift up the flap at the forward edge of the rubber grommet base and remove the self-tapping screw.

7. Undo and remove the two Phillips head screws securing the radio speaker grille to the console unit. These screws are to be found between the petrol reserve control and choke control. Lift away the speaker grille.

8. Remove the gearchange lever sleeve (52).

9. Slide both front seats as far back as they will go and keep the locking levers in their raised position.

10 Carefully roll back the handbrake rubber grommet and to assist removal of the grommet smear the handbrake handle and the grommet with a little silicone grease.

11 Lift the forward edge of the cover over and off the gearchange lever.

12 Apply the handbrake and slide the cover forward and upwards so as to enable the leading edge to protrude into the aperture at the console. At the same time carefully push the handbrake grommet off the handbrake handle.

13 Release the handbrake fully and lift away the cover assembly.

14 Undo and remove the three bolts that secure the retaining cap assembly and then lift away the gear lever and retaining cap from the inside of the car.

15 The gearchange lever may now be separated from the support plate once the four bolts and self-locking nuts have been removed.

16 Refitting the gearchange lever is the reverse sequence to removal. It will, however, be necessary to check the alignment of the gearchange lever. Details of this operation are given in Section 11.

17 It is important that the reverse stop sleeve clears the shoulder on the reverse stop when pulled upwards, so as to enable reverse gear to be selected. Adjustment may be made by unscrewing the spring retaining sleeve (54) until the stop sleeve clears the reverse stop shoulder.

11. Gearchange Shaft — Removal, Refitting & Adjustment

1. Jack up the rear of the car and position on firmly based axle stands located at the body jacking points or, alternatively, position the rear of the car over a pit or on a ramp.

2. If the rear of the car is jacked up always supplement the jack with supporting axle stands or blocks so that danger is minimised should the jack collapse.

3. If the rear wheels are off the ground, place the car in gear, or put the handbrake on to ensure that the propeller shaft does not turn when an attempt is made to loosen the nuts securing the propeller shaft universal joint flanges to the rear of the gearbox and to the final drive extension shaft flange.

4. The propeller shaft is carefully balanced to fine limits and it is important that it is replaced in exactly the same position it was in prior to its removal. Scratch a mark on the propeller shaft and mating flanges to ensure accurate refitting when the time comes for reassembly.

5. Undo and remove the four nuts and bolts which hold the flange of the propeller shaft to the flange on the final drive extension shaft.

6. Push the propeller shaft forwards, lower the rear end and place on the floor.

7. Undo and remove the four nuts which hold the flange of the propeller shaft to the flange on the rear of the gearbox.

8. Push the propeller shaft rearwards and lift it away from the underside of the car.

9. If the car is a TC model it will be necessary to remove the centre exhaust pipe. Further details and a layout of the exhaust system will be found in Chapter 3, Section 21.

10 Undo and remove the two nuts and bolts that secure the gearchange shaft and selector lever retainer cap, bush and plate to the support plate, (Fig.6.24).

11 Carefully push the reverse selector shaft forward so as to engage gear. Rotate the selector shaft through 90° in an anti-clockwise direction so as to clear the selector gate.

12 Lower the selector shaft to clear the gearchange lever and then withdraw the shaft rearwards.

13 If it is necessary to remove the selector lever from the shaft, it will be necessary to reset the adjustment as detailed later in this Section.

14 To remove the support plate, undo and remove the four bolts that secure the bottom plate, and lift away the plate and rubber block, working underneath the car.

15 By referring to the introduction to Section 10, details were given of the modification to the gearchange lever mounting. If the owner

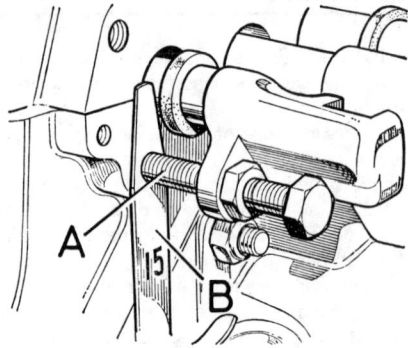

Fig.6.21. TOP GEAR STOP BOLT ADJUSTMENT
A Stop bolt   B 0.015 inch feeler gauge

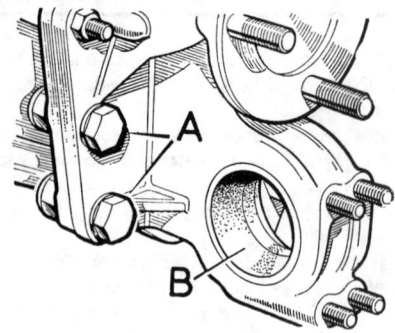

Fig.6.22. CORRECT POSITIONING OF BOLT HEADS AT REAR OF GEARBOX
A Securing bolts   B Snub rubber

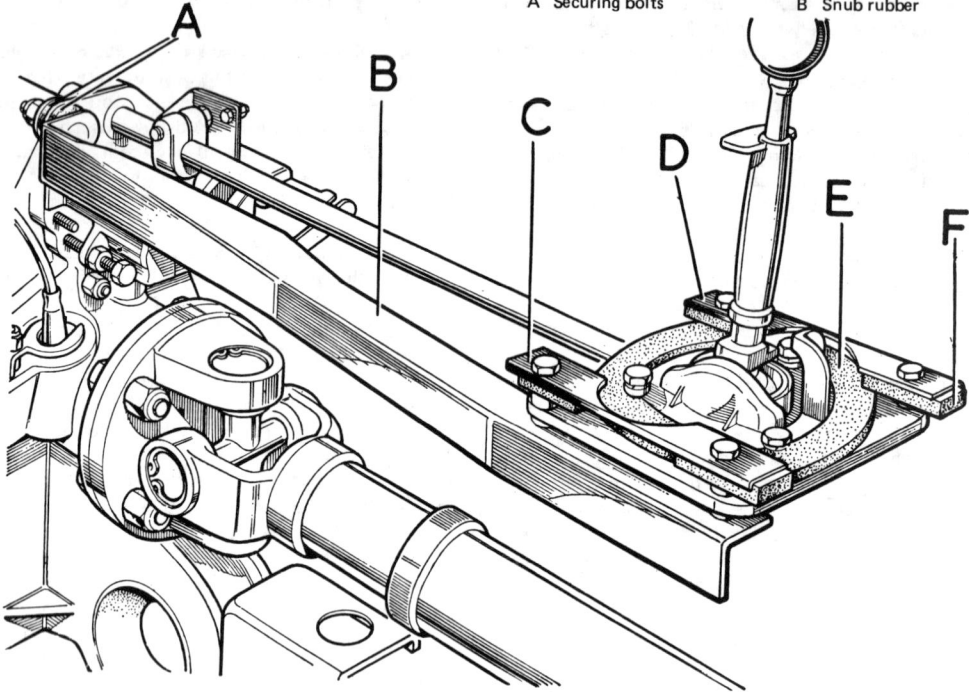

Fig.6.23. THE GEAR CHANGE LEVER SYSTEM

A Bush, rubber fixing tie   B Tie bracket, gearbox to   C Top plate, left-hand side   E Seal, neoprene sponge
bracket to gearbox   gear change   D Top plate, right-hand side   F Pad, neoprene sponge

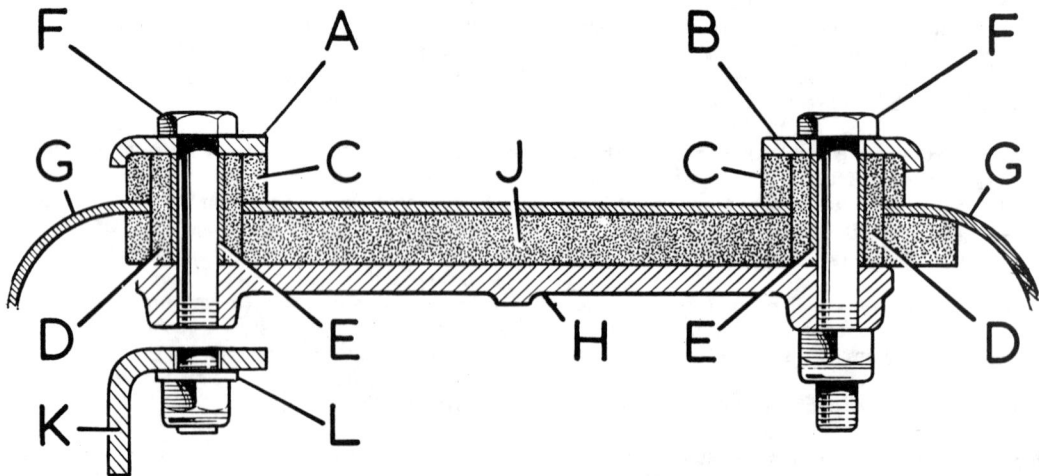

Fig.6.24. CROSS SECTION THROUGH GEAR LEVER FIXINGS

A Top plate-left-hand side   D Neoprene sleeve   G Body propeller shaft tunnel   J Neoprene sponge seal
B Top plate-right-hand side   E Distance tube   H Gear change lever support   K Tie bracket
C Neoprene sponge pad   F Bolt   plate   L Plain washer

wishes to modify an earlier type gearbox to the later specification a kit having a Part No.601577 may be obtained and fitted. Full fitting instructions are supplied with the kit.

16 Refitting is the reverse sequence to removal. It is important that the gearchange lever ball and spherical seating are not lubricated.

17 If the selector lever setting relative to the selector rod has been disturbed, it will be necessary to adjust the position of the selector lever.

18 Refer to Fig.6.25, and make sure that there is a clearance between the gearchange lever and tunnel finisher when first and reverse gears are selected.

19 Should it be noticed that dimensions A and B are not equal the gearchange lever support plate must be moved until equidistant movement is obtained.

20 Move the gearchange lever to the central position of neutral and very gently push it forwards until the detent is felt. Do not move the lever forwards any further.

21 Note the position of the gearchange lever relative to the vertical and this should be 10° as shown in Fig.6.26.

22 Should the angle be incorrect, remove the reverse switch access hole rubber grommet and with a socket or 'T' spanner slacken the selector lever clamp bolt.

23 Place the gearchange lever in the vertical position and then move it forwards in the same plane until it is at 10° to the vertical. Tighten the clamp bolt on the selector lever. Make sure that the selector lever is in a vertical position relative to the gearchange shaft.

24 Move the gearchange lever to the first gear position.

25 Slacken the selector lever clamp bolt again and move the gearchange lever to the left until it contacts the reverse stop. Then lift the reverse stop and move the gearchange lever approximately 1/8 inch to the left.

26 Tighten the selector lever clamp bolt and check for correct selection of all gears by road testing.

12. Manual Gearbox — Fault Finding

Faults in the gearbox can range from small noises and minor deficiencies in engagement of gears and operation of synchromesh, to serious faults consisting of loud whines serious vibrations or inability to engage or remain in one or more gears. For serious faults there is no alternative to removing the gearbox and either overhauling it completely or fitting another. For minor faults, other than those which can be detected in the change mechanism rather than the gearbox, it is more a question of how long can the fault be tolerated before taking action. Once something starts to wear to a degree which is noticeable, things usually start to deteriorate rapidly. Unfortunately, the amount of trouble to rectify a minor fault will be the same as for a major one — removal and dismantling of the gearbox. One may save something on spare parts but even this is problematical as it is not until the gearbox is stripped that many faults can be diagnosed accurately. Some faults can go on for thousands of miles without further deterioration to the whole unit - a worn synchro cone for example. Failure of the mainshaft bearing could, however, completely ruin the whole assembly in a few hundred miles.

The following list is intended as a guide to aid decisions on WHEN to take action:—

Fault	Cause
Ineffective synchromesh on one or more gears.	Worn synchro cones.
	Worn blocker bars.
Jumps out of one or more gears.	Worn selector forks.
	Weak detent springs.
	Worn gear engagement dogs.
	Worn selector hub fork groove.
	Selector fork loose on rail (rare).
Noisy - rough - whining, vibration	Worn bearings and/or laygear thrust washers (initially) resulting in extended wear generally due to

Noisy and difficult engagement of gear.

Difficult selecting forward or reverse gears and moving change lever out of gear.

play and backlash.
Clutch not disengaging properly.

Worn change lever linkage, particularly on steering column controls. General wear on remote control.
General wear on remote control.
Maladjusted reverse lever stop on early remote control.

13. Automatic Transmission — General Description

The Borg Warner type 35 automatic transmission unit may be fitted as a factory production optional extra to models covered by this manual. Cars produced before October 1966 did not have automatic transmission offered as an optional extra.

Automatic transmissions have been fitted to medium and large sized cars for many years and have now been accepted as a desirable feature to have fitted by many motorists. It takes the place of the clutch and gearbox, which are, of course, mounted behind the engine.

The system comprises two main components:—
1. A three element hydrokinetic torque converter coupling capable of torque multiplication at an indefinitely variable ratio between 2:1 and 1:1.
2. A torque/speed responsive and hydraulic epicyclic gearbox, comprising a planetary gearset providing three forward ratios and one reverse ratio.

Due to the complexity of the automatic transmission unit, if performance is not up to standard or overhaul is necessary, it is imperative that rectification be left to the local main agents who will have the special equipment and knowledge for fault diagnosis and rectification.

The content of this Chapter is therefore confined to supplying general information and any service information and instruction that can be used by the owner.

14. Automatic Transmission — Driving Technique

The selector lever is mounted on a console placed between the two front seats and controls the operation of the automatic transmission. There are six positions marked on the quadrant and these are:— 'P', 'R', 'N', 'D2', 'D1' and 'L'. As a safety factor to prevent accidental engagement it is necessary to depress the button in the centre of the selector lever to engage all positions except between 'D2' and 'D1'. Also the lever can be moved from 'L' onto 'D1' or 'D2' and from 'R' into 'N' without depressing the button.

'P'   This is the park position, whereby no engine torque is transmitted to the driving wheels and the transmission is locked by mechanical means. For safety reasons it is recommended that this position be used whenever the car is parked or when the engine is to be run for tuning or adjustment. Serious damage will result if this position is selected whilst the car is moving.

'R'   Reverse position, whereby the car can be driven in reverse, and to assist control, full engine braking is available. As with the 'P' position it is important not to select 'R' whilst the car is moving forwards.

'N'   This is the neutral normal position, whereby no engine torque is transmitted to the driving wheels. Always apply the handbrake when the selector lever is in the 'N' position and the car is stationary.

'D2'   For normal leisurely driving conditions this is the usual position of the selector lever and dispenses with the first gear condition. This position should also be used when driving on slippery road surfaces.

'D1'   This is the normal driving condition and is the usual position of the selector lever. It gives a fully automatic range of three

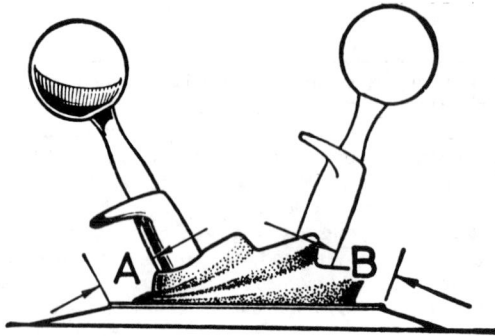

Fig.6.25. GEAR LEVER CLEARANCE CHECK
A Check distance between gear   B Check distance between gear
   lever and tunnel finisher when   lever and tunnel finisher when
   first gear is selected.   reverse gear is selected.

Dimension A = Dimension B

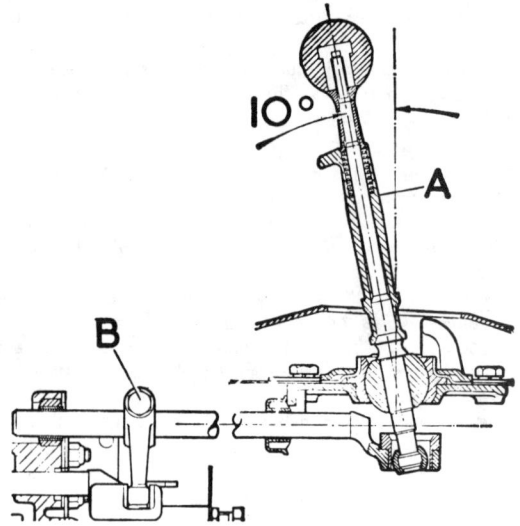

Fig.6.26. GEAR LEVER SETTING IN NEUTRAL POSITION
A Set gear lever to an angle of 10° forward of the vertical
B Tighten clamp bolt of selector lever to a torque wrench setting
   of 17 lb/ft. once gear lever position has been set.

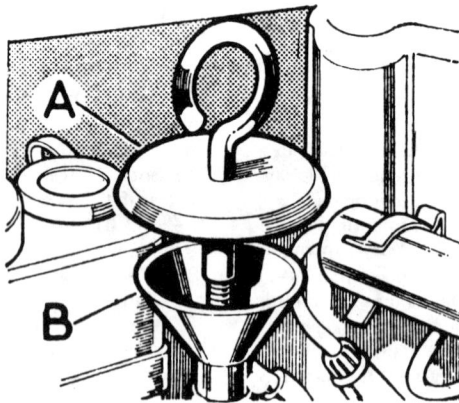

Fig.6.27. AUTOMATIC TRANSMISSION DIPSTICK LOCATION
A Dipstick
B Tube for dipstick

forward ratios, all of which are progressively engaged up and down depending upon the position of the accelerator and the speed of the car.

'L' In this position the automatic ratio train is over-ridden for first and second ratios. It also gives full engine braking. It must not be selected at speeds of 70 miles per hour or above as otherwise the engine will over-speed causing serious mechanical damage.

Starting the Engine

The starter motor may only be operated when the selector lever is in the 'P' or 'N' position, this being controlled by a micro switch fitted to the underside of the automatic transmission unit. For safety reasons always apply either the handbrake or footbrake before starting the engine.

Care should be taken when starting the engine from cold using the choke control. Stalling should be avoided if this control is left out sufficiently to increase engine speed until it has reached its normal operating temperature. At the fast idle speed when the selector is moved to the 'L' or 'D^1' position a firm engagement will be obtained but this has no ill effects on the automatic transmission unit.

On cars fitted with automatic transmission units, the rubber button on the starter solenoid is blanked off so that the engine cannot be started from the engine compartment region for obvious safety reasons.

Normal Driving Conditions

When 'D^2' position is selected the automatic transmission covers an automatic range of two ratios commencing with second gear which will operate in conjunction with the torque converter. The ratios will be progressively engaged according to the car speed and accelerator pedal position. Top gear will then be retained until the car speed falls below 10 m.p.h. whereupon second gear will automatically be engaged. This is, of course, providing that the 'kick-down' position of the accelerator pedal is not used

If the road speed is below 50 mph, second gear may be obtained by using the 'kick-down' position of the accelerator pedal and can be held in this condition until a maximum speed of 70 mph is obtained whereupon top gear will automatically be engaged. It should be remembered that in the 'D^2' position first gear is not engaged at any time.

When the selector is moved to the 'D^1' position a fully automatic change throughout the range of the three forward speeds is achieved, commencing with a first gear start in conjunction with the torque converter. The second and third gear ratios are automatically obtained as the car speed increases.

Should it be necessary to retain top gear it may automatically be held in this position until about 10 mph, whereupon second gear will automatically be engaged. When the speed falls to about 3 mph, first gear will then be automatically engaged.

If the road speed is below 55 mph it is possible to obtain second gear by depressing the accelerator pedal to the 'kick-down' position and can then be held until a road speed of 70 mph is achieved, whereupon it will automatically change to top gear. Conversely, first gear can be obtained below 20 mph with the accelerator pedal in the 'kick-down' position and can be held until a road speed of 40 mph is achieved whereupon it will automatically change to second gear.

With the selector in the 'L' position, it is possible to hold the automatic transmission in either first or second gear and driving technique is similar to that for a conventional gearbox with the exception of the torque converter. Full over-run braking is available in either first or second gear, which is of considerable assistance when descending long hills. The 'L' position must not be engaged at speeds above 70 mph. If the 'L' position is selected when starting the car from rest the automatic transmission will remain locked in first gear regardless of the position of the accelerator pedal or road speed. The car must not exceed a speed of 45 mph in first gear. When necessary to change from first gear to second gear 'L' position, move the selector lever to either 'D^1' or 'D^2' to effect

the second gearchange and then return the selector to the 'L' position. The maximum road speed in second gear must not exceed 70 mph. To effect a gear change from second speed in the 'L' position move the selector lever to the 'D^1' or 'D^2' position. When the automatic transmission is in top gear with the selector in either 'D^1' or 'D^2' position, movement of the selector lever to the 'L' position will automatically give second gear, and then when the road speed falls to below 18 mph first gear will automatically be obtained.

When the automatic transmission is in second gear, first gear may be engaged at road speeds below 20 mph by depressing the accelerator pedal to the 'kick-down' position, but then to change up to second gear the lever must be moved to the 'D^1' or 'D^2' position and then returned to the 'L' position as previously stated.

Special Driving or Recovery Conditions

1. To slow down or stop, remove the foot from the accelerator pedal and depress the footbrake in the usual way. The engine will not stall.
2. Parking. With the car stationary, move the selector to the 'P' position and apply the handbrake. If the car has been parked on a steep gradient, move the selector to the 'L' or 'D^1' position and increase the engine speed slightly if facing uphill, or if facing downhill, move the selector to the 'R' position and increase the speed slightly. Then release the handbrake.
3. Soft surfaces. When the rear wheels will not grip the road surface due to snow, ice or mud conditions, rock the car forwards and backwards by moving the selector alternatively to the 'R' and 'L' or 'D^1' positions and raising the engine speed slightly.
4. Towing. If a caravan, boat or trailer is being towed, always select the 'L' position before ascending or descending steep hills, to stop overheating of the special transmission fluid, and also to receive benefit from the engine braking assistance.
5. Recovery towing. Should it be necessary to have the car towed to a garage, the distance must not exceed 20 miles or the speed 30 m.p.h. Towing is permitted providing the transmission is not damaged and that the oil level is correct. Put the selector lever in the 'N' position. If there are noises emitting from the transmission, or the towing distance is greater than 20 miles, the propeller shaft should be disconnected and completely removed, and the end of the transmission sealed to prevent oil loss and dirt ingress. As an alternative, the car can be suspended and towed with the rear wheels off the ground.
6. The car may be push or tow started. Move the selector to the 'L' position and switch on the ignition. If the engine is cold, pull out the choke control and then release the handbrake. The car should then be towed until the engine fires and starts to run. This should occur at a road speed of below 25 mph. An extra long tow rope must be used unless the car is being pushed and very great care taken not to run into the back of the towing vehicle once the engine starts.

15. Automatic Transmission Fluid Level

It is important that transmission fluids manufactured only to the correct specification, such as Castrol TQ, are used. The capacity of the unit is approximately 12 pints when dry, but for a drain and refill, which is not actually necessary except during repairs, the capacity will be approximately 6 pints as the converter cannot be completely drained.

16. Automatic Transmission — Maintenance

1. Ensure that the exterior of the converter housing and gearbox is always kept clean of dust or mud, otherwise overheating will occur.
2. Every 5,000 miles or more frequently, check the automatic transmission fluid level. With the engine at its normal operating temperature, move the selector to the 'P' position and allow to idle for 2 minutes. Remove the dipstick (Fig.6.27) wipe it clean and with the

Fig.6.28. The Borg-Warner Model 35 Automatic Transmission

Fig.6.29. The Torque Converter

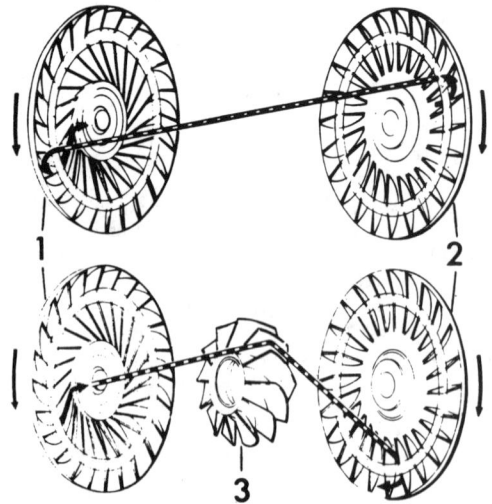

Fig.6.30. DIAGRAMMATIC OPERATION OF TORQUE CONVERTER

1. Turbine   3. Stator
2. Impeller

engine idling, insert the dipstick and quickly withdraw it again. If necessary add enough oil of the correct grade to bring the level to the 'HOT' mark on the dipstick if the transmission is hot or if it is cold top up to the 'COLD' mark (Fig.6.31). If a large quantity of fluid is required to bring the level up to the required mark, inspect the automatic transmission unit for signs of hydraulic fluid leakage.

3. If the unit has been drained, it is recommended that only new fluid is used. Fill up to the correct level on the dipstick by gradually refilling the unit, the exact amount will depend on how much·was left in the converter after draining.

17. Automatic Transmission Unit — Removal & Replacement

1. Any suspected faults must be referred to the main agent before unit removal, as with this type of transmission, the fault must be confirmed using specialist equipment before it has been removed from the car.

2. As the automatic transmission unit is relatively heavy it is best if the car is raised from the floor on ramps, but it is also possible to remove the unit if the car is placed on high axle stands.

3. Open the engine compartment lid and place old blankets over the wings to prevent accidental scratching of the paintwork.

4. Disconnect the battery earth terminal.

5. Undo and remove the carburetter installation heat shield securing nuts and bolts and lift away the heat shield.

6. Soak the three nuts and bolts securing the exhaust front pipe to the manifold. Undo and remove the nuts, bolts and spring washers and separate the joint.

7. Place a clean and dry container having a capacity of at least 8 pints under the location of the oil filler tube and undo the large union nut securing the filler tube to the oil pan. Push the filler tube clear of the oil pan and allow all the oil to drain out. Take care if the car has just been run as the oil can be very hot.

8. Disconnect the engine tie-rod bracket from the cylinder head by undoing and removing the two bolts with spring and plain washers.

9. Refer to Fig.6.32, and disconnect the downshift outer cable at the bracket D. Also disconnect the control rod outer ball joint from the coupling shaft lever by releasing the spring retainer and pulling the cup off the ball joint.

10 Disconnect the coupling shaft from the carburetter fork.

11 Refer to Fig.6.32, and release the spring clip that secures the inner cable clevis to the coupling shaft lever. Withdraw the clevis. Finally remove the accelerator pedal coupling shaft.

12 Mark the flange of the propeller shaft rear universal joint and the mating flange of the final drive unit. Undo and remove the four nuts and bolts and separate the two flanges. Lower the end of the propeller shaft to the floor.

13 Refer to Chapter 3, Section 21 and either disconnect the front exhaust pipe from the intermediate silencer or alternatively remove the complete exhaust system.

14 Place a piece of flat soft wood on the saddle of the garage hydraulic jack and place on the rear portion of the engine sump. Carefully raise the jack until the weight of the engine is just being taken by the jack.

15 Refer to Fig.6.33, and remove the rear engine mounting, the location of the bolts, spring washers and plain washers being clearly shown.

16 Very carefully lower the engine until it is just possible to gain access to the underside of the selector lever and also to the top of the bellhousing.

17 Refer to Fig.6.34, and disconnect the tie-rod 'A' from the pivot housing by undoing and removing the nut and spring washer. Pull the ball joint off the pivot housing.

18 Disconnect the operating rod 'D', Fig.6.34, at the end of the selector lever 'C', by undoing and removing the nut and spring washer. Pull the ball joint off the end of the selector lever.

19 Refer to Fig.6.35, and disconnect the lower control rod from the side of the automatic transmission unit. Undo and remove the nut and spring washer and separate the lower control rod or joint

from the lower selector lever.

10 Undo and remove the three bolts and spring washers that secure the compensator bracket to the top of the bellhousing. This bracket is shown in Fig.6.36. Carefully lift away the compensator and rods.

21 Undo the knurled cap nut that secures the speedometer outer cable to the right angle drive. Withdraw the cable and nut from the right angle drive.

22 Make a note of the electrical cable connections at the inhibitor switch and disconnect the wires from the inhibitor switch. Release the cables from the clips on the bellhousing.

23 Disconnect the two oil cooler pipes from the automatic transmission unit and release them from the securing clip. Swing the two pipes to one side out of the way of the unit.

24 Disconnect the nylon oil filler breather pipe and release from the clip at the bellhousing if the torque converter is to be removed. Otherwise leave in place.

25 Place a container under the transmission unit and undo the six nuts and bolts that secure the transmission unit to the bellhousing whilst the weight of the unit is being taken by an assistant. Remove the six bolts and spring washers.

26 Very carefully ease the automatic transmission unit rearwards out of engagement of the torque converter and then lift away from the underside of the car. Oil will drain out of the torque converter so catch it with the container previously placed under the transmission unit.

27 If it is necessary to remove the torque converter and bellhousing, undo and remove the securing nuts and bolts that hold the bellhousing to the engine backplate.

28 Disconnect the heavy duty cable at the starter motor endplate and lift away the starter motor.

29 Remove the sparking plugs to facilitate rotation of the crankshaft. Turn the crankshaft and, working through the starter motor aperture in the engine backplate, undo and remove the four bolts and washers that secure the torque converter to the engine drive plate. Whilst these bolts are being undone an assistant should take the weight of the torque converter.

30 When the torque converter is being lifted away, bear in mind that it still contains a little hydraulic fluid which should be tipped into the container previously used to catch the hydraulic fluid.

31 Refitting the automatic transmission unit is the reverse sequence to removal but there are several additional points which should be noted to ensure satisfactory refitting and subsequent reliable operation. These points are given in the following paragraphs.

32 When refitting the unit to the rear of the engine, it is recommended that the weight be supported with a garage hydraulic jack so as not to place undue strain on the front pump drive flanges or the front oil seal.

33 The driving flanges on the torque converter and corresponding drive slots on the transmission front pump should be carefully positioned in relative alignment before actually lifting the automatic transmission unit into place, so as to ensure easy and correct alignment to the torque converter.

34 The nuts and bolts securing the automatic transmission case to the bellhousing should be tightened to a torque wrench setting of between 8 to 10 lb/ft.

35 When refilling the unit with transmission fluid, make sure that the car is standing on level ground. Select the 'P' position and allow the engine to idle for two minutes and then add the fluid in small quantities until the correct level is obtained as indicated by the 'COLD' mark on the dipstick. The capacity of the unit from dry is 11 pints, or 10 pints if there is residual fluid in the torque converter.

36 Make sure that the rear mounting cross shaft is central in the snub rubber and also that the support spring is in a vertical position.

37 Adjust the gear selector linkage as detailed in Section 18 of this Chapter.

38 Adjust the starter inhibitor/reverse light switch as detailed in Section 19 of this Chapter.

39 Adjust the downshift valve cable as detailed in Section 20 of this Chapter.

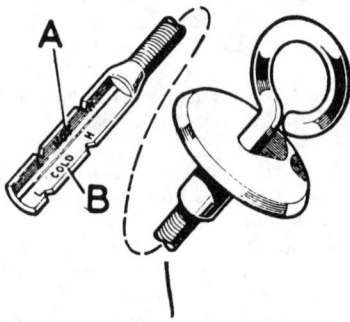

Fig.6.31. AUTOMATIC TRANSMISSION DIPSTICK MARK-
INGS
A. Transmission hot, top up to upper mark on HOT side of
   dipstick.
B. Transmission cold, top up to upper mark on COLD side of
   dipstick.

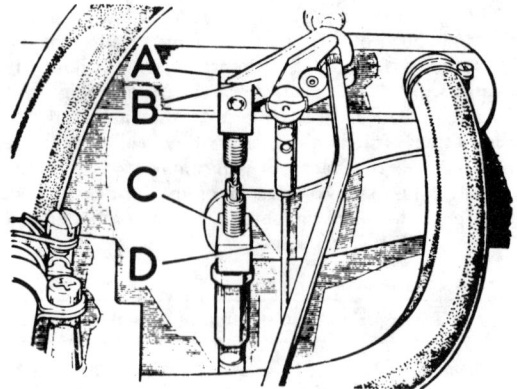

Fig.6.32. DOWNSHIFT VALVE CABLE—ENGINE END

A Clevis for inner cable	C Fixing for outer cable
B Lever for coupling shaft	D Bracket for outer cable

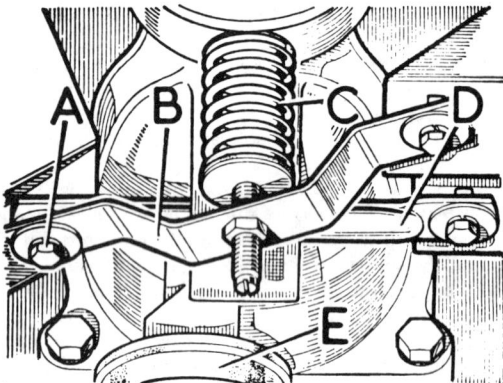

Fig.6.33. REAR ENGINE MOUNTING (CARS FITTED WITH
AUTOMATIC TRANSMISSION)

A Bolt fixing rear engine mounting	mounting
B Support crossmember	D Shaft for rear engine mounting
C Spring for rear engine	E Mounting rubber for front exhaust pipe

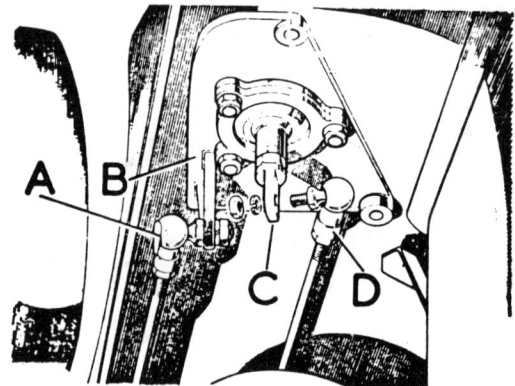

Fig.6.34. SELECTOR LINKAGE RODS

A Tie rod	C Selector lever
B Pivot housing	D Operating rod

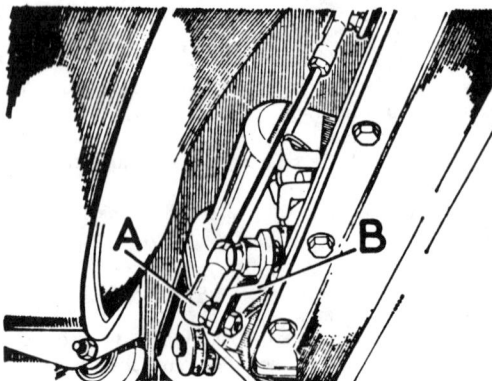

Fig.6.35. LOWER CONTROL ROD
A Lower control rod   B Selector lever - lower

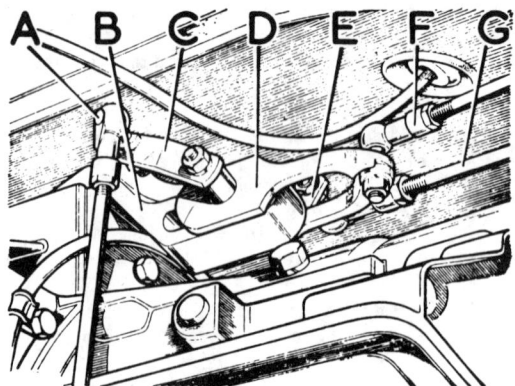

Fig.6.36. GEAR LINKAGE COMPENSATOR BRACKET

A Lower control rod	E Selector lever and shaft
B Compensator bracket	F Tie-rod
C Selector lever-upper	G Control rod
D Compensator block	

18. Selector Linkage — Adjustment

1. It is important that the selector linkage is adjusted if it has been disturbed due to automatic transmission unit removal or the fitting of new parts.
2. The component parts of the linkage, together with the important dimensions are shown in Fig.6.37. Check and adjust the length of each rod until the dimensions indicated in the illustration compare with those of the actual linkages. The dimensions are taken between the centres of the ball joints.
   The control rod length should be 18½ inches.
   The tie-rod length should be 13½ inches.
   The vertical rod length should be $7^{15}/16$ inches.
3. Apply the handbrake and place the selector in the 'N' position.
4. Refer to Fig.6.35 and Fig.6.38, and adjust the lower control rod to give the final adjustment. Make sure that the ball joint can be reconnected to the selector lever WITHOUT strain.
5. Finally check the quadrant gating in all the selector positions making sure that the linkage does not over-ride the transmission detent.

19. Starter Inhibitor/Reverse Light Switch — Removal, Replacement & Adjustment

1. To gain access to the switch, remove the carburetter installation heat shield and the front exhaust pipe.
2. Make a note of the electrical cable connections on the switch and then disconnect the terminals from the switch.
3. Using a small open-ended spanner slacken the switch locknut and unscrew the switch from the transmission case.
4. Refitting is the reverse sequence to removal. 'It will, however, be necessary to adjust the switch as detailed in the subsequent paragraphs. DO NOT refit the carburetter installation heat shield or the exhaust pipe until the switch has been correctly adjusted.
5. Move the selector lever to position 'D2', 'D1' or 'L' and working under the car disconnect the four leads from the switch, having first made a note of their location.
6. Slacken the switch locknut and undo but do not remove the switch.
7. Connect a 12-volt test lamp and battery circuit across the two reverse light terminals (C), Fig.6.39. Gradually screw in the switch until the light goes out. Make a pencil mark on the switch and casing.
8. Disconnect the test lamp circuit from the reverse terminals and re-connect them to the starter inhibitor terminal (D), Fig.6.39. The test lamp bulb should now be off.
9. Screw the switch in approximately one turn until the test lamp bulb ignites. Make a new mark on the transmission case opposite to the pencil mark on the switch.
10 Disconnect the test lamp circuit. Unscrew the switch until the switch pencil mark is in the mid-way position between the two previously made marks on the casing.
11 Tighten the locknut and connect all four cables to the switch cable.
12 Re-connect the front exhaust pipe and the carburetter installation heat shield.
13 Chock the wheels and apply the handbrake firmly. Test that the starter only operates when the selector lever is at the 'P' or 'N' position.

20. Downshift Valve Cable Adjustment

Before the cable is adjusted it is necessary to confirm that it is the cable that is maladjusted and not some other fault. Generally, if difficulty is experienced in obtaining downshift in the 'kick-down' position at just below 31 mph, it is an indication that the outer cable is short. If there is a bumpy or delayed shift at low throttle openings it is an indication the outer cable is too long.

During production of the car, the adjustment is set by a crimped stop on the carburetter end of the inner cable and it is unusual for this setting to change except at high mileages when the inner cable can stretch. To adjust proceed as follows:—
1. Apply· the handbrake firmly and chock the front wheels for safety reasons.
2. Run the engine until it reaches normal operating temperature. Adjust the engine idle speed to approximately 500 rpm with the selector in the 'D2' or 'D1' position.
3. Stop the engine and with an open ended spanner slacken the locknut and adjust the outer cable control to the crimped stop on the inner cable. Should the stop have been moved or be loose, it will be necessary to remove the transmission sump pans.
4. Reset the engine idle to normal speed with the selector in the 'N' position. Stop the engine.
5. Wipe the area around the drain plug and sump. Place a clean container of at least 8 pints capacity under the pan drain plug. Undo the plug and allow the oil to drain into the container.
6. Undo and remove the 15 sump pan retaining bolts and spring washers. Take care not to damage the joint between the transmission casing and the sump pan.
7. Refer to Fig.6.40, and check that the position of the downshift cam is in the idling position as shown in the illustration.
8. Adjust the length of the outer cables so as to remove all the slack from the inner cables.
9. Again refer to Fig.6.40, and check the position of the downshift cam with the throttle pedal in the 'kick-down' position as shown in the illustration.
10 Refit the sump pan joints, sump pan and retaining bolts with spring washers. Tighten the bolts in a diagonal pattern.
11 Refill the transmission with correct grade hydraulic fluid or use the fluid that was drained originally if it is clean with no streaks showing signs of contamination.

21. Automatic Transmission — Modified Type

A modified system of selection and operation is fitted to the later produced cars, whereby the selection quadrant has positions marked as follows:— 'P', 'R', 'N', 'D', '2', '1'.

This allows manual control over both up and down changes.

Fitted to the selector lever is a button which must be depressed to allow selector lever movement except between positions 'D' and '2' and also from '1' to '2' or 'D', or from 'R' to 'N'. Movement of the selector lever to 'P', 'R', and 'N' is as on the early type of transmission.

The following points should be noted about a slight difference in driving technique:—
1. 'D' position. This is used for all normal driving conditions and the 'kick-down' is also available to engage second speed between 30 and 55 mph. It should hold up to a maximum speed of 70 mph. If the accelerator pedal is depressed into the 'kick-down' position at speeds below 30 mph first speed should be engaged and held up to a speed of 40 mph.
2. '2' position. With the selector in the '2' position and the car stationary, the car will start in second speed and remain in this speed until the selector lever is moved. If 'D' is selected and then moved to the '2' position, second speed will be engaged and will be held, with either 'D or '1' position selected. NOTE: Do not select a lower gear when the car is travelling above 70 mph as this will cause the engine to overspeed resulting in possible mechanical damage. If the '2' position is selected with the car ascending a hill the car may be stopped and the brake pedal released without fear of the car rolling back down the hill.
3. '1' position. The transmission shifts into first speed and will then remain in this speed until the selector lever is moved regardless of road speed or position of the accelerator pedal.
4. Tow starting. It is not possible to push or to start a car fitted with the later type of automatic transmission.
5. Recovery towing. The car must not be towed for more than ½

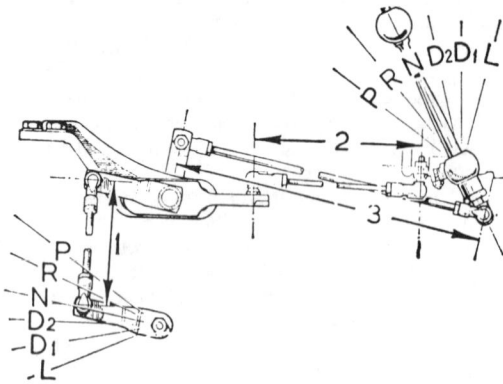

Fig.6.37. SELECTOR LINKAGE ROD
1 Vertical rod 7.15/16 inch
2 Tie rod 13½ inch
3 Control rod 18½ inch

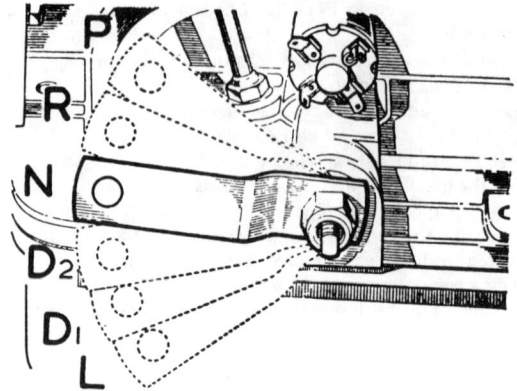

Fig.6.38. Selector lever positions on the side of the transmission unit.

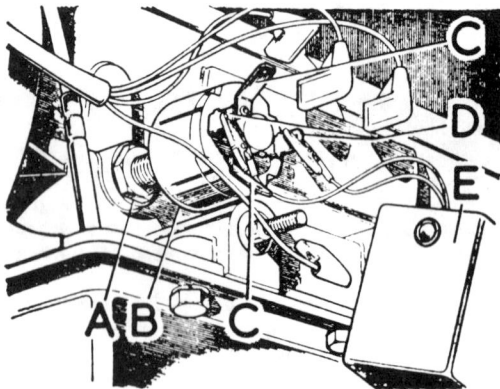

Fig.6.39. ADJUSTMENT OF INHIBITOR SWITCH
A Switch locknut   D Engine isolation terminals
B Starter inhibitor switch E Test lamp
C Reverse light terminals

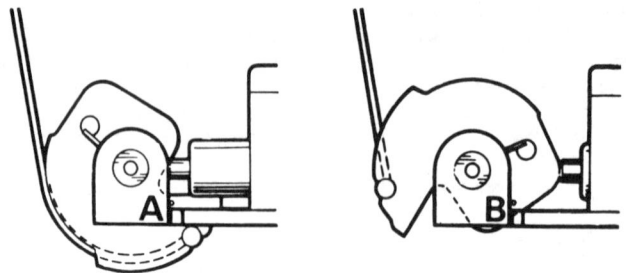

Fig. 6.40. Downshift valve cable adjustment (Borg-Warner)
A Idling position
B Kickdown position

mile without disconnecting the propeller shaft or lifting the rear wheels clear of the road.

22. Automatic transmission (early type) - fault finding

As has been mentioned elsewhere in this Chapter, no service repair work to the automatic transmission should be considered due to the complexity of its design and the need for specialist knowledge. A table and fault diagnosis procedure is given in this Chapter so that if a fault should appear the owner can carry out a little diagnostic work to show the area in which the fault could be existant, and possibly alleviate the fear of expensive repair.

Stall Test Procedure

The function of a stall test is to determine that the torque converter and gearbox are operating satisfactorily.
1. Check the condition and state of tune of the engine. An engine which is not developing full power will affect the stall test reading.
2. Allow the engine and transmission to reach normal operating temperatures.
3. Connect a tachometer to the engine.
4. Chock the wheels and apply the hand and foot brake.
5. Select the 'L' position, and depress the throttle to the 'kick-down' position. Note the reading on the tachometer which should be between 2,000 and 2,500 rpm. If the reading is down to between 1,300 and 1,600 rpm the engine requires tuning. However, if the stall speed is below 1,200 rpm suspect the converter for stator slip in which case a new torque converter must be fitted. NOTE: Do not carry out a stall test for longer than 10 seconds, otherwise the transmission will become overheated.

Converter Diagnosis

Inability to start on steep gradients, combined with poor acceleration from rest and low stall speeds (1,200 rpm), indicates that the converter stator uni-directional clutch is slipping. This condition permits the stator to rotate in an opposite direction to the impeller and turbine, and torque multiplication cannot occur.

Poor acceleration in third gear above 30 mph and reduced maximum speed, indicates that the stator uni-directional clutch has seized. The stator will not rotate with the turbine and impeller, and the 'fluid flywheel' phase cannot occur. This condition will also be indicated by excessive overheating of the transmission although the stall speed will be correct.

Static Test Procedure

1. Refer to Section 15 of this Chapter and check the automatic transmission unit fluid level. Top up as necessary.
2. Chock the wheels and apply the handbrake firmly.
3. The temperature of the fluid should not exceed $110^{\circ}C$ so if this test is following the previous stall test procedure allow the temperature to drop.
4. Check that the starter motor only operates in the 'P' and 'N' selector lever positions and NOT in 'D^1', 'D^2', 'L' and 'R' positions.

5. Check that the reverse light comes on when 'I' is selected. DO NOT leave the driving seat, but check by reflection or with the help of an assistant.
6. Return the selector to the 'N' position and check that when the engine speed is increased there is no tendency for the engine to drive the car.
7. With the foot off the accelerator pedal move the selector lever as follows:– 'N' – 'D^1'; 'N' – 'D^2'; 'N' – 'L' and finally 'N' – 'R'. At each movement of the selector lever a definite engagement of the transmission should be felt.

Road Test Procedure

It is recommended that these tests be carried out on a long straight road free of too much traffic. Then proceed as follows:—
1. With the engine and transmission at normal operating temperature move the selector to the 'D^1' position and start from rest using light accelerator pedal pressure. Gently accelerate and it should be noted that the transmission should change from 1 to 2 at approximately 6–10 mph and then from 2 to 3 at approximately 11–17 mph. Stop the car.
2. With the selector still in the 'D^1' position, press the accelerator pedal hard so as to reach full throttle position as soon as possible. The transmission should now change from 1 to 2 at 26–39 mph and then from 2 to 3 at 43–58 mph.
3. Under 'kick-down' conditions with the selector lever still in 'D^1' position, the transmission should change from 2 to 1 at 37–45 mph and from 3 to 2 at about 62–76 mph. Stop the car.
4. With the selector lever still in the 'D^1' position and the car travelling at 25 mph in top gear with light accelerator pedal pressure, the transmission should not change down at 'kick-down'. Now increase the speed to 40 mph and depress the accelerator pedal to 'kick-down' and the transmission should change to 2 speed. Next release the accelerator and the transmission should change up.
5. Slow down to 20 mph with the selector in 'D^1' and light accelerator pedal pressure, then press the accelerator pedal to the 'kick-down' position and the transmission should change to first speed. Release the accelerator pedal and the transmission should change up to third speed. Stop the car.
6. Select 'D^1' or 'D^2' and drive at 30 mph in third speed. Move the selector 'L' and the transmission should change to second and give engine braking assistance. Slow down and stop by depressing the brake pedal. Under 18 mph the transmission should change to first with a noticeable increase in braking assistance.
7. With the selector still in 'L' position depress the accelerator pedal and increase the car speed to 30 mph. Close the throttle and it should be observed that the transmission does not change up.
8. Now travelling at 30 mph down a hill move the selector to the 'N' position and then switch off the ignition. Allow the car to coast. When the speed drops to 30 mph switch on the ignition and the engine should re-start through the transmission.
9. Drive the car to a steep hill and stop. Select 'P' and with the car facing either uphill or downhill the car should not move.
10 Finally move the selector to 'R' with the car stationary. Release the brakes and reverse uphill using full throttle. There should be no noise or signs of slip from the transmission.

23. Automatic Transmission (modified later type) — Fault Diagnosis

Stall Test Procedure

The function of a stall test is to determine that the torque converter and gearbox are operating satisfactorily.

1. Check the condition of the engine. An engine which is not developing full power will affect the stall test readings.
2. Allow the engine and transmission to reach correct working temperatures.
3. Connect the tachometer to the vehicle.
4. Chock the wheels and apply the handbrake and footbrake.
5. Select L or R and depress the throttle to the 'kick-down' position. Note the reading on the tachometer which should be 1,800 r.p.m. If the reading is below 1,000 r.p.m. suspect the converter for stator slip. If the reading is down to 1,200 r.p.m. the engine is not developing full power. If the reading is in excess of 2,000 r.p.m. suspect the gearbox for brake band or clutch slip.

NOTE: Do not carry out a stall test for a longer period than 10 seconds, otherwise the transmission will become overheated.

Converter Diagnosis

Inability to start on steep gradients, combined with poor acceleration from rest and low stall speed (1,000 r.p.m.), indicates that the converter stator uni-directional clutch is slipping. This condition permits the stator to rotate in an opposite direction to the impeller and turbine, and torque multiplication cannot occur.

Poor acceleration in third gear above 30 m.p.h. and reduced maximum speed, indicates that the stator unidirectional clutch has seized. The stator will not rotate with the turbine and impeller and the 'fluid flywheel' phase cannot occur. Ths condition will also be indicated by excessive overheating of the transmission although the stall speed will be correct.

Road Test Procedure

1. Check that the engine will only start with the selector lever in P or N and that the reverse lights operate only in R.
2. Apply the handbrake and with the engine idling select N–D, N–R and N–L. Engagement should be positive.
3. With the transmission at normal running temperature, select D, release the the brakes, and accelerate with minimum throttle. Check 1–2 and 2–3 shift speeds and quality of change.
4. At a minimum road speed of 30 m.p.h. select N and switch off ignition. Allow the road speed to drop to approximately 28 m.p.h. switch on the ignition, select D and the engine should start.
5. Stop the vehicle, select D and re-start, using 'full throttle'. Check 1–2 and 2–3 shift speeds and quality of change.
6. At 25 m.p.h. apply 'full throttle'. The vehicle should accelerate in third gear and should not downshift to second.
7. At a maximum of 57 m.p.h. 'kickdown' fully. The transmission should downshift to second.
8. At a maximum of 31 m.p.h. in third gear 'kickdown' fully. The transmission should downshift to first gear.
9. Stop the vehicle, select D and re-start using 'kickdown'. Check the 1–2 and 2–3 shift speeds.
10 At 40 m.p.h. in third gear, select L and release the throttle. Check 2–3 downshift and engine braking.
11 With L still engaged stop the vehicle and accelerate to over 25 m.p.h. using 'kickdown'. Check for slip, 'sqawk' and absence of upshifts.
12 Stop the vehicle and select R. Reverse using 'full throttle' if possible. Check for slip and clutch 'sqawk'.
13 Stop the vehicle on a gradient. Apply the handbrake and select P. Check the parking pawl hold when the handbrake is released. Turn the vehicle around and repeat the procedure. Check that the selector lever is held firmly in the gate in P.

Fault Finding Chart - Standard Gearbox

Symptom	Reason/s	Remedy
Weak or ineffective synchromesh General wear	Synchronising cones worn, split or damaged.	Dismantle and overhaul gearbox. Fit new gear wheels and synchronising cones.
	Baulk ring synchromesh dogs worn, or damaged.	Dismantle and overhaul gearbox. Fit new baulk ring synchromesh.
Jumps out of gear General wear or damage	Broken gearchange fork rod spring.	Dismantle and replace spring.
	Gearbox coupling dogs badly worn.	Dismantle gearbox. Fit new coupling dogs.
	Selector fork rod groove badly worn	Fit new selector fork rod.
	Selector fork rod securing screw and locknut loose.	Remove side cover, tighten securing screw and locknut.
Excessive noise Lack of maintenance	Incorrect grade of oil in gearbox or oil level too low.	Drain, refill, or top up gearbox with correct grade of oil.
	Bush or needle roller bearings worn or damaged.	Dismantle and overhaul gearbox. Renew bearings.
	Gearteeth excessively worn or damaged.	Dismantle, overhaul gearbox. Renew gearwheels.
	Laygear thrust washers worn allowing excessive end play.	Dismantle and overhaul gearbox. Renew thrust washers.
Excessive difficulty in engaging gear Clutch not fully disengaging	Clutch pedal adjustment incorrect.	Adjust clutch pedal correctly.

Chapter 7 Propeller shaft and universal joints

Contents

Specifications

Type	Hardy Spicer, open one piece propeller shaft type 1310
Nominal length	$45^{1}/16$ inch (face to face)
Journal bearings	Pre-packed needle roller

Torque Wrench Setting

Flange nuts	30 lb/ft. (4 m.Kg.)

1. General Description

Drive is transmitted from the gearbox to the final drive extension housing flange by means of a finely balanced tubular propeller shaft. Fitted at each end of the shaft is a universal joint, which allows for vertical movement of the rear axle. Each universal joint comprises a four-legged centre spider, four-needle roller bearings and two yokes. Fore and aft movement of the rear axle is absorbed by a sliding spline at the front of the propeller shaft which slides over a mating spline on the rear of the front universal joint splined sleeve.

All models are fitted with sealed type universal joint yoke bearings, but the splined sleeve has a grease nipple which must be lubricated every 5,000 miles.

The propeller shaft is a relatively simple component and to overhaul and repair is fairly easy.

2. Propeller Shaft -- Removal & Replacement

1. Jack up the rear of the car and position on firmly based axle stands located at the body jacking points. Alternatively, position the rear of the car over a pit or on a ramp.
2. If the rear of the car is jacked up always supplement the jack with supporting axle stands or blocks so that danger is minimised should the jack collapse.
3. If the rear wheels are off the ground, place the car in gear, or put the handbrake on to ensure that the propeller shaft does not turn when an attempt is made to loosen the nuts securing the propeller shaft universal joint flanges to the rear of the gearbox and to the final drive extension shaft flange.
4. The propeller shaft is carefully balanced to fine limits and it is important that it is replaced in exactly the same position it was in prior to its removal. Scratch a mark on the propeller shaft and mating flanges to ensure accurate refitting when the time comes for reassembly.
5. Undo and remove the four nuts and bolts which hold the flange of the propeller shaft to the flange on the final drive extension shaft.
6. Push the propeller shaft forwards and lower the rear end of the

propeller shaft and place on the floor.
7. Undo and remove the four nuts which hold the flange of the propeller shaft to the flange on the rear of the gearbox. The bolts are a press fit into the gearbox mainshaft flange so they should be left in place.
8. Push the propeller shaft rearwards and lift the propeller shaft away from the underside of the car.
9. Replacement of the propeller shaft is a reversal of the above procedure. Ensure that the mating mark scratched on the mating flanges line up correctly.

3. Universal Joints -- Inspection & Repair

1. Wear in the needle roller bearings is characterised by vibration in the transmission, clonks' on taking up the drive, and in extreme cases of lack of lubrication, metallic squeaking and ultimately grating and shrieking sounds as the bearings break up.
2. It is easy to check if the needle roller bearings are worn with the propeller shaft in position, by trying to turn the shaft with one hand, the other hand holding the flange on the final drive extension shaft when the rear universal joint is being checked, and the front half coupling when the front universal joint is being checked. Any movement between the propeller shaft and the front and rear half couplings is indicative of considerable wear. If worn, the old bearings and spiders will have to be discarded and a repair kit, comprising new universal joint spiders, bearings, oil seals, and retainers purchased. Check also by trying to lift the shaft and noticing any movement in the joints.
3. Examine the propeller shaft splined sleeve and propeller shaft splines for wear. Also check if the yokes are badly worn. If wear is evident, an exchange propeller shaft must be fitted. It is not possible to fit oversize bearings and journals to the trunnion bearing holes.

4. Universal Joints -- Dismantling

1. Clean away all traces of dirt and grease from the circlips located on the ends of the bearing cups, and remove the clips by pressing their open ends together with a pair of pointed pliers or circlip

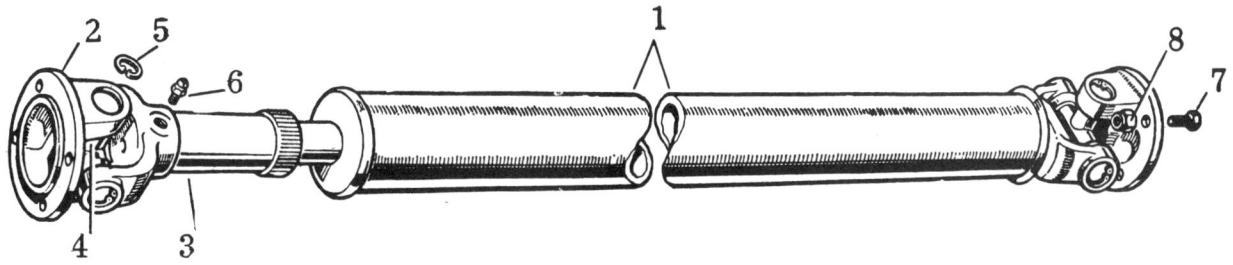

Fig.7.1. PROPELLER SHAFT & UNIVERSAL JOINTS — EXPLODED VIEW

1 Propeller shaft assembly	3 Sleeve yoke	5 Circlip for journal	7 Bolt
2 Flange yoke	4 Journal	6 Grease nipple for sleeve yoke	8 Self locking nut

4.1

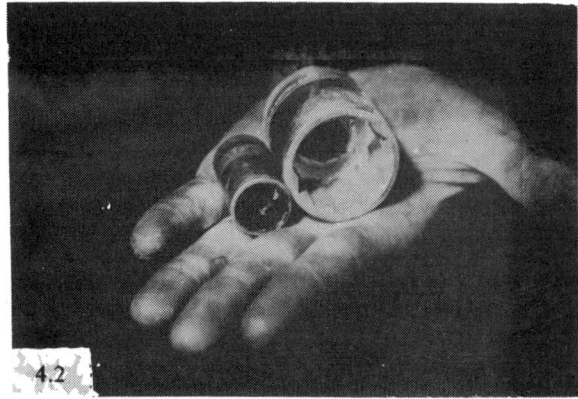

4.2

4.3

4.4

4.5

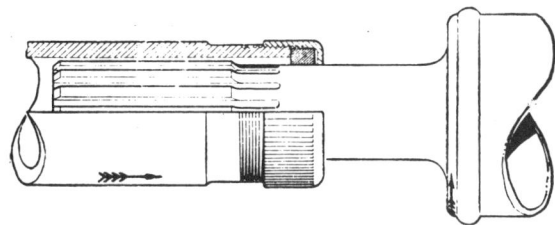

Fig.7.2. Sliding joint alignment arrows.

pliers (photo) and lever them out with a screwdriver. NOTE: If they are difficult to remove, tap the bearing cup face resting on top of the spider with a mallet which will ease the pressure on the circlip.

2. Take off the bearing cups on the propeller shaft yoke. To do this select two sockets from a socket spanner set, one large enough to fit completely over the bearing cup and the other smaller than the bearing cup (photo).

3. Open the jaws of the vice and with the sockets opposite each other and the universal joint in between, tighten the vice and so force the narrower socket to move the opposite cup partially out of the yoke into the larger socket (photo).

4. Remove the cup with a pair of pliers. Remove the opposite cup, and then free the yoke from the propeller shaft (photo).

5. To remove the remaining two cups, now repeat the instructions given in paragraph 3, or use a socket and hammer as illustrated (photo).

6. To separate the splined sleeve from the propeller shaft, undo the knurled collar and withdraw the splined sleeve from the propeller shaft.

5. Universal Joints — Reassembly

1. Thoroughly clean out the yokes and journals.

2. Fit new oil seals and retainers onto the spider journals, place the spider onto the propeller shaft yoke, and assemble the needle rollers in the bearing races with the assistance of some thick grease. Fill each bearing about a third full with Castrolease LM or similar, and fill the grease holes in the journal spider making sure all air bubbles are eliminated.

3. Refit the bearing cups onto the spider and tap the bearings home so they lie squarely in position. Replace the circlips.

4. Check the felt seal within the knurled collar and if it shows signs of leaking or damage fit a new seal.

5. Align the arrow on the propeller shaft with the arrow on the sliding yoke as shown in Fig.7.2, and fit the two parts together. Screw the knurled collar onto the sliding yoke and lubricate the splines by applying a grease gun to the grease nipple in the sliding yoke.

Chapter 8 Rear axle

Contents

Specifications

Type	Hypoid
Ratio	3.54 : 1
Capacity	2½ Imperial pints (3 US pints, 1.5 litres)
Backlash (crown wheel to pinion)	.005 to .008 in (0.12 to 0.20 mm)
Crown wheel bearing pre-load	.003 to .005 in (0.07 to 0.12 mm)
Pinion bearing pre-load (2000 models)	9 to 14 lb/in. (10 to 16 cm/kg)
Pinion bearing pre-load (2200 models)	8 to 16 lb/in. (9 to 20 cm/kg))
Pinion height (nose of pinion to crown wheel axis)	1.990 in. (50.5 mm)
Hub bearing pre-load	5 to 10 lb. (2.2 to 4.5 kg)
Pinion housing and pinion housing cover clearance (2000 models) ...	.003 to .005 in. (0.07 to 0.12 mm)
Pinion housing and pinion housing cover clearance (2200 models) ...	.005 to .010 in. (0.12 to 0.25 mm)
Brake disc run-out	Maximum .007 in. at 10 in. (0.17 mm at 254 mm)
Dunlop handbrake pads to disc minimum clearance	.002 in. (0.05 mm)

Torque Wrench Settings	lb/ft.	Kgm.
Crown wheel bolts (5/16 in.)	25	3.5
Crown wheel bolts (3/8 in.)	45	6.2
Pinion nut	75	10
Drive shaft flanges to disc bolts	68	9.3
On later models	85	11.9
Bearing housing to pinion housing bolts	30	4
Cover to pinion housing bolts — 5/16 inch nuts	15	2
3/8 inch nuts	30	4
Extension housing to pinion housing bolts	30	4
Brake callipers to bearing housing,bolts	60	8.5
Inspection cover to pinion housing, bolts	8	1
Coupling flange to extension shaft, bolts	35	4.9
Hub to De Dion tube bolts	20	2.7
Panhard rod to final drive fixing	30	4

1. General Description

The hypoid final drive and differential unit is rubber mounted to the underside of the car body by means of a crosswise mounting bracket which is part of the De Dion rear suspension.

The final drive casing comprises two parts which are bolted together. Each half casing has a detachable bearing retainer which also acts as an end cover. Located on the right-hand casing is an extension in which is placed the final drive pinion running in two taper roller bearings. Attached to the front end of the final drive pinion housing is an extension shaft which transmits the drive of the relatively short propeller shaft to the drive pinion. The extension shaft is located at its rear end by means of a splined femal which engages with the externally splined drive pinion shaft. At the front end it is supported in a single ball bearing located in the forward end of the extension housing. A flange is splined to the forward end of the shaft and this acts as a coupling to the rear universal joint of the propeller shaft.

Fitted to the front end of the pinion extension housing is a special harmonic damper which keeps transmission noise to a minimum.

The front end of the extension housing is attached to the underside of the car by a special rubber cushioned mounting bracket.

Attached to each differential side gear by means of splines is a two flanged half shaft, each being supported by a single ball bearing which is situated in the detachable bearing retainer. The latter also acts as an anchor for the calliper units of the inboard disc brakes which are fitted to either side of the final drive unit.

It should be noted that on cars produced with final drive units having a suffix D and onwards incorporated in the number, final drive units of the 401 series as opposed to the 400 series were modified to incorporate the Girling type braking system.

The main advantage of mounting the final drive unit to the underside of the body is to reduce the unsprung weight, therefore contributing to the road holding and general comfort of the driver and passengers.

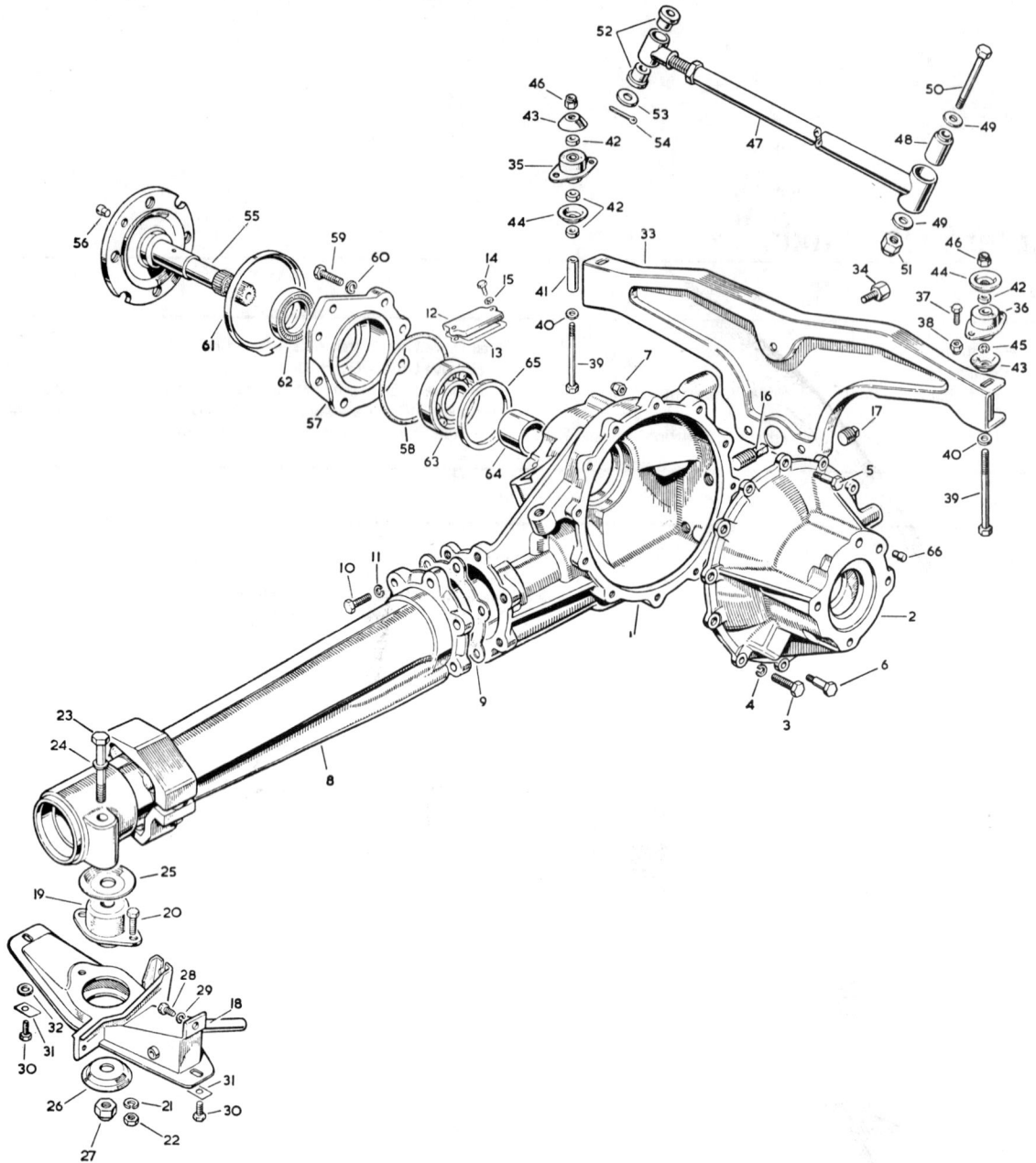

Fig.8.1. FINAL DRIVE CASING COMPONENT PARTS

1 Housing for pinion and drive shaft
2 Cover for pinion and drive shaft housing
3 Set bolt
4 Spring washer
5 Fitting bolt, top
6 Fitting bolt, bottom
7 Self-locking nut
8 Extension case and damper for final drive
9 Joint washer for extension case
10 Set bolt
11 Spring washer
12 Inspection cover for pinion housing
13 Joint washer for inspection cover
14 Set bolt
15 Spring washer
16 Filler plug
17 Drain plug
18 Mounting bracket, front, for final drive
19 Flexible mounting, front, for final drive
20 Set bolt
21 Spring washer
22 Nut
23 Bolt
24 Special washer, flat
25 Special washer, coned
26 Plain washer
27 Self-locking nut
28 Set bolt
29 Spring washer
30 Set bolt
31 Tab washer
32 Plain washer
33 Mounting bracket, rear, for final drive
34 Special countersunk bolt fixing rear mounting bracket
35 Flexible mounting, RH rear, for final drive
36 Flexible mounting, LH rear, for final drive
37 Bolt
38 Self-locking nut
39 Bolt
40 Plain washer
41 Distance piece
42 Distance washer
43 Coned washer
44 Dished washer
45 Spring washer
46 Self-locking nut
47 Rear stabiliser rod assembly
48 Bush for rear stabiliser rod
49 Thrust washer for rear stabiliser rod
50 Bolt
51 Self-locking nut
52 Rubber bush fixing rod to final drive
53 Plain washer
54 Split pin
55 Differential drive shaft
56 Dowel locating brake disc
57 Bearing housing, RH
58 'O' ring for bearing housing
59 Set bolt
60 Spring washer
61 Oil catcher
62 Oil seal for drive shaft
63 Bearing for drive shaft
64 Thrust collar for bearing
65 Spacer (.255 in.) for drive shaft bearing
66 Dowel, bearing housings to pinion housing and cover

2. Routine Maintenance

Every 5,000 miles clean the area around the combined filler and level plug located at the rear of the unit housing. Undo and remove the plug. Top up with Castrol Hypoy until the oil is level with the bottom of the filler plug hole when the car is standing on level ground. It is important that the unit is not overfilled.

Every 20,000 miles undo and remove the combined filler and level plug and also the drain plug and allow the oil to drain out. Preferably this should be done when the oil is warm. Refit the drain plug and refill with 2½ pints of Castrol Hypoy oil.

The oil level of the De Dion tube of the rear suspension should be checked every 10,000 miles and topped up with Castrol GTX oil until the level of oil is at the bottom of the combined filler/level plug hole. This plug is located at the top centre of the De Dion tube.

It is recommended that every 10,000 miles the rubber boots be inspected for damage or signs of perishing and if evident, new ones fitted.

3. Rear Hub & External Drive Shaft — Removal, Overhaul & Re-Fitting

1. If it is required to overhaul the rear hub it will be necessary to have the use of a press or a large engineer's vice and a selection of suitable packing pieces. Make sure that these are available before commencing work.
2. Remove the wheel trim and slacken the road wheel nuts. Chock the front wheels, jack up the rear of the car (Fig.8.3) and support on axle stands as shown in Fig.8.4. Remove the road wheel nuts and lift away the road wheel.
3. Undo and remove the six bolts and self locking nuts that secure the rear hub bearing housing to the De Dion tube assembly.
4. Undo and remove the four bolts and lock plates that secure the drive shaft flange yoke to the differential drive shaft.
5. The hub and drive shaft assembly may now be lifted away from the underside of the car.
6. Should it be necessary to overhaul the drive shaft journals this is similar to the overhaul of the propeller shaft universal joints and full information will be found in Chapter 7. Note, however, that the journals on the drive shafts are fitted with lip seals which are designed to prevent dirt ingress. Care must be taken in removing and refitting of these seals.
7. To overhaul the rear hub first release the lockwasher from the yoke shaft nut and then undo and remove the yoke retaining nut and lockwasher. A cross sectional view of the hub is shown in Fig.8.5. and an exploded view in Fig.8.6.
8. Withdraw the external drive shaft from the hub assembly.
9. Using either the table of a press or the open jaws of an engineer's vice support the rear hub as shown in Fig.8.7, and with a brass drift and hammer carefully drift the driving flange from the bearing housing.
10 Lift away the collapsible spacer.
11 The inner bearing must next be removed and for this a medium size two leg puller with long flat feet will be required. Locate the feet behind the bearing and with a thrust block in the end of the screw thread, carefully remove the inner bearing.
12 The two oil seals may now be removed from the bearing housing by carefully using a copper drift.
13 Using a suitable sized drift carefully remove the two roller races from the bearing housing noting which way round they are fitted.
14 Using a sharp knife and a little wet or dry paper clean all traces of 'Loctite' from the splines.
15 Inspect the bearings for signs of overheating as indicated by discolouration, and the rollers and tracks for signs of wear or pitting and if suspect obtain new parts. A new collapsible spacer will be required also new oil seals.
16 Using suitably sized drifts carefully press the new roller bearing races into the bearing housing. Make sure that they are the correct

way round and that they are pressed fully home.
17 Insert a new oil seal to the outer side of the outer hub with the lip facing inwards and pack with a little grease.
18 Carefully press the outer roller bearing onto the driving flange making sure that it is the correct way round and that it is pressed fully home.
19 Slide a new collapsible spacer over the driving flange and position the driving flange onto the bearing housing.
20 Place the roller bearing onto the driving flange and with a suitable sized drift drive it on as far as possible.
21 Carefully fit a new oil seal to the inner side of the bearing housing with the lip facing inwards.
22 Thoroughly clean the splines of the yoke shaft using methylated spirits to remove any trace of grease and then sparingly apply Loctite sealant grade AVV.
23 Fit the yoke shaft into the hub assembly.
24 Refit the lockwasher and lightly tighten the nut.
25 If the existing bearings are being re-used mount the hub assembly in a vice as shown in Fig.8.8., and tighten the nut until the new collapsible spacer is just trapped. There should be approximately 0.060 inch endfloat in the assembly.
26 Using a spring balance as will be found in many kitchens note the torque required to rotate the hub by pulling on a piece of string attached to the hub as shown in Fig.8.8.
27 Slowly tighten the nut until the torque required to rotate the hub is between 3 and 8 lbs. above the seal friction reading as taken in the previous paragraph. It is important that care is taken in tightening the nut as the required reading must not be exceeded.
28 When new bearings are being fitted hold the hub assembly in a vice as shown in Fig.8.8, and tighten the nut until the load on the bearings is such that a pull of between 5 and 10 lbs is required to rotate the hub.
29 When the required pre-load has been obtained lock the nut by bending over the lockwasher tab.
30 To refit the hub and external drive shaft assembly, position the assembly onto the De Dion tube whilst at the same time locating the drive shaft flange onto the brake disc and differential drive shaft.
31 Refit the six nuts and bolts that secure the hub bearing housing to the De Dion tube and tighten to a torque wrench setting of 20 lb/ft.
32 Secure the drive shaft flange to the brake disc and differential drive shaft with the four bolts and new locking washers and tighten to a torque wrench setting of 85 lb/ft. Make sure that there is a minimum clearance of 0.010 inch between the ends of the bolts and the oil catcher.
33 Lock the bolts by bending over the locking washers.
34 Refit the road wheel and replace the road wheel nuts.
35 Raise the rear of the car, remove the stands and lower the car. Tighten the road wheel nuts and refit the wheel trim.
36 Do not use the car for a period of 12 hours so that the 'Loctite' can fully cure.

4. Differential Drive Shaft — Removal, Overhaul & Refitting

1. It is first necessary to remove the rear discs and the method for this will depend on the braking system fitted. For Dunlop type brakes follow the subsequent paragraphs but where a Girling system is fitted start at paragraph 15 and proceed to paragraph 27 and then 8 onwards.
2. Remove the wheel trim and slacken the road wheel nuts. Chock the front wheels, jack up the rear of the car and support on axle stands as shown in Fig.8.4. Remove the road wheel nuts and lift away the road wheel.
3. Undo and remove the four bolts and lock plates that secure the flange of the drive shaft to the final drive output flange Expand the De Dion tube and allow the shaft to fall clear.
4. With a pair of pliers straighten the split pin locking the adjuster bolt of the handbrake calliper unit and extract the split pin. Slacken

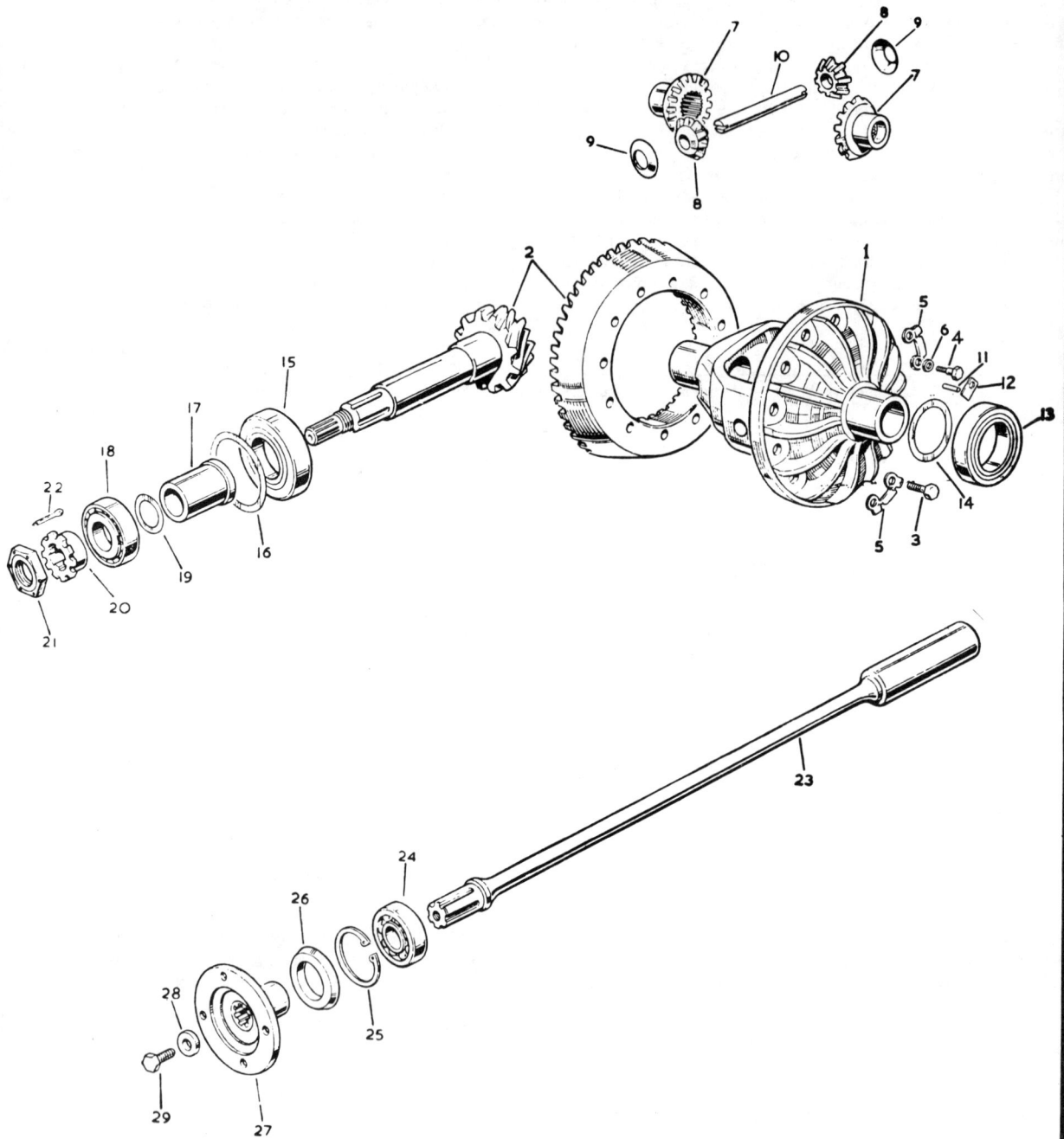

Fig.8.2. DIFFERENTIAL & EXTENSION SHAFT

1 Differential case	8 Differential pinion	15 Bearing, pinion end	23 Extension shaft
2 Crownwheel and hypoid pinion	9 Thrust washer	16 Shim, pinion end	24 Bearing
3 Special bolt	10 Spindle for pinion	17 Spacer	25 Circlip
4 Fitting bolt	11 Locking pin for spindle	18 Bearing, front end	26 Oil seal
5 Double locker	12 Retainer for locking pin	19 Shim, front end	27 Coupling flange
6 Plain washer	13 Bearing for differential	20 Serrated locking collar	28 Plain washer
7 Differential wheel	14 Shim for differential bearing	21 Special locking nut	29 'Wedglock' bolt
		22 Split pin	

off the adjuster bolt and also the outer pad retaining nut. Remove the pad. These parts are shown in Fig.9.7.

5. If the car is fitted with a dowelled disc it will be necessary to remove the outer footbrake pad. To do this undo and remove the nut, washer and bolt, that secures the brake pad keep plate and lift away the plate.

6. Lift out the pads noting to which side they are fitted so that they can be replaced in their original positions.

7. Undo and remove the four bolts that secure the disc to the hub and lift away the disc and any shims that may be placed behind the disc.

8. Remove the connecting pipe from between the callipers and plug the end to prevent leakage. Undo and remove the nut to release the clip on the differential housing bolt. If the right-hand side drive shaft is being removed disconnect the flexible brake hose, and plug to prevent leakage.

9. Next disconnect the clevis pin connecting the automatic adjuster unit to the operating linkage.

10 To stop oil dripping onto the floor place a drip tray under the final drive assembly.

11 Undo and remove the four bolts and spring washers that secure the bearing housing to the pinion housing. It may be necessary to rotate the flange to gain access to the bolts.

12 Withdraw the differential drive shaft and bearing housing complete with the brake calliper and also the 'O' ring if one is fitted.

13 Keep the drive shaft bearing spacer in a safe place as it must be refitted.

14 Undo and remove the two bolts and spring washers and separate the calliper from the housing. Retain the shims for re-use.

15 To remove the Girling type disc raise the rear of the car and remove the road wheel as detailed in paragraph 2.

16 Knock back the lockwasher tab on the forward locker of the pad retainer plate bolts and undo and remove the bolt. Lift away the retainer plate and anti-rattle spring.

17 Swing the top of the inner pad forwards and withdraw the pad towards the rear of the car.

18 Knock back the tabs on the locker at the rear position and slacken the bolt to release the anti-rattle spring tension on the outer pad.

19 Pull the calliper outwards and remove the outer pad from the drag pins and withdraw the pad.

20 Remove the four bolts and lock plates securing the drive shaft flange to the final drive output flange, expand the De Dion tube and allow the shaft to fall clear.

21 Rotate the disc until the dowel holes are parallel with the callipers and ease the disc off the dowels. Lift away the disc.

22 Disconnect the handbrake linkage at the calliper lever. For the left-hand calliper remove the two bolts that secure the bell crank bracket to the differential casing and move the bracket to one side.

23 Remove the stop pin for the handbrake lever and rotate the lever inwards as far as it will go. Secure the lever in position with a piece of string to make sure that it is not accidentally withdrawn. Should this occur the handbrake tappet may drop down so preventing the lever being inserted into its correct position.

24 Using a socket on the spring loaded plug undo and remove the plug and the spring. These may be seen in Fig.8.9.

25 With an Allen key rotate the pivot pin until it is unscrewed from the bearing at the other end.

26 Remove the bearing from the rear of the calliper and push the pivot pin out towards the front of the vehicle. This will release the calliper which may now be suspended out of the way on a piece of string or wire. By using this method it is not necessary to disconnect the hydraulic system.

27 Replace the handbrake lever stop screw so preventing lever displacement and remove the string.

28 Continue removal as detailed in paragraphs 8 to 13 inclusive.

29 To overhaul the differential drive shafts, first remove the bearing spacer from the housing and ensure that it is retained for refitting into the appropriate housing.

30 It should be noted that on early produced models fitted with plain thrust collars, before removing the collar it should be turned off on a lathe until only a thin skin remains. Cut through the skin with a sharp chisel which will allow the remaining portion of the collar to tbe removed by hand.

31 Using a drift of suitable size drive the shaft through the bearing. Do not attempt this operation without reducing the thickness of the collar as otherwise the bearing housing can be irrepairably distorted.

32 Later produced models have a different thrust washer with a machined groove in it. Use a three leg puller and suitable thrust block to remove the collar.

33 The drive shaft should next be drifted or pressed from the bearing housing.

34 Using a suitable sized drift drive out the old oil seal from the bearing housing followed by the bearing.

35 Provided that the oil catcher is not damaged or loose there is no need to remove it.

36 Inspect the bearing for signs of wear, pitting or signs of overheating and if suspect obtain a new one.

37 If the old oil catcher has been removed a new one must be fitted. Carefully tap it into position using a soft wood block making sure that the lip is adjacent to the oil drain hole on the underside of the housing. It should be tapped fully home so that the differential drive shaft is not in contact with it.

38 Apply a little Bostik 1776 to the outside diameter of the new seal and using a drift of suitable size, carefully drive the new seal into position with the lip facing inwards.

39 Smear the oil seal contact circumference of the drive shaft with a little Silicone Compound MS4 to provide lubrication to the oil seal lip.

40 Using an engineer's vice or a press and a drift, press the new bearing into the housing. Next place the bearing and housing over the drive shaft and using a tubular drift drive it fully home.

41 Obtain a modified thrust collar and check that the little breather slots are clean. Place the thrust collar over the differential drive shaft with the small slots facing the bearing face and press home. This could present a little problem because a minimum pressure of two tons will be required. With a large engineer's vice a figure near to this can be obtained otherwise access to a press will be required.

42 To refit the differential drive shaft first fit the original bearing spacer over the bearing and offer the drive shaft assembly to the pinion housing or cover.

43 Before refitting the securing bolts check that there is a clearance of 0.003 to 0.005 between the face of the drive shaft housing and the pinion housing. This clearance is shown in Fig.8.10. If the clearance is too great or not sufficient, adjustment may be made by fitting a spacer of different thickness.

44 Cars fitted with Dunlop brakes proceed in the following manner, otherwise for the Girling braking system refer to paragraph 47.

45 Once the correct clearance has been obtained remove the drive shaft housing to allow for fitment of the brake calliper and the original shims. Secure with two bolts and spring washers and tighten to a torque wrench setting of 60 lb/ft.

46 Refit the assembly to the pinion housing together with an 'O' ring seal if originally fitted. Use Hylomar SQ 32M sealing compound on ball joint faces. Tighten to a torque wrench setting of 30 lb/ft.

47 For cars fitted with Girling brakes refit the drive shaft and bearing housing as detailed previously. The calliper must then be refitted to the housing. Full details of this will be found in Chapter 9, Section 14.

48 For the Dunlop braking system refit the brake disc and packing washers and secure with four bolts. Whilst on the Girling system it will be necessary to rotate the disc and drive shaft until the dowel holes are parallel with the calliper, then ease the disc between the calliper pads and onto the dowels.

49 Using a dial indicator gauge or feeler gauges check the disc run-out at a 10 inch diameter and this should not exceed 0.007 inch otherwise a new disc should be fitted, if there is no dirt between the disc mating face and the hub.

50 On Dunlop braking systems check that the slot between each side of the disc and the calliper slot face does not exceed

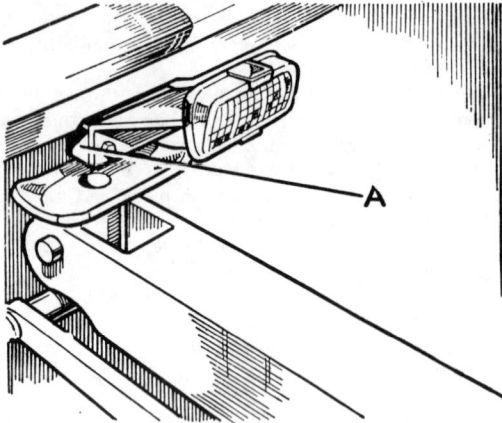

Fig.8.3. REAR JACKING POINT
A. Jacking bracket

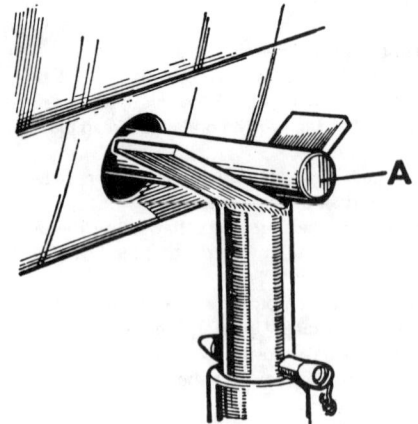

Fig.8.4. CORRECT METHOD OF SUPPORTING BODY ON AXLE STANDS
A. 7/8 inch diameter rod inserted into jacking tube.

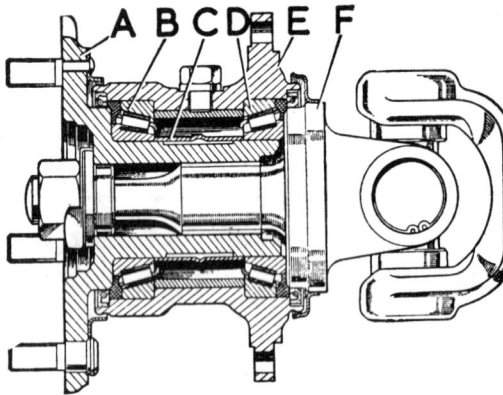

Fig.8.5. CROSS SECTIONAL VIEW OF REAR HUB

A Driving flange for road wheel	D Bearing, inner
B Bearing, outer	E Bearing housing for hub
C Collapsible tube	F Drive shaft for rear hub

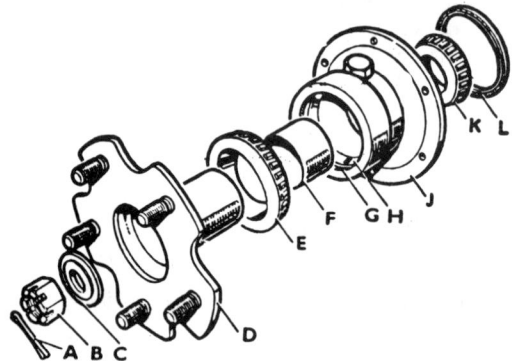

Fig.8.6. EXPLODED VIEW OF REAR HUB

A Split pin	F Collapsible tube
B Castle nut	G Oil seal
C Special washer	H Outer track for bearing
D Driving flange for road wheel	J Bearing housing for hub
E Bearing, outer	K Bearing, inner
	L Oil seal

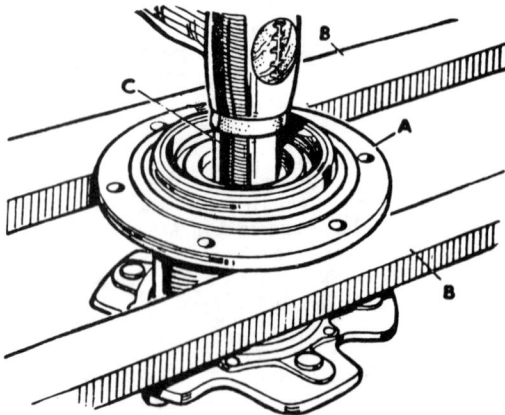

Fig.8.7. REAR HUB DISMANTLING

A Rear hub	C Brass drift
B Metal support blocks	

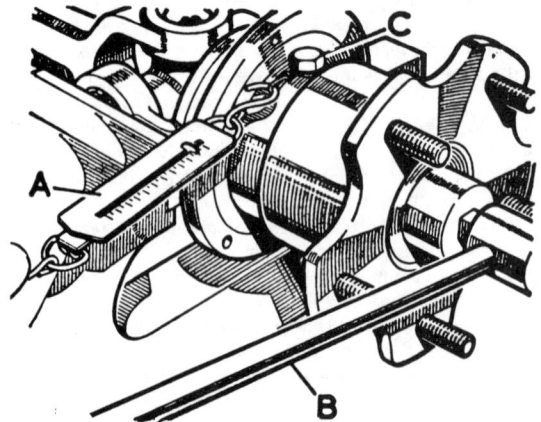

Fig.8.8. DETERMINATION OF REAR HUB BEARING PRE-LOAD

A Spring balance	C String attached to plug and wound around the hub
B Lever attached to socket spanner	

155

0.010 inch. Should any adjustment be necessary alter the number of shims placed between the calliper housing and the bearing housing. For this adjustment it will be necessary to remove the drive shaft bearing housing. Re-tighten the calliper fixing bolts to a torque wrench setting of 60 lb/ft.

51 Replace the outer footbrake and handbrake pads.

52 Any hydraulic pipes that have been previously removed should next be refitted. Make sure that the ends are clean so that there is no possibility of dirt ingress into the hydraulic system.

53 On models fitted with Dunlop brakes replace the washer and split pin on the linkage pivot pin if these were previously disconnected.

54 On models fitted with Girling brakes reconnect the handbrake linkage. Further information will be found in Chapter 9 if required.

55 Undo and remove the four bolts and packing washers that secure the brake disc and place the external drive shaft assembly onto the brake disc.

56 Refit the four bolts with new lock plates that secure the drive shaft flange yoke to the disc and differential drive assembly and tighten these bolts to a torque wrench setting of 85 lb/ft. Ensure that there is a clearance of at least 0.010 inch between the bolts and the oil catcher.

57 To assist removal at a later date the ends of the bolts should be painted with a rust proof paint when finally in position.

58 Refer to Chapter 9, Section 20 and bleed the brake hydraulic system.

59 Replace the road wheel and refit the wheel nuts.

60 Refer to Chapter 9, Section 13, and adjust the handbrake calliper. Refit the adjuster split pin and open the ends.

61 Remove the axle stands and lower the car to the ground. Tighten the wheel nuts fully and refit the wheel trims.

62 Check the level of oil in the final drive unit and top up as necessary. Finally road test the car to ensure satisfactory operation of the drive shaft.

5. Final Drive Unit — Removal & Refitting

1. Remove the rear wheel trims and slacken the wheel nuts. Chock the front wheels, jack up the rear of the car and support on stands as shown in Fig.8.4. Remove the rear wheels.

2. As the propeller shaft is carefully balanced to fine limits it is important that it is refitted to the final drive unit in exactly the same position as it was in prior to its removal. Scratch a mark on the mating flanges of the propeller shaft and final drive extension shaft.

3. Undo and remove the four nuts and bolts which hold the flange of the propeller shaft on the final drive extension shaft.

4. Push the propeller shaft forwards, lower the rear end and place on the floor.

5. Undo and remove the four special bolts and two lockwashers from each side securing the left-hand and right-hand hub drive shafts to the brake discs.

6. On models fitted with Dunlop brakes disconnect the handbrake rod clevis pin at the forward support bracket.

7. On models fitted with Girling brakes disconnect the handbrake cable at the handbrake lever. For further information see Chapter 9, Section 24.

8. Disconnect the brake flexible hose at the right-hand calliper banjo and plug the end to prevent leakage. Wrap the exposed ends in a clean non-fluffy rag to prevent dirt ingress.

9. Slacken the exhaust pipe clamp and re-position so that the forward support bracket bolt is accessible.

10 Undo and remove the one side bolt and spring washer and slacken the two bottom bolts and tab washers that secure the final drive forward mounting bracket.

11 Place the saddle of a garage hydraulic jack and support its weight.

12 On early produced models undo and remove the three bolts and spring washers that secure the final drive assembly to the rear mounting bracket.

13 Carefully draw the rear mounting bracket rearwards so as to clear the filler plug.

14 Now remove the two bolts and tab washers that secure the front mounting bracket. These two bolts were previously slackened.

15 Lower the jack whilst a second person supports the final drive unit on the jack and withdraw from beneath the rear of the car. Lift the unit off the jack.

16 If the unit is to be dismantled wash in paraffin or 'Gunk' and wipe dry.

17 It should be noted that on later produced models special countersunk bolts are used as shown in Fig.8.11. The final drive housing has its fixing bolts countersunk and used in conjunction with a countersunk type bolt. The reason for this is that when the new type of bolt is tightened it bends the final drive rear mounting bracket bolt hole lip into the housing. When using this type of bolt make sure that all the threads are clear of grease or oil and apply a little 'Loctite' sealant grade AVV.

If it is necessary to convert an early produced model to the later type a kit is available for this conversion.

18 The mountings have been mounted from models having serial numbers from 40034642D, 40102305D, 40308255D and 41801038A onwards. These mountings are of Styrene Butadiene rubber and may be fitted to earlier produced models in complete sets only.

19 To refit the final drive unit, first place on the saddle of a garage hydraulic jack and place under the rear of the car.

20 Carefully raise the jack and fit the two bolts and tab washers that secure the front support bracket to the body. Also refit the one side bolt and spring washer.

21 Refit the three bolts and spring washers or the new type countersunk bolts and tighten securely.

22 Raise each hub drive shaft assembly onto the disc brake location and secure with four bolts and two lockwashers. When tight make sure that there is a clearance of at least 0.010 inch between the bolt ends and the oil catcher.

23 Lower the jack and remove from the rear of the car.

24 If the exhaust pipe clamp was disturbed it should be repositioned so that the rubber mounting is not under stress.

25 Reconnect the flexible brake hose to the right-hand brake calliper having first removed the plug and rag.

26 On models fitted with Dunlop brakes, reconnect the handbrake rod clevis at the forward support bracket.

27 On models fitted with Girling brakes refit the cable to the handbrake lever.

28 Refit the propeller shaft to the extension shaft coupling flange in the same position as originally fitted by lining up the previously made marks.

29 It will now be necessary to bleed the brake hydraulic system as detailed in Chapter 9, Section 20.

30 Refit the road wheels and lightly tighten the nuts. Lower the rear end of the car and tighten the wheel nuts fully. Replace the wheel trims.

31 If the final drive unit has been overhauled or the oil drained out it should now be refilled. The capacity is 2½ pints.

6. Final Drive Unit — Overhaul

To dismantle the differential unit several special tools are necessary and without these the job is impossible. Before commencing work the author recommends that this section be studied and the various items not usually found in the home garage be obtained.

1. Undo and remove the self locking nut, plain washers and bolt that secures the front mounting bracket to the extension casing.

2. Refer to Section 4 and remove the handbrake linkage, brake discs and drive shaft assemblies from the final drive unit.

3. Extract the split pin and plain washer that attaches the handbrake linkage to the pivot pin on the pinion housing.

4. Disconnect one end of the hydraulic bridge pipe and remove the clip retaining nut.

5. From each brake calliper, remove the outer footbrake pad. Also remove the split pin and slacken the handbrake adjusting bolts on each calliper unit.

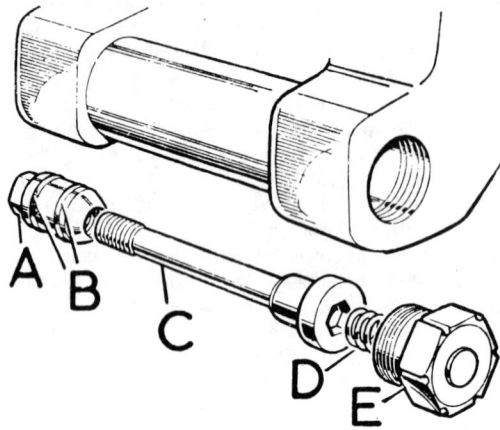

Fig.8.9. CALLIPER PIVOT PIN

A Bearing   D Spring for plug
B Seals for bearing   E Plug
C Pivot pin

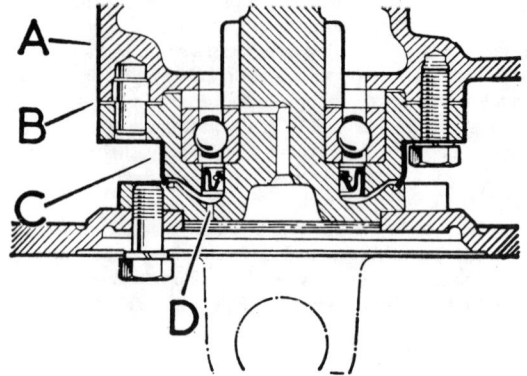

Fig.8.10. CHECKING CLEARANCE BETWEEN DRIVE SHAFT
HOUSING & PINION HOUSING

A Pinion housing   C Drive shaft bearing housing
B Clearance 0.003 to 0.005 in.   D Breather passages

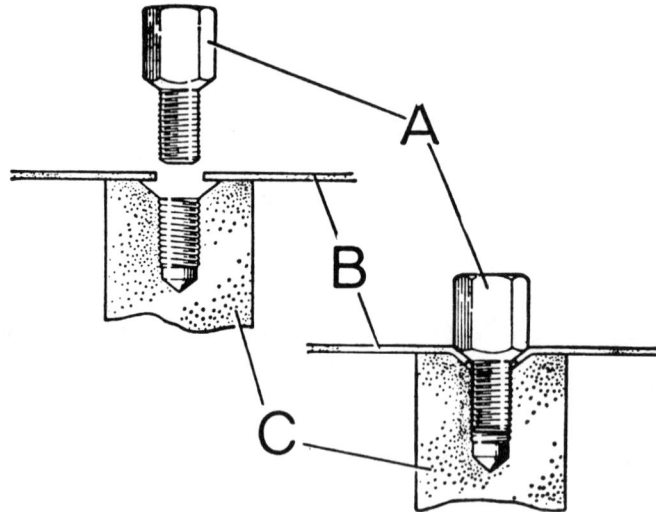

Fig.8.11. THE FITTING OF SPECIAL COUNTERSUNK BOLTS TO FINAL DRIVE REAR MOUNTING

A Countersunk bolt
B Mounting bracket
C Final drive housing

6. Undo and remove the six bolts and spring washers that secure the final drive extension to the pinion and drive shaft housing and separate the two parts.

7. Undo and remove the ten bolts and spring washers that secure the pinion housing cover and lift off the cover.

8. Two bolts with shakeproof washers were fitted from final drive unit number 40003732A otherwise two fitted bolts and self locking nuts are located at the top and bottom of the cover.

9. Lift the crownwheel and differential assembly from the pinion housing.

10 Using a soft metal drift carefully remove the differential races from the pinion housing and cover.

11 Using a pair of pliers extract the split pin locking the pinion nut.

12 Make up a lever using a piece of flat metal about 2 feet long with two bolts inserted, the pitch being the same as the extension shaft drive flange holes and suitably placed so it is possible to fit a spanner onto the nut. Hold the flange with the tool and undo the pinion nut. Remove the nut.

13 Lift away the serrated locking collar and the taper roller bearing. Also remove the pinion, shims and spacing sleeve from the housing. Keep the shims in a safe place so that they can be used during reassembly.

14 Using a soft metal drift remove both the pinion bearing races making sure that the shims under the pinion head bearing race are not damaged.

15 The front bearing race may be removed with a long soft metal drift inserted through the drain and filler plug holes and gently tapping the race circumference.

16 The pinion head roller bearing may next be removed using a three leg puller fitted with flat feet. Lift away the bearing and the adjustment shims. Keep in a safe place for re-use.

17 Again using the three leg puller withdraw the differential bearings from the differential case and retain any shims with the respective bearings.

18 With a flat chisel bend back the tabs of the locking plates and remove the crownwheel bolts. Note the position of the two special fitted bolts. Scratch identification marks on the crownwheel and differential case to ensure they are correctly matched in their original relative positions and separate the crownwheel from the differential case.

19 With a suitable diameter parallel pin punch drift out the differential pinion shaft locating peg.

20 Using a soft metal drift, drive out the differential pinion shaft.

21 Lift out the differential pinions and side wheels together with their fibre thrust washers. From final drive unit number 4003811B the fibre thrust washers were discontinued.

22 Thoroughly wash all parts in paraffin and wipe dry using a non-fluffy rag. Carefully examine all parts for wear, cracks or chips. Examine the races for excessive play or loose rollers in the cages; check that the rollers are not pitted. Inspect the differential pinion thrust face for signs of ridging or scoring and the bearing locations for scoring. If any part is damaged or suspect new parts must be fitted.

23 To reassemble the crownwheel and differential case, if fibre thrust washers were previously used place these in position and insert the differential wheels into the carrier.

24 Place the differential pinions and thrust washers, where applicable into the carrier and insert the spindle the correct way round so it will locate with the locking peg when it is inserted.

25 Check that there is just a slight amount of backlash between the differential pinions and each differential wheel. If the backlash is excessive or not detectable thrust washers of four different thicknesses are available.

26 When the correct setting has been obtained lock the spindle with the spindle locking peg.

27 Locate the two previously made marks on the crownwheel and differential case and refit the crownwheel to the differential case. Screw in the ten bolts with plain washers and lock plates but do not tighten yet.

28 The two special fitted bolts should be placed diagonally opposite

to each other. Tighten the bolts in a diagonal manner using several passes and then tighten fully to a torque wrench setting of 25 lb/ft. Lock the bolts by bending up the locking tab.

29 The outer circumference of an old bearing outer pinion head race track should be ground down until it is an easy sliding fit in the pinion housing. The old bearing should not be badly worn.

30 Using a micrometer or dial indicator gauge compare the width of the slave bearing race against the new race. The difference in width should not exceed 0.008 inch.

31 With either a press or a piece of suitable diameter tube and a hammer position the front pinion bearing race in the pinion housing.

32 Fit the prepared pinion head slave bearing race into the housing but at this stage omitting the shims. Refit the front roller bearing, the slotted locking collar and the pinion nut.

33 Tighten the pinion nut until a force of between 9 and 14 lb/in. is required to rotate the pinion. This may be determined by using a small spring scale or a suitably calculated torque wrench. If the correct tool kit is available the special tool for this job has a part number of 600968.

34 On later produced models the recess for the differential bearing location in both the pinion housing and cover for the pinion housing has been increased in size to permit the differential bearing races to creep round. The reason for this modification is to give a more even distribution of wear on the bearing track.

As a result of this the pinion height gauge had to be modified and the one required for subsequent operating will have to be determined from the details below:

a) Gauge Number 605004. This is a double-ended height gauge and is suitable for both press fit and push fit bearings.

b) Gauge Number 601998. This is designed for push fit bearings and this height gauge will NOT fit the earlier produced differential units.

c) Gauge Number 600299. This is designed for press fit bearings and this height gauge must NOT be used on the later produced differential units with the push fit bearings.

35 Place the correct pinion height gauge (C), Fig.8.14 in the pinion and secure in place.

36 Position the slip gauge (B) on the face of the pinion and press firmly into position. Using a feeler gauge determine the clearance between the height gauge and slip gauge. Make a note of this measurement.

37 Determine the markings on the face of the pinion and referring to the charts detailed below determine the final feeler gauge clearance required between the height gauge and slip gauge. To assist identification of the pinion markings refer to Fig.8.15 and Fig.16.

It will be seen from the illustrations that in addition to the production batch number marked on the face of all pinions, there may also be a pinion height dimension which can be $\pm$ 0.005 inch.

On later produced pinions a further dimension is added and has a prefix letter of H or HD which indicates the 'head depth' which can be from zero to −0.004 inch. These dimensions must be taken into account when setting the pinion height regardless of which type of pinion setting gauge is being used. Where the pinion height has no dimensional marking use the pinion height 'O' column and head depth 'O' on the charts for feeler gauge clearance.

a) This chart is to be used when height gauge numbered 600299 or 601998 is being used.

Final Feeler Gauge Clearance

		in.	in.	in.	in.	in.
Pinion Height Markings	+5	.012	.011	.010	.009	.008
	+4	.011	.010	.009	.008	.007
	+3	.010	.009	.008	.007	.006
	+2	.009	.008	.007	.006	.005
	+1	.008	.007	.006	.005	.004
	0	.007	.006	.005	.004	.003
	−1	.006	.005	.004	.003	.002
	−2	.005	.004	.003	.002	.001
	−3	.004	.003	.002	.001	.000
	−4	.003	.002	.001	.000	.001✳
	−5	.002	.001	.000	.001✳	.002✳
		−4	−3	−2	−1	0

Head depth (H or HD) markings

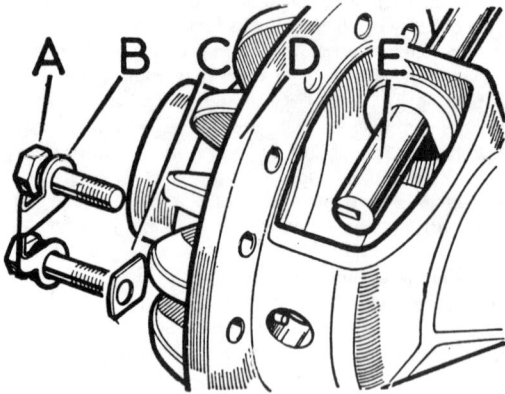

Fig.8.12. THE FITTING OF THE PINION SPINDLE

A Crownwheel fixing bolt plate
B Lock plate D Differential case
C Pinion spindle locking peg E Pinion spindle

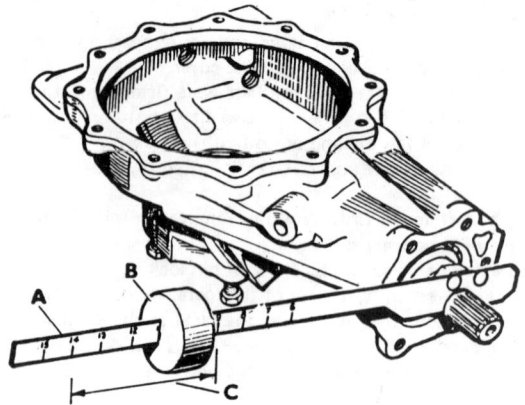

Fig.8.13. CHECKING PINION BEARING PRE-LOAD

A Arm gauge)
B 1 lb. sliding weight) Tool Part Number 600968
C Tolerance 9 to 14 lb/in.)

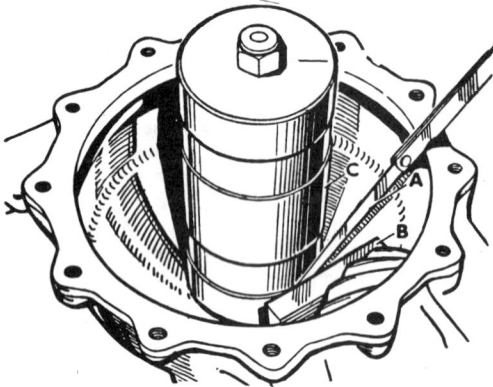

Fig.8.14. PINION HEIGHT CHECK

A Feeler gauge C Pinion height gauge
B Slip gauge

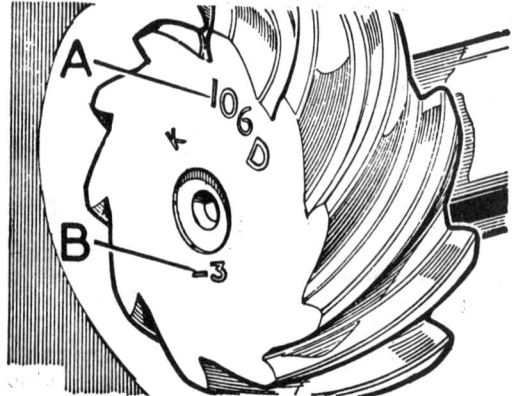

Fig.8.15. PINION HEIGHT MARKINGS

A Batch number B Height dimension ± 0.005 in.

NOTE: This illustration shows the batch number.
−3 pinion height indicates −0.003 in pinion height

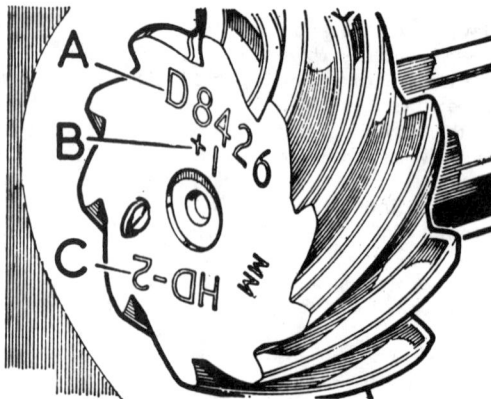

Fig.8.16. PINION HEIGHT & HEAD DEPTH MARKINGS

A Batch number
B Height dimension
C Head depth dimension zero to −0.004 inch

NOTE: This illustration shows the batch number.
+ 1 pinion height indicating + 0.001 inch pinion height.
HD −2 indicates − 0.002 inch head depth.

NOTE: Any pinion marking dimensions falling within the space marked with an asterisk (✱) add the figure shown to the initial measurement taken between height gauge and slip gauge.

b) This chart is to be used when height gauge number 605004 is being used.

		Final Feeler Gauge Clearance				
		in.	in.	in.	in.	in.
	+5	.020	.019	.018	.017	.016
	+4	.019	.018	.017	.016	.015
	+3	.018	.017	.016	.015	.014
	+2	.017	.016	.015	.014	.013
	+1	.016	.015	.014	.013	.012
Pinion Height Markings	0	.015	.014	.013	.012	.011
	−1	.014	.013	.012	.011	.010
	−2	.013	.012	.011	.010	.009
	−3	.012	.011	.010	.009	.008
	−4	.011	.010	.009	.008	.007
	−5	.010	.009	.008	.007	.006
		−4	−3	−2	−1	0
		Head depth (H or HD) markings				

38 From the dimension previously noted subtract the figure previously determined with the feeler gauge from the figure obtained in the chart and the result is the thickness of the shims to be inserted beneath the pinion head race.

39 NOTE: Final drive units produced having a suffix D in the number and before, the pinion height was adjusted by using two shims. From suffix E numbers only one shim was used and shims are available in increments of 0.001 inch between 0.051 and 0.068 inch.

40 Remove the pinion height gauge pinion nut and slotted collar and lift out the pinion assembly.

41 Remove the pinion head slave race and locate the selected shims. Replace the slave race and reassemble the pinion into the pinion housing. Adjust the pre-load to between 9 and 14 lb/in. as detailed in paragraph 33 of this Section.

42 Replace the pinion height gauge and with the clip gauge in position ensure that the clearance between the height gauge and the slip gauge agrees with the figure obtained in the chart with a tolerance of ± 0.001 inch.

43 If any further adjustment is necessary add or subtract the required shim thickness from beneath the pinion head slave race.

44 Remove the gauge and once again withdraw the pinion assembly together with the slave pinion head race. Adjust the value of the shims in accordance with the variation in width of the slave bearing and the new bearing.

45 Drift the new pinion head outer race, together with the selected shims into the pinion housing and put the pinion assembly to one side.

46 Before proceeding further study the following paragraphs to ensure the correct method of working is determined, as applicable to the type of bearings fitted.

47 On models fitted with press fit bearings, locate shims of thickness 0.050 inch on each side of the differential case followed by the slave differential race.

48 Insert the differential assembly into the pinion housing and then place the pinion cover into position.

49 On later produced models with push fit bearings new taper roller bearings should be fitted to each side of the differential case. Then place shims to the value of 0.050 inch into the differential race location in both the pinion housing and cover followed by the outer races of the new bearings.

50 Insert the differential assembly into the pinion housing and then replace the pinion cover but do not fit any securing bolts.

51 Apply a steady pressure to the pinion housing cover and insert two feeler gauges of equal thickness and diagonally opposite to each other. Determine the clearance between the pinion housing cover and pinion housing.

52 This clearance should be 0.003 to 0.005 inch and may only be obtained by altering the value of the shims at the upper position as checked at the pinion cover.

53 Once this clearance has been obtained place the crownwheel and differential assembly to one side, retaining the selected shims carefully.

54 Refit the pinion into the housing, positioning shims to the approximate value of 0.060 inch between the distance collar and the front roller bearing.

55 Tighten the pinion nut to a torque wrench setting of 75 lb/ft.

56 Using the method described in paragraph 33 of this Section check that the pre-load is between 9 and 14 lb/in. This may be adjusted by adding or subtracting shims. When the required setting has been obtained lock the pinion nut with a new split pin.

57 Place the crownwheel assembly into the pinion housing and attach the pinion housing cover holding it in position with four bolts and also the two special fitting bolts all evenly spaced around the cover.

58 It is now necessary to determine the backlash between the crownwheel and pinion and for this a dial indicator gauge and mounting bracket will be required. This is shown in Fig.8.20.

59 Mount the dial indicator gauge with a rod through the pinion hole as shown in Fig.8.20 so that the probe is 1 inch from the centre of the pinion (Dimension B).

60 The backlash when correctly adjusted should be between 0.005 and 0.008 inch. It is controlled by adding or subtracting shims from the pinion housing only. It is important to note that the differential case pre-load must remain constant so shims of identical value must be added or subtracted from the pinion housing cover.

61 Note also that final drive units produced with numbers incorporating suffix E and onwards one shim only is used instead of two or more. The new shims are available in thickness from 0.042 to 0.074 inch in increments of 0.001 inch.

As well as a dimensional change in shim thickness the shims are now fitted behind the outer race of the differential bearing, i.e. in the pinion housing and the cover.

62 On early produced models remove the crownwheel assembly and replace the slave roller races with the new roller races, and check for any bearing height variation with a micrometer or dial indicator gauge. Any slight variation should be adjusted by using thicker or thinner shims as necessary. The crownwheel can then be refitted.

63 Make sure that the faces of both halves of the pinion housing are clean and free of grease or oil and apply a little Hylomar SQ/32M sealing compound to each face and secure with the fixing bolts. Make sure that the two special fitted bolts are in their correct positions as noted during dismantling. Tighten all the bolts in a diagonal manner using several passes finishing up at a torque wrench setting of 30 lb/ft.

64 Refer to Section 3 and replace the drive shaft assemblies.

65 Should it be necessary to overhaul the extension housing proceed as follows otherwise continue reassembly starting at paragraph 78.

66 Undo and remove the bolt and special shaped washer securing the extension shaft drive coupling. For this it will be necessary to hold the flange securely. Remove the flange using a three leg puller and thrust block.

67 With a screwdriver withdraw the oil seal noting which way round it is fitted.

68 Remove the circlip that retains the special self aligning bearing with a pair of circlip pliers.

69 Using a soft faced hammer or soft metal drift carefully drive the extension shaft and bearing from the rear of the extension housing.

70 With a soft metal drift or three leg puller and thrust block remove the bearing from the shaft.

71 All parts should be cleaned and inspected for signs of damage or wear. Remove all traces of Loctite from the splines on the extension shaft and threads of the coupling flange bolt.

72 It should be noted that the harmonic damper positioned at the forward end of the extension case must not be disturbed as it is specially adjusted to match the extension housing.

73 To reassemble fit the bearing onto the extension shaft using a tubular drift of suitable size.

74 Insert the extension shaft into the extension casing and drift into position with a soft faced hammer and soft metal drift.

75 Refit the bearing retaining circlip making sure that it is seating

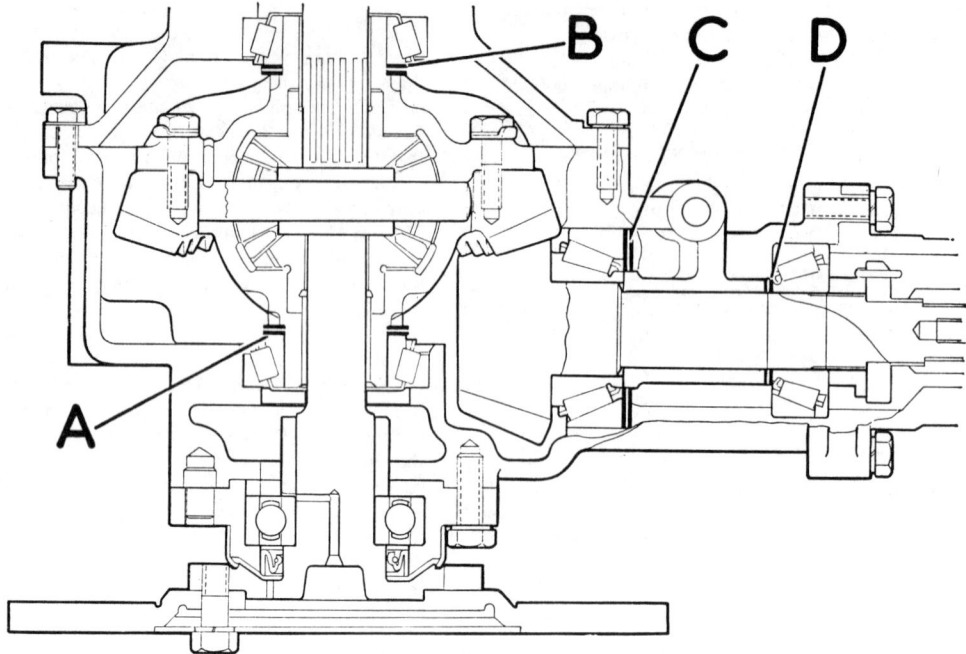

Fig.8.17. POSITION OF DIFFERENTIAL AND PINION BEARING SHIMS, FINAL DRIVE SUFFIX LETTERS A, B, C AND D

A Shims between bearing and differential carrier for crownwheel backlash adjustment
B Shims between bearing and differential carrier for bearing pre-load adjustment
C Shims between bearing and pinion housing for pinion height adjustment
D Shims between pinion tail bearing and spacer for pinion pre-load adjustment

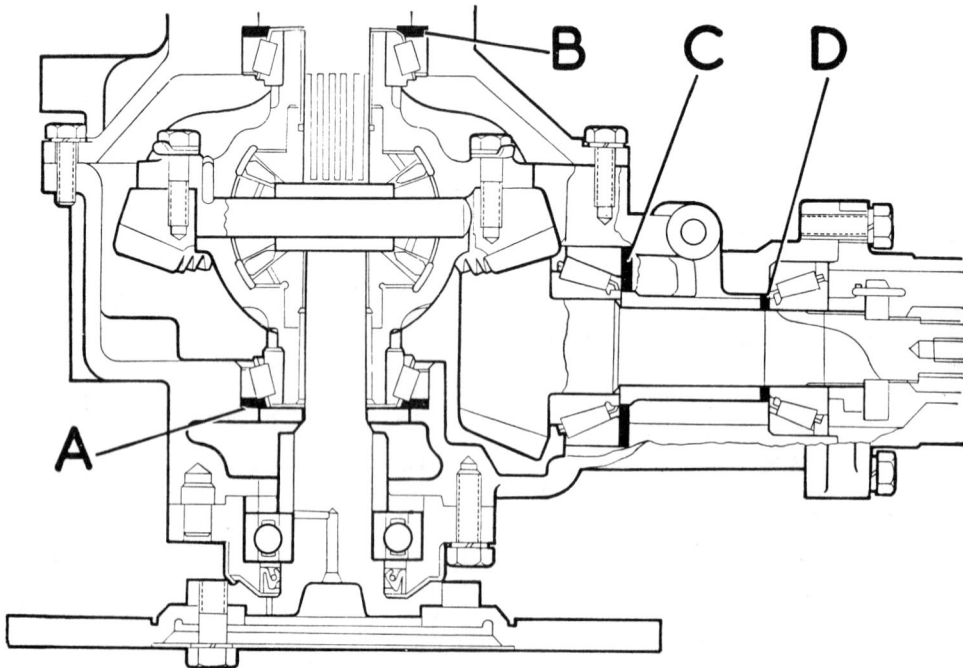

Fig.8.18. POSITION OF DIFFERENTIAL AND PINION BEARING SHIMS, FINAL DRIVE SUFFIX LETTER E AND ONWARDS

A Shim between bearing and pinion housing for crownwheel backlash adjustment
B Shim between bearing and bearing cover for bearing pre-load adjustment
C Shim between bearing and pinion housing for pinion height adjustment
D Shim between pinion tail bearing and spacer for pinion pre-load adjustment

correctly.

76 Carefully fit a new oil seal with the lip facing inwards. Tap into position using a tubular drift of suitable diameter.

77 Apply a little Loctite sealant grade AVV to the splines of the extension shaft and thread of the coupling flange fixing bolt. Assemble the coupling flange to the extension shaft and secure with the bolt and plain washer. Tighten the bolt to a torque wrench setting of 35 lb/ft. and leave for 12 hours to cure.

78 Refit the final drive extension casing to the final drive housing with a new gasket in between the two faces and secure with six bolts and spring washers. Tighten the bolts to a torque wrench setting of 30 lb/ft.

79 Replace the bolt, plain washer and self locking nut that secures the front mounting bracket to the extension casing and tighten fully.

80 The final drive assembly is now ready for refitting. Do not forget to refill the unit with fresh oil. It has a capacity of 2½ pints.

7. Final Drive Rear Flexible Mountings — Removal & Refitting

1. Chock the front wheels, remove the rear wheel trims and slacken the wheel nuts. Jack up the rear of the car and position on axle stands as shown in Fig.8.4. Remove the wheel nuts and road wheels.

2. Remove the contents of the rear luggage compartment including the spare wheel.

3. Very carefully peel back the luggage compartment trim above the access cover plates for the mountings.

4. Undo and remove the screws securing the cover plates and lift away the cover plates.

5. Place the saddle of a garage hydraulic jack under the final drive unit and just support its weight. NOTE: It is recommended that one flexible mounting is removed and refitted at a time so that the final drive position is not disturbed.

6. Undo and remove the centre support nut and bolt (Fig.8.21).

7. Undo and remove the two nuts and bolts that secure the flexible mounting to the underside of the car body.

8. The mounting may now be eased away together with its dished and cone shaped washers and also the distance pieces.

9. Cars produced since the numbers detailed below have modified mountings of a Styrene Butadiene rubber fitted. The modified mountings may be fitted in sets to earlier produced models provided that the front flexible mounting for the extension case is also fitted.

40034642D	40102305D
40308258D	41801038A

10 Refitting is the reverse sequence to removal. Fig.8.21 shows the correct refitting order of the component parts of the mountings.

8. Pinion Extension Case Assembly, Removal, Overhaul & Refitting

1. Chock the front wheels, remove the rear wheel trims and slacken the wheel nuts. Jack up the rear of the car and position on axle stands as shown in Fig.8.4. Remove the wheel nuts and road wheels.

2. Undo and remove the final drive unit drain plug and allow the oil to drain into a container having a capacity of 2½ pints.

3. Mark the propeller shaft rear flange and final drive unit flange so that they may be refitted in their original positions. Undo and remove the four flange nuts and bolts, ease the propeller shaft forwards and lower the rear end onto the floor.

4. On cars with Girling braking systems follow the subsequent operations, but if the car is fitted with a Dunlop braking system proceed directly to paragraph 8.

5. Refer to Fig.8.22 and with a pair of pliers extract the handbrake cable retaining clip.

6. Remove the split pin and clevis pin from the handbrake relay lever.

7. Slacken the exhaust mounting bracket and pull the rubber mountings clear of the tube on the front mounting bracket of the

final drive unit.

8. Place the saddle of a garage hydraulic jack under the forward end of the final drive casing and just support its weight.

9. Undo and remove the side bolt and also the two bolts and tab washers from the mounting bracket.

10 Undo and remove the six bolts and spring washers that secure the extension casing to the final drive unit.

11 The extension casing may now be removed complete with the front mounting bracket.

12 To detach the front mounting bracket from the casing, undo and remove the nut, bolt and washer. Separate the two parts.

13 If it is necessary to overhaul the extension casing, first undo and remove the bolt and special shaped washer securing the extension shaft drive coupling. For this it will be necessary to hold the flange securely. Remove the flange using a three leg puller and thrust block.

14 With a screwdriver withdraw the oil seal noting which way round it is fitted.

15 Remove the circlip that retains the special self aligning bearing with a pair of circlip pliers.

16 Using a soft faced hammer or soft metal drift carefully drive the extension shaft and bearing from the rear of the extension housing.

17 With a soft metal drift or three leg puller and thrust block remove the bearing from the shaft.

18 All parts should be cleaned and inspected for signs of damage or wear. Remove all traces of Loctite from the splines on the extension shaft and threads of the coupling flange bolt.

19 It should be noted that the harmonic damper positioned at the forward end of the extension case must not be disturbed as it is specially adjusted to match the extension housing.

20 To reassemble fit the bearing onto the extension shaft using a tubular drift of suitable size.

21 Insert the extension shaft into the extension casing and drift into position with a soft faced hammer and soft metal drift.

22 Refit the bearing retaining circlip making sure that it is seating correctly.

23 Carefully fit a new oil seal with the lip facing inwards. Tap into position using a tubular drift of suitable diameter

24 Apply a little Loctite sealant grade AVV to the splines of the extension shaft and thread of the coupling flange fixing bolt. Assemble the coupling flange to the extension shaft and secure with the bolt and plain washer. Tighten the bolt to a torque wrench setting of 35 lb/ft. and leave for 12 hours to cure.

25 To refit the extension case assembly is the reverse sequence to removal. The following two additional points should be noted.

26 The extension casing bolts should be tightened to a torque wrench setting of 30 lb/ft.

27 Do not forget to refill the final drive unit with oil. It has a capacity of 2½ pints.

9. Rear Stabiliser Rod — Removal & Refitting

1. To remove the rear stabiliser rod, undo and remove the bolt and self locking nut that secures the stabiliser to the final drive unit.

2. With a pair of pliers straighten and extract the split pin and then lift away the plain washer that secures the stabiliser bar to the underside of the body. The stabiliser may then be lifted away.

3. Should it be necessary the rubber bushes may be removed and new ones pressed into position. The best way to do this is to use a piece of tubing of the same diameter as the outside of the bush and a large bench vice.

4. To refit the stabiliser rod settle the rear of the car by rocking it up and down several times and then refit the rod to the underside of the body. It will be necessary to compress the rubber but this is not too difficult to do.

5. Adjust the length of rod so that the bolt just fits easily at the final drive unit and insert the bolt. Refit the self locking nut and tighten securely.

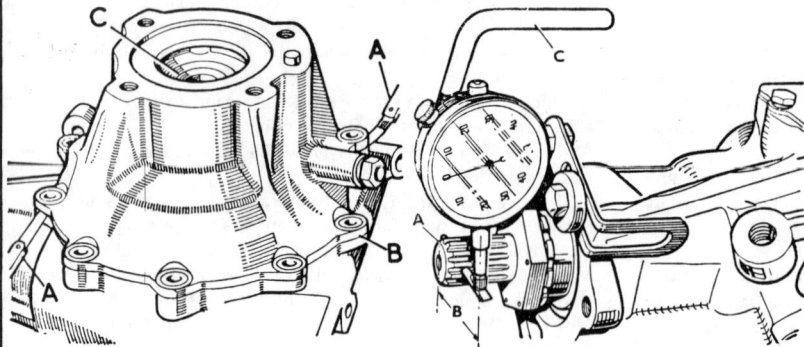

Fig.8.19. Using feeler gauges to determine differential bearing pre-load
A Feeler gauges
B Housing faces
C Differential bearing

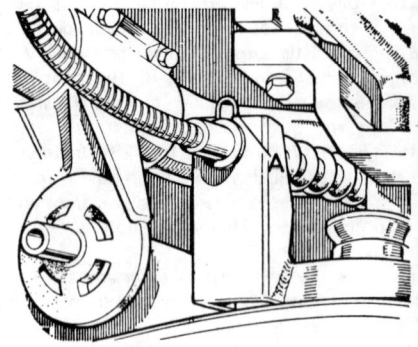

Fig.8.20. Use of dial indicator gauge to determine backlash between pinion and crownwheel
A Pinion
B Adaptor rod, 1 inch centre
C Dial indicator gauge bracket

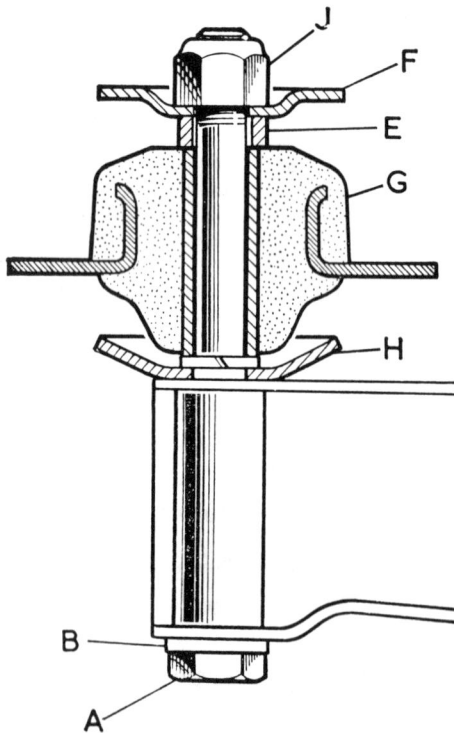

Fig.8.22. Handbrake linkage spring clip location
A Spring clip

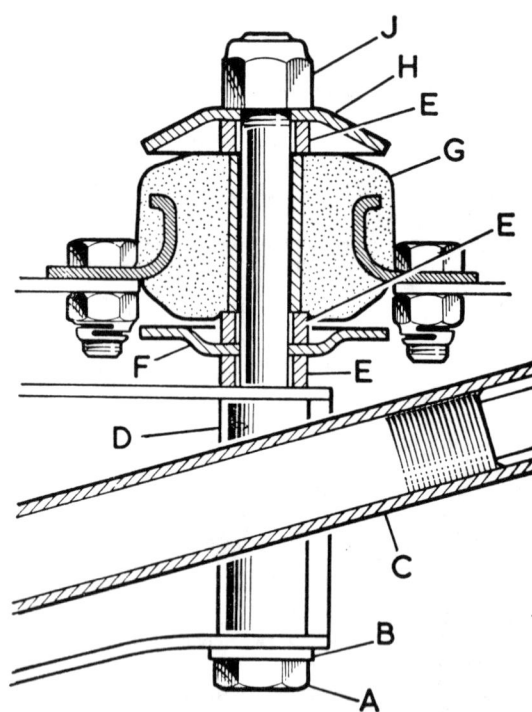

Fig.8.21. FINAL DRIVE REAR FLEXIBLE MOUNTINGS

A Bolt
B Washer
C Stabiliser rod
D Distance piece
E Distance washer
F Dished washer
G Flexible mounting
H Coned washer
J Self-locking nut

Chapter 9 Braking system

Contents

Specifications

Brake System

Footbrake	Hydraulic
Front	Outboard discs
Rear	Inboard discs
Handbrake	Dunlop or Girling disc
Handbrake lever ratio	80 : 1 overall
Master cylinder diameter	0.875 in.
Master cylinder stroke at pushrod	1.43 in.
Master cylinder rod free play	0.020 in.
Pedal spindle endfloat	Zero taken up by each spring

Brake Disc

	Dunlop	Girling
Standard diameter - Front	10.75 in.	10.312 in.
Rear	10.26 in.	10.690 in.
Standard thickness	0.39 in.	Front 0.505 in.
		Rear 0.380 in.
Pad area - Front	4.025 in^2	5.2 in^2
Total area	16.10 in^2	20.8 in^2
Rear	4.025 in^2	3.5 in^2
Total area	16.10 in^2	14.0 in^2
Pad area total	32.2 in^2	34.8 in^2
Swept area - Front brakes	248 in^2	214 in^2
Rear brakes	436 in^2	356 in^2
Calliper cylinder internal diameter - Front	2.125 in.	2.142 in.
Rear	1.563 in.	0.75 in.
Brake fluid	Dunlop brake fluid (Specification SAE 70 R3)	
	Castrol Girling 'Crimson' Brake Fluid (Specification SAE 70 R3)	

Vacuum Servo Unit

	Type 5.5	Type 7
Effective vacuum cylinder diameter	5.5 in.	7 in.
Vacuum cylinder stroke	2.06 in.	2.18 in. (max)
Slave cylinder displacement	0.610 cu.in.	0.620 cu.in.
Slave cylinder diameter		0.625 in.
Hydraulic reaction piston diameter		0.375 in.

Torque Wrench Settings

	lb.ft.	kgm.
Bearing housing to pinion housing	30	4
Brake calliper to front suspension member	60	8.5
Brake calliper to final drive bearing housing	60	8.5
Disc to front hub	44	6
Disc to rear drive flange (early models)	68	9.3
Disc to rear drive flange (later models)	85	11.9
Rear hub to De Dion tube	20	2.8
Dunlop cylinder calliper...	8	1.0

1. General Description

All models covered by this manual are fitted with disc brakes at the front and inboard disc brakes at the rear. They are hydraulically operated with vacuum servo assistance, whilst the handbrake operates through a mechanical linkage to the rear brakes only.

If the servo unit should fail, although assistance will be lost, the hydraulic system will still be functional but a greater pedal pressure will be required to stop the car.

It will be seen from the specifications two brake systems were used. Initially Dunlop brakes were used on SC models having numbers incorporating suffix letters A,B,C and D and TC models with suffix letter A. All other models, plus cars fitted with automatic transmission, were fitted with Girling brakes.

Although the principle of the operation is basically identical in both cases there are slight design differences. The Dunlop braking system has separate handbrake friction pads and operating gear which swings from the fixed calliper footbrake housing, but the Girling system uses one set of friction pads for both the footbrake and the handbrake, the pads being mounted in a swinging calliper housing.

The handbrake is automatically adjusted to take up clearance caused by pad wear.

2. Routine Maintenance

1. Every month or 5,000 miles whichever is earlier, carefully clean the top of the brake master cylinder, remove the cap and inspect the level of the fluid which should be at the rib on the reservoir. Check that the breathing holes in the cap are clear.
2. If the fluid is below this level top up the reservoir with Castrol Girling Brake fluid, specification SAE J170 R3a or SAE 70 R3. Use of a non-standard fluid will result in brake-failure caused by the perishing of the special seals in the master and brake cylinders. If topping up becomes frequent then check the metal piping and flexible hosing for leaks. Also check the master cylinder or calliper units for leaks which will cause this loss of fluid.
3. Every 5,000 miles check the correct operation of the brake fluid level safety switch and warning light. This is incorporated in the reservoir cap and is tested by switching on the ignition and lifting the cap up until the little float is clear of the hydraulic fluid. The amber warning light should be on.
4. Every 5,000 miles examine the wear on the brake disc pads and change them round if one is very much more worn on one side of the rotating disc than the other.
5. Every 5,000 miles lubricate the handbrake linkage and pivot points to ensure freedom of movement.
6. Every 40,000 miles or 3 years, the rubber seals in the master cylinder and calliper pistons should be renewed and then filled with fresh brake fluid.

3. Front Brake Pads (Dunlop) — Removal, Inspection & Refitting

1. Apply the handbrake, remove the wheel trim, loosen the front wheel nuts, jack up the front of the car and support on axle stands at the front jacking points. Lift away the road wheels.
2. Undo and remove the nut, washer and bolt that secures the brake pad keep plate in position. Withdraw the keep plate (B) Fig.9.3.
3. The brake pads may now be removed by sliding upwards off the spigot (Fig.9.4). The pads must be renewed when the thickness of the material has worn down to ¼ inch.
4. Carefully clean the recesses in the calliper in which the friction pad assemblies lie and the exposed face of each piston backing plate, from all traces of dirt and rust.
5. Remove the cap from the hydraulic fluid reservoir and place a large rag underneath the unit. Press the pistons in each half of the calliper right in with a piece of tapered hardwood - this will cause the fluid level in the reservoir to rise and possibly to spill over the brim onto the protective rag.
6. Insert the pads ensuring that the pad locating slotted plate engages with the spigot on the piston backing plate.
7. Refit the keep plate and secure in position with the bolts, washer and nut.
8. Refit the road wheels and the wheel nuts, remove the axle stands and lower the car to the ground. Tighten the wheel nuts and refit the wheel trims.
9. Press the brake pedal down several times to adjust the brakes. Top up the master cylinder as necessary.

4. Front Brake Pads (Girling) - Removal, Inspection & Refitting

1. Apply the handbrake, remove the wheel trim, loosen the front wheel nuts, jack up the front of the car and support on axle stands at the front jacking points. Lift away the road wheels.
2. Extract the pin retaining clip (B), Fig.9.5, and withdraw the pad retaining pins (A).
3. The brake pads may now be removed by sliding them out of the calliper together with the anti-rattle springs (D) and damping shims. Note which way round the shim is fitted.
4. Mark each pad (E) so that if it is to be refitted it may be replaced in its original position. The pads must be renewed when the thickness of the material has worn down to 1/8 inch.
5. Carefully clean the recesses in the calliper in which the friction pad assemblies lie and the exposed face of each piston, from all traces of dirt and rust.
6. Remove the cap from the hydraulic fluid reservoir and place a large rag underneath the unit. Press the pistons in each half of the calliper right in with a piece of tapered hardwood - this will cause the fluid level in the reservoir to rise and possibly to spill over the brim onto the protective rag.
7. Carefully slide the pads into position together with the damping shims. The cut-out arrow in the shim must point in the direction of normal forward rotation.
8. Replace the anti-rattle springs, one to each pad, and insert the pad retaining pins so that the anti-rattle springs are clipped under the pins. Lock the pins with the special clips.
9. Refit the road wheels and wheel nuts, remove the axle stands and lower the car to the ground. Tighten the wheel nuts and refit the wheel trims.
10 Press the brake pedal down several times to adjust the brakes. Top up the master cylinder as necessary.

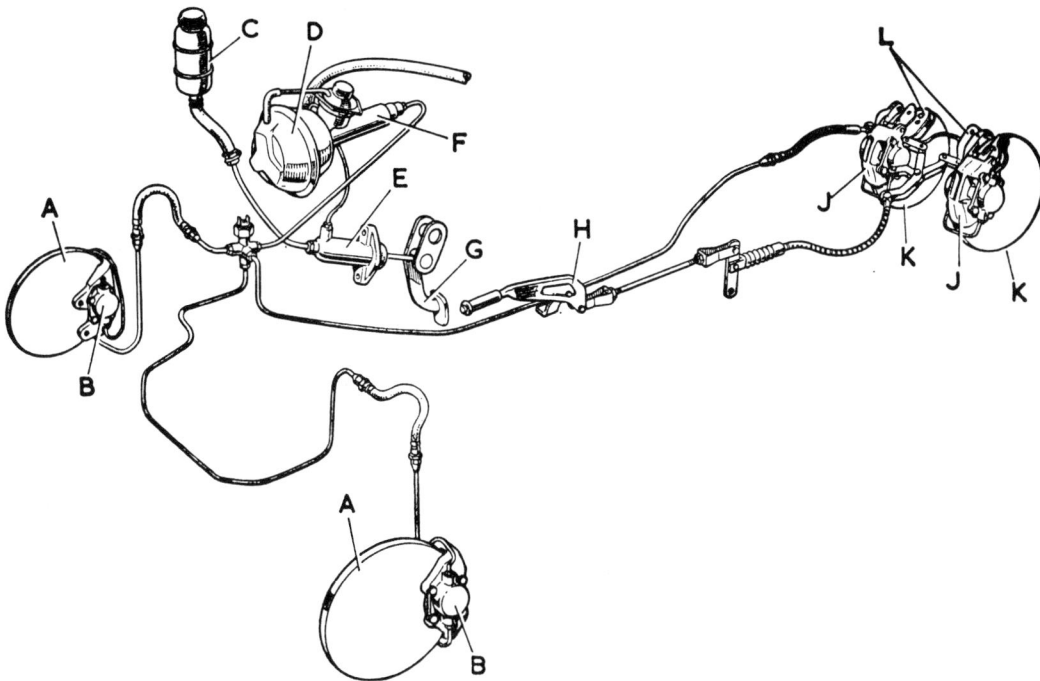

Fig.9.1. LAYOUT OF DUNLOP BRAKING SYSTEM

A Front discs	D Servo unit	G Foot pedal	K Rear discs
B Front callipers	E Master cylinder	H Handbrake	L Auto adjuster units
C Brake reservoir	F Servo slave cylinder	J Rear callipers	

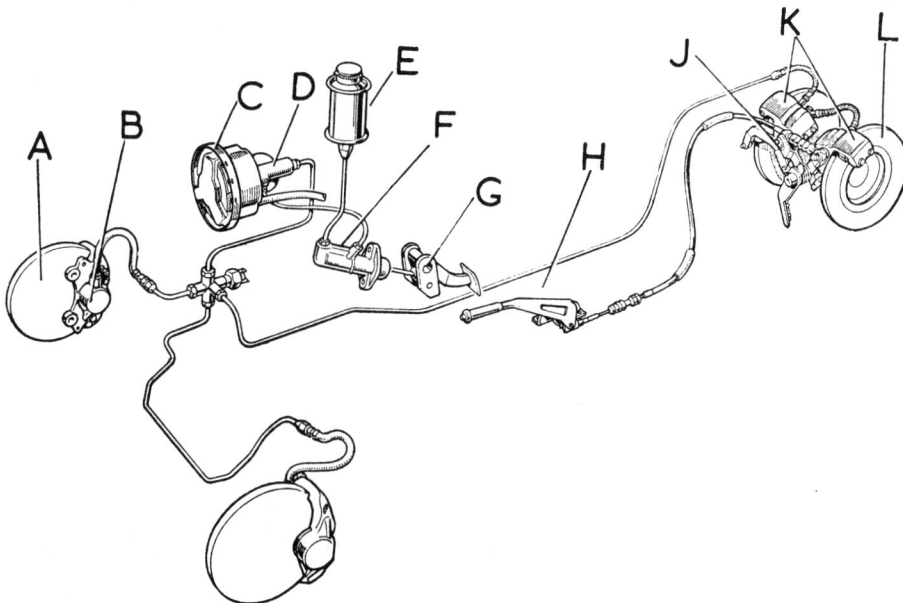

Fig.9.2. LAYOUT OF GIRLING BRAKING SYSTEM

A Front discs	D Servo slave cylinder	G Foot pedal	K Swinging calliper
B Front calliper	E Brake reservoir	H Handbrake	L Rear discs
C Servo unit	F Master cylinder	J Handbrake linkage	

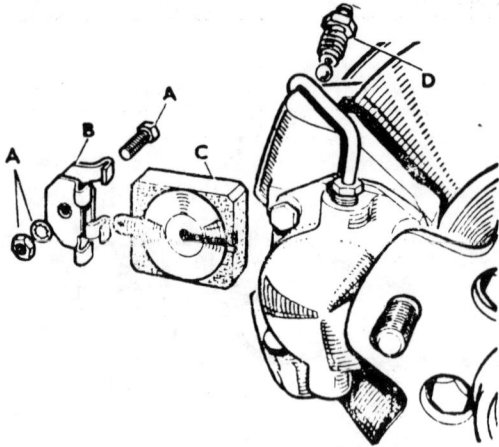

Fig.9.3. FRONT BRAKE PAD & KEEP PLATE (DUNLOP)
A Fixing bolt, nut & washer   C Brake pad
B Keep plate   D Bleed nipple

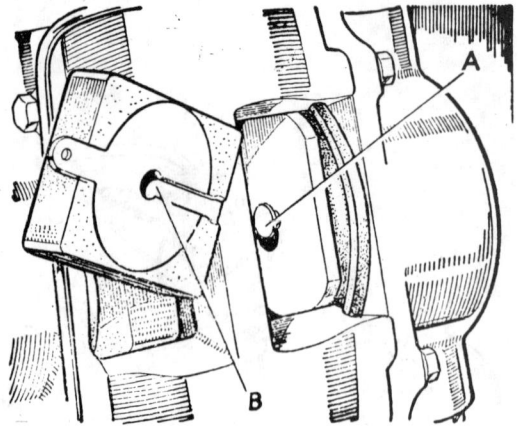

Fig.9.4. REMOVAL OF BRAKE PAD FROM SPIGOT
A Piston spigot   B Brake slot

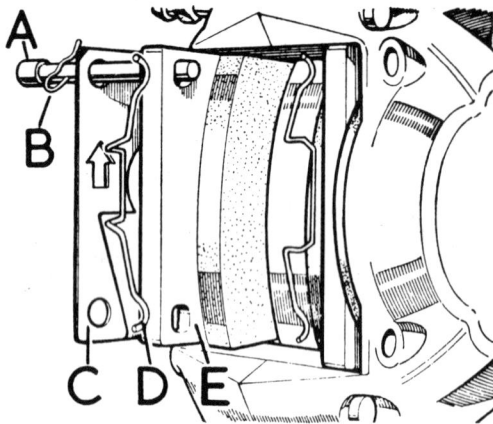

Fig.9.5. FRONT BRAKE PAD & SHIMS (GIRLING)
A Pad retaining pins   D Anti-rattle spring
B Special clip for pin   E Brake pad
C Damping shim

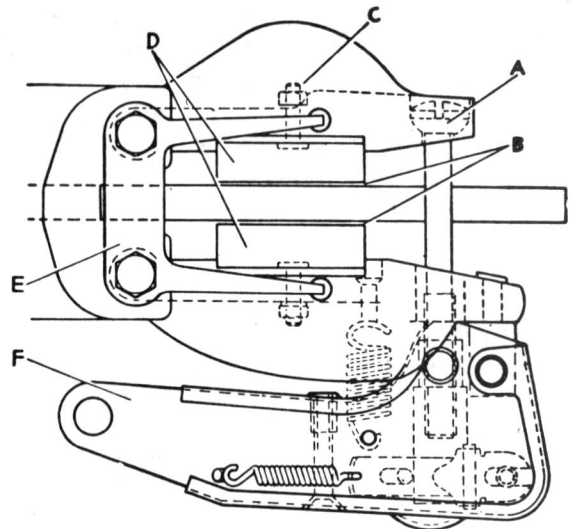

Fig.9.6. REAR HANDBRAKE PADS (DUNLOP)
A Adjuster bolt   D Handbrake pads
B .010 in. (0.25 mm) clearance E Retractor plate
   at these points   F Auto adjuster unit
C Pad locating bolt

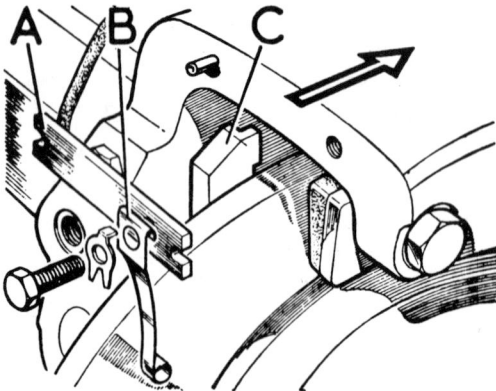

Fig.9.7. REAR INNER BRAKE PAD REMOVAL (GIRLING)
A Retainer plate   C Withdraw inner pad in
B Anti-rattle spring   direction arrowed

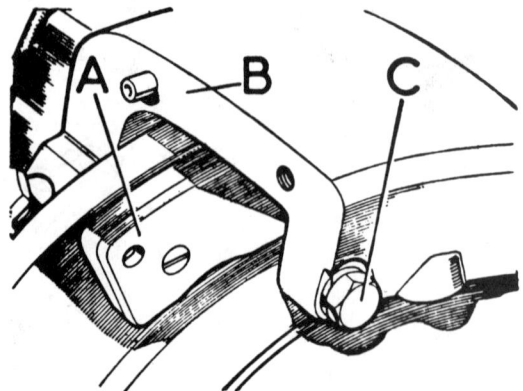

Fig.9.8. REAR OUTER BRAKE PAD REMOVAL (GIRLING)
A Outer brake pad   C Drag pin
B Calliper pulled outwards

5. Rear Brake Pads (Dunlop) — Footbrake — Removal, Inspection & Refitting

1. For reference to the various parts see Fig.9.9. Chock the front wheels, remove the rear wheel trim, slacken the wheel nuts, jack up the rear of the car and support on axle stands at the rear jacking points. Lift away the road wheels.

2. Undo and remove the nut, washer and bolt that secures the brake pad keep plate in position and withdraw the keep plate.

3. The brake pads may now be removed by sliding upwards off the spigot. The pads must be renewed when the thickness of the material has worn down to ¼ inch.

4. Carefully clean the recesses in the calliper in which the friction pad assemblies lie and the exposed face of each piston backing plate, from all traces of dirt and rust.

5. Remove the cap from the hydraulic fluid reservoir and place a large rag underneath the unit. Press the pistons in each half of the calliper right in with a piece of tapered hardwood - this will cause the fluid level in the reservoir to rise and possibly to spill over the brim onto the protective rag.

6. Insert the pads ensuring that the pad locating slotted plate engages with the spigot on the piston backing plate.

7. Refit the keep plate and secure in position with the bolt, washer and nut.

8. Refit the road wheels and wheel nuts, remove the axle stands and lower the car to the ground. Tighten the wheel nuts and refit the wheel trims.

9. Press the brake pedal down several times to adjust the brake pad position. Top up the master cylinder as necessary.

6. Rear Brake Pads (Dunlop) — Handbrake — Removal, Inspection & Refitting

1. Chock the front wheels, remove the rear wheel trims, slacken the wheel nuts, jack up the rear of the car and place on axle stands at the rear jacking points. Lift away the road wheels.

2. Place the saddle of a garage hydraulic jack under the final drive and support its weight. Undo and remove the three bolts that secure the final drive to its rear mountings. Also remove the filler and level plug.

3. Slacken the locknut that secures the brake hose to its bracket, and lower the hose.

4. Carefully lower the final drive unit, and support at the end of the extension casing.

5. Apply the handbrake and using a 2BA box spanner slacken the pad locating nuts (C) Fig.9.6. Now release the handbrake.

6. Extract the split pin and slacken the auto adjuster unit bolt 'A', Fig.9.6.

7. The handbrake pads may now be lifted clear.

8. Inspect the thickness of the pads and if they are less than ¼ inch thick new pads should be fitted.

9. Refitting the pads is the reverse procedure to removal. There are, however, several additional points to be noted.

10 Make sure that the head of the locating bolt is correctly positioned in the slot of the brake pad.

11 The pad clearance should be adjusted by using the adjuster bolt until there is 0.010 inch gap between the pad and disc.

12 Fit a new split pin and then operate the handbrake firmly several times. Recheck the clearance as detailed in paragraph 11.

13 Jack up the final drive casing and replace the three bolts securing it to the mounting bracket.

14 Check the level of oil in the final drive unit and replace the filler level plug.

15 Refit the road wheels, lower the car to the ground, tighten the wheel nuts and replace the wheel trims.

7. Rear Brake Pads (Girling) — Removal, Inspection & Refitting

1. A special piston resetting tool is necessary for this operation. It has a Rover part number of 601962. Also this operation is best performed if it is on a garage type lift or the rear wheels on individual ramps.

2. With a chisel, bend back the tabs on the locker at the front position. Unscrew the bolt and withdraw the retainer plate and anti-rattle spring.

3. Swing the top of the inner pad forward and withdraw the pad towards the rear of the vehicle (Fig.9.7).

4. With a chisel bend back the tabs on the locker at the rear position and slacken the bolt to release the anti-rattle spring tension on the outer pad.

5. Carefully pull the calliper outwards and remove the outer pad from the drag pins and withdraw the pad (Fig.9.8).

6. Disconnect the calliper handbrake lever at the link lever and link plates respectively.

7. Remove the bolts fixing the bracket for the bellcrank lever to the pinion housing.

8. Withdraw the complete handbrake mechanism to hang clear of the callipers. This operation is necessary so as to give clearance for the special piston setting tool.

9. Push the calliper towards the centre and then, from the front, fit the special piston fitting tool over the projecting piston (Fig.9.10).

10 First movement of the tool will lock in onto the piston. Next operate the tool by pushing the handle inwards so as to engage on the serrations and turn in the direction required

11 Rotate the piston in an anti-clockwise direction one complete turn. Remove the tool and clear the projection area of the piston free of dust or dirt. Then smear the end of the piston with a little brake grease.

12 Refit the tool and turn back the piston in a clockwise direction until it is right back and the clicking of the ratchet can be heard, (Fig.9.11).

13 When the piston is right in make sure that the lever on the piston is pointing upright and then remove the tool.

14 Inspect the ends of the drag pins for the outer pad. If they are round and true do not disturb them. If they are worn then they should be renewed.

15 Refitting is the reverse sequence to removal but the following additional points should be noted.

16 Make sure that the inner anti-rattle spring is fitted at the forward position with the dome outwards. The outer pad anti-rattle spring should be fitted at the rear position.

17 Tighten the pad retaining bolts to a torque wrench setting of 9 lb/ft., and bend up the lockwasher tab.

8. Front Disc Brake Calliper (Dunlop) — Removal, Overhaul & Refitting

1. Apply the handbrake, remove the wheel trim, loosen the front wheel nuts, jack up the front of the car and support on axle stands at the front jacking points. Lift away the road wheels.

2. Unscrew the reservoir cap and place to one side. Wrap a piece of polythene over the top of the reservoir and tie securely in position so as to make an air tight seal thus preventing loss of hydraulic fluid.

3. Wipe the hydraulic pipe union at the swivel pillar free of dust and dirt.

4. Disconnect the hydraulic fluid feed pipe at the swivel pillar and wrap the open ends with clean rag to prevent dust ingress into the system.

5. Bend back the locking plate, undo and remove the two bolts and plain washers and lift away the calliper unit.

6. Remove the pad keep plate having first removed the bolt, nut and washer and lift away the two pads.

7. Wipe the unions clean and remove the hydraulic fluid feed pipe and bridge pipe from the calliper unit.

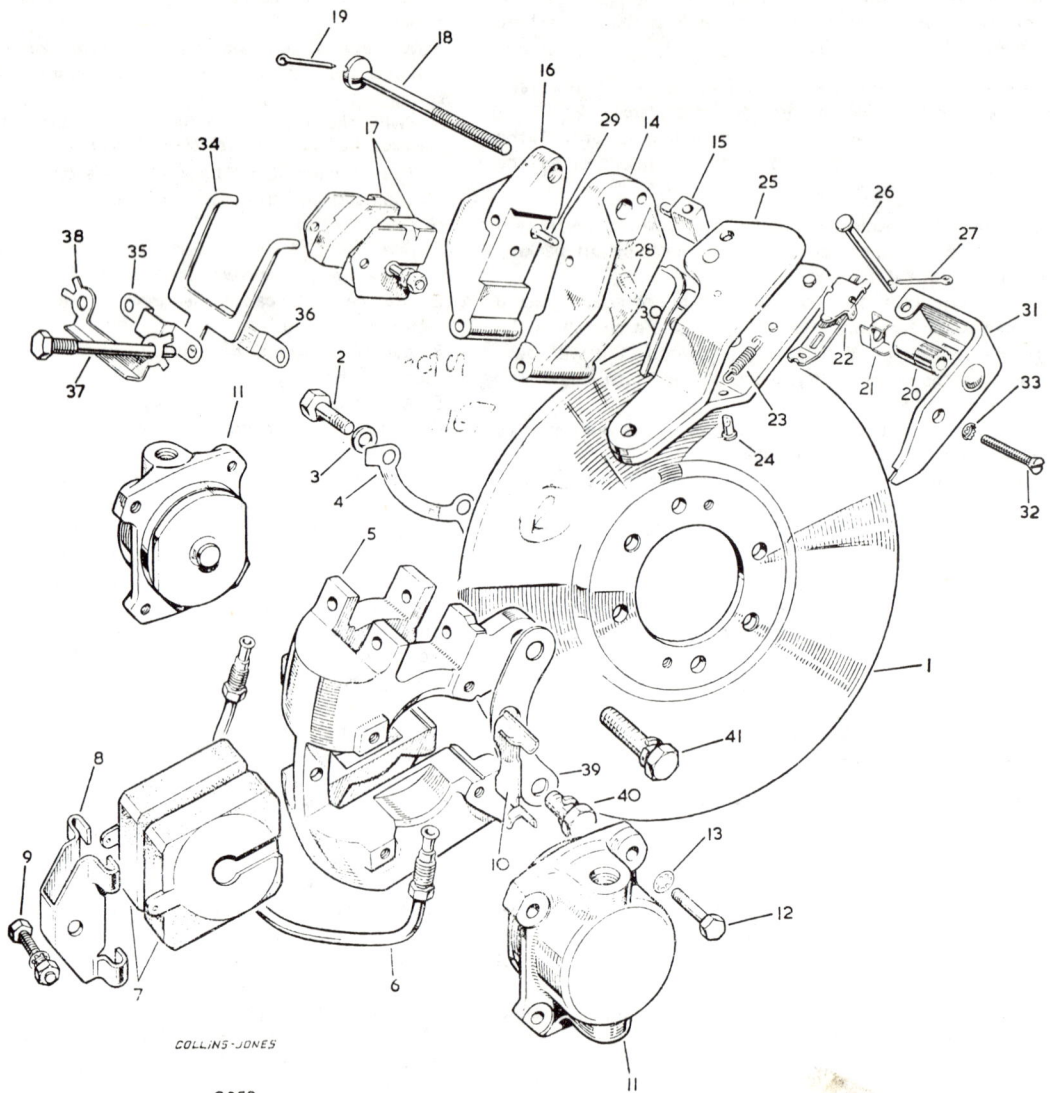

COLLINS-JONES

G959

Fig.9.9. REAR DISC BRAKE CALLIPER (DUNLOP)

1 Disc for rear brake	12 Special bolt	23 Spring for pawl	32 Special countersunk screw
2 Set bolt	13 Shakeproof washer	24 Anchor for pawl spring	33 Special countersunk washer
3 Shim washer	14 Inner pad carrier	25 Operating lever for hand-brake	34 Reaction plate
4 Lockwasher	15 Pivot seat		35 Top locating plate
5 Rear footbrake calliper assembly, RH	16 Outer pad carrier	26 Hinge pin for operating lever	36 Bottom locating plate
6 Bridge pipe	17 Friction pad	27 Split pin for hinge pin	37 Special bolt fixing reaction plate and pad carrier
7 Friction pad	18 Operating bolt	28 Return spring for operating lever	38 Tab washer for reaction plate bolt
8 Keep plate for friction pad	19 Split pin for operating bolt	29 Anchor pin for return spring	39 Shim
9 Special bolt, nut & washer fixing keep plate	20 Adjusting nut for pad carrier	30 Protection cover, outer, for operating lever	40 Special bolt (7/16in UNF)
10 Support plate for friction pad	21 Friction spring for adjusting nut	31 Protection cover, inner, for operating lever	41 Special bolt (7/16in UNF x 1.1/8in long)
11 Piston & cylinder complete	22 Pawl complete for adjusting nut		

8. Undo and remove the eight bolts (18) Fig.9.12. There are four bolts each side that secure the two cylinder and piston assemblies to the calliper.

9. Separate the cylinder and piston assemblies from the calliper bridge.

10 Carefully disengage the dust seal (A), Fig.9.14, from the groove around the cylinder bore face.

11 The piston (B) may now be eased from the cylinder. If it is a tight fit it may be removed by either applying a low pressure air line to hydraulic pipe connection or alternatively reconnecting the hydraulic pipe to the cylinder assembly and depressing the brake pedal.

12 The dust seal and piston seal (C) may now be removed from the piston.

13 It is not necessary to dismantle the piston further or to remove the retractor pin from the cylinder bore.

14 Thoroughly wash all parts in hydraulic fluid and wipe dry using a clean non-fluffy rag. Inspect the pistons and cylinders for signs of scoring and, if evident, a new assembly should be obtained and fitted. Also check that none of the threads have stripped either in the bridge or on the bolts.

15 To reassemble soak the new piston seals in clean brake fluid for several minutes.

16 Engage the collar of a new dust seal with the lip of the backing plate making sure that it is not stretched.

17 Fit the piston seal to the piston face. Apply a little clean brake fluid to the cylinder bore and locate the piston assembly over the end of the retractor pin.

18 Carefully apply an even pressure to the piston backing plate; at the same time making sure that the piston is fitting squarely so avoiding damage to the seal.

19 Once the piston has entered the bore correctly, smear the cavity around the piston with clean brake fluid and fit the new dust seal over the rim of the cylinder flange.

20 Push the piston fully home down the bore.

21 Repeat the above procedure for the second cylinder and piston assembly as detailed in paragraphs 15 to 20 inclusive above.

22 Refit the two piston and cylinder assemblies to the calliper bridge and tighten the eight securing bolts to a torque wrench setting of 8 lb/ft.

23 Insert the pads ensuring that the pad locating slotted plate engages with the spigot on the piston backing plate.

24 Refit the keep plate and secure in position with the bolt, washer and nut.

25 Refit the calliper unit to the swivel pillar and tighten the bolts to a torque wrench setting of 60 lb/ft. Lock the bolts by bending over the locking plate tabs.

26 Reconnect the bridge pipe and feed pipe to the calliper unit taking care not to cross thread the unions upon initial tightening.

27 It will now be necessary to bleed the hydraulic system, details of which are given in Section 20 of this Chapter.

28 Refit the road wheels and wheel nuts, remove the axle stands and lower the car to the ground. Tighten the wheel nuts and refit the wheel trims.

29 Press the brake pedal down several times to adjust the brake pad position. Top up the master cylinder as necessary.

9. Front Disc Brake Calliper (Girling) — Removal, Overhaul & Refitting

1. Apply the handbrake, remove the wheel trim, loosen the front wheel nuts, jack up the front of the car and support on axle stands at the front jacking points. Lift away the road wheels.

2. Unscrew the reservoir cap and place to one side, wrap a piece of polythene over the top of the reservoir and tie securely in position so as to make an air tight seal thus preventing loss of hydraulic fluid.

3. Wipe the hydraulic pipe union at the calliper free of dust and dirt. Remove the pipe clip at the swivel pillar.

4. Disconnect the hydraulic fluid feed pipe (A), Fig.9.15, at the

calliper and wrap the open end with clean rag to prevent dust ingress into the system.

5. Extract the pin retaining clip (B), Fig.9.5, and withdraw the pad retaining pins (A).

6. The brake pads may now be removed by sliding them out of the calliper together with the anti-rattle springs (D) and damping shims. Note which way round the shim is fitted.

7. Mark each pad so that if it is refitted it may be replaced in its original position.

8. Undo and remove the two bolts (C), Fig.9.15, spring washers and plain washers that attach the brake shield to the calliper.

9. Bend back the tabs on the locking plate and remove the two bolts (B), locking plate and calliper unit.

10 Do not under any circumstances remove the bolts that secure the two halves of the calliper. The pistons and seals may be removed without separating the two halves.

11 Undo and remove the bleed screw.

12 Carefully remove the rubber boot (H), Fig.9.16, from the piston (G) and the calliper housing (F).

13 Apply a low pressure air line to the bleed screw hole or alternatively reconnect the hydraulic pipe to the calliper and depress the brake pedal so as to ease out the pistons.

14 Remove the inner sealing rings with a screwdriver taking care not to scratch the bores or locating groove.

15 Thoroughly wash all parts in hydraulic fluid and wipe dry using a clean non-fluffy rag. Inspect the pistons and cylinders for signs of scoring and, if evident, a new assembly should be obtained and fitted. Also check that none of the threads have stripped either in the calliper or on the bolts.

16 To reassemble soak new piston seals in clean brake fluid for several minutes.

17 Make quite sure that the grooves are clean in the calliper housing and fit the new sealing rings into the longer of the two grooves.

18 Smear a little Castrol Girling Brake Fluid onto the bore and the exterior of the piston.

19 Fit the rubber boot to the housing making sure that the lip of the boot is seated in the small groove.

20 Insert the piston squarely into the bore and press in gently. Engage the sealing lip of the rubber boot in the groove in the piston and push the piston in fully.

21 Repeat the above procedure for the second piston.

22 Replace the bleed screw in the calliper body.

23 Refitting the calliper unit is the reverse sequence to removal. Take care that the union is not cross threaded when replacing in the calliper unit.

24 The calliper mounting bolts should be tightened to a torque wrench setting of 60 lb/ft.

25 It will now be necessary to bleed the brake hydraulic system, details of which will be found in Section 20 of this Chapter.

10. Front Disc (Dunlop) — Removal & Refitting

1. Apply the handbrake, remove the wheel trim, loosen the front wheel nuts, jack up the front of the car and support on axle stands at the front jacking points. Lift away the road wheels.

2. Unscrew the reservoir cap and place to one side. Wrap a piece of polythene over the top of the reservoir and tie securely in position so as to make an air tight seal thus preventing loss of hydraulic fluid.

3. Wipe the hydraulic pipe union at the swivel pillar free of dust and dirt.

4. Disconnect the hydraulic fluid feed pipe at the swivel pillar and wrap the open ends with clean rag to prevent dust ingress into the system.

5. Bend back the locking plate, undo and remove the two bolts and plain washers and lift away the calliper unit.

6. Carefully prise off the hub cap with a wide bladed screwdriver and then extract the split pin and slotted nut from the stub axle.

7. Note that on later produced models having a suffix letter 'C'

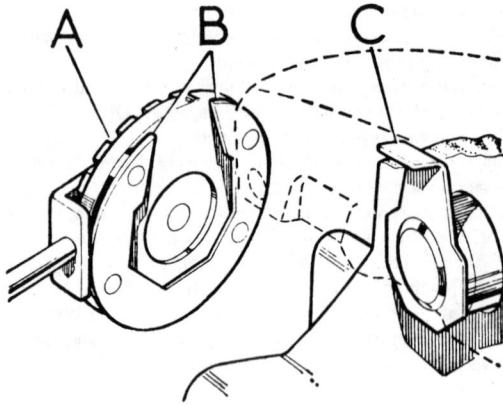

Fig.9.10. PISTON SETTING TOOL (GIRLING)

A Piston setting tool   piston
B Slots in tool for lever on   C Lever in piston

NOTE: This illustration shows the relationship of the tool
      relative to the lever on the piston

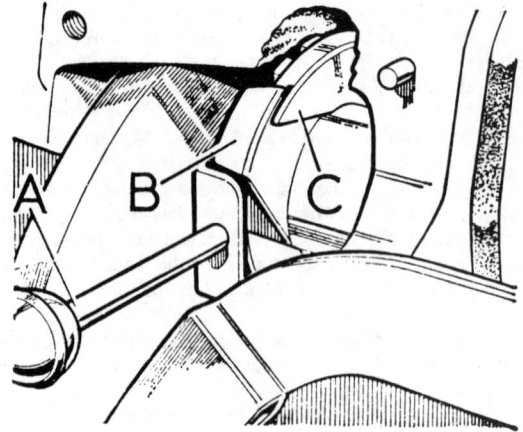

Fig.9.11. PISTON SETTING TOOL IN POSITION ON CALLI-
PER PISTON

A Piston setting tool   C Lip of tool locked on piston
B Lever on piston   lever

NOTE: This illustration shows the piston being screwed inwards.

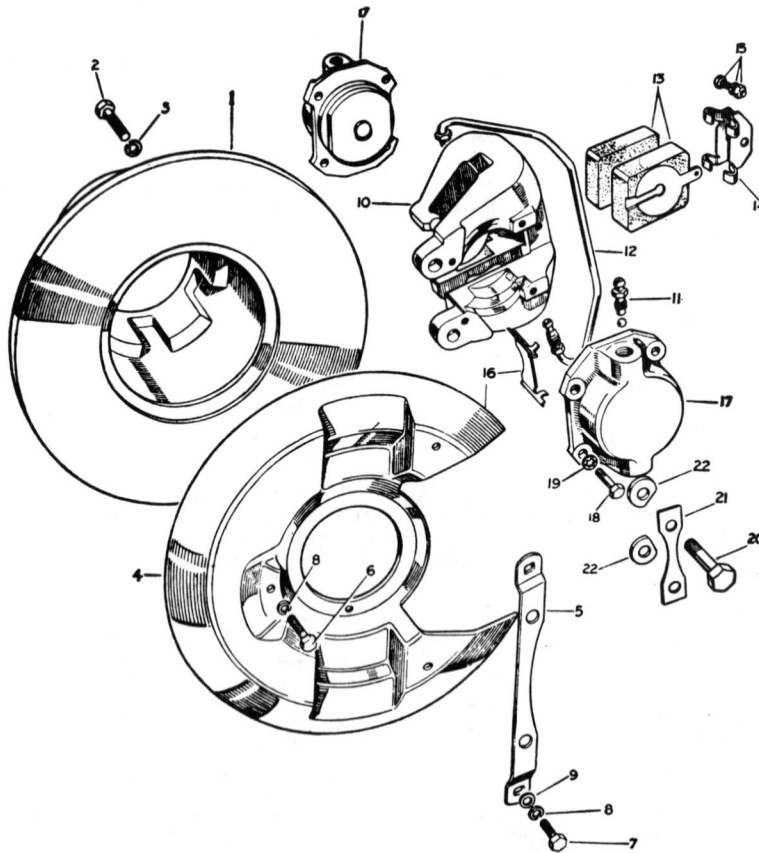

Fig.9.12. FRONT CALLIPER COMPONENT PARTS (DUNLOP)

1 Disc for front brake	7 Set bolt	13 Friction pad	18 Special bolt
2 Set bolt	8 Spring washer	14 Keep plate	19 Shakeproof washer
3 Spring washer	9 Plain washer	15 Special bolt, nut and	20 Special set bolt
4 Shield and dust cover	10 Front calliper assembly	washer	21 Tab washer
5 Strap for shield	11 Bleed screw and ball	16 Support plate	22 Plain washer
6 Set bolt	12 Bridge pipe RH	17 Piston and cylinder	

and onwards it will be necessary to remove the locking cap and special nut as shown in Fig.11.3.

8. Remove the special washer and then the complete hub assembly.

9. Undo and remove the five bolts securing the disc to the hub flange face and separate the two parts using a soft faced hammer.

10 To refit the disc make quite sure that the mating faces of the disc and hub flange are clean and free from burrs. Place the disc onto the hub flange and secure with the five bolts, tightening them to a torque wrench setting of 44 lb/ft.

11 Refit the hub and adjust the nut to give a zero endfloat. If available a dial indicator gauge and mounting bracket will give an accurate indication of the endfloat.

12 Check the brake disc run out with a dial indicator gauge suitably mounted as shown in Fig.9.17. The run out must not exceed 0.003 inch at the outer circumference as shown. If the run out is excessive re-position the disc on the hub flange and re-check.

13 On early produced models adjust the hub nut to give an endfloat of between 0.003 and 0.005 inch by using one of a range of three thrust washer thicknesses.

14 On later produced models position the locking cap onto the nut in such a manner that the split pin can be inserted through the serrations without altering the position of the special hub nut.

15 Fit a new split pin and bend over the legs. Repack the hub cap with Castrol LM grease and replace the hub cap.

16 Refit the calliper unit to the swivel pillar and tighten the bolts to a torque wrench setting of 60 lb/ft. Lock the bolts by bending over the locking plate tabs.

17 Reconnect the feed pipe to the calliper unit taking care not to cross thread the unions upon initial tightening.

18 It will now be necessary to bleed the hydraulic system, details of which are given in Section 20 of this Chapter.

19 Refit the road wheels and wheel nuts, remove the axle stands and lower the car to the ground. Tighten the wheel nuts and refit the wheel trims.

20 Press the brake pedal down several times to adjust the brake pad position. Top up the master cylinder as necessary and refit the cap.

11. Front Disc (Girling) — Removal & Refitting

1. Apply the handbrake, remove the wheel trim, loosen the front wheel nuts, jack up the front of the car and support on axle stands at the front jacking points. Lift away the road wheels.

2. Unscrew the reservoir cap and place to one side. Wrap a piece of polythene over the top of the reservoir and tie securely in position so as to make an air tight seal thus preventing loss of hydraulic fluid.

3. Wipe the hydraulic pipe union at the calliper free of dust and dirt. Remove the pipe clip at the swivel pillar.

4. Disconnect the hydraulic fluid feed pipe (A), Fig.9.15, at the calliper and wrap the open end with clean rag to prevent dust ingress into the system.

5. Extract the pin retaining clip (B) Fig.9.5, and withdraw the pad retaining pins (A).

6. The brake pads may now be removed by sliding them out of the calliper together with the anti-rattle spring (D) and damping shims. Note which way round the shim is fitted.

7. Mark each pad so that if it is to be refitted it may be replaced in its original position.

8. Undo and remove the two bolts (C), Fig.9.15, spring washers and plain washers that attach the brake shield to the calliper.

9. Bend back the tabs on the locking plate and remove the two bolts (B), locking plate, and finally the calliper unit.

10 Carefully prise off the hub cap with a wide bladed screwdriver and then extract the split pin and slotted nut from the stub axle.

11 Note that on later produced models having a suffix letter 'C' and onwards, it will be necessary to remove the locking cap and special nut as shown in Fig.11.3.

12 Remove the special washer and then the complete hub assembly.

13 Undo and remove the five bolts securing the disc to the hub flange face and separate the two parts using a soft faced hammer.

14 To refit the disc make quite sure that the mating faces of the disc and hub flange are clean and free from burrs. Place the disc onto the hub flange and secure with the five bolts tightening them to a torque wrench setting of 44 lb/ft.

15 Refit the hub and adjust the nut to give a zero endfloat. If available a dial indicator gauge and mounting bracket will give an accurate indication of the endfloat.

16 Check the brake disc run-out with a dial indicator gauge suitably mounted as shown in Fig.9.17. The run-out must not exceed 0.003 inch at the outer circumference as shown. If the run-out is excessive reposition the disc on the hub flange and re-check.

17 On early produced models adjust the hub nut to give an endfloat of between 0.003 and 0.005 inch by using one of a range of three thrust washer thicknesses.

18 On later produced models position the locking cap onto the nut in such a manner that the split pin can be inserted through the serrations without altering the position of the special hub nut.

19 Fit a new split pin and bend over the legs. Repack the hub cap with Castrol LM grease and replace the hub cap.

20 Refit the calliper unit and secure in position with two bolts and the locking plate. Lock the bolts by bending up the tabs.

21 Refit the calliper brake shield and retain in position with the two bolts, spring and plain washers.

22 Replace the pads in their original positions if the original ones are being fitted otherwise fit new pads. Also refit the damping shims making sure that they are the correct way round and finally the anti-rattle springs.

23 Insert the pad retaining pins and secure with the specially shaped pin retaining clips.

24 Reconnect the hydraulic fluid feed pipe to the calliper taking care not to cross the threads when first tightening the union.

25 Reconnect the hydraulic pipe clip to the swivel pillar.

26 It will now be necessary to bleed the hydraulic system, details of which are given in Section 20 of this Chapter.

27 Refit the road wheels and wheel nuts, remove the axle stands and lower the car to the ground. Tighten the wheel nuts and refit the wheel trims.

28 Press the brake pedal down several times to adjust the brake pad position. Top up the master cylinder as necessary and refit the cap.

12. Rear Disc Brake Calliper (Dunlop) — Removal, Overhaul & Refitting

1. Remove the wheel trim and slacken the road wheel nuts. Chock the front wheels, jack up the rear of the car and support on axle stands as shown in Fig.9.18. Remove the road wheel nuts and lift away the road wheel.

2. Undo and remove the four bolts and lock plates that secure the flange of the drive shaft to the final drive output flange. Expand the De Dion tube and allow the shaft to fall clear.

3. With a pair of pliers straighten the split pin locking the adjuster bolt of the handbrake calliper unit and extract the split pin. Slacken off the adjuster bolt and also the outer pad retaining nut. Remove the pad. These parts are shown in Fig.9.6.

4. If the car is fitted with a dowelled disc it will be necessary to remove the outer footbrake pad. To do this undo and remove the nut, washer and bolt that secures the brake pad keep plate and lift away the plate.

5. Lift out the pads noting which side they are fitted so that they can be replaced in their original positions.

6. Undo and remove the four bolts that secure the disc to the hub and lift away the disc and any shims that may be placed behind the disc.

7. Remove the connecting pipe between the callipers and plug the end to prevent leakage. Undo and remove the nut to release the clip on the differential housing bolt. If the right-hand side calliper is to be removed disconnect the flexible brake hose and plug to prevent leakage.

8. Next disconnect the clevis pin connecting the automatic adjuster

Fig.9.14. Piston and cylinder assembly (Dunlop)

A   Dust seal
B   Piston
C   Piston seal
D   Cylinder

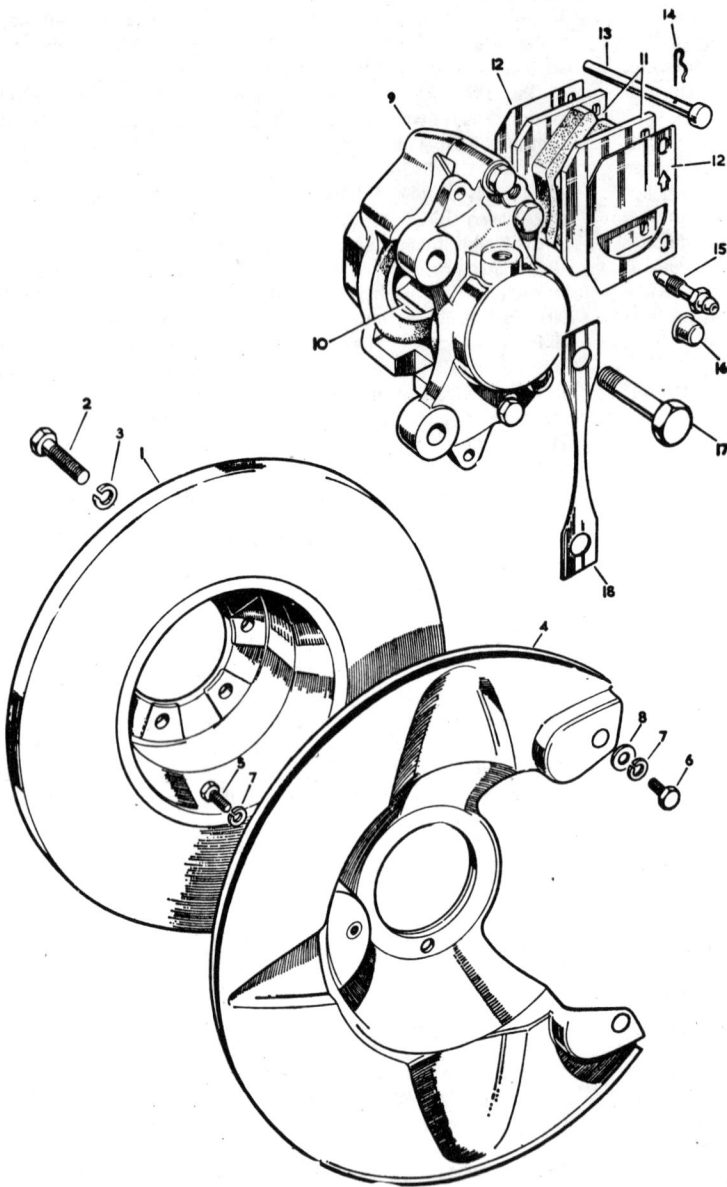

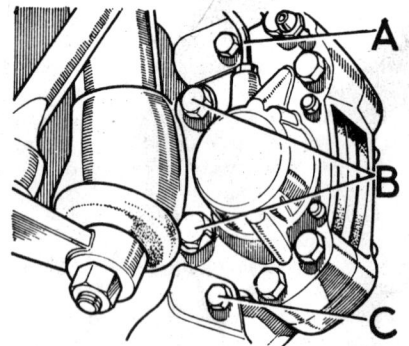

Fig.9.13. FRONT CALLIPER COMPONENT PARTS (GIRLING)

1	Disc for front brake	10 Piston for calliper
2	Set bolt	11 Friction pad
3	Spring washer	12 Damping shim
4	Shield & dust cover for disc	13 Retaining pin for pad
5	Set bolt	14 Clip retaining pin
6	Set bolt	15 Bleed screw
7	Spring washer	16 Dust cap for bleed screw
8	Plain washer	17 Special set bolt
9	Front brake calliper assembly	18 Tab washer

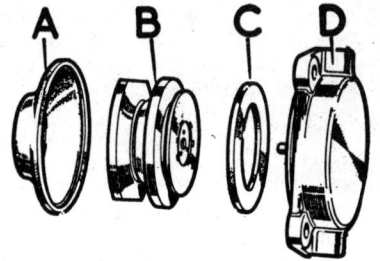

Fig.9.15. Front calliper securing bolts (Girling)

A   Hydraulic fluid feed pipe
B   Bolts securing calliper
C   Bolts fixing shield to calliper

unit to the operating linkage.

9. To stop oil dripping onto the floor, place a drip tray under the final drive assembly.

10 Undo and remove the four bolts and spring washers that secure the bearing housing to the pinion housing. It may be necessary to rotate the flange to gain access to the bolts.

11 Withdraw the differential drive shaft and bearing housing complete with the brake calliper and also the 'O' ring if one is fitted.

12 Keep the drive shaft bearing spacer in a safe place as it must be refitted.

13 Undo and remove the two bolts and spring washers and separate the calliper from the housing and retain the shims for re-use.

14 If the pads have not been removed this should now be done. First remove the bolt, nut and washer and lift away the two pads.

15 Wipe the unions clean and remove the hydraulic feed pipe and bridge pipe from the calliper unit.

16 Undo and remove the eight bolts, (18), Fig.9.12. There are four bolts each side that secure the two cylinder and piston assemblies to the calliper.

17 Separate the cylinder and piston assemblies from the calliper bridge.

18 Carefully disengage the dust seal (A), Fig.9.14, from the groove around the cylinder bore face.

19 The piston (B) may now be eased from the cylinder. If it is a tight fit it may be removed by either applying a low pressure air line to the hydraulic pipe connection or alternatively reconnecting the hydraulic pipe to the cylinder assembly and depressing the brake pedal.

20 The dust seal and piston seal (C) may now be removed from the piston.

21 It is not necessary to dismantle the piston further or to remove the retractor pin from the cylinder bore.

22 Thoroughly wash all parts in clean hydraulic fluid and wipe dry using a clean non-fluffy rag. Inspect the pistons and cylinders for signs of scoring and, if evident, a new assembly should be obtained and fitted. Also check that none of the threads have stripped either in the bridge or on the bolts.

23 To reassemble soak the new piston seals in clean brake fluid for several minutes.

24 Engage the collar of a new dust seal with the lip of the backing plate making sure that it is not stretched.

25 Fit the piston seal to the piston face. Apply a little clean brake fluid to the cylinder bore and locate the piston assembly over the end of the retractor pin.

26 Carefully apply an even pressure to the piston backing plate at the same time making sure that the piston is fitting squarely so avoiding damage to the seal.

27 Once the piston has entered the bore correctly, smear the cavity around the piston with clean brake fluid and fit the new dust seal over the rim of the cylinder flange.

28 Push the piston fully home down the bore.

29 Repeat the above procedure for the second cylinder and piston assembly as detailed in paragraphs 24 to 28 inclusive.

30 Refit the two piston and cylinder assemblies to the calliper bridge and tighten the eight securing bolts to a torque wrench setting of 8 lb/ft.

31 Insert the pads ensuring that the pad locating slotted plate engages with the spigot on the piston backing plate.

32 Refit the keep plate and secure in position with the bolt, washer and nut.

33 To refit the calliper hold it in its approximate location, together with its shims, secure with two bolts and spring washers and tighten to a torque wrench setting of 60 lb/ft.

34 Refit the assembly to the pinion housing together with an 'O' ring seal if originally fitted. Use Hylomar SQ 32M sealing compound on the ball joint faces. Tighten to a torque wrench setting of 30 lb/ft.

35 Refit the brake disc and packing washers and secure with four bolts.

36 Using a dial indicator gauge or feeler gauges check the disc run-out at a 10 inch diameter and this should not exceed 0.007 inch other-

wise a new disc should be fitted if there is no distance between the disc mating face and the hub.

37 Check that the slot between each side of the disc and the calliper slot face does not exceed 0.010 inch. Should any adjustment be necessary alter the number of shims placed between the calliper housing and the bearing housing. For this adjustment it will be necessary to remove the drive shaft bearing housing. Re-tighten the calliper fixing bolts to a torque wrench setting of 60 lb/ft.

38 Replace the outer footbrake and handbrake pads if not already in position.

39 Any hydraulic pipes that have been previously removed should next be refitted. Make sure that the ends are clean so there is no possibility of dirt ingress into the hydraulic system.

40 Replace the washer and split pin on the linkage pivot pin if these were previously disconnected.

41 Undo and remove the four bolts and packing washers that secure the brake disc and place the external drive shaft assembly onto the brake disc.

42 Refit the four bolts with new lock plates that secure the drive shaft flange yoke to the disc and differential drive assembly and tighten these bolts to a torque wrench setting of 85 lb/ft. Ensure that there is a clearance of 0.010 inch between the bolts and the oil catcher.

43 To assist removal at a later date the ends of the bolts should be painted with a rustproof paint when finally in position.

44 It will now be necessary to bleed the hydraulic system and details of this will be found in Section 20 of this Chapter.

45 Replace the road wheel and refit the wheel nuts.

46 Refer to Section 23 of this Chapter and adjust the handbrake calliper. Refit the adjuster split pin and open the ends.

47 Remove the axle stands and lower the car to the ground. Tighten the wheel nuts fully and refit the wheel trims.

48 Check the level of oil in the final drive unit and top up as necessary. Operate the brake pedal several times to automatically adjust the pad clearance. Finally road test the car to ensure satisfactory operation of the braking system.

13. Rear Disc Brake Handbrake Calliper (Dunlop) — Removal, Overhaul & Refitting

1. Remove the rear wheel trim and slacken the road wheel nuts. Chock the front wheels, jack up the rear of the car and support on axle stands as shown in Fig.9.18. Remove the road wheel nuts and lift away the road wheel.

2. Place the saddle of a garage hydraulic jack under the final drive unit and support its weight.

3. Remove the locknut that secures the brake hose to the bracket and then lower the hose.

4. Undo and remove the bolts and spring washers that secure the final drive assembly to the rear support bracket.

5. Carefully pull the rear support bracket rearwards so as to clear the filler plug.

6. Gradually lower the final drive assembly sufficiently to allow access to the handbrake calliper securing bolts.

7. Disconnect the automatic adjuster unit from the linkage by removing the split pin, washer and clevis pin.

8. Remove the split pin from the handbrake calliper adjuster bolt and slacken the adjuster bolt to give a greater clearance between the pad and the disc.

9. Bend back the tabs of the lockplates and remove the bolts, lockplates, locating plates and calliper retractor plates.

10 The handbrake calliper may now be lifted away from the disc.

11 To overhaul the rear calliper handbrake automatic adjusting unit refer to Fig.9.19, and remove the countersunk screw (A) from the side of the outer protection cover.

12 Extract the hinge pin locking split pin and withdraw the hinge pin (C). Lift away the cover (B).

13 Disconnect the large return spring (E) and separate the operating lever from the pad carrier.

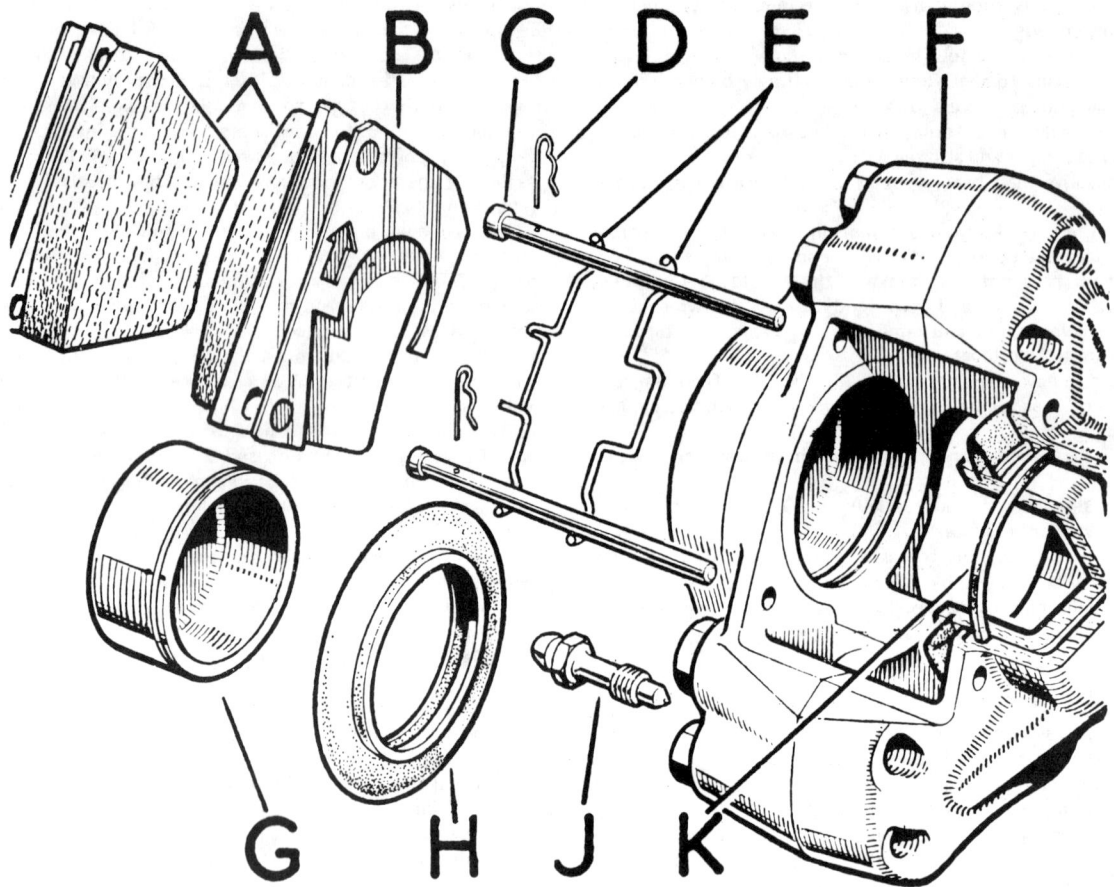

Fig.9.16. INTERNAL COMPONENTS OF FRONT CALLIPER (GIRLING)

A Brake pads
B Damping shim
C Pin retaining pads
D Special clip for pin
E Anti-rattle spring
F Calliper housing
G Piston
H Boot
J Bleed screw
K Piston seal

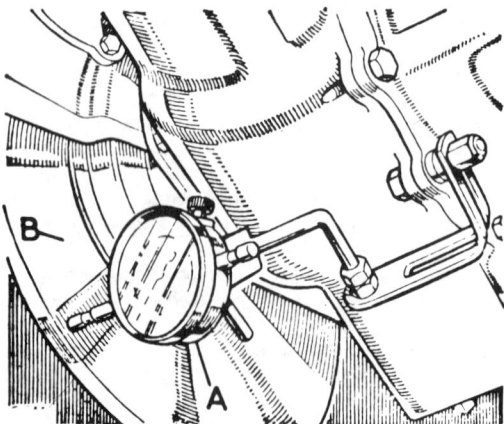

Fig.9.17. CHECKING DISC RUN-OUT USING A DIAL
INDICATOR GAUGE

A Gauge and bracket   B Disc

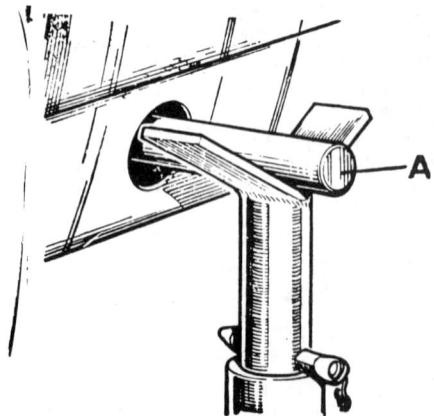

Fig.9.18. CORRECT METHOD OF SUPPORTING THE BODY
USING AXLE STANDS AT THE JACKING POINTS
A 7/8 inch diameter steel rod

14 Release the spring and spring anchor and remove the adjusting nut (G) and friction spring (H). Remove the adjusting nut pawl assembly.

15 Inspect the pad linings and if they have worn down to less than ¼ inch of material release the pads by undoing and removing the securing nuts and spring washers and lifting away the pads.

16 Inspect all moving parts for wear and obtain new parts as necessary. Check that the springs have not rusted badly as this will affect their efficiency.

17 To reassemble fit the pads and secure in position with the nut and spring washer.

18 Refit the adjusting nut pawl, spring (H) and anchor pin (F) to the operating lever (D).

19 Place the operating lever on the inner pad carrier together with the inner protection plate. Insert the large spring through the orifice and with a pair of pointed pliers carefully hook the end of the spring over the spring locating pin.

20 Clip the friction spring (H) onto the base of the adjusting nut and fit to the lever making sure that the friction spring seats on the trunnion and the nut engages with the pawl.

21 Refit the outer protection cover, and secure with the hinge pin (C), countersunk screw (A) and washers. Lock the hinge pin with a new split pin and bend over the legs.

22 Fit the adjuster bolt connecting the two pad carriers, but do not fit the split pin as the final adjustment must be made with the unit in position.

23 To refit the calliper replace in its correct position and install the retractor plates, locating plates, lockplates and bolts. Tighten the bolts and bend over the lockplate tabs.

24 Reconnect the automatic adjuster unit to the operating linkage and insert the clevis pin. Lock with a new split pin and bend over the legs.

25 Carefully raise the final drive assembly and ease the rear support bracket forwards into position.

26 Refit the rear support bracket to final drive housing bolts and spring washers and tighten securely.

27 Refit the locknut that secures the brake hose to the bracket.

28 Remove the jack from under the car and adjust the pad clearance to 0.010 inch by rotating the special adjuster bolt. Use feeler gauges to determine this measurement. Operate the handbrake lever several times and re-check the pad clearance.

29 Replace the road wheels and refit the wheel nuts.

30 Remove the axle stands and lower the car to the ground. Tighten the wheel nuts fully and refit the wheel trims.

14. Rear Disc Brake Calliper (Girling) — Removal, Overhaul & Refitting

1. Remove the rear wheel trim and slacken the road wheel nuts. Chock the front wheels, jack up the rear of the car and support on axle stands as shown in Fig.9.18. Remove the road wheel nuts and lift away the road wheel.

2. Knock back the tabs on the lockwasher at the front position and unscrew the bolt. Lift away the retainer plate and anti-rattle spring. These parts are shown in Fig.9.7.

3. Swing the top of the inner pad forwards and withdraw the pad towards the rear of the car.

4. Bend back the tabs on the lockwasher at the rear position and slacken the bolt enough to release the spring tension of the anti-rattle spring on the outer pad.

5. Ease the calliper outwards and release the outer pad from the drag pins. Lift away the pad.

6. Release the handbrake cable from the calliper lever, this being shown in Fig.9.2. Extract the split pins and clevis pins that connect the linkage to the levers on each calliper.

7. Undo and remove the two bolts that hold the bracket to the final drive unit and remove the complete handbrake linkage system.

8. Wipe the unions of the hydraulic feed pipe and pipe connecting the two callipers, to stop dirt ingress into the system and disconnect the two pipes at the unions. Plug the end of the pipes.

9. Remove the stop pin (F) Fig.9.20, and then turn the lever (E) as far as it will go towards the centre line of the car body. Do not pull it out of the calliper unit but lie a piece of string or fit a thick elastic band around the unit to keep it in place. It should be noted that if the lever is pulled out the handbrake tappet will drop down and the lever cannot be reassembled without dismantling the unit.

10 With the stop pin out and the lever in its furthermost position it will be just possible to get a socket onto the hexagonal headed plug (E), Fig.9.21. Unscrew and remove the plug together with the coil spring behind it. For information this coil spring may be seen in Fig.9.25.

11 Fit an Allen key into the head of the pivot pin (C), Fig.9.21, and unscrew it from the bearing (A).

12 Push the bearing out from the rear of the calliper, and withdraw the pivot pin from the front. The calliper at this stage will be free to be lifted away ready for dismantling.

13 To dismantle the calliper first undo and remove the two self locking nuts that secure the cover in position. Lift away the cover and the large rubber seal, also the two smaller rubber seals and the special anti-corrosive paper.

14 Undo and remove the two nuts (D), Fig.9.22, that retain the beam in position.

15 With a pencil or scriber, mark the strut so that it will be fitted in its original position and then remove by lifting the lever and pulling the strut forwards (Fig.9.23).

16 Depress the lever and withdraw it complete with the pawl.

17 Next push the piston upwards from below and ease off the main spring (A), Fig.9.24. over the two studs. Lift off the beam (B).

18 Suitably mark one sleeve (C), Fig.9.26 and stud, and remove both the sleeves.

19 Carefully detach the 'S' shaped spring (B).

20 Unscrew the serrated head pushrod (A), Fig.9.27, and withdraw the piston (B) from below. With a suitable sized Allen key undo and remove the Allen screw and location plate (B), Fig.9.28, followed by the stop washer (C).

21 Rotate the handbrake lever (C), Fig.9.29, so as to eject the tappet (E), Fig.9.28.

22 Apply a low pressure air jet to the tappet bore and with a piece of clean rag placed over the hydraulic piston eject the hydraulic piston. Take care that it does not fly out.

23 Unscrew and remove the stop pin (B), Fig.9.29, and completely withdraw the handbrake lever and shaft (C).

24 Carefully ease out the remaining 'O' rings and their retainers located as shown in Fig.9.30. Also remove the drag pins and spring washers (E). Finally remove the bleed screw.

25 During reassembly it will be necessary to obtain a complete set of rubber parts and also two new drag pins and two cover nuts.

26 Thoroughly wash all parts in clean hydraulic fluid and wipe dry with a clean non-fluffy rag. Inspect the piston and cylinder for signs of scoring and, if evident, a new assembly should be obtained and fitted. Also check that none of the threads have stripped either in the calliper body or the bolts.

27 The procedure for reassembly is the reverse sequence to dismantling but the following additional points must be noted. First soak all rubber seals in clean hydraulic fluid.

28 A new seal must be fitted to the hydraulic piston and so placed that the smaller diameter of the seal is nearest to the pointed end of the piston.

29 The handbrake tappet (E), Fig.9.28, should be positioned in the calliper so that the pointed end is uppermost.

30 Screw in the serrated head pushrod (A), Fig.9.27, three complete turns only.

31 Place the beam (A), Fig.9.26 in its original position as shown in the illustration.

32 Refit the pawl to the lever and insert the assembly slantwise, as shown in Fig.9.31, so that it is between the beam and the head of the pushrod. To assist this operation pull the piston down from below and then swing the lever square and press into position.

33 The nuts that secure the main spring and beam should be tightened to a torque wrench setting of 28 lb/ft.

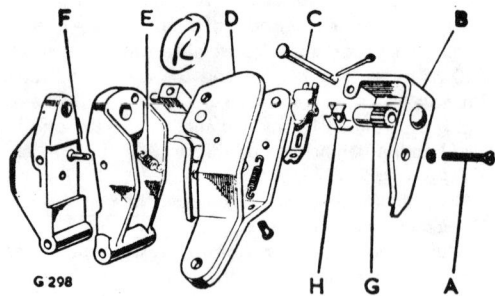

Fig.9.19. AUTOMATIC ADJUSTER UNIT (DUNLOP)

A Countersunk screw
B Protection cover
C Hinge pin
D Operating levers
E Return spring
F Anchor pin
G Adjusting nut
H Friction spring

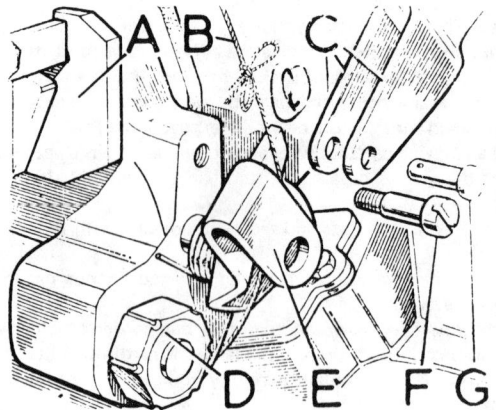

Fig.9.20. HANDBRAKE LINKAGE (GIRLING)

A Inner brake pad
B String retaining handbrake lever
C Link lever
D Spring loaded plug
E Handbrake lever
F Stop pin for handbrake lever
G Clevis pin for handbrake lever

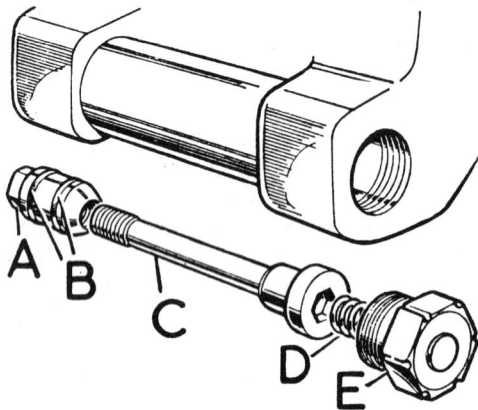

Fig.9.21. PIVOT PIN FOR CALLIPER (GIRLING)

A Bearing
B Seals for bearing
C Pivot pin
D Spring for plug
E Plug

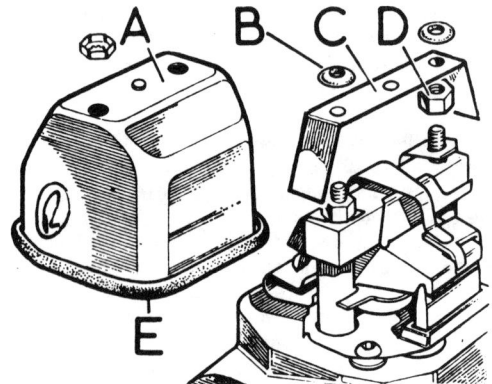

Fig.9.22. CALLIPER COVER REMOVAL

A Cover
B Small rubber seal
C Anti-corrosive paper
D Nut for beam
E Large rubber seal

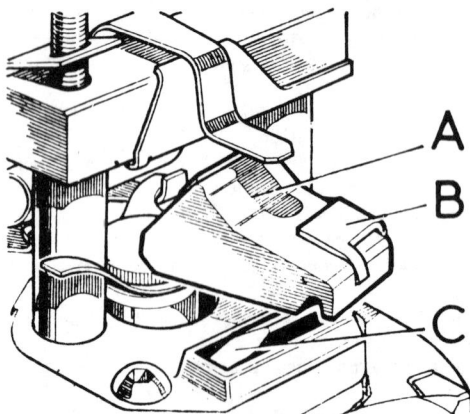

Fig.9.23. STRUT AND LEVER

A Strut
B Pawl
C Lever

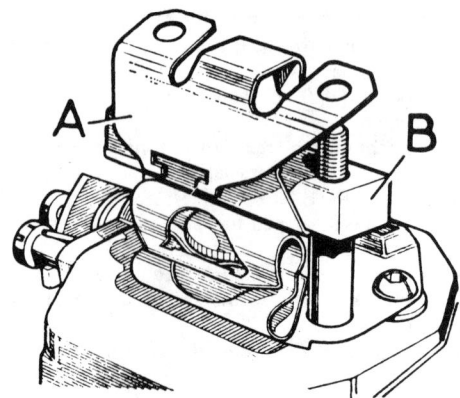

Fig.9.24. MAIN SPRING

A Main spring
B Beam

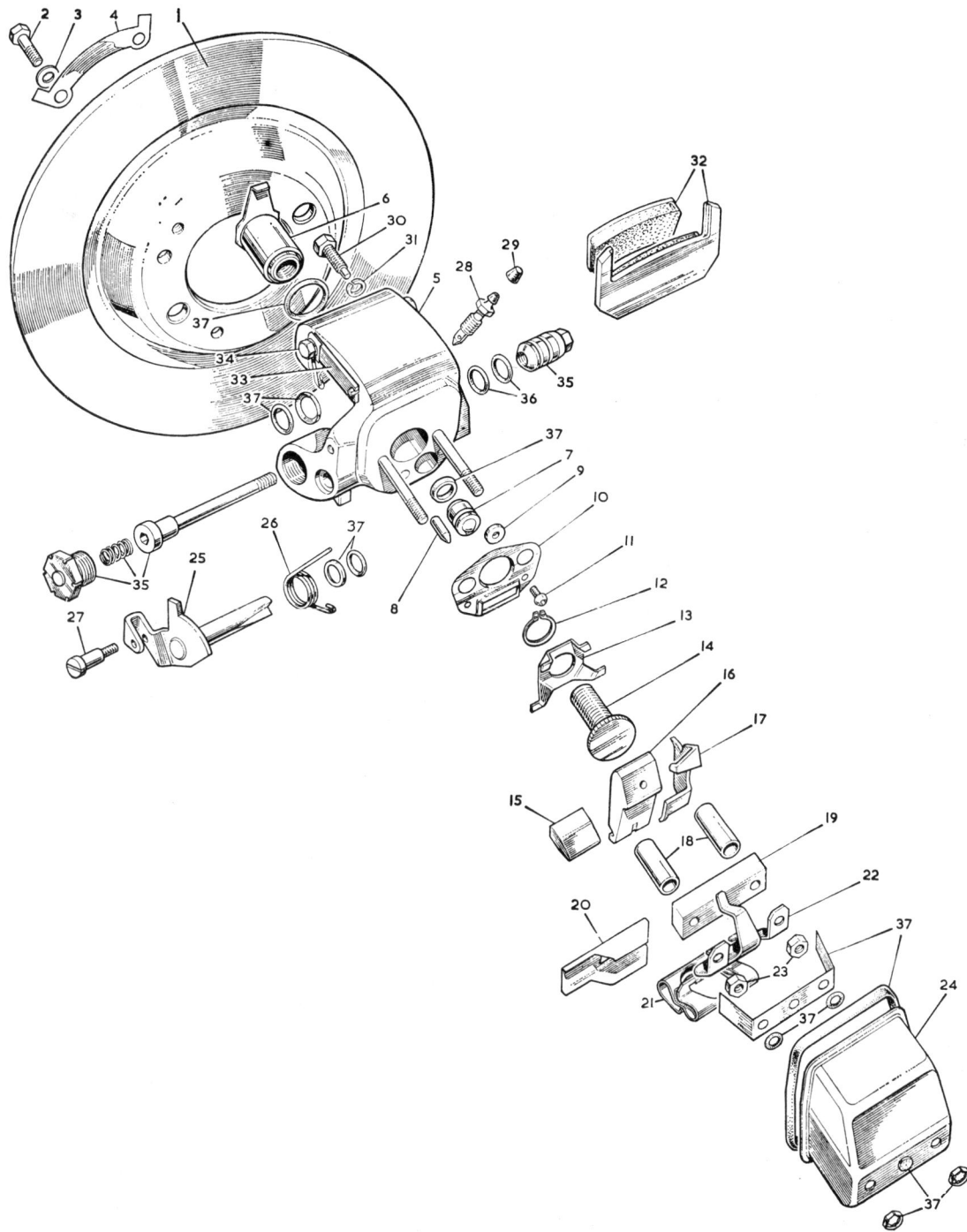

Fig.9.25. REAR FOOTBRAKE & HANDBRAKE CALLIPER COMPONENTS (GIRLING)

1 Disc for rear brake	12 Circlip for pushrod	25 Cam lever for handbrake,
2 Special bolt	13 Collar for pushrod	RH
3 Shim washer, thick	14 Pushrod	26 Return spring for cam
4 Locking washer	15 Strut	lever, RH
5 Rear brake calliper	16 Lever for strut	27 Stop pin for cam
assembly, RH	17 Pawl	lever
6 Piston cup assembly	18 Sleeve	28 Bleed screw
7 Piston	19 Beam	29 Dust cap for bleed
8 Tappet for handbrake	20 Lever locator	screw
9 Stop washer for piston	21 'S' spring	30 Drag pin
10 Location plate	22 Main spring	31 Spring washer
11 Special screws fixing	23 Special nut	32 Friction pads, set of four,
location plate	24 Cover	(includes locking tabs and

spring plates)	
33 Retaining plate for pad	
34 Special bolt for pad	
retainer plate	
35 Hinge pin assembly	
36 Seal for hinge pin scaling	
nut	
37 Seal repair kit for rear	
callipers	

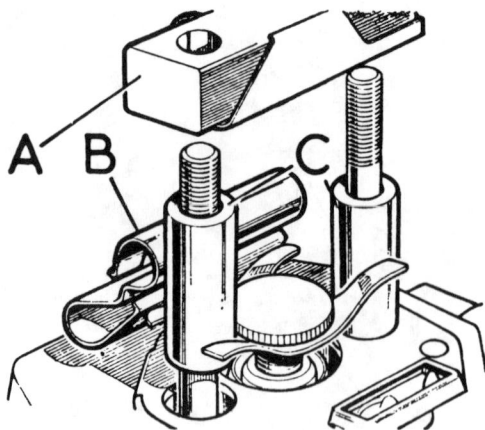

Fig.9.26. SLEEVES AND 'S' SHAPED SPRING
A Beam
B 'S' spring
C Sleeves

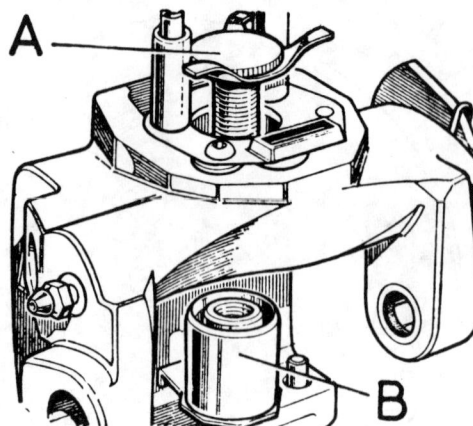

Fig.9.27. PUSHROD AND PISTON
A Serrated head pushrod   B Piston

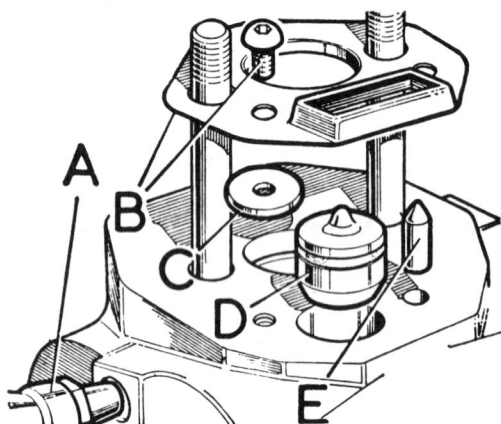

Fig.9.28. HYDRAULIC PISTON, LOCATION PLATE & STOP WASHER

A Air line
B Location plate and fixings
C Stop washer for piston
D Hydraulic piston
E Tappet for handbrake

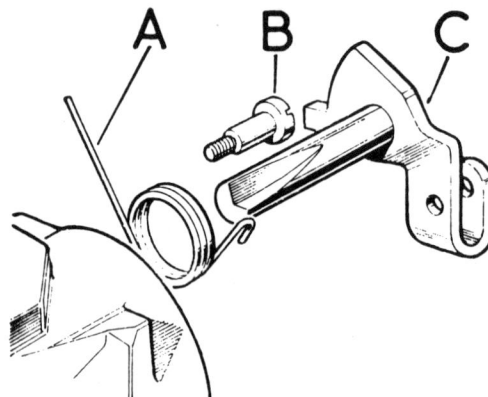

Fig.9.29. HANDBRAKE LEVER
A Return spring
B Stop pin
C Handbrake lever and shaft

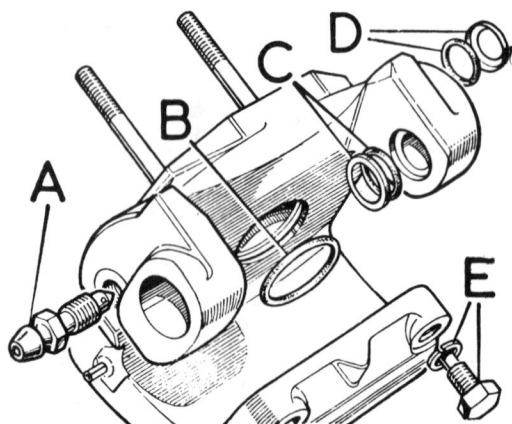

Fig.9.30. LOCATION OF THE RUBBER 'O' RINGS
A Bleed screw
B Rubber 'O' ring for piston
C Rubber 'O' ring and retainer for pivot pin
D Rubber 'O' ring and retainer for handbrake lever shaft
E Drag pin and spring washer

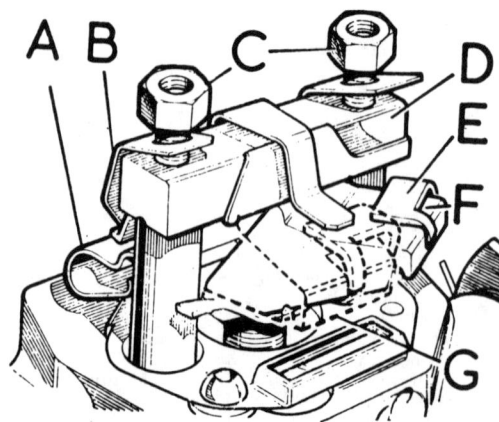

Fig.9.31. LEVER FOR CALLIPER
A 'S' spring
B Main spring
C Nuts for beam loosely assembled
D Beam
E Pawl
F Strut
G Strut and pawl in final position

34 At this stage check the action of the unit as shown in Fig.9.32 by operating the handbrake lever. The pawl should click as the lever moves and the serrated head of the pushrod should rotate one tooth only on return. Should this not occur the lever with the pawl is incorrectly located.

35 Screw in the piston fully and turn the lever so that it is in the position shown in Fig.9.33.

36 The calliper unit is now ready for refitting to the car.

37 Refitting the calliper is the reverse sequence to removal as detailed in paragraphs 1 to 12 but the following additional points should be noted.

38 Fit new 'O' rings to 'the bearing and then pull it into position by screwing in the pivot pin with an Allen key of suitable size. By doing it this way the two 'O' rings will not be damaged. Tighten the bearing to a torque wrench setting of 35 lb/ft.

39 Tighten the spring loaded plug to a torque wrench setting of between 28 and 35 lb/ft.

40 The bolts that secure the drive shaft flange should be tightened to a torque wrench setting of 85 lb/ft.

41 It will now be necessary to bleed the hydraulic system and details of this operation will be found in Section 20 of this Chapter.

42 Replace the road wheel and refit the wheel nuts.

43 Remove the axle stands and lower the car to the ground. Tighten the wheel nuts fully and refit the wheel trims.

44 Road test the car and ensure that the braking system is operating satisfactorily. Do not forget to check the operation of the handbrake.

15. Rear Disc (Dunlop) — Removal & Refitting

1. Remove the rear wheel trim and slacken the road wheel nuts. Chock the front wheels, jack up the rear of the car and support on axle stands as shown in Fig.9.18. Remove the road wheel nuts and lift away the road wheel.

2. Bend back the lock tabs and undo and remove the four bolts and lockplates that secure the drive shaft flange to the final drive output flange. Mark the two flanges so that they are refitted in their original positions.

3. Expand the De Dion tube and lower the shaft.

4. Extract the split pin and slacken off the adjuster bolt of the handbrake calliper unit. Also slacken the outer pad retaining nut and lift away the pad.

5. On cars fitted with a dowelled brake disc remove the outer footbrake pad as well. Further information will be found in Section 5 of this Chapter.

6. Undo and remove the four bolts securing the disc and with a soft faced hammer carefully remove the disc. Lift away the packing washers at the back of the disc.

7. To refit the disc position it with the previously removed packing washers on the back of the disc and secure with the four bolts.

8. Using a dial indicator gauge mounted as shown in Fig.9.17, check the run-out of the disc at a 10 inch diameter. This should not exceed 0.007 inch. If this limit is exceeded remove the four disc retaining bolts and reposition the disc. If this still does not produce the required results it is an indication that either the mating faces are dirty or the disc is distorted.

9. Check that the disc is central in the caliper and that a gap of 0.010 inch exists between the disc and brake pads on each side (Fig. 9.6). Referring to Fig. 9.34 ensure that the gap between the disc and caliper inner walls does not vary by more than 0.010 inch.

10 Refitting thereafter is the reverse sequence to removal. It will be necessary, however, to expand the De Dion tube so that the drive shaft may be reconnected.

16. Rear Disc (Girling) — Removal & Refitting

1. Remove the rear wheel trim and slacken the road wheel nuts. Chock the front wheels, jack up the rear of the car and support on axle stands as shown in Fig.9.18. Remove the road wheel nuts and lift away the road wheel.

2. Refer to Section 7 and remove the rear brake pads.

3. Bend back the lock tabs and undo and remove the four bolts and lockplates that secure the drive shaft flange to the final drive output flange. Mark the two flanges so that they are refitted in their original positions.

4. Expand the De Dion tube and lower the shaft.

5. Rotate the disc until the dowel holes are parallel with the callipers and then ease off the dowels and withdraw the disc.

6. To refit the disc is the reverse sequence to removal. It is advisable, however, to use a dial indicator gauge mounted as shown in Fig.9.17 and check the run-out of the disc at a 10 inch diameter. This should not exceed 0.007 inch. If this limit is exceeded, remove the four disc retaining bolts and reposition the disc. If this still does not produce the required results it is an indication that either the mating faces are dirty or the disc is distorted.

17. Master Cylinder — Removal & Refitting

1. Wipe the union free of dust and disconnect the hydraulic fluid feed pipe from the reservoir at the master cylinder. Raise the pipe so as to prevent leakage.

2. Undo and remove the vacuum pipe banjo bolt at the servo unit and carefully move the pipe to one side.

3. Wipe the unions clean, slacken off and disconnect the fluid feed pipe at both the master cylinder and also the servo unit. Ease the pipe from its locations and blank off the servo unit connections to stop dirt ingress.

4. Undo and remove the nuts and spring washers from the master cylinder mounting studs on the engine bulkhead but do not yet remove the master cylinder.

5. Disconnect the footbrake pedal return spring.

6. Refer to Fig.9.36, and release the locknut from the operating rod at the foot pedal. With a wide bladed screwdriver screw the rod through the trunnion, at the same time withdrawing the master cylinder.

7. To refit the master cylinder place it on the mounting studs at the same time inserting the operating rod into the threaded trunnion in the foot pedal assembly. If difficulty is found in aligning the operating rod try using a long thin screwdriver to guide the rod into the trunnion.

8. Screw the rod through the trunnion until approximately 1 inch protrudes from the end.

9. Check that the rod and brake pedal have a free movement and then refit the two master cylinder securing nuts and spring washers.

10 Refit the brake pedal return spring and adjust the height of the pedal by screwing the master cylinder pushrod in or out. The correct setting is when a vertical distance of between 6½ and 6¾ inch exists between the underside of the pedal rubber and the floor panel, with the carpets removed.

11 Reconnect the hydraulic fluid reservoir pipe to the master cylinder. Also refit the hydraulic fluid pipe between the master cylinder and the servo unit.

12 Reconnect the vacuum pipe to the servo unit.

13 It will now be necessary to bleed the hydraulic system and details of this will be found in Section 20 of this Chapter.

18. Master Cylinder Overhaul — Dunlop

If a replacement master cylinder is to be fitted it will be necessary to lubricate the seals before fitting to the car as they have a protective coating when originally assembled. Remove the blanking plug from the hydraulic pipe union seating. Ease back and remove the pushrod dust cover so that clean brake fluid can be injected at these points. Operate the piston several times so that the fluid will spread over all internal working surfaces.

1. The internal parts of the master cylinder are shown in Fig. 9.35.

2. Carefully ease the dust cover (B) out from its location groove on the master cylinder body.

3. With a pair of pliers or circlip pliers remove the circlip (C) and

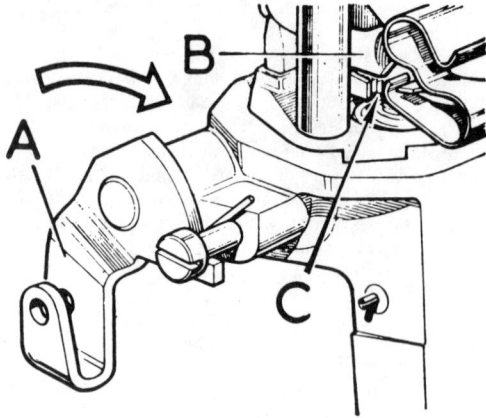

Fig.9.32. CHECKING OPERATION OF HANDBRAKE MECH-
ANISM
A Handbrake lever   C Serrated head of pushrod
B Pawl

Fig.9.33. CORRECT POSITION OF PISTON LEVER
A Piston lever

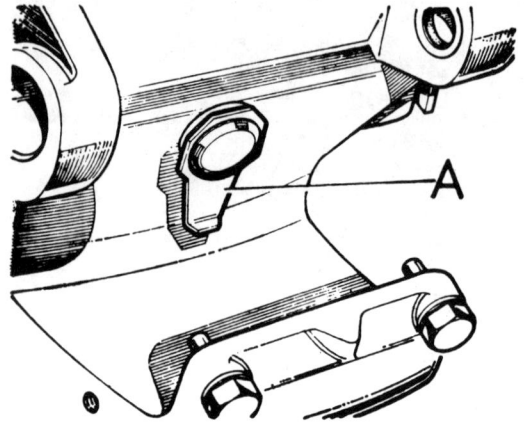

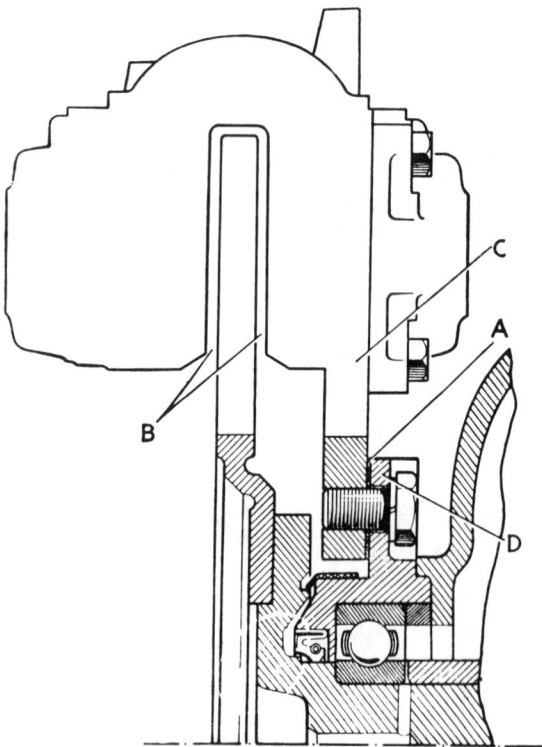

Fig.9.34. POSITION OF BRAKE CALLIPER SHIMS
A Shim   C Calliper housing
B This gap must not vary more   D Bearing housing
   than 0.010 inch

Fig.9.35. BRAKE MASTER CYLINDER COMPONENTS
(DUNLOP)
A Rod   H Support
B Dust cover   J Spring
C Circlip   K Valve spring support
D Dished washer   L Spring
E Seal   M Valve
F Piston   N Seal
G Seal

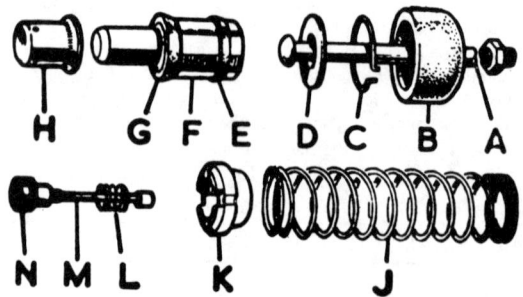

withdraw the operating rod (A) complete with the dished washer (D).

4. The piston assembly (F) may now be removed by applying a low pressure air jet to the master cylinder body inlet port. Take great care as the piston may fly out.

5. Carefully remove the piston seals (E and G) noting which way round the seals are fitted.

6. Ease out the valve assembly (M) which will include the springs (J and L) and support (K). Note which way round the valve seal is fitted and carefully remove the seal.

7. Examine the bore of the cylinder for any signs of scores or ridges and if this is found to be smooth all over new seals may be fitted. If there is any doubt of the condition of the bore then a new master cylinder must be fitted.

8. If examination of the seals shows them to be apparently oversize, swollen or very loose on the piston or valve, suspect oil contamination in the system. Oil will swell these rubber seals, and if one is found to be swollen it is reasonable to assume that all seals in the braking system will need attention.

9. Thoroughly clean all parts in either hydraulic fluid or Industrial Methylated Spirits. Ensure that the ports are free of dirt.

10. All components should be assembled wet by dipping in clean brake fluid.

11. Fit the seal onto the end of the valve making sure that the lip registers with the groove. Then refit the smaller diameter spring (L).

12. Refit the seals (E and G) to the grooves in the piston (F) making sure that they are fitted the correct way round as shown in Fig.9.36.

13. Refit the spring (J) and insert the piston into the spring support (H) making sure that the lead of the valve (M) engages in the piston bore.

14. Well lubricate the valve and piston assembly and slide the complete assembly into the cylinder body taking care not to damage the piston seals or rolling the seals upon initial entry into the bore.

15. Insert the pushrod and depress the piston sufficiently to allow the dished washer to seat onto the shoulder on the head of the cylinder. Refit the circlip and check that it is seating in its groove correctly.

16. Pack the dust excluder with rubber grease and refit to the master cylinder body.

17. The master cylinder is now ready for refitting.

19. Master Cylinder Overhaul – Girling

If a replacement master cylinder is to be fitted it will be necessary to lubricate the seals before fitting to the car as they have a protective coating when originally assembled. Remove the blanking plug from the hydraulic pipe union seating. Ease back and remove the pushrod dust cover so that the clean brake fluid can be injected at these points. Operate the piston several times so that the fluid will spread over all internal working surfaces.

1. The internal parts of the master cylinder are shown in Fig.9.37.

2. Carefully ease the dust seal cap (E) and seal (D) from the body of the master cylinder.

3. With a pair of circlip pliers remove the circlip (C) and withdraw the operating pushrod (B) complete with the dished washer.

4. The piston assembly (N) may now be removed by applying a low pressure air jet to the master cylinder body inlet port. Take great care as the piston may fly out.

5. With a small screwdriver ease the locking lip of the spring retainer (L) clear of the shoulder on the piston and separate the piston.

6. Compress the return spring (K) and position the valve stem so as to align with the larger hole in the spring retainer (L). Remove the spring (K) and retainer (L).

7. Slide the valve spacer (J) over the valve stem (G).

8. Remove the spring washer (H) noting which way round it is fitted, and then the valve seal (F) from the valve stem.

9. Carefully remove the piston seal (M) from the piston noting which way round it is fitted.

10. Examine the bore of the cylinder carefully for any signs of scores or ridges, and if this is found to be smooth all over new seals can be fitted. If there is any doubt of the condition of the bore then a new cylinder must be fitted.

11. If examination of the seals shows them to be apparently oversize, swollen, or very loose on the plunger, suspect oil contamination in the system. Oil will swell these rubber seals, and if one is found to be swollen it is reasonable to assume that all seals in the braking system will need attention.

12. Thoroughly clean all parts in either clean hydraulic fluid or Industrial Methylated spirits. Ensure that the ports are clean.

13. All components should be assembled wet by dipping in clean brake fluid.

14. Fit a new valve seal (F) the correct way round so that the flat side is correctly seating on the valve head (G). Fig.9.37 shows this in detail.

15. Place the dished washer (H) with the dome against the underside of the valve head (Fig.9.37). Hold it in position with the valve spacer (J) ensuring that the legs face towards the valve seal (F).

16. Replace the plunger return spring (K) centrally on the spacer (J), insert the spacer retainer (L) into the spring (K) and depress until the valve stem (G) engages in the keyhole of the spacer retainer (L).

17. Ensure that the spring is central on the spacer before fitting a new piston seal (M) onto the piston (N) with the flat face against the face of the plunger. This is shown in Fig.9.37.

18. Insert the reduced end of the piston into the spring retainer (L) until the lip engages under the shoulder of the piston and press home the lip.

19. Check that the master cylinder bore is clean and smear with clean brake fluid. With the piston suitably wetted with brake fluid insert the assembly into the bore with the valve end first. Ease the lip of the piston seal carefully into the bore.

20. Replace the pushrod (B) and refit the circlip (C) into the groove in the cylinder body. Smear the sealing into the areas of the dust seal (D and E) and pack the interior of the seal with rubber grease. Refit the seal to the master cylinder body.

21. The master cylinder is now ready for refitting to the car.

20. Bleeding the Hydraulic System

1. Removal of all the air from the hydraulic system is essential to the correct working of the braking system, but before undertaking this examine the fluid reservoir cap to ensure that both vent holes, one on top and the second underneath but not in line, are clear; check the level of fluid and top up if required.

2. Check all brake line unions and connections for possible seepage, and at the same time check the condition of the rubber hoses which may be perished.

3. If the condition of the wheel cylinders is in doubt, check for possible signs of fluid leakage.

4. If there is any possibility of incorrect fluid having been put into the system drain all the fluid out and flush through with methylated spirits. Renew all piston seals and cups since they will be affected and could possibly fail under pressure.

5. Gather together a clean jam jar, a 9 inch length of tubing which fits tightly over the bleed nipple, and a tin of the correct brake fluid, i.e. Girling Crimson SAE 70R3.

6. For reference the bleed nipple locations are shown in Fig.9.39 and Fig.9.40.

7. To bleed the system clean the areas around the bleed valve, and start on the rear brakes first by removing the rubber cup over the bleed valve and fitting a rubber tube in position. The nipple location is shown in Fig.9.40.

8. Place the end of the tube in a clean glass jar containing sufficient fluid to keep the end of the tube underneath during the operation.

9. Open the bleed valve with a spanner and quickly press down the brake pedal. After slowly releasing the pedal, pause for a moment to allow the fluid to recoup in the master cylinder and then depress

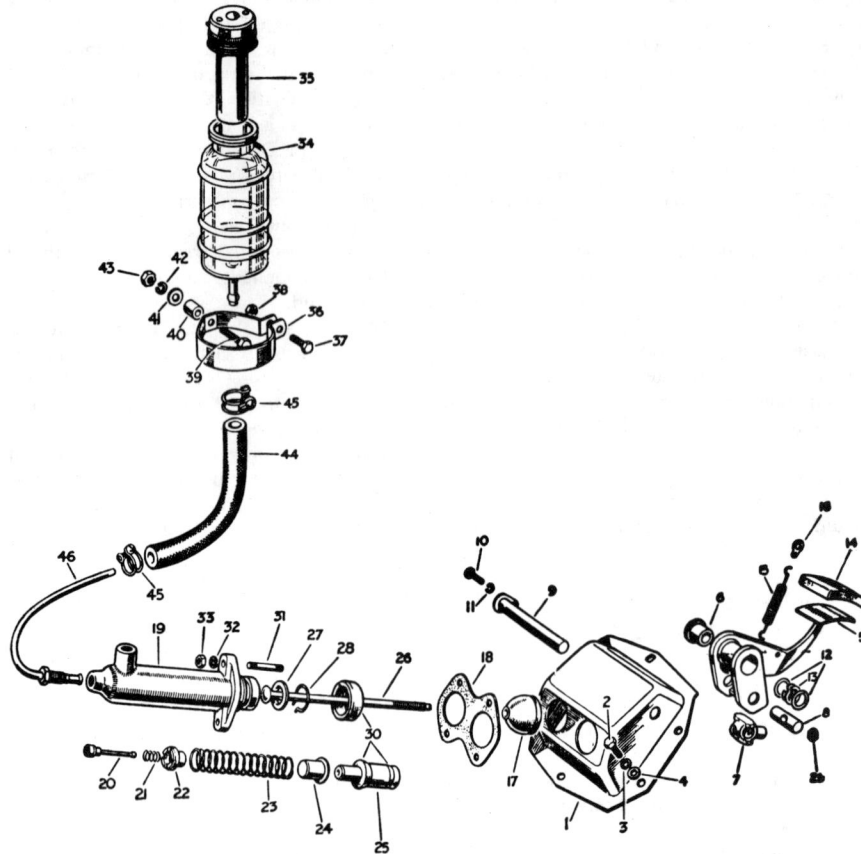

Fig.9.36. BRAKE RESERVOIR' MASTER CYLINDER & PEDAL (DUNLOP)

1	Brake & clutch pedal box	13	Spring washer, double coil	24	Support for main spring	35	Cap and switch
2	Set bolt	14	Rubber pad	25	Piston	36	Bracket for supply tank
3	Spring washer	15	Return spring	26	Push rod	37	Bolt
4	Plain washer	16	Anchor plate	27	Washer for push rod	38	Nut
5	Brake pedal assembly	17	Grommet	28	Circlip retaining push rod	39	Bolt
6	Bush for brake pedal	18	Packing plate	29	Nut for push rod	40	Spacer
7	Adjuster for brake pedal	19	Brake master cylinder assembly	30	Repair kit for master cylinder	41	Plain washer
8	Trunnion for adjuster	20	Valve	31	Stud	42	Spring washer
9	Shaft	21	Spring for valve	32	Spring washer	43	Nut
10	Set bolt	22	Support for valve spring	33	Nut	44	Hose
11	Spring washer	23	Main spring	34	Brake fluid supply tank	45	Clip for hose
12	Shim washer					46	Brake pipe complete

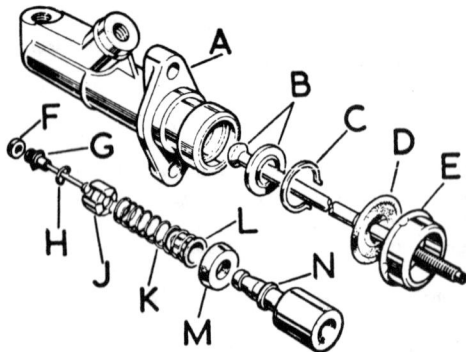

Fig.9.37. BRAKE MASTER CYLINDER COMPONENTS (GIRLING)

A	Master cylinder body	G	Valve stem
B	Push rod and retaining washer	H	Spring washer
C	Circlip	J	Valve spacer
D	Dust seal	K	Return spring
E	Cap for dust seal	L	Spacer retainer
F	Valve seal	M	Piston seal
		N	Piston

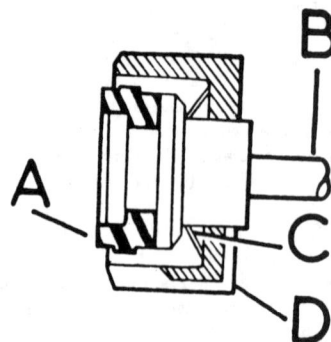

Fig.9.38. VALVE ASSEMBLY (GIRLING)

A	Valve seal	C	Spring washer
B	Valve stem	D	Valve spacer

again. This will force air from the system. Continue until no more air bubbles can be seen coming from the tube. At intervals make certain that the reservoir is kept topped up, otherwise air will enter at this point again.

10 Repeat this operation on all four brakes, and when completed, check the level of the fluid in the reservoir and then check the feel of the brake pedal. This should be firm and free from any 'spongy' action which is normally associated with air in the system.

21. Flexible Hose – Inspection, Removal & Replacement

Inspect the condition of the flexible hydraulic hoses leading from the chassis mounted metal pipes to the brake backplates. If any are swollen, damaged, cut, or chafed they must be renewed.

1. Unscrew the metal pipe union nut from its connection to the hose, and then holding the hexagon on the base with a spanner, unscrew the attachment nut and washer.

2. The chassis end of the hose can now be pulled from the chassis mounting brackets and will be quite free.

3. Disconnect the flexible hydraulic hose from the calliper unit. NOTE: When releasing the hose from the calliper unit the chassis end must always be freed first.

4. Replacement is a straightforward reversal of the above procedure.

22. Handbrake Lever – Removal, Overhaul & Refitting

1. The handbrake lever and linkage for the Dunlop system is shown in Fig.9.1, whereas the Girling system may be seen in Fig.9.2.

2. The procedure for the removal, overhaul and refitting of the handbrake lever is identical for both types of system.

3. Chock the rear wheels securely to prevent car movement during removal of the console cover.

4. Remove the front and rear ashtrays and undo the two nuts located under the rear ashtray and the nut under the front ashtray.

5. Refer to Fig.9.41 and remove the two Phillips screws at the front of the cover.

6. Carefully raise the flat on the forward edge of the handbrake grommet base and remove the drive screw.

7. Locate the two Phillips head screws securing the speaker grille to the console unit and remove these two screws. Lift away the speaker grille. If a radio set is installed it will be necessary to disconnect the two speaker cables.

8. Release the gearchange lever knob locknut and remove the knob, spring retaining sleeve and the gearchange lever sleeve.

9. Move the front seats as far to the rear as possible by sliding on their runners. Raise the seat locking levers.

10 Carefully roll back the handbrake grommet and apply a smear of MS4 Silicone grease to both the grommet and the handbrake handle.

11 Gently lift the forward edge of the cover over and off from the gearchange lever.

12 Pull the handbrake lever until it is in the fully 'on' position. Do not, however, force for extra movement.

13 Slide the cover forwards and upwards to enable the forward edge to protrude into the aperture at the top of the console and at the same time, push the handbrake grommet off the handbrake handle.

14 Release the handbrake and withdraw the cover assembly.

15 Extract the split pin and remove the clevis pin for the handbrake rod at the relay linkage.

16 Undo and remove the two bolts that secure the handbrake lever assembly to the propeller shaft tunnel.

17 Note which way round the handbrake switch cables are fitted to the rear of the switch and disconnect the cables.

18 The handbrake lever and operating rod may now be removed.

19 To overhaul the handbrake lever, first extract the split pin and remove the clevis pin that secures the brake rod to the handbrake lever.

20 Extract the split pin and withdraw the clevis pin from the ratchet pawl. Also remove the special plain steel washer.

21 Hold the handbrake lever in the normal 'off' position and depress the plunger so that the pawl may be drawn away in a downwards direction.

22 Examine all moving parts for wear, especially the pawl, and obtain new parts as required.

23 To reassemble place the handbrake lever on its side and depress the release plunger.

24 Insert the pawl into position and align the clevis pin holes with a small screwdriver.

25 Fit the clevis pin, plain steel washer and secure with a new split pin. Bend over the legs to lock.

26 Fit the handbrake rod to the lever and secure with the clevis pin. Lock the clevis pin with a new split pin and bend over the legs to lock it.

27 To refit the handbrake lever and the console cover is the reverse sequence to removal. Check the operation of the handbrake 'on' position warning light to ensure that it operates correctly.

28 Should the handbrake warning light switch require adjustment refer to Chapter 10, Section 51.

23. Handbrake Linkage (Dunlop) – Removal & Refitting

1. To remove the handbrake linkage extract the split pins and withdraw the clevis pins from the handbrake calliper to operating links and separate the linkage from the calliper.

2. Extract the split pin and remove the plain washer from the pivot pin at the final drive casing.

3. Extract the split pin and withdraw the clevis pin located at the forward end of the brake cable.

4. Refer to Fig.9.42, and ease the rubber boot from the torque reaction bracket. Remove the spring clip that secures the handbrake outer cable.

5. The cable and linkage may now be lifted away from the underside of the car.

24. Handbrake Linkage (Girling) – Removal & Refitting

1. The linkage is shown in Fig.9.44. Undo and remove the two Phillips head screws and remove together with the trunnion retainers (F), from the inner and outer bellcrank levers.

2. Remove the handbrake cable from the inner and outer bellcrank levers (C and E).

3. Extract the split pins and withdraw the clevis pins so that the link lever (A) and the link plates (L) may be disconnected from the bellcrank levers (C and E).

4. Extract the split pin (D) and withdraw the clevis pin that secures the bellcrank lever and return spring to the pivot pin. The parts may be lifted away as an assembly.

5. If considered necessary remove the pivot pin and abutment plate from the bracket and then the bracket from the final drive unit.

6. Detach the handbrake cable at the handbrake lever. Ease back the inner cable rubber sleeve and remove the nut, now exposed. The handbrake cable may now be withdrawn.

7. To refit the handbrake linkage is the reverse sequence to removal. It is important, however, that the inner cable clevis must fit to the handbrake lever without any tension in the cable. The outer cable nuts should be in the midway position on the thread.

25. Servo Unit – Removal & Refitting

1. Disconnect the battery terminals and on pre 1970 models release the battery clamp and lift away the battery from its location in the engine compartment.

2. Wipe the unions clean on the five way brake hydraulic pipe junction and remove the servo unit feed pipe. Plug the end of the union on the junction to stop loss of hydraulic fluid.

3. Disconnect the vacuum pipe at the union on the servo unit.

4. Disconnect the pipe from the master cylinder to the servo unit

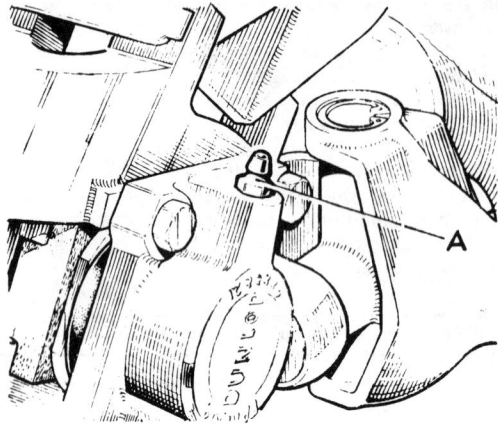

Fig.9.39. BLEED NIPPLE POSITION (DUNLOP)
A Bleed nipple

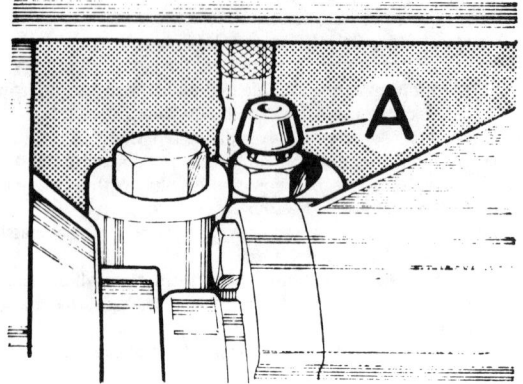

Fig.9.40. BLEED NIPPLE POSITION (GIRLING)
A Rear bleed screw

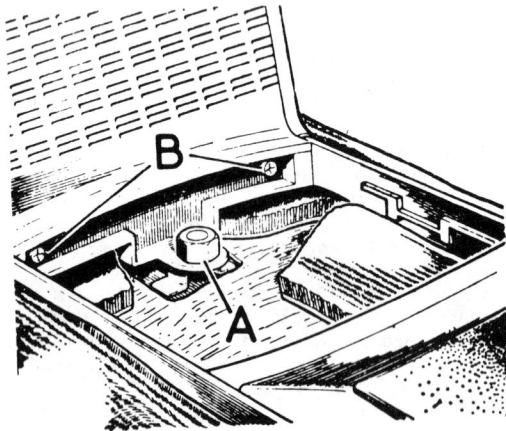

Fig.9.41. GEARBOX CONSOLE FRONT FIXINGS
A Front fixing nut   B Phillips screws

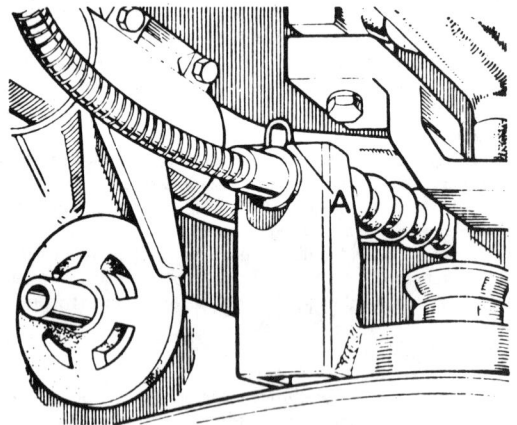

Fig.9.42. LOCATION OF HANDBRAKE LINKAGE SPRING
CLIP
A Spring clip

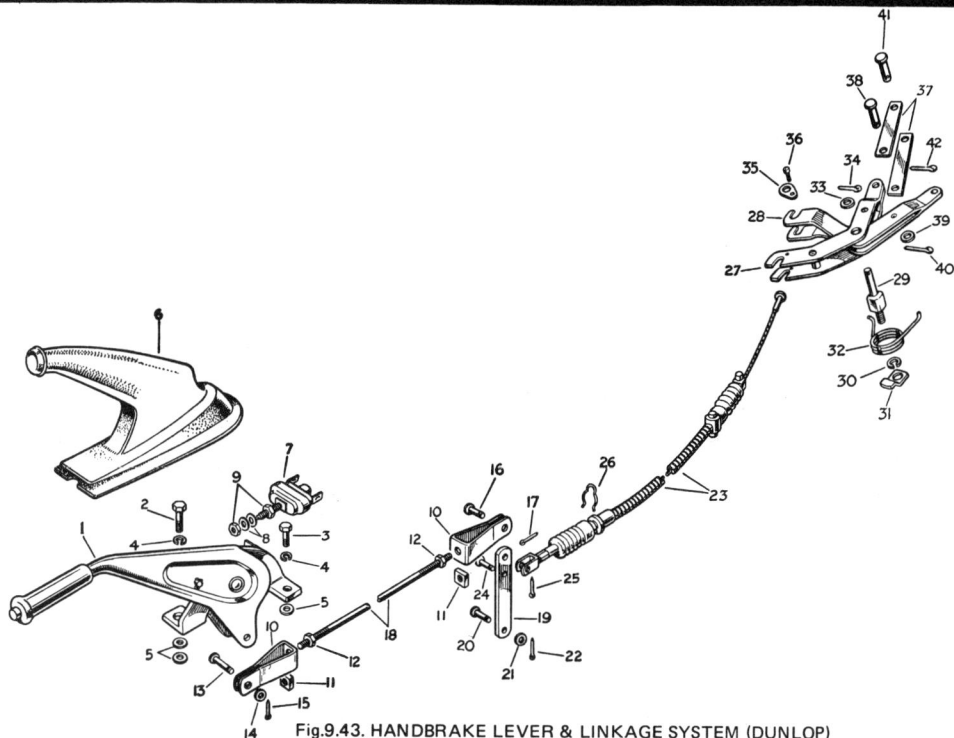

Fig.9.43. HANDBRAKE LEVER & LINKAGE SYSTEM (DUNLOP)

1	Handbrake lever complete	12	Locknut for fork end	23	Handbrake cable complete
2	Set bolt	13	Clevis pin	24	Clevis pin
3	Set bolt	14	Plain washer	25	Split pin
4	Spring washer	15	Split pin	26	Clip for handbrake cable
5	Packing washer	16	Clevis pin	27	Bellcrank lever, outer
6	Grommet for handbrake lever	17	Split pin	28	Bellcrank lever, inner
7	Switch for warning light	18	Brake rod, handbrake lever to relay lever	29	Pivot pin for bellcrank lever
8	Plain washer	19	Relay lever for handbrake	30	Spring washer
9	Nut	20	Clevis pin	31	Abutment plate for return spring
10	Fork end for brake rod	21	Plain washer	32	Return spring for bellcrank
11	Square nut in fork end	22	Split pin		

	levers	
33	Plain washer	
34	Split pin	
35	Trunnion retaining plate	
36	Self-tapping screw	
37	Operating link	
38	Clevis pin	
39	Plain washer	
40	Split pin	
41	Clevis pin	
42	Split pin	

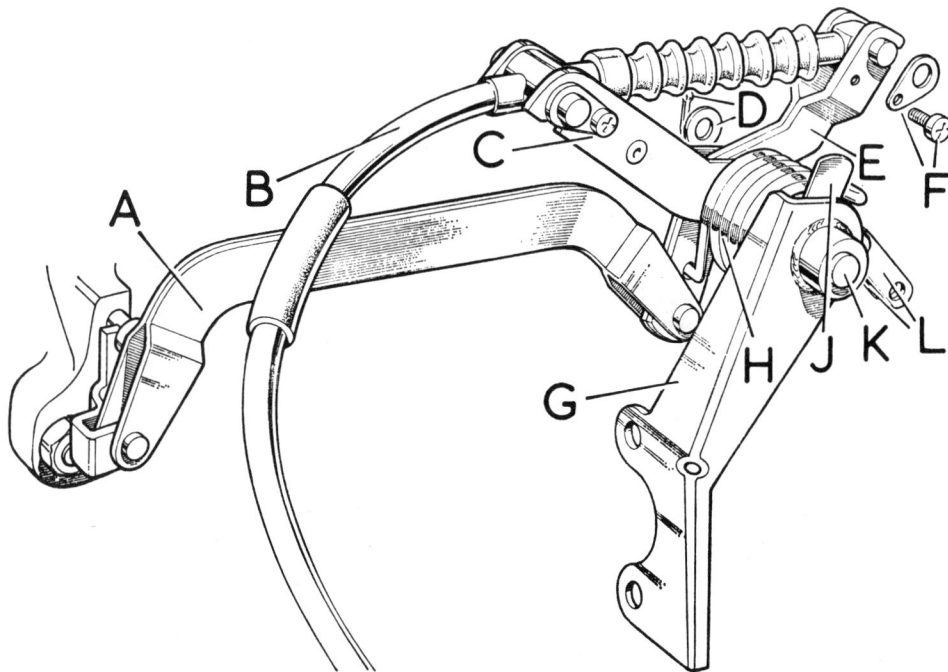

Fig.9.44. LAYOUT OF HANDBRAKE LINKAGE (GIRLING)

A	Link lever		ing bellcrank levers	G	Bracket for bellcrank lever
B	Handbrake cable	E	Bellcrank lever, inner	H	Return spring for lever
C	Bellcrank lever, outer	F	Trunnion retainer and fixing	J	Abutment plate for
D	Washer & split pin retain-				

	return spring
K	Pivot pin, threaded into bracket
L	Link plates

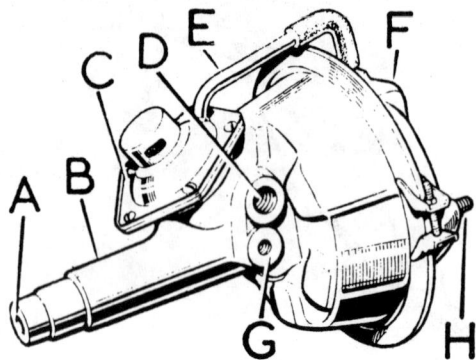

Fig.9.45. SERVO UNIT EXTERNAL DETAILS – 5.5 INCH
EARLY TYPE

A Brake fluid outlet (to   E Air inlet connecting pipe
   wheels)   F Vacuum chamber
B Servo cylinder   G Brake fluid inlet (from
C Air valve assembly   master cylinder)
D Manifold vacuum connection H Fixing stud

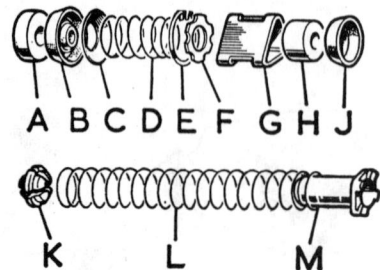

Fig.9.46. PISTON ASSEMBLY (5.5 INCH SERVO UNIT)

A Guide piece   G Distance piece
B Secondary cup   H Hydraulic piston
C Cup spreader   J Main cup
D Spring   K Spring guide
E Circlip   L Spring
F Washer   M Spring retainer

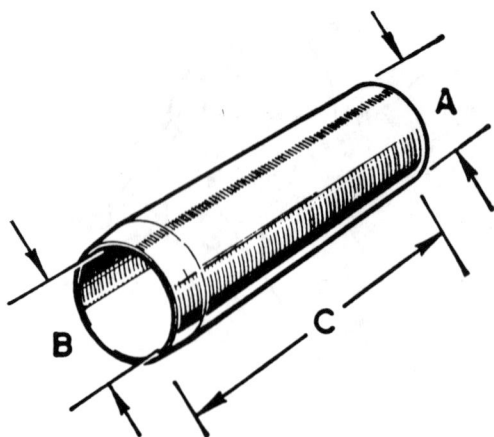

Fig.9.47. FITTING SLEEVE (5.5 INCH SERVO UNIT)

A Outside diameter   0.725 inch
B Inside diameter   0.625 inch
C Length   1.75 inch

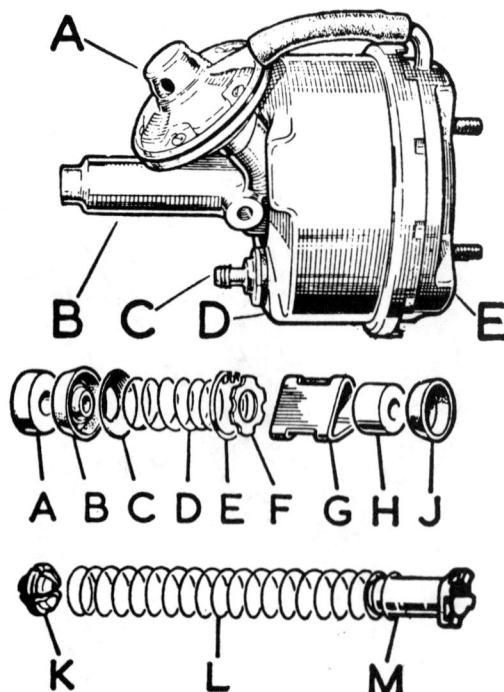

Fig.9.48. SERVO UNIT EXTERNAL DETAILS – 7 INCH
LATER TYPE

A Air valve assembly   D Vacuum chamber
B Slave cylinder   E Cover for vacuum
C Non-return valve   chamber

at the servo.

5. Undo and remove the two nuts and spring washers that secure the servo unit to the front bracket.

6. Undo and remove the two nuts and spring washers that secure the rear bracket to the inner wing valance. Also undo and remove the bracket to servo unit pinch bolt.

7. On some models there may be a nut and spring washer securing the brake fluid reservoir bracket which should also be removed.

8. The servo unit may now be lifted away from the engine compartment.

9. If necessary remove the mounting bracket from the servo unit.

10 Refitting the servo unit is the reverse sequence to removal. It will, however, be necessary to bleed the brake hydraulic system. Details of this operation will be found in Section 20 of this Chapter.

26. Servo Unit (5.5 Inch Type) - Overhaul

1. Mount the servo unit between soft faces in an engineer's vice so that it is held at the slave cylinder body. Take care not to overtighten so as to distort the casting.

2. Remove the rubber elbow on the end of the air manifold connecting pipe.

3. Undo and remove the five screws securing the air valve cover and lift away the air valve cover and control valve diaphragm assemblies.

4. Remove the valve housing and then apply a low pressure air jet to the hydraulic system inlet connection. Also place a thumb over the hydraulic outlet connection and by doing this the valve piston assembly will be ejected. Take care that it does not fly out.

5. Carefully remove the seal from the valve piston.

6. Undo the clamping ring bolt and remove the clamping ring. Carefully release the end cover together with the booster diaphragm as this will be under the influence of the big spring.

7. Carefully remove the rubber buffer from the pushrod.

8. With a screwdriver or small chisel bend back the tabs of the locking plates and remove the four bolts that secure the vacuum shell and abutment plate to the slave cylinder. Note the gasket between the two mating faces.

9. With a piece of wire with the end bent into the shape of a hook extract the guide piece and secondary cup from the slave cylinder. Also recover the cup spreader and spring. These parts are shown in Fig.9.46.

10 Depress the hydraulic piston against the action of the spring by using the pushrod or a suitable piece of 5/16 inch diameter brass or copper rod. The circlip may then be released using a pair of circlip pliers.

11 Recover the washer, distance piece, hydraulic piston, main cup and spring complete with spring guide and spring retainer.

12 Separate the operating rod from the diaphragm taking extreme care not to damage the high quality surface finish. Also part the diaphragm and the plates.

13 With the servo unit dismantled inspect the following parts for wear and if suspect obtain new parts as necessary:

    Valve piston;   Pushrod;

    Valve piston bore;   Distance piece;

    Slave cylinder main bore.

14 All other parts should be washed in Industrial grade methylated spirits and left to dry.

15 It is important that all rubber cups and seals are assembled wet by dipping in brake fluid and allowing to soak before fitting.

16 Before commencing reassembly a special fitting sleeve will be required and details of this are shown in Fig.9.47. A piece of shim brass with the sharp edge removed may be used if workshop facilities are not available.

17 Fit the spring retainer into one end of the spring and the spring guide into the other end.

18 Insert the spring assembly into the slave cylinder bore with the retainer end first.

19 Refit the main cup to the servo unit bore using the tool as detailed in paragraph 16.

20 Next fit the hydraulic piston with the flat face leading into the bore and by holding the piston against the spring pressure with a piece of suitable brass rod 9/16 inch diameter or the pushrod. Insert the distance piece and washer and secure with the circlip. Make sure that the circlip seats correctly in its groove.

21 Insert the spring into the slave cylinder bore followed by the cup spreader — the dished side should be facing inwards.

22 Also insert the pushrod gland seal cup with the hollow side facing inwards. Ensure that it locates correctly on the cup spreader.

23 Fit the guide piece in the end of the bore with the smooth side facing inwards.

24 Refit the vacuum shell and a new gasket to the slave cylinder with the abutment plate and secure using the locking plates and four bolts. Tighten the four bolts to a torque wrench setting of 150 to 170 lb/in. Bend up the locking plate tabs.

25 Next build up the diaphragm assembly by fitting the large plate, lip downwards onto the threaded end of the pushrod. Replace the rubber diaphragm with the hollow face towards the large plate and then the small plate with the lip facing upwards. Finally secure with the nut and lock the nut by centre punching in two places 180° opposite to each other.

26 Refit the rubber buffer.

27 Engage the smaller end of the return spring under the tabs of the locking plate.

28 Attach the large end of the return spring to the diaphragm and enter the end of the pushrod into the slave cylinder bore by compressing the spring.

29 Hold the assembly in this position and refit the end cover and secure the latter with the clamping ring. Do not, however, fully tighten the nut and bolt yet.

30 Refit the seal onto the valve and position so that the lip is facing away from the piston. Insert the piston seal end first into the bore of the slave cylinder.

31 Replace the valve housing and its gasket and secure in position with the four screws.

32 Position the control valve diaphragm assembly onto the valve housing with the narrow stem inserted into the piston.

33 Fit a new air valve cover assembly complete with rubber elbow and secure in position. The air valve cover assembly is designed so that it must be renewed instead of being overhauled.

34 Move the position of the end cover so that the connecting pipe is in line with the rubber elbow. The nut and bolt that secures the clamping ring can now be fully tightened.

35 Reconnect the rubber elbow to the connecting pipe.

36 The unit is now ready for fitting to the car.

27. Servo Unit (7 Inch Type) — Overhaul

1. Secure the servo unit in an engineer's bench vice with soft faces between the jaws at the slave cylinder. Do not overtighten otherwise the slave cylinder can be distorted.

2. Carefully insert the blade of a screwdriver in one of the cover holes of the air filter and prise the cover off. Lift away the sorbo rubber washer, filter and spring. These parts are shown in Fig.9.49.

3. Undo and remove the five screws that secure the valve cover to the housing and withdraw the cover from the rubber hose, lift off the reaction valve diaphragm (A), Fig.9.50 and support (B) and separate from the housing (C).

4. Undo and remove the three countersunk head screws (A), Fig. 9.51 and separate the valve housing (B) together with the gasket (C) from the slave cylinder body (D).

5. Lift away the cup seal (B), Fig.9.52 from the valve piston (A).

6. Carefully prise the vacuum non-return valve (E), Fig.9.52, from the vacuum shell (D). Lift away the seal (F).

7. Reposition the servo unit in the vice so that the vacuum shell is placed uppermost.

8. It will now be necessary to make up a special tool so that the end cover can be removed. The best method is to obtain a piece of flat metal bar and drill two holes to match the stud locations as shown

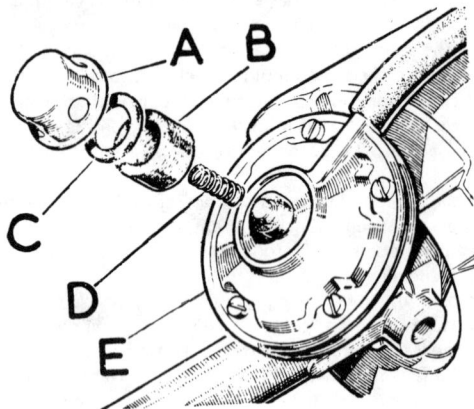

Fig.9.49. FILTER & COVER REMOVAL (7.0 INCH SERVO
UNIT)

A Air filter cover   D Spring for valve
B Filter   E Valve cover
C Sorbo washer

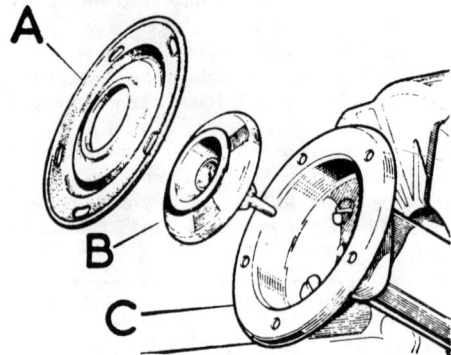

Fig.9.50. REACTION VALVE DIAPHRAGM SEPARATED
FROM SUPPORT (7.0 INCH SERVO UNIT)

A Reaction valve diaphragm
B Diaphragm support
C Valve housing

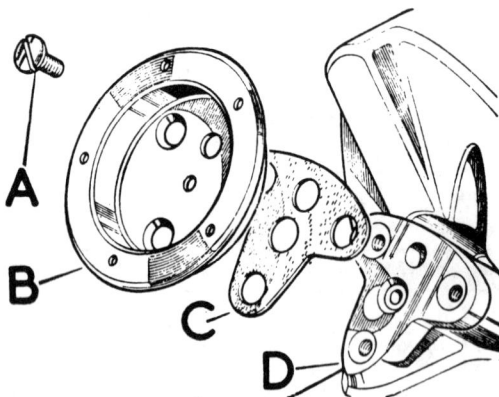

Fig.9.51. AIR VALVE BODY REMOVAL (7.0 INCH SERVO
UNIT)

A Body securing screw   C Gasket
B Air valve body   D Slave cylinder body

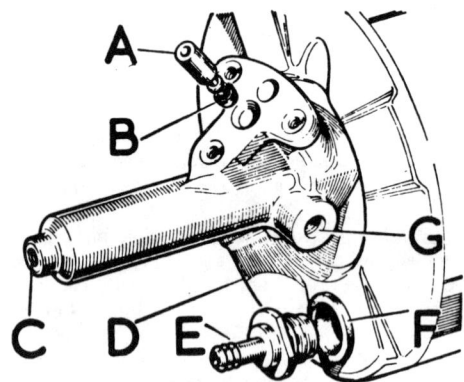

Fig.9.52. AIR VALVE PISTON & NON-RETURN VALVE
REMOVAL (7.0 INCH SERVO UNIT)

A Air valve piston   E Non-return valve
B Seal for air valve piston   F Seal for non-return
C Outlet connection   valve
D Vacuum chamber   G Inlet connection

in Fig.9.53. Fit the tool and secure with two 5/16 inch UNF nuts and turn the tool in an anti-clockwise direction. It will be necessary to apply considerable pressure to complete this operation.

9. Release the rubber diaphragm (A), Fig.9.54, from the diaphragm support (C) by peeling it from the rim of the vacuum shell, and then lifting off the groove (B) of the support.

10 Press the diaphragm support (A), Fig.9.55 downwards and shake the key (B) from the diaphragm support (A). Once the key is free remove the support (A) and the large return spring (C).

11 With a screwdriver bend back the tabs on the locking plate (A), Fig.9.56 and remove the three set bolts. Lift away the locking plate (A) and abutment plate (E). Separate the vacuum chamber (B), together with the gasket (C) from the slave cylinder body (F).

12 Withdraw the pushrod and internal parts from the slave cylinder as shown in Fig.9.57.

13 Remove the guide (F), Fig.9.58, large gland seal (E) and spacer (D) from the pushrod (C). Also remove the small piston seal (A) from the piston (B).

14 Should it be necessary to remove the piston from the rod hold the pushrod between soft faces in a vice and with a small screwdriver expand the spring clip (D), Fig.9.59 on the piston (B) and carefully ease the clip off the piston. It is important that the piston is not scratched.

15 The piston (B) may now be separated from the pushrod (A) by pressing out the small pin (C).

16 The servo unit is now completely dismantled and all the parts should be carefully inspected for signs of wear, damage or rusting and if any parts are suspect new ones should be obtained.

17 An overhaul repair kit is available and will include all rubber parts as well as a new piston.

18 To refit the slave cylinder piston to the pushrod first secure the pushrod (D), Fig.9.60, in between soft faces in a vice and then slide the slave cylinder piston over the tapered end of the pushrod.

19 Hold the small spring within the piston back towards the diaphragm end of the pushrod and insert the small pin into the hole in the pushrod, making sure that the end of the spring rests against the pin and that it does not pass through the coil of the spring.

20 Once the pin has been refitted satisfactorily, expand the spring clip and pass it over the piston to secure the pin. Again care must be taken not to scratch the piston.

21 Remove the pushrod from the vice. Soak a small 'U' section seal onto the end of the slave cylinder piston so that the groove in the seal is facing towards the head of the piston.

22 Reassemble the spacer with the larger diameter against the head of the piston, and follow up with the larger gland seal suitably wetted, with the grooved face leading onto the pushrod.

23 Mount the slave cylinder body between soft faces in a vice, and then fit the pushrod assembly into the bore of the slave cylinder taking care not to nip or damage the seals in any way.

24 Next refit the pushrod guide into the slave cylinder so that its flat face is innermost in the bore.

25 Position a new gasket over the pushrod guide and then refit the vacuum shell with the abutment plate and the locking plates. With a small screwdriver line up the holes with the tapped holes in the slave cylinder and insert the three securing bolts. Tighten these bolts to a torque wrench setting of between 12 to 14 lb/ft. and lock by bending up the locking tabs.

26 Make sure that the pushrod is in the fully withdrawn position and place the return spring over the pushrod and locate the diaphragm support on the end of the pushrod. Compress the support and secure by fitting the key into the slot in the side of the diaphragm support. Ensure that the key engages with the groove in the pushrod and that it is pushed right in.

27 The smaller diameter of the diaphragm should now be stretched into position on the diaphragm support making sure that it is correctly fitted into its groove. Next locate the outer edge of the diaphragm in the vacuum shell.

28 If the flat face of the diaphragm should have a buckled attitude it is an indication that the diaphragm has not been assembled

correctly. Recheck that the inner and outer edge of the diaphragm are seating correctly.

29 The end cover may now be refitted. With the special tool fitted, press down and turn in a clockwise direction until it is locked. It will be necessary to initially place the end cover so that when it is locked the air pipe is in the correct position relative to the face of the air valve.

30 Undo the two nuts securing the tool to the end cover and lift away the tool.

31 Release the slave cylinder from the grip of the vice and reposition it so that the air valve face is uppermost.

32 Next ease the cup into the groove in the air valve piston so that the lip of the cup faces the shouldered end of the piston. Insert the piston into the valve bore of the slave cylinder.

33 Place a new gasket into the slave cylinder and then position the valve housing in the gasket carefully aligning three holes with a small screwdriver. Refit the three countersunk headed screws and tighten them to a torque wrench setting of between 5 and 7 lb/ft.

34 Stretch the reaction valve diaphragm onto the diaphragm support and insert the pushrod portion of the diaphragm support through the hole in the valve housing.

35 The valve rubber may now be stretched and fitted with the groove around its inside diameter onto the valve stem flange using the fingers only. Do not use any metal or wooden tools to do this.

36 Insert the valve stem through the hole in the valve cover and fit the second valve rubber over the valve stem. Secure by fitting on the snap-on cap. If this is difficult it is permissible to warm up the cup in hot water.

37 Inspect the original hose and if necessary fit a new rubber hose. Insert the valve cover end into the hose and then position the cover onto the valve housing. Secure the cover with the five self tapping screws. It is important that the reaction valve diaphragm is not trapped between the valve cover bosses and the valve housing.

38 It is recommended that the air filter cover valve and seals be renewed as a new assembly, as the valve stem and seals are a selective assembly.

39 If the air filter is dirty it should be either washed out with methylated spirits and blown dry with an air line, or alternatively, a new filter fitted.

40 Place the air filter over the air valve and then position the metal spring over the snap-on cap.

41 Refit the sorbo rubber washer in the air filter cover and snap the assembly into the air valve cover.

42 Inspect the non-return valve assembly sealing rubber, and if necessary renew. Place the sealing rubber into the valve and push the valve into its location in the end cover.

28. Footbrake Pedal — Removal & Refitting

The brake and clutch pedals are mounted on a common fulcrum point attached to a bracket on the toe board. To remove the pedal assembly proceed as follows:—

1. Undo and remove the two bolts, nuts and spring washers that secure the accelerator cross-shaft mounting bracket to the body. These two bolts are accessible from beneath the front wing. NOTE: On LHD models these two bolts are accessible from within the engine compartment and in fact also secure the pedal bracket.

2. Unhook the two pedal return springs from the pedal.

3. Working inside the car, undo and remove the two bolts, nuts, plain and spring washers that secure the clutch pedal stop and bracket, these being shown in Fig.9.61. Lift away the bracket.

4. Undo and remove the four bolts with plain and spring washers that secure the pedal box (C) to the bracket.

5. Release and undo the two locknuts from the clutch and brake pushrods and with a screwdriver screw the rods through the pedal trunnions, whilst the pedal box assembly is being withdrawn. The two master cylinder pushrods may be left in position in the master cylinders. NOTE: On LHD models the accelerator mounting bracket will have to be held clear during this operation.

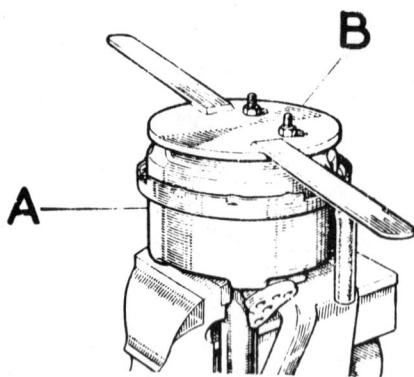

Fig.9.53. REMOVAL OF SERVO END COVER (7.0 INCH
SERVO UNIT)

A   End cover   B   Special tool or equivalent

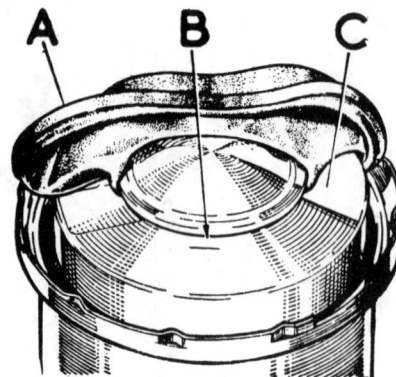

Fig.9.54.RUBBER DIAPHRAGM REMOVAL (7.0 INCH SERVO
UNIT)
A   Diaphragm
B   Groove
C   Diaphragm support

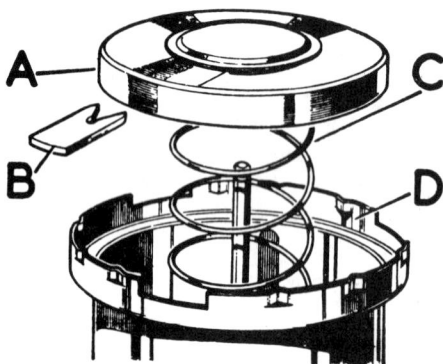

Fig.9.55. REMOVAL OF DIAPHRAGM SUPPORT & SPRING
A   Diaphragm support   C   Return spring
B   Key securing diaphragm support D   Vacuum chamber

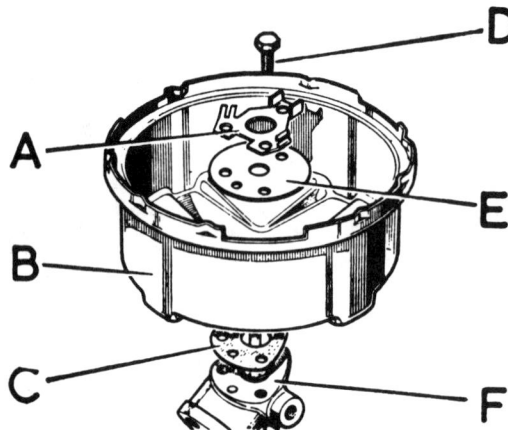

Fig.9.56. REMOVAL OF VACUUM CHAMBER (7.0 INCH
SERVO UNIT)

A   Lockplate   D   Vacuum chamber securing bolt
B   Vacuum chamber   E   Abutment plate
C   Gasket   F   Slave cylinder

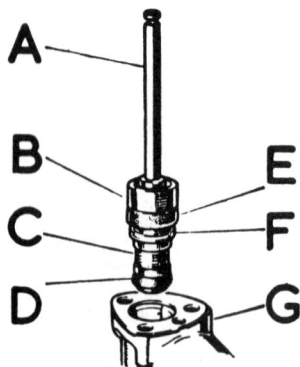

Fig.9.57 PUSHROD & INTERNAL PARTS REMOVAL FROM
SLAVE CYLINDER (7.0 INCH SERVO UNIT)

A   Pushrod   E   Gland seal
B   Pushrod guide   F   Spacer
C   Piston   G   Slave cylinder body
D   Piston seal

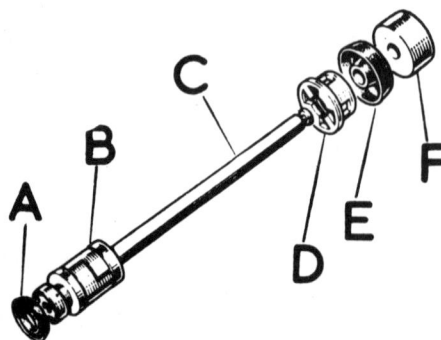

Fig.9.58. PUSHROD COMPONENTS (7.0 INCH SERVO)

A   Piston seal   D   Spacer
B   Piston   E   Gland seal
C   Pushrod   F   Pushrod guide

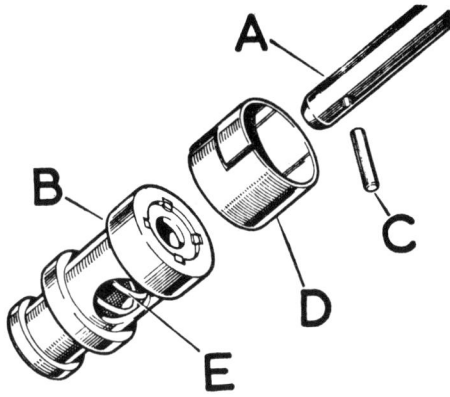

Fig.9.59. PISTON REMOVAL FROM PUSHROD (7.0 INCH
SERVO UNIT)

A Pushrod   D Spring clip
B Piston   E Piston spring
C Pin

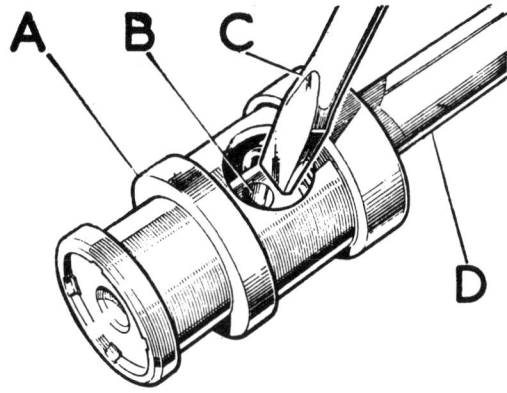

Fig.9.60. REFITTING PISTON TO PUSHROD (7.0 INCH
SERVO UNIT)

A Piston   C Screwdriver
B Hole for pin   D Pushrod

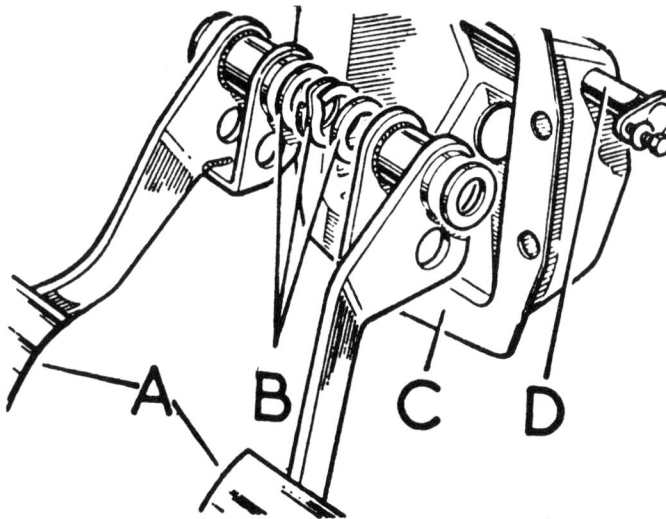

Fig.9.61. FOOTBRAKE PEDAL ASSEMBLY

B Shim washers & double spring washer   C Pedal bracket   D Pivot spindle

6. Undo and remove the bolt and spring washer that retains the pedal shaft to the pedal box and withdraw the shaft from the two pedals.

7. Lift away the two pedals from the pedal box and recover the two shim washers and double coil spring washers.

8. To reassemble first apply a little molybdenum disulphide grease to the pedal bushes and the shaft and assemble to the two pedals, shim washers, and double spring washer to the pedal box, and insert the pedal shaft. Secure the shaft in position with the lock bolt and spring washer.

9. Apply a little Bostik 692 or equivalent non-setting sealer to the pedal box flange and offer in position, whilst at the same time locating the two pushrods in the trunnions using a small thin screwdriver. Screw the pushrods in an anti-clockwise direction until approximately one inch of thread is protruding from the trunnions.

10 Replace the pedal box and clutch stop bracket bolts with spring and plain washers. Do not tighten the bolts until all are in position.

11 Attach the accelerator cross-shaft mounting bracket to the body and secure in position with the two bolts, nuts and spring washers. NOTE: On LHD models, this bracket is located by two of the bolts that secure the pedal box.

12 Reconnect the two pedal return springs.

13 Adjust the brake pedal height by screwing the master cylinder pushrod in or out. The correct setting is when a vertical distance of between 6½ and 6¾ inch exists between the underside of the pedal rubber and the floor panel, with the carpets removed

14 It will now be necessary to adjust the clutch pedal and linkage and full details of this will be found in Chapter 5, Section 11.

29. Hydraulic Fluid Reservoir — Removal & Refitting

1. Undo and remove the bolts that secure the support bracket to the wing valance.

2. Make a note of the electrical cable connections at the switch on the reservoir cap and disconnect the cables.

3. Disconnect the main feed cap to the master cylinder and blank off the master cylinder union to stop any dirt ingress. Also plug the end of the flexible pipe with a sharpened pencil or other means so that hydraulic fluid does not spill onto the bodywork.

4. Refitting the hydraulic fluid reservoir is the reverse sequence to removal. It will however, be necessary to bleed the hydraulic system, details of which will be found in Section 20 of this Chapter.

Symptom	Reason/s	Remedy
Leaks and air bubbles in hydraulic system	Brake fluid level too low.	Top up master cylinder reservoir. Check for leaks.
	Calliper leaking.	Dismantle calliper, clean, fit new rubber seals and bleed brakes.
	Master cylinder leaking. (Bubbles in master cylinder fluid).	Dismantle master cylinder, clean, and fit new rubbers. Bleed brakes.
	Brake flexible hose leaking.	Examine and fit new hose if old hose leaking. Bleed brakes.
	Brake line fractured.	Replace with new brake pipe. Bleed brakes.
	Brake system unions loose.	Check all unions in brake system and tighten as necessary. Bleed brakes.
Normal wear	Pad linings over 75% worn.	Fit replacement pads.
Incorrect adjustment	Brakes badly out of adjustment.	Check calliper for correct operation.
	Master cylinder pushrod out or adjustment causing too much pedal free movement.	Reset to manufacturer's specification.
Brake pedal feels springy		
Pad lining renewal	New linings not yet bedded-in.	Use brakes gently until springy pedal feeling leaves.
Excessive wear or damage	Brake discs badly worn and weak or cracked.	Fit new brake discs.
Lack of maintenance	Master cylinder securing nuts loose.	Tighten master cylinder securing nuts. Ensure spring washers are fitted.
Brake pedal feels spongy and soggy		
Leaks or bubbles in hydraulic system	Calliper leaking.	Dismantle calliper, clean, fit new rubber seals and bleed brakes.
	Master cylinder leaking (bubbles in master cylinder reservoir).	Dismantle master cylinder, clean, and fit new rubber seals and bleed brakes. Replace cylinder if internal walls scored.
	Brake pipe line or flexible hose leaking.	Fit new pipe line or hose.
	Unions in brake system loose.	Examine for leaks, tighten as necessary.
Excessive effor trequire to brake car		
Lining type or condition	Pads badly worn.	Fit replacement pads.
	New pads recently fitted - not yet bedded in.	Use brake gently until braking effort normal.
	Harder pads fitted than standard causing increase in pedal pressure.	Remove pads and replace with correct specified pads.
Oil or grease leaks	Pads and brake discs contaminated with oil, grease, or hydraulic fluid.	Rectify source of leak, clean brake discs, fit new pads.
Brakes uneven & pulling to one side		
Oil or grease	Pads and brake discs contaminated with oil, grease, or hydraulic fluid.	Ascertain and rectify source of leak, clean brake discs, fit new pads.
Lack of maintenance	Tyre pressures unequal.	Check and inflate as necessary.
	Radial ply tyres fitted at one end of car only.	Fit radial ply tyres of the same make to all four wheels.
	Brake calliper or disc loose.	Tighten calliper or disc securing nuts and bolts.
	Brake pads fitted incorrectly.	Remove and fit pads correct way round.
	Different type of pads fitted at each wheel.	Fit the pads specified by the manufacturers all round.
	Anchorages for front or rear suspension.	Tighten front and rear suspension pick-up points inclduing spring anchorages.
	Brake discs badly worn, cracked or distorted.	Fit new brake discs.
Brakes tend to bind, drag or lock-on		
Incorrect adjustment	Brake pads or pistons seized, adjusted too tightly.	Check callipers.

Chapter 10 Electrical system

Contents

Specifications

Electrical System Type

Cars prior to suffix letter 'D'	Positive earth
Cars with suffix letter 'D' onwards and TC	Negative earth
Voltage	12 volts

Battery Capacity ... ... — 60 A/H at 20 hour rate

Dynamo

Type	Lucas C42—22910
Output	30 amps at 13.5 volts
Minimum brush length	¼ inch
Brush spring tension	16—33 oz.
Commutator insulation undercut	1/32 inch
Field coil resistance	4½ ohm.
Identification:—	
Black moulding on output terminal	Positive earth system
Red moulding on ouput terminal	Negative earth system

Regulator & Control Box

Type...	Lucas RB340—37517

Cut-in voltage	12.7 to 13.3 volts
Drop-off voltage	4.5 to 11.0 volts
Voltage setting at 3,000 rpm	10°C (50°F) 14.9 to 15.5 volts
	20°C (68°F) 14.7 to 15.3 volts
	30°C (86°F) 14.5 to 15.1 volts
	40°C (104°F) 14.3 to 14.9 volts
Reverse current	3.0 to 5.0 amps
Current regulator	22 + or − 1 amp

Alternator

Type	Lucas 11AC (or 18ACR. See Chapter 13)
Nominal voltage	12 volts
Nominal DC output	43 amps
Resistance of field coil at 68°F (20°C)	3.8 ohms.
Stator phases	3
Stator connection	Star
Number of rotor poles	8
Number of field coils	1
Slip ring brushes - New length	0.625 inch (15.9 mm)
Replace at	0.156 inch (4.0 mm)
Brush spring tests - Load at 25/32 inch (19.9 mm)	4 to 5 oz. (113 to 142 gms)
- Load at 13/32 inch (10.3 mm(...	7.5 to 8.5 oz (212 to 241 gms)

Control Unit

Type	Lucas 4 TR

Field Isolating Relay

Type	Lucas 6 RA

Warning Light Control

Type	Lucas 3 AW

Starter Motor

Type - Single carburetter engine	Lucas M418G—25521D
- Twin carburreter engine	Lucas M45G—26164A
Number of drive pinion teeth	10
Commutator insulation undercut	NIL
Lock torque	17 lb/ft. with 430—450 amp at 7.4—7.0 volts
Torque at 1,000 rpm	8.0 lb/ft. with 250—270 amp at 9.4—9.0 volts
Light running speed and current	5,800 — 6,500 rpm on 12 volts at 45—60 amp
Pre-engaged type	Lucas LU M418G
Brush spring tension	30 to 40 oz. (850 gm. to 1.13 kg.)

Windscreen Wiper

Type	Lucas 6W — angle of wipe 105°
Cars produced from suffix letter 'D' onwards	Lucas DL3A — angle of wipe 115°

Screen Washer

Type	Lucas 4SJ

Bulbs (2000 models) — See Chapter 13 for 2200 models

	Lucas Part Number	Wattage
Headlamps:—		
Inner headlamp sealed beam	LU 54522973	37.5
Outer headlamp sealed beam	LU 54521806	50—37.5
Sidelamp	989	6
Stop/tail lamp	380	6—21
Direction indicator lamp	382	21
Rear number plate lamp	989	6
Instrument panel light	987	2.2
Warning lights, suffix 'D' onwards	984	3.6
Warning lights	643	2.2
Interior lights, festoon bulb	254	6
Map-reading lamp	254	6
Clock	281	2
Reverse lamp	382	21
Rear luggage boot lamp	209	6
Tachometer	987	2.2
Selector light	254	6

1. General Description

The electrical system is of the 12 volt type and the major components comprise a 12 volt battery; a voltage regulator and cut-out; a Lucas dynamo or alternator (special equipment models) which is fitted to the front left-hand side of the engine and is driven by the fan belt from the cranksahft pulley wheel; and a starter motor which is fitted to the end plate and clutch housing on the left-hand side of the engine.

The battery earth connection has been varied between models and it is very important that before starting work on the car which entails electrical equipment, the battery polarity is determined. This is particularly important when any transistorised equipment is being used or installed, e.g. radio, tachometer etc.

It will be found that on vehicles having a serial number incorporating a suffix D onwards the negative terminal of the battery is earthed. Before this, all vehicles had positive earth. The two systems are also distinguished by the colour of the nylon moulding beneath the output terminal of the dynamo. Negative earth system dynamos have a red coloured moulding and positive earth systems have a black moulding. The two types are NOT interchangeable. The ignition coil is also marked with a '+' or '−'.

The 12 volt battery supplies a steady amount of current for the ignition, lighting, and other electrical circuits, and provides a reserve of electricity when the current consumed by the electrical equipment exceeds that being produced by the dynamo.

The dynamo is of the two brush type and works in conjunction with the voltage regulator and cut-out. The dynamo is cooled by a multi-bladed fan behind the dynamo pulley, and blows air through the cooling holes in the dynamo end bracket. The output from the dynamo is controlled by the voltage regulator which ensures a high output if the battery is in a low state of charge, or the demands from the electrical equipment high, and a low output if the battery is fully charged and there is little demand from the electrical equipment.

The fuel and water temperature gauges are controlled by a bi-metal resistance which stabilises the power supply to them, ensuring accurate readings over a wide range of voltage supply due to the state of charge of the battery.

2. Battery Removal & Replacement

1. The battery is in a special carrier fitted on the right-hand side of the engine compartment. It should be removed once every three months for cleaning and testing. Disconnect the positive and then the negative leads from the battery terminals by undoing the retaining screws and lifting away the battery leads.
2. Remove the battery clamp wing nuts and lift away the battery clamp bar. Lift the battery out of its compartment. Hold the battery vertical to ensure that none of the electrolyte is spilled.
3. Replacement is a direct reversal of the above procedure. Smear the terminals with petroleum jelly (vaseline) to prevent corrosion. NEVER use an ordinary grease as applied to other parts of the car.

3. Battery Maintenance & Inspection

1. Normal weekly battery maintenance consists of checking the electrolyte level in each cell to ensure that the separators are covered by ¼ inch of electrolyte. If the level has fallen, top up the battery using distilled water only. Do not overfill. If a battery is overfilled or any electrolyte spilled, immediately wipe away the excess as electrolyte attacks and corrodes any metal it comes into contact with very rapidly.
2. As well as keeping the terminals clean and covered with petroleum jelly, the top of the battery, and especially the tops of the cells, should be kept clean and dry. This helps prevent corrosion and ensures that the battery does not become partially discharged by leakage through dampness and dirt.
3. Once every three months, remove the battery and inspect the battery securing wing nuts, the battery clamp plate, tray and battery leads for corrosion (white fluffy deposits on the metal which are brittle to touch). If any corrosion is found, clean off the deposit with ammonia and paint over the clean metal with an anti-rust, anti-acid paint.
4. At the same time inspect the battery case for cracks. If a crack is found, clean and plug it with one of the proprietary compounds marketed by firms such as Holts, for this purpose. If leakage through the crack has been excessive, then it will be necessary to refill the appropriate cell with fresh electrolyte as detailed later. Cracks are frequently caused to the top of the battery cases by pouring in distilled water in the middle of winter AFTER instead of BEFORE a run. This gives the water no chance to mix with the electrolyte and so the former freezes and splits the battery case.
5. If topping up the battery becomes excessive and the case has been inspected for cracks that could cause leakage, but none are found, the battery is being overcharged and the voltage regulator will have to be checked and reset.
6. With the battery on the bench at the three monthly interval check, measure the specific gravity with a hydrometer to determine the state of charge and condition of the electrolyte. There should be very little variation between the different cells and if a variation in excess of 0.025 is present it will be due to either:—

a) Loss of electrolyte from the battery at some time caused by spillage or a leak, resulting in a drop in the specific gravity of the electrolyte when the deficiency was replaced with distilled water instead of fresh electrolyte.

b) An internal short circuit caused by buckling of the plates or a similar malady pointing to the likelihood of total battery failure in the near future.

7. The specific gravity of the electrolyte for fully charged conditions at the electrolyte temperature indicated, is listed in Table A. The specific gravity of a fully discharged battery at different temperatures of the electrolyte is given in Table B.

TABLE A

Specific gravity − battery fully charged

1.268 at 100°F or 38°C electrolyte temperature	
1.276 at 80°F or 27°C	ditto
1.280 at 70°F or 21°C	ditto
1.284 at 60°F or 16°C	ditto
1.288 at 50°F or 10°C	ditto
1.292 at 40°F or 4°C	ditto
1.296 at 30°F or -1.5°C	ditto

TABLE B

Specific gravity − battery fully discharged

1.098 at 100°F or 38°C electrolyte temperature	
1.102 at 90°F or 32°C	ditto
1.106 at 80°F or 27°C	ditto
1.110 at 70°F or 21°C	ditto
1.114 at 60°F or 16°C	ditto
1.118 at 50°F or 10°C	ditto
1.122 at 40°F or 4°C	ditto
1.126 at 30°F or -1.5°C	ditto

4. Battery − Electrolyte Replenishment

1. If the battery is in a fully charged state and one of the cells maintains a specific gravity reading which is 0.025 or more lower than the others, and the check of each cell has been made with a voltage meter to check for short circuits (a four to seven second test should give a steady reading of between 1.2 and 1.8 volts), then it is likely that the electrolyte has been lost from the cell with the low reading at some time.
2. Top the cell up with a solution of 1 part sulphuric acid to 2.5

parts of water. If the cell is already topped up draw some electrolyte out of it with a pipette. The total capacity of each cell is approximately ¾ pint.

3. When mixing the sulphuric acid and water NEVER ADD WATER TO SULPHURIC ACID - always pour the acid slowly onto the water in a glass container. IF WATER IS ADDED TO SULPHURIC ACID IT WILL EXPLODE.

4. Continue to top up the cell with a freshly made electrolyte and then re-charge the battery and check the hydrometer readings.

5. Battery — Charging

1. In winter time when heavy demand is placed upon the battery, such as when starting from cold and much electrical equipment is continually in use, it is a good idea to occasionally have the battery fully charged from an external source at the rate of 3.5 to 4 amps.

2. Continue to charge the battery at this rate until no further rise in specific gravity is noted over a four-hour period.

3. Alternatively, a trickle charger, charging at the rate of 1.5 amps can be safely used overnight.

4. Specially rapid 'boost' charges which are claimed to restore the power of the battery in 1 to 2 hours are most dangerous as they can cause serious damage to the battery plates through overheating.

5. While charging the battery note that the temperature of the electrolyte should never exceed 100°F.

6. Dynamo — Maintenance

1. Routine maintenance consists of checking the tension of the fan belt, and lubricating the dynamo rear bearing once every 6,000 miles.

2. The fan belt should be tight enough to ensure no slip between the belt and the dynamo pulley. If a shrieking noise comes from the engine when the unit is accelerated rapidly, it is likely that the fan belt is slipping. On the other hand, the belt must not be too taut or the bearings will wear rapidly and cause dynamo failure or bearing seizure. Ideally 5/16 inch of total free movement should be available at the fan belt mid-way between the fan and crankshaft pulleys.

3. To adjust the fan belt tension, slightly slacken the three dynamo retaining bolts, and swing the dynamo outwards to increase the tension, and inwards to decrease it.

4. It is best to leave the bolts fairly tight so that considerable effort has to be used to move the dynamo, otherwise it is difficult to get the correct setting. If the dynamo is being moved outwards to increase the tension and the bolts have only been slackened a little, a long spanner acting as a lever placed behind the dynamo with the lower end resting against the block works very well in moving the dynamo outwards. Retighten the dynamo bolts and check that the dynamo pulley is correctly aligned with the fan belt.

5. Lubrication of the dynamo consists of inserting three drops of SAE 30 engine oil in the centre of the commutator end bracket. This lubricates the rear bearing. The front bearing is pre-packed with grease and requires no attention.

7. Dynamo — Testing in Position

1. If, with the engine running, no charge comes from the dynamo, or the charge is very low, first check that the fan belt is in place and is not slipping, then check that the leads from the control box to the dynamo are firmly attached and that one has not come loose from its terminal.

2. The lead from the 'D' terminal on the dynamo should be connected to the 'D' terminal on the control box, and similarly the 'F' terminal on the dynamo and control box should also be connected together. Check that this is so and that the leads have not been incorrectly fitted. The cable between the two 'D' terminals is coloured yellow and the cable between the two 'F' terminals should be coloured yellow with a green tracer.

3. Make sure none of the electrical equipment, such as the lights or radio, is on, and then pull the leads off the dynamo terminals marked 'D' and 'F'. Join the terminals together with a short length of wire.

4. Attach to the centre of this length of wire one lead of a 0—20 volts voltmeter and run the other clip to earth on the dynamo yoke. Start the engine and allow it to idle at approximately 750 r.p.m. At this speed the dynamo should give a reading of about 15 volts on the voltmeter. There is no point in raising the engine speed above a fast idle as the reading will then be inaccurate.

5. If no reading is recorded, then check the brushes and brush connections. If a very low reading of approximately 1 volt is observed, then the field winding may be suspect.

6. If a reading of between 4 to 6 amps is recorded it is likely that the armature is at fault.

7. On early dynamos it was possible to remove the dynamo cover band and check the dynamo and brushes in position. With the Lucas C42 windowless yoke dynamo, it must be removed and dismantled before the brushes and commutator can be attended to.

8. If the voltmeter shows a good reading, then with the temporary link still in position, connect both leads from the control box to 'D' and 'F' to the dynamo ('D' to 'D' and 'F' to 'F'). Release the lead from the 'D' terminal at the control box end and clip one lead of the voltmeter to the end of the cable, and the other lead to a good earth point. With the engine running at the same speed as previously, an identical voltage to that recorded at the dynamo should be noted on the voltmeter. If no voltage is recorded, there is a break in the wire. If the voltage is the same as recorded at the dynamo then check the 'F' lead in a similar manner. If both readings are the same as at the dynamo then it will be necessary to test the control box.

8. Dynamo — Removal & Replacement

1. Slacken the two lower dynamo retaining bolts and the bolt on the sliding link. Move the dynamo in towards the engine, so that the fan belt can be removed.

2. Disconnect the two leads from the dynamo terminals.

3. On later produced models with a rubber bushed support bracket, also remove the earthing lead.

4. Remove the three bolts and lift the dynamo from the engine.

5. Replacement is the reverse sequence to removal. Do not fully tighten the retaining bolts until the fan belt has been tensioned correctly.

9. Dynamo — Dismantling & Inspection

1. Remove the two nuts and bolts with spring washers that secure the strap to the dynamo heat shield. Lift away the strap and heat shield.

2. Mount the dynamo in a vice and unscrew and remove the two through bolts, (Fig.10.1), from the commutator end bracket (see photo).

3. Mark the commutator end bracket and the dynamo casing so the end bracket can be replaced in its original position. Pull the end bracket off the armature shaft. NOTE: Some versions of the dynamo may have a raised pip on the end bracket which locates in a recess on the edge of the casing. If so, marking the end bracket and casing is unnecessary. A pip may also be found on the drive end bracket at the opposite end of the casing (photo).

4. Lift the two brush springs and draw the brushes out of the brush holders (arrowed in photo).

5. Measure the brushes and if worn down to 9/32 inch or less, unscrew the screws that hold the brush leads to the end brackets. Take off the brushes complete with leads. Old and new brushes are compared in the photograph.

6. If no locating pip can be found, mark the drive end bracket and the dynamo casing so the drive end bracket can be replaced in its

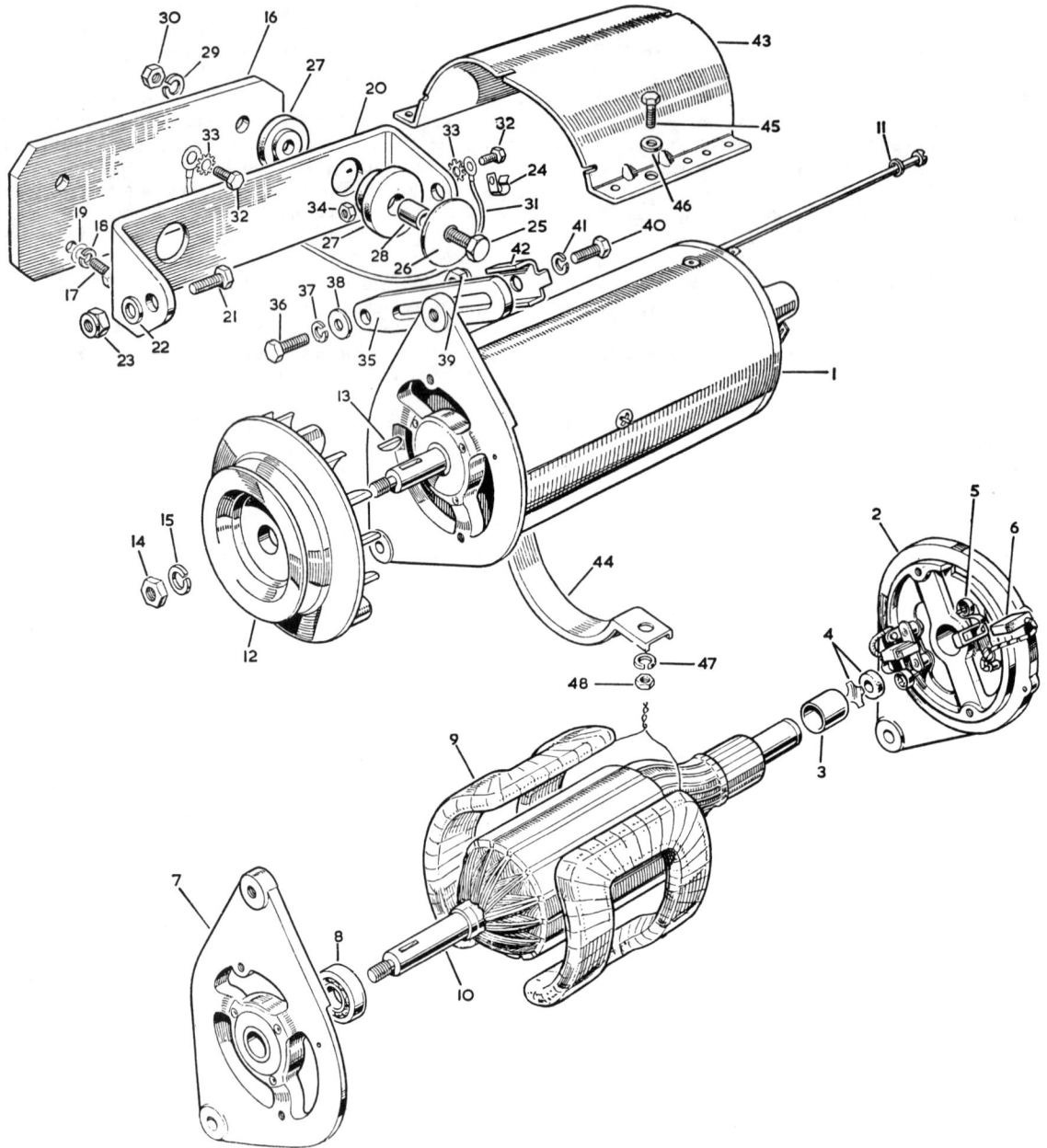

Fig.10.1. EXPLODED VIEW OF LUCAS C42 DYNAMO

1	Dynamo complete	12	Pulley for dynamo	24	Clip for harness	37	Spring washer
2	Bracket, commutator end	13	Woodruff key	25	Bolt	38	Plain washer
3	Bush for armature, commutator end	14	Special nut	26	Plain washer	39	Special locknut
4	Oiler for dynamo	15	Special washer	27	Rubber bush	40	Set bolt
5	Springs, set, for bush tension	16	Adjustable mounting plate for dynamo	28	Sleeve for bush	41	Spring washer
6	Brushes, set, for dynamo	17	Set bolt	29	Spring washer	42	Clamping washer
7	Bracket, drive end	18	Spring washer	30	Nut	43	Heat shield for dynamo
8	Ball bearing, drive end	19	Plain washer	31	Earth lead for dynamo	44	Strap for heat shield
9	Field coil for dynamo	20	Support plate for dynamo	32	Bolt	45	Bolt
10	Armature for dynamo	21	Bolt	33	Fan disc washer	46	Plain washer
11	Bolt for bracket	22	Plain washer	34	Nut	47	Spring washer
		23	Special locknut	35	Adjustable link for dynamo	48	Nut
				36	Set bolt		

original position. Then pull the drive end bracket complete with armature out of the casing, (photo).

7. Check the condition of the ball bearing in the drive end plate, by firmly holding the plate and noting if there is visible side movement of the armature shaft, in relation to the end plate. If play is present, the armature assembly must be separated from the end plate. If the bearing is sound there is no need to carry out the work described in the following two paragraphs.

8. Hold the armature in one hand (mount it carefully in a vice if preferred) and undo the nut holding the pulley wheel and fan in place. Pull off the pulley wheel and fan.

9. Next remove the woodruff key (arrowed in photo) from its slot in the armature shaft and also the bearing locating ring.

10 Place the drive end bracket across the open jaws of a vice with the armature downwards and gently tap the armature shaft from the bearing (see photo), in the end plate with the aid of a suitable drift.

11 Carefully inspect the armature and check it for open or short circuited winding. It is a good indication of an open circuited armature when the commutator segments are burnt. If the armature has short circuited, the commutator segments will be very badly burnt, and the overheated armature windings badly discoloured. If open or short circuits are suspected then test by substituting the suspect armature for a new one (see photo).

12 Check the resistance of the field coils. To do this, connect an ohmmeter between the field terminal and the yoke and note the reading on the ohmmeter which should be about 6 ohms. If the ohmmeter reading is infinitely above, this indicates an open circuit in the field winding. If the ohmmeter reading is below 5 ohms, this indicates that one of the field coils is faulty and must be replaced.

13 Field coil replacement involves the use of a wheel operated screwdriver, a soldering iron, caulking and riveting and this operation is considered to be beyond the scope of most owners. Therefore, if the field coils are at fault, either purchase a rebuilt dynamo, or take the casing to a Rover dealer or electrical engineering works for new field coils to be fitted.

14 Next check the condition of the commutator. If it is dirty and blackened, as shown in the photo, clean it with a petrol dampened rag. If the commutator is in good condition the surface will be smooth and quite free from pits or burnt areas, and the insulated segments clearly defined.

15 If, after the commutator has been cleaned, pits and burnt spots are still present, wrap a strip of glass paper around the commutator taking great care to move the commutator one quarter of a turn every 10 rubs until it is thoroughly cleaned (photo).

16 In extreme cases of wear, the commutator can be mounted in a lathe and with the lathe turning at a high speed, a very fine cut be taken off the commutator. Then polish the commutator with glass paper. If the commutator has worn so that the insulators between the segments are level with the top of the segments, then undercut the insulators to a depth of 1/32 inch (8 mm), see Fig.10.2. The best tool to use for this purpose is half a hacksaw blade ground to the thickness of the insulator, and with the handle end of the blade covered with insulating tape to make it comfortable to hold. The sort of finish the surface of the commutator should have when completed is shown in the photo.

17 Check the brush bearing in the commutator end bracket for wear by noting if the armature spindle rocks when placed in it. If worn, it must be renewed (photo).

18 The bush bearing can be removed by a suitable extractor, or by screwing a 5/8 inch tap four or five times into the bush. The tap, complete with bush is then pulled out of the end bracket.

19 NOTE: The bush bearing is of the porous bronze type and, before fitting a new one, it is essential that it is allowed to stand in SAE 30 engine oil for at least 24 hours before fitment. In an emergency the bush can be immersed in hot oil (100°C) for 2 hours.

20 Carefully fit the new bush into the end plate, pressing it in until the end of the bearing is flush with the innerside of the end plate. If available, press the bush in with a smooth shouldered mandrel, the same diameter as the armature shaft.

10. Dynamo – Repair & Reassembly

1. To renew the ball bearing fitted to the drive end bracket drill out the rivets which hold the bearing retainer plate to the end bracket and lift off the plate.

2. Press out the bearing from the end bracket and remove the corrugated and felt washers from the bearing housing.

3. Thoroughly clean the bearing housing and the new bearing, and pack with high melting point grease.

4. Place the felt washer and corrugated washer in that order in the end bracket bearing housing (photo).

5. Then fit the new bearing as shown (photo).

6. Gently tap the bearing into place with the aid of a suitable drift, (photo).

7. Replace the bearing plate and fit three new rivets (photo).

8. Open up the rivets with the aid of a suitable cold chisel (photo).

9. Finally peen over the open end of the rivets with the aid of a ball pin hammer as illustrated.

10 Refit the drive end bracket to the armature shaft. Do not try and force the bracket on but with the aid of a suitable socket abutting the bearing, tap the bearing on gently, so pulling the end bracket down with it (photo).

11 Slide the spacer up the shaft and refit the woodruff key (photo).

12 Replace the fan pulley wheel and then fit the spring washer and nut and tighten the latter. The drive bracket end of the dynamo is now fully reassembled as shown (photo).

13 If the brushes are a little worn and are to be used again, then ensure that they are placed in the same holders from which they were removed. When refitting brushes either new or old, check that they move freely in their holders. If either brush sticks, clean with a petrol moistened rag and if still stiff, lightly polish the sides of the brush with a very fine file until the brush moves quite freely in its holder.

14 Tighten the two retaining screws and washers which hold the wire leads to the brushes in place (photo).

15 It is far easier to slip the end plate with brushes over the commutator, if the brushes are raised in their holders, as shown in the photo and held in this position by the pressure of the springs resting against their flanks.

16 Refit the armature to the casing and then the commutator end plate, and screw up the two through bolts.

17 Finally, hook the ends of the two springs off the flanks of the brushes and onto their heads, so that the brushes are forced down into contact with the armature.

11. Control Box – General Description

1. The control box comprises three units, two separate vibrating armature–type single contact regulators and a cut-out relay. One of the regulators is sensitive to changes in current and the other to changes in voltage.

2. Adjustments can only be made with a special tool which resembles a screwdriver with a multi-toothed blade. This can be obtained through Lucas agents.

3. The regulators control the output from the dynamo, depending on the state of the battery and the demands of the electrical equipment and ensure that the battery is not overcharged. The cut-out is really an automatic switch and connects the dynamo to the battery when the dynamo is turning fast enough to produce a charge. Similarly it disconnects the battery from the dynamo when the engine is idling or stationary so that the battery does not discharge through the dynamo.

12. Cut-Out & Regulator Contacts – Maintenance

1. Every 10,000 miles check the cut-out and regulator contacts. If they are dirty or rough or burnt, place a piece of fine glass paper (DO NOT USE EMERY PAPER OR CARBORUNDUM PAPER)

9.2

9.3

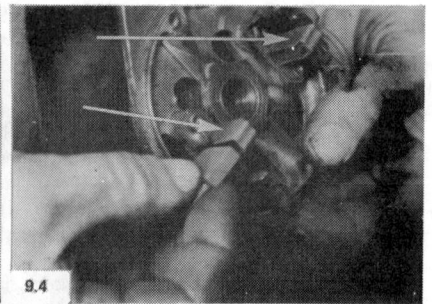
9.4

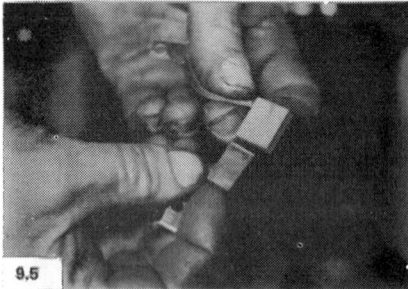
9.5

9.6

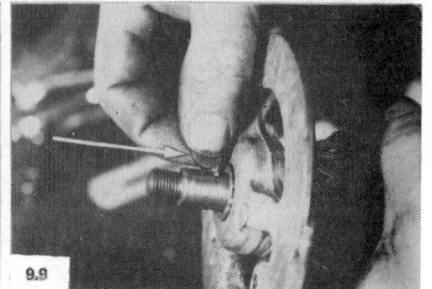
9.9

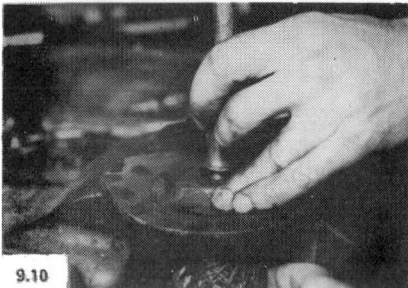
9.10

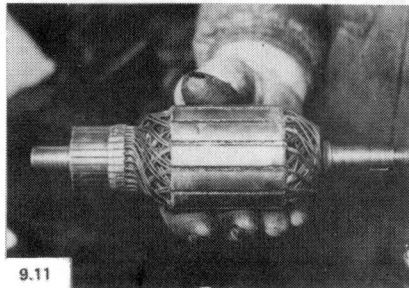
9.11

9.14

9.15

9.16

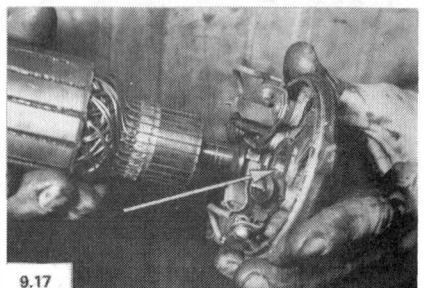
9.17

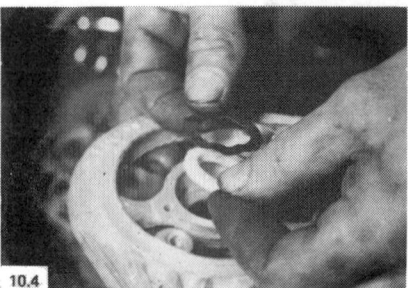
10.4

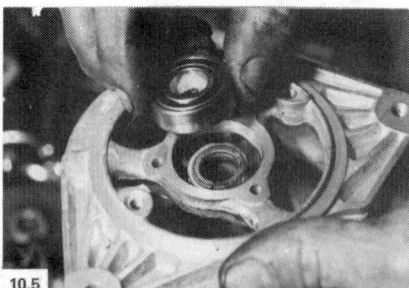
10.5

10.6

10.7

10.8

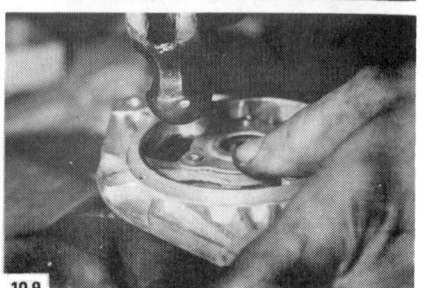
10.9

between the cut-out contacts, close them manually and draw the glass paper through several times.

2. Clean the regulator contacts in exactly the same way, but use emery or carborundum paper and not glass paper. Carefully clean both sets of contacts from all traces of dust with a rag moistened in methylated spirit.

13. Voltage Regulator Adjustment

1. The regulator requires very little attention during its service life, and should there be any reason to suspect its correct functioning, tests of all circuits should be made to ensure that they are not the reason for the trouble.

2. These checks include the tension of the fan belt, to make sure that it is not slipping and so providing only a very low charge rate. The battery should be carefully checked for possible low charge rate due to a faulty cell, or corroded battery connection.

3. The leads from the generator may have been crossed during replacement and if this is the case, then the regulator points will have stuck together as soon as the generator starts to charge. Check for loose or broken leads from the generator to the regulator.

4. If, after a thorough check it is considered advisable to test the regulator, this should only be carried out by an electrician who is well acquainted with the correct method, using test bench equipment.

5. Pull off the Lucar connections from the two adjacent control box terminals 'B'. To start the engine it will now be necessary to join together the ignition and battery leads with a suitable wire.

6. Connect a 0–20 volt voltmeter between terminals 'D' on the control box and the terminal 'W'. Start the engine and run it at 3,000 r.p.m. The reading on the voltmeter should be steady and lie between the limits detailed in the specification.

7. If the reading is unsteady, this may be due to dirty contacts. If the reading is outside the specified limits, stop the engine and adjust the voltage regulator in the following manner.

8. Take off the control box cover and start and run the engine at 3,000 r.p.m. Using the correct tool turn the voltage adjustment cam anti-clockwise to raise the setting and clockwise to lower it. To check that the setting is correct, stop the engine and then start it and run it at 3,000 r.p.m, noting the reading. Refit the cover and the connections to the 'W' and 'D' terminals.

14. Current Regulator – Adjustment

1. The output from the current regulator should equal the maximum output from the dynamo which is 30 amps. To test this it is necessary to by-pass the cut-out by holding the contacts together.

2. Remove the cover from the control box and with a bulldog clip hold the cut-out contacts together (see Fig. 10.3).

3. Pull off the wires from the adjacent terminals 'B' and connect a 0–40 moving coil ohmmeter to one of the terminals and to the leads.

4. All the other load connections including the ignition, must be made to the battery.

5. Turn on all the lights and other electrical accessories and run the engine at 3,000 r.p.m. The ohmmeter should give a steady reading of approximately 30 amps. If the needle flickers, it is likely that the points are dirty. If the reading is too low turn the special Lucas tool clockwise to raise the setting and anti-clockwise to lower it.

15. Cut–Out Adjustment

1. Check the voltage required to operate the cut-out by connecting a voltmeter between the control box terminals 'D' and 'W'. Remove the control box cover, start the engine and gradually increase its speed until the cut-outs close. This should occur when the reading is between 12.7 – 13.3 volts.

2. If the reading is outside these limits, turn the cut-out adjusting

cam by means of the adjusting tool, a fraction at a time clockwise to raise the voltage, and anti-clockwise to lower it.

3. To adjust the drop off voltage, bend the fixed contact blade carefully. The adjustment to the cut-out should be completed within 30 seconds of starting the engine as otherwise heat build-up from the shunt coil will affect the reading.

4. If the cut-out fails to work, clean the contacts, and, if there is still no response renew the cut-out and regulator unit.

16. Lucas 11AC Alternator – General Description

Rover 2,000 models fitted with air conditioning or other specialist equipment are fitted with an alternator. The main advantage of the alternator lies in its ability to provide a high charge at low revolutions. This is especially welcome to city dwellers as driving slowly in heavy traffic with a dynamo invariably leads to little or no charge reaching the battery. In similar conditions, even with the wiper, lights, heater and perhaps radio switched on, the 11AC alternator will ensure a charge reaching the battery.

An important feature of the alternator system is its output control, this being based on thick film hybrid integrated micro-circuit techniques.

The alternator is of the rotating field, ventilated design. It comprises, principally a laminated stator on which is wound a star connected three-phase output and an eight-pole rotor carrying the field winding. The front end of the rotor shaft runs in a ball race bearing and the rear in a needle roller race, each of which is lubricated for life, and natural finish aluminium diecast end brackets incorporating the mounting lugs.

The rotor is belt driven from the engine through a pulley keyed to the rotor shaft and a pressed steel fan adjacent to the pulley draws cooling air through the machine. This fan forms an integral part of the alternator specifications. It has been designed to provide adequate air flow with a minimum of noise and to withstand the high stresses associated with maximum speeds.

The brush gear for the field system is mounted on the slip ring end bracket. Two carbon brushes bear against a pair of concentric brass slip rings carried on a moulded disc attached to the end of the rotor. Also attached to the slip ring end brackets are six silicone diodes connected in a three-phase bridge to rectify the generated alternating current to direct current for use in charging the battery and supplying power to the electrical system.

The alternator output is controlled by an electrical voltage regulator unit and a warning light control unit to indicate to the driver when all is not well.

17. Alternator – Routine Maintenance

1. The equipment has been designed for the minimum amount of maintenance in service, the only items subject to wear being the brushes and bearings.

2. Brushes should be examined after about 75,000 miles, and renewed if necessary. The bearings are pre-packed with grease for life, and should not require further attention.

3. Check the fan belt every 5,000 miles for correct adjustment, which should be 5/16 inch total movement between the crankshaft and fan pulley.

18. Alternator – Special Procedures

Whenever the electrical system of the car is being attended to or external means of starting the engine are used, there are certain precautions that must be taken otherwise serious and expensive damage can result.

1. Always make sure that the negative terminal of the battery is earthed. If the terminal connections are accidentally reversed, or if

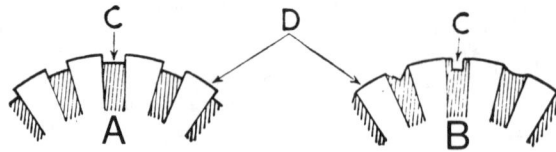

Fig.10.2. CORRECT METHOD OF UNDERCUTTING THE COMMUTATOR

A Correct way   B Incorrect way   C Insulator   D Segments

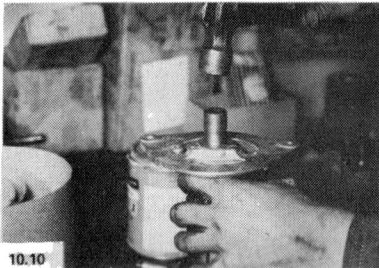

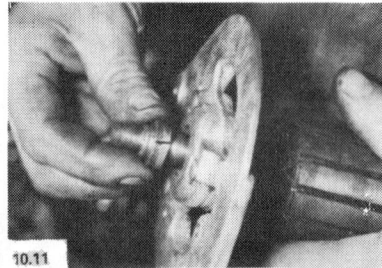

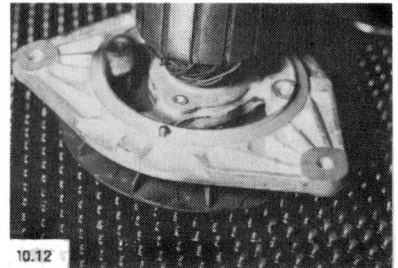

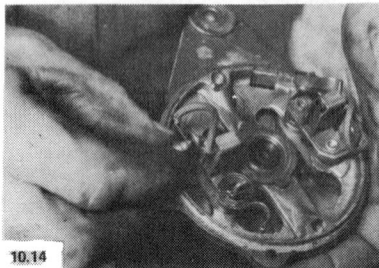

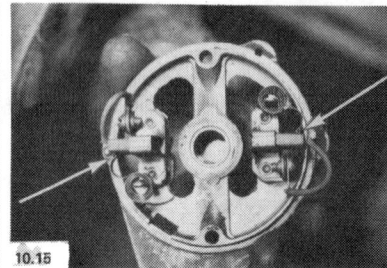

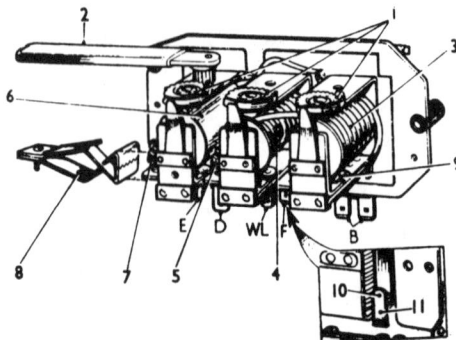

Fig.10.3. CONTROL BOX (COVER REMOVED)

1	Adjustment cams	4	Current regulator	7	Voltage regulator	9	Armature back stop
2	Setting tool	5	Current relay contacts		contacts	10	Cut-out contacts
3	Cut-out relay	6	Voltage regulator	8	Clip - contacts	11	Fixed contact bracket

the battery has been reverse charged, the alternator diodes will burn out.

2. The output terminal on the alternator marked 'BAT' must never be earthed, but should always be connected directly to the positive terminal of the battery.

3. Whenever the alternator is to be removed or when disconnecting the terminals of the alternator circuit, always disconnect the battery earth terminal first.

4. The alternator must never be operated without the battery to alternator cable connected.

5. If the battery is to be charged by external means always disconnect both battery cables before the external charger is connected.

6. Should it be necessary to use a booster charger or booster battery to start the engine always double check that the negative cables are connected to negative terminals and positive cables to positive terminals.

19. Alternator — Removal & Refitting

1. Refer to Chapter 2, Section 5, and remove the radiator and oil cooler.
2. Undo the two battery terminal securing screws and disconnect the terminals.
3. Undo but do not remove the three alternator mounting bolts and push the alternator towards the engine. Lift away the fan belt.
4. Remove the four bolts, nuts and spring washers that secure the fan to the hub and lift away the fan blades.
5. Remove the four nuts and washers that secure the fan pulley to the hub. Lift off the reinforcing plate, pulley and shim.
6. Disconnect the 35 amp Lucar terminal and the two field cables from the terminal block at the rear of the alternator. Remove the Lucar connection from the 'AL' connector on the alternator rear cover.
7. Remove the nut and bolt that secures the alternator adjusting link to the top compressor brackets. Also remove the bolt, spring and flat washer securing the adjusting link to the alternator. Lift away the adjusting links.
8. Undo and remove the two bolts, nuts and washers that secure the alternator support bracket to the compressor bottom bracket. The alternator and bracket may now be withdrawn forwards.
9. To separate the alternator from the support bracket, undo and remove the two bolts and nuts.
10 To refit the alternator is the reverse sequence to removal.

20. Alternator — Fault Finding & Repair

Due to the specialist knowledge and equipment required to test or service an alternator it is recommended that if the performance is suspect, the car be taken to an automobile electrician, who will have the facilities for such work. Because of this recommendation no further details of service information are given other than the exploded view of the unit, Fig.10.4, and the control unit wiring diagram Fig.10.5, as well as technical information at the beginning of this chapter.

21. Warning Light Control — General Description

With an alternator, a warning light is fitted and its indication is for similar reasons to the ignition warning light fitted with dynamo charging systems. The warning light is illuminated when the car is stationary or is being driven slowly. The light is extinguished when the output voltage begins to rise. The light control unit is a thoroughly operated relay for controlling the switching on and off of a facia panel warning light. It is connected through the alternator terminal AL to the centre point of one pair of the six alternator control diodes and to earth.

Should the warning light indicate lack of charge, check this unit

before the alternator. If it is suspect it must be replaced with a similar new unit. Although similar in design to the direction indicator flasher unit, it is not interchangeable.

22. Starter Motor — General Description

There are two types of starter motor to be found on models of car covered by this manual. The inertia starter motor is fitted to all cars of right-hand drive specification. The pre-engaged starter is fitted to some cars built for the left-hand drive export market.

Both starter motors are, in fact, interchangeable and engaged with a common flywheel starter wing gear or torque converter ring gear (automatic transmission). With the first type the starter solenoid switch is mounted within the engine compartment whilst the second type has the solenoid switch mounted on top of the motor itself.

23. Starter Motor — Testing on Engine

1. If the starter motor fails to operate then check the condition of the battery, by turning on the headlamps. If they glow brightly for several seconds and then gradually dim, the battery is in an uncharged condition.
2. If the headlamps glow brightly and continue to glow, and it is obvious that the battery is in good condition, then check the tightness of the battery wiring connections (and in particular the earth lead from the battery terminal to its connection on the bodyframe). If the positive terminal on the battery becomes hot when an attempt is made to operate the starter, this is a sure sign of a poor connection on the battery terminal. To rectify remove the terminal, clean the inside of the cap and the terminal post thoroughly and reconnect. Check the tightness of the connections at the relay switch and at the starter motor.
3. If the wiring is in order, then check that the starter motor is operating. To do this press the rubber covered button in the centre of the solenoid under the bonnet. (Manual transmission cars only). If it is working the starter motor will be heard to click as it tries to rotate. Alternatively, check it with a voltmeter.

If the battery is fully charged, the wiring in order, and the switch working and the starter motor fails to operate, then it will have to be removed from the car for examination. Before this is done, however, ensure that the starter pinion has not jammed in mesh with the flywheel. Check by turning the square end of the armature shaft with a spanner. This will free the pinion if it is stuck in engagement with the flywheel teeth. On some models the square on the end of the shaft will be covered by a metal cap.

24. Inertia Type Starter Motor — General Description

The starter motor is held in position by two bolts which also clamp the gearbox bellhousing flange.

The motor is of the four field coil, four pole piece type, and utilises four spring-loaded commutator brushes. Two of these brushes are earthed, and the other two are insulated and attached to the field coil ends.

When the ignition switch is turned on current flows from the battery to the starter motor solenoid switch, which causes it to become energised. Its internal plunger moves inwards and closes an internal switch so allowing full starting current to flow from the battery to the starter. This causes a powerful magnetic field to be induced into the field coils which causes the armature to rotate.

Mounted on helical splines is the drive pinion which, because of the sudden rotation of the armature, is thrown forwards along the armature shaft and into engagement with the flywheel wing gear. The engine crankshaft will then be rotated until the engine starts to operate on its own and at this point the drive pinion is thrown out of mesh with the flywheel wing gear.

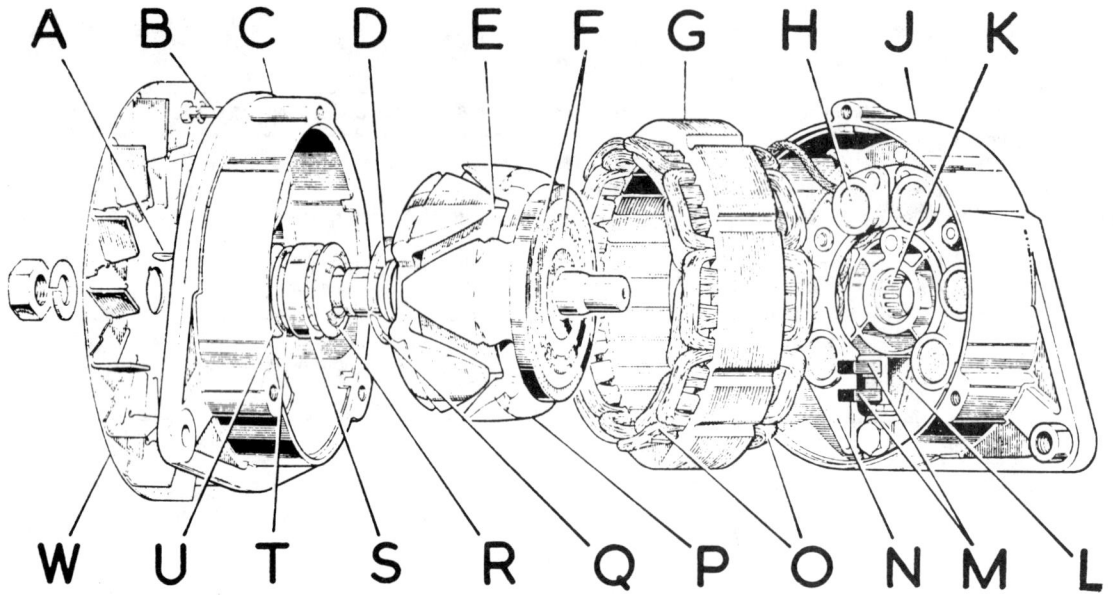

A B C D E F G H J K

W U T S R Q P O N M L

Fig.10.4. EXPLODED VIEW OF LUCAS 11AC ALTERNATOR

A Woodruff key
B Through bolt (3)
C Drive end bracket
D Jump ring shroud
E Rotor (field) winding
F Slip rings
G Stator laminations
H Silicon diodes (6)
J Slip-ring end bracket
K Needle roller bearing
L Brush box
M Brushes (2)
N Diode heat sink (2)
O Stator winding
P Rotor
Q Circlip
R Bearing retaining plate
S Ball bearing, drive end
T 'O' ring
U 'O' ring retaining washer
W Fan

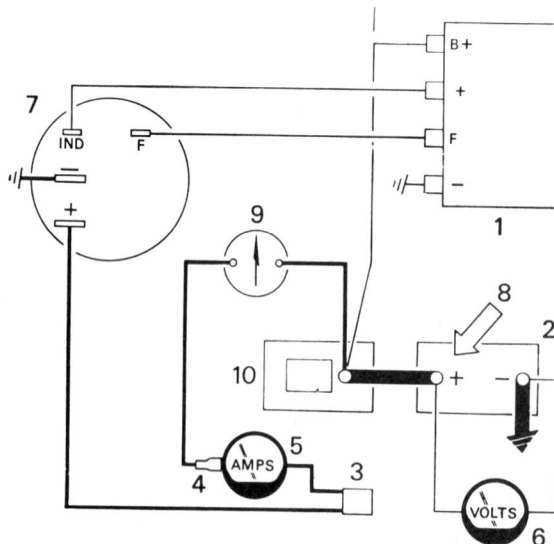

Fig.10.5. ALTERNATOR CONTROL UNIT WIRING DIAGRAM

1 Alternator control unit
2 Battery
3 Connector block
4 Brown/white wire
5 Ammeter (circuit under test)
6 Voltmeter (circuit under test)
7 Alternator
8 Apply-or remove-electrical load here (circuit under test)
9 Ammeter (vehicle unit on facia panel)
10 Starter motor

connector

25. Starter Motor — Removal & Replacement

1. Disconnect the battery earth lead from the battery terminal post.
2. Disconnect the starter motor cable from the terminal on the starter motor end plate.
3. Undo and remove the upper starter motor securing nut and bolt.
4. Working under the car, loosen and then remove the one lower starter motor securing nut and bolt, taking care to support the motor so as to prevent damage to the drive component.
5. Lift the starter motor out of engagement with the flywheel ring gear and lower it out of the car.
6. Replacement is a straightforward reversal of the removal procedure.

26. Starter Motor & Drive Gear (Inertia Type) — Dismantling & Reassembly

1. With the starter motor on the bench, loosen the screw on the cover band and slip the cover band off. An exploded view of the starter motor is shown in Fig.10.6. With a piece of wire bent into the shape of a hook, lift back each of the brush springs in turn and check the movement of the brushes in their holders by pulling on the flexible connectors.
3. If the brushes are so worn that their faces do not rest against the commutator, or if the ends of the brush leads are exposed on their working face, they must be renewed.
4. If any of the brushes tend to stick in their holders, then wash them with a petrol moistened cloth and, if necessary, lightly polish the sides of the brush with a very fine file, until the brushes move quite freely in their holders.
5. If the surface of the commutator is dirty or blackened, clean it with a petrol dampened rag. Secure the starter motor in a vice and check it by connecting a heavy gauge cable between the starter motor terminal and a 12 volt battery.
6. Connect the cable from the other battery terminal to earth in the starter motor body. If the motor turns at high speed it is in good order.
7. If the starter motor still fails to function or if it is wished to renew the brushes, then it is necessary to further dismantle the motor.
8. Start by lifting the brush spring with the aid of a wire hook, off the brushes, and then take out the brushes from their holders one at a time.
9. Working from the drive end of the starter motor using a pair of pliers close the legs of the split pin and extract the split pin from the shaft nut (1), Fig.10.7.
10 Using a pair of pliers carefully unscrew the shaft nut (1) (photo).
11 Lift away the shaft nut (1) followed by main spring (2), washer (3), screwed sleeve and pinion (4), collar (5), pinion restraining spring (6) and the spring restraining sleeve (7) from the end of the armature (photo).
12 Undo the terminal nuts and washers from the terminal post and unscrew and remove the two through bolts and spring washers.
13 The commutator end bracket, the drive end bracket, and the armature can now be removed.
14 At this stage if the brushes are to be renewed, their flexible connectors must be unsoldered from the connectors and the new brushes soldered in their place. Check that the new brushes move freely in their holders. If cleaning the commutator with petrol fails to remove the burnt areas and spots, then wrap a piece of glass paper round the commutator and rotate the armature.
15 If the commutator is very badly worn, mount the armature in a lathe and with the lathe turning at high speed, take a very fine cut-out of the commutator and finish the surface by polishing with glass paper. DO NOT UNDERCUT MICA INSULATORS BETWEEN THE COMMUTATOR SEGMENTS.
16 With the starter motor dismantled, test the four field coils for an open circuit. Connect a 12 volt battery with a 12 volt bulb in one of the leads between the field terminal post and the tapping point of the field coil, to which the brushes are connected. An open circuit is proved by the bulb not lighting. If the bulb lights, it does not necessarily mean that the field coils are in order, as there is a possibility that one of the coils will be earthing to the starter yoke or pole shoe. To check this, remove the lead from the brush connector and place it against a clean portion of the starter yoke. If the bulb lights the field coils are earthing.
17 Replacement of the field coils calls for the use of a wheel operated screwdriver, a soldering iron, caulking and riveting operations, and is considered beyond the scope of the majority of owners. The starter yoke should be taken to an automobile electrical engineering works for new field coils to be fitted. Alternatively, purchase an exchange Lucas starter motor.
18 If the armature is damaged this will be evident after visual inspection. Look for signs of burning, discolouration, and for conductors that have lifted away from the commutator. Ensure that if any parts of the drive gear are worn or damaged, they are renewed.
19 Reassembly is a straightforward reversal of the dismantling procedure.

27. Starter Motor Bushes — Inspection, Removal & Replacement

1. With the starter motor stripped down, check the condition of the bushes. They should be renewed when they are sufficiently worn to allow visible side movement of the armature shaft.
2. The old bushes are simply driven out with a suitable drift and new bushes inserted by the same method. As the bearings are of the phosphor bronze type it is essential that they are allowed to stand in SAE 30 engine oil for at least 24 hours before fitment. In an emergency the bush can be immersed in hot oil (100°C) for 2 hours.

28. Pre-Engaged Starter (Moving Pole Shoe Solenoid) — General Description

When the ignition switch is turned, current flows from the latter to the starter motor solenoid switch which becomes energised. Its internal plunger moves inwards and closes an internal switch so allowing full starting current to flow from the battery to the starter.

The starter motor heavy duty terminal is attached to the field coils, one of which is directly earthed through a pair of contact points. This field coil receives a large current and the magnetic field induced in the winding pulls down a pole shoe that is pivoted above it. Attached to one side of the pole shoe is a lever, and this engages with the drive pinion. Any movement of the pole shoe is therefore transmitted to the drive pinion which is able to slide along the armature shaft and into engagement with the starter ring gear on the flywheel or torque converter.

When the pinion is in mesh fully with the starter ring gear teeth, and the pole shoe is fully seated it opens the earthing contact points and full starting current is able to flow through all four field coils. The armature is then able to rotate the crankshaft so starting the engine.

A special one-way clutch is fitted to the starter drive pinion, so that when the engine just fires and starts to operate on its own, it does not drive the starter motor.

29. Starter Motor — Removal & Replacement

1. Disconnect the battery earth lead from the battery terminal post.
2. Make a special note of the starter motor cable connections at the rear of the solenoid and disconnect the cables.
3. Remove the upper starter motor securing nut and bolt.
4. Working under the car, loosen and then remove the one lower

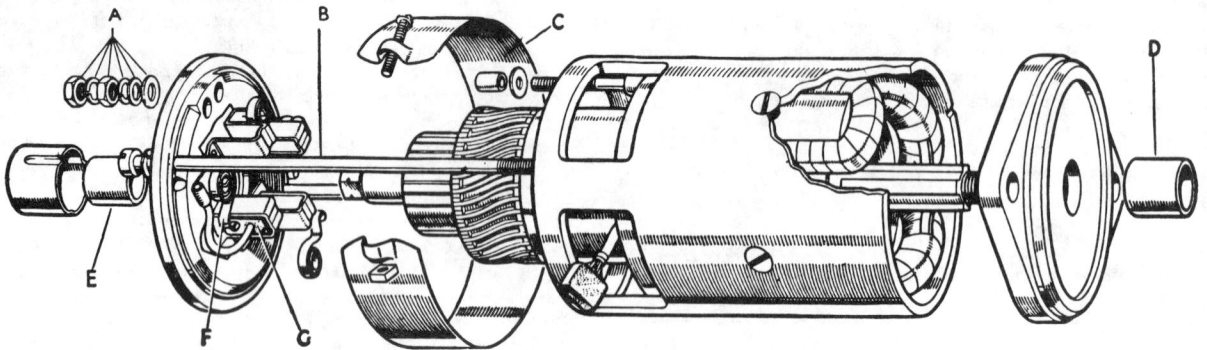

Fig.10.6. EXPLODED VIEW OF LUCAS INERTIA TYPE STARTER MOTOR

A Terminal nuts and washers	C Cover band	E Bearing bush	G Brush
B Through bolts	D Bearing bush	F Brush spring	

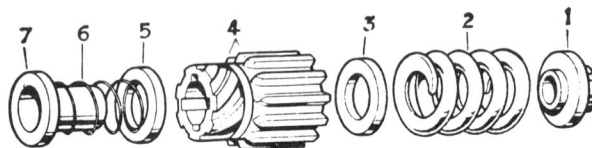

Fig.10.7. COMPONENT PARTS OF STARTER DRIVE

1 Shaft nut	3 Washer	5 Collar	7 Spring restraining
2 Main spring	4 Screwed sleeve and pinion	6 Pinion restraining spring	sleeve

26.10

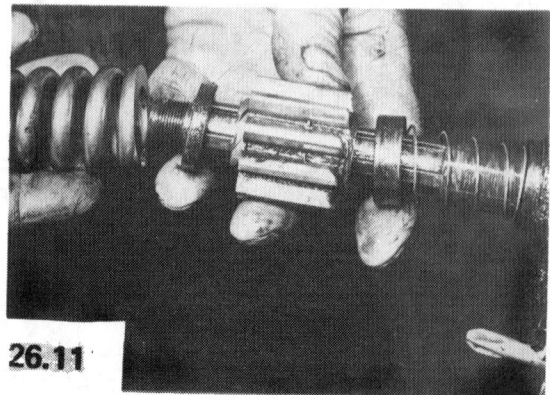

26.11

starter motor securing nut and bolt taking care to support the motor so as to prevent damage to the drive component.

5. Lift the starter motor out of engagement with the flywheel ring gear and lower it from the car.

6. Replacement is a straightforward reversal of the removal procedure. Take extreme care to ensure that the cables on the back of the solenoid are reconnected correctly.

30. Starter Motor — Dismantling & Reassembly

1. With the starter motor on the bench, loosen the screw on the cover band and slip the cover band off. An exploded view of this starter motor is shown in Fig.10.8.

2. Disconnect the cable link between the lower solenoid terminal and the starter motor casing by undoing and removing the terminal nut and spring washer at the rear of the solenoid.

3. Undo and remove the two solenoid securing nuts and spring washers and withdraw the solenoid from the drive end bracket.

4. Move the starter pinion away from the armature to the end of its travel, then disengage the solenoid plunger from its engagement lever and withdraw the plunger and spring.

5. With a piece of wire bent into the shape of a hook lift back each of the brushes in their holders by pulling on the flexible connectors. If the brushes are so worn that their faces do not rest against the commutaotr, or if the ends of the brush leads are exposed on their working face, they must be renewed.

6. If any of the brushes tend to stick in their holders, then wash them with a petrol moistened rag and if necessary lightly polish the sides of the brush with a very fine file until the brushes move quite freely in their holders.

7. If the surface of the commutator is dirty or blackened, clean it with a petrol moistened rag. Secure the starter motor in a vice and check it by connecting a heavy gauge cable between the starter motor cable and a 12 volt battery.

8. Connect the cable from the other battery terminal to earth on the starter motor body. If the motor turns at high speed it is in good order.

9. If the starter motor still fails to function, or if it is wished to renew the brushes, it is necessary to further dismantle the motor.

10 Lift the brush spring with the wire hook, and lift all four brushes out of their holders one at a time.

11 Undo and remove the two long through bolts from the commutator end of the starter motor body, and pull off the commutator end bracket.

12 Remove the drive end bracket from the starter motor body.

13 Refer to Fig.10.8, and carefully push out the moving pole shoe pivot pin and lift away the pole shoe.

14 Undo and remove the two screws that secure the earth leads to the starter motor body. One lead is also soldered to one side of the contact points and must be cut as near to the connection as possible using a pair of side cutters.

15 Remove the brushes from the starter motor body.

16 Using the pair of side cutters, cut the insulated field coil brush leads as near to the field coil connections as possible and remove the brushes.

17 If new brushes are to be fitted, check that the new brushes move freely in their holders, as detailed previously. If cleaning the commutator with petrol fails to remove all the burnt areas and spots, then work a piece of glass paper round the commutator. If the commutator is very badly worn, remove the drive gear as detailed in the following Section. Then mount the armature in a lathe and with the lathe turning at high speed, take a very fine cut out of the commutator and finish the surface by polishing with glass paper. DO NUT UNDERCUT THE MICA INSULATORS BETWEEN THE COMMUTATOR SEGMENTS.

18 With the starter motor dismantled, test the four field coils for an open circuit. Connect a 12 volt battery with a 12 volt bulb in one of the leads between the two ends of each field coil. An open circuit is proved by the bulb not lighting.

19 If the bulb lights, it does not necessarily mean that the field coils are in order, as there is a possibility that one of the coils will be earthing at the yoke or pole shoes.

20 To check this, remove the lead from the brush connector and place it against a clean portion of the starter motor body. If the bulb lights, the field coils are earthing. Replacement of the field coils calls for the use of a wheel operated screwdriver, a soldering iron, caulking and riveting operations and is considered beyond the scope of the majority of owners. The starter motor body should be taken to a reputable electrical engineering works for new field coils to be fitted. Alternatively, purchase an exchange starter motor

21 If the armature is damaged, it will be evident after visual inspection. Look for signs of burning, discolouration and for conductors that have lifted from the commutator.

22 Reassembly is a straightforward reversal of the dismantling procedure.

31. Starter Motor Drive Pinion Assembly — Removal & Refitting

1. Refer to Section 30 and dismantle the starter motor.

2. Using a small screwdriver or a pair of circlip pliers, remove the circlip that retains the drive pinion assembly onto the armature shaft. Slide the drive pinion assembly from the armature shaft.

3. Carefully hold the drive pinion assembly, but not by holding the one-way clutch, in a vice, and remove the circlip behind the spring retainer plate.

4. It should be noted that the drive pinion and one-way clutch assembly is serviceable as a complete unit and individual parts are not available.

5. To refit, first place the spring and retainer plate onto the drive pinion and one-way clutch unit and secure in position with the circlip.

6. Refit the drive pinion assembly onto the armature shaft with the spring retainer placed nearest to the starter motor body. Secure in position with the circlip.

7. Check that the retaining ring is fitted over the circlip before refitting the drive end housing to the starter motor. Refer to Fig. 10.9, and reset the pinion clearance using feeler gauges and rotating the eccentric pivot pin D.

32. Fuses — General

The fuse box is mounted on the right-hand side of the engine, above the steering box as shown in Fig.10.10. On early produced models a two-amp line fuse contained in a plastic carrier is inserted into the cable just below the fuse box and its function is to protect the panel lights. To fit a new fuse into the carrier, push on one end of the carrier and twist, whilst the other part of the carrier is firmly held.

The A2 fuse in the carrier is rated at 35 amps and protects the horns, cigar lighter and interior light units. The A4 fuse in the carrier is also rated at 35 amps and protects the electric screen washer, stop lights and flasher unit.

Later produced cars have all the fuses contained in a box and are all rated at 35 amps. The fuse holders are identified as follows:—

1—2	Horns, cigar lighter illumination and interior lights.
3—4	Windscreen washer, stop lights and flasher lights.
5—6	Cigar lighter, clock and panel illumination.
7—8	Heater and wiper motor.

33. Flasher Circuit — Fault Finding & Rectification

1. The flasher unit is in a small cylindrical metal container located behind the instrument panel to the right. Unfortunately it is only accessible once the instrument panel has been removed. The unit is actuated by the direction indicator switch.

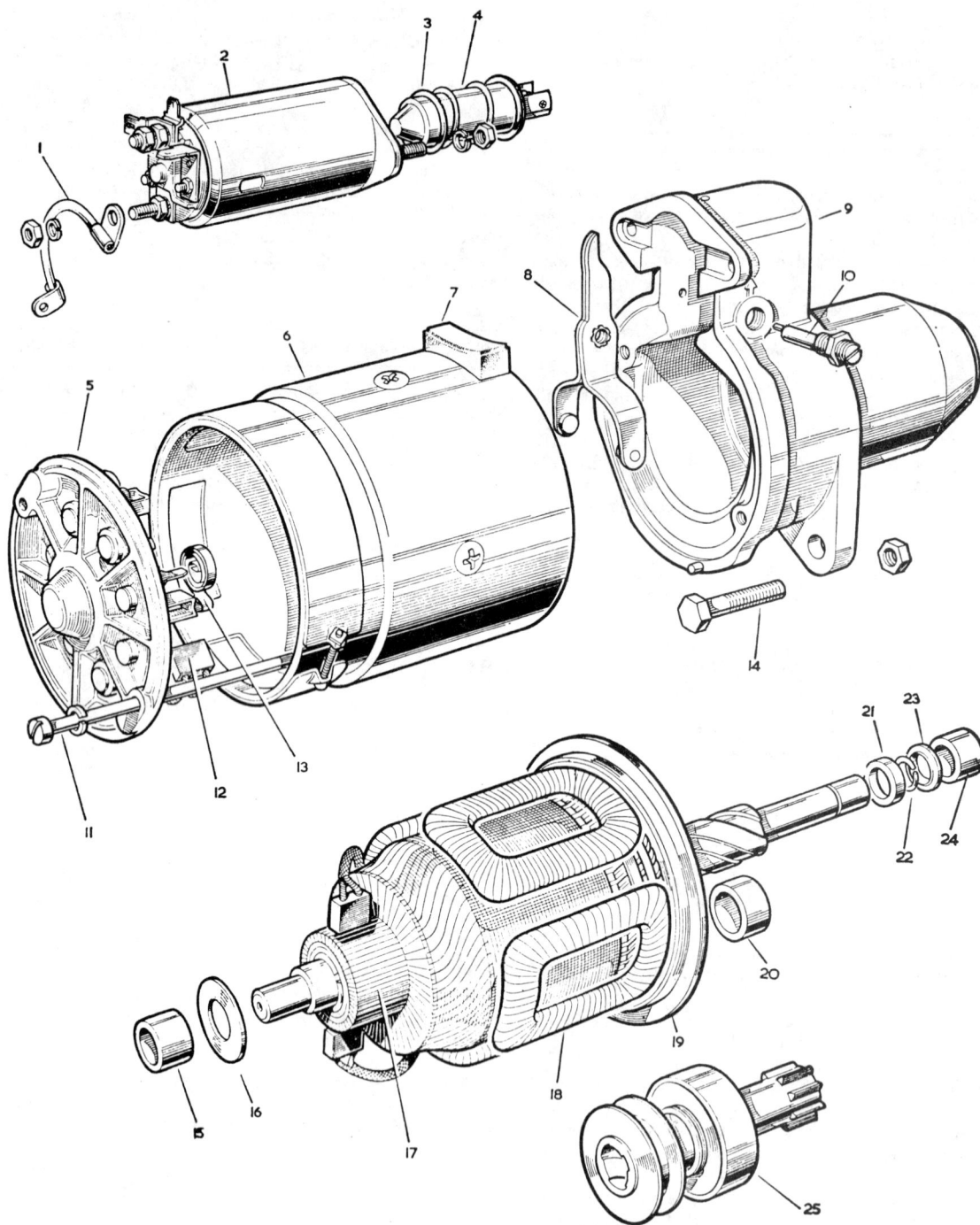

Fig.10.8. EXPLODED VIEW OF LUCAS PRE—ENGAGED STARTER

1	Cable link	8	Pre-engaged fork	15	Bush	21	Collar
2	Solenoid	9	Drive end bracket	16	Thrust washer	22	Jump ring
3	Return spring	10	Fork adjuster	17	Armature	23	Thrust washer
4	Solenoid plunger	11	Through bolt	18	Field coil	24	Bush, drive end
5	Commutator end bracket	12	Brush	19	Intermediate bracket		bracket
6	Yoke	13	Brush spring	20	Bush, intermediate	25	Drive assembly
7	Seal	14	Bolt fixing starter		bracket		

2. If the flasher unit fails to operate, or works very slowly or rapidly, check the flasher indicator circuit as detailed below before assuming there is a fault in the unit itself.
a) Examine the direction indicator bulbs, front and rear for broken filament.
b) If the external flashers are working, but the internal flasher warning light has ceased to function, check the filament in the warning light bulb and replace with a new bulb if necessary.
c) If a flasher bulb is sound, but does not work, check all the flasher circuit connections with the aid of the wiring diagram.
d) In the event of total indicator failure, check the fuse applicable, (see Section 32). It will be fairly obvious if this fuse has blown, as it also protects the stop lamps and electric screen washer.
e) With the ignition switched on, check that the current is reaching the flasher unit by connecting a voltmeter between the '+' or 'B' terminal and earth. If it is found that current is reaching the unit, connect the two terminals '+' or 'B' and 'L' and operate the flasher switch. If the warning light comes on, this proves that the flasher unit itself is at fault and must be replaced, as it is not possible to dismantle and repair it. Before removing make a special note of the electrical connections to ensure correct refitting to the unit.

34. Windscreen Wiper Mechanism — Maintenance

1. Renew the windscreen wiper blades at intervals of 12,000 miles or more frequently if necessary.
2. The washer around the wiper arm spindles can be lubricated with several drops of glycerine every 6,000 miles.
3. The later type link drive pivots can be lightly oiled every 6,000 miles.

35. Windscreen Wiper Blades — Removal & Replacement

1. Lift the wiper arm away from the windscreen and remove the old blade by returning it slowly towards the arm and then disengage the arm from the slot in the blade.
2. To fit a new blade, slide the end of the wiper arm into the slotted spring fastening in the centre of the blade. Push the blade firmly onto the arm, until the raised portion of the arm is fully home in the hole in the blade.

36. Windscreen Wiper Arms — Removal & Replacement

1. Before removing a wiper arm, turn the windscreen wiper switch on and off to ensure the arms are in their normal parked position, parallel to the bottom of the windscreen.
2. To remove an arm, pivot the arm back and pull the wiper arm head off the splined sleeve. If the arm proves difficult to remove, a screwdriver with a wide blade can be used to lever the wiper arm head off the splined sleeve. Care must be taken not to damage the spline.
3. When replacing an arm, position it so that it is in the correct relative parked position and then press the arm head onto the splined drive until it is fully home on the splines.

37. Windscreen Wiper Mechanism — Fault Diagnosis & Rectification

Early Rack & Pinion Type
1. When operating correctly, the wiper blades should operate at between 40 to 50 cycles per minute when the wiper switch is set to the slow speed position and between 60 to 70 cycles per minute in the fast speed position.
2. If the required speeds are not reached, the cause will probably be found in the rack cable or wheel boxes.
3. When the rack cable is disconnected from the motor and the wiper blades are away from the windscreen glass, the maximum

permissible force required to move the cable rack should not exceed 6 lb. If this force is greater, further investigation will be necessary, probably requiring removal of the system, thoroughly cleaning, and re-packing with Ragosine Listate 225 grease.
4. It is recommended that before the end cover is refitted after completion of the previous test, the limit switch contacts ('A', Fig.10.12) be inspected for signs of burning which would be the reason for inconsistent self parking.
5. Should signs of burning be evident at the limit switch contacts and no other visible sign of trouble be apparent, the limit switch should be adjusted. Clean the contact points with a very fine contact file or glass paper. Reconnect the rack and reset the limit switch by turning the knurled nut 'D' positioned near to the wiper motor gearbox cable outlet, half a turn at a time until the wiper blades just reach the correct parking position.

Later Link Drive Type
1. Should the windscreen wipers fail, or work very slowly, then check the terminals of the motor for loose connections and make sure the insulation of all the wiring is not cracked or broken, thus causing a short circuit. If this is in order, then check the current the motor is taking by connecting an ohmmeter in the circuit and turning on the wiper switch. Consumption should be between 2.3 and 3.1 amps.
2. If no current is passing through the motor, check that the switch is operating correctly. If the wiper motor takes a very high current, check the wiper blades for freedom of movement. If this is satisfactory, check the gearbox cover and gear assembly for damage.
3. If the motor takes a very low current ensure that the battery is fully charged. Check the brush gear and ensure the brushes are bearing on the commutator. If not, check the brushes for freedom of movement and, if necessary, renew the tension springs. If the brushes are very worn they should be replaced with new ones. Check the armature by substitution if this unit is suspect.

38. Windscreen Wiper Mechanism, Rack & Pinion Type — Removal & Refitting

1. Disconnect the earth terminal from the battery terminal posts.
2. Remove the wiper arms and blades from the spindle.
3. Refer to Chapter 12, Section 31, and remove the air intake valance.
4. Undo and remove the locknut and distance pieces from the wheel boxes.
5. Remove the nuts that attach the wiper motor to the mounting bracket.
6. Make a note of the electrical cable connections at the screen wiper motor and disconnect the cables from the block connector.
7. Slacken the nut that secures the flexible drive outer tube to the gearbox.
8. The wiper motor and rack cable may now be withdrawn by carefully drawing the motor back away from the outer tube.
9. Refitting the assembly is the reverse sequence to removal. Take great care when inserting the rack cable not to cause it to kink or buckle.

39. Windscreen Wiper Motor, Rack & Pinion Type - Removal & Refitting

1. Refer to Chapter 12, Section 31,, and remove the air intake valance.
2. Undo and remove the nuts that secure the wiper motor to the mounting bracket.
3. Disconnect the battery earth terminal from the terminal posts.
4. Make a note of the electrical cable connections at the screen wiper motor and disconnect the cables from the block connector.
5. Undo and remove the six screws that secure the cover to the motor and lift away the cover.

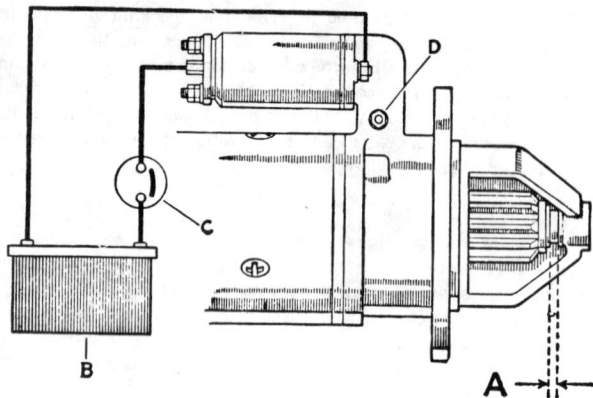

Fig.10.9. PINION CLEARANCE ADJUSTMENT WITH SOLE-
NOID ENERGISED

A Clearance 0.005 to 0.015 in.   C Switch
B Battery   D Eccentric pivot pin

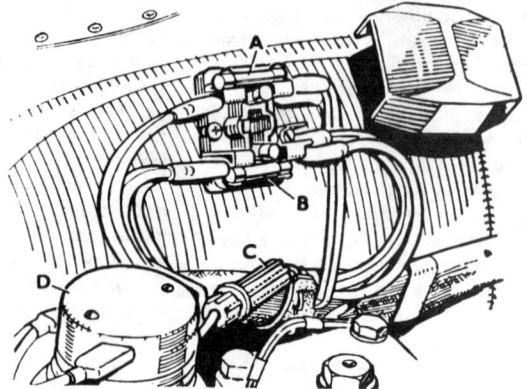

Fig.10.10. LOCATION OF FUSE BOX (EARLY TYPE)

A A2 fuse   fuse
B A4 fuse   D Brake fluid reservoir
C Panel illumination   cap

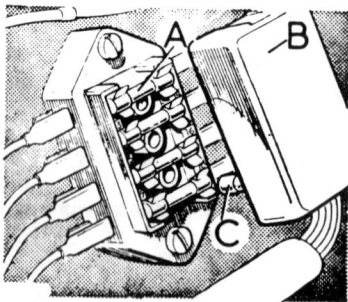

Fig.10.11. LATER TYPE FUSE BOX

A Fuse   C Spare fuse
B Cover for fuse box

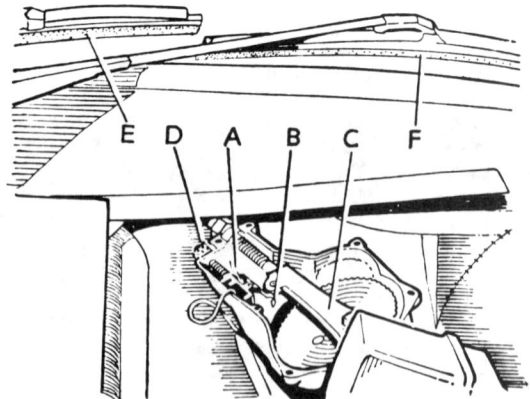

Fig.10.12. WINDSCREEN WIPER MOTOR PARK POSITION
ADJUSTMENT

A Contacts   D Knurled nut adjuster
B Cam   E RH wiper
C Cross arm   F LH wiper

6. Using a pair of circlip pliers or a small screwdriver, remove the circlip and plain washer from the cross arm spindle and remove the cross arm from the cable.
7. Separate the cable from the wiper motor gearbox and lift away the wiper motor.

40. Windscreen Wiper Motor, Rack & Pinion Type — Dismantling, Inspection & Reassembly

1. Undo the screws that hold the gearbox cover in place and lift away the cover.
2. Undo and remove the two through bolts from the commutator end bracket. Pull out the connector and free the end bracket from the yoke.
3. Carefully remove the brush gear as a unit from the commutator and then withdraw the yoke.
4. Clean the commutator and brush gear and if worn fit new brushes. The resistance between adjacent commutator segments should be 0.34 to 0.41 ohm.
5. Carefully examine the internal wiring for signs of chafing, breaks or charring which would lead to a short circuit. Insulate or replace any damaged wires.
6. Measure the value of the field resistance which should be between 12.8 to 14 ohms. If a lower reading than this is obtained it is likely that there is a short circuit and a new field coil should be fitted.
7. Renew the gearbox gear if the teeth are damaged, chipped or worn.
8. Reassembly is a straightforward reversal of the dismantling sequence, but ensure the following items are lubricated:—
a) Immerse the self-aligning armature bearing in SAE 20 engine oil for 24 hours before assembly.
b) Oil the armature bearings in SAE 20 engine oil.
c) Soak the felt lubricator in the gearbox with SAE 20 engine oil.
d) Grease generously the worm wheel bearings, crosshead, guide channel, connecting rod, crankpin, worm, cable rack and wheel boxes and the final gear shaft.

41. Windscreen Wiper Drive Cable & Wheelboxes, Rack & Pinion Type — Removal & Refitting

1. Refer to Section 39, and remove the wiper motor and rack cable.
2. Undo and remove the six screws that secure the cover to the motor and lift away the cover.
3. Using a pair of circlip pliers or a small screwdriver extract the circlip from the cross arm spindle. Lift away the plain washer and finally remove the cross arm from the cable.
4. Remove the cable from the wiper motor.
5. The wheelboxes may now be removed from the rack cable.

42. Windscreen Wiper Mechanism, Link Type — Removal & Refitting

1. Disconnect the battery earth terminal from the battery terminal post.
2. Refer to Chapter 12, Section 31, and remove the air intake valance.
3. Slacken the locknut that clamps the link drive and spacer to the base unit.
4. Remove the locknut on the wiper motor bracket that is held in position on the steering box cover plate.
5. Make a note of the electrical cable connections at the screen wiper motor and disconnect the cables from the block connector.
6. The complete system may now be withdrawn from its location by very carefully manipulating the assembly between the heater box and the base unit. Once free, lift away the assembly from the engine compartment.
7. Release the spring circlip from the link to the driver's side (E), Fig.10.14) at the motor end and lift up clear of the bush.
8. Undo and remove the three screws that fix the wiper motor to

the bracket and remove the motor.
9. Reassembling and refitting is the reverse sequence to removal. As the links incorporate 'Oilete' bushes at the pivot points, no further lubrication will be required.

43. Windscreen Wiper Motor, Link Type — Dismantling & Reassembly

This is similar to that used in the early rack and pinion system and full details are given in Section 40 of this chapter.

44. Headlamps — Removal & Refitting

The headlamp units fitted are of the sealed beam type and due to their design they may be serviced only as a complete unit.
1. Undo the wing nuts at the rear of the centre badge on the radiator grille and lift away the badge.
2. Remove the plastic caps over the Phillips screws on the side of the grille to be removed, undo and remove the three screws, spring washers and plain washers that secure the half radiator grille to the body.
3. Ease the top of the grille away, lift up the grille so that the locating clips ('A', Fig.10.15) lift out of the rubber mountings and then remove forwards from the front of the car.
4. Undo and remove the three Phillips screws that secure the headlamp rim and light unit in position.
5. Disconnect the wiring adaptor from the rear of the light unit and lift away the light unit.
6. Refitting is the reverse sequence to the above.

45. Headlamp — Beam Adjustment

The twin beam headlights may be adjusted but because special equipment is required it is recommended that this be left to the local Rover agents, who will have the necessary equipment. The procedure for alignment of twin beam headlights is not the same as that for single beam headlamp systems, and if attempted will give unsatisfactory results.

46. Side & Flasher Light Unit — Removal & Refitting

1. Undo and remove the four Phillips screws that secure the light lens to the light body.
2. Lift away the light lens and the foam rubber seal.
3. Undo and remove the three screws that secure the light body to the front wing.
4. The light body may now be withdrawn until the three-way wiring connector is visible. Make a note of the cable connections and disconnect the three cables. Finally lift away the light body.
5. Refitting is the reverse sequence to removal.

47. Tail Light Unit — Removal & Refitting

1. Undo and remove the Phillips screws that secure the light lens to the light body.
2. Lift away the light lens and the foam rubber seal.
3. Undo and remove the screws that secures the light body to the rear wing.
4. Make a note of the light unit cable connections at the main wiring harness and disconnect the cable. Attach a piece of string or wire to the tail light wiring when withdrawing it from the body, as it will facilitate the refitting of the wiring through the grommet in the side panel.
5. Carefully withdraw the light unit body and at the same time ease the cables through the grommet.

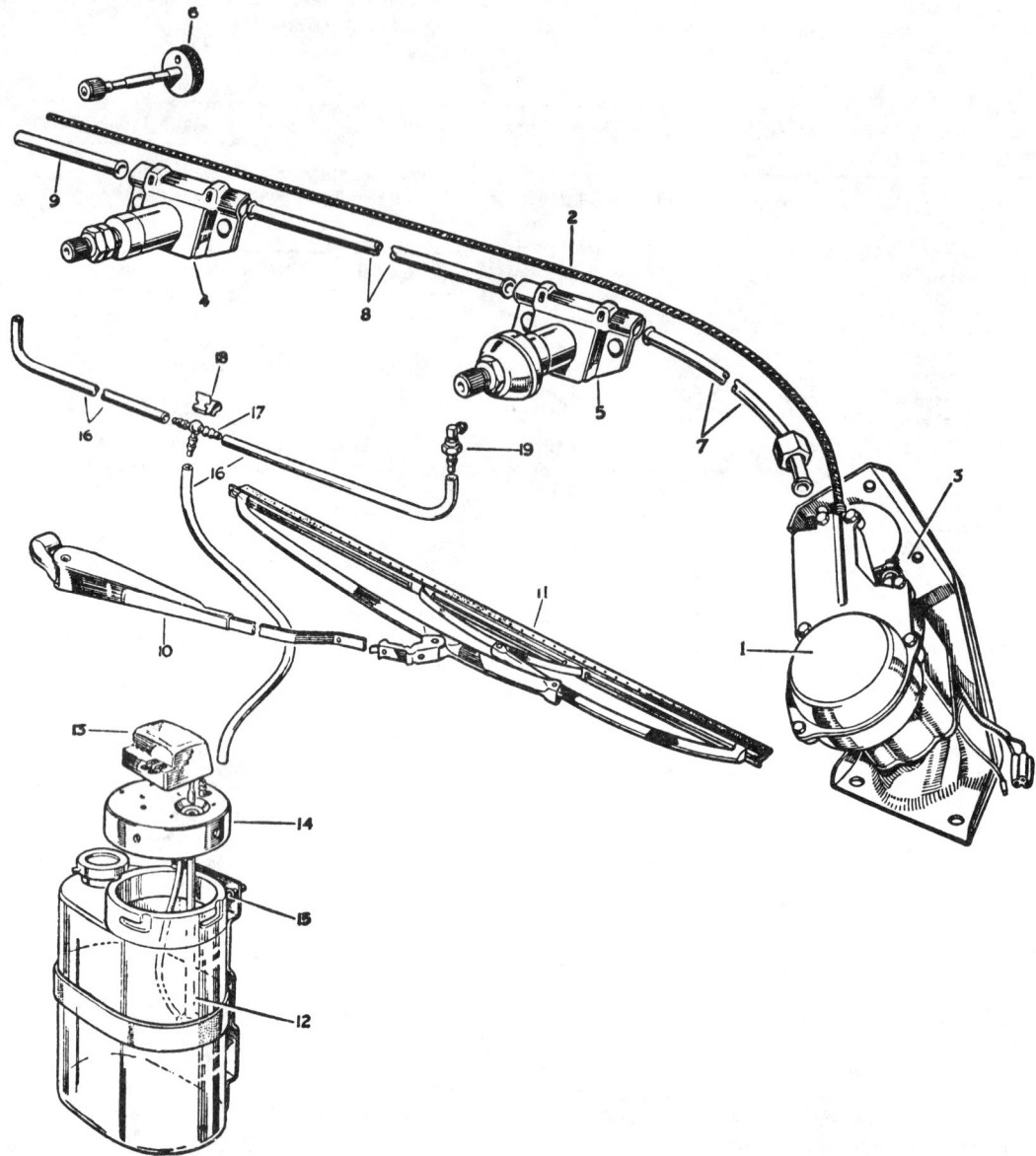

Fig.10.13. RACK & PINION TYPE WINDSCREEN WIPER MECHANISM

1 Screen wiper motor complete
2 Cable for wiper motor
3 Bracket for wiper motor
4 Wheelbox for wiper, RH
5 Wheelbox for wiper, LH
6 Spindle and gear for wheelbox
7 Outer casing, motor to wheelbox
8 Outer casing, wheelbox to wheelbox
9 Outer casing, wheelbox end
10 Wiper arm
11 Wiper blade
12 Windscreen washer reservoir and pump
13 Motor for screen washer
14 Cover and pump for screen washer
15 Pop rivet fixing reservoir to base unit
16 Plastic tubing for windscreen washer
17 'T' piece connector for tubing
18 Clip, 'T' piece and tubing to stiffener
19 Windscreen washer nozzle complete

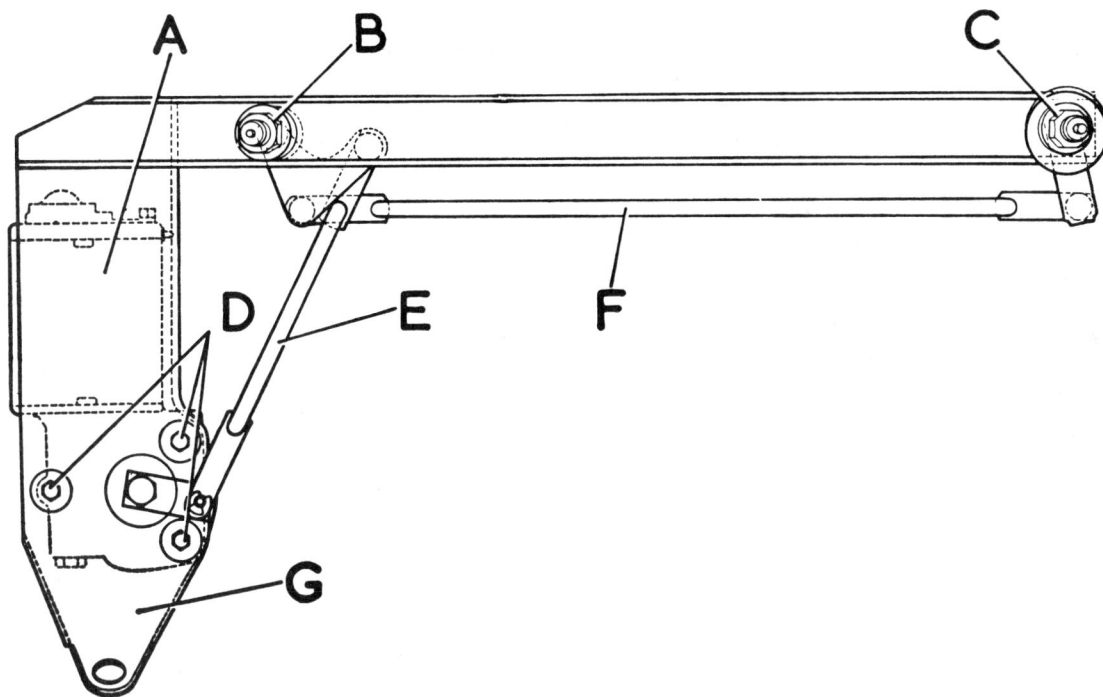

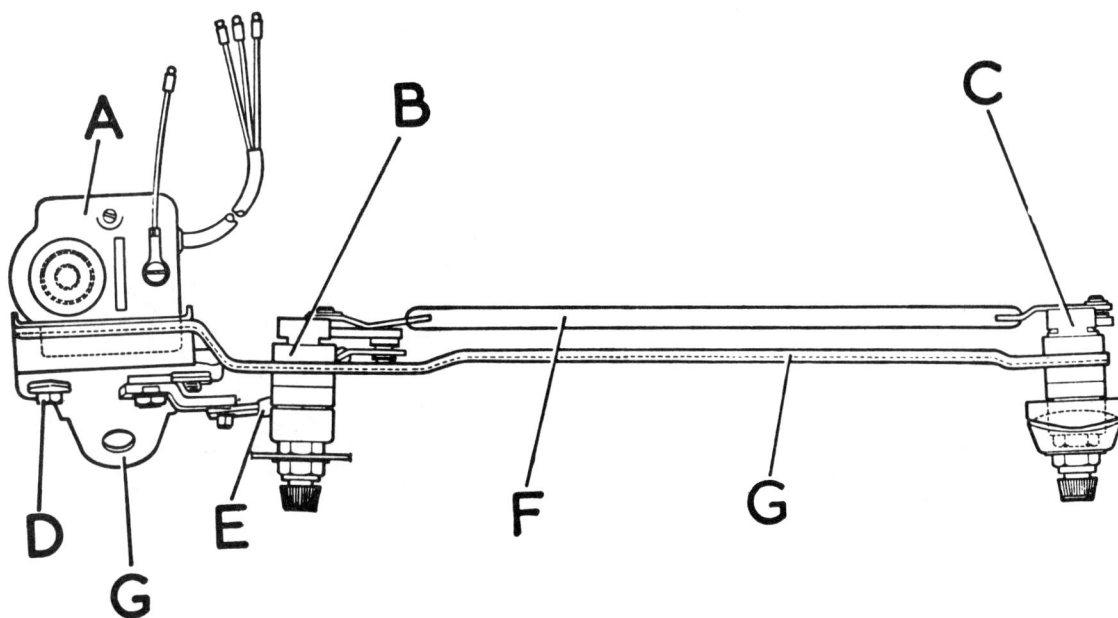

Fig.10.14. LINK TYPE WINDSCREEN WIPER MECHANISM SIDE & PLAN VIEWS

A Wiper motor
B Link drive, driver's side
C Link drive, passenger's
   side
D Bolts fixing wiper
   motor to bracket
E Link, wiper motor to
   driver's side
F Link, driver's to passenger's
   side
G Bracket for wiper motor
   and link drives

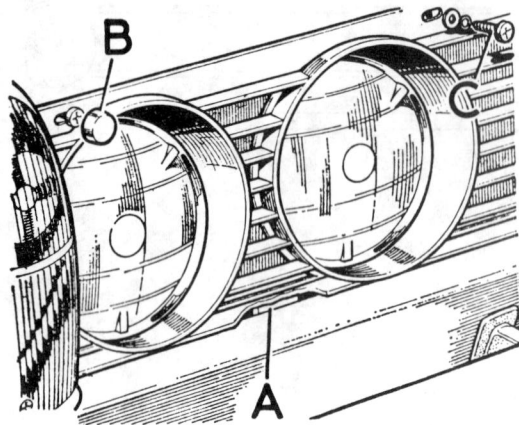

Fig.10.15. FRONT GRILLE FIXINGS

A Clip
B Plastic cap
C Fixing screw and
   washers

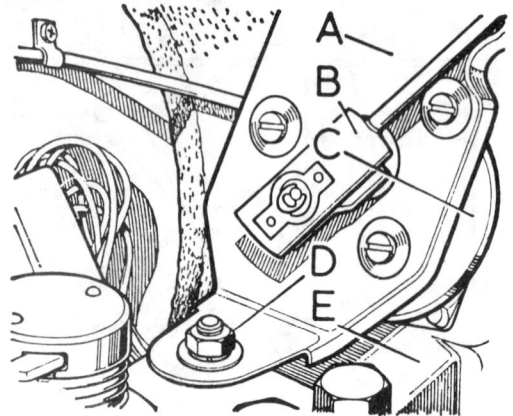

Fig.10.16. WINDSCREEN WIPER MOTOR MOUNTING LOCA-
TION

A Bracket for wiper motor   C Wiper motor
   and link drives   D Locknut fixing bracket to
B Link, wiper motor to   steering box
   driver's side   E Steering box

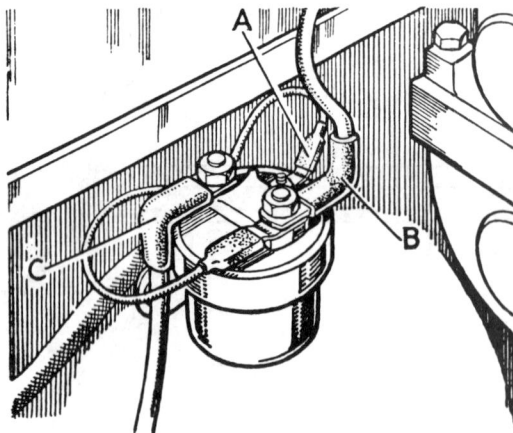

Fig.10.17. ENGINE STARTER SOLENOID — EARLY TYPE
A — Switch cable
B — Battery connection
C — Starter connection

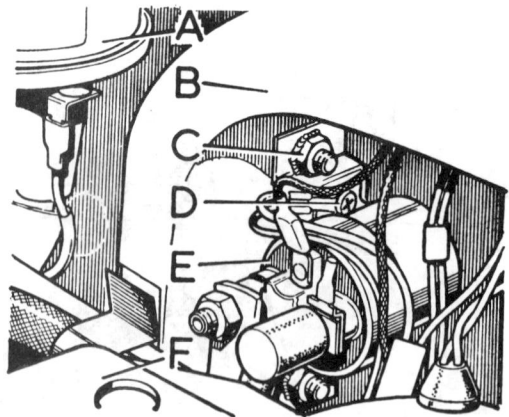

Fig.10.18. ENGINE STARTER SOLENOID — LATER TYPE
A Ignition coil   D Screw fixing solenoid to
B Wing valance   bracket
C Bracket and weld nut   E Starter solenoid
   for solenoid   F Radiator

6. Refitting is the reverse sequence to removal.

48. Headlamp or Horn & Flasher Switch — Removal & Refitting

1. Undo and remove the two Allen screws (early produced cars) or the two self-locking screws that secure the steering wheel finisher to the steering wheel. Lift away the finisher.
2. Undo and remove the nut and spring washer that secures the steering wheel to the inner column. Mark the steering wheel hub and inner column to ensure correct refitting in its original position and remove the steering wheel by thumping on the back of the spokes with the palms of the hands.
3. Carefully spring off the plastic cover from the steering column nacelle.
4. Make a note of the switch electrical cable connections and disconnect the cables from the connectors.
5. The switch may now be removed by undoing the self-tapping screws and then lifting away the switch from its location.
6. Refitting the switch is the reverse sequence to removal. Check that switch operates correctly when all reassembled.

49. Horn — Removal & Refitting

The horn is mounted onto the body beneath the battery. Should it not operate correctly or it completely fails, check the wiring leading to it for short circuiting or loose connection. Make sure that it is firmly attached to the body and that there is nothing lying on the horn body. To remove the horn, proceed as follows:—
1. Make a note of the electrical cable connections to the horn and disconnect from the horn.
2. Undo and remove the two bolts, nuts and spring washers that secure the horn to the base unit, and lift away the horn.
3. Refitting is the reverse sequence to removal.

50. Electrical Clock — Removal, Adjustment & Refitting

1. Undo and remove the two nuts and washers that secure the clock shroud to the facia top rail.
2. Make a note of the electrical cable connections to the rear of the clock and then disconnect the connectors.
3. The clock and shroud may now be removed from the facia top rail.
4. To separate the clock from the shroud, slacken the brass set screw and remove the clock from the shroud.
5. It is only considered necessary to adjust the clock if it gains or loses more than three minutes per week. To adjust, turn the little screw at the rear of the clock as follows:—

    Clock gains ... ... Turn towards the '—' mark.
    Clock loses ... ... Turn towards the '+' mark.

6. Refitting is the reverse procedure to removal.

2200 TL Models

7. Remove the instrument panel front section.
8. Unscrew and remove the clock retaining screws and extract the clock. Detach the wire connector.
9. Refer to paragraphs 5 and 6 for adjustment and installation procedures.

51. Switches — General

Brake Fluid Level Warning Light Switch

This switch is located in the brake fluid reservoir cap which is to be found on the right-hand side of the engine above the steering box.

To check the switch for correct operation, select a gear or move the selector lever to 'P' (automatic transmission) and release the handbrake. Switch on the ignition, but do not start the engine. Unscrew the reservoir filler cap and lift it one inch from the top of the filler neck. The warning light should come on. Replace the cap and the light should go out. If this test is negative, make sure that the float moves freely and that all electrical connections are clean and tight.

Courtesy Light Switches

Courtesy light switches are fitted to all four doors and operate automatically when a door is opened. If a switch should fail, it must be renewed as a complete unit. It is important that if a new switch is to be fitted, the shims positioned between the existing switch and the door post are retained and re-used with the new switch.

Reverse Light Switch

The reverse light switch is located on the right-hand side of the manual gearbox and access to it is gained through a little inspection cover on the right-hand side of the floor tunnel.

The switch is adjustable by removing the 'set' of the striker arm until, with reverse gear selected, the reverse light comes on. The light should extinguish when neutral is selected.

Stop Light Switch

The stop light switch is located on the right-hand side of the engine compartment, just below the brake servo unit. It is of the hydraulic pressure design and is non-adjustable. Should renewal be necessary, unscrew the original switch and fit the new one, after which it will be necessary to bleed the brake hydraulic systems.

Handbrake Switch

The handbrake warning light switch is located under the moulded handbrake surround and is attached to the rear handbrake mounting bracket. The switch is adjustable by means of two locknuts. Undo the locknuts and apply the handbrake until the ratchet pole is on the second notch. Adjust the switch until the warning light is just alight and tighten the locknuts. Re-check the adjustment.

Starter Solenoid

The solenoid is located on the right-hand side of the engine compartment beneath the battery. On later produced models having a serial number suffix 'D' onwards the solenoid was repositioned behind the left-hand inner headlamp. Fig.10.17 shows the early type solenoid and Fig.10.18 the later type solenoid.

Heated Rear Window Switch and Air Conditioning Switch (where fitted)

Open the glove box and unscrew the switch knob. Extract the bulb and spring from the switch. On late model 2200's compress the switch location tabs at the sides and withdraw the switch from the switch from the panel. To remove the switch completely on the earlier models unscrew and remove the lock ring. Disconnect the wires.

Installation for both types of switch is a reversal of the removal procedure.

WIRING DIAGRAMS COMMENCE OVERLEAF

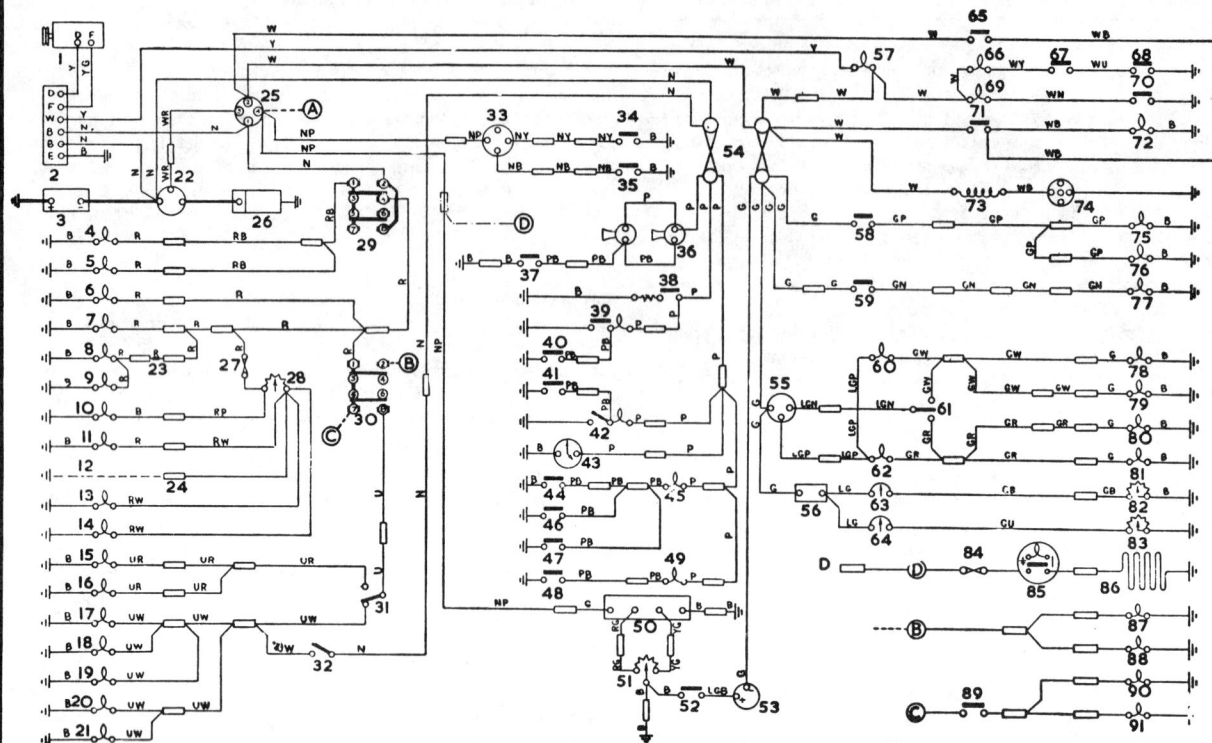

Fig.10.19. CIRCUIT DIAGRAM RHD MODELS WITH POSITIVE EARTH ELECTRICAL SYSTEM

1 Dynamo, C42	29 Switch, side & park	53 Screen washer	81 Front direction indicator, LH
2 Control box, RB340	30 Switch, headlamp	54 Fuse unit	82 Tank unit
3 Battery, 60 A/H	31 Switch, headlamp, dip	55 Direction indicator unit	83 Water temperature transmitter
4 Side & park lamp, RH	32 Switch, headlamp, flash	56 Bi-metal voltage regulator	
5 Tail & park lamp, RH	33 Heater blower unit, two-speed	57 Warning light, ignition	84 In-line fuse
6 Side lamp, LH		58 Switch, stop light	85 Illuminated switch
7 Tail lamp, LH	34 Switch, fast speed heater blower unit	59 Switch, reverse light	86 Backlight heater
8 Number plate lamp		60 Warning light, indicator, LH	87 Fog light
9 Number plate lamp	35 Switch, low speed heater blower unit	61 Switch, direction indicator	88 Fog light
10 Cigar lighter illumination		62 Warning light, indicator, RH	89 Long range driving light switch
11 Clock illumination	36 Twin horns	63 Fuel gauge	
12 Spare cable	37 Horn push	64 Temperature gauge	90 Long range driving lamp
13 Panel light	38 Switch, cigar lighter	65 Switch, handbrake	91 Long range driving lamp
14 Panel light	39 Switch, map and courtesy lamp, LH	66 Warning light, choke	
15 Headlamp dip beam, LH		67 Switch, choke	
16 Headlamp dip beam, RH	40 Switch, front door, LH	68 Switch, choke thermometer	
17 Headlamp main beam, RH	41 Switch, front door, RH	69 Warning light, oil pressure	
18 Headlamp main beam, RH	42 Switch, map and courtesy lamp, RH	70 Switch, oil pressure	
19 Main beam warning light		71 Switch, brake fluid	
20 Headlamp main beam, LH	43 Clock	72 Warning light, brake fluid level and handbrake	Earth terminals
21 Headlamp main beam, LH	44 Switch, interior lamp		A Radio and illumination feed) Feed
22 Starter solenoid	45 Interior lamp	73 Coil	B Fog lamp) pick-up
23 Cable identification tag	46 Switch, rear door, LH	74 Distributor	C Auxiliary driving lamps) points
24 Spare cable pick-up point	47 Switch, rear door, RH	75 Stop lamp, RH	
25 Switch, ignition & starter	48 Switch, boot light	76 Stop lamp, LH	
26 Starter motor	49 Boot lamp	77 Reverse lamp	
27 In-line fuse	50 Screenwiper motor	78 Front direction indicator, RH	
28 Rheostat for panel illumination	51 Rheostat for wiper motor	79 Rear direction indicator, RH	
	52 Switch screen washer	80 Rear direction indicator, LH	

Key to Cable Colours

B—Black	G—Green	LG—Light green	N—Brown	O—Orange	P—Purple
R—Red	S—Slate	U—Blue	W—White	Y—Yellow	

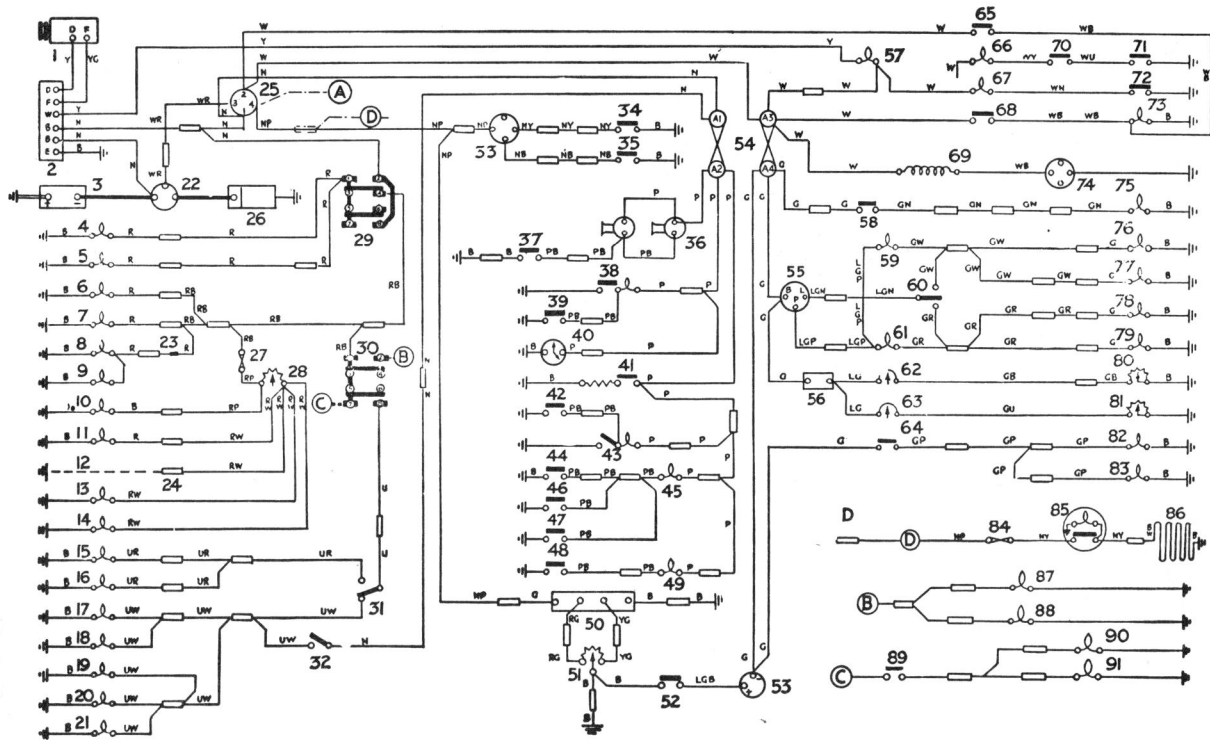

Fig.10.20. CIRCUIT DIAGRAM LHD MODELS WITH POSITIVE EARTH ELECTRICAL SYSTEM

1 Dynamo	29 Switch, side & park	54 Fuse unit (35-amp fuse)	79 Front direction indicator,LH
2 Control box	30 Switch, headlamp	55 Direction indicator unit	80 Tank unit
3 Battery, 60 A/H	31 Switch, headlamp dip	56 Bi-metal voltage regulator	81 Water temperature transmitter
4 Side & park lamp,LH	32 Switch, headlamp flasher	57 Warning light, ignition.Brake fluid level & handbrake on late models	82 Stop lamp, LH
5 Tail & park lamp,LH	33 Heater blower unit, two-speed		83 Stop lamp, RH
6 Side lamp, RH	34 Switch, fast speed, heater blower unit	58 Switch, reverse light	84 In-line fuse for heated backlight
7 Tail lamp, RH	35 Switch, slow speed, heater blower unit	59 Warning light, indicator,LH	85 Switch, illuminated, for heated backlight
8 Number plate lamp	36 Twin horns	60 Switch, direction indicator	86 Backlight heater
9 Number plate lamp	37 Horn switch	61 Warning light, indicator,RH	87 Fog lamp, RH
10 Cigar light illumination	38 Switch, map and courtesy lamp, LH	62 Fuel gauge	88 Fog lamp, LH
11 Clock illumination	39 Switch, front door, LH	63 Temperature gauge	89 Switch, long range driving lamp
12 Spare cable	40 Clock	64 Switch, stop light	90 Long range driving lamp, RH
13 Panel light	41 Switch, cigar lighter	65 Switch, handbrake	
14 Panel light	42 Switch, front door,RH	66 Warning light, choke	91 Long range driving lamp, LH
15 Headlamp dip beam,LH	43 Switch, map and courtesy lamp, RH	67 Warning light, oil pressure	
16 Headlamp dip beam,RH	44 Switch, interior lamp	68 Switch, brake fluid	
17 Headlamp main beam,RH	45 Interior lamp	69 Coil	
18 Headlamp main beam,RH	46 Switch,rear door,LH	70 Switch, choke	
19 Main beam warning light	47 Switch,rear door,RH	71 Switch, choke thermometer	
20 Headlamp main beam,LH	48 Switch, boot lamp	72 Switch, oil pressure	
21 Headlamp main beam,LH	49 Boot lamp	73 Warning light, brake fluid level and handbrake, ignition on late models	Earth terminals
22 Starter solenoid	50 Screenwiper motor		A Radio & illumination feed) Feed
23 Cable identification tag	51 Switch for wiper motor		B Fog lamp) pick-
24 Spare cable pick-up point	52 Switch, screen washer	74 Distributor	C Auxiliary driving lamps) up
25 Switch,ignition & starter	53 Screen washer	75 Reverse lamp	D Heated backlight) points
26 Starter motor		76 Front direction indicator,RH	
27 In-line fuse (2-amp) for panel rheostat switch		77 Rear direction indicator,RH	
28 Switch for panel illumination		78 Rear direction indicator,LH	

Key to Cable Colours

B—Black	G—Green	LG—Light green	N—Brown	O—Orange	P—Purple
R—Red	S—Slate	U—Blue	W—White	Y—Yellow

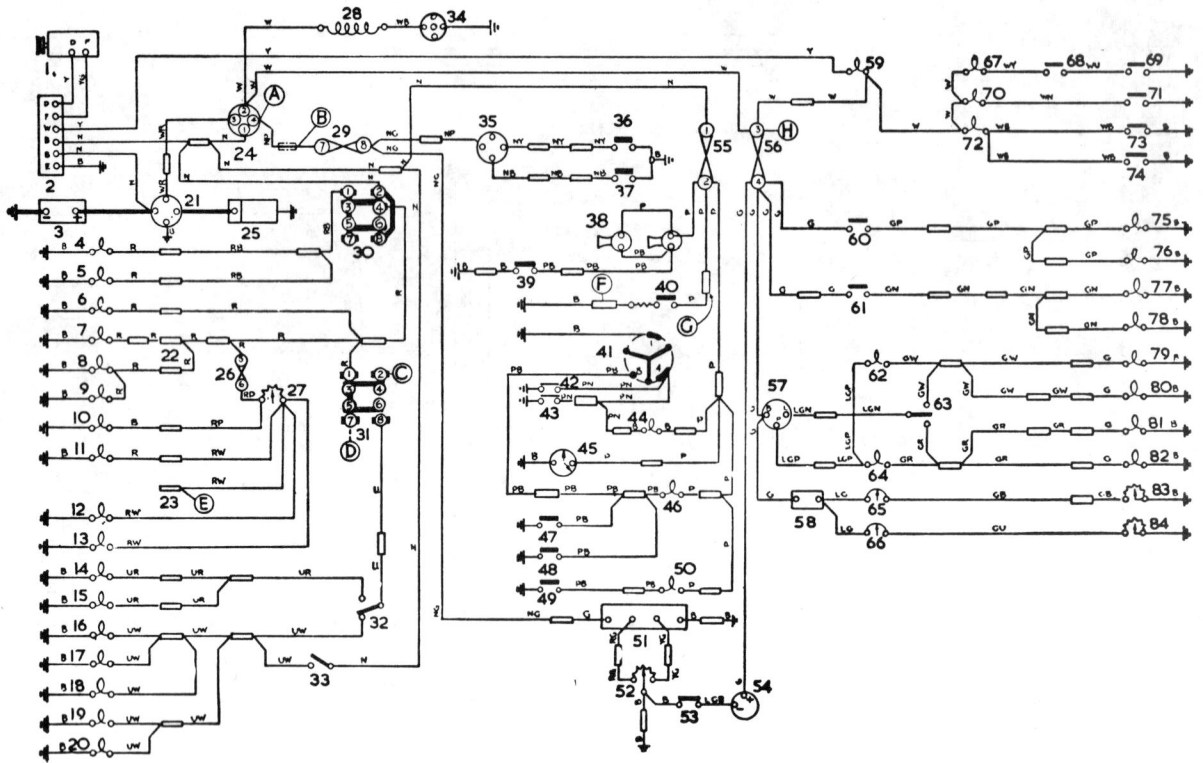

Fig.10.21. CIRCUIT DIAGRAM RHD MODELS WITH NEGATIVE EARTH WITH INERTIA TYPE STARTER SYSTEM

1 Dynamo, C42
2 Control box, RB340
3 Battery, 60 A/H
4 Side & park light, RH
5 Tail & park light, RH
6 Side lamp, LH
7 Tail lamp, LH
8 Number plate lamp
9 Number plate lamp
10 Cigar lighter illumination
11 Clock illumination
12 Panel light
13 Panel light
14 Headlamp dip beam, LH
15 Headlamp dip beam, RH
16 Headlamp main beam, RH
17 Headlamp main beam, RH
18 Main beam warning light
19 Headlamp main beam, LH
20 Headlamp main beam, LH
21 Starter solenoid
22 Cable identification tag
23 Spare cable pick-up point
24 Switch, ignition & starter
25 Starter motor
26 Fuse, 5 & 6, 35-amp
27 Switch for panel illumination
28 Ignition coil
29 Fuse, 7 & 8, 35-amp
30 Switch, side & park
31 Switch, headlamp
32 Switch, headlamp, dip
33 Switch, headlamp flash
34 Distributor
35 Heater blower unit, two-speed
36 Switch, fast speed heater blower
37 Switch, slow speed heater blower
38 Twin horns
39 Switch, horn
40 Switch, cigar lighter
41 Switch, interior lamps
42 Switch, front door, LH
43 Switch, front door, RH
44 Interior lamp, front
45 Clock
46 Interior lamp, rear
47 Switch, rear door, LH
48 Switch, rear door, RH
49 Switch, boot light
50 Boot light
51 Screen wiper motor
52 Switch, screen wiper
53 Switch, screen washer
54 Screen washer
55 Fuse, 1 & 2, 35-amp
56 Fuse, 3 & 4, 35-amp
57 Direction indicator unit
58 Bimetal voltage regulator
59 Warning light, ignition
60 Switch, stop lamp
61 Switch, reverse light
62 Warning light indicator, LH
63 Switch, direction indicator
64 Warning light indicator, RH
65 Fuel gauge
66 Temperature gauge
67 Warning light, choke
68 Switch, choke
69 Switch, choke thermometer
70 Warning light, oil pressure
71 Switch, oil pressure
72 Warning light, brake fluid level and handbrake
73 Switch, handbrake
74 Switch, brake fluid
75 Stop lamp, RH
76 Stop lamp, LH
77 Reverse lamp, RH
78 Reverse lamp, LH
79 Front direction indicator, RH
80 Rear direction indicator, RH
81 Rear direction indicator, LH
82 Front direction indicator, LH
83 Tank unit
84 Water temperature transmitter

A Radio feed & illumination pick-up point
B Heated backlight pick-up point
C Fog lamps pick-up point
D Auxiliary driving lamps pick-up point
E Spare pick-up point
F) Rear passengers' headrest
G) Light, pick-up point
H Spare pick-up point

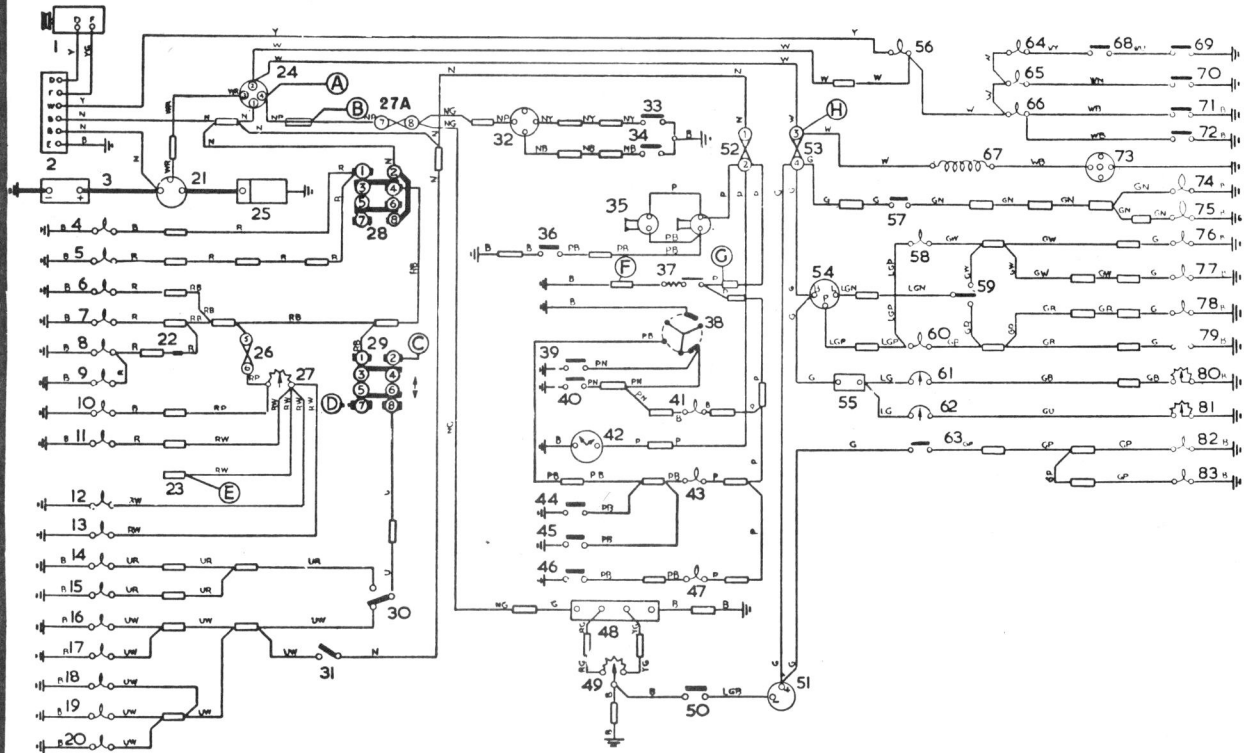

Fig.10.22. CIRCUIT DIAGRAM LHD MODELS WITH NEGATIVE EARTH WITH INERTIA TYPE STARTER SYSTEM

1 Dynamo, C42
2 Control box, RB340
3 Battery, 60 A/H
4 Side & park light, LH
5 Tail & park light, LH
6 Side lamp, RH
7 Tail lamp, RH
8 Number plate lamp
9 Number plate lamp
10 Cigar lighter illumination
11 Clock illumination
12 Panel light
13 Panel light
14 Headlamp dip beam, LH
15 Headlamp dip beam, RH
16 Headlamp main beam, RH
17 Headlamp main beam, RH
18 Main beam warning light
19 Headlamp main beam, LH
20 Headlamp main beam, LH
21 Starter solenoid
22 Cable identification tag
23 Spare cable pick-up point
24 Switch, ignition & starter
25 Starter motor
26 Fuse, 5 & 6, 35-amp
27 Switch for panel illumination

27a Fuse, 7 & 8, 35-amp
28 Switch, side & park
29 Switch, headlamp
30 Switch, headlamp dip
31 Switch, headlamp flash
32 Heater blower unit, two-speed
33 Switch, fast speed heater blower
34 Switch, slow speed heater blower
35 Twin horns
36 Switch, horn
37 Switch, cigar lighter
38 Switch, interior lamps
39 Switch, front door, LH
40 Switch, front door, RH
41 Interior lamp, front
42 Clock
43 Interior lamp, rear
44 Switch, rear door, LH
45 Switch, rear door, RH
46 Switch, boot light
47 Boot light
48 Screen wiper motor
49 Switch, screen wiper
50 Switch, screen washer

51 Screen washer
52 Fuse, 1 & 2, 35-amp
53 Fuse, 3 & 4, 35-amp
54 Direction indicator unit
55 Bi-metal voltage regulator
56 Warning light, ignition
57 Switch, reverse light
58 Warning light, indicator, LH
59 Switch, direction indicator
60 Warning light, indicator, RH
61 Fuel gauge
62 Temperatue gauge
63 Switch, stop lamp
64 Warning light, choke
65 Warning light, oil pressure
66 Warning light, brake fluid level and handbrake
67 Ignition coil
68 Switch, choke
69 Switch, choke thermometer
70 Switch, oil pressure
71 Switch, handbrake
72 Switch, brake fluid
73 Distributor
74 Reverse lamp, RH
75 Reverse lamp, LH
76 Front direction indicator, RH

77 Rear direction indicator, RH
78 Rear direction indicator, LH
79 Front direction indicator, LH
80 Tank unit
81 Water temperature transmitter
82 Stop lamp, RH
83 Stop lamp, LH

A Radio feed and illumination pick-up point
B Heated backlight pick-up point
C Fog lamps pick-up point
D Auxiliary driving lamps pick-up point
E Spare pick-up point
F) Rear passengers' headrest
G) Light, pick-up point
H Spare pick-up point

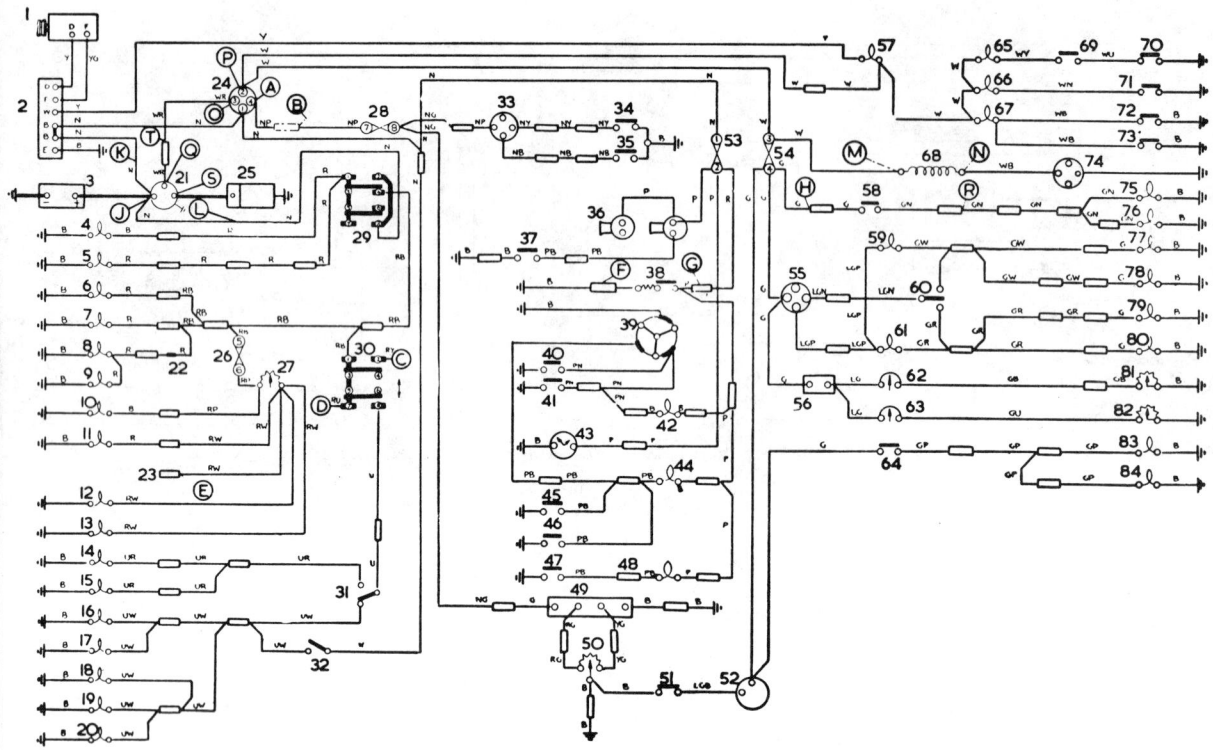

Fig.10.23. CIRCUIT DIAGRAM LHD MODELS WITH PRE--ENGAGED STARTER MOTOR

1 Dynamo, C42
2 Control box, RB340
3 Battery, 60 A/H
4 Side & park light, LH
5 Tail & park light, LH
6 Side lamp, RH
7 Tail lamp, RH
8 Number plate lamp
9 Number plate lamp
10 Cigar lighter illumination
11 Clock illumination
12 Panel illumination
13 Panel illumination
14 Headlamp dip beam, LH
15 Headlamp dip beam, RH
16 Headlamp main beam, RH
18 Main beam warning light
19 Headlamp main beam, LH
20 Headlamp main beam, LH
21 Starter solenoid
22 Cable identification tag
23 Spare cable pick-up point

24 Switch, ignition & starter
25 Starter motor
26 Fuse, 5 & 6, 2-amp
27 Switch for panel illumination
28 Fuse, 7 & 8, 15-amp
29 Switch, side & park
30 Switch, headlamp
31 Switch, headlamp dip
32 Switch, headlamp flash
33 Heater blower unit, two-speed
34 Switch, fast speed heater blower
35 Switch, slow speed heater blower
36 Twin horns
37 Switch, horn
38 Switch, cigar lighter
39 Switch, interior lamps
40 Switch, front door, LH
41 Switch, front door, RH
42 Interior lamp, front

43 Clock
44 Interior lamp, rear
45 Switch, rear door, LH
46 Switch, rear door, RH
47 Switch, boot light
48 Boot light
49 Screen wiper motor
50 Switch, screen wiper
51 Switch, screen washer
52 Screen washer
53 Fuse, 1 & 2, 35-amp
54 Fuse, 3 & 4, 35-amp
55 Direction indicator unit
56 Bi-metal voltage regulator
57 Warning light, ignition
58 Switch, reverse light
59 Warning light, indicator, LH
60 Switch, direction indicator
61 Warning light, indicator, RH
62 Fuel gauge
63 Temperatue gauge
64 Switch, stop lamp

65 Warning light, choke
66 Warning light, oil pressure
67 Warning light, brake fluid level and handbrake
68 Coil
69 Switch, choke
70 Switch, choke thermometer
71 Switch, oil pressure
72 Switch, handbrake
73 Switch, brake fluid level
74 Distributor
75 Reverse lamp, RH
76 Reverse lamp, LH
77 Front direction indicator, RH
78 Rear direction indicator, RH
79 Rear direction indicator, LH
80 Front direction indicator, LH
81 Tank unit
82 Water temperature transmitter
83 Stop lamp, RH
84 Stop lamp, LH

Encircled letters on circuit diagram show pick-up points for additional and optional equipment

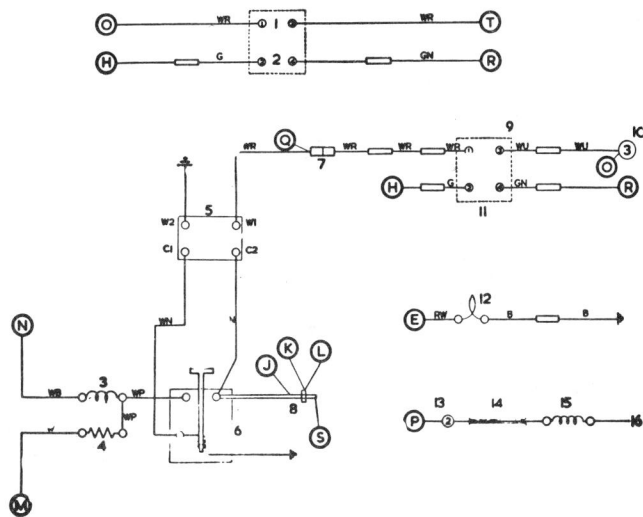

Fig.10.24. AUTOMATIC TRANSMISSION CIRCUIT DIAGRAM

1	Inhibitor switch)	All LHD automatic models with	12 Gear change illumination
2	Reverse light switch)	inertia-type starter motors	13 Ignition switch terminal number)
3	Ignition coil)		14 Ignition switch) Germany
4	Ballast resistor)	All LHD 2000	15 Ignition coil) only
5	Starter relay)	automatic	16 To distributor)
6	Starter motor solenoid)	models	
7	In-line connector)	with pre-	
8	Terminal post)	engaged	
9	Inhibitor switch)	starter	
10	Ignition and starter switch terminal number)	motor	
11	Reverse light switch)		

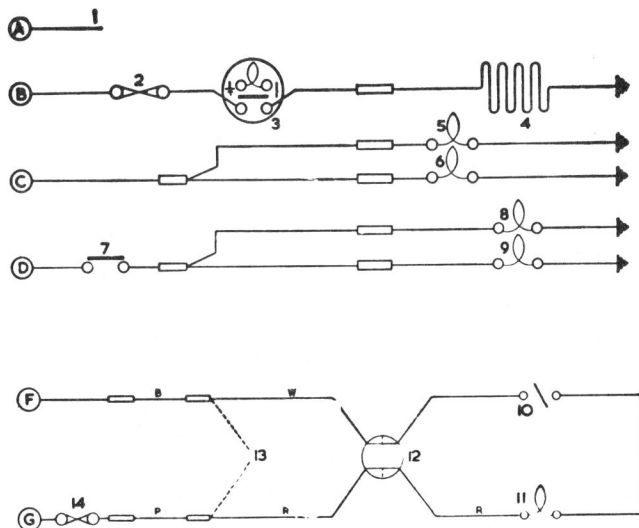

Fig.10.25. OPTIONAL EXTRAS CIRCUIT DIAGRAM

1	Radio feed and illumination pick-up point	8	Auxiliary lamp, RH
2	In-line fuse (10-amp) for heated backlight	9	Auxiliary lamp, LH
3	Illuminated switch for heated backlight	10	Switch for headrest lamp
4	Heated backlight	11	Headrest lamp
5	Fog lamp, RH	12	Plug and socket for headrest lamp
6	Fog lamp, LH	13	Pick-up points when two lamps are fitted
7	Switch, auxiliary lamp	14	In-line fuse (10-amp) for rear seat light

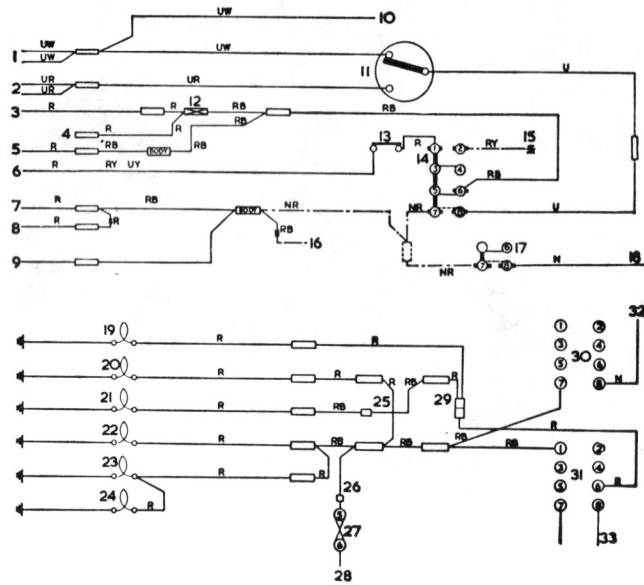

Fig.10.26. MODIFIED CIRCUIT DIAGRAM FOR CARS PRODUCED NORTH AMERICA DOLLAR AREA SPECIFICATION

1 Headlamp main beam	)	
2 Headlamp dip beam	)	
3 Side lamp, LH	)	
4 Spare lead	)	
5 Side lamp, RH	)	
6 Connected to auxiliary lamp lead in LHD harness	)	
7 Tail lamp, RH	)	
8 Number plate illumination	)	
9 Tail lamp, LH	)	Up to chassis
10 Connected to headlamp flasher switch (No.32 in LHD circuit diagram)	)	serial numbers 41804512B and
11 Foot dipper switch	)	40800166E
12 Lucar connection	)	
13 Switch, auxiliary driving lamp, when fitted	)	
14 Headlamp switch	)	
15 Connected to pick-up point 'C' in LHD circuit diagram	)	
16 Connected to fuse for panel rheostat switch (No.26 in LHD circuit diagram)	)	
17 Side lamp switch	)	
18 Connected to side light switch in LHD circuit diagram	)	

19 Side lamp, LH	)	
20 Tail lamp, LH	)	
21 Side lamp, RH	)	
22 Tail lamp, RH	)	
23 Number plate illumination	)	
24 Number plate illumination	)	
25 Cable identification tag, green	)	From chassis serial
26 Cable identification tag, yellow	)	numbers 41804513B and
27 Fuse, 5 and 6	)	4800167E onwards
28 To panel light switch	)	
29 In-line Lucar connection	)	
30 Side lamp switch	)	
31 Headlamp switch	)	
32 To starter motor solenoid	)	
33 To headlamp dip switch	)	

Fault Finding Chart - Electrical System

Symptom	Reason/s	Remedy
Starter motor fails to turn engine No electricity at starter motor	Battery discharged. Battery defective internally Battery terminal leads loose or earth lead not securely attached to body. Loose or broken connections in starter motor circuit. Starter motor switch or solenoid faulty.	Charge battery. Fit new battery. Check and tighten leads. Check all connections and tighten any that are loose. Test and replace faulty components with new.
Electricity at starter motor: faulty motor	Starter motor pinion jammed in mesh with flywheel gear ring. Starter brushes badly worn, sticking, or brush wires loose. Commutator dirty, worn, or burnt. Starter motor armature faulty. Field coils earthed.	Disengage pinion by turning squared end of armature shaft. Examine brushes, replace as necessary, tighten down brush wires. Clean commutator, recut if badly burnt. Overhaul starter motor, fit new armature. Overhaul starter motor.
Starter motor turns engine very slowly Electrical defects	Battery in discharged condition. Starter brushes badly worn, sticking, or brush wires loose. Loose wires in starter motor circuit.	Charge battery. Examine brushes, replace as necessary, tighten down brush wires. Check wiring and tighten as necessary.
Starter motor operates without turning engine Dirt or oil on drive gear	Starter motor pinion sticking on the screwed sleeve.	Remove starter motor, clean starter motor drive.
Mechanical damage	Pinion or flywheel gear teeth broken or worn.	Fit new gear ring to flywheel, and new pinion to starter motor drive.
Starter motor noisy or excessively rough engagement Lack of attention or mechanical damage	Pinion or flywheel gear teeth broken or worn. Starter drive main spring broken. Starter motor retaining bolts loose.	Fit new gear teeth to flywheel, or new pinion to starter motor drive. Dismantle and fit new main spring. Tighten starter motor securing bolts. Fit new spring washer if necessary.
Battery will not hold charge Wear or damage	Battery defective internally. Electrolyte level too low or electrolyte too weak due to leakage. Plate separators no longer fully effective. Battery plates severely sulphated.	Remove and fit new battery. Top up electrolyte level to just above plates. Remove and fit new battery. Remove and fit new battery.
Insufficient current flow to keep battery charged	Fan/dynamo belt slipping. Battery terminal connections loose or corroded. Dynamo not charging properly. Short in lighting circuit causing continual battery drain. Regulator unit not working correctly.	Check belt for wear, replace if necessary, and tighten. Check terminals for tightness, and remove all corrosion. Remove and overhaul dynamo. Trace and rectify. Check setting, clean, and replace if defective.
Ignition light fails to go out, battery runs flat Dynamo not charging	Fan belt loose and slipping, or broken. Brushes worn, sticking, broken or dirty. Brush springs weak or broken. Coomutator dirty, greasy, worn, or burnt. Armature badly worn or armature shaft bent.	Check, replace, and tighten as necessary. Examine, clean, or replace brushes as necessary. Examine and test. Replace as necessary. Clean commutator and undercut segment separators. Fit new or recondition armature.

Fault Finding Chart - Electrical System

Symptom	Reason/s	Remedy
Ignition light fails to go out, battery runs flat in a few days Dynamo not charging	Commutator bars shorting. Dynamo bearings badly worn. Dynamo field coils burnt, open, or shorted. Commutator no longer circular. Pole pieces very loose.	Undercut segment separations. Overhaul dynamo, fit new bearings. Remove and fit rebuild dynamo. Recut commutator and undercut segment separators. Strip and overhaul dynamo. Tighten pole pieces.
Regulator or cut-out fails to work correctly	Regulator incorrectly set. Cut-out incorrectly set. Open circuit in wiring of cut-out and regulator unit.	Adjust regulator correctly. Adjust cut-out correctly. Remove, examine, and renew as necessary.
Alternator not charging	Internal fault in alternator of control circuit.	Seek specialists advice.

Failure of individual electrical equipment to function correctly is dealt with alphabetically, item by item, under the headings listed below.

Symptom	Reason/s	Remedy
Fuel gauge gives no reading	Fuel tank empty! Cable between tank unit and gauge broken or disconnected Fuel gauge case not earthed. Fuel gauge supply cable interrupted. Fuel gauge unit broken.	Fill fuel tank. Check cable and repair as necessary Ensure case is well earthed. Check and replace cable if necessary. Replace fuel gauge.
Fuel gauge registers full all the time	Cable between tank unit and gauge earthed.	Check cable for earthing and repair as necessary.
Horn operates all the time	Horn push either earthed or stuck down. Horn cable to horn push earthed.	Disconnect battery earth. Check and rectify source of trouble. Disconnect battery earth. Check and rectify source of trouble.
Horn fails to operate	Blown fuse. Cable or cable connection loose, broken or disconnected. Horn has an internal fault.	Check and renew if broken. Ascertain cause. Check all connections for tightness and cables for breaks. Remove and overhaul horn.
Horn emits intermittent or unsatisfactory noise	Cable connections loose. Horn incorrectly adjusted.	Check and tighten all connections. Adjust horn until best note obtained.
Lights do not come on	If engine not running, battery discharged. Light bulb filament burnt out or bulbs broken. Wire connections loose, disconnected or broken. Light switch shorting or otherwise faulty.	Push-start car, charge battery. Test bulbs in live bulb holder. Check all connections for tightness and wire cable for breaks. By-pass light switch to ascertain if fault is in switch and fit new switch as appropriate.
Lights come on but fade out	If engine not running battery discharged.	Push-start car, and charge battery.
Lights give very poor illumination	Lamp glasses dirty. Reflector tarnished or dirty. Lamps badly out of adjustment. Incorrect bulb with too low wattage fitted. Existing bulbs old and badly discoloured. Electrical wiring too thin not allowing full current to pass.	Clean glasses. Fit new reflectors. Adjust lamps correctly. Remove bulb and replace with correct grade. Renew bulb units. Re-wire lighting system.
Lights work erratically - flashing on and off especially over bumps	Battery terminals or earth connection loose. Lights not earthing properly.	Tighten battery terminals and earth connection. Examine and rectify.

Fault Finding Chart - Electrical System

Symptom	Reason/s	Remedy
	Contacts in light switch faulty.	By-pass light switch to ascertain if fault is in switch and fit new switch as appropriate.
Wiper motor fails to work	Blown fuse.	Check and replace fuse if necessary.
	Wire connections loose, disconnected, or broken.	Check wiper wiring. Tighten loose connections.
	Brushes badly worn.	Remove and fit new brushes.
	Armature worn or faulty.	If electricity at wiper motor, remove and overhaul and fit replacement armature.
	Field coils faulty.	Purchase reconditioned wiper motor.
Wiper motor works very slowl and takes excessive current	Commutator dirty, greasy, or burnt.	Clean commutator thoroughly.
	Drive to wheelboxes too bent or unlubricated.	Examine drive and straighten out severe curvature. Lubricate.
	Wheelbox spindle binding or damaged.	Remove, overhaul, or fit replacement.
	Armature bearings dry or unaligned.	Replace with new bearings correctly aligned.
	Armature badly worn or faulty.	Remove, overhaul, or fit replacement armature.
Wiper motor works slowly and takes little current	Brushes badly worn.	Remove and fit new brushes.
	Commutator dirty, greasy, or burnt.	Clean commutator thoroughly.
	Armature badly worn or faulty.	Remove and overhaul armature or fit replacement.
Wiper motor works but wiper blades remain static	Driving cable rack disengaged or faulty.	Examine and if faulty, replace.
	Wheelbox gear and spindle damaged or worn.	
	Wiper motor gearbox parts badly worn.	Overhaul or fit new gearbox.

Chapter 11 Suspension, dampers and steering

Contents

Specifications

Front Suspension

Type ... ... Independant front suspension

Road Spring Data

	2000 models prior to suffix 'B'	2000 models suffix 'B' onwards	2200 models
Number of working coils..	7	8	6 3/8
Free length...	16.5 inch	17.5 inch	16.3 in.
Rate	170 lb/in.	150 lb/in.	170 lb/in.

Hydraulic Dampers

Type	Telescopic, double acting
Bore	1 inch
Mounting	Rubber bushes

Front Hub

Front hub endfloat ... ... 0.003 to 0.005 in.

Rear Suspension

Type ... ... Independant rear suspension

Road Spring Data

	Early 2000 models	Late 2000 Models	2200 models
Free length...	13.250 in.	13.562 in.	13.312
Identification	Green stripe ½ in.wide	Red stripe ½ in.wide	Green or white stripe ½ in. wide

De Dion Tube

Type of oil	SAE 20W
Oil capacity	1/3rd Imperial pint

Rear Stabiliser Rod

Type ... ... Rubber insulated (adjustable)

Shock Absorbers

Type ... ... Hydraulic (non-adjustable)

Steering

Type	Hourglass worm and roller or Burman system (later models)
Camshaft endfloat..	Pre-load set by shimming
Front wheel alignment	1/16th inch toe-in plus or minus 1/16th inch

Ratio	20.3:1 lock to lock
Relay lever endfloat (mechanical type)	Zero endfloat but still free to rotate; set by screwing up the flanged tube
Rocker shaft endfloat	Zero. Correct by adjusting screw in cover
Steering column shaft ball race assembly lubrication	Keenol Grease KG15 before assembly into column housing
Steering unit - type	Adamant Marles hourglass cam and roller, follower type
Steering wheel diameter...	17 inch
Steering wheel turns, lock to lock	3¾ turns approximately
Tightening torque - relay nut, suffix 'A' models..	60 lb/ft.
Turning circle (between kerbs)...	31.5 ft. (between walls), 35ft. 7 in.

Steering Angles

Camber angle	$0^o \pm 1^o$
Castor angle (2000 models)	$\frac{1}{2}^o$ positive $\pm \frac{1}{2}^o$
Castor angle (2200 models)	$\frac{3}{4}^o$ positive $\pm \frac{1}{2}^o$
Swivel pin inclination	8°
Wheel alignment (2000 models)	1/16th inch toe-in ± 1/16th inch tolerance
Wheel alignment (2200 models)	1/8th inch toe-in ± 1/16th inch tolerance

NOTE: Check with car in static unladen position; that is, with water, oil and five gallons of fuel. Rock car up and down at the front to allow it to take up a static position.

Torque Wrench Settings

Front Suspension	lb.ft.	mkg.
Front calliper to front suspension member	60	8.5
Top ball swivel nut	55 to 85	7.5 to 11.5
Bottom ball swivel nut	60 to 75	8.5 to 10
Bottom link strut to bottom link ball joint	60 to 75	8.5 to 10
Bottom link to base unit	54	7.5
Bottom link strut to base unit	54	7.5
Bottom link to swivel pillar...	60 to 75	8.5 to 10
Top link securing bolts	30	4.0
Anti-roll bar cap bolts	30	4.0

Rear Suspension		
Bottom link bolts...	54	7.5
De Dion tube/elbows...	8	1.0
Top link bolts	54	7.5
Wheel hub bearing housing to De Dion tube/elbow..	20	2.7
Axle flange to disc..	85	11.5

Steering		
Steering drop arm securing nut torque	130 + 0–5	17.9

1. General Description

Upon inspection of the front suspension system as shown in Fig.11.1 it will be seen that it is of a rather unusual design whereby coil springs are mounted horizontally in the wheel arch and are assisted by double acting telescopic shock absorbers.

The long front wheel swivels carry the disc brake assemblies and at their lower ends are located by transverse wishbone type suspension arms which are rubber mounted to the underbody at their inner ends. The upper ends of the front wheel swivels are attached to bellcrank shaped leading upper suspension arms which pivot on very long transverse bearings on the bulkhead.

The coil springs are anchored in the bulkhead at their outer ends and located at the front end on the bellcrank pushrods of the upper suspension arms.

The shock absorbers are fitted between the centre of the upper arms and at their lower ends to the body. They are so mounted that their main working parts and oil recuperation chambers remain stationary. This positioning eliminates any possibility of aeration and frothing.

The bearing bosses of the upper suspension arms are joined across the car by means of a single hectagonal bar which serves to act as an anti-roll bar.

The rear suspension is of the semi-independent De Dion design with stabiliser rods and double acting shock absorbers. From Fig. 11.2 it will be seen that the De Dion tube is of a fixed length and locates the rear wheels laterally and that the drive shafts have specially designed sliding members.

The De Dion tube itself is located by a Watts linkage which has long trailing links fitted at the front and short leading links at the rear. The transverse location for the suspension is provided by the solid hub drive shafts on early produced models and the tubular shafts on later models, in conjunction with a Panhard stabiliser rod fitted laterally between the final drive and underside of the body.

Because of its design the rear suspension system gives the advantages of both the beam axle and also independent rear suspension systems. The unsprung weight is reduced and the alteration of road wheel angle and track variation minimised.

The steering box is of the Adamant hour glass worm and roller follower type having a ratio of 20.3 : 1.

A universal joint is placed between the steering box inner column and the steering column shaft on the end of which is a 17 inch diameter steering wheel. The steering box is located close to the bulkhead and positioned such that it cannot be easily damaged if the front of the car is subjected to a collision.

On early produced models the steering linkage incorporates a steering relay lever assembly, but on later models an Armstrong steering idler damper is used. Like the steering box, these are positioned so that they are well protected in the event of an accident.

The swivel pillars are anchored to the top link assemblies and the bottom link strut assembly by means of ball joints which do not require any maintenance attention.

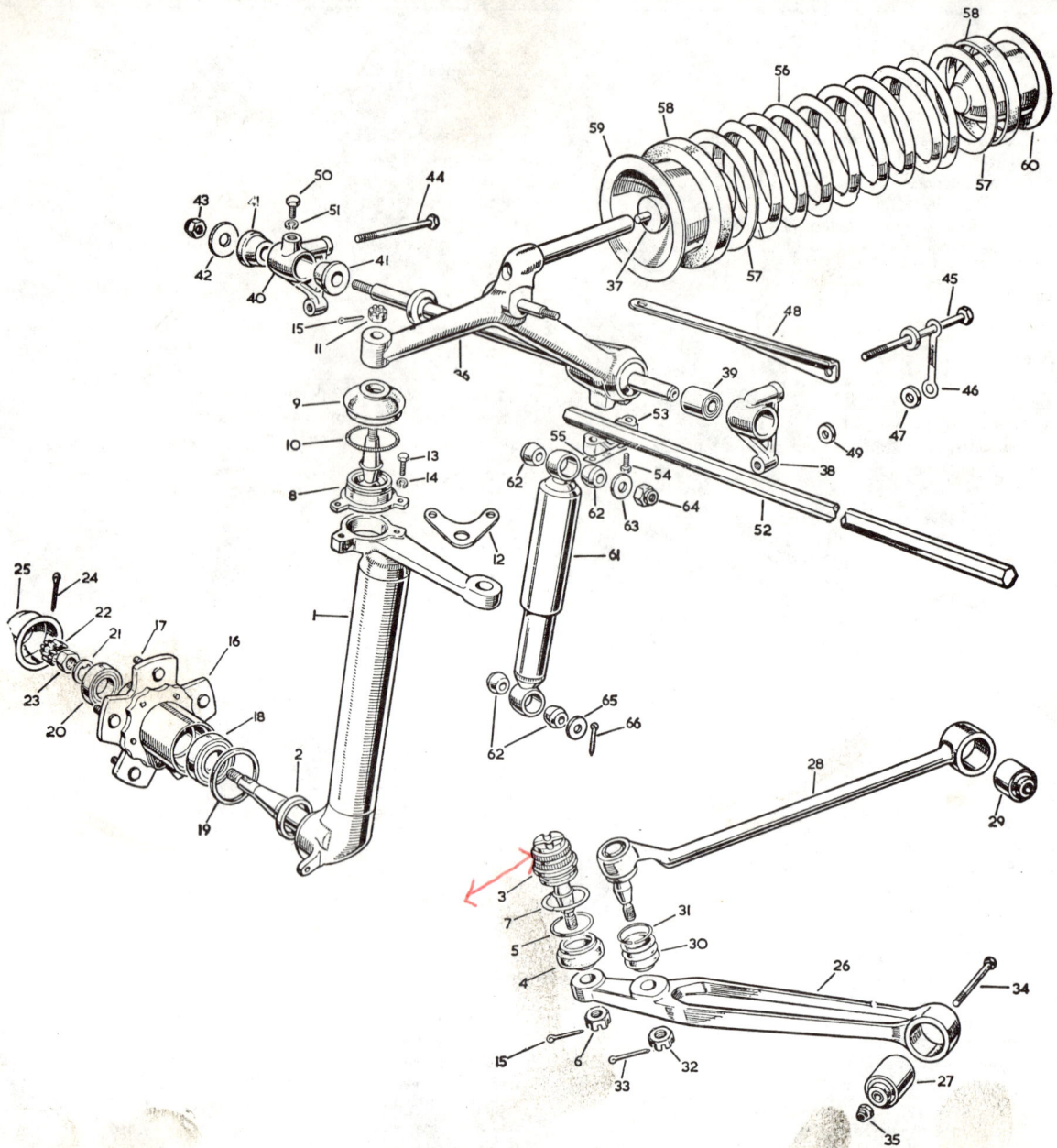

Fig.11.1. THE FRONT SUSPENSION SYSTEM

1 Swivel pillar assembly RH	16 Front hub assembly	33 Split pin fixing strut to link	49 Spacing washer
2 Distance piece for front hub bearing	17 Stud for road wheel	34 Bolt	50 Set bolt
3 Bottom ball joint complete	18 Bearing for hub, inner	35 Self-locking nut	51 Spring washer
4 Flexible boot for bottom ball joint	19 Oil seal for inner bearing	36 Top link assembly, RH	52 Anti-roll bar
5 Retaining ring for flexible boot	20 Bearing for hub, outer	37 Rubber-covered ball end for top link	53 Cap for anti-roll bar
6 Special slotted nut	21 Special washer fixing hub to stub axle	38 Top link mounting bracket, inner	54 Set bolt
7 Retaining ring for bottom ball joint	22 Locking cap	39 Bush for top link mounting bracket, inner	55 Locking plate
8 Top ball joint complete	23 Slotted nut	40 Top link mounting bracket, outer	56 Road spring, front
9 Flexible boot for top ball joint	24 Split pin	41 Bush for top link mounting bracket, outer	57 Shim for front road spring
10 Retaining ring for flexible boot	25 Hub cap	42 Special washer	58 Cushion for front road spring, front and rear
11 Special slotted nut	26 Bottom link assembly, RH	43 Self-locking nut	59 Support cap for front road spring
12 Mounting plate for front brake hose	27 Bush for bottom link	44 Set bolt	60 Bump rubber
13 Set bolt	28 Bottom link strut assembly, RH	45 Set bolt	61 Shock absorber, front
14 Spring washer	29 Bush for bottom link strut	46 Locking plate	62 Rubber bush for front shock absorber
15 Split pin for top & bottom ball joint nuts	30 Rubber boot for ball joint	47 Packing washer	63 Plain washer
	31 Retaining ring for boot	48 Stiffener, RH, at top link	64 Self-locking nut
	32 Special slotted nut fixing strut to link		65 Plain washer
			66 Split pin

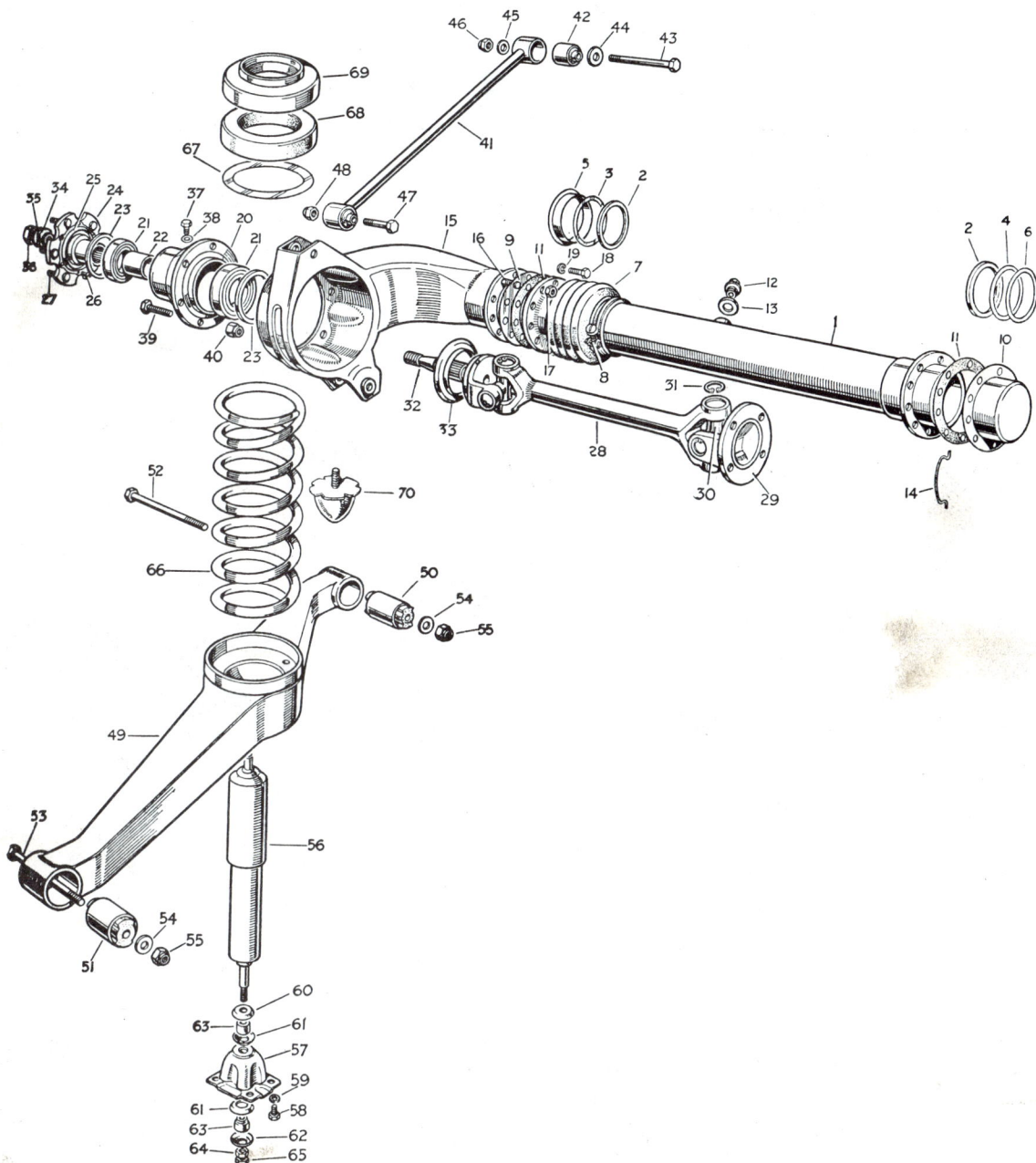

Fig.11.2. THE REAR SUSPENSION SYSTEM

1 De Dion tube assembly	19 Spring washer	35 Lockwasher	53 Bolt, front
2 Oil seal for De Dion tube	20 Bearing housing	36 Special nut	54 Plain washer
3 Packing washer	21 Bearing for rear hub	37 Plug for rear hub	55 Self-locking nut
4 Packing washer	22 Collapsible spacer	38 Joint washer for plug	56 Shock asborber, rear
5 Retainer	23 Oil seal for rear hub	39 Bolt	57 Lower mounting
6 Retainer ring	24 Driving flange assembly	40 Self-locking nut	58 Set bolt
7 Dust extractor	25 Dust excluder, outer	41 Top link assembly	59 Spring washer
8 Clip for dust excluder	26 Drive screw	42 Bush for top link	60 Retainer, large
9 Blanking plate, RH	27 Stud for road wheel	43 Bolt	61 Guide washer
10 Blanking plate, LH	28 Drive shaft assembly for	44 Plain washer, large	62 Retainer, small
11 Joint washer	rear hub up to final drive	45 Plain washer, small	63 Rubber cushion
12 Filler plug	number 40022259A	46 Self-locking nut	64 Nut
13 Joint washer for filler plug	29 Flange yoke for drive shaft	47 Bolt	65 Locknut
14 Spring clip for inner tube	30 Journal complete	48 Self-locking nut	66 Road spring, rear
15 De Dion elbow assembly	31 Circlip for journal	49 Bottom link assembly	67 Shim
16 Stud for De Dion elbow	32 Yoke shaft for rear hub	50 Bush for bottom link	68 Cushion for rear road spring
17 Nut	33 Dust excluder, inner	51 Bush for bottom link	69 Top support cup
18 Set bolt	34 Special washer	52 Bolt	70 Bump rubber

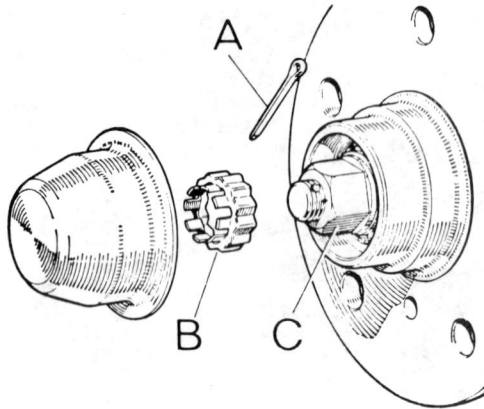

Fig.11.3. FRONT HUB FIXING

A Split pin   C Nut for front hub
B 'Bottle' top

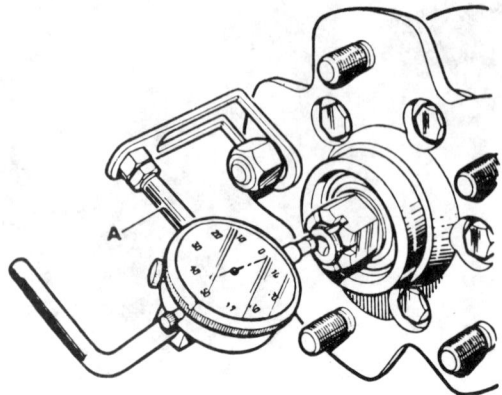

Fig.11.4. USING A DIAL INDICATOR GAUGE TO DETER-
MINE FRONT HUB END FLOAT
A Dial gauge and bracket

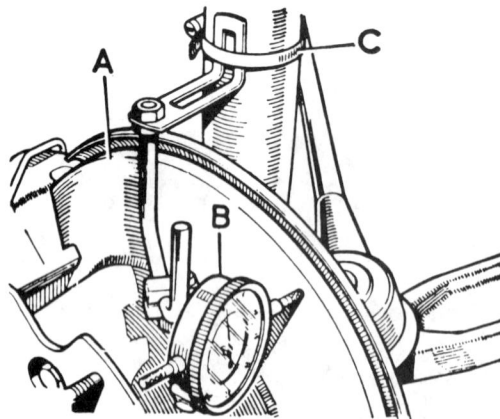

Fig.11.5. USING A DIAL INDICATOR GAUGE TO DETERMINE DISC RUN–OUT

A Disc
B Dial gauge and bracket
C Jubilee clip

2. Front Hub — Removal, Overhaul & Refitting

1. Before removing the front hub it will be necessary to remove the front brake callipers. Details of this operation will be found in Chapter 8, Section 8 (Dunlop braking system) or Section 9 (Girling braking system).

2. Remove the hub cap, split pin and slotted nut from the stub axle.

3. On later produced models, remove the locking cap and special nut as shown in Fig.11.3. This will be found on models produced having a suffix letter 'C' and onwards.

4. Remove the special washer and withdraw the hub assembly.

5. It may be found necessary on some of the early models to remove the brake disc shield as well.

6. To remove the hub bearing, place the hub on a bench vice jaws and with a soft metal drift carefully drive out the bearing. Also remove the oil seal.

7. Inspect the bearing for signs of wear by holding the inner track and rotating the outer track, checking for roughness of movement. Again hold the inner track and rock the outer track to check for sideways movement.

8. Look at the inner diameter of the inner track and the outer diameter of the outer track for signs of movement on its location. If the bearing is suspect always fit a new one.

9. If the oil seal has been disturbed it must always be renewed as most likely it will have been distorted upon removal.

10 To reassemble the front hub bearing, first carefully replace the bearing distance piece and oil seal using a tubular drift of a suitable diameter to contact the outer track.

11 If the brake disc shield was removed on early produced models remove all traces of sealing compound and then place a little Prestic 5686 sealing compound on the mating face of the shield to stub axle. Make sure that the oil seal, distance piece and bearing are correctly in position.

12 Carefully pack the hub with Castrol LM grease.

13 Replace the hub and adjust the nut so as to give a zero endfloat. Do not overtighten the nut. The best method of determining endfloat is to use a dial indicator gauge mounted as shown in Fig.11.4.

14 Reposition the dial indicator gauge as shown in Fig.11.5 and position the probe on the outer diameter of the disc. Slowly rotate the disc and check that the run-out does not exceed 0.003 inch. If the run-out exceeds this limit, the disc should be repositioned on the hub and the run-out rechecked. Should this still not produce a satisfactory result, a distorted disc should be suspected and a new disc obtained and fitted.

15 On early produced models, adjust the hub nut so that an endfloat of 0.003 to 0.005 inch is obtained by using one of three available thrust washer sizes.

16 On later produced models, place the locking cap onto the nut in such a position that the split pin can be inserted through the serrations without altering the position of the special hub nuts.

17 Lock the special hub nut with a new split pin and bend over the legs to secure it. Repack the hub cap with Castrol LM grease and gently tap the cap into position with a soft faced hammer.

18 It will now be necessary to refit the front calliper and details of this will be found in Chapter 8, Section 8 (Dunlop braking system) or Section 9 (Girling braking system).

3. Front Suspension Swivel Pillar & Bottom Ball Joint — Removal & Refitting

1. Refer to Section 2 of this Chapter and remove the front hub assembly.

2. Extract the split pin and slacken the slotted nut to be found at the bottom of the ball joint of the swivel pillar at the bottom link.

3. It will be necessary to use a special tool part No.601476 as shown in Fig.11.6, or alternatively a two legged puller and suitable metal thrust block to break the taper of the ball joint. Remove the nut

once the joint has been broken.

4. The swivel pillar may now be separated from the bottom link.

5. Extract the split pin from the slotted nut of the swivel pillar top ball joint at the top link. Also extract the split pin from the slotted nut of the steering side rod ball joint at the swivel pillar end. The two nuts should now be slackened but not yet removed.

6. Refer to paragraph 3 above and break the taper of both the ball joints. Remove the two nuts once both the joints have been broken.

7. The swivel pillar may now be completely removed.

8. Using a small screwdriver carefully remove the flexible rubber boot on the swivel pillar bottom ball joint. Take care not to jab the screwdriver through the rubber boot.

9. Extract the retaining ring from the bottom ball joint.

10 A special ball joint extracter, part number 600962 will now be required to remove the ball joint from the swivel pillar. An illustration of this is shown in Fig.11.7, and if the tool is not available, one can be made from a piece of tube, 'U' shaped angle iron and a piece of plain steel bar, suitably drilled and welded to the tube as shown.

11 If it is necessary to remove the top ball joint from the swivel pillar, full information will be found in Section 8 of this Chapter.

12 To refit the bottom ball joint using a suitable sized tubular drift, drive the ball joint into the swivel pillar housing.

13 Refit the bottom ball joint retaining ring.

14 Ease the flexible boot into position with the screwdriver, again taking care not to puncture the rubber boot. Obviously if the original one was damaged a new one must be fitted.

15 Refitting the swivel pillar is the reverse sequence to removal. The ball joint nuts must be tightened to a torque wrench setting of 55 to 85 lb/ft. (Top ball joint) and 60 to 75 lb/ft. (Bottom ball joint).

16 Refit the hub as detailed in Section 2 of this Chapter.

4. Front Shock Absorbers — Removal & Refitting

1. Remove the wheel trim and slacken the wheel nuts. Chock the rear wheels, apply the handbrake, jack up the front of the car and support the body on axle stands as shown in Fig.11.8. Remove the road wheels.

2. Place a jack under the suspension making sure that it will not slip off and carefully raise it so as to take the weight off the shock absorber.

3. Extract the split pin from the bottom mounting with a suitable parallel pin punch.

4. Lift away the plain washer and prise out the outer rubber bush with a wide bladed screwdriver.

5. Undo and remove the nut from the top shock absorber fixing and lift away the washer and outer rubber bush.

6. The shock absorber may now be lifted away from the underside of the wing.

7. Remove the inner bushes and inspect the bushes for signs of oil contamination or perishing. Obtain new bushes if the original ones are suspect.

8. Refitting the shock absorber is the reverse sequence to removal. If the bushes are a little tight and difficult to insert into the shock absorber they may be lubricated with a little rubber grease.

5. Front Road Spring & Top Link Assembly — Removal, Overhaul & Refitting

1. Before commencing work it will be necessary to obtain three special spring retaining rods. These have a part number of 600304 and are shown in Fig.11.9. These can be made up of high tensile steel rod but difficulty may be experienced in forming the ends if forging facilities are not available. Do not try to compromise as serious damage or injury can result in the spring running wild.

2. Some owners have found it beneficial to remove the front wing. This is an easy operation and full details will be found in Chapter 12.

3. With the assistance of three heavy persons press down on the front of the car so as to compress the spring as much as possible so

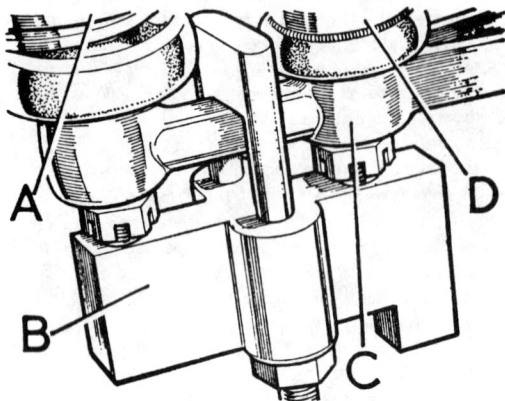

Fig.11.6. BALL JOINT SEPARATOR IN POSITION FOR
BOTTOM BALL JOINT

A Swivel column   C Bottom link
B Ball joint separator 601476   D Bottom link strut

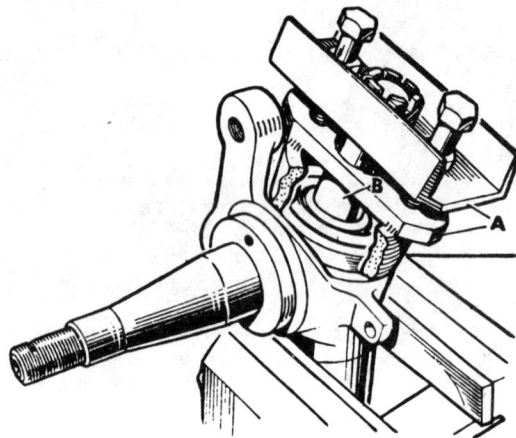

Fig.11.7. REMOVAL OF BOTTOM BALL JOINT
A Extractor part number 600962   B Ball joint

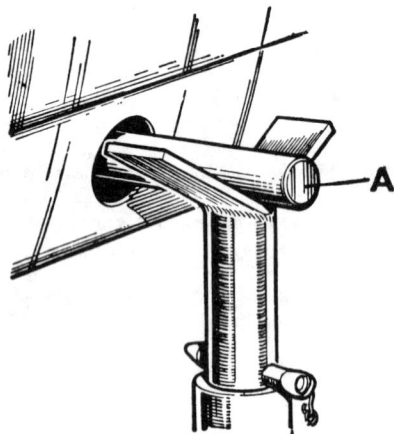

Fig.11.8. CORRECT LOCATION OF AXLE STANDS AT
BODY JACKING POINTS
A 7/8 inch diameter rod

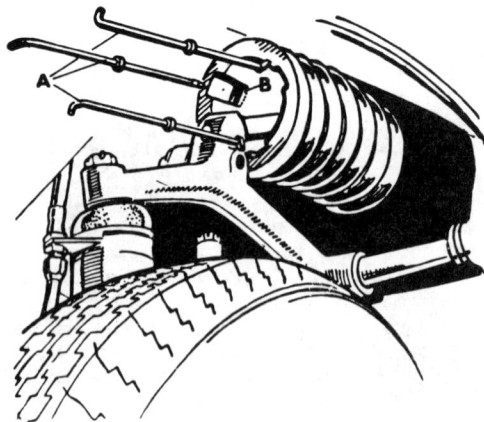

Fig.11.9. THE FITTING OF SPRING RETAINERS INTO THE
FRONT COIL SPRING
A Spring retainers   B Slots in spring end cap

that the three spring retaining rods can be inserted. This operation is shown in Fig.11.9. The rods should be inserted through the road spring front support cup and into the slots in the bump rubber rear support.

4. IMPORTANT' The retainers must be turned through exactly 90° so as to prevent the spring from expanding. Rotate the spring through one complete turn so as to ensure that the retainer rods have seated correctly.

5. Remove the wheel trim and slacken the wheel nuts. Chock the rear wheels, apply the handbrake, jack up the front of the car and support on axle stands as shown in Fig.11.8. Remove the road wheel.

6. Undo and remove the upper shock absorber securing nut. Lift away the washer and outer rubber bush.

7. The top swivel pillar ball joint should next be removed from the top link. To do this extract the split pin and slacken the slotted nut that secures the top ball joint to the top link.

8. Remove the three bolts that secure the brake hose mounting plate and top ball joint to swivel pillar.

9. Using a suitable lever on the bottom link, hold the bottom link downwards and then, using a drift carefully tap the top ball joint from the swivel column.

10 It will now be necessary to use a special tool, part number 601476 or alternatively a two legged puller and suitable metal thrust block as shown in Fig.11.10 to break the taper of the ball joint. Remove the nut and ball joint.

11 Remove the bolts and lock plates that secure the anti-roll bar cap to the top link and lift away the cap.

12 Remove the locker lid and cut and bend the bulkhead insulation panel as illustrated in Fig.11.11 working from inside the right-hand side of the car. NOTE: If the left-hand suspension assembly is being worked upon, the insulation of the left-hand side will have to be cut.

13 Release the lock plate tabs and remove the two bolts that secure the top link inner mounting bracket. This is readily accessible when the door is fully opened.

14 Release the lock plate tabs and remove the two bolts that secure the top link outer mounting bracket. Like the inner mounting bracket, this is readily accessible when the door is fully opened.

15 Remove the top link assembly stiffener, spacing washers and coil spring.

16 To check and overhaul the spring, compress the spring, making sure it is firmly supported and will not fly out of a press, and remove the three spring retainer rods. Release the pressure on the spring.

17 The spring coils should be checked for signs of excessive rusting, fractures or splitting, and, if evident a new pair of springs must be fitted. If only one spring is fitted the car may be slightly higher on one side than the other.

18 Inspect the rubber cushions and bump rubber for signs of oil contamination or deterioration and obtain new parts as necessary.

19 Compare the length of the spring with the spring data in the specifications at the beginning of this chapter. If it has settled unduly, new springs must be fitted.

20 Reassemble the shims, rubber cushions, bump rubber and support cap to the spring. Turn the support cap until the slots in the cap and bump rubber are in line ready to accept the retainer rods.

21 Compress the spring and insert the three retainer rods and turn through just 90°. Release the spring from the press once you are satisfied that the three retainer rods are correctly located. This is shown in Fig.11.12.

22 To overhaul the top link assembly, undo and remove the self locking nut and plain washer that secures the top link to the outer mounting bracket. Then undo and remove the bolt that secures the stiffener to the bracket.

23 Withdraw the mounting bracket together with the two rubber bushes and press of the inner mounting bracket and bush.

24 Inspect all parts for wear and fit new parts as necessary.

25 When pressing the inner mounting bracket complete with bush back onto the top link, make sure that the bracket mounting face is correctly aligned at 90° to the anti-roll bar cap mounting face as shown in Fig.11.13.

26 Refit the outer mounting bracket together with the rubber bushes making sure that the mounting face lines up with the corresponding face on the inner mounting bracket.

27 Refit the plain washer and self locking nut.

28 To refit the spring and top link assembly is the reverse sequence to removal. The following additional points should however be noted.

29 Before the retainer rods are removed, make sure that the road spring is correctly seating against the bulkhead location.

30 Before refitting the top link brackets to the body, slightly bend the tabs of new lock plates so that they can be easily bent to their locked positions when required.

31 The anti-roll bar cap should be refitted once the spring retainer rods have been removed.

32 Tighten the top link and anti-roll bar fixing bolts to a torque wrench setting of 30 lb/ft.

33 Always fit a new split pin to the top of the swivel pillar ball joint slotted nut.

6. Front Suspension Bottom Link Strut — Removal & Refitting

1. Remove the wheel trim and slacken the wheel nuts. Chock the rear wheels, apply the handbrake, jack up the front of the car and support the body on axle stands as shown in Fig.11.8. Remove the road wheel.

2. Extract the split pin and remove the slotted nut that secures the bottom link strut to the bottom link.

3. Undo and remove the nut and bolt that secures the bottom link strut to the body. Lift away the strut.

4. Inspect the ball joint for wear and if worn it will be necessary to renew the complete strut.

5. Check the bush for signs of ovality or wear. This may be drifted out and a new one fitted using a drift of suitable size.

6. Refitting the bottom link strut is the reverse sequence to removal. Always fit new split pins and bend open the legs.

7. It is important that the bolts securing the strut to the body and the bottom link are tightened once the road wheel has been refitted and the car is on the ground in the normal unladen condition.

8. The bottom link strut to bottom link (ball joint) should be tightened to a torque wrench setting of 60 to 75 lb/ft. and the bottom link strut to body 54 lb/ft.

7. Front Suspension Bottom Link — Removal & Refitting

1. Remove the wheel trim and slacken the wheel nuts, chock the rear wheels, jack up the front of the car and place on axle stands located as shown in Fig.11.8. Remove the road wheel.

2. Extract the split pins and then slacken the two slotted nuts that secure the bottom link to the swivel pillar and strut to the bottom link.

3. It will now be necessary to use a special tool, part number 601476 as shown in Fig.11.14, or alternatively a two legged puller and suitable metal thrust block to break the taper of the ball joints Remove the nut once the joint has been broken.

4. Undo and remove the self locking nut and bolt that secures the bottom link to the body. The link may now be lifted away.

5. Inspect the bottom link bush for wear and renew if necessary by drifting out the old one and fitting a new bush.

6. Refitting the bottom link is the reverse sequence to removal. It is however necessary to tighten up the bolt that fixes the bottom link to the body once the car has been lowered to the ground and is in its normal static unladen condition. This bolt should be tightened to a torque wrench setting of 54 lb/ft.

8. Front Suspension Top Ball Joint — Removal & Refitting

1. Remove the wheel trim and slacken the wheel nut. Chock the rear wheels, apply the handbrake, jack up the front of the car and

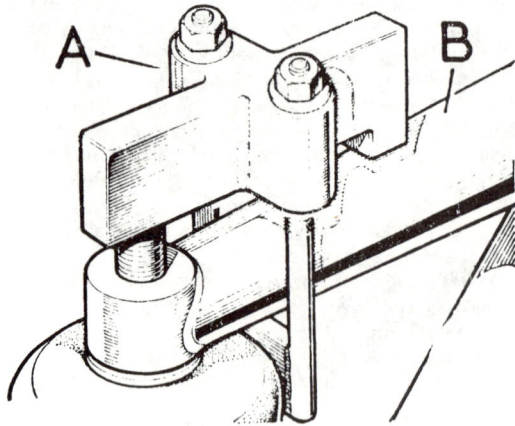

Fig.11.10. BALL JOINT SEPARATOR IN POSITION FOR TOP
BALL JOINT

A   Separator part number 601476   B   Top link

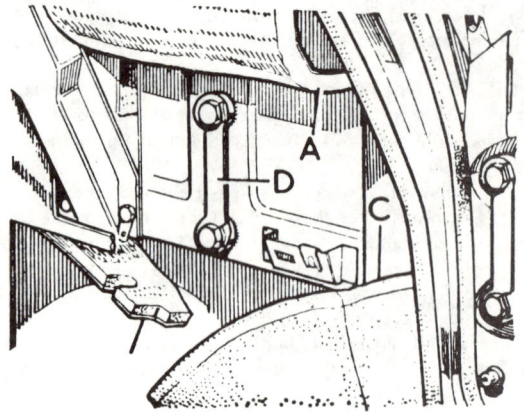

Fig.11.11. TOP LINK SECURING BOLTS

A   Cut in insulation   D   Bracket securing bolts and
B   Cut in insulation   lock plates
C   Cut in insulation

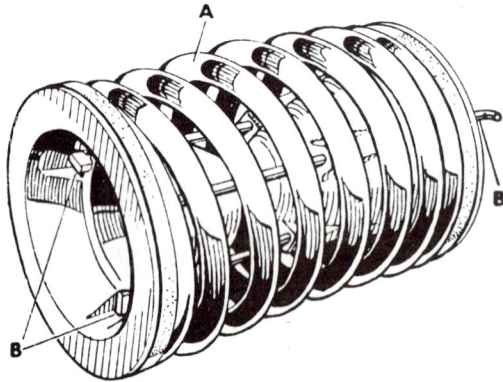

Fig.11.12. ROAD SPRING WITH RETAINERS CORRECTLY
POSITIONED

A   Spring held in compressed   B   These rods are to be turned
    state   through 90° only once inserted
                                             through the bump rubber plate

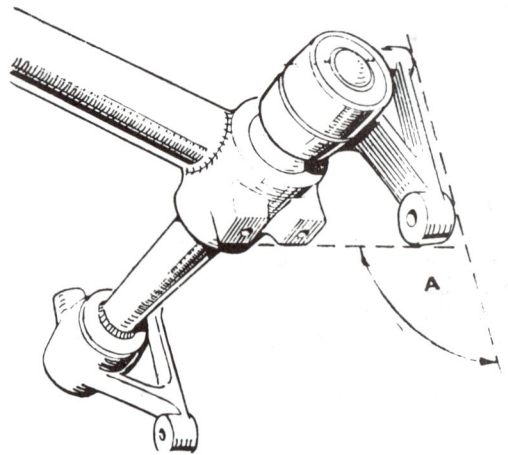

Fig.11.13. THE CORRECT SETTING ANGLE OF THE TOP
LINK OUTER MOUNTING BRACKET
A 90°

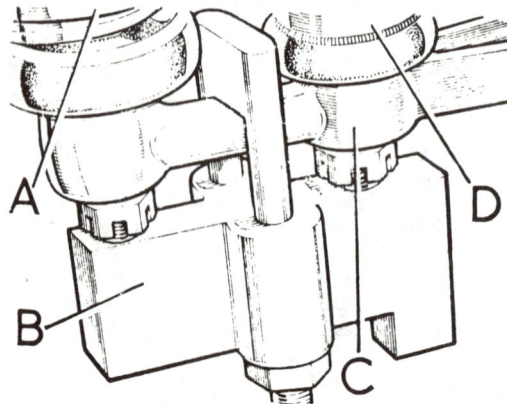

Fig.11.14. USE OF SPECIAL BALL JOINT SEPARATOR TO REMOVAL BOTTOM LINK STRUT BALL JOINT

A   Swivel column   B   Separator part No.601476   C   Bottom link   D   Bottom link strut

support the body on axle stands as shown in Fig.11.8. Remove the road wheel.

2. Extract the split pin and slacken the slotted nut that secures the top ball joint to the top link.

3. Undo and remove the three bolts that secure the brake hose mounting plate and top ball joint to the swivel pillar.

4. With a suitable lever on the bottom link, hold the bottom link downwards and with a drift of suitable size drive the top ball joint from the swivel column.

5. It will be necessary to use a special tool, part number 601476 as shown in Fig.11.15, or alternatively a two legged puller and suitable metal thrust block to break the taper of the ball joint. Remove the nut once the joint has been broken and then lift away the ball joint.

6. To refit the top ball joint, first make sure that the bolt holes are correctly lined up and then fit the top ball joint mounting for the top brake hose and the three set bolts onto the swivel pillar.

7. Whilst the bolts are being tightened lightly tap the ball joint.

8. Inspect the flexible rubber boot for signs of perishing or damage and obtain a new one if suspect. Fit the rubber boot easing it into position with a small screwdriver.

9. Refitting is the reverse sequence to removal. The top ball joint slotted nut must be tightened to a torque wrench setting of 55 to 85 lb/ft. Fit a new split pin to the slotted nut and open the legs so as to secure it in position.

9. Anti-Roll Bar — Removal & Refitting

1. Remove both front wheel trims and slacken the wheel nuts. Chock the rear wheels, apply the handbrake, jack up the front of the car and support the body on axle stands as shown in Fig.11.8. Remove the road wheels.

2. Undo and remove the four bolts and lock plates that secure the anti-roll bar caps to the top links. Lift away the anti-roll bar caps.

3. The anti-roll bar may now be lifted away from the underside of the car.

4. To refit the anti-roll bar, first make sure that the contact surfaces of the anti-roll bar and also those of the locating housing and cap, are clean.

5. Refit the caps and secure in position with the lock plate and bolts.

6. Tighten the bolts to a torque wrench setting of 30 lb/ft. and lock by bending up the locking tabs.

10. Rear Coil Spring — Removal & Refitting

1. Remove the wheel trim and slacken the road wheel nuts.

2. Chock the front wheels and jack up the rear of the car until the rear wheels are approximately 12 inches from the ground. Support the rear of the body on axle stands at the rear jacking points as shown in Fig.11.8.

3. Remove the wheel nuts and lift away the road wheel.

4. Position a jack under the bottom link as shown in Fig.11.16. For this it is preferable that a garage hydraulic jack be used.

5. Raise the bottom link just sufficiently to allow the lower end of the shock absorber fixing to be released by undoing and removing the nuts and rubber cushions.

6. Remove the nut and bolt that secures the bottom link to the De Dion tube.

7. Gradually lower the jack, so lowering the bottom link, and lift away the coil spring and its support plate.

8. Inspect the spring coils for signs of excessive rusting, fractures or splitting and, if evident, a new pair of springs must be fitted. If only one spring is fitted the car may be slightly higher on one side than the other.

9. Compare the length of the spring with the spring data in the specifications at the beginning of this Chapter. If it has settled unduly, new springs must be fitted.

10 Refitting the rear spring is the reverse sequence to removal with the exception that the bottom link must not be tightened until the car is on the ground and in the normal unladen condition. The bolt should then be tightened to a torque wrench setting of 54 lb/ft.

11 Make quite sure that the spring is correctly seating at its top and bottom positions so that there is no possibility of it moving.

11. Rear Shock Absorber — Removal & Refitting

1. Lift out rear seat cushion. Undo and remove the two self tapping screws that secure the bottom of the rear seat squab to the body, and lift away the squab from inside the car.

2. Undo and remove the two nuts that secure the retainer for the rubber cushion, the rubber cushion and the top of the shock absorber to the body panel.

3. Chock the front wheels, remove the rear wheel trim and slacken the wheel nuts. Jack up the rear of the car and support on axle stands placed at the rear body jacking points as shown in Fig.11.8. Remove the wheel nuts and lift away the road wheel.

4. Undo and remove the four bolts and spring washers that secure the lower shock absorber mounting to the bottom link. The shock absorber may now be lifted away from the rear suspension.

5. If necessary remove the shock absorber lower mounting.

6. Inspect the shock absorber for leaks and, if evident, a new unit must be fitted.

7. To check the operation of the shock absorber, secure one end in a vice and then push and pull the free end throughout its complete operating stroke. It should be observed that greatest resistance is felt when the shock absorber is being pulled outwards. Should this condition not be felt a new shock absorber must be fitted as non-adjustable.

8. To refit the shock absorber first assemble it to the lower mounting.

9. Carefully jack up the bottom link and guide the shock absorber into its location in the body panel mounting. Secure the lower mounting to the bottom link.

10 Refit the rubber cushion and nuts to the top of the shock absorber and lock in position.

11 Refit the road wheel and replace the wheel nuts. Lower the car to the ground and tighten the wheel nuts securely.

12 Replace the squab and secure with the two self tapping screws. Refit the rear seat cushion.

12. Rear Suspension Top Link - Removal & Refitting

1. Remove the wheel trim and slacken the wheel nuts. Chock the rear wheels, apply the handbrake, jack up the front of the car and support the body on axle stands as shown in Fig.11.8. Remove the road wheel.

2. Position a jack under the rear end of the bottom link and raise a few inches so as to relieve the load on the top link.

3. Undo and remove the two nuts and bolts that secure the top link to the De Dion tube and the body. The link may be lifted away.

4. If the left-hand link is being removed, it will be necessary to lift away the spare wheel and rear luggage compartment trim so as to expose the link rear bolts.

5. If the bushes are worn they may be drifted out and new ones fitted using a suitable sized metal drift.

6. To refit the top link is the reverse sequence to removal. The securing bolts must however, be tightened to a torque wrench setting of 54 lb/ft. once the car has been lowered to the ground and is in the normal static unladen condition.

13. Rear Suspension Lower Link — Removal & Refitting

1. Refer to Section 10 and remove the rear coil spring.

2. Undo and remove the nut, bolt and two plain washers from the front end of the lower link. Lift away the link.

3. If the bushes have worn they may be drifted out using a link of suitable size and then new ones fitted. It is important that they are

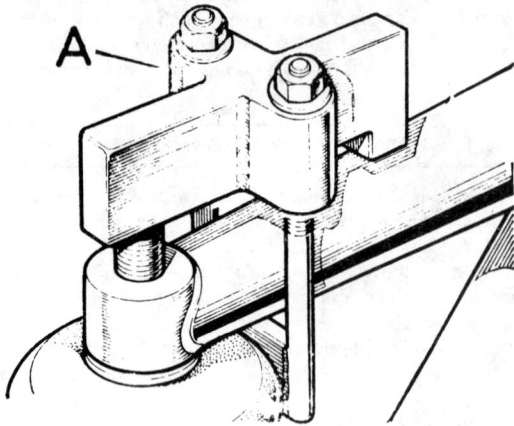

Fig.11.15. REMOVAL OF TOP BALL JOINT
A Separator, Part number 601476

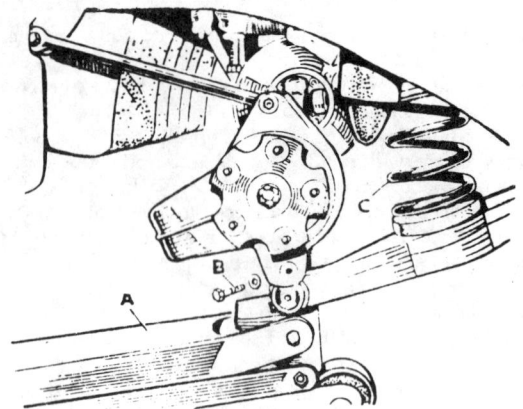

Fig.11.16. REMOVAL OF REAR SPRING
A Lifting jack   bolt
B Bottom link securing   C Road spring

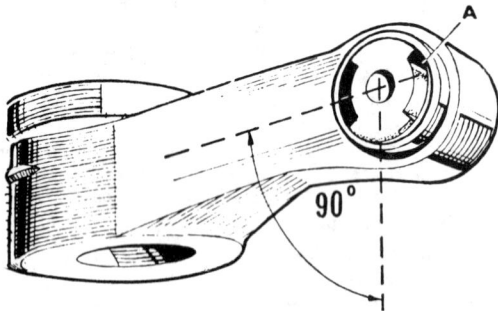

Fig.11.17. CORRECT FITTING POSITION FOR BOTTOM
LINK BUSHES
A Bush cut-outs

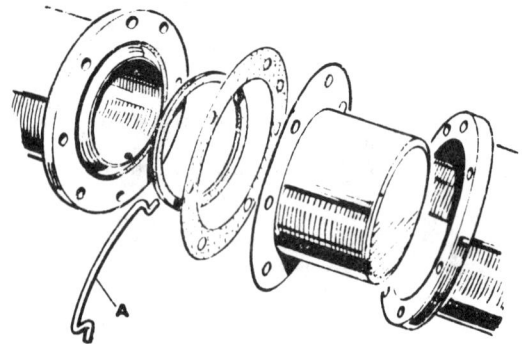

Fig.11.18. DE DION TUBE RETAINING CLIP
A Retaining clip

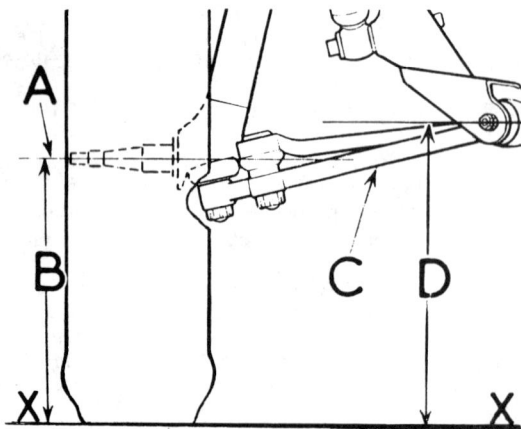

Fig.11.19. FRONT SUSPENSION HEIGHT CHECK DIMEN-
SIONS

A Centre line for road   C Bottom link
  wheel   D 13.7/8 in. $\pm$ ¼ inch
B 11.5/16 inch   xx Level floor surface

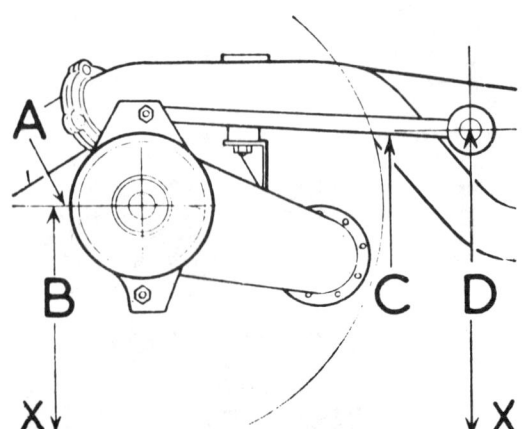

Fig.11.20. REAR SUSPENSION HEIGHT CHECK DIMENSIONS

A Centre line of road wheel	) For early suspension.
B 11.5/16 inch	) Rear springs denoted
C Top link, rear suspension	) by a green stripe.
D 16.5/8 inch $\pm$ ¼ inch	)
A Centre line of road wheel	) For late suspension.
B 11.5/16 inch	) Rear springs denoted
C Top link, rear suspension	) by a red stripe
D 17.1/8 inch $\pm$ ¼ inch	)

positioned as shown in Fig.11.17.

4. Refitting of the lower link is the reverse sequence to removal. The securing bolts must be tightened to a torque wrench setting of 54 lb/ft. once the car has been lowered to the ground and is in the normal static unladen condition.

14. De Dion Tube — Removal, Overhaul & Refitting

1. Remove the rear wheel trims and slacken the rear wheel nuts. Chock the front wheels and jack up the rear of the car and support on axle stands located under each of the bottom links below the coil springs. Remove the road wheels.

2. Undo and remove the eight bolts and lock plates that secure the hub drive shaft flange yokes to the differential drive shafts. Mark the respective flanges so that they are correctly refitted upon reassembly.

3. Undo and remove the twelve bolts and self locking nuts that retain the bearing housings for the rear hubs to the De Dion tube. Remove the hub and drive shaft as a complete assembly.

4. Undo and remove the bolts that secure the top links to the De Dion tube and disconnect the links from the elbow.

5. Slacken the bolts that secure the lower links to the De Dion tube and allow the De Dion tube to pivot downwards. When this position has been reached the bolt may then be completely removed.

6. Lift away the De Dion tube from the underside of the car.

7. Before overhauling the De Dion tube it should be noted that a modified type of De Dion tube was fitted to models with a final drive number incorporating the suffix letter 'D' and onwards. On TC models the final drive is identified by the prefix letter 'T'. The unit serial number of the final drive was also changed from the 400 series to the 401 series. Later type new parts can be used on cars prior to final drive suffix 'D' provided that they are fitted as a set and not individually.

8. Undo and remove the brass drain plug and allow the oil to drain out into a container having a capacity of approximately 1/3rd pint.

9. With a scriber or file mark the De Dion tube and elbow at the connecting flanges to ensure correct reassembly.

10 Undo and remove the four nuts and twelve set bolts with spring washers and detach the right-hand and left-hand De Dion tube elbows.

11 The blanking plates and packing washer (if fitted) may now be removed.

12 Extract the retaining clip (A), Fig.11.18 from the left-hand end of the inner tube.

13 Slacken the dust excluder clip and ease out the dust excluder and garter spring from its location. The inner tube assembly may now be removed from the outer tube assembly.

14 Lift away the dust excluder, garter spring and clip.

15 If further dismantling is necessary the left-hand seal, packing washer (when fitted) and retainer may next be removed by carefully prising it out of its housing.

16 The right-hand seal and retainer may be removed by carefully drifting out with a long soft metal drift.

17 All parts should be thoroughly washed and dried on a non-fluffy rag. Any part showing signs of wear or damage should be replaced bearing in mind the comments made in paragraph 7 of this Section.

18 To reassemble the De Dion tube first slide the gaiter, garter spring and clip onto the right-hand side of the outer tube.

19 Carefully fit a new seal and flexible packing washer (if originally fitted) into the retainer and smear with MS4 Silicone grease. Fit the seal and retainer to the right-hand end.

20 Fit the seal and retainer to the left-hand end of the outer tube in a similar manner.

21 Replace the respective cup using a suitable oil resisting jointing compound on the mating faces.

22 Refit the inner tube assembly into the outer tube assembly.

23 Refit the retaining clip to the left-hand end of the inner tube.

24 Replace the De Dion tube elbows, locating the four studs correctly and tightening the bolts to a torque wrench setting of 8 lb/ft. Make sure that when the right-hand elbow is being fitted, the dust excluder is located before the bolts are fitted. Tighten the dust excluder clip.

25 Refill the De Dion tube with 1/3rd pint of oil and refit the brass drain plug.

26 To refit the De Dion tube assembly is the reverse sequence to removal. It is however, important that the top and bottom link bolts are tightened to the required torque wrench setting once the car has been lowered to the ground and is in the normal static unladen condition.

27 The recommended torque wrench setting for the bottom link to De Dion tube, bottom link to body, top link to De Dion tube and top link to body is 54 lb/ft. The wheel bearing housing bolts should be tightened to a torque wrench setting of 20 lb/ft. and the drive shaft flange yoke to differential drive shaft 85 lb/ft.

15. Front Suspension Height Check

If the car is leaning to one side or the other, it is possible for the suspension height to be checked. Upon reference to Fig.11.19 it will be seen that various height dimensions are given and these are only applicable to a car in a normal unladen condition with five gallons of petrol in the tank.

The tyre pressures should next be checked and adjusted as necessary. Finally the tyre radius 'B' should be checked and with a normal tyre in good condition this will be approximately 11.15/16th inch. If the height differs an allowance must be made when measuring dimension 'D'.

If the result of the dimensional check differs from the measurement given in the caption, Fig.11.19, additional shims should be placed under the coil springs. It is important that the total thickness of the shims does not exceed 3/8 inch as otherwise the coil spring seating will be affected and the spring may become dislodged under adverse road conditions.

Any difficulty in obtaining the correct height after shiming to the maximum limit indicates that the coil spring has settled and a new pair of springs should be fitted.

16. Rear Suspension Height Check

If the car is leaning to one side or the other it is possible for the suspension height to be checked. Upon reference to Fig.11.20 it will be seen that various height dimensions are given and these are only applicable to a car in a normal unladen condition with five gallons of petrol in the tank.

The tyre pressures should next be checked and adjusted as necessary. Finally the tyre radius 'B' should be checked and with a normal tyre in good condition this will be approximately 11.15/16th inch. If the height differs an allowance must be made when measuring dimension 'D'.

If the result of the dimensional check differs from the measurement given in the caption Fig.11.20, additional shims should be placed under the coil springs. It is important that the total thickness of the shims does not exceed 3/8 inch as otherwise the coil spring seating will be affected and the spring may become dislodged under adverse road conditions.

Any difficulty in obtaining the correct height after shiming to the maximum limit indicates that the coil spring has settled and a new pair of springs should be fitted.

17. Steering Box — Removal, Overhaul & Refitting

1. On cars fitted with the link drive type windscreen wipers, release the wiper arms and blades from the spindles. Further information will be found in Chapter 10 — specifications and also Section 36.

2. Open the bonnet and support in the open position as far back as it will go.

3. For safety reasons disconnect the earth cable from the battery

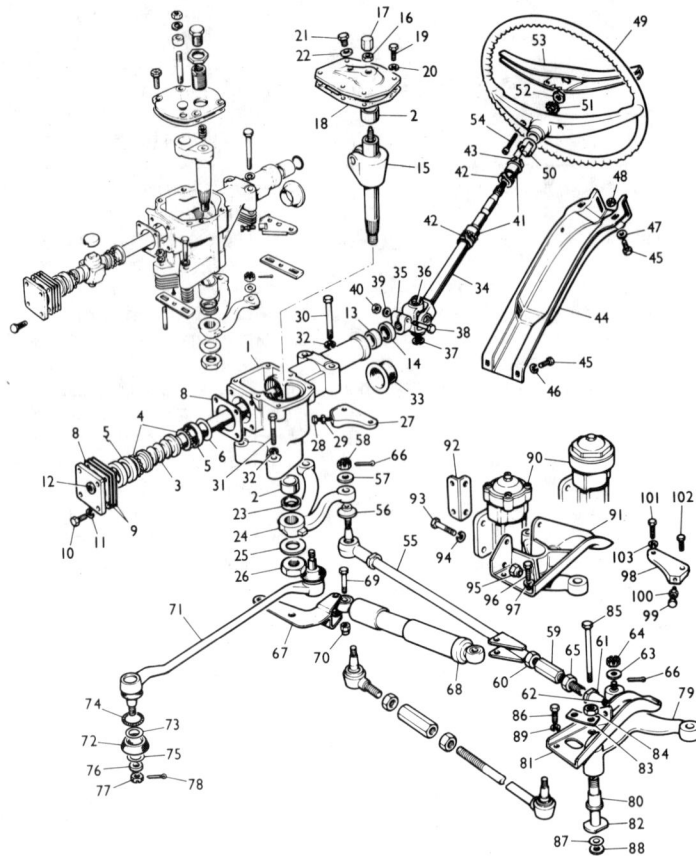

Fig.11.21. STEERING BOX & SYSTEM COMPONENT PARTS

1 Steering box
2 Bush for rocker shaft
3 Inner column and cam
4 Cage & balls for cam
5 Cup for cage & balls
6 Shim for bearing
7 Spacer washer for cam
8 Joint washer for front cover plate
9 Nylon shim for front cover plate
10 Set bolt
11 Spring washer
12 Special rubberised washer
13 Top bush for inner column
14 Oil seal for inner column
15 Rocker shaft complete
16 Special locknut for adjusting screw
17 Domed nut for adjusting screw
18 Joint washer for top cover plate
19 Set bolt
20 Spring washer
21 Oil filler plug
22 Joint washer for oil filler plug
23 Oil seal for rocker shaft
24 Drop arm
25 Tab washer
26 Special nut

27 Lock stop bracket, driver's side
28 Special bolt
29 Locknut
30 Set bolt
31 Set bolt
32 Spring washer
33 Grommet, steering box to base unit
34 Steering column shaft assembly
35 Splined yoke
36 Journal complete for steering column shaft
37 Circlip for journal
38 Pinch bolt
39 Plain washer
40 Nut
41 Bearing for steering column shaft
42 Spring washer
43 Circlip
44 Support bracket for steering column
45 Bolt
46 Spring washer
47 Plain washer
48 Nut
49 Steering wheel
50 Striker for flasher switch
51 Shakeproof washer
52 Special nut

53 Finisher for steering wheel
54 Special screw fixing finisher to wheel
55 Steering track rod assembly
56 Rubber boot for ball joint
57 Plain washer
58 Special slotted nut
59 Adjuster for track rod
60 Locknut for adjuster, RH thread
61 Ball joint assembly, LH thread
62 Rubber boot for ball joint
63 Plain washer
64 Special slotted nut
65 Locknut for ball joint, LH thread
66 Split pin for slotted nut
67 Damper mounting bracket
68 Steering damper
69 Bolt
70 Self-locking nut
71 Steering side rod assembly
72 Rubber boot
73 Boot ring
74 Garter spring
75 Boot retainer
76 Plain washer
77 Special slotted nut
78 Split pin for slotted nut
79 Steering relay lever assembly
80 Bush ro relay lever
81 Mounting plate

82 Flanged tube
83 Locking plate
84 Locknut
85 Set bolt
86 Set bolt
87 Shim
88 Plain washer
89 Spring washer
90 Steering idler damper complete
91 Mounting bracket for damper
92 Mounting angle for accelerator bracket
93 Bolt
94 Plain washer
95 Self-locking nut
96 Set bolt
97 Spring washer
98 Lock stop bracket, passenger's side
99 Special bolt
100 Locknut
101 Set bolt
102 Set bolt
103 Spring washer

Note: The standard worm and roller steering box as fitted to most models is shown as an exploded veiw. The Burman type steering box as fitted to later 2200 models is shown above it.

terminal.

4. Disconnect the screen washer hoses from the windscreen washer reservoir. Make a note of the electrical cable connections observing that the green cable is connected to the right-hand (−VE) terminal and disconnect the two cables. Remove the windscreen washer unit.

5. On early produced models the brake hydraulic fluid reservoir was adjacent to the steering box and it is necessary to reposition this. Note the two switch terminal connections on the cap and disconnect the two cables.

6. Undo and remove the nut, plain and spring washers that secure the reservoir mounting bracket to the wing valance and distance piece. Temporarily tie the reservoir onto the servo unit mounting bracket with a piece of string or wire.

7. On cars fitted with the link drive type windscreen wipers it is necessary to remove the complete wiper assembly. Full details of this operation will be found in Chapter 10, Section 42.

8. Jack up the front of the car just sufficiently to allow the road wheels to turn and support on axle stands located at the front jacking points.

9. Extract the split pins from the two ball joints located at the steering box drop arm and remove the two nuts and washers that secure the ball joint. Using a universal ball joint separator or tool number 601763 as shown in Fig.11,22, disconnect the ball joints so freeing the track rod and steering side rod.

10 With a sharp knife or side cutters, cut away the rubber boot for the track rod ball joint and fit a nut temporarily onto the threads to prevent damage. Grease the jaws of the ball joint separator and insert it between the heater unit and steering box. The jaws should face the ball joint.

11 Make quite sure that the extractor is located correctly over the ball joint before screwing down so as to extract the bolt. When free, remove the nut and separate the ball joint.

12 Again using a sharp knife or side cutters, cut away the rubber boot from the ball joint of the steering side rod assembly.

13 The steering side rod ball joint may now be removed using the ball joint separator suitably greased to prevent damage.

14 Remove the glove box lid strap located under the steering column which will then give better access to the steering column splined yoke and journal.

15 Slacken the bolt and nut that secure the splined yoke to the inner column.

16 NOTE:—

a) On left-hand drive SC models and automatics it is now necessary to remove the bracket for the accelerator shaft from its three locations on the steering box.

b) The electrical wiring harness should next be unclipped from its location at the base of the steering box and then moved to one side so that it does not interfere with the steering box when it is being removed.

17 NOTE:—

a) On left-hand drive TC models it is necessary to remove the carburetter air cleaner installation. Full details of this operation are given in Chapter 3, Section 2.

b) The electrical wiring harness should next be unclipped from its location at the base of the steering box and then moved to one side so that it does not interfere with the steering box when it is being removed.

c) Next unclip the choke control cable from the top water heater-pipe and with string or wire, tie back to one side so as to clear the steering box whilst it is being removed.

d) The accelerator shaft should be removed from its two locations on the steering box.

18 Undo and remove the four bolts and spring washers that secure the steering box to the body and withdraw the unit together with the steering lock stop. This is located under the back of the steering box.

19 If it is necessary to remove the drop arm, bend back the tab washer and undo the nut from the end of the rocker shaft. With a scriber mark the relative position of the drop arm at the rocker shaft

so that they may be correctly refitted and then withdraw the drop arm using a universal two legged puller.

20 Before overhauling the steering box, thoroughly wash the exterior in paraffin or 'Gunk' and wipe dry using a non-fluffy rag.

21 Undo and remove the steering box oil filler plug and allow the oil to drain out.

22 Undo and remove the special cap nut (E) Fig.11.23 and lock nut (D) from the rocker shaft adjusting screw (C).

23 Remove the six bolts and spring washers that secure the top cover of the steering box. On later produced models a stud replaces one of the bolts so that the link drive type windscreen wiper motor may be attached to it.

24 The top cover may now be lifted away at the same time screwing the adjuster in a clockwise direction with a screwdriver as shown in Fig.11.23. Lift away the gasket.

25 The rocker shaft assembly may now be lifted away from the interior of the steering box.

26 Remove the four bolts, spring washers and rubberised washer from the front cover. Note that the rubber washer is fitted to the top left-hand bolt.

27 Lift off the front cover together with the nylon shims and two paper gaskets. Note the assembly order of the shims and gaskets.

28 The steering box mounting bolt and spring washer may now be removed.

29 With a soft faced hammer lightly tap the rear end of the steering camshaft so as to extract the spacer washer, cup and caged balls.

30 The inner column and cam together with the caged balls may now be withdrawn from the steering box.

31 Remove the caged balls and cup together with any shims that may have been previously fitted. Keep the shims in a safe place as they will be required during reassembly.

32 Place the complete steering box in a container of very hot water and when it is really warm, the rear bearing cup should be drifted out using a soft metal drift.

33 The steering box and component parts may now be inspected. Check all moving parts for signs of wear, especially the bushes and rocker shaft. If the steering box previously showed signs of an oil leak, inspect the oil seals for signs of damage or wear and fix new as necessary. Should it be necessary to fit new rocker shaft bushes, this is best left to the local Rover agents as a special drift and reaming equipment will be required.

34 To reassemble the steering box, first make sure that all new parts have been obtained as necessary and then refit the shims that were previously removed or alternatively if a new inner column and cam box have been obtained, fit shims to a value of 0.015 inch.

35 Next refit the rear bearing cup and with a suitable sized soft metal drift make quite sure that it is fully seating.

36 The reason for the fitting of the shims in paragraph 34 is to centralise the cam in the steering box housings.

37 Position the caged balls over the rear end of the inner column.

38 Place the camshaft together with the caged ball race into the steering box and position the caged ball race into the outer ball cup.

39 Fit the front caged ball race onto the front of the inner column and cam, and with a soft metal drift lightly tap the cup into the steering box so as to locate over the caged ball race.

40 It is very important that when fitting the cup it is not allowed to tilt otherwise it will lock solid into the casing.

41 Place the spacer washer onto the end of the outer cup and fit the mounting bolt and spring washer for locating the steering box to the body into the front outer hole.

42 Fit the four bolts with spring washers into the front cover. Note that a new rubberised washer must be fitted to the top left-hand bolt.

43 Refit the shims, with the paper joint washers to the outside of the shim pack, onto the front cover assembly and replace the steering box front cover onto the steering box. Tighten the four bolts to a torque wrench setting of 15 lb/ft.

44 Refer to Fig.11.25 and mount a dial indicator gauge onto the steering box as shown, so that the endfloat may be determined. Push and then pull on the camshaft (A) and note the full needle movement.

45 Undo and remove the four bolts and washers securing the front

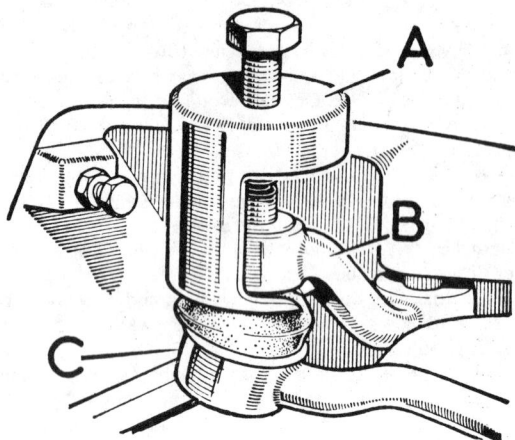

Fig.11.22. BALL JOINT SEPARATOR MOUNTED ONTO
STEERING DROP ARM

A Separator tool number   B Steering drop arm
   601763   C Ball joint

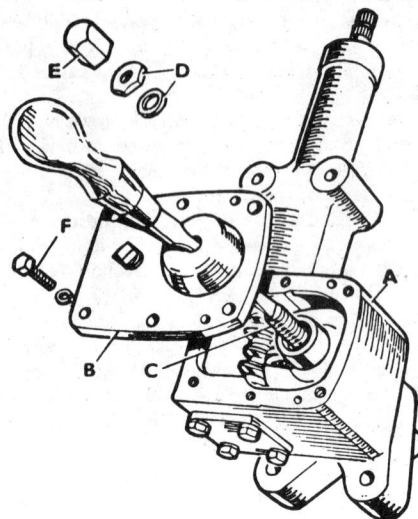

Fig.11.23. REMOVAL OF TOP COVER FROM STEERING BOX

A Steering box   D Washer and locknut for
B Steering box top cover   adjuster screw
C Adjuster screw for   E Domed nut
   rocker shaft   F Bolt for top cover

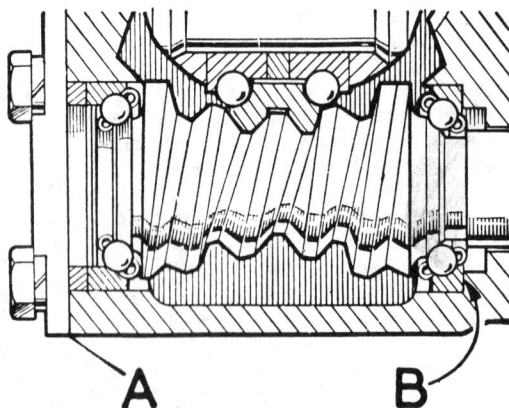

Fig.11.24. LOCATION OF SHIMS IN THE STEERING BOX

A Shims under front   B Shims under rear for cage
   cover   and balls cup

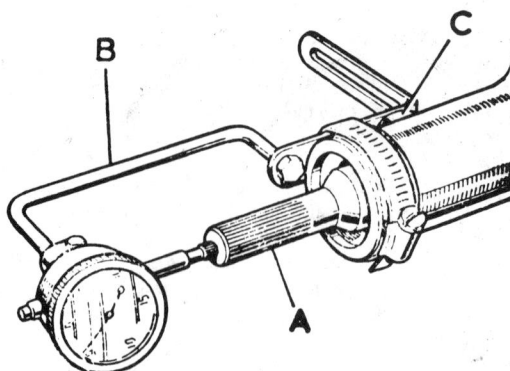

Fig.11.25. USE OF DIAL INDICATOR GAUGE TO CHECK
STEERING BOX END FLOAT

A Inner column & cam   C Packing for mounting
B Dial indicator gauge   bracket

cover and lift away the front cover and shim pack. Remove the number of shims equivalent in value to the endfloat as determined in paragraph 44, plus a further 0.005 inch so as to give a preload on the camshaft.

46 Refit the front cover and secure with the bolts, spring washers and one rubberised washer. Tighten the bolts to a torque wrench setting of 15 lb/ft.

47 Lubricate the rocker shaft assembly and slide it into position in the steering box and locate intermesh with the camshaft.

48 Fit a new joint washer for the top cover of the steering box. Locate the top cover over the rocker shaft adjustment screw and turn the adjustment screw in an anti-clockwise direction until the cover is just in position on the steering box.

49 Replace the six top cover securing bolts and spring washers, and tighten to a torque wrench setting of 15 lb/ft.

50 Replace the rocker shaft adjusting screw lock nut but do not tighten yet.

51 Refit the drop arm to the rocker shaft splines so that with the cam and rocker shaft set for the straight ahead position the track rod arm lies in line with the inner column and cam and points to the rear. If the original parts are being refitted line up the marks as previously made in paragraph 19 of this Section.

52 Fit a new lock washer and nut but do not yet bend up the lock washer tab.

53 It is now necessary to make up a test wheel as shown in Fig.11.26. The material is wood and ideally the diameter should be about 12 inches. Drill a hole exactly in the centre just smaller in diameter than the splines in the inner column and tap the wheel onto the splines.

54 With a piece of bent wire make up a pointer and mount it as shown in Fig.11.26.

55 Turn the wheel as far as it will go in one direction and then back in the other direction as far as it will go, counting the number of revolutions. This will give the number of turns from one steering lock to the other. Turn the wheel back by exactly half this amount so as to give the straight ahead position.

56 Adjust the rocker shaft until there is no play between the roller and the cam. Next check for zero backlash by trying to move the drop arm whilst the camshaft is being held rigidly in the hand. There should be no sign of any movement between the two parts.

57 Next rotate the test wheel away from the straight ahead position until signs of backlash are just evident. Mark the test wheel with a pencil in line with the straight ahead position. (Fig.11.26). Repeat this procedure with the wheel being turned in the opposite direction and again mark the test wheel when backlash just occurs. This will give an area of zero backlash.

58 Upon inspection this area should cover a range of between three-quarters and one and a half turns. If this is not evident adjust the rocker shaft again till this condition is met, without any signs of a tight spot.

59 Mark the test wheel at the point of equal distance between the two marks, indicating the total area of zero backlash. This point should be in the straight ahead position with an equal amount of travel each side of the straight ahead position before backlash occurs and should not be more than half a turn from the straight ahead position.

60 If it is necessary to equalise the zero backlash area each side of the straight ahead position, shims will have to be added or subtracted from behind the rear bearing cup and an identical value of plastic shims added or subtracted from the end cover so as to maintain the already established amount of preload.

61 To determine the position of zero backlash centre, rotate the test wheel to the right-hand side of the straight ahead position until backlash occurs and note the position of the mark indicating the centre of zero backlash area (Fig.11.27). If this is greater than half a turn from the straight ahead position ADD to the shims behind the rear bearing cup in increments of 0.005 inch until a condition of less than half a turn is obtained, an identical value of plastic shims being added to the end cover so as to maintain the correct pre-load.

62 Now rotate the test wheel to the left-hand side of the straight ahead position till backlash occurs and note the position of the mark indicating the centre of the zero backlash area (Fig.11.28). Should this be greater than half a turn from the straight ahead position REMOVE shims from behind the bearing cup until a condition of less than half a turn is obtained, an identical value of plastic shims being removed from the end cover to maintain the preload.

63 Once the correct backlash has been determined, smear a little Hylomar SQ32M sealing compound onto the end cover gaskets and secure the end cover with the four bolts, tightening them to a torque wrench setting of 15 lb/ft.

64 Hold the steering box firmly in a vice, remove the wooden test wheel and tighten the drop arm securing nut to a torque wrench setting of 130 lb/ft.

65 Lock the nut by bending over the tab washer onto the nut and also down onto the drop arm.

66 Refit the rocker shaft domed nut onto the adjuster screw.

67 Refill the steering box with the correct grade of oil and replace the filler/level plug.

68 The steering box is now ready for refitting to the car.

69 Refitting the steering box is the reverse sequence to removal, but the following additional points should be noted.

70 Always fit new rubber boots to the steering ball joints and new split pins to the slotted nuts. Bend over the legs to lock in place.

71 Make sure that the steering wheel spokes are positioned horizontally when the front wheels are in the straight ahead positions. It may be necessary to remove the steering wheel and reposition it on the splines to obtain this condition.

72 Refer to Section 26 and check the steering lock stop adjustment.

73 The front wheel alignment should be checked and further information on this will be found in Section 25 of this Chapter.

74 Finally check the oil level in the steering box and adjust as necessary.

18. Steering Column Shaft Assembly — Removal & Refitting

1. It will first be necessary to remove the right-hand glove box (right-hand drive cars) or the left-hand glove box (left-hand drive cars). To do this, open the glove box lid and detach one check strap end (right-hand box) or both strap ends (left-hand box) from the spring clips, these being shown in Fig.11.29.

2. Undo and remove the two bolts that secure the hinges. The glove box may now be withdrawn from its location.

3. Slacken the bolt and nut that secure the journal to the steering box inner column.

4. Unscrew the two Allen screws (used on earlier produced cars) or the two self locking screws that secure the steering wheel finisher to the steering wheel. Lift away the finisher.

5. Undo and remove the nut and spring washer that secure the steering wheel to the inner column and by using the palms of the hands on the rear of the steering wheel rim next to the horizontal spokes thump the wheel from the splines on the inner column.

6. Next disconnect the two pedal return springs from the anchor plates.

7. Undo and remove the two bolts, nuts, plain and spring washers that secure the support bracket to the bulkhead next to the panel.

8. Remove the two bolts that secure the support bracket as well as the clutch and brake return spring anchor plates to the bulkhead.

9. Make a note of the electrical cable connections at the steering column to the headlights and flashers so that they may be reconnected in the correct manner, and disconnect the cables.

10 The steering column shaft may now be lifted away, but take great care not to touch the headlining or trim which could be accidentally damaged.

11 Now spring off the plastic cover from the steering column nacelle, use a wide bladed screwdriver, hacksaw blade or knife so as not to break the plastic cover.

12 Extract the circlip and lift away the double spring washer from

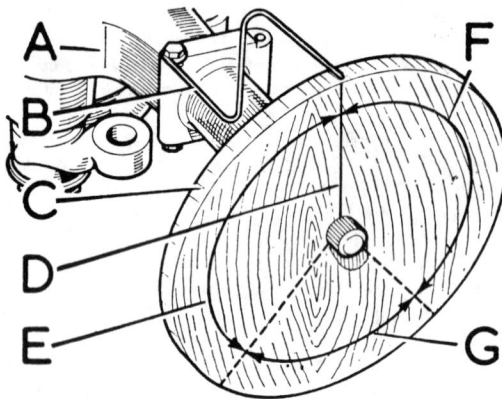

Fig.11.26. STEERING GEARBOX BACKLASH CHECK

A Steering box
B Pointer
C Test wheel, wood
D Centre of zero backlash area
E Area of zero backlash, LH
F Area of zero backlash, RH
G Backlash area

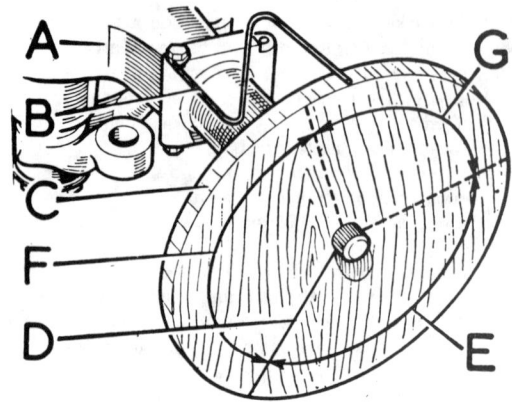

Fig.11.27. CENTRE OF BACKLASH AREA EXCEEDING
HALF A TURN RH LOCK—ADD SHIMS

A Steering box
B Pointer
C Test wheel
D Centre of zero backlash area
E Area of zero backlash
F Area of backlash
G Backlash area

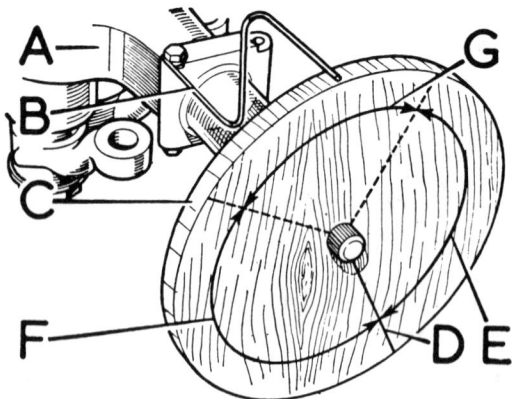

Fig.11.28. CENTRE OF BACKLASH AREA EXCEEDING
HALF A TURN, LH LOCK—REMOVE SHIMS

A Steering box
B Pointer
C Test wheel
D Centre of zero backlash area
E Area of zero backlash
F Area of backlash
G Backlash area

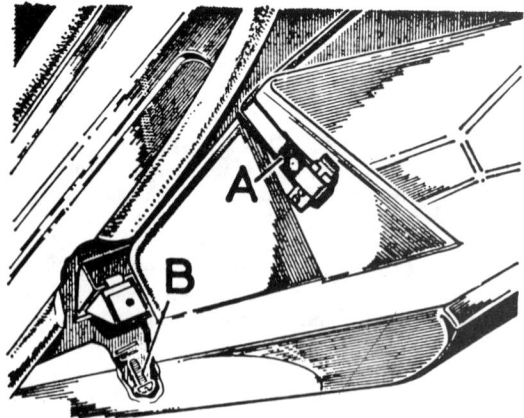

Fig.11.29. GLOVE BOX REMOVAL

A Check strap
B Hinge fittings

the top end of the steering column and withdraw it from the assembly.

13 Remove the lower double spring washer and circlip.

14 Note that on early produced models the steering column journal can be serviced and overhauled in the same manner as the universal joints on the propeller shaft. Full details will be found in Chapter 7, Sections 3 to 5 inclusive.

15 On later produced models the steering column shaft is supplied complete with the journal and cannot be serviced.

16 Refitting the column shaft is the reverse sequence to removal but there are several additional points to be noted.

17 Take care to reconnect the electrical cables correctly and when the job has been completed, test the headlamps and flashers for correct operation.

18 When refitting the steering wheel, make sure the front wheels are in the straight ahead position and the steering wheel spokes in the horizontal plane.

19 If the car is a left-hand drive model the glove box compartment has a larger radius at the upper end so as to provide a clearance for the speedometer cable.

19. Steering Column Shaft Bearings — Removal & Refitting

1. Refer to Section 18 of this Chapter and remove the steering column shaft assembly from the car.
2. Refer to Chapter 10, Section 48 and remove the headlight and direction indicator switch from the column assembly.
3. The special clip (B) Fig.11.30 should next be removed from the steering column rake adjuster followed by the tufnol washer.
4. Unscrew the adjuster and remove the square shaped nut, plain washer, double coil spring washer and tufnol washer.
5. The bearings may now be easily removed from the steering column nacelle.
6. Note that on later produced models the retaining collar for the lower bearing has been replaced by a circlip so that both bearings are retained by a circlip. These changes took place from models with serial number 40016279B, 40100758B and 40304613B onwards.
7. Refitting and reassembly is the reverse sequence to removal. It is however important that the bearings are well lubricated before fitting to the column nacelle.

20. Steering Relay (Mechanical Type) — Removal, Overhaul & Refitting

1. Open the bonnet and support in the fully open position.
2. Chock the rear wheels, apply the handbrake and jack up the front of the car until the front wheels are just off the ground. Support the body on axle stands as shown in Fig.11.8.
3. Extract the split pin from the steering side rod and also from the track rod ball joints. Undo and remove the nuts and plain washer.
4. With a pair of side cutters or a sharp knife, cut away the rubber boot from the ball joint. It will now be necessary to use a universal ball joint separator and a thrust block on the ball joint to be released.
5. Apply a little grease to the jaws of the ball joint separator and fit the tool so that it is positioned centrally. Screw down the centre bolt and separate the ball joint.
6. Knock back the locking plate on the relay and move the bolt that supports the steering relay lever.
7. Undo and remove the special bolts that secure the mounting plate to the body and lift away the relay, shims and washer as well as the steering lock stop located under the rear of the mounting plate.
8. For reference a cross section view of the steering relay is shown in Fig.11.31.
9. To overhaul the relay assembly, first knock back the lock plate and remove the nut. Lift away the lock plate.
10 Unscrew the flanged tube from the mounting bracket and withdraw the tube from the relay.

11 If the bushes are worn they may be drifted out using a suitable diameter soft metal drift.

12 To fit new bushes, press them into position in the relay body using a large vice. Make sure that the bushes are initially entered squarely.

13 Smear the tube with a little engine oil and place in the relay body with the flanged end away from the arms.

14 Thread the tube into the mounting plate and lightly tighten so as to eliminate all endfloat.

15 Fit a new lock plate followed by the nut and tighten to a torque wrench setting of 60 lb/ft.

16 Make sure that the relay body is free to rotate on the tube without any endfloat.

17 Bend over the ends of the lock plate so as to lock the nut onto the mounting plate and then fold the lock plate over so as to allow the mounting bolt to be passed through the centre of the flanged tube.

18 Refitting is the reverse sequence to removal. Always fit new rubber boots and split pins to the ball joints.

19 It will now be necessary to check the steering lock stop bolt adjustment as detailed in Section 26 of this Chapter.

20 The front wheel alignment must next be checked and further information on this subject will be found in Section 25 of this Chapter.

21. Steering Relay (Idler Damper, Hydraulic Type) — Removal & Refitting

1. It should be noted that the steering damper must not be dismantled and under normal circumstances requires no service attention.
2. If signs of oil leaks are evident it is necessary to fit a completely new unit. Also it is important that the steering relay lever must not be removed as the lever shaft is accurately set so that the internal vanes of the damper are in their critical operating position. For reference the steering idler damper is shown in Fig.11.32.
3. To remove the unit, first open the bonnet and support in the fully opened position.
4. Chock the rear wheels and jack up the front until the front wheels are just free of the ground. Support the body on axle stands at the forward jacking point as shown in Fig.11.8.
5. Extract the split pin from the steering side rod and track rod ball joint. Undo and remove the nuts and lift away the plain washers.
6. The ball joint should next be removed from the relay using a ball joint separator. Before the actual tool is used it will be necessary to cut away the rubber boots with a pair of side cutters or a sharp knife. This will allow the ball joint separator to be fitted centrally.
7. On right-hand drive cars it will be necessary to undo and remove the bolts that secure the accelerator bracket to the angle bracket.
8. Undo and remove the bolt that secures the mounting bracket to the base unit. The complete steering relay unit may now be lifted away.
9. If a new unit is to be fitted, remove the mounting and angle brackets from the idler damper.
10 To refit the idler damper is the reverse sequence to removal, but the following additional points should be noted.
11 The ball joint should always be checked for correct fitting in the drop arm before finally securing the mounting bracket.
12 Always fit new split pins to the slotted nuts.
13 It will be necessary to check the steering lock stop adjustment as detailed in Section 26 of this Chapter.
14 The front wheel alignment must be checked and further information on this subject will be found in Section 25 of this Chapter.

22. Steering Linkage — Removal & Refitting

Track Rod

1. Open the bonnet and support in the fully opened position.
2. Chock the rear wheels, apply the handbrake, jack up the front of

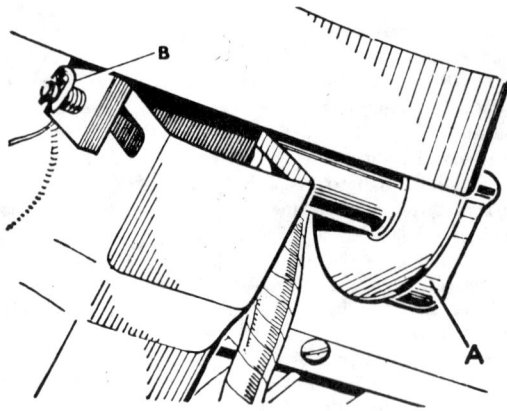

Fig.11.30. RETAINING CLIP FOR STEERING COLUMN
RAKE ADJUSTER

A Adjuster   B Special retaining clip

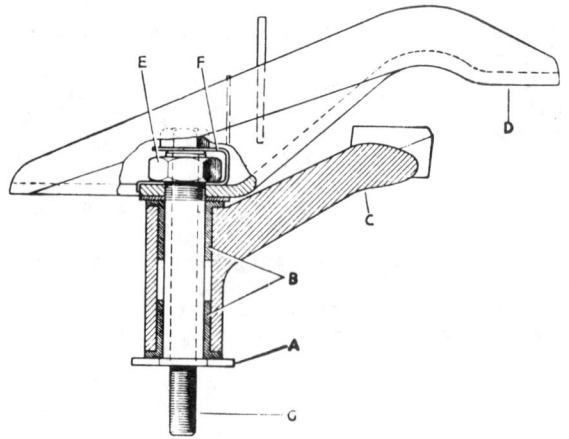

Fig.11.31. CROSS SECTIONAL VIEW OF STEERING RELAY

A Flanged tube   E Locknut
B Bushes   F Lockplate
C Relay lever   G Mounting bolt
D Mounting plate

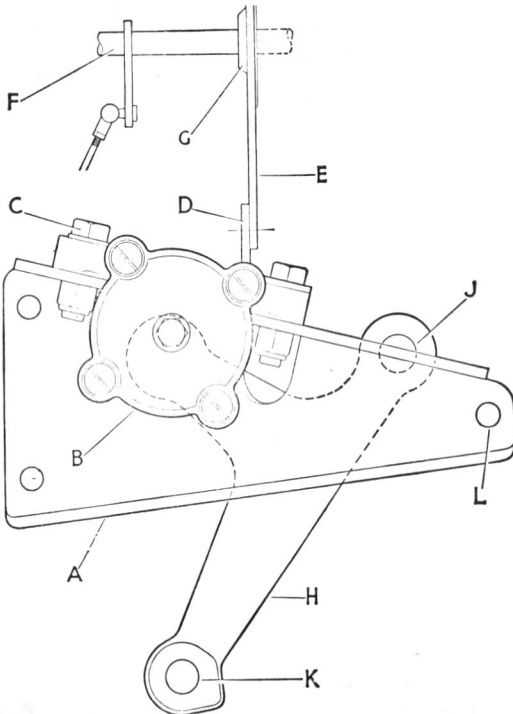

Fig.11.32. STEERING IDLER DAMPER (HYDRAULIC TYPE)

A Steering idler damper   F Coupling shaft
  mounting bracket   G Nylon bearing for
B Steering idler damper   shaft
C Bolt fixings—steering   H Idler relay lever
  idler damper   J Track rod connection
D Mounting angle bracket   K Side rod connection
E Bracket—accelerator   L Mounting bracket fixing
  coupling shaft   holes

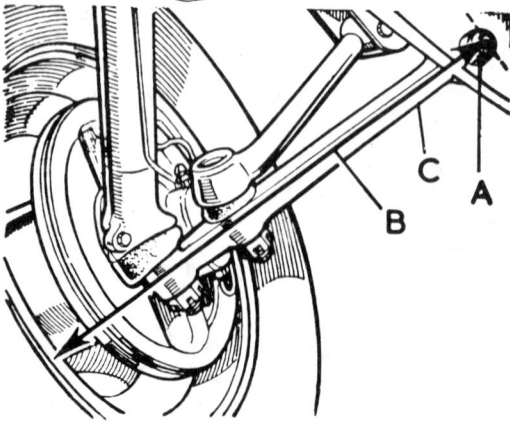

Fig.11.33. STEERING LOCK STOP MEASUREMENT

A Bottom link bolt   C Bottom link
B Line of measurement

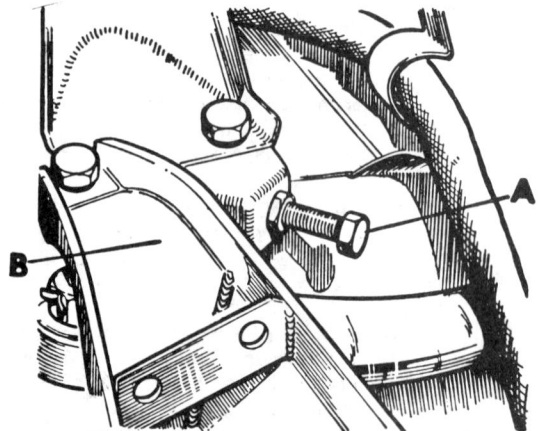

Fig.11.34. LOCATION OF STEERING LOCK STOP

A Adjustable stop bolt and locknut
B Relay arm (LH side illustrated but RH side is similar)

the car and place on axle stands located at the front jacking points as shown in Fig.11.8.

3. Knock back the lock plates and remove the two bolts that secure each end of the anti-roll bar.

4. With a pair of side cutters or a sharp knife, cut the rubber boot from each of the track rod ball joints so as to give adequate clearance for the jaws of the ball joint separator to be fitted centrally and correctly.

5. Extract the split pins that lock the track rod ball joints securing nuts. Undo and remove the nuts.

6. On early produced models it will be necessary to disconnect the horizontal steering damper and move it to one side.

7. For left-hand drive cars remove the steering relay mounting bracket to gain access to the ball joint.

8. On right-hand drive cars, turn the steering wheel fully onto one lock so that the ball joint passes under the relay mounting bracket.

9. Locate the ball joint separator between the steering relay and heater box with the separator jaws facing the ball joint on the steering relay end of the track rod. Now turn the steering wheel back until the ball joint separator can be fitted over the ball joint. Check that the ball joint separator is seating correctly and then tighten the centre bolt so breaking the taper joint.

10 Now turn the steering onto a lock so that the ball joint on the steering box end of the track rod passes under the steering box.

11 Locate the ball joint separator between the steering box and heater box with the separator jaws facing the ball joint. Now turn the steering wheel back until the ball joint separator can be fitted over the ball joint. Check that the ball joint separator is seating correctly and then tighten the centre bolt so breaking the taper joint.

12 The track rod may now be lifted away from under either the right-hand or left-hand wing valance.

13 If the ball joint separator being used is not the official Rover one having a part number of 601763, difficulty may be experienced in placing it over the ball joint due to lack of clearance between the bulkhead and the steering arms. If this is the case, undo and remove the bolts that secure the steering box or relay unit to the body, so giving a greater clearance. On later produced models with the link drive type windscreen wiper motor, it may be necessary to remove the air intake valance as well as the wiper motor itself. Further information will be found in Chapter 10, Section 42.

14 To refit the track rod is the reverse sequence to removal, but the following additional points should be noted.

15 If it was found necessary to remove the steering box make sure that the mounting bolts are really tight.

16 Always use new rubber boots and split pins.

17 It will be necessary to reset the front wheel alignment and further information on this subject will be found in Section 25 of this Chapter.

Steering Side Rod

1. Chock the rear wheels and apply the handbrake. Remove the front wheel trim and slacken the wheel nuts, jack up the front of the car and support on axle stands located at the front jacking points as shown in Fig.11.8. Remove the wheel.

2. Extract the split pin and remove the slotted nut and plain washer from the ball joint at either end of the steering side rod.

3. With a pair of side cutters or a sharp knife cut away the rubber boots at each end of the rod and with a ball joint separator break the taper joint of each ball joint.

4. The steering rod may now be lifted away.

5. Refitting is the reverse sequence to removal. Always fit new rubber boots and split pins.

6. It will be necessary to reset the front wheel alignment and further information on this subject will be found in Section 25 of this Chapter.

23. Steering Hydraulic Damper — Removal & Replacement

1. To remove the steering hydraulic damper, first open the bonnet and support in the fully opened position.

2. Make a note of the electrical cable connections at the top of the windscreen washer reservoir (the green cable goes to the −VE terminal) and disconnect the two cables. Also remove the water pipe connection and then lift away the washer assembly from its mounting bracket.

3. Disconnect the throttle linkage located adjacent to the heater.

4. Undo and remove the bolt and nut located at each end of the damper at the mounting bracket.

5. Rotate the steering wheel until the bolt on the track rod end of the hydraulic damper does not foul the anti-roll bar and then remove the hydraulic damper.

6. Refitting the hydraulic damper is the reverse sequence to removal.

24. Steering Box Adjustment

1. These instructions are only relevant when the steering box is still in position on the car. They should not be followed if the steering box is away from the car as detailed in Section 17 of this Chapter.

2. Chock the rear wheels, apply the handbrake, jack up the front of the car and support on axle stands located at the front jacking point as shown in Fig.11.8.

3. Undo and remove the rocker shaft adjuster cap nut.

4. With the steering wheel very lightly held between two fingers, turn the steering wheel slightly to the left and right so as to ascertain the amount of backlash present in the steering box.

5. An assistant should now release the adjuster lock nut and then with a screwdriver very slowly screw in the adjusting screw whilst the steering wheel is still being rocked, until a condition of zero backlash is achieved. This is when no free movement is felt on the steering wheel.

6. Tighten the lock nut securely.

7. Turn the steering wheel slowly from one lock and back to the other lock so as to check if there is any excessive tightness throughout the steering wheel movement range. If this is evident either the adjuster has been screwed in too far, or the steering box is too worn and requires overhaul as detailed in Section 17 of this Chapter.

8. Refit the adjuster screw cap nut and finally road test the car.

25. Wheel Alignment

The front wheels are correctly aligned when they are turning in at the front 1/16th inch with a tolerance of + or − 1/16th inch. It is important that this measurement is taken on a centre line drawn horizontally and parallel with the ground through the centre line of the hub. The exact point should be in the centre of the side wall of the tyre and not on the wheel rim which could be distorted and so give inaccurate readings.

The adjustment is affected by loosening the lock nut on each track rod adjuster at the rear of the engine and turning the rod so as to obtain the correct alignment.

This is a job best left to your local Rover dealer as accurate alignment requires the use of specialist equipment. If the wheels are not in alignment, tyre wear will be heavy and uneven, and the steering will be stiff and unresponsive.

26. Steering Lock Stops — Adjustment

1. Chock the rear wheels and apply the handbrake, jack up the front of the car and support on axle stands located at the front jacking points as shown in Fig.11.8.

2. Turn the wheels slowly onto one full lock position and with a long rule or steel tape measure the distance from the centre of the bolt securing the bottom link to the body along the line of the link to the front rim of the road wheel as shown in Fig.11.33. This dimension should be exactly 18¾ inches. Take this measurement at several positions on the wheel rim to eliminate any error caused by

a distorted rim.

3. If any adjustment is necessary refer to Fig.11.34 and adjust the steering lock stop, working through the wing valance, until the required dimension is obtained.

4. Repeat the instructions given in paragraphs 2 and 3 for the opposite lock stop.

WHEEL & TYRE SPECIFICATIONS

Tyre sizes	165 x 14 inch Dunlop tubless
	165 x 14 inch Pirelli, Cinturato, tubed
Wheels	5J x 14 inch
Wheel nuts	7/16 inch UNF, ball-faced; right-hand threads all round

Tyres, Single Carburetter Models

Size ... ...   Pirelli Cinturato 165 x 14 with inner tubes
                                               Dunlop SP41. 165 x 14 tubeless

Pressures - check with tyres cold:

All speeds and normal loads	Front	Rear
lb/sq.in.	26	28

Tyres, Twin Carburetter Models

Size ... ...   Pirelli Cinturato 165 x 14 with inner tubes
                                               Dunlop SP41. 165 x 14 tubeless

Pressures - check with tyres cold:

Up to speeds of 105 mph. and normal loads:	Front	Rear
lb/sq.in	26	28
When driving consistently at speeds of over 105 mph. and normal loads:	30	32

NOTE: When the car is driven fully laden, the rear tyre pressures should be increased by 4 lb/sq.in. When high-speed touring, the tyre pressures should be checked much more frequently, even to the extent of a daily check.

Fault Finding Chart - Suspension - Dampers - Steering

Symptom	Reason/s	Remedy
Steering feels vague, car wanders and floats at speed General wear or damage	Tyre pressures uneven. Dampers worn or require topping up. Steering gear ball joints badly worn. Suspension geometry incorrect. Steering mechanism free play excessive. Front suspension and rear suspension pick-up points out of alignment.	Check pressures and adjust as necessary. Top up dampers, test, and replace if worn. Fit new ball joints. Check and rectify. Adjust or overhaul steering mechanism. Normally caused by poor repair work after a serious accident. Extensive re-building necessary.
Stiff and heavy steering Lack of maintenance or accident damage	Tyre pressures loo low. No grease in suspension joints where required. No oil in steering gear. No grease in steering and suspension ball joints. Front wheel toe-in incorrect. Suspension geometry incorrect. Steering gear incorrectly adjusted too tightly. Steering column badly misaligned.	Check pressures and inflate tyres. Clean nipples and grease thoroughly. Top up steering gear. Clean nipples and grease thoroughly. Check and reset toe-in. Check and rectify. Check and re-adjust steering gear. Determine cause and rectify. (Usually due to bad repair after severe accident damage and difficult to correct).
Wheel wobble and vibration General wear or damage	Wheel nuts loose. Front wheels and tyres out of balance. Steering ball joints badly worn. Hub bearings badly worn. Steering gear free play excessive. Front springs, weak or broken.	Check and tighten as necessary. Balance wheels and tyres and add weights as necessary. Replace steering gear ball joints. Remove and fit new hub bearings. Adjust and overhaul steering gear. Inspect and overhaul as necessary.

Chapter 12 Bodywork and underframe

Contents

1. General Description

The all steel body and chassis frame is of a welded construction and is of a design whereby a strong base unit is used to which doors, panels, bonnet and boot lid are bolted. This means that any superficial panel damage can be easily rectified by simply unbolting the existing panel and fitting a new one.

It is also possible for a considerable amount of the base unit to be repaired using simple welding equipment. Fig.12.1 and Fig.12.2 show the construction of the base unit; all parts that are unshaded may be renewed. From inspection of the design of the base unit it can be seen that most of the strength and rigidity of the basic construction is incorporated in the body platform with particular additional support by the use of deep section members under the door sills. The bulkhead is of a rigid box section which is able to accommodate the demands of the front suspension as well as adding to the overall strength of the base unit.

The rear suspension coil springs are located forward of the rear wheel centre line and also below the rear seating so that any stress caused by high speed motoring or by driving over very rough road is distributed to the strong central section of the body. This also means that by using this type of construction, none of the external body panels or the roof panel is subjected to stress and therefore not required to contribute to the overall rigidity of the fully panelled body.

Whilst the car is being produced all the mechanical parts are assembled to the base unit and it is only at the last stage of production that fully painted panels are in fact fitted. These are jig prepared so that service supplied panels are already painted.

The underside of the base unit is painted in a slipper bath and then completely coated with a special anti-corrosive sealing compound. In addition to this all mating body panels up to a height of 15 inches are treated with a Zinc rust primer.

The interior upholstery and fittings are all of top quality. The seats on the 2000 models are upholstered in prime hide whilst on the 2200 range the seats are covered with a hard wearing, stain resistant, non slip and non shine double corded brushed nylon. If preferred however leather covered seats could be had as an option. The front seats are individual 'bucket' type being fully adjustable including the back rest.

Individual rear seats have a wide centre folding arm rest and heavy pile floor carpeting with thick felt underlay on both the front and rear floors.

There is a comprehensive range of interior accessories and these include front and rear courtesy lights operated by either opening the doors or by individual switches, ashtrays on the transmission tunnel, twin collapsible sun visors which are fully adjustable and able to swing round to the front doors, electric clock, cigar lighter, full width parcel shelf, two glove boxes and provision to fit a radio set.

Available as an optional extra is a laminated glass windscreen and electrically heated rear screen. To add to passenger safety, provision is made for the fitting of safety harness for both front and rear passengers.

2. Maintenance - Bodywork & Underframe

The general condition of a car's bodywork is the one thing that significantly affects its value. Maintenance is easy but needs to be regular. Neglect, particularly after minor damage, can lead quickly

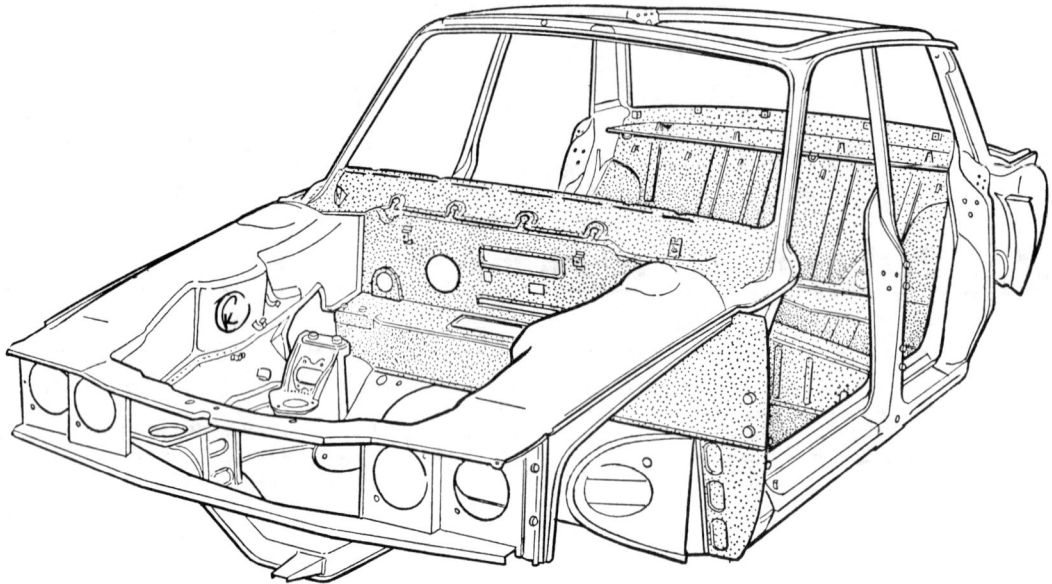

Fig.12.1. THREE QUARTER FRONT VIEW OF BASE UNIT
NOTE: Shaded panels are non-serviceable

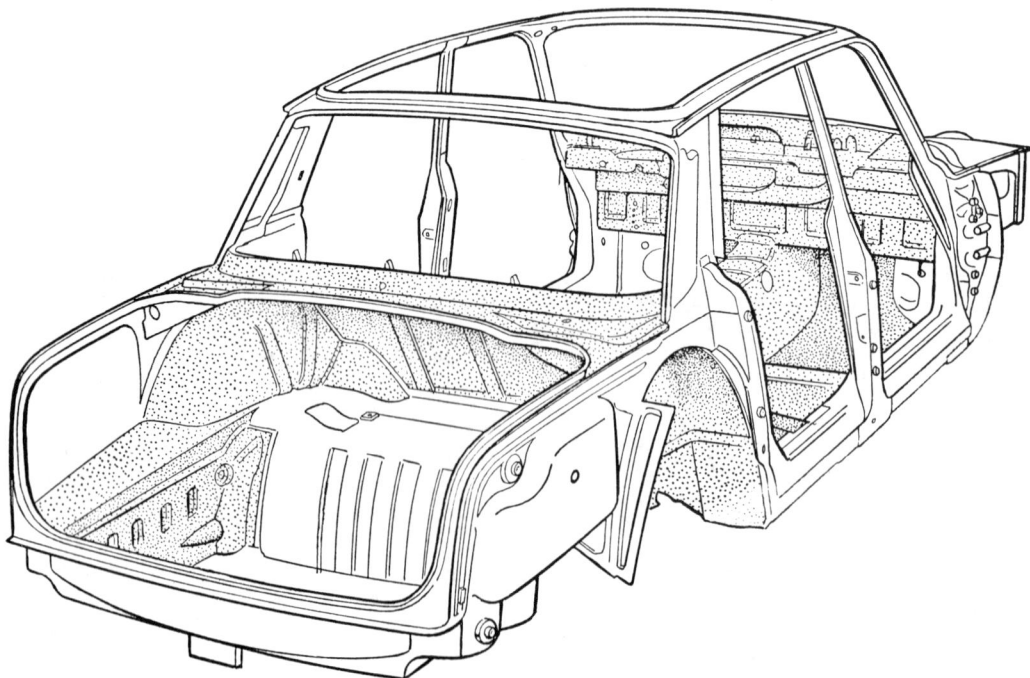

Fig.12.2. THREE QUARTER REAR VIEW OF BASE UNIT
NOTE: Shaded panels are non-serviceable

to further deterioration and costly repair bills. It is important also to keep watch on those parts of the car not immediately visible, for instance the underside, inside all the wheel arches and the lower part of the engine compartment.

The basic maintenance routine for the bodywork is washing — preferably with a lot of water, from a hose. This will remove all the loose solids which may have stuck to the car. It is important to flush these off in such a way as to prevent grit from scratching the finish.

The wheel arches and underbody need washing in the same way to remove any accumulated mud which will retain moisture and tend to encourage rust. Paradoxically enough, the best time to clean the underbody and wheel arches is in wet weather when the mud is thoroughly wet and soft. In very wet weather the underbody is usually cleaned of large accumulations automatically and this is a good time for inspection.

Periodically it is a good idea to have the whole of the underside of the car steam cleaned, engine compartment included, so that a thorough inspection can be carried out to see what minor repairs and renovations are necessary. Steam cleaning is available at many garages and is necessary for removal of accumulations of oily grime which sometimes is allowed to cake thick in certain areas near the engine, gearbox and back axle. If steam facilities are not available, there are one or two excellent grease solvents available which can be brush applied. The dirt can then be simply hosed off.

After washing paintwork, wipe off with a chamois leather to give an unspotted clear finish. A coat of clear protective wax polish will give added protection against chemical pollutants in the air. If the paintwork sheen has dulled or oxidised, use a cleaner/polisher combination to restore the brilliance of the shine. This requires a little effort, but is usually caused because regular washing has been neglected. Always check that the door and ventilator opening drain holes and pipes are completely clear so that water can drain out. Bright work should be treated the same way as paintwork. Windscreens and windows can be kept clear of the smeary film which often appears, if a little ammonia is added to the water. If they are scratched, a good rub with a proprietary metal polish will often clear them. Never use any form of wax or other body or chromium polish on glass.

3. Maintenance - Upholstery & Carpets

Mats and carpets should be brushed or vacuum cleaned regularly to keep them free of grit. If they are badly stained remove them from the car for scrubbing or sponging and make quite sure they are dry before replacement. Seats and interior trim panels can be kept clean by a wipe over with a damp cloth. If they do become stained (which can be more apparent on light coloured upholstery) use a little liquid detergent and a soft nail brush to scour the grime out of the grain of the material. Do not forget to keep the head lining clean in the same way as the upholstery. When using liquid cleaners inside the car do not over-wet the surfaces being cleaned. Excessive damp could get into the seams and padded interior causing stains, offensive odours or even rot. If the inside of the car gets wet accidentally it is worthwhile taking some trouble to dry it out properly particularly where carpets are involved. Do not leave oil or electric heaters inside the car for this purpose.

4. Maintenance - PVC External Roof Covering

Under no circumstances try to clean any external PVC roof covering with detergents, caustic soaps or spirit cleaners. Plain soap and water is all that is required with a soft brush to clean dirt that may be ingrained. Wash the covering as frequently as the rest of the car.

5. Minor Body Damage - Repair

The photograph sequence on pages 254 and 255 illustrates the operations detailed in the following sub-Sections.

Repair of minor scratches in the car's bodywork

If the scratch is very superficial, and does not penetrate to the metal of the bodywork, repair is very simple. Lightly rub the area of the scratch with a paintwork renovator, or a very fine cutting paste, to remove loose paint from the scratch and to clear the surrounding bodywork of wax polish. Rinse the area with clean water.

Apply touch-up paint to the scratch using a thin paint brush, continue to apply thin layers of paint until the surface of the paint in the scratch is level with the surrounding paintwork. Allow the new paint at least two weeks to harden; then, blend it into the surrounding paintwork by rubbing the paintwork, in the scratch area with a paintwork renovator, or a very fine cutting paste. Finally apply wax polish.

An alternative to painting over the scratch is to use a paint patch. Use the same preparation for the affected area; then simply pick a patch of a suitable size to cover the scratch completely. Hold the patch against the scratch and burnish its backing paper; the patch will adhere to the paintwork, freeing itself from the backing paper at the same time. Polish the affected area to blend the patch into the surrounding paintwork. Where the scratch has penetrated right through to the metal of the bodywork, causing the metal to rust, a different repair technique is required. Remove any loose rust from the bottom of the scratch with a penknife, then apply rust inhibiting paint to prevent the formation of rust in the future. Using a rubber or nylon applicator fill the scratch with bodystopper paste. If required, this paste can be mixed with cellulose thinners to provide a very thin paste which is ideal for filling narrow scratches. Before the stopper-paste in the scratch hardens, wrap a piece of smooth cotton rag around the top of a finger. Dip the finger in cellulose thinners and then quickly sweep it across the surface of the stopper-paste in the scratch; this will ensure that the surface of the stopper-paste is slightly hollowed. The scratch can now be painted over as described earlier in this section.

Repair of dents in the car's bodywork

When deep denting of the car's bodywork has taken place, the first task is to pull the dent out, until the affected bodywork almost attains its original shape. There is little point in trying to restore the original shape completely, as the metal in the damaged area will have stretched on impact and cannot be reshaped fully to its original contour. It is better to bring the level of the dent up to a point which is about 1/8 inch (3 mm) below the level of the surrounding bodywork. In cases where the dent is very shallow anyway, it is not worth trying to pull it out at all.

If the underside of the dent is accessible, it can be hammered out gently from behind, using a mallet with a wooden or plastic head. Whilst doing this, hold a suitable block of wood firmly against the impact from the hammer blows and thus prevent a large area of bodywork from being 'belled-out'.

Should the dent be in a section of the bodywork which has a double skin or some other factor making it inaccessible from behind, a different technique is called for. Drill several small holes through the metal inside the dent area — particularly in the deeper sections. Then screw long self-tapping screws into the holes just sufficiently for them to gain a good purchase in the metal. Now the dent can be pulled out by pulling on the protruding heads of the screws with a pair of pliers.

The next stage of the repair is the removal of the paint from the damaged area, and from an inch or so of the surrounding 'sound' bodywork. This is accomplished most easily by using a wire brush or abrasive pad on a power drill, although it can be done just as effectively by hand using sheets of abrasive paper. To complete the preparations for filling, score the surface of the bare metal with a

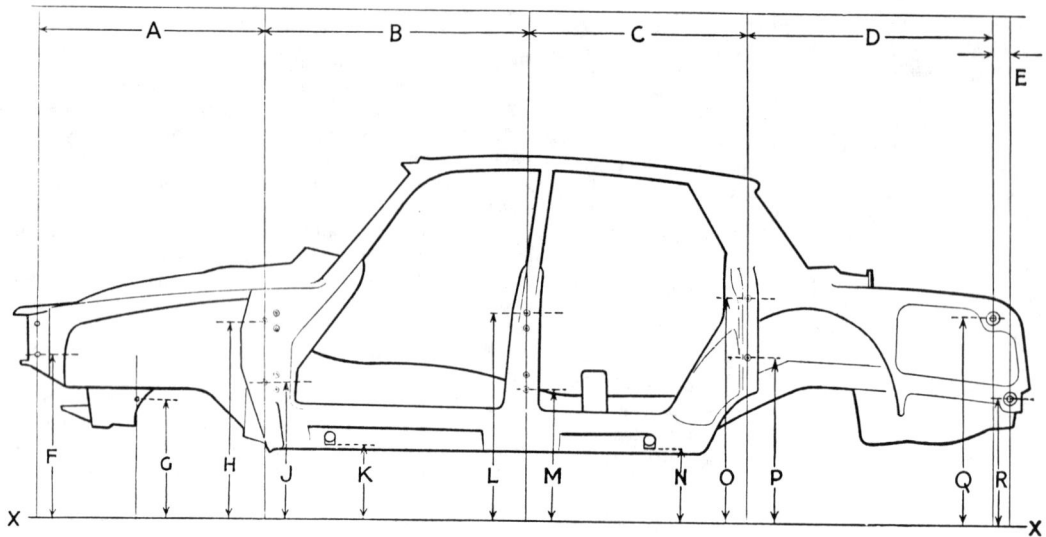

Fig.12.3. DIAGRAMMATIC SIDE VIEW OF BASE UNIT SHOWING DATUM POSITIONS

A 36.29/32 in.	F 29 in.	L 35.31/32 in.	Q 35.21/64 in.
B 41.3/32 in.	G 20.13/32 in.	M 25.15/32 in.	R 22.61/64 in.
C 33.7/8 in.	H 34.27/64 in.	N 15.55/64 in.	XX Floor level
D 38.3/8 in.	J 25.11/64 in.	O 38.33/64 in.	
E 3.7/16 in.	K 16.13/64 in.	P 29.35/64 in.	

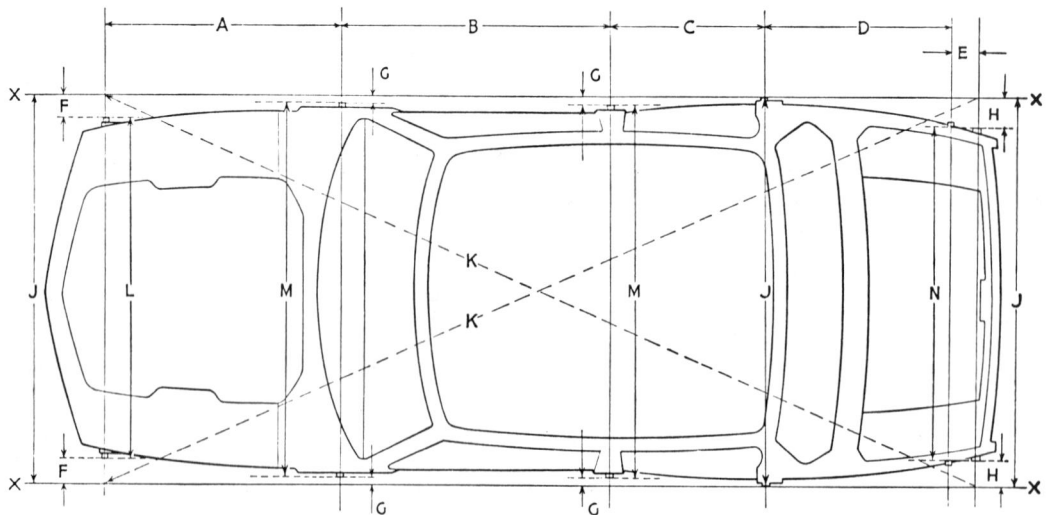

Fig.12.4. DIAGRAMMATIC PLAN ELEVATION OF BASE UNIT SHOWING DATUM POSITIONS

A 36.29/32 in.	E 3.7/16 in.	J 62.1/16 in.	N 50.5/16 in.
B 41.3/32 in.	F 4.25/32 in.	K 165.25/32 in.	
C 33.7/8 in.	G 5/8 in.	L 52½ in.	
D 38.3/8 in.	H 5.7/8 in.	M 60.13/16 in.	

screwdriver or the tang of a file, or alternatively, drill small holes in the affected area. This will provide a really good 'key' for the filler paste.

To complete the repair see the Section on filling and respraying.

Repair of rust holes or gashes in the car's bodywork

Remove all paint from the affected area and from an inch or so of the surrounding 'sound' bodywork, using an abrasive pad or a wire brush on a power drill. If these are not available a few sheets of abrasive paper will do the job just as effectively. With the paint removed you will be able to gauge the severity of the corrosion and therefore decide whether to replace the whole panel or to repair the affected area. Replacement body panels are not as expensive as most people think and it is often quicker and more satisfactory to fit a new panel than to attempt to repair large areas of corrosion.

Remove all fittings from the affected area except those which will act as a guide to the original shape of the damaged bodywork (eg: headlamp shells etc.). Then, using the tin snips or a hacksaw blade, remove all loose metal and any other metal badly affected by corrosion. Hammer the edges of the hole inwards in order to create a slight depression for the filler paste.

Wire brush the affected area to remove the powdery rust from the surface of the remaining metal. Paint the affected area with rust inhibiting paint; if the back of the rusted area is accessible treat this also.

Before filling can take place it will be necessary to block the hole in some way. This can be achieved by the use of one of the following materials: Zinc gauze, Aluminium tape or Polyurethane foam.

Zinc gauze is probably the best material to use for a large hole. Cut a piece to the approximate size and shape of the hole to be filled, then position it in the hole so that its edges are below the level of the surrounding bodywork. It can be retained in position by several blobs of filler paste around its periphery.

Aluminium tape should be used for small or very narrow holes. Pull a piece off the roll and trim it to the approximate size and shape required, then pull off the backing paper (if used) and stick the tape over the hole; it can be overlapped if the thickness of one piece is insufficient. Burnish down the edges of the tape with the handle of a screwdriver or similar, to ensure that the tape is securely attached to the metal underneath.

Polyurethane foam is best used where the hole is situated in a section of bodywork of complex shape, backed by a small box section (eg: where the sill panel meets the rear wheel arch — most cars). The usual mixing procedure for this foam is as follows: put equal amounts of fluid from each of the two cans provided in the kit, into one container. Stir until the mixture begins to thicken, then quickly pour this mixture into the hole, and hold a piece of cardboard over the larger apertures. Almost immediately the Polyurethane will begin to expand, gushing out of any small holes left unblocked. When the foam hardens it can be cut back to just below the level of the surrounding bodywork with a hacksaw blade.

Bodywork repairs - filling and re-spraying

Before using this Section, see the Sections on dent, deep scratch, rust hole, and gash repairs.

Many types of bodyfiller are available, but generally speaking those proprietary kits which contain a tin of filler paste and a tube of resin hardener are best for this type of repair. A wide, flexible plastic or nylon applicator will be found invaluable for imparting a smooth and well contoured finish to the surface of the filler.

Mix up a little filler on a clean piece of card or board — use the hardener sparingly (follow the maker's instructions on the packet) otherwise the filler will set very rapidly.

Using the applicator, apply the filler paste to the prepared area; draw the applicator across the surface of the filler to achieve the correct contour and to level the filler surface. As soon as a contour that approximates the correct one is achieved, stop working the paste — if you carry on too long the paste will become sticky and begin to 'pick-up' on the applicator. Continue to add thin layers of filler paste at twenty-minute intervals until the level of the filler is just 'proud' of the surrounding bodywork.

Once the filler has hardened, excess can be removed using a Surform plane or Dreadnought file. From then on, progressively finer grades of abrasive paper should be used, starting with a 40 grade production paper and finishing with a 400 grade 'wet-and-dry' paper. Always wrap the abrasive paper around a flat rubber, cork, or wooden block — otherwise the surface of the filler will not be completely flat. During the smoothing of the filler surface the 'wet-and-dry' paper should be periodically rinsed in water. This will ensure that a very smooth finish is imparted to the filler at the final stage.

At this stage the dent should be surrounded by a ring of bare metal, which in turn should be encircled by the finely 'feathered' edge of the good paintwork. Rinse the repair area with clean water, until all of the dust produced by the rubbing-down operation is gone.

Spray the whole repair area with a light coat of grey primer — this will show up any imperfections in the surface of the filler. Repair these imperfections with fresh filler paste or bodystopper, and once more smooth the surface with abrasive paper. If bodystopper is used, it can be mixed with cellulose thinners to form a really thin paste which is ideal for filling small holes. Repeat this spray and repair procedure until you are satisfied that the surface of the filler, and the feathered edge of the paintwork are perfect. Clean the repair area with clean water and allow to dry fully.

The repair area is now ready for spraying. Paint spraying must be carried out in a warm, dry, windless and dust free atmosphere. This condition can be created artificially if you have access to a large indoor working area, but if you are forced to work in the open, you will have to pick your day very carefully. If you are working indoors, dousing the floor in the work area with water will 'lay' the dust which would otherwise be in the atmosphere. If the repair area is confined to one body panel, mask off the surrounding panels; this will help to minimise the effects of a slight mis-match in paint colours. Bodywork fittings (eg: chrome strips, door handles, etc.) will also need to be masked off. Use genuine masking tape and several thicknesses of newspaper for the masking operation.

Before commencing to spray, agitate the aerosol can thoroughly, then spray a test area (an old tin, or similar) until the technique is mastered. Cover the repair area with a thick coat of primer; the thickness should be built up using several thin layers of paint rather than one thick one. Using 400 grade 'wet-and-dry' paper, rub down the surface of the primer until it is really smooth. While doing this, the work area should be thoroughly doused with water, and the 'wet-and-dry' paper periodically rinsed in water. Allow to dry before spraying on more paint.

Spray on the top coat, again building up the thickness by using several thin layers of paint. Start spraying in the centre of the repair area and then, using a circular motion, work outwards until the whole repair area and about 2 inches of the surrounding original paintwork is covered. Remove all masking material 10 to 15 minutes after spraying on the final coat of paint.

Allow the new paint at least 2 weeks to harden fully; then, using a paintwork renovator or a very fine cutting paste, blend the edges of the new paint into the existing paintwork. Finally, apply wax polish.

6. Major Body Damage - Repair

Where serious damage has occurred or large areas need renewal due to neglect, it means certainly that completely new sections or panels will need welding in and this is best left to professionals. If the damage is due to impact it will also be necessary to completely check the alignment of the bodyshell structure. Due to the principle of construction the strength and shape of the whole can be affected by damage to a part. In such instances the services of a Rover agent with specialist checking jigs are essential. If a body is left misaligned it is first of all dangerous as the car will not handle properly, and secondly uneven stresses will be imposed on the steering, engine and transmission, causing abnormal wear or complete failure. Tyre wear may also be excessive.

7. Maintenance — Locks & Hinges

Regularly lubricate the bonnet, boot and door hinges with a few drops of engine oil from an oil can. The door striker plates should be given a thin smear of grease so as to reduce wear and ensure free movement.

8. Door Rattles — Tracing & Rectification

1. The commonest cause of door rattles is a misaligned, loose or worn striker plate but other causes may be:—
a) Loose door handles, window winder handles or door hinges.
b) Loose, worn or misaligned door lock components.
c) Loose or worn remote control mechanism.
2. It is quite possible for door rattles to be the result of a combination of the above faults so a careful examination must be made to determine the cause of the fault.
3. If the nose of the striker plate is worn as a result of door rattles, renew it and adjust the plate as described later in this Chapter.
4. If the nose of the door lock wedge is badly worn and the door rattles as a result, then fit a new lock as described later in this Chapter.
5. Should the hinges be badly worn then they must be renewed as a complete assembly.

9. Door – Removal & Refitting

1. Remove the locking cap from the check strap locating peg (A) Fig.12.5 on the body.
2. Slacken the bottom hinge pin nut (D) and screw up the hinge pin (B) far enough to allow the door to be lifted off the top hinge pin. For this an Allen key will be required.
3. Do not slacken or remove the top hinge pin as this will locate the door when it is being refitted.
4. Very carefully lift the door from the hinge pin. Lay a blanket on the door and place the door so that it is leaning up against a wall out of the way to prevent any possible damage to it.
5. To refit the door, first locate the door on the top hinge pin and position the check strap onto its peg. Fit a new locking cap (A), Fig.12.5.
6. With an Allen key screw down the lower hinge pin until all play has been eliminated. Make sure that the door closes correctly and make any adjustment necessary as detailed in Section 10 of this Chapter.
7. Lubricate the hinge pins and check strap pivots with a little Castrol GTX.

10. Door Adjustment

1. To ensure that it is possible to fit the door correctly to its aperture there are three separate adjustments:—
a) Shims may be added or subtracted between the door hinge and the body so as to move the door either into or out of the door aperture, Fig.12.6.
b) Shims may be added or subtracted between the door and hinge so as to move the door either forwards or rearwards in the door aperture, Fig.12.7.
c) Raising or lowering the hinge pin which will raise or lower the door in the door aperture, Fig.12.5.
2. The correct method of adjusting the door position is to first check that the striker plate has not been distorted by placing a metal rule or straight edge across the two outside faces as shown in

Fig.12.8.
3. If distortion is evident, undo and remove the three crosshead screws and lift away the striker plate. Lower the seating face on the pillar so as to allow the plate to sit squarely.
4. If there is any distortion evident the sliding wedge will foul the bottom of the striker. Refit the plate and lightly tighten the screws to hold it in an approximately vertical position on the pillar.
5. With the door push button fully depressed, gently close the door on the striker. If necessary move the striker up or down until the dovetail does not foul either the nylon block or the bottom of the sliding wedge.
6. If movement of the striker is required but is not possible because the striker is at the limit of its movement, the door must be raised or lowered by adjusting the height of the hinge pins.
7. Tighten the three crosshead screws in the striker plate and close the door fully. Next check that overtravel exists by pushing the door in against the door aperture sealing rubber so that a little movement is felt after the rotary arm has been engaged. This movement should be about 0.060 inch which may be adjusted by moving the striker inwards or outwards relative to the door pillar.
8. The vertical and horizontal alignment of the lock and striker faces is independent and these should be kept as near parallel as possible.
9. To make sure that the rotary cam of the door lock is fully engaged with the latch plate, ensure that there is push button free play. With the door open make a pencil mark on the side of the bottom adjacent to the escutcheon.
10 Close the door and make a second mark on the side of the button. Open the door again and check if the two pencil marks coincide which is in fact what they should do.
11 If the clearance when the door is closed is more than when the door is open, the rotary cam of the lock is not fully engaged with the latch of the striker plate. Move the striker plate outwards slightly until this is rectified.
12 Make sure that the lock is fully engaged with the striker plate and also that the striker plate does not foul any part of the lock. Any further adjustment may be made by adding shims between the striker plate and the door pillar.

11. Door Sealing Rubbers — Removal & Refitting

1. Before the door sealing rubbers can be removed it is necessary to remove the doors.
2. First remove the locking cap from the check strap locating peg (A), Fig.12.5 on the body.
3. Slacken the bottom hinge pin nut and screw up the hinge pin (B) far enough to allow the door to be lifted off the top hinge pin. For this an Allen key will be required.
4. Do not slacken or remove the top hinge pin as this will locate the door when it is being refitted.
5. Very carefully lift the door from its top hinge pin. Lay a blanket on the floor and place the door so that it is leaning up against a wall out of the way to prevent possible damage.
6. Undo and remove the screws securing the sill plate and lift away the sill plate.
7. Undo and remove the screws and metal strip that secure the door aperture sealing rubber to the sill.
8. The door sealing rubber may now be carefully pulled out working from each end and meeting in the centre.
9. To refit the door sealing rubber, prepare it first by applying a little Silicone MS4 to the seating face of the rubber.
10 Position the rubber at the door sill channel and secure it to the sill with the metal strip and screws.
11 The remainder of the door sealing rubbers may now be refitted using either the special tool as shown in Fig.12.9 or a piece of tapered wood with the corners rounded. If the latter method is used, lubricate the wood with a little Silicone grease MS4.
12 Wipe away any excess Silicone grease and refit the sill plate.
13 It will now be necessary to refit the door in the reverse sequence

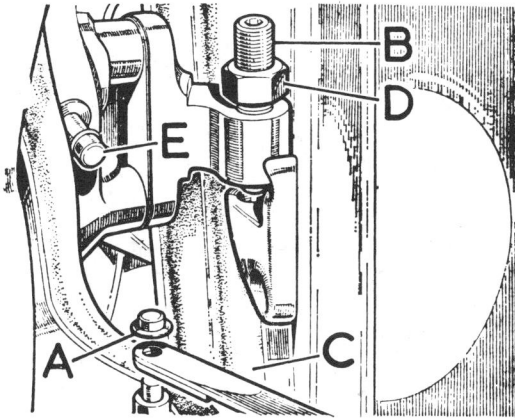

Fig.12.5. DOOR BOTTOM HINGE PIN

A Door check strap post cap
B Hinge pin
C Check strap arm
D Hinge pin locknut
E Courtesy light switch

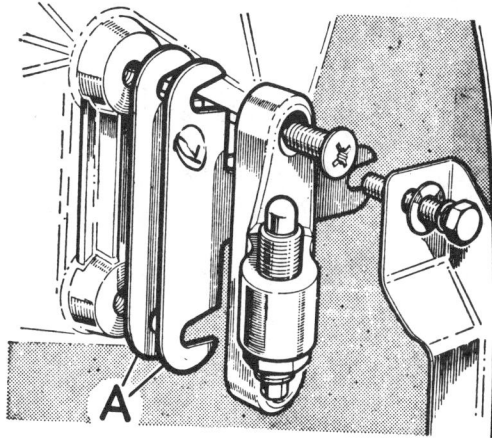

Fig.12.6. LOCATION OF SHIMS BETWEEN DOOR HINGE & BASE UNIT
A Shims

Fig.12.7. LOCATION OF SHIMS BETWEEN HINGE & DOOR
A Shims

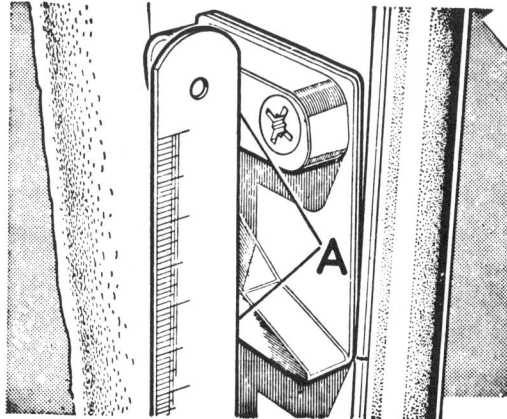

Fig.12.8. USING A STEEL RULE TO CHECK FOR STRIKER PLATE DISTORTION
A Steel rule

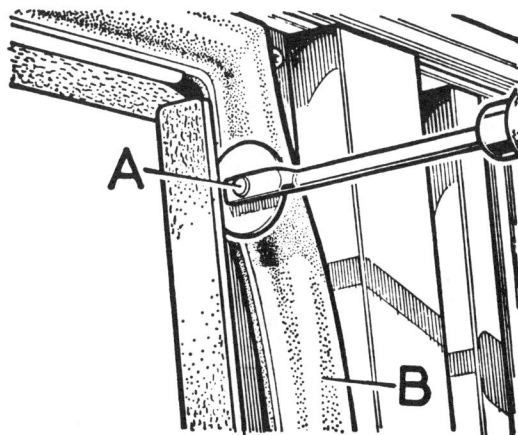

Fig.12.9. SPECIAL TOOL BEING USED TO REFIT DOOR APERTURE SEALING RUBBER
A Special tool
B Sealing rubber

This sequence of photographs deals with the repair of the dent and paintwork damage shown in this photo. The procedure will be similar for the repair of a hole. It should be noted that the procedures given here are simplified — more explicit instructions will be found in the text

In the case of a dent the first job — after removing surrounding trim — is to hammer out the dent where access is possible. This will minimise filling. Here, the large dent having been hammered out, the damaged area is being made slightly concave

Now all paint must be removed from the damaged area, by rubbing with coarse abrasive paper. Alternatively, a wire brush or abrasive pad can be used in a power drill. Where the repair area meets good paintwork, the edge of the paintwork should be 'feathered', using a finer grade of abrasive paper

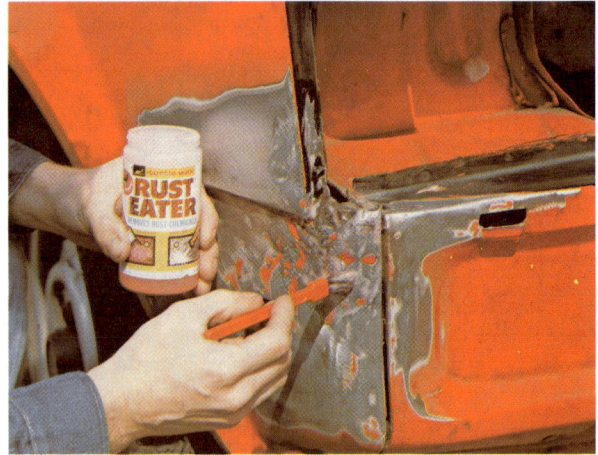
In the case of a hole caused by rusting, all damaged sheet-metal should be cut away before proceeding to this stage. Here, the damaged area is being treated with rust remover and inhibitor before being filled

Mix the body filler according to its manufacturer's instructions. In the case of corrosion damage, it will be necessary to block off any large holes before filling — this can be done with zinc gauze or aluminium tape. Make sure the area is absolutely clean before...

...applying the filler. Filler should be applied with a flexible applicator, as shown, for best results; the wooden spatula being used for confined areas. Apply thin layers of filler at 20-minute intervals, until the surface of the filler is slightly proud of the surrounding bodywork

Initial shaping can be done with a Surform plane or Dread-nought file. Then, using progressively finer grades of wet-and-dry paper, wrapped around a sanding block, and copious amounts of clean water, rub down the filler until really smooth and flat. Again, feather the edges of adjoining paintwork

The whole repair area can now be sprayed or brush-painted with primer. If spraying, ensure adjoining areas are protected from over-spray. Note that at least one inch of the surrounding sound paintwork should be coated with primer. Primer has a 'thick' consistency, so will fill small imperfections

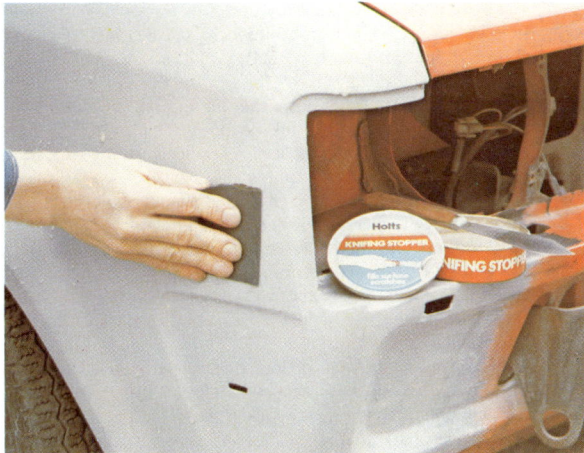

Again, using plenty of water, rub down the primer with a fine grade of wet-and-dry paper (400 grade is probably best) until it is really smooth and well blended into the surrounding paintwork. Any remaining imperfections can now be filled by carefully applied knifing stopper paste

When the stopper has hardened, rub down the repair area again before applying the final coat of primer. Before rubbing down this last coat of primer, ensure the repair area is blemish-free – use more stopper if necessary. To ensure that the surface of the primer is really smooth use some finishing compound

The top coat can now be applied. When working out of doors, pick a dry, warm and wind-free day. Ensure surrounding areas are protected from over-spray. Agitate the aerosol thoroughly, then spray the centre of the repair area, working outwards with a circular motion. Apply the paint as several thin coats

After a period of about two weeks, which the paint needs to harden fully, the surface of the repaired area can be 'cut' with a mild cutting compound prior to wax polishing. When carrying out bodywork repairs, remember that the quality of the finished job is proportional to the time and effort expended

to removal. Any adjustment to its positioning in the aperture may be made as detailed in Section 10 of this Chapter.

14 Lubricate the hinge pins and check strap pivots with a little Castrol GTX.

12. Door Trim – Removal & Refitting

1. Carefully slide the veneer out of the waist moulding if the car is an early produced model. On later produced models remove the retaining clips.

2. Undo and remove the Phillips head screws that retain the waist moulding.

3. Unscrew the remote control lock knob and lift away the moulding.

4. Make up a piece of hooked wire as shown in Fig.12.10, note the position of the window winder and with a wide bladed screwdriver ease back the bezel so as to gain access to the retaining spring clip. Extract the spring clip as shown.

5. Repeat the previous operation for the door lock handle.

6. Undo and remove the two Phillips head set screws that secure the arm rest to the door panel. Lift away the arm rest.

7. With a wide bladed screwdriver very carefully ease the door trim panel so as to release the clips from the door panel. When all are free, lift away the door trim and the plastic waterproof sheeting.

8. Refitting the door trim is the reverse sequence to removal, but the following additional points should be noted:—

a) With Bostik or other suitable adhesive secure the plastic water-proof sheet to the door inner panel.

b) Care must be taken in refitting the veneer retaining clips on the later produced model.

9. Place the veneer retaining clips with the convex side outwards and the chamfered sides facing towards the rear over the waist moulding fixing screw. The veneer may now be slid into position.

13. Door Lock & Remote Control System – Removal, Refitting & Adjustment

1. Refer to Section 12 and remove the door trim. The component parts of the door lock system are shown in Fig.12.12.

2. Once the door trim has been removed a closing panel will be found on the inside face of the door inner panel. Undo and remove the securing screws and lift away the panel.

3. Disconnect the remote control arm (E) Fig.12.11 by extracting the clip at the remote control. Next disconnect the lower link from the private key lock (B) and finally the link to the locking knob (C).

4. Undo and remove the screws securing the lock assembly to the door end panel. Carefully lift away the dovetail and lock assembly together with the lower link.

5. Separate the lower link from the lock by extracting the spring clip.

6. Should it be necessary to remove the lock remote control assembly, undo and remove the three retaining screws securing it to the door panel and lift away the remote control assembly.

7. To remove the door push button, carefully lever the retaining clip (A) upwards which will release the push button housing. This may now be removed by withdrawing inwards into the door assembly.

8. On early produced cars the key lock barrel is held in position with a clip similar in shape to the push button housing clip. This is shown in Fig.12.13. Lever the retaining clip upwards which will release the key lock barrel. This can be removed by withdrawing inwards into the door assembly.

9. On later produced cars the key lock barrel is held in position by wires as shown in Fig.12.14. To remove the barrel it is necessary to raise the angled part of the wires and then with a pair of pliers withdraw them. The barrel may then be removed.

10 Refitting the door lock system is the reverse sequence to removal. It is, however, necessary to adjust the lock as detailed in the subsequent paragraph. This should be done before the interior trim is refitted.

11 The remote control handle and push button must have the same amount of free movement before they contact the rotary cam. Although this is a small amount, if it does not exist the door will open by the slightest touch and move onto the safety catch.

12 To adjust the remote control, slide it along its fixing hole slots so that the lever connecting the remote control with the lock has a slight amount of free movement before the lock begins to operate. This means that the lever (D) Fig.12.15 has a slight amount of movement and therefore the lock system is not loaded.

13 The push button adjustment bolt governs the clearance between the bolt head (A) Fig.12.16 and the lock contact plate (C). Clearance at this point should be between 1/16 and 3/32 inch. Once this condition has been achieved the push button should be fully depressed.

14 With the door in the open position check that the rotary cam of the lock is fully retracted to within 3°. This will ensure clearance of the striker plate latch when the door is opened.

15 To adjust the linkage for the key lock, first disconnect the link that connects the push button to the lock and also the lower link. This may be seen in Fig.12.12, Item 6.

16 Position the index hole in the push button backplate with the hole in the operating arm by inserting a 1/8th inch diameter rod as shown in Fig.12.17 (early models) or 12.18 (later models).

17 Now with the key turn the arm on the key lock to the fully locked position. Then push the sill locking knob to the locked position and engage the linkage on the lock arm using the most appropriate holes. Three holes are provided on the ends of the links to give the best possible assembly (Fig.12.19).

18 On later produced cars this condition is achieved by adjusting the nylon eye located in the end of the single link.

19 When refitting the lower link do not depress the return spring as this will affect synchronisation.

20 To adjust the remote control safety lock on the rear door handles first slacken the three handle securing bolts and move the handle out towards the lock.

21 Next engage the interior locking knob and move the handle away from the lock until it reaches its stop. Tighten the three handle securing bolts. Disengage the locking knob.

22 Recheck that there is still free movement before the remote control handle operates the rotary cam.

14. Front Door Window Regulator – Removal & Replacement

1. Refer to Section 12 and remove the door trim.

2. Undo and remove the nine closing panel retaining screws found on the inner door panel and lift away the panel.

3. Temporarily replace the window regulator handle and raise the glass to its fully up position.

4. Undo and remove the four bolts and spring washers that secure the window regulator mechanism. These bolts (A) are shown in Fig.12.20.

5. The window regulator may now be parted from the glass support channel and lifted away through the top of the door.

6. Refitting is the reverse sequence to removal. Make sure that the anti-rattle pad (B) is in position. It is recommended that all moving parts are lubricated with a little Castrol LM grease to ensure free movement.

15. Front Door Glass Frame – Removal & Replacement

1. Refer to Section 12 and remove the door trim.

2. Undo and remove the nine self tapping screws that secure the closing panel at the top of the door. Lift away the panel.

3. Undo and remove the four Phillips head set screws with star

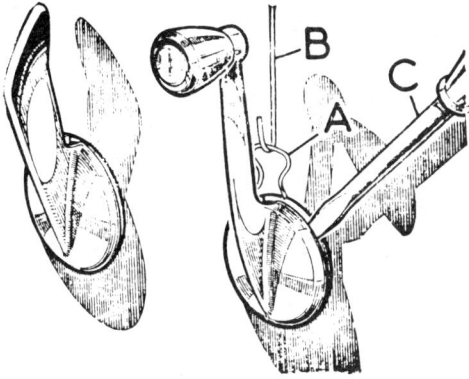

Fig.12.10. REMOVAL OF INTERIOR DOOR HANDLES
A Retaining spring clip   C Screwdriver
B Wire hook

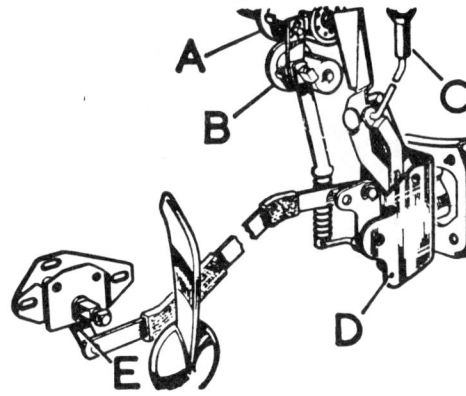

Fig.12.11. DOOR LOCK MECHANISM
A Push button   D Door lock
B Private lock   E Remote control and link
C Interior locking knob

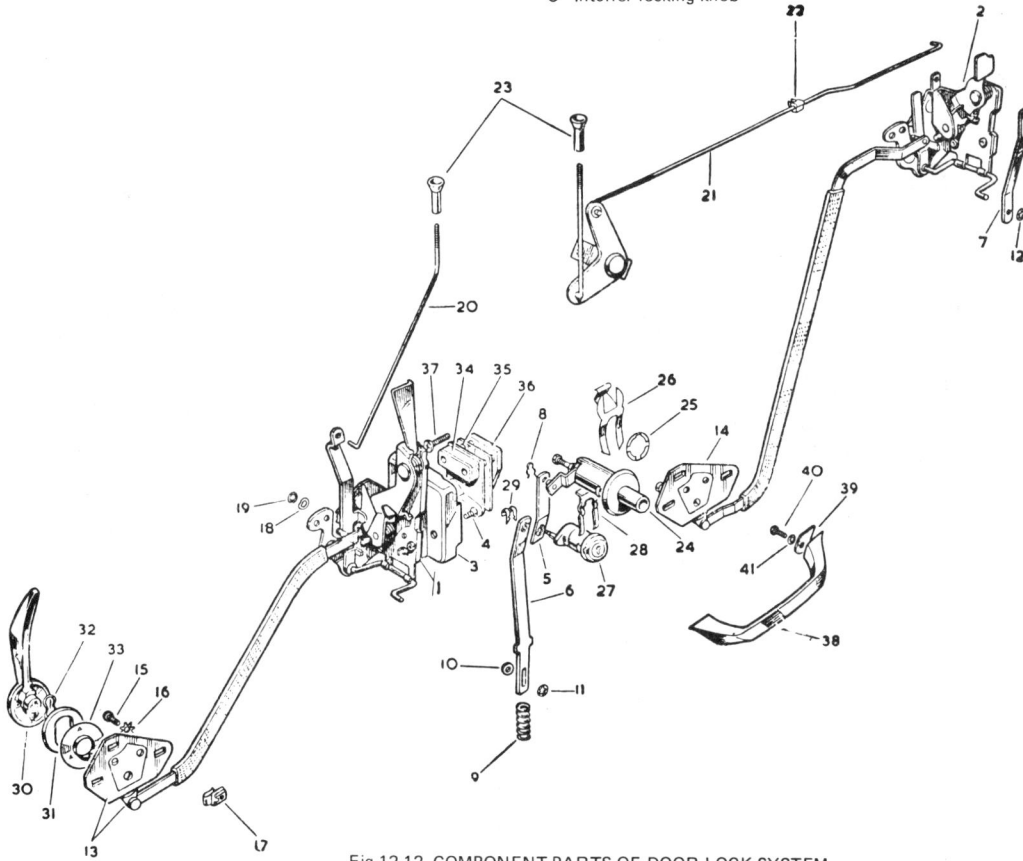

Fig.12.12. COMPONENT PARTS OF DOOR LOCK SYSTEM

1   Lock complete, front door, L.H.
2   Lock complete, rear door, L.H.
3   Dovetail for L.H. door locks
4   Special screw fixing lock to door
5   Upper link for L.H. front door lock
6   Lower link for L.H. front door lock
7   Connecting link for rear door lock
8   Retaining clip, link to push button
9   Spring for links, front door
10 Plain washer
11 'Starlock' washer
12 'Starlock' washer, link to rear door lock
13 Remote control and link, front door, L.H.
14 Remote control and link, rear door, L.H.
15 Screw
16 Shakeproof washer
17 Spire nut
18 Waved washer
19 Circlip
20 Locking rod, front door, L.H.
21 Bell crank and link for rear door safety catch, L.H.
22 Nylon steady bracket for rear door links
23 Interior locking knob, front and rear door
24 Push button, front and rear door, L.H.
25 Seating washer for push button
26 Retaining clip for push button
27 Private lock, front door, L.H.
28 Retaining clip for private lock
29 Spring clip, link to private lock
30 Inside door handle assembly
31 Escutcheon for inside door handle
32 Spring clip fixing inside door handle
33 Wearing plate for inside door handle
34 Striker for door lock, L.H.
35 Shim
36 Tapping plate
37 Screw fixing strikers to 'B' and 'D' posts
38 Outside door handle
39 Seating washer for outside handle
40 Set bolt
41 Shakeproof washer

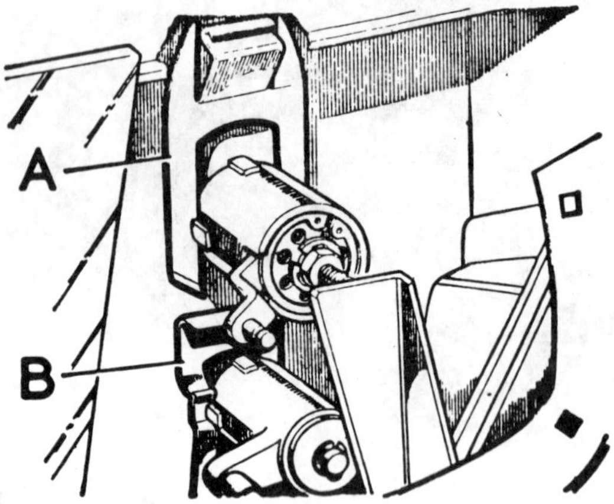

Fig.12.13. PUSH BUTTON & LOCK RETAINERS (EARLY MODELS)

A Push button clip retainer   B Private lock clip retainer

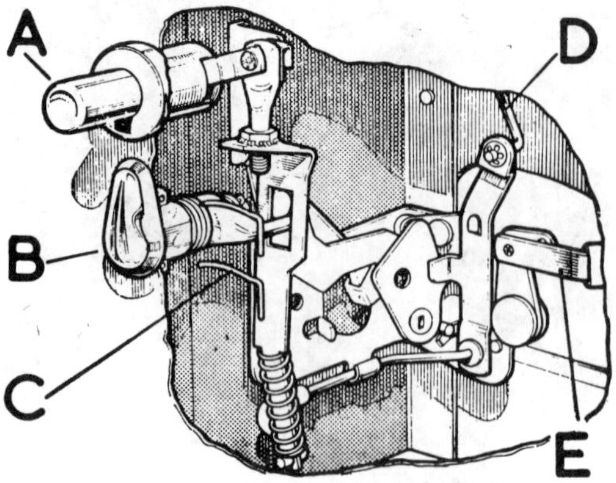

Fig.12.14. PRIVATE KEY LOCK (LATER MODELS)

A Push button   D Control rod for sill
B Private key lock   knob
C Retaining wires   E Remote control

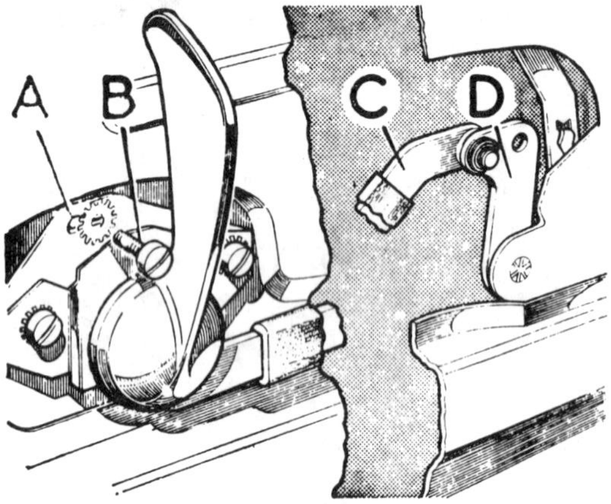

Fig.12.15. REMOTE CONTROL ADJUSTMENT

A Adjustment slots, move the   B Screws fixing remote control
   remote control towards the   to door
   door lock to increase clearance C Link for remote control
                                  D Remote control

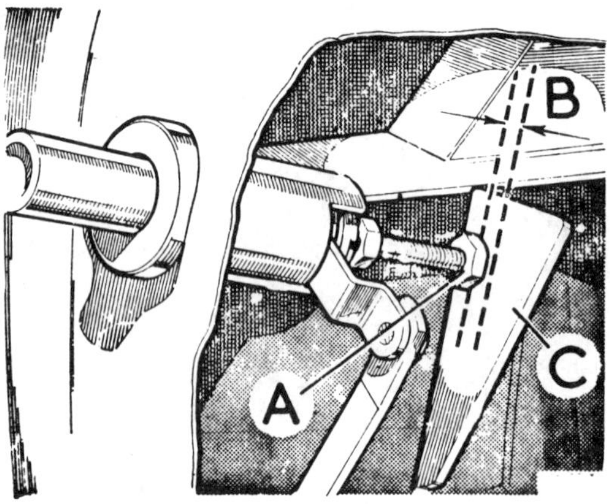

Fig.12.16. PUSH BUTTON ADJUSTMENT

A Head of adjustment bolt   C Lock contact plate
B 1/16 to 3/32 inch

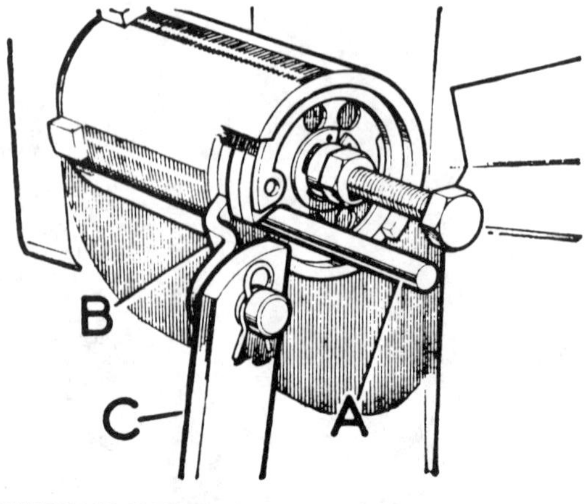

Fig.12.17. ALIGNMENT OF OPERATING ARM WITH PUSH BUTTON (EARLY MODELS)

A Rod 1/8 inch diameter
B Operating arm
C Upper connecting link

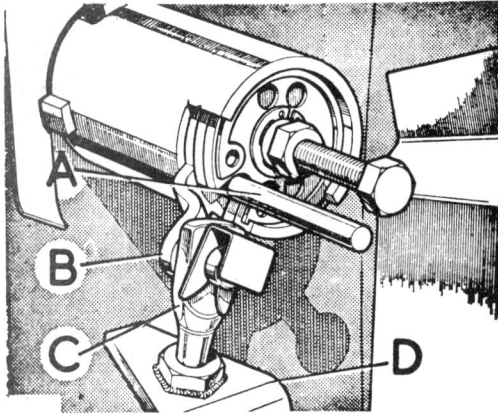
Fig.12.18. ALIGNMENT OF OPERATING ARM WITH PUSH BUTTON (LATER MODELS)

A Rod 1/8 inch diameter   C Link adjuster
B Push button lever   D Link

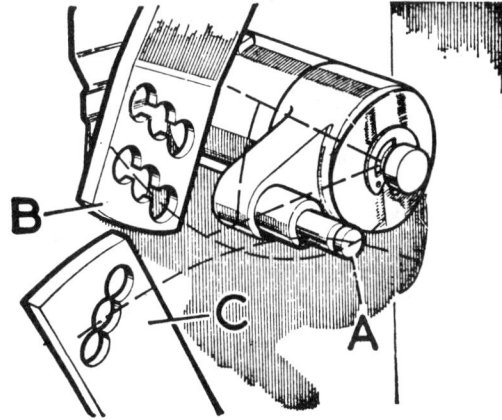
Fig.12.19. ALIGNMENT OF PRIVATE LOCK LINKS

A Operating arm   C Lower link, (spring
B Upper link   loaded).

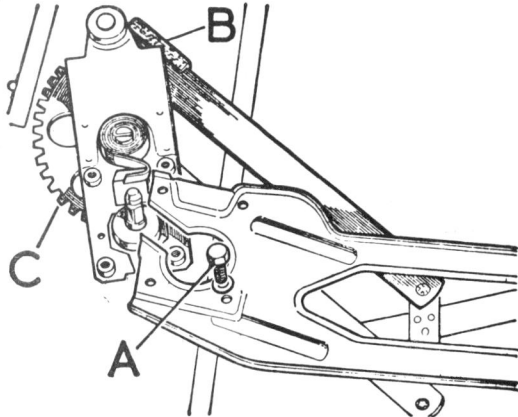
Fig.12.20. WINDOW REGULATOR MECHANISM

A Fixing bolts   C Window regulator
B Anti-rattle pad

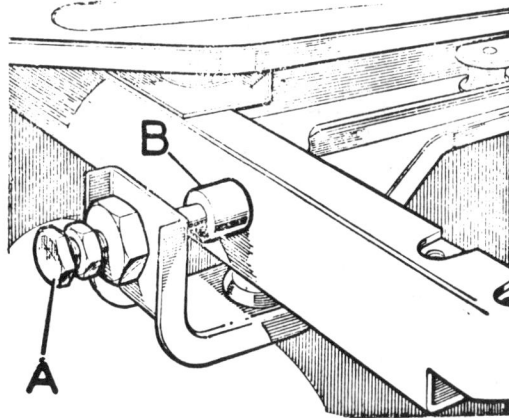
Fig.12.21. GLASS STEADY PAD

A Steady pad bolt   B Nylon steady pad

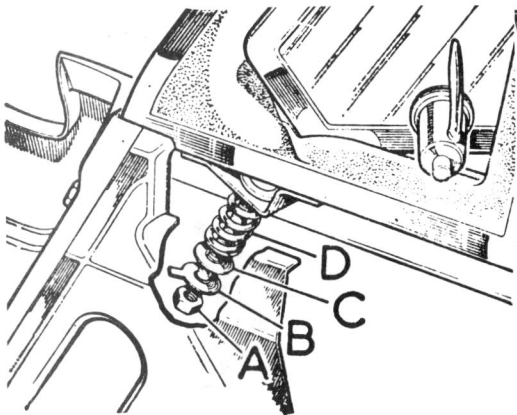
Fig.12.22. FRONT QUARTER LIGHT REMOVAL

A Nut   C Plain washer
B Tab washer   D Spring

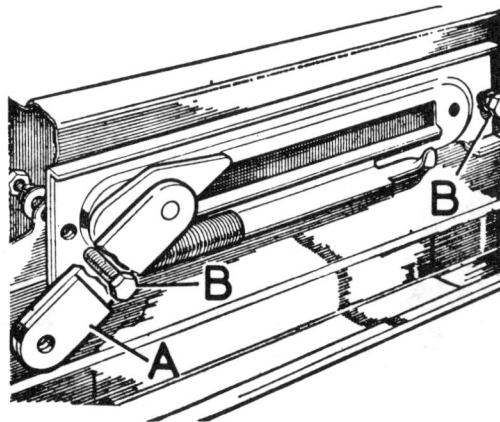
Fig.12.23. FRONT & REAR DOOR CHECK STRAP

A Check strap arm   B Fixing bolts

washers that secure the glass stop to the bottom of the door.

4. Temporarily replace the window regulator handle and lower the glass as far as it will go without straining the regulator. This will give access to the five Phillips head set screws with plain and spring washers, that secure the window frame cross rail to the top edge of the door.

5. Undo and remove the two Phillips head set screws and shakeproof washers that retain the window frame channel to the rear edge of the door and the two set bolts, flat and spring washers retaining the channel at the front edge.

6. Undo and remove the four set bolts, flat and spring washers retaining the bottom of the window channel, access to which will be gained through the aperture in the bottom of the door.

7. Undo and remove the two long through bolts, flat washers and cage nuts located at the front top of the inside of the door. Access to these is gained through the aperture in the door.

8. Remove the complete window frame, mechanism and rubber weather seal from the door.

9. Wind up the window again and remove the four bolts and spring washers that secure the window regulator. Also slacken off the glass steady pad locknut and unscrew the bolt. Do not however, completely remove. This is shown in Fig.12.21.

10 Remove the window regulator from the door. Take care that the glass does not fall down by supporting with a piece of wood.

11 Carefully slide the glass down the channel and remove from the inside of the door.

12 If necessary the glass support channel and glazing strip may be removed from the glass.

13 To refit the door glass carefully manoeuvre the complete assembly into position together with the weatherseal.

14 Refit the regulator assembly and connect it to the glass frame. Raise the glass and refit the glass regulator securing bolts loosely

15 Lower the glass and fit the four self tapping screws and star washers to the top of the frame.

16 Replace all other bolts with their plain and spring washers as were used and noted upon removal, but do not tighten fully yet.

17 With the window frame height carefully adjusted so that it is a good fit in the bodyframe tighten the four set bolts into the two brackets located at the bottom of the glass runners.

18 Adjust the frame inwards so as to apply a little tension to the weatherstrip seal at the top of the door and then tighten all securing bolts.

19 Refer to Fig.12.21 and adjust the nylon glass steady pad so as to minimise door glass movement therefore checking glass vibration.

20 Replace the window glass stop bracket and rubber pad and secure in position with the four set bolts, plain and spring washers.

21 Fit the top closing panel and secure with the self tapping screws.

22 Refit the waist moulding with four self tapping screws and slide the veneer strip into position.

23 Refit the locking knob to the threaded rod.

24 Apply a little Castrol LM grease to all lock and window regulator moving parts to ensure adequate lubrication.

25 With Bostik or other suitable adhesive secure the plastic waterproof sheet to the door inner panel.

26 Refit the door trim panel and secure in position by pushing the clips fully home.

27 Refit the arm rest and secure with two Phillips head set screws.

28 Refit the window winder handle and interior lock handle in their correct positions as was noted upon removal and secure with the retaining wire spring clips.

16. Front Door Quarter Light — Removal & Refitting

1. Refer to Section 12 and remove the door trim.

2. Undo and remove the nine self tapping screws that secure the closing panel at the top of the door. Lift away the panel.

3. Refer to Fig.12.22 and bend back the tab washer lock tab (B) undo the nut (A) and lift away the tab washer (B) plain washer (C), and spring (D) securing the front quarter light to the door. These are accessible through the door aperture.

4. The quarter light may now be lifted away from its location.

5. Refitting is the reverse sequence to removal. When the retaining nut for the quarter light has been locked in position apply a little Castrol LM grease to the spring washers and nut to prevent corrosion in the future.

17. Front & Rear Door Check Strap — Removal & Refitting

1. Refer to Section 12 and remove the door trim.

2. Remove the cap from the check strap pin and remove the check strap arm from the pin.

3. Remove one bolt and one nut and bolt located as shown in Fig. 12.23.

that secure the door check strap to the door and lift away the check strap.

4. Note that on later produced cars both door and trim panels were modified and the securing clip holes were raised by 3/8th inch from their original positions. If new trim panels are being fitted to the older type doors it will be necessary to drill new holes for the trim spring clips.

5. Refitting is the reverse procedure to removal. Lubricate all moving parts with Castrol GTX oil.

18. Rear Door Window Regulator — Removal & Replacement

The sequence for this operation is identical to that for the front door window regulator and full details will be found in Section 14 of this Chapter.

19. Rear Door Glass Frame — Removal & Replacement

1. Refer to Section 12 and remove the door trim.

2. Unscrew and remove the nine self tapping screws and also the two Phillips head screws with star washers that secure the closing panel to the door locking mechanism and lift away the closing panel.

3. Undo and remove the four Phillips head set screws with star washers that secure the glass stop to the door and lift away the stop.

4. Temporarily replace the window regulator handle and lower the glass to its fully down position.

5. Wind the window down to give access to the six Phillips head screws, plain washers and spring washers that secure the channel rails to the top of the door.

6. Undo and remove the two bolts, plain and spring washers that secure the side frame at the rear side of the door.

7. Undo and remove the two Phillips head screws and shakeproof washers next to the lower door hinge.

8. With a screwdriver ease out the rubber grommet (B) Fig.12.25. Undo and remove the nut, spring and plain washer adjacent to the top hinge.

9. Withdraw the spring clip that secures the bell crank link and disconnect the link from the door lock mechanism.

10 The complete window and mechanism may now be lifted away from the door together with the weather seal rubber.

11 Wind up the window glass and remove the bolts that secure the window winding mechanism, which may be lifted away.

12 Carefully slide the glass down its channel and lift away the glass.

13 The support channel and glazing strip may be removed from the glass.

14 To refit the glass, first reassemble it to the channel and then refit the window winding mechanism.

15 Slide the glass assembly into position with the top external weather seal rubber in place.

16 Wind the glass down so as to give access to the six Phillips head

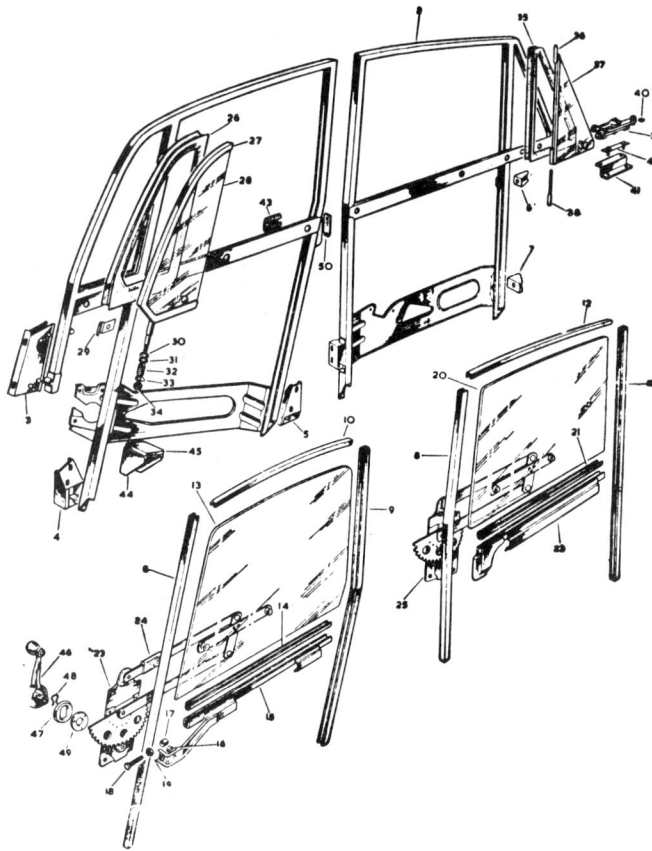

Fig.12.24. DOOR FRAME, GLASS & WINDOW WINDER COMPONENTS

1 Frame, front door, LH
2 Frame, rear door, LH
3 Bracket for door frame, (at waist), front door, LH
4 Bracket for door frame, front lower, front door, LH
5 Bracket for door frame, rear lower, front door, LH
6 Bracket for door frame, rear upper, rear door
7 Bracket for door frame, rear lower, rear door
8 Channel, front and rear door, front
9 Channel, front door, rear
10 Channel front door, top
11 Channel, rear door, rear
12 Channel, rear door, top
13 Glass assembly for front door, LH
14 Glazing strip
15 Support channel for glass, front door, LH
16 Self-sealing grommet
17 Steady pad for glass lifting channel, front door
18 Bolt
19 Locknut
20 Glass assembly for rear door, LH
21 Glazing strip
22 Support channel for glass, rear door, LH
23 Window regulator, front door, LH
24 Anti-rattle pad for front window regulator
25 Window regulator, rear door, LH
26 Vent seal, front door, LH
27 Ventilator assembly front door LH
28 Glass only for front door ventilator
29 Vent pivot clamping plate, front door, LH
30 Plain washer, brass
31 Plain washer, steel
32 Spring
33 Tab washer
34 Nut
35 Vent seal, rear door, LH
36 Ventilator assembly, rear door, LH
37 Glass only for rear door ventilator
38 Pivot pin for ventilator
39 Ventilator catch, rear door L.H.
40 Fibre washer for catch
41 Support angle for catch
42 Stud plate fixing support angle
43 Window steady pad
44 Glass stop bracket
45 Pad for glass stop bracket
46 Window regulator handle assembly
47 Escutcheon
48 Spring clip
49 Wearing plate
50 Shim, front door frame to inner panel

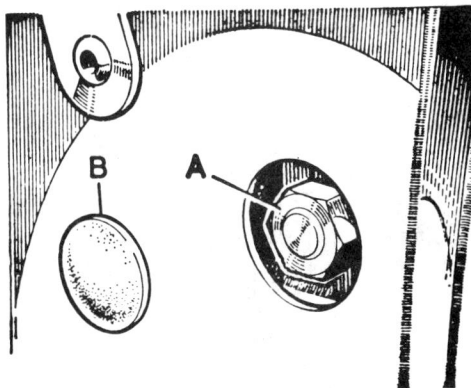

Fig.12.26. REAR DOOR GLASS FRAME BOTTOM FIXING
A Frame securing screws   B Cap

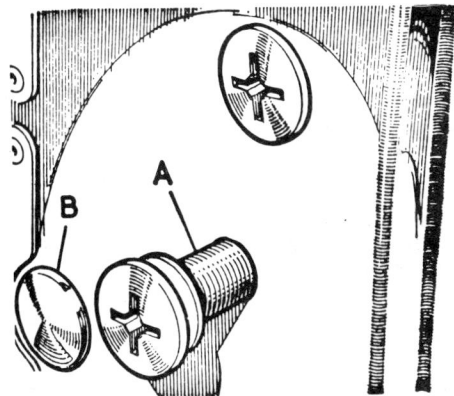

Fig.12.25. REAR DOOR GLASS FRAME TOP FIXING
A Bolt   B Rubber grommet

screws in the channel cross rail.

17 Replace all bolts, Phillips head screws, nuts and washers located as noted during dismantling but do not tighten at this stage.

18 Adjust the length of the window so as to be a correct fit in the body panel aperture and then tighten the four set bolts into the two brackets located at the bottom of the runners. Adjust the position of the frame inwards slightly so it will apply tension to the seal at the top of the door and now tighten all securing bolts.

19 Apply a little Castrol LM grease to all mechanical moving parts and check the window for ease of movement.

20 Refit the window glass stop bracket and secure with the four set bolts, plain and spring washers.

21 Replace the top closing panel and secure in position with the nine self tapping screws, and the door locking mechanism secured by Phillips head screws and start washer to the closing panel.

22 Refit the door trim panel as detailed in Section 12 of this Chapter.

20. Rear Door Quarter Light – Removal & Refitting

1. Remove the door trim as detailed in Section 12.
2. Undo and remove the nine self tapping screws, two Phillips head screws and star washers securing the closing panel to the door locking mechanism. Lift away the closing panel.
3. Unscrew the plastic knob from the door lock remote control and lift away the door frame bracket.
4. Slacken the pinch bolt that secures the bottom of the quarter light spindle located as shown in Fig.12.27.
5. Remove the spring clip that secures the remote control lever to the lock.
6. Unscrew the spindle from the bracket in the glass frame.
7. Undo and remove the screw and fibre washer that secures the catch to the quarter light. This screw is shown in Fig.12.27.
8. The quarter light may now be removed from the frame in the door.
9. Refitting the quarter light is the reverse sequence to removal. The bottom hinge pin should be adjusted so there is no up or down movement and then locked in position with the bolt.
10 Apply a little Castrol LM grease to the moving parts of the hinge and pivot to ensure ease of movement.

21. Bonnet – Removal & Replacement

1. Open the bonnet and secure in the open position. Place some old blankets over the rear of the wings and below the windscreen so that the paintwork is not damaged.
2. Disconnect the screen washer jet hose end. With the assistance of a second person take the weight of the bonnet (it is made of aluminium so it is not very heavy but take care because it is easily scratched or damaged). Undo the two retaining bolts to each hinge and lift away the bolts, spring and plain washers. These are located as shown in Fig.12.28.
3. Note that the forward hinge securing bolt also secures the front wing rear mounting bracket which is 'Pop' riveted to the wing panels.
4. With the bolts free, carefully slide the bonnet rearwards about 2 inches from the hinges to clear the wing upper mounting brackets. Lift the rear of the bonnet up and then lift away the complete bonnet from the front of the car. Put in a safe place where it will not be damaged.
5. Refitting is the reverse sequence to removal. Inspect the sealing around the hinge mounting plate and if rusted clean off and re-seal with Bostik 692.

22. Boot Lid, Hinges & Torsion Bars – Removal & Refitting

1. Open the boot and remove the two metal hinge covers on the boot lid.
2. An assistant at this stage must support the weight of the boot lid as otherwise it can be easily damaged by the securing bolts.
3. Place an old blanket under the rear screen and along the forward edges of the rear wings so that they will not be scratched.
4. Undo and remove the four bolts and plain washers that secure the hinge to the boot lid. (Fig.12.29.).
5. Very carefully lift away the boot lid.
6. To remove the hinge undo and remove the three bolts which secure the rear edge of the lower decker panel, so as to allow the panel to be eased out of its normal position.
7. Slacken the hinge bracket steady bolts.
8. Undo and remove the four bolts that secure the hinge to the body and lift away the hinges and torsion bars as a complete assembly.
9. Refitting the hinge and torsion bar assembly and also the boot lid is the reverse sequence to removal. To adjust the position of the boot lid in the aperture, the bolts securing the hinge bracket to the base should be slackened and adjusted as necessary.

23. Front Valance & Bumper – Removal & Refitting

1. Undo and remove the six bolts with spring and plain washers that secure the bumper bar to the brackets. Lift away the bumper.
2. Undo and remove the two bolts, spring and plain washers and nuts that secure the two outer brackets to the body.
3. It will now be necessary to remove the radiator grille. Undo the wing nuts and remove the badge from the centre of the grille.
4. Remove the plastic screw caps (B), Fig.12.30.
5. Undo and remove the six Phillips head screws and shakeproof washers that secure the two sections of the grille to the frame and lift away the grille.
6. Remove the six self tapping screws that secure the valance to the front member of the base unit.
7. Undo and remove the four nuts, plain and spring washers that secure the wing to the valance. (Fig.12.31). Remove the stud plates.
8. The front valance may now be removed from the base unit.
9. Refitting the valance and the bumper bar is the reverse sequence to removal. When refitting the two grille halves mount them loosely in position and then centralise to suit the badge clips.

24. Rear Valance & Bumper – Removal & Refitting

1. Undo and remove the six Phillips head set screws that secure the rear valance to the base unit. Also undo and remove the two special bolts (A) Fig.12.32 that secure the valance to the rear wing.
2. On early produced models note the reverse light cable colours at their connections as shown in Fig.12.33 and disconnect the cables.
3. Undo and remove the reverse lamp brackets (early models only).
4. Remove the two drive screws that secure the rear valance panel to the base unit behind the reverse light mounting bracket.
5. Undo and remove the four bolts, nuts and washer (A) Fig.12.33 that secure the bumper to the mounting bracket.
6. The bumper bar and valance may now be lifted away whilst taking care that the two cables without the connectors are fed through the rubber grommet.
7. Refitting is the reverse sequence to removal.

25. Front Windscreen – Removal & Refitting

1. Refer to Section 21 and remove the bonnet.
2. Refer to Section 31 and remove the air intake valance.
3. The stainless steel finishes must next be removed. It will be necessary to drill out the 'Pop' rivets securing the finishes to the base unit before they may be removed. Finally remove the stainless steel finisher at the top of the screen by sliding to one side.
4. Undo and remove the centre windscreen support bracket securing bolts, spring and plain washers and then lift away the support

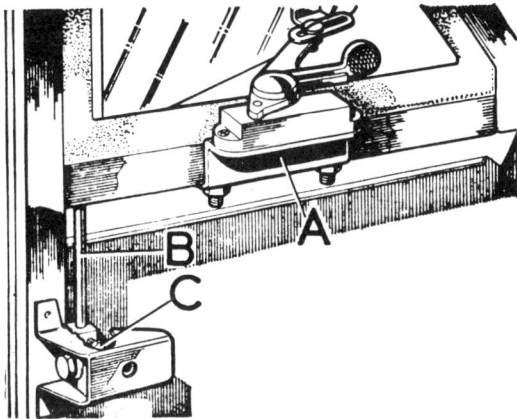

Fig.12.27. REAR QUARTER LIGHT FIXINGS

A Catch
B Pivot pin
C Set screw locking pivot
   pin

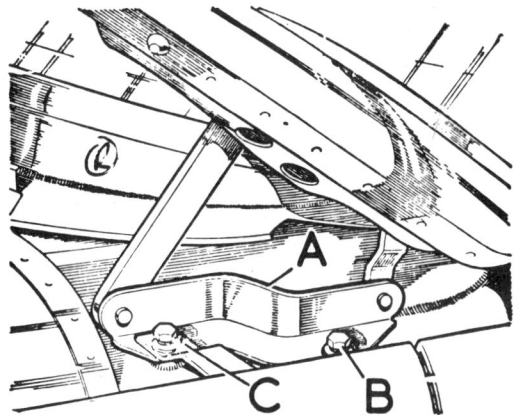

Fig.12.28. BONNET FIXINGS

A Bonnet hinge
B Bonnet fixings
C Bonnet and wing
   fixings

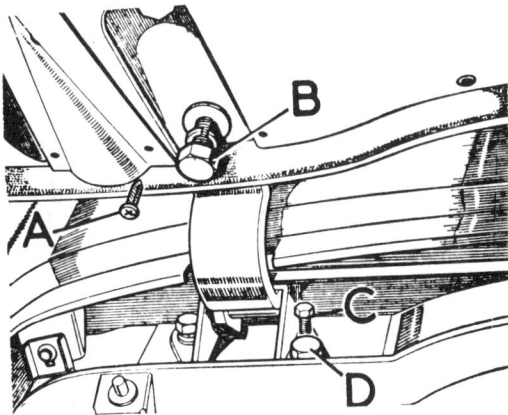

Fig.12.29. BOOT LID HINGE FIXINGS

A Drive screw fixing hinge
   cover
B Fixings, hinge to boot
   lid
C Steady post for hinge
D Fixings, hinge to base
   unit

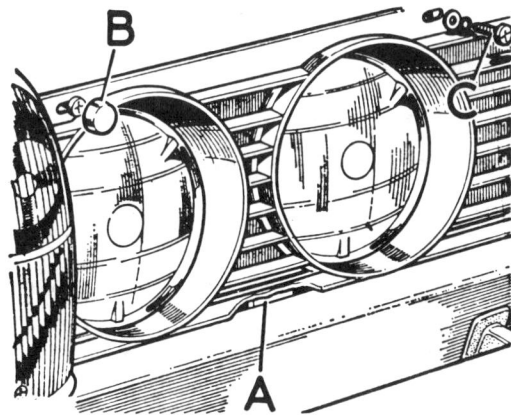

Fig.12.30. FRONT GRILLE FIXINGS

A Clip
B Plastic cap
C Fixings

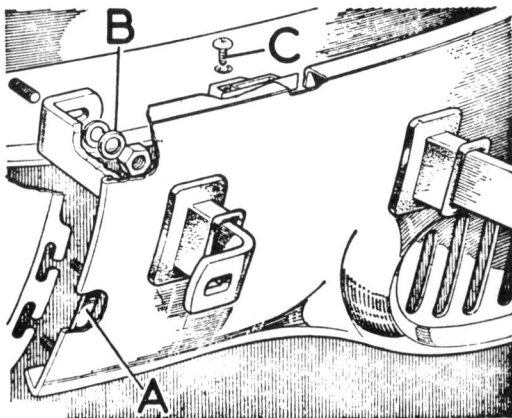

Fig.12.31. FRONT VALANCE REMOVAL
A Valance to front wing fixings B Fixings, bumper to base unit

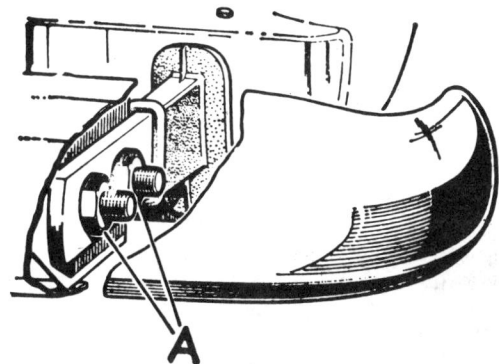

Fig.12.32. REAR BUMPER FIXINGS
A Securing nuts and bolts

bracket.

5. Release the lock nuts and lower the left and right-hand side support brackets.

6. The windscreen glass may now be removed together with the rubber surround. If the glass is to be renewed inspect the rubber surround for signs of perishing or damage and, if evident, a new rubber surround must be obtained and refitted. This is also applicable if the windscreen glass has shattered.

7. Now is the time to remove all pieces of glass if the screen has shattered. Use a vacuum cleaner to extract as much as possible. Switch on the heater boost motor but watch out for flying pieces of glass which might be blown out of the ducting.

8. Thoroughly clean off all traces of any sealing compound that may have been used on the glass and rubber seal.

9. Insert a little sealing compound such as Sealastik SR51 in the glass channel of the rubber seal and fit it to the glass.

10 Insert a length of cord to the rubber seal which will assist the fitting of the seal over the edge of the base unit.

11 Refit the bottom support channel to the glass.

12 Apply a little Sealastik SR51 to the screen channel in the base unit.

13 Mix up a little soft soap solution to act as a lubricant and apply to the exterior of the seal and insert the assembled screen into the aperture of the base unit.

14 Refer to Fig.12.36 and fit the neoprene blocks (A) between the base unit and windscreen support channel at each jacking point so as to maintain the correct clearance between the windscreen glass and base unit.

15 Loosely fit the right-hand and left-hand side mounting plates with the jacking bracket to the base unit.

16 Adjust the brackets upwards to the angle support of the screen using the hinges only.

17 Check that the rubber seal is in position round the glass and lift the lip of the seal over the base unit using the cord previously inserted into the rubber surround.

18 Refit the centre clamp bracket to the base unit with the nylon spacer correctly fitted and tighten just sufficiently to support the glass.

19 The left-hand and right-hand brackets should be adjusted until the glass is fully seating in the rubber seal.

20 It is important that a gap of 1/8th inch exists between the rubber seal and the edge of the channel as shown in Fig.12.37. The glass will be in a state of stress if the left-hand and right-hand brackets are over-tightened which could, in adverse weather conditions, cause it to break.

21 Lightly tighten the centre clamp bracket and lock in position.

22 Mask the area of the body next to the rubber surround to prevent scratching and fit the finisher along the top edge of the screen. Next refit the two screen side finishers and corner finishers and 'Pop' rivet the finishers so that they are secured in place.

23 Remove the masking tape and any excess sealing compound from around the rubber seal. Clean the windscreen both inside and out.

24 Refit the air intake valance as detailed in Section 31 and finally the bonnet as detailed in Section 21.

26. Rear Windscreen — Removal & Refitting

1. Refer to Section 33 and remove the filler unit and rear decker panel.

2. Undo the bolt (A) Fig.12.38 securing the centre clamp bracket to the base unit and lift away the clamp bracket.

3. Slacken the left-hand and right-hand jacking bracket lock nuts and lower the brackets (Fig.12.39).

4. With the help of an assistant push the windscreen from the inside of the car in a downwards direction and then outwards.

5. Remove the rubber seal.

6. Inspect the rubber seal for signs of perishing or damage, and if evident, a new seal should be obtained.

7. Clean all traces of old sealing compound from the screen glass and channel.

8. Smear a little Sealastik SR51 onto the rubber seal and fit the seal to the glass.

9. Insert a length of cord to the rubber seal which will assist in fitting it over the edge of the stainless steel trim.

10 Refit the bottom glazing seal to the glass.

11 Mix up a little soft soap solution to act as a lubricant and apply to the exterior of the screen and insert the assembled glass into the aperture of the base unit.

12 Position the angle support channel centrally on the base of the glass.

13 Refit the left-hand and right-hand side retaining brackets to the base unit and adjust the position of the brackets so as to just take the weight of the glass.

15 Refit the centre clamp bracket to the base unit with the nylon spacer and tighten just sufficiently to nip the glass.

15 Check that the rubber seal is in position round the glass and lift the lip over the stainless steel trim using the previously positioned cord.

16 Carefully adjust the left-hand and right-hand bracket evenly until the glass is fully home in the rubber seal. Take extreme care not to overtighten the brackets as the glass will be stressed which could, in adverse weather conditions, cause it to break.

17 Lightly tighten the centre clamp bracket to the glass and lock the bracket in position.

18 Refer to Section 33 and refit the rear decker panel and petrol filler neck.

19 Remove any excess sealing compound from around the rubber seal and then clean the windscreen both inside and out.

27. Moulded Cover Gearbox Tunnel — Removal & Refitting

1. Slacken the gearchange lever knob lock nut. Unscrew the gearchange lever knob.

2. Unscrew and remove the knob lock nut and spring retaining sleeve. Lift away the spring.

3. Remove the front and rear ashtrays from the gearbox tunnel moulded cover.

4. Locate and remove the two nuts to be found under the rear ashtray location and the single nut under the front ashtray location. (Fig.12.40).

5. Undo and remove the two Phillips head screws at the front of the moulded cover.

6. Lift up the flap at the forward edge of the rubber grommet base and remove the self tapping screw.

7. Undo and remove the two Phillips head screws securing the radio speaker grille to the console unit. (Fig.12.41). These screws are to be found between the petrol reserve control and choke control. Lift away the speaker grille. If a radio is fitted the loud speaker cables must be disconnected.

8. Remove the gearchange lever sleeve.

9. Slide both front seats as far back as they will go and keep the locking levers in their raised position.

10 Carefully roll back the handbrake rubber grommet and to assist removal of the grommet smear the handbrake handle and the grommet with a little Silicone grease.

11 Lift the forward edge of the cover over and off the gearchange lever.

12 Apply the handbrake and slide the cover forward and upwards so as to enable the leading edge to protrude into the aperture at the front of the console. At the same time carefully push the handbrake grommet off the handbrake handle.

13 Release the handbrake fully and lift away the cover assembly.

14 Refitting the gearbox cover tunnel is the reverse sequence to removal. Take care to remove all traces of Silicone grease from the handbrake lever.

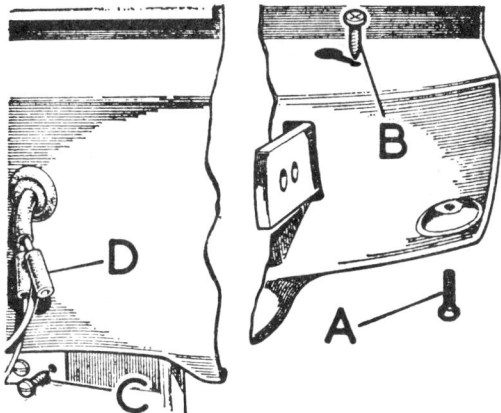

Fig.12.33. REAR VALANCE FIXINGS

A Valance to wing fixing
B Valance to base unit fixing
C Valance to rear jacking
   point fixing
D Reverse lamp wiring
   connectors (early models)

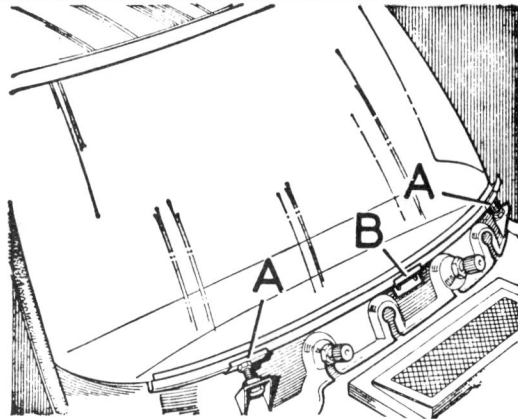

Fig.12.34. WINDSCREEN MOUNTING DETAILS

A Windscreen jacking points   B Centre retaining bracket

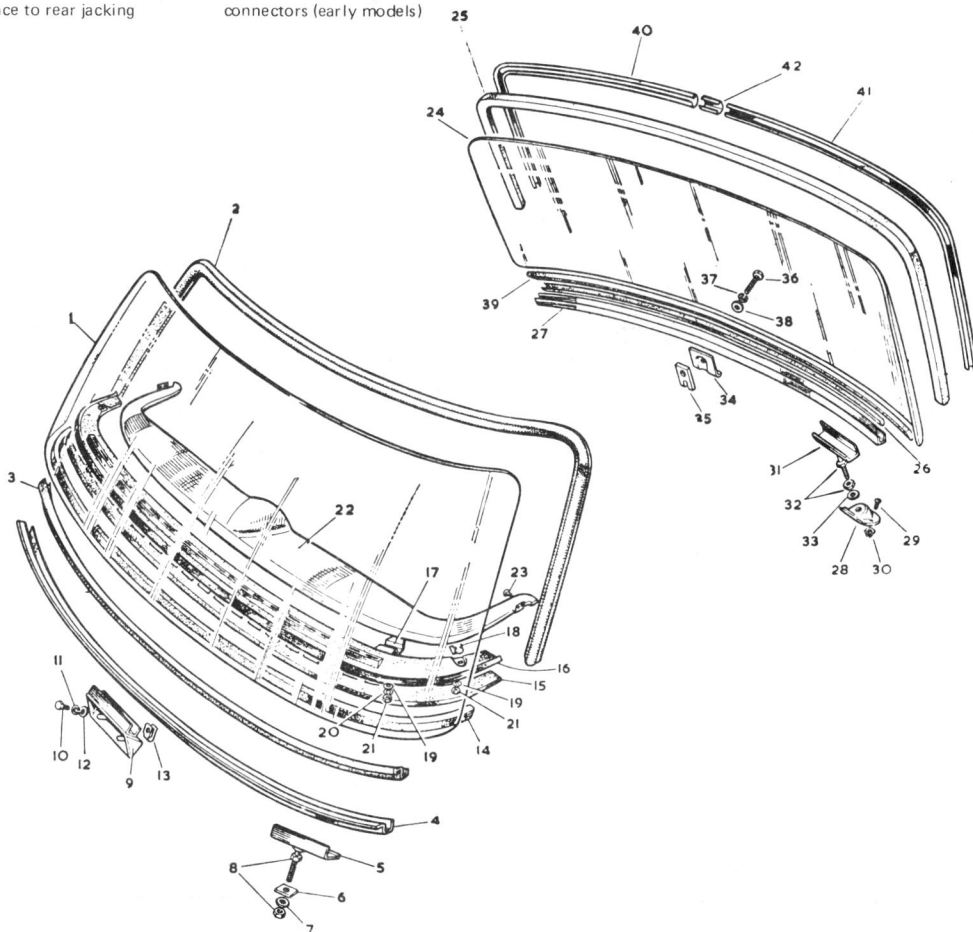

Fig.12.35. FRONT & REAR WINDSCREEN COMPONENT PARTS

1 Glass for windscreen	12 Plain washer	33 Plain washer
2 Seal for windscreen, top and sides	13 Spire nut	34 Centre clamp for backlight
	14 Seal, windscreen to base unit	35 Spacer for centre clamp
3 Glazing rubber, for windscreen, lower	15 Dust seal	36 Set bolt
4 Support channel for windscreen, lower	16 Finisher	37 Spring washer
	17 Retainer for screen demister finisher	38 Plain washer
5 Jacking bracket complete, for windscreen	18 Clip, screen finisher end, to dash	39 Seal, backlight to base unit
6 Plate for jacking bracket	19 Plain washer	40 Stainless steel finisher, R.H. for backlight
7 Plain washer	20 Spring washer	41 Stainless steel finisher, L.H. for backlight
8 Nut	21 Nut	42 Joint cover clip for backlight finishers
9 Centre clamp for windscreen	22 Screen rail complete	
10 Bolt	23 Drive screw fixing screen rail	
11 Spring washer	24 Glass for backlight	
	25 Seal for backlight, top and sides	
	26 Glazing rubber for backlight, lower	
	27 Support channel for backlight	
	28 Mounting plate for backlight jacking bracket	
	29 Drive screw	
	30 Nylon clinch nut	
	31 Jacking bracket complete for backlight	
	32 Nut	

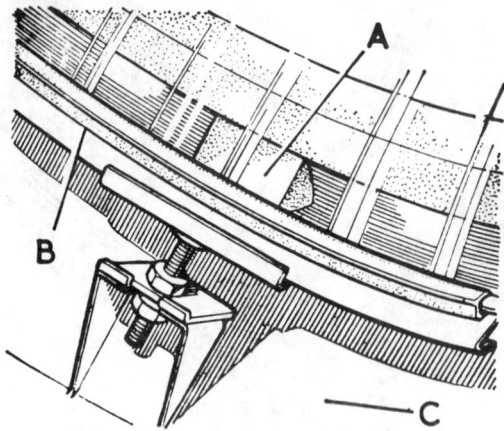

Fig 12.36. WINDSCREEN LOCATION NEOPRENE BLOCKS
A Neoprene block   C Base unit
B Support channel

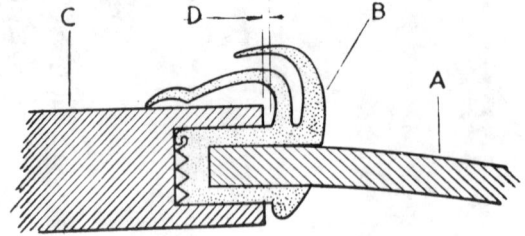

Fig.12.37. GAP BETWEEN RUBBER SEAL & EDGE OF CHANNEL
A Screen glass   C Base unit channel
B Rubber seal   D 1/8 inch gap

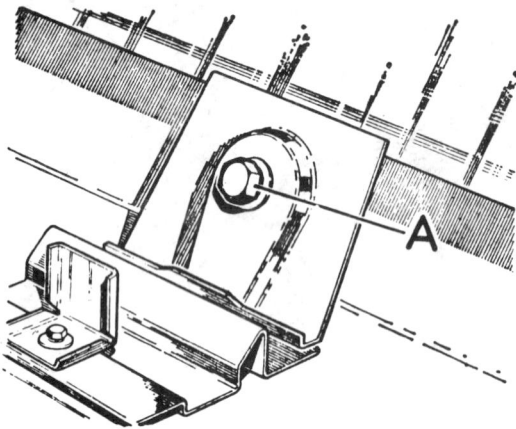

Fig.12.38. REAR SCREEN CENTRE FIXING BRACKET
A Bolt securing clamp to base unit

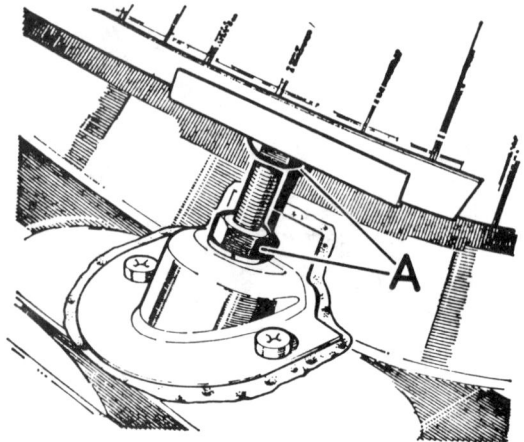

Fig.12.39. REAR SCREEN JACKING POINT
A Adjustment nuts

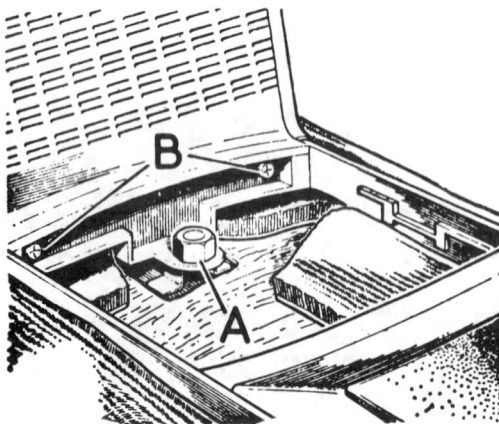

Fig.12.40. GEARBOX COVER FRONT FIXINGS
A Fixing nuts   B Console screws

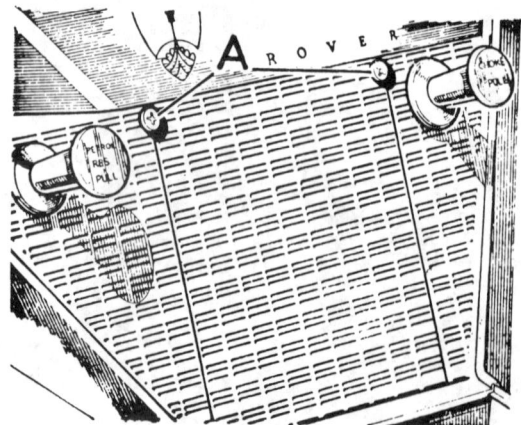

Fig.12.41. RADIO SPEAKER GRILLE FIXINGS
A Phillips head screws

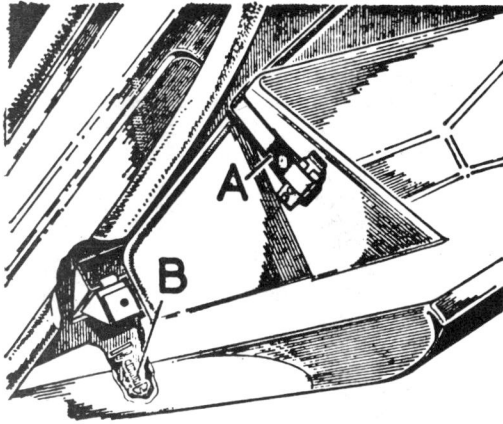

Fig.12.42. GLOVE BOX COMPARTMENT—REMOVAL
A Check strap   B Hinge fixings

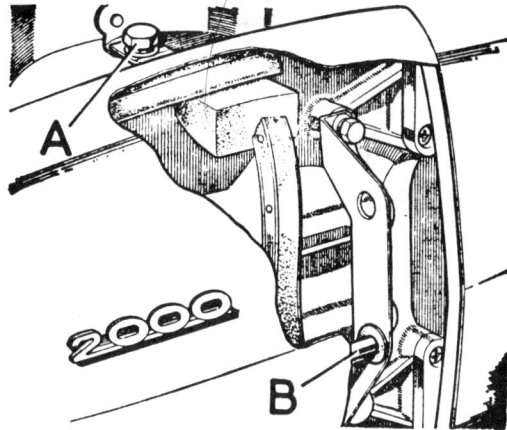

Fig.12.43. FRONT WING REAR FIXING POINTS
A Top rear fixing   B Dowel

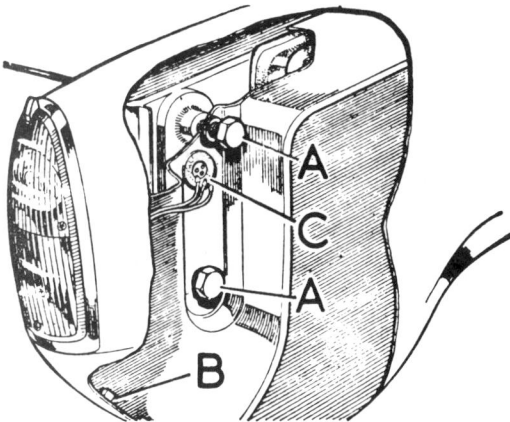

Fig.12.44. FRONT WING FRONT FIXING POINT
A Front fixing bolts   C Flasher and side light wiring
B Wing to valance fixings   connector

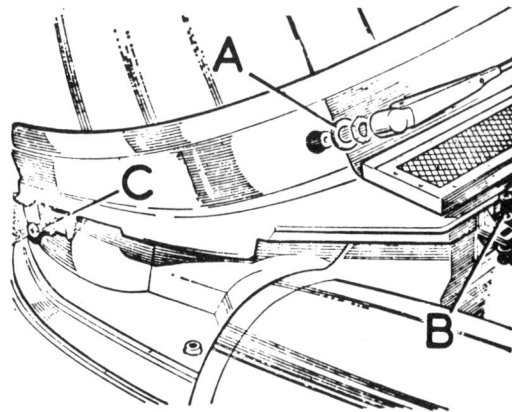

Fig.12.45. AIR INTAKE VALANCE FIXING POINTS
A Windscreen wiper fixings   C Air intake valance to base
B Air intake valve to heater   unit fixings
   fixings

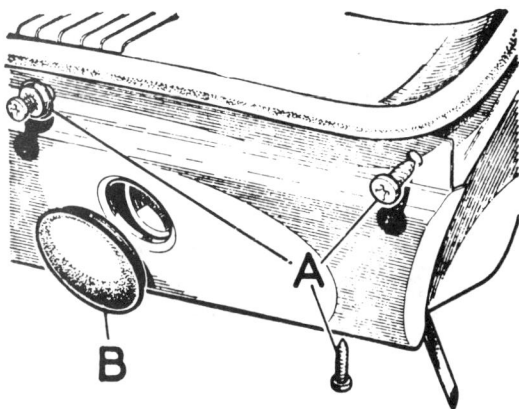

Fig.12.46. BODY SILL PANEL
A Sill panel to base unit fixings B Rubber jacking point plug

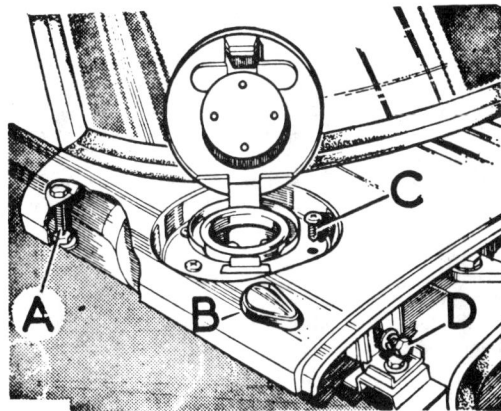

Fig.12.47. REAR DECKER PANEL & PETROL FILLER CAP
FIXINGS
A Decker panel fixing - front   C Petrol cap fixings
B Fuel filler cap lock   D Decker panel fixing - rear

28. Glove Box — Removal & Refitting

1. Open the glove box lid and detach one strap end for the right-hand box and two strap ends for the left-hand box from the spring clips as shown in Fig.12.42.
2. Undo and remove the two bolts that retain the hinges on both the right-hand and left-hand glove boxes. These hinges are shown in Fig.12.42.
3. The glove box may now be lifted away.
4. Refitting is the reverse sequence to removal. If a new glove box is to be fitted to the driver's side of a LHD car make sure that the new glove box has a larger radius at the upper end of the large compartment so as to give the necessary clearance for the speedometer cable.

29. Radiator Grille - Removal & Refitting

1. Open the bonnet and support in the fully open position.
2. Remove the badge from the centre of the radiator grille assembly.
3. Remove the six plastic screw caps (B) Fig.12.30.
4. Undo and remove the six Phillips head screws and shakeproof washers that secure the two sections of the grille to the frame. Lift away the two sections of the grille.
5. Refitting is the reverse sequence to removal. Care must, however, be taken when refitting the two halves of the grille as they should be assembled loosely until the badge is in position.

30. Front Wing — Removal & Refitting

1. Should it be necessary to remove the front wing because of corrosion subsequent to the fitting of a new panel (photo) or to give better access to the front suspension as detailed in Chapter 11, first open the bonnet and support in the fully open position.
2. Disconnect the battery earth terminal for safety reasons.
3. Clean the electrical cables and connections located behind the front wing and identify the cable coding. If this is difficult, use strips of insulation tape so that the cables may be reconnected correctly. Release the three cables (photo).
4. Undo and remove the bolt, spring washer and flat washer (A) Fig.12.43 that secure the rear top edge of the panel to the base unit. It will be seen that this bolt is also used to secure the hinge.
5. Remove the nuts, plain washers and spring washers together with stud plate from the valance.
6. Undo and remove the two bolts fixing the top front of the wing, working underneath the wheel arch (photo).
7. Refer to Fig.12.44 and undo and remove the two screws (A) from the underside of the wing. It is quite possible that at this point there will be evidence of serious corrosion on an early produced car so it will probably be easier to rip the wing off if it is to be renewed and then remove the two securing screws. (See photo 30:9).
8. Ease the wing forwards so as to bring it clear of the dowel (B), Fig.12.43 and lift it away from the side of the car (photo). If the panel is being removed to give better access to the front suspension system take great care not to scratch the wing on the front bumper by suitably marking off the area with masking tape or wrapping the end of the bumper bar in a little cloth.
9. This photo shows the two front wing fixings left in position when a badly corroded wing is to be renewed and the original one was ripped off.
10 The rear edge of the front wing is located by a dowel in a rubber grommet. (photo). Soak the dowel in penetrating oil and remove the securing nut and spring washer.
11 Fit the dowels to the new wing panel (photo).
12 Undo and remove the four Phillips head screws that secures the front light lens to the light body. Lift away the lens and foam rubber seal.
13 Undo and remove the three screws that secure the light body to the front wing. The light body may now be withdrawn from the front wing.

14 Fit the wing into position on the body taking care not to scratch the paintwork on the bumper bar (photo). If necessary wrap a little cloth around the end of the bumper bar.
15 Insert the special nuts into the wing as shown in this photo. These nuts are a nylon equivalent to the speed nut variety. They are positioned in the wing so that when the bolt is entered and screwed up the nut will grip tighter.
16 Refit the wing securing bolts, screws and nuts.
17 It will be seen from the previous photos that a wing painted in primer was used. This is because a new wing panel may be obtained either factory painted in a standard colour or finished in primer. It will be found to be cheaper if either a factory painted panel is obtained or a new panel in primer obtained and sprayed when fitted to the car.
18 It is recommended that all exposed bolts and nuts are coated with an anti-corrosive paint.
19 Rub down the primer with some wet and dry flatting paper and any bare metal areas should be given a coat of undercoat. Further information on preparing the panel for respraying and applying the paint is given in Section 5.
20 Insert the three nylon caps into the front light aperture (photo).
21 Refit the light body and foam rubber backing and secure with the three screws (photo). Replace the light lens and foam rubber backing and secure with the four Phillips head screws.
22 Reconnect the light cables in the same positions as were noted upon removal from the connectors under the front wheel arch.

31. Air Intake Valance — Removal & Refitting

1. Open the bonnet and support in the fully open position.
2. The windscreen wiper arms must next be removed but before removing a wiper arm turn the windscreen wiper switch on and off to ensure that the arms are in their normal parked position, parallel to the bottom of the windscreen.
3. To remove the arms, pivot the arm back and pull the wiper arm head off the spline sleeve. If the arm proves difficult to remove a screwdriver with a wide blade can be used to lever the wiper arm head off the spline. Care must be taken not to damage the spline.
4. Refer to Fig.12.45 and remove the drive screws (C) securing the valance to the base unit, located at the left-hand and right-hand sides. Also the two screws (B) with spring and plain washers and nuts that secure the air intake valance to the heater.
5. Undo and remove the nuts and washers securing the windscreen wiper wheelboxes to the air intake valance.
6. Lift away the air intake valance.
7. Refitting is the reverse sequence to removal. Make sure that when replacing the windscreen wiper arms they are positioned so that they are in the correct relative parked position and then press the arm head onto the spline drive until it is fully home on the spline.

32. Body Sill Panels — Removal & Refitting

1. Refer to Fig.12.46 and remove the Phillips head set screws and also the drive screws that secure the valance to the base unit.
2. Lift away the body sill panel.
3. Refitting is the reverse sequence to removal.

33. Rear Decker Panel — Removal & Refitting

1. Open the boot compartment lid. Undo and remove the four screws that secure the trimmed boot inner panel covering the petrol tank. Lift away the panel.
2. Slacken the hose clips that secure the top petrol filler hose and cut the hose to remove it.
3. Undo and remove the four screws (C) that secure the petrol filler unit. These are visible once the filler cap has been opened as

30.8

30.14

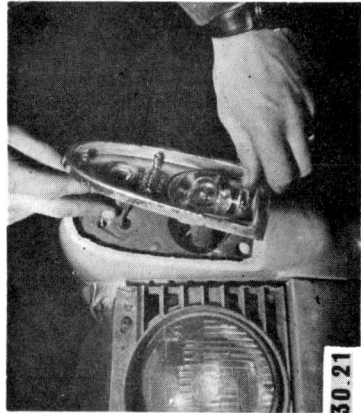

30.21

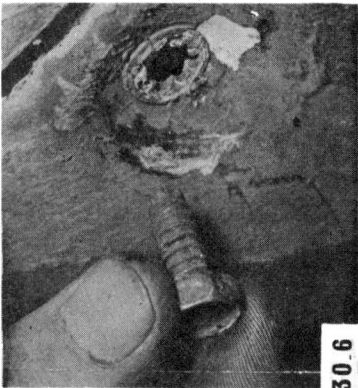

30.6

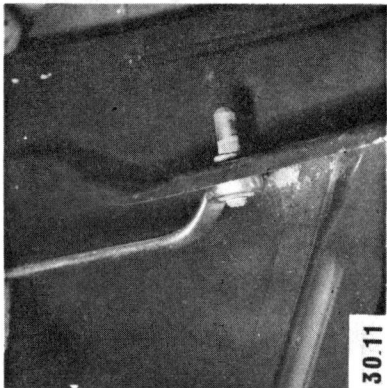

30.11

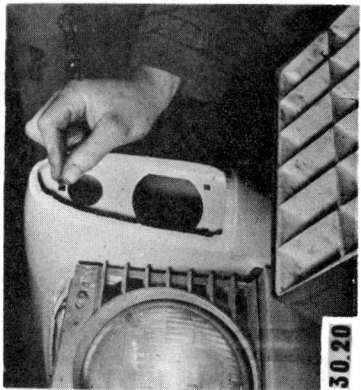

30.20

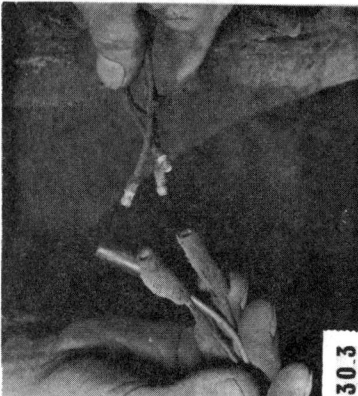

30.3

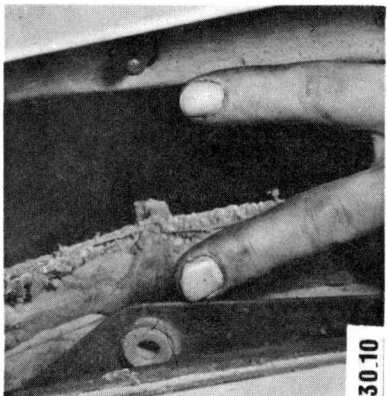

30.10

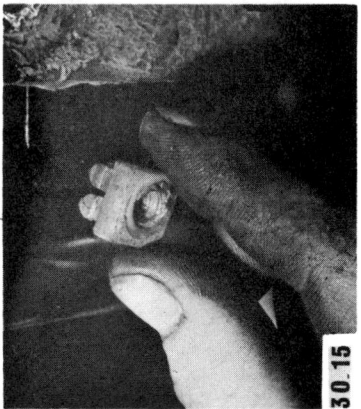

30.15

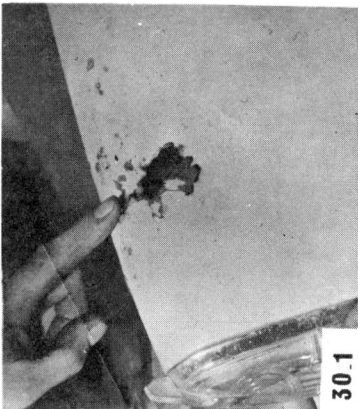

30.1

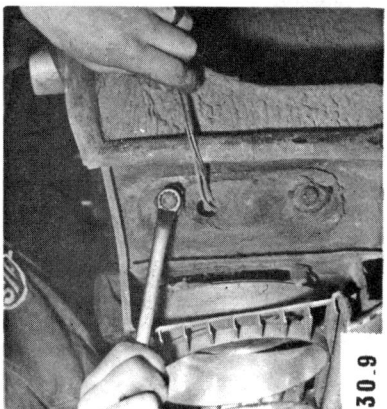

30.9

shown in Fig.12.47.

4. Remove the complete filler unit from the rear decker panel.

5. Release the rubber grommet retaining spring clip and remove the rubber grommet from the filler cap orifice.

6. Undo and remove the two nuts with plain and spring washers that secure the decker panel to the base unit. These are located at the right-hand and left-hand corners of the decker panel and are readily accessible through the boot.

7. Undo and remove the three nuts and bolts (D), Fig.12.47 that secure the rear edge of the decker panel and carefully lift away the panel.

8. Refitting is the reverse sequence to removal. It will be necessary to fit a new petrol filler hose.

9. To give a good seal apply a little Bostik 1753 sealing compound to the filler end of the top hose and a little Bostik 692 round the mounting bolts.

34. Fuel Filler Cap Lock — Removal & Refitting

1. Refer to Section 33 and remove the rear decker panel.

2. Open the fuel filler cap and place a large rag in the filler pipe neck to stop dirt ingress.

3. Undo and remove the special set bolt (H), Fig.12.48 and shakeproof washer (G) that secures the lever (F) to the lock. Lift away the lever and shaped washer (E).

4. Remove the large nut (D) that secures the lock (A) to the decker panel and withdraw the lock (A) washers (B) and distance piece (C) from the panel.

5. To refit the lock place it in the decker panel with a washer each side of the panel and the distance piece on the underside and secure in position with the large nut.

6. Refit the special washer and the lever making sure that it will engage in the filler cap catch. To do this temporarily fit the filler cap to the decker panel.

7. Lock the lever in position with the shakeproof washer and special set bolt.

8. The rear decker panel should now be refitted.

9. Lubricate the lock by placing a little Castrol GTX oil on the key and inserting and withdrawing it several times.

35. Rear Quarter Panel — Removal & Refitting

1. Remove the complete rear seat assembly by first lifting out the rear seat cushion. Undo and remove the two self tapping screws that secure the bottom of the rear seat squab to the body, and lift away the squab from inside the car.

2. Undo and remove the two Phillips head drive screws that retain the rear quarter trim. Carefully ease the trim panel forwards so as to release it from its retaining clips. When free lift the trim panel away.

3. Undo and remove the three Phillips head screws adjacent to the edge of the rear screen (Fig.12.49).

4. Undo and remove the three chrome plated Phillips head screws that are located in the body adjacent to the rear edge of the door glass surround.

5. Carefully lift away the rear quarter panel.

6. Refitting is the reverse sequence to removal. It is necessary to seal the three rear screw heads with a little Sealastik SR51 or similar sealing compound.

36. Rear Wing — Removal & Refitting

1. Open the boot lid and support in the fully open position.

2. Disconnect the battery earth terminal for safety reasons.

3. Make a note of the cable connections at the connectors, located within the boot compartment, to ensure correct reassembly. Disconnect the cables at this point.

4. Remove the trim from the inside panel within the boot compart-

ment which will give access to the rear wing mounting bolts.

5. Undo and remove the two bolts with spring and plain washers that secure the wing to the body side panel. One will be found inside the boot (photo), and the second one located on the underside of the car at the rear corner. These are shown in Fig.12.50.

6. Note that on later produced models studs mounted onto plates are used instead of bolts. It may be necessary to soak the nuts in penetrating oil as they will probably be well rusted in position.

7. Undo and remove the special bolt and shakeproof washer that secures the rear valance to the rear wing (photo).

8. Remove the two bolts, spring and plain washers that secure the forward edge of the rear wing to the rear door pillar. These are accessible once the rear door is opened and shown in Fig.12.50 and photo.

9. Refer to Fig.12.50 and remove the nut and bolt (B) adjacent to the mud flap.

10 Remove the rear wing (photo) and at the same time withdraw the rear light cluster cables through the rubber grommet in the side of the boot inner panel.

11 Next remove the Phillips head screws that secure the lens to the light cluster and lift away the lens and foam rubber seal.

12 Undo and remove the screws that secure the lamp body to the rear wing and lift away the lamp body and foam rubber seal (photo).

13 The new wing panel may be obtained either factory painted in the standard colours or finished in primer. It will be found cheaper if either a factory painted panel is obtained or the new panel, in primer and sprayed when fitted to the car.

14 A new weatherstrip should be fitted to the rear wing and for this a drill and 'Pop' rivet gun will be necessary. If necessary self tapping screws can be used instead of the 'Pop' rivets.

15 Place the weatherstrip in position and starting at the ends drill the holes in the panel and secure the little bracket with a self tapping screw or rivet (photo), as each hole is drilled.

16 Proceed along the length of the weatherstrip until the last mounting bracket at the centre has been secured.

17 Carefully ease the wing panel in position making sure that the rear quarter panel, rear decker panel or doors are not accidentally scratched (photo).

18 Refitting is now the reverse sequence to removal. It is recommended that all exposed bolts and nuts are coated with an anti-corrosive paint.

19 As will be seen from the photographs a wing panel in primer was used so it will be necessary to mask up the surrounding panels using masking tape and newspaper as shown, so as to prevent overspray on the panels (photo).

20 Rub down the primer with some wet and dry flatting paper and any bare metal areas should be given a coat of undercoat. Further information on preparing the panel for respraying and applying the paint is given in Section 5 (photo).

37. Heater & Ventilation System — General

A cross sectional view of the heater is shown in Fig.12.54. It will be seen that the air flows through a built-in grille, assisted as necessary by a blower and passes to an air mixing chamber with various valves to control the temperature and direction of air movement.

The 'air inlet valve' is opened by means of the main control lever (A), Fig.12.52 in the right-hand side of the console and will allow air to pass into the air mixing chamber.

There is a 'wind blown' flap which is automatically opened by the ram effect of the air entering the mixture chamber as the car travels along the road. This air flow bypasses the blower fan.

The electric blower fan, when switched on, takes its air supply from the mixing chamber and increases the air flow above that effected by the forward motion of the car. The blower fan is controlled by a three position switch so as to give: off, half-speed and full-speed conditions. When the blower is operating the wind-blown flap will close owing to the greater internal pressure.

The heater distribution (C), Fig.12.52 and temperature control

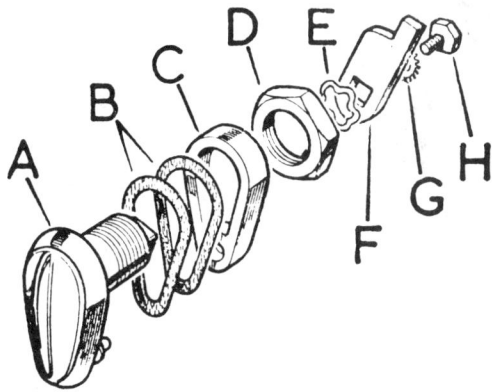

Fig.12.48. FUEL FILLER CAP LOCK FIXINGS

A Private lock
B Washers for lock
C Distance piece
D Nut fixing lock
E Special washer for lever
F Lever
G Shakeproof washer
H Special set bolt

Fig.12.49. FIXING POINTS FOR REAR QUARTER PANELS
A Fixing screws

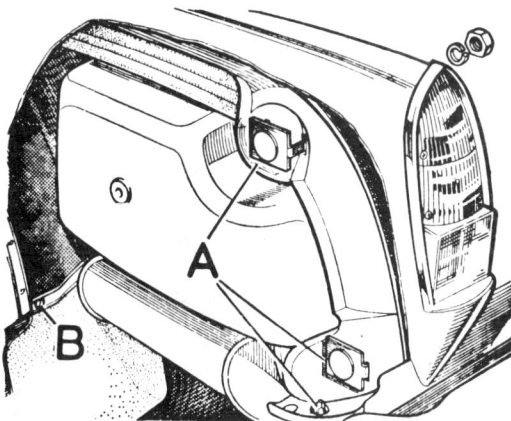

Fig.12.50. REAR WING REAR ATTACHMENT POINTS

A Wing to base unit fixings   B Mud flap fixing

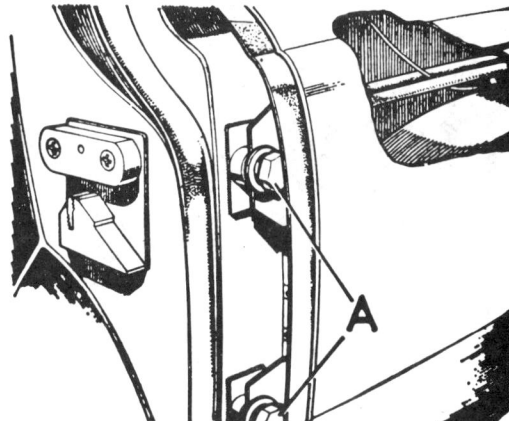

Fig.12.51. REAR WING FRONT ATTACHMENTS
A Bolts securing wing to door pillar

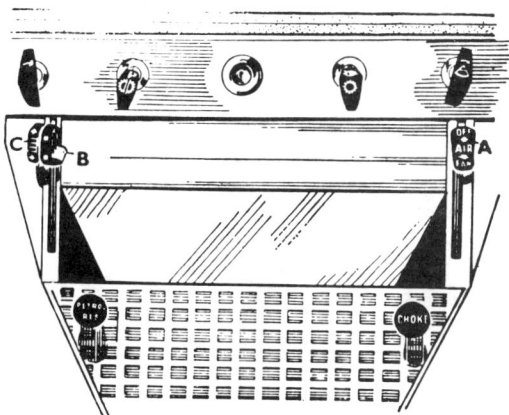

Fig.12.52. HEATER CONTROLS

A Main control   C Distribution control
B Temperature control

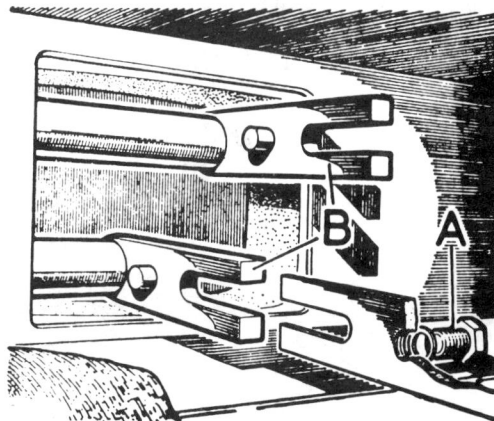

Fig.12.53. HEATER CONTROL CONNECTIONS
A Lever fixing bolt   B Levers

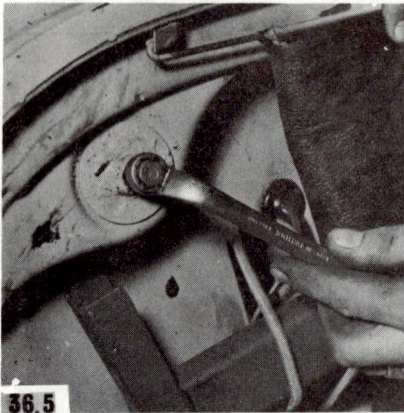

36.5

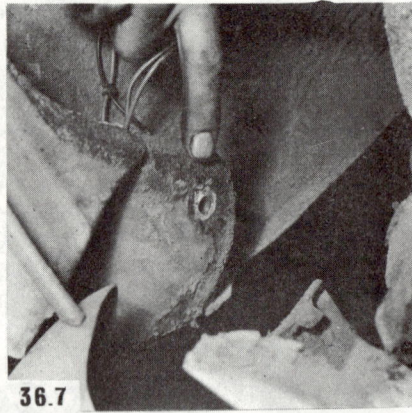

36.7

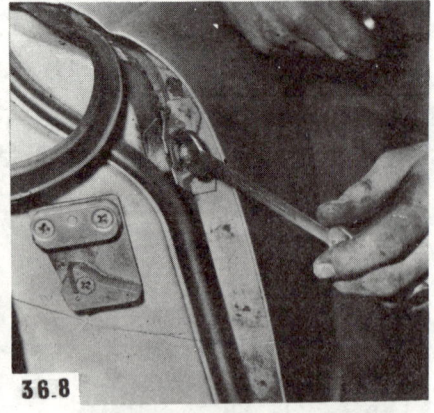

36.8

36.10

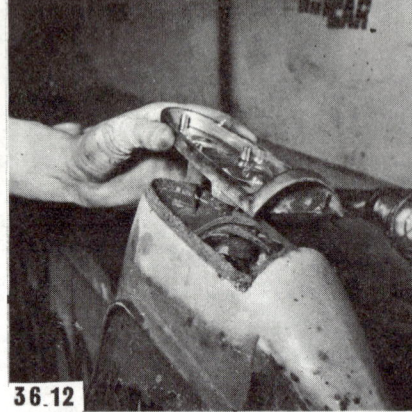

36.12

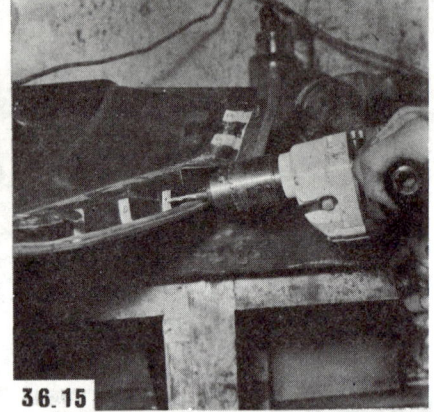

36.15

36.17

36.19

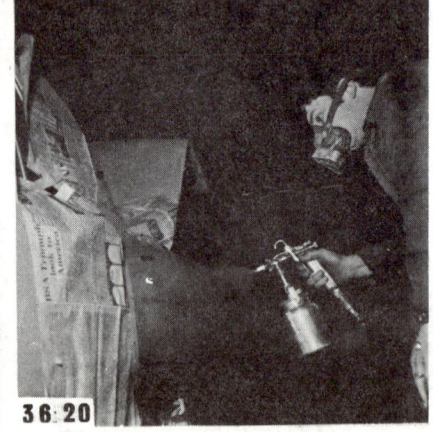

36.20

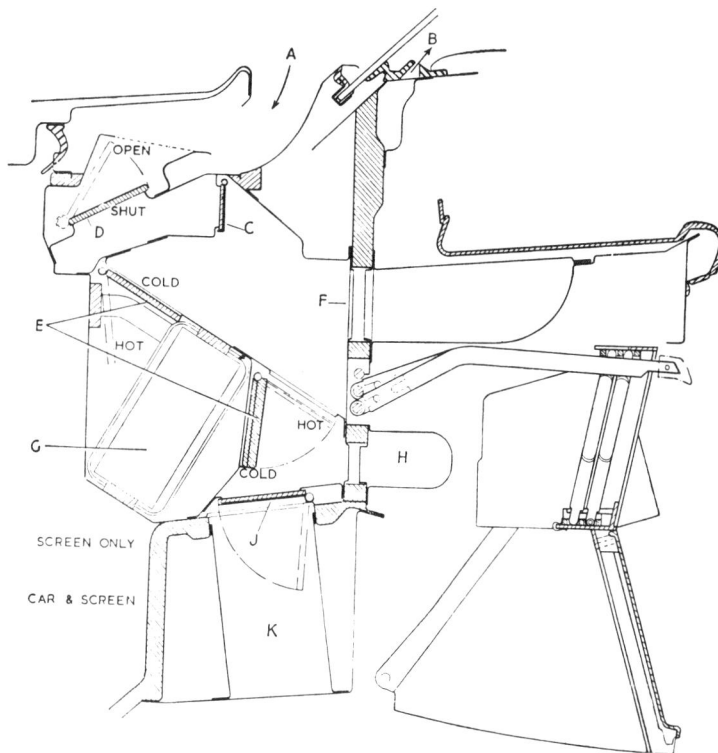

Fig.12.54. CROSS SECTIONAL VIEW THROUGH HEATER & DEMISTER UNIT

A Fresh air inlet	D Main valve	position shown dotted	H Inlet to demister duct
B Outlet from demister unit	E Mixing valves, shown in	F Inlet to face-level vents	J Distribution valve
C Windblown valve	'Cold' position, full heat	G Heater matrix	K Inlet to car heater

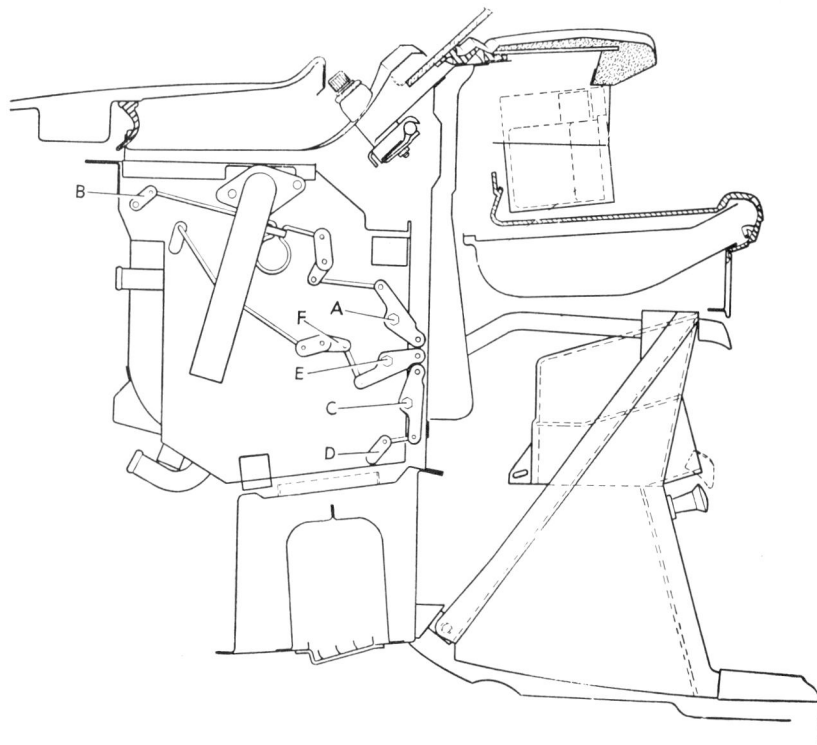

Fig.12.55. HEATER & VENTILATION SYSTEM LINKAGES

A Locking screw, upper lever	C Locking screw, lower	D Link, lower	lever
B Link, upper	lever	E Locking screw, centre	F Link, centre

(B) are located on the left-hand side of the heater control panel and control the air blending valves, mixing the hot and cold air ready for passing to the car interior. These valves are positioned on either side of the heat exchanger radiator and are so connected that when one is open the other one is closed.

The air outlet valve is able to shut off the air flow into the car through the outlets at floor level. It is closed to increase the air flow through the demist nozzles when the car is being used during very cold conditions.

One of the features of the heater and ventilation system is the built-in face level ventilation ducts whereby a large outlet in the cold air passage allows fresh air to be directed to the instrument fascia panel ducting.

38. Heater — Removal & Refitting

1. Refer to Section 28 and remove both the glove boxes.
2. Disconnect the heater controls from the adjustment forks underneath the dashboard. These fixing bolts are shown in Fig.12.53.
3. Refer to Chapter 2, Section 2 and drain the cooling system.
4. The windscreen wiper arms should next be removed. Turn the windscreen wiper switch on and off to ensure the arms are in their normal parked position parallel to the bottom of the windscreen.
5. To remove the arm pivot it back and pull the wiper arm lead off the spline sleeve. If an arm proves difficult to remove, a screwdriver with a wide blade can be used to lever the wiper arm head off the spline but take care not to damage the spline.
6 Refer to Section 31, and remove the air intake valance.
7 Make a note of the electrical cable connections to the electrical screen washer pump. The green cable is connected to the right-hand (—VE) terminal. Disconnect the two cables.
8. The screen washer may now be lifted from its bracket and rubber retaining strap.
9. Disconnect the accelerator coupling shaft bracket from the relay.
10 Make a note of the electrical cable connections to the booster motor, and disconnect the electrical cables.
11 Disconnect the vacuum advance system and brake servo pipe from the top of the engine top cover.
12 Undo and remove the three shaped nuts that secure the engine top cover in place. Lift away the sealing washers noting the assembly order and finally lift away the engine top cover.
13 Lock two nuts onto the rear stud on the engine that secure the top cover, and unscrew the rear stud.
14 Slacken the hose clips at the hose connections to the heater unit and disconnect the hoses.
15 Undo and remove the four bolts, plain washers and spring washers that secure the heater to the bulkhead panel.
16 Hold the air intake flap (Fig. 12.54) in the closed position and carefully lift out the complete heater unit.
17 To refit the heater unit is the reverse sequence to removal. It will

be necessary to hold the air intake flap in the closed position before finally positioning the heater unit.
18 Make sure that the heater unit seats correctly on the seating rubbers and also that the blower motor cables are not trapped.
19 Refill the cooling system as detailed in Chapter 2, Section 4 and then run the engine to check for cooling system leaks at the heater unit.

39. Heater Control - Adjustment

Upon reference to Fig.12.55 it will be seen that the heater control linkages are all on the left-hand side of the unit so that if the performance is not satisfactory the linkage may be checked in the following manner:—
1. Slacken off the upper lever locking screw and move the main control lever on the control console (Fig. 12.52) approximately ¼ inch below the upper detent position.
2. Move the upper link on the heater box in a clockwise direction and hold in this position with firm finger pressure so making sure that the valve is well seating onto the rubber pad. Tighten the locking screw.
3. Move the control knob to the 'warm air only' detent position. This will be approximately half way down the full travel. Look through the intake grille to see if the metal back of the inlet valve is almost touching, or actually touching, the small piece of foam rubber pad which acts as a stop.
4. If it is observed that the inlet valve is not in the correct position slacken the adjusting screw and slide the end of the spring link into the trunnion so as to increase the effective length of the link by between 1/16 to 1/8 inch. Retighten the screw firmly.
5. Now repeat the operation in paragraphs 1, 2 and 3. It is important that the length of the spring link is not increased more than necessary as otherwise there will be insufficient adjustment at the screw (A), Fig.12.55 to ensure that the flap can be shut when the control is in the 'off' position.
6. If the distribution of air is not corresponding to the control setting, slacken off the locking screw on the lower lever and then set the distribution lever on the console (Fig.12.52), approximately ¼ inch below the upper detent position.
7. Apply firm finger pressure to the lower link on the heater box in a clockwise direction so making sure that the heater valve is well seating onto the rubber pad. Tighten the locking screw.
8. If the temperature of the air entering the car does not correspond to the position selected by the temperature control lever on the console, slacken the locking screw and set the temperature control lever to approximately ¼ inch below the upper detent position.
9. Apply firm finger pressure to the centre link on the heater box in a clockwise direction and, maintaining this pressure, tighten the locking screw.

Chapter 13 Supplement

Contents

1 Introduction

Unless otherwise stated, it can be assumed that those specifications not given for the 2200 models are as per the 2000 range (see relevant Chapter).

Since the introduction of the Rover 2000, the modifications carried out have generally been of a minor nature and are described in the appropriate sections of this Chapter.

Major changes include the installation of emission control equipment and on 1974 models the uprating of the engine capacity to 2205 cc (designated Rover 2200).

Modifications to vehicles operating in North America are also fully described in the individual sections of this Chapter.

2 Specifications

Engine (model SC/TC 2200):

Capacity	134.6 in.^{3} (2205 cc)
Bore	3.563 in. (90.5 mm)
Stroke	3.375 in. (85.7 mm)
Compression ratio	9 1
Max. torque (DIN)	SC 126 lb/in. at 2500 rev/min.
	(TC 135 lb/in. at 3000 rev/min.)

Cooling System

Coolant capacity	14 pints (8 litres)

Fuel system and carburation:

Models	SC/TC 2200
Fuel tank capacity	15 gals. (68 litres)
Carburettor type	SC and automatic transmission — one
	SU HIF6
	TC — two SU HIF6

Braking system:

Revised specification (all models including 2200)
Girling type

Friction pad swept area	Front 204 in.^{2}
	Rear 152 in.^{2}
	Total 356 in.^{2}
Front brake diameter	10.366 in.
Dual circuit specification	
Vacuum servo units	Two Lockheed 7 in. dia. with 5/8 in.
	(15.5 mm) slave cylinder
Tandem master cylinder	Girling 7/8 in. (22 mm) dia.
	maximum stroke 1.22 in. (31 mm)
Hydraulic fluid	Castrol - Girling Crimson

Electrical system:

Alternator

Type	Lucas 18 ACR
Nominal output	45 amps
Field coil resistance	3.2 Ohms
Minimum permissible brush length	0.300 in (8 mm)

Starter motor

Type	Lucas 2 M 100 (pre-engaged)
Windscreen wiper motor	Lucas 15 W

Bulbs (2200 models)

The bulbs given below are those that differ from the earlier 2000 models - (see Specifications in Chapter 10)

	Wattage
Side lights	4
Rear licence plate	4
Instrument panel lights (SC models)	3.6
Interior light	10
Map light	4
Switch panel	6
Automatic selector illumination	3
Hazard warning	2
Rear screen heater switch light (where fitted)	2

Suspension and steering:

Front road springs (North America 1968 onwards)

Number of working coils	7.35 (nominal)
Free length	17.12 in. (434.8 mm) nominal
Spring rate	170 lb/in. ± 5%

3 Engine

Crankcase emission control

1 The layout of the systems for single and twin carburettor installations have been modified as shown in Figs. 13.1, 13.2.
2 The locations of the top cover breather and the flame trap are shown in Figs. 13.3 and 13.4.
3 Servicing procedure for the latter components remains as described in Chapter 1 Section 60.

Starter ring gear - revised renewal procedure

1 The instructions given in Chapter 1, Section 37 for the removal and refitting of flywheel starter ring gear are superseded by the following operations. The procedure for the renewal of the drive plate starter ring gear on vehicles equipped with automatic transmission remains as given.
2 Secure the flywheel securely in a vice fitted with jaw protectors.
3 Drill a 3/16 in (4 mm) diameter hole mid-way between the root of the uppermost tooth and the outer edge of the fly-wheel. Drill carefully ensuring that the drill does not foul the flywheel.
4 Driving a sharp cold chisel directly downward from above the hole, split the ring gear from the flywheel. During this operation, stand directly behind and above the flywheel in case the ring gear should fly out sideways when split.
5 Heat the new ring gear to between 225 and 250°C (437 and 482°F). These temperatures are normally attainable in a domestic oven and should not be exceeded.
6 Position the flywheel on a flat surface and then drop the ring gear onto the flywheel with the square edges of the teeth against the flywheel flange. When correctly heated there will be a gap

between the inner diameter of the ring gear and the flywheel of at least 1/16 inch (1.6 mm).
7 Keep the ring gear pressed against the flange and allow it to cool naturally.

Modifications (chassis nos. 43600001A and 44500001A onwards)

Oil pressure gauge

An electrically operated oil pressure gauge is fitted as standard. The transmitter is located in the coupling at the lower end of the oil feed pipe on the right-hand of the cylinder block.

Additional oil pressure switch (TC models 10.0 : 1.0 compression ratio)

These models when fitted with emission control have an additional oil pressure switch as an essential component of the anti-run-on valve circuit. This transmitter switch is located towards the rear of the cylinder block.

4 Cooling system

Radiator filler cap - change of location

Later model vehicles are fitted with a shallower radiator necessitated by a lower bonnet line. In consequence the filler cap is located on the upper corner of the radiator side tank.

Anti-freeze solution

It is recommended that a solution containing 33 1/3% of recommended anti-freeze is used in the cooling system to provide protection down to -25°F (-32°C). This will also reduce corrosion within the system and the coolant should be renewed annually.

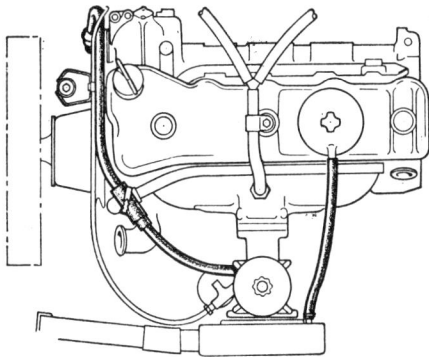

Fig. 13.1. Layout of SC crankcase emission control system (Sec. 3)

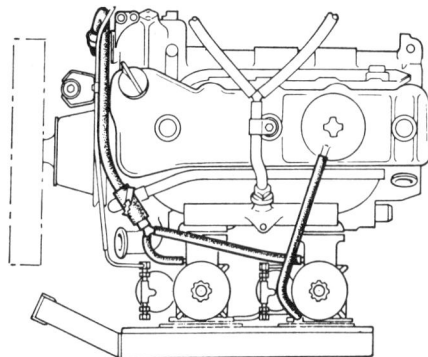

Fig. 13.2. Layout of TC crankcase emission control system (Sec. 3)

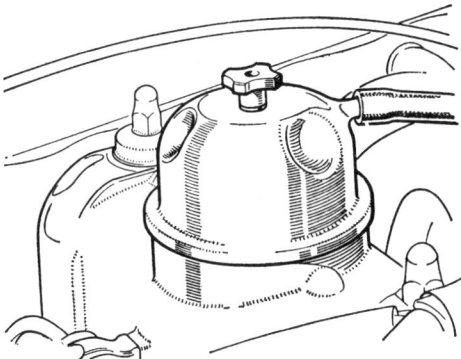

Fig. 13.3. Rocker box cover breather cap (crankcase emission control) (Sec. 3)

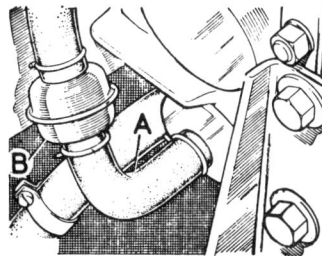

Fig. 13.4. Location of flame trap (crankcase emission control) (Sec. 3)

A Hose   B Trap

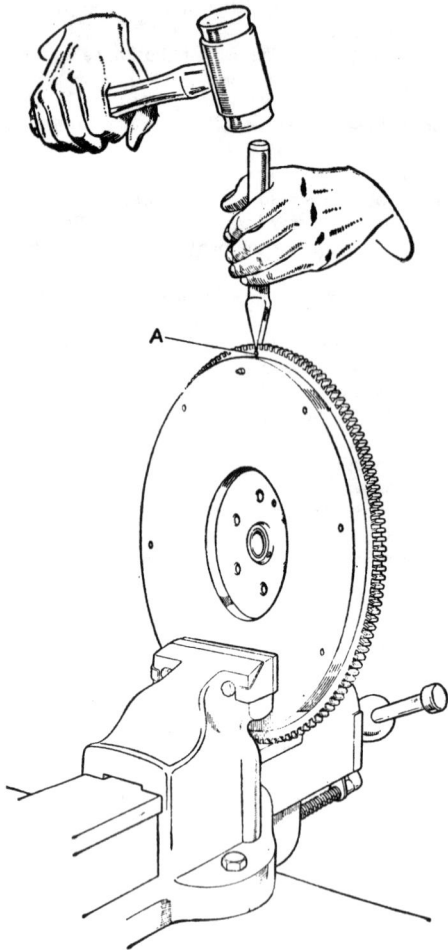

Fig. 13.5. Removing starter ring gear from flywheel A drilled hole

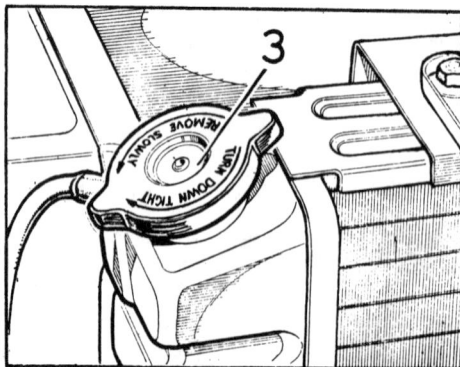

Fig. 13.7a   SC type air cleaner (emission control)

2   Air intake
3   Engine breather and temperature compensator hoses
4   Non-return valve and vacuum capsule pipes

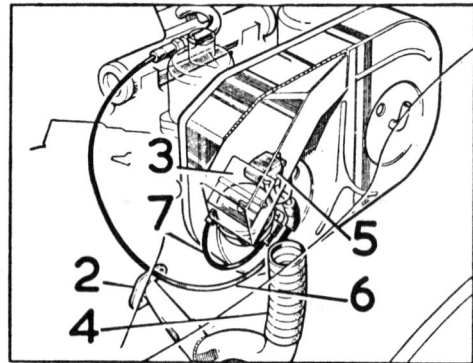

Fig. 13.7b   TC type air cleaner (emission control)

2   Hot box
3   Flap valve
4   Hose (hot box to flap valve)
5   Temperature sensor
6   Pipe from inlet manifold
7   Pipe to vacuum capsule which operates flap valve

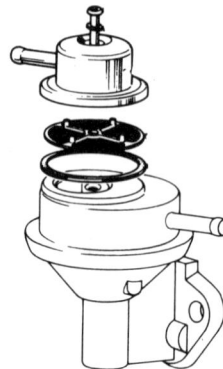

Fig. 13.6. Re-location of radiator filler cap
3   Pressure cap

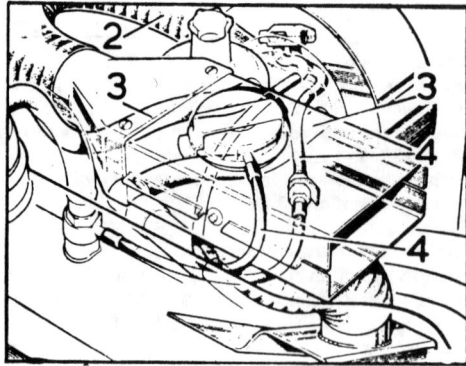

Fig. 13.8 Exploded view of Unitac type fuel pump

5 Fuel system and carburation

Air cleaner - single carburettor type with emission control

1 This type of air cleaner, fitted to vehicles operating in North America and other territories incorporates a device for maintaining air intake temperatures at 100°F (38°C) when ambient temperatures are below this level.

2 The air cleaner element should be renewed every 12000 miles (20000 km) by carrying out the following procedure.

3 Disconnect the air intake trunking at the cleaner body.

4 Disconnect the engine breather and temperature compensator hoses at the cleaner body.

5 Disconnect the vacuum pipes from the non-return valve and vacuum capsule.

6 Detach the air cleaner from the carburettor flange.

7 Remove the air cleaner cover by unscrewing the wing nut.

8 Renew the element and gaskets (where necessary). Reassembly is a reversal of dismantling.

9 Occasionally check for satisfactory operation of the flap valve by starting the engine from cold and checking that the valve starts to open slowly within a few minutes of engine operation. If it fails to do so, then either the operating vacuum capsule or vacuum switch is faulty.

Air cleaner - twin carburettor type with emission control

1 The operating principle is similar to that for the single carburettor type described in the preceding section and servicing should be carried out at a similarly recommended interval.

2 Disconnect the vacuum pipe from the cleaner body.

3 Disconnect the evaporative emission hose from the cleaner body.

4 Remove the two sleeve nuts and washers.

5 Withdraw the air cleaner far enough to enable the hot box hose to be disconnected.

6 Pull the lid from the cleaner body and then remove the two elements and wipe the interior of the cleaner body free from oil and dirt.

7 Refitting is a reversal of dismantling but use new sealing gaskets if required.

8 Periodically test the operation of the flap valve as described for the SC air cleaner.

SC type temperature compensator - emission control system

1 Single carburettor vehicles are fitted with an independently mounted temperature compensator which allows an air bleed to by-pass the carburettor jets to give a weaker mixture at high air intake temperatures. It gives precise mixture control over a wide variation in intake temperature levels.

2 This component cannot be serviced and if it develops a fault then it must be renewed.

Fuel pump (Unitac type)

1 This fuel pump is mechanically operated in the same manner as the early type but it differs in design as can be seen in Fig. 13.8. It is not possible completely to dismantle it and therefore should it malfunction, apart from checking the filter and cover seal, there is little one can do and the unit must be renewed.

2 To inspect the seal and clean the filter, unscrew the top cover retaining screw and remove the cover, seal and filter. Wash the filter and cover in clean petrol. If the seal ring is damaged or suspect renew it and ensure that it seats correctly when the cover is refitted. Do not overtighten the cover screw on assembly.

Carburettor throttle damper - application and adjustment

1 This component is fitted to both SC and TC models with emission control systems.

2 Every 6000 miles (10000 km) carry out the following check and adjust if necessary.

3 With the throttle butterfly valves fully closed, the nylon roller will just be making contact with the damper plunger.

4 Depress the damper plunger fully towards the engine and the nylon roller will no longer maintain contact with the plunger but will have a gap of from 0.120 to 0.130 in. (3.0 to 3.3 mm) between the points of contact.

5 If the gap is incorrect, slacken the nylon roller lever pinch bolt and set the lever correctly with the damper plunger fully depressed.

6 Retighten the pinch bolt and re-check the setting.

Anti-run-on valve - filter renewal (SC and TC emission control carburettors)

1 This device operates automatically after the ignition is switched off and it allows air to flow directly into the inlet manifold to ensure that the engine does not continue to run as a result of the retarded ignition and high idle speed which are inherent features of engines on which an emission control system is installed.

2 The valve is energised through an additional electrical circuit which is connected to the ignition switch and current flows through a relay when the ignition switch is moved to the OFF position.

3 Earthing is through an engine oil pressure switch.

4 When the engine comes to rest, the oil pressure switch contacts open, thus breaking the circuit and the anti-run-on valve closes.

5 Every 12000 miles (20000 km) either wash the filter elements in fuel or renew them if they are badly contaminated.

6 Disconnect the air pipe at the valve, remove the nuts and disc.

7 Withdraw the filter cover and extract the filter elements.

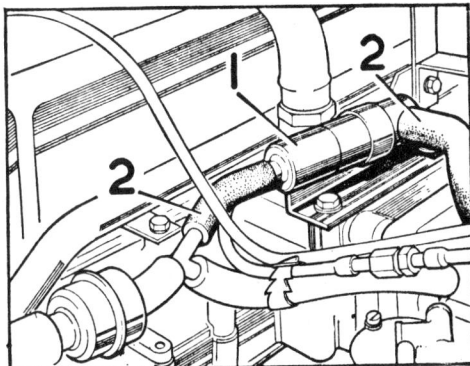

Fig. 13.9. SC type temperature compensator

1 Temperature compensator
2 Connecting pipes

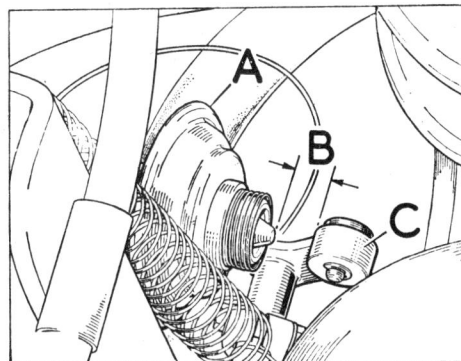

Fig. 13.10. Throttle damper on SC & TC types with emission control

A Damper
B Clearance when damper fully depressed
C Nylon roller

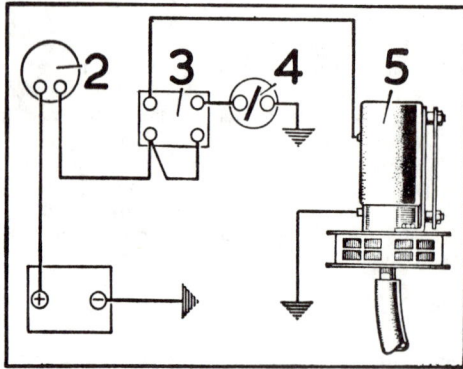

Fig. 13.11. Circuit for emission control anti-run-on valve

2 Ignition switch   4 Engine oil pressure switch
3 Relay   5 Valve

Fig. 13.12. 5 Components of the emission control anti-run-on valve

4 Air pipe   7 Filter cover
5 Securing nut   8 Filter elements
6 Disc   9 Valve assembly

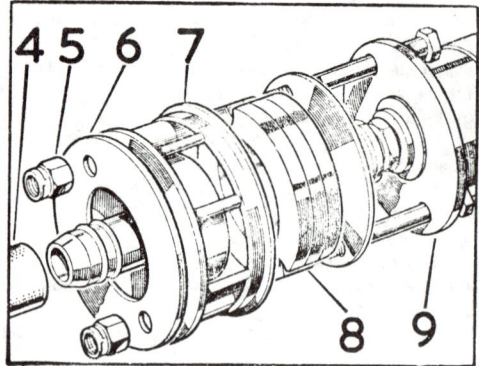

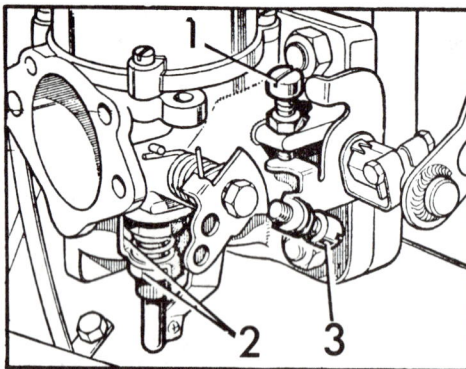

Fig. 13.13. Location of adjusting screws — emission control type single carburettor

1 Idling speed screw
2 Jet adjusting nut (mixture)
3 Fast idle screw

Fig. 13.14. Location of adjusting screws — emission control type twin carburettors

6 Idle speed screw   7 Mixture screw

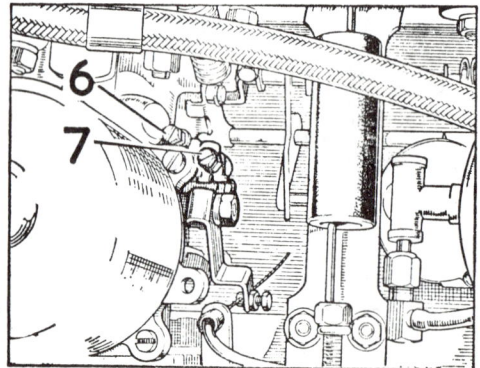

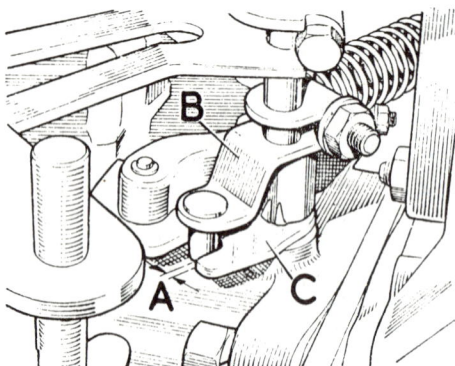

Fig. 13.15. TC type lost motion linkage adjustment

A Gap (0.025 to 0.030 in.   0.70 to 0.80 mm)
B Slotted link
C Lost motion lever

Fig. 13.16. TC type throttle lever and roller

A Lever   C Lost motion
B Roller   linkage gap

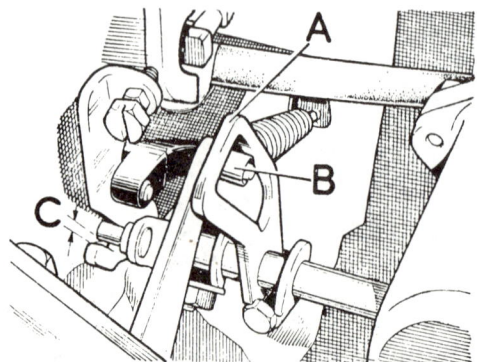

Carburettor adjustment - SC and automatic transmission models fitted with emission control system - revised procedure

1 This operation should be carried out at intervals of 6000 miles (10000 km) with an ambient temperature of between 60 and 80°F, (15.5 and 26.5°C).

2 Run the engine until normal operating temperature is attained.

3 Adjust the idling speed screw to give an engine speed of between 650 and 700 rev/min.

4 If the idling quality is poor and the engine is lumpy or uneven, rotate the jet adjusting nut within the confines of travel permitted by the limiter device. Under no circumstances should this device be tampered with.

5 Re-adjust the idling speed screw if necessary and tighten its locknut.

6 Failure to obtain smooth idling may be the result of a leak in the brake servo unit hose or crankcase ventilation hoses assuming that all other engine and ignition adjustments are correct.

7 The fast idle cam screw is pre-set and will not require alteration.

Carburettor adjustment - TC models with emission control

1 Run the engine until normal operating temperature is attained.

2 Blank off the vacuum pipe (inlet manifold to air cleaner).

3 Balance the carburettors to give an engine idling speed of between 850 and 900 rev/min using a proprietary balancer and tachometer. To achieve this screw the slow running screw in or out as necessary.

4 If the quality of the idling speed is poor, rotate the mixture control screws within the confines of the limiter devices. On no account must these be removed.

5 When adjustment is correct, tighten the screw locknuts.

6 If the correct idling cannot be achieved, carry out the tests described for single carburettor installations in the preceding section.

In addition to the foregoing details, vehicles fitted with emission control systems also have modified ignition settings and reference should be made to the appropriate section later in this Chapter.

TC carburettors - revised linkage adjustment

1 The clearance between the slotted lost motion link adjacent to the front carburettor should be between 0.25 and 0.30 in. (0.70 and 0.80 mm). The gap being measured from the pin to the slot edge on the engine side as shown in Fig. 13.15.

2 When this adjustment is correct, ensure that the countershaft lever is at the end of the slot on the front carburettor throttle lever and is approximately central, with its roller not touching the sides of the slot (Fig. 13.16). Slacken the countershaft lever pinch bolt if necessary to obtain the correct setting.

Carburettor needles - removal and refitting of fixed and spring-loaded types (HS6, HD8 and HS8 carburettors).

1 Fixed needles are simply removed from the air valve pistons by loosening the retaining screw A, Fig. 13.17.

2 Spring-loaded needles are removed after loosening the retaining screw and withdrawing the bias sleeve, Fig. 13.18.

3 To refit the fixed type needle, insert it into the air valve piston until its shoulder is level with the bottom face of the piston.

4 To refit the spring-loaded type needle, assemble the components exactly as shown in Fig. 13.20. It is most important that the needle is correctly aligned as indicated and that its shoulder is flush with the piston bottom face otherwise the emission control characteristics of the engine will be adversely affected.

Evaporative emission control

1 In order to prevent discharge of fuel vapour from the fuel tank directly to atmosphere, a charcoal canister is located under the front left-hand wing.

2 The unit should be renewed at 40000 mile (64000 km)

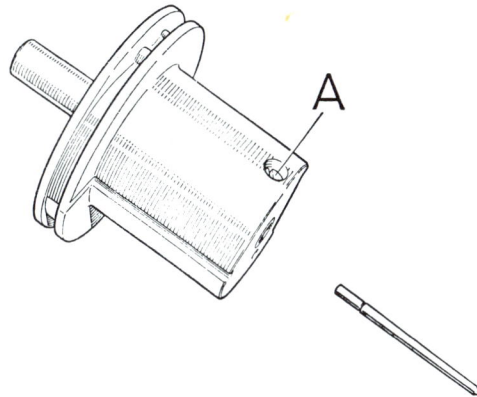

Fig. 13.17. Method of securing fixed type carburettor needle

A Screw

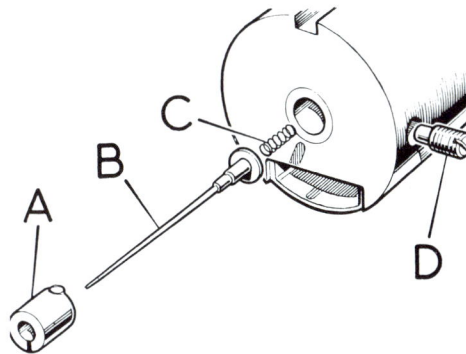

Fig. 13.18. Method of securing spring-loaded type carburettor needle

A Bias sleeve
B Needle
C Spring
D Screw

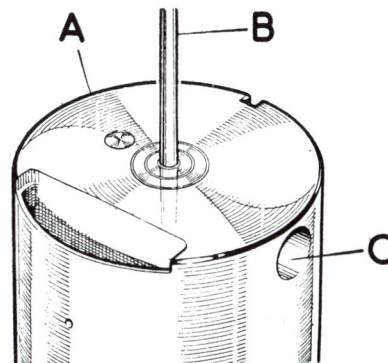

Fig. 13.19. Method of fitting fixed type carburettor needle to air valve piston

A Piston
B Needle
C Screw aperture

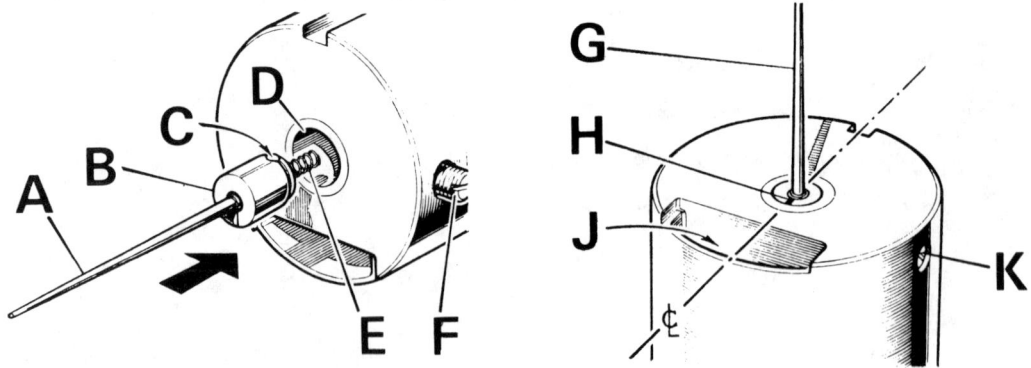

Fig. 13.20. Method of fitting spring-loaded type carburettor needle

A Needle
B Bias sleeve
C Correct location of sleeve (end face boss towards piston)
D Recess
E Spring
F Needle fixing screw
G Needle correctly installed with shoulder flush with piston
H Alignment mark on bias sleeve
J Air passage
K Needle fixing screw

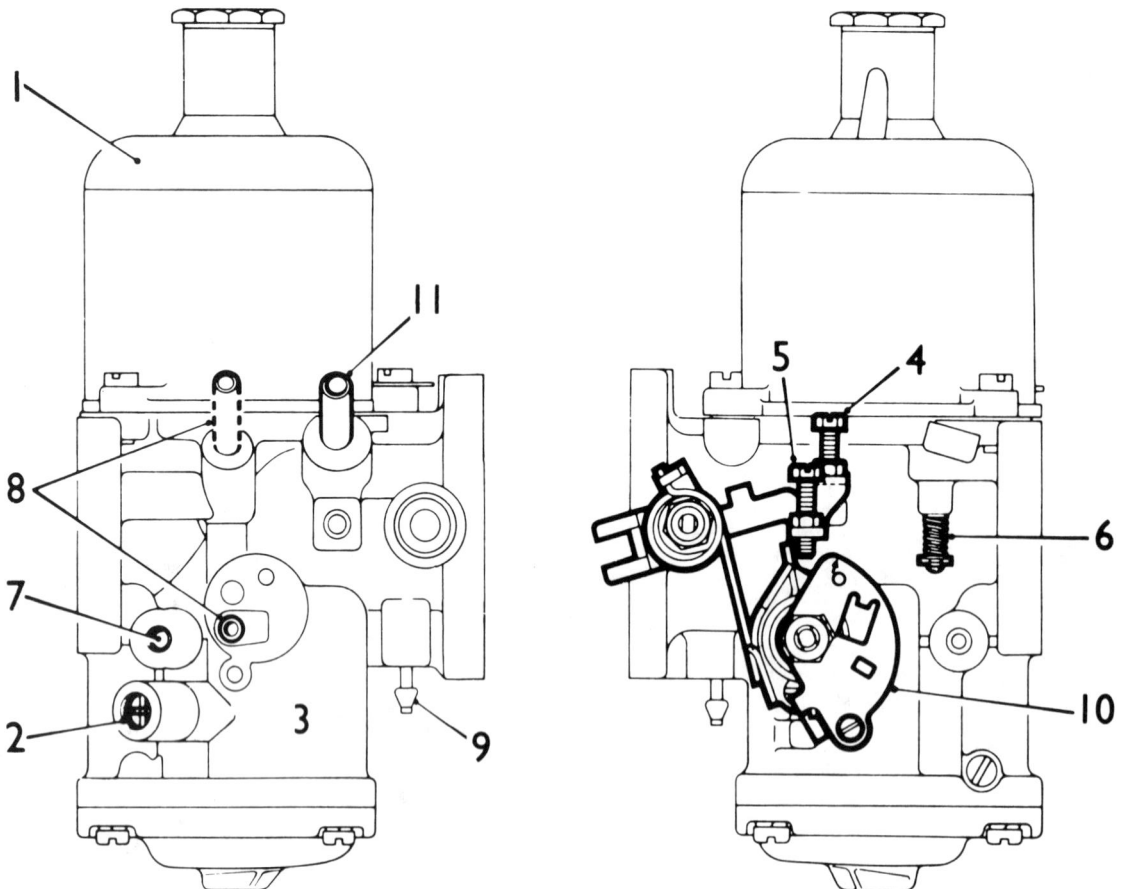

Fig. 13.21A The SU HIF6 carburettor (typical)

1 Piston/suction chamber
2 Jet adjusting screw
3 Float chamber
4 Throttle adjusting screw
5 Fast idle adjusting screw
6 Piston lifting pin
7 Fuel inlet
8 Vent tube (alternative positions)
9 Auto ignition connection
10 Cold start enrichment lever (cam lever)
11 Crankcase ventilation tube

intervals otherwise maintenance consists of checking the condition of the connecting pipes and the security of the clips.
3 Should the unit start to flood causing discharge through the breather pipe (D) (Fig. 13.22a) or weeping of fuel from the non-vented filler cap, renew the filter pad in the base of the canister and if the fault is not rectified, renew the unit complete.

Modifications to 1974 models

The 1974 Rover 2200 models are fitted with 15 gallon (68 litres) fuel tanks. SC and automatic transmission versions are fitted with one SU type HIF6 (swing needle) carburettor while the TC version has two carburettors of the same type.

Carburettor (SUHIF6) - general description

The SUHIF6 carburettor is used on late SC and TC models. These carburettors still work on the same principle as all SU carburettors with dashpots holding the pistons to regulate the airflow, and needles to control the fuel flow from the jet. From above, the HIF6 carburettors look much the same as other types, but there is no float chamber beside the piston; instead this is concentric with the jet and gives the bottom of the carburettor a fatter shape. By placing the float chamber centrally it limits fuel level changes when braking, accelerating and cornering.

The jet is held in place by a horizontal arm. This is made of a bi-metallic spring, so will vary the jet height to give compensation for temperature changes. These would otherwise give mixture variation due to fuel viscosity changes. This jet mounting arm is connected through a pivot to a lever. The lever is moved by a screw in the side of the carburettor body to adjust the mixture. The screw head will normally be hidden by a seal.

The rich mixture needed for starting is provided by a special jet. This has a progressive control to allow partial enrichment and is worked by turning a cam lever on the carburettor side opposite to that having the mixture control screw. This lever has the cam so that as it is moved to enrich the mixture, the cam will push up the fast idle screw to open the throttle. The valve that controls this cold start mixture is a hollow inner core that is twisted with a cylindrical sleeve to bring a hole in it in line with one in the sleeve.

An emulsion bypass passage runs from the jet bridge to the throttle. At small throttle openings unevaporated fuel droplets will be drawn along this passage, and mixed better with this faster travelling air. To match this passage, there is a slot cut out of the base of the piston.

The HIF6 carburettor has a spring biased needle and incorporates an overrun valve in the throttle disc. The spring biased needle (biased to one side of the jet) is used to provide reputability of emission values from one vehicle to another, since with this arrangement the shape, size and position of the metering orifice will always remain the same for any particular carburettor specification. The throttle disc overrun valve prevents the emission of excessive hydro-carbons in the exhaust during the engine overrun phase, by permitting a quantity of fuel/air mixture to be drawn through the closed throttle valve.

Carburettor (SUHIF6) - removal and refitting

There are no special instructions for removal and refitting the HIF6 carburettor, other than those listed for other carburettors. Take great care that the linkage is refitted in its original position and, where applicable, that the necessary running adjustments are made.

Carburettor (SUHIF6) - running and adjustments

Running adjustments (idle mixture, idle speed, fast idle speed and linkage adjustments) are basically the same as described previously in this Chapter and Chapter 3 for other SU carburettors. However, it must be remembered that jet adjustment is by means of a screw (which may be sealed) in the side of the carburettor body. The screw is rotated clockwise to enrich the mixture and anticlockwise to weaken the mixture, but before any adjustment is attempted, a check should be made to ensure that local emission control regulations are not being contravened.

Carburettor (SUHIF6) - dismantling, inspection and reassembly

1 Assuming that you have the carburettor on the workbench, start by cleaning the exterior thoroughly with paraffin (kerosene), or a detergent such as Gunk, using a stiff brush where necessary.
2 Undo the cap at the top of the carburettor and withdraw it complete with the small damper piston. Empty the oil from the dashpot.
3 Remove the suction chamber fixing screws, take off the suction chamber and spring, then lift the piston and needle assembly straight out of the carburettor body.
4 Mark the position of the float chamber cover relative to the body and remove it by unscrewing the four screws holding it down. Empty out any fuel still in the fuel chamber.
5 The float is held to the body by a pivot having a screw head on it. Unscrew and remove the pivot, with its sealing washer and remove the float, followed by the needle.
6 Dismantle the various control linkages, being sure by studying Figs. 13.15, 13.16 and 13.21C that you know how they fit together. It is an easy matter to sort this out before you take them apart but much more difficult when they are in bits.
7 Unscrew the nut holding the fast idle cam - having first straightened its tab washer, take off the cam and its spring which is contained in a small housing behind it. Undo the two screws holding down this housing and pull on the spindle which held the fast idle cam and the whole cold start assembly will come out of the body.
8 Undo the screws holding the throttle disc into its shaft, being careful not to put too much pressure on the shaft in the process (support it with the other hand). Remove the disc and withdraw the throttle shaft.
9 Unscrew the jet retaining (pivot) screw and remove the bi-metal assembly holding the jet.
10 If considered necessary unscrew the float needle seat.
11 The carburettor is now sufficiently dismantled for inspection to be carried out. One or two adjusting screws and the like have been left in the body, but it is recommended that these are only removed when you are actually ensuring that the various channels are clear. Generally speaking, the HIF6 carburettor is very reliable but even so it may develop faults which are not readily apparent unless a careful inspection is carried out, yet may nevertheless effect engine performance. So it is well worthwhile giving the carburettor a good look over when you have got it dismantled.
12 Inspect the carburettor needle for ridging. If this is apparent you will probably find corresponding wear on the inside of the jet. If the needle is ridged, it must be replaced. Do not attempt to rub it down with abrasive paper as carburettor needles are made to very fine tolerances.
13 When installing the needle locate it in the piston as shown in Fig. 13.21D. The shoulder should be flush with the piston face and the engraved line should point directly away from the channel in the piston sidewall. Note that this makes the needle incline in the direction of the carburettor air cleaner flange when the piston is fitted.
14 Inspect the jet for wear. Wear inside the jet will accompany wear on the needle. If any wear is apparent on the jet, replace it. It may be unhooked from the bi-metal spring and this may be used again.
15 Inspect the piston and the carburettor body (suction chamber) carefully for signs that these have been in contact. When the carburettor is operating the main piston should not come into contact with the carburettor body. The whole assembly is supported by the rod of the piston which slides in the centre guide tube, this rod being attached to the cap in the top of the carburettor body. It is possible for wear in the centre guide to allow the piston to touch the wall of the body. Check for this by assembling the small piston in the carburettor body and sliding the large one down, rotating it about the centre guide tube at the same time. If contact occurs and the cause is worn parts, replace them. In no circumstances try to correct piston sticking by altering the tension of the return spring, though very slight contact with the body may be cured - as a temporary

3a Removing the suction chamber

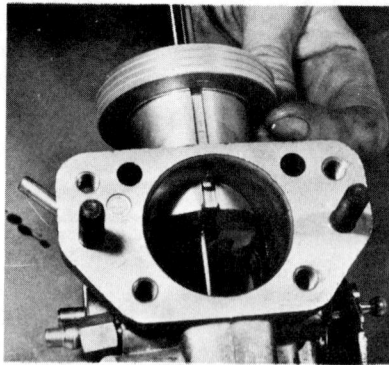

3b Carefully remove the piston assembly

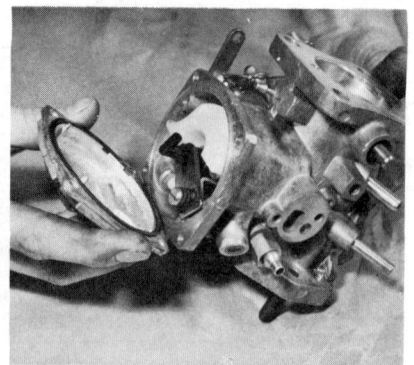

4 Float chamber cover plate removed

9a Removing bimetal and jet assembly

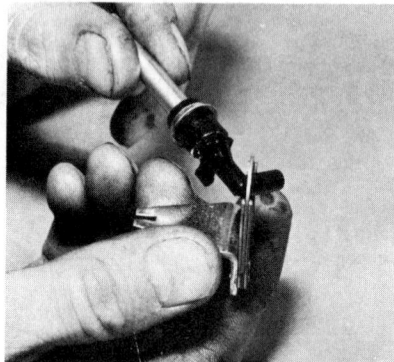

9b How to separate jet from bimetal

5 Removing the float pivot pin

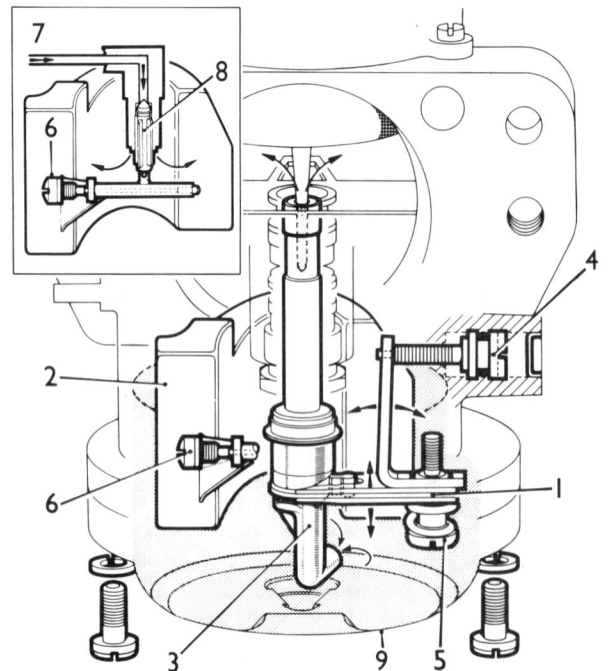

Fig. 13.21B. The float chamber and jet adjustment arrangement on the HIF6 carburettor

1 Bi-metal assembly
2 Concentric float
3 Jet head
4 Jet adjusting screw
5 Bi-metal pivot screw
6 Float pivot screw
7 Fuel inlet
8 Needle valve
9 Bottom cover

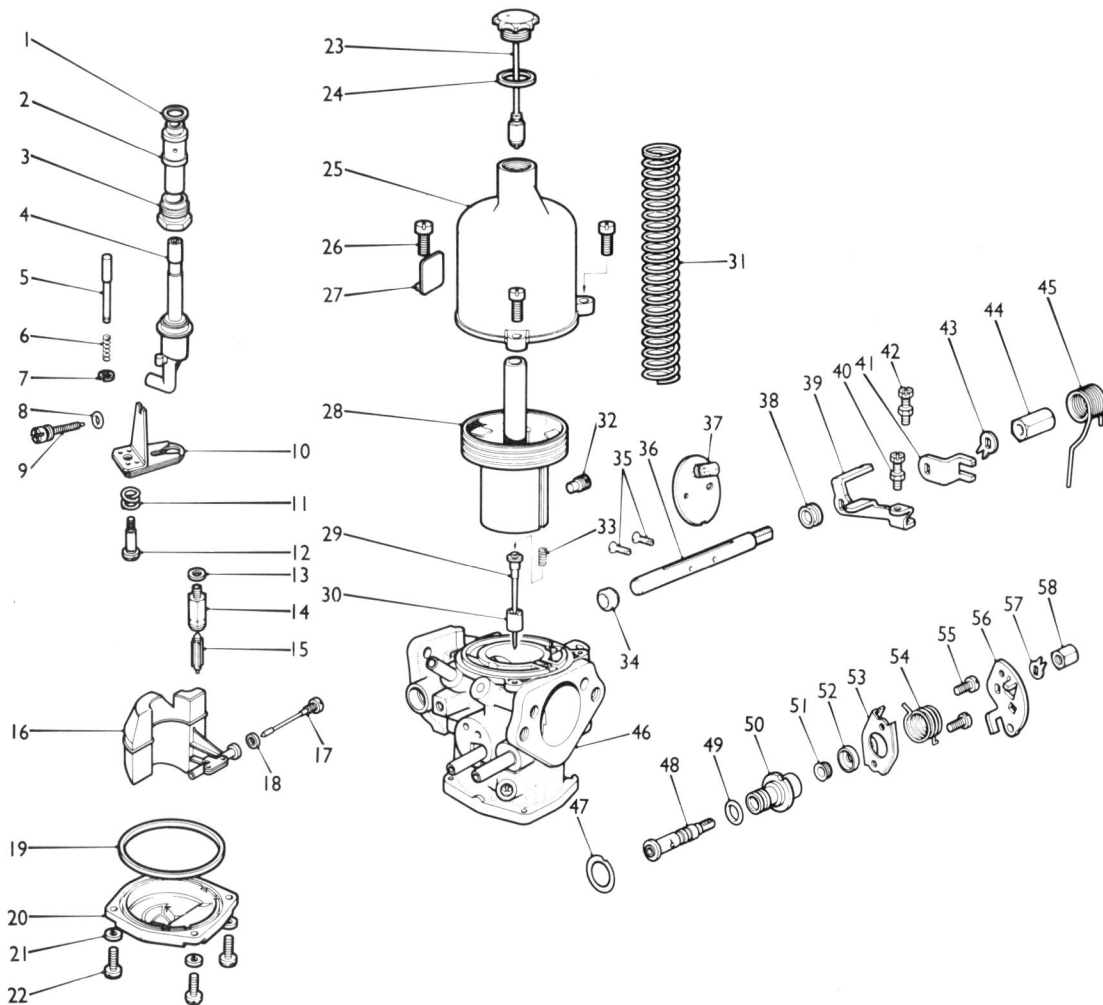

Fig. 13.21C. HIF6 carburettor - exploded view (typical)

1	Jet bearing washer	21	Spring washer	40	Fast idle screw and nut
2	Jet bearing	22	Screw (4)	41	Throttle lever
3	Jet bearing nut	23	Piston damper	42	Throttle adjusting screw and nut
4	Jet assembly	24	Damper washer	43	Tab washer
5	Lifting pin	25	Suction chamber	44	Nut
6	Lifting pin spring	26	Screw (3)	45	Throttle spring
7	Circlip	27	Identity tag	46	Body
8	Adjusting screw seal	28	Piston	47	Cold start seal
9	Jet adjusting screw	29	Jet needle	48	Cold start spindle
10	Bi-metal jet lever	30	Needle guide	49	'O' ring
11	Jet spring	31	Piston spring	50	Cold start body
12	Jet retaining (pivot) screw	32	Needle retaining screw	51	Spindle seal
13	Needle seat washer (if required)	33	Needle spring	52	End cover
14	Float needle seat	34	Throttle spindle seal	53	Retaining plate
15	Float needle	35	Throttle disc screws	54	Cold start spring
16	Float	36	Throttle spindle	55	Retaining screw
17	Float pivot	37	Throttle disc	56	Fast idle cam
18	Pivot seal	38	Throttle spindle seal	57	Tab washer
19	Float chamber cover seal	39	Throttle actuating lever	58	Nut
20	Float chamber cover				

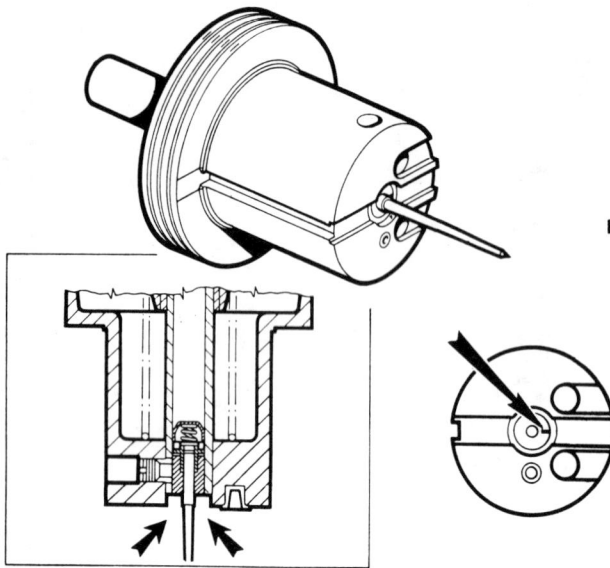

Fig. 13.21D. The correct position of the needle. The arrows indicate the needle position in the piston

Fig. 13.21E. Checking the piston
The plugged holes are arrowed

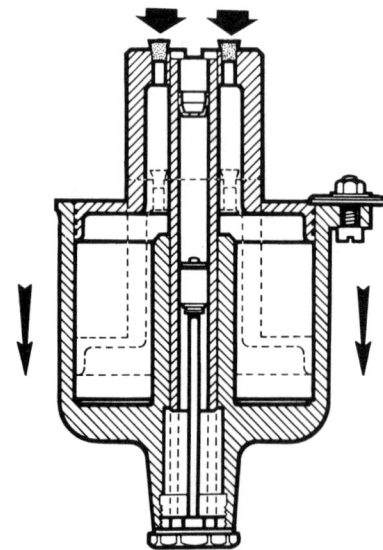

measure - by polishing the offending portion of the body wall with metal polish or extremely fine emery cloth.

16 The fit of the piston in the suction chamber can be checked by plugging the air hole in the body and assembling the piston in the chamber without its return spring, fitting the damper piston without filling the dashpot with oil. If the assembly is now turned upside down as shown in Fig. 13.21E, the piston should sink to the bottom in 5-7 seconds. If the time is appreciably less than this, the piston and suction chamber should both be replaced since they are matched to each other.

17 Check for wear on the throttle shaft and bushes through which it passes. Apart from the nuisance of a sticking throttle, excessive wear here can cause air leaks in the induction system adversely affecting engine performance. Worn bushes can be extracted and new bushes fitted if necessary. The cold start device can be dismantled for cleaning, and new parts used where necessary when reassembling.

18 Reassembly is a straightforward reversal of the dismantling process. During reassembly the float level can be checked and adjusted if necessary by inverting the carburettor body so that the needle valve is held shut by the weight of the float. Using a straight edge across the face of the float chamber measure the gap at the point arrowed (Fig. 13.21F). It should be 0.04 ± 0.02 in $(1.0 \pm 0.5$ mm). The arm can be bent carefully to obtain this dimension.

19 When assembling the jet, position the adjusting screw so that the upper edge of the jet is level with the bridge. This gives the initial position for jet adjustment.

20 When the carburettor is assembled, the dashpot should be filled with engine oil until it is ½ inch (13 mm) above the top of the hollow piston rod. Check that the piston is operating properly by lifting it with the lifting pin and letting it fall. It should hit the bridge of the carburettor with an audible click. If it does not, the needle may be fouling the jet (it is supposed to touch it lightly on one side). This should not occur with careful assembly; there is not provision for centering the jet but if it is properly assembled, this is not necessary.

41(f)

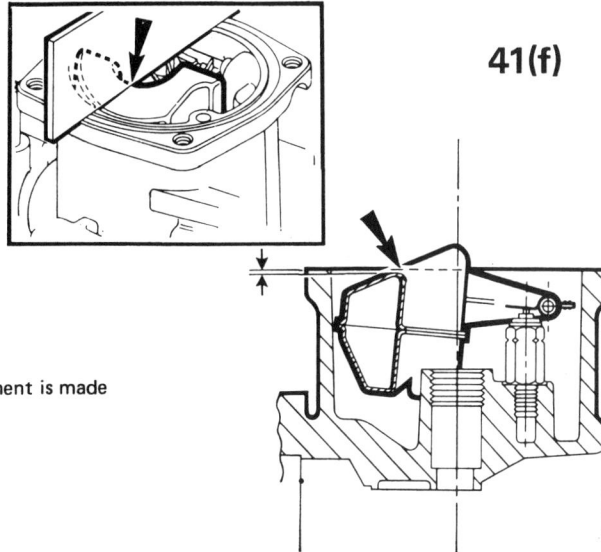

Fig. 13.21F. Float adjustment
The arrows indicate the point at which measurement is made

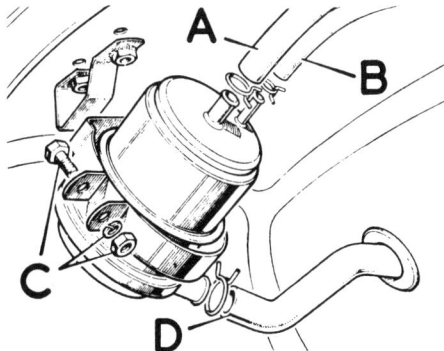

Fig. 13.22A. Charcoal canister for evaporative emission control

A and B   Hoses
C   Pinch bolt
D   Breather pipe

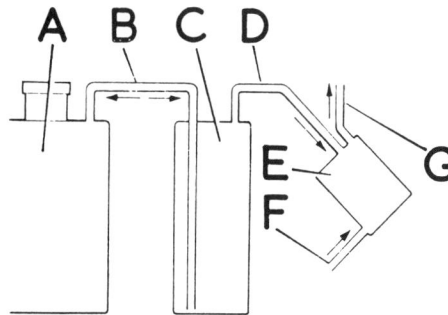

Fig. 13.22B. Layout of evaporative emission control system

A Fuel tank   E Charcoal canister
B Breather pipe   F Air inlet pipe
C Expansion tank   G Pipe to carburettor
D Breather pipe   air cleaner

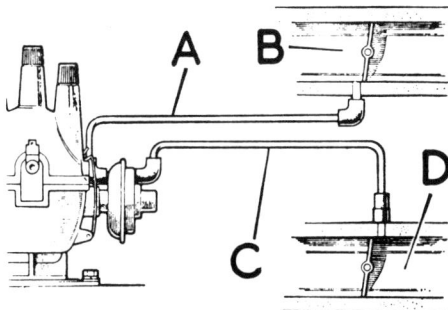

Fig. 13.23. Dual action distributor vacuum capsule used in conjunction with emission control system

A Vacuum pipe (engine side of throttle butterfly (B) to vacuum capsule)
B Throttle butterfly valve
C Vacuum pipe (air cleaner side of throttle butterfly (D) to vacuum capsule)

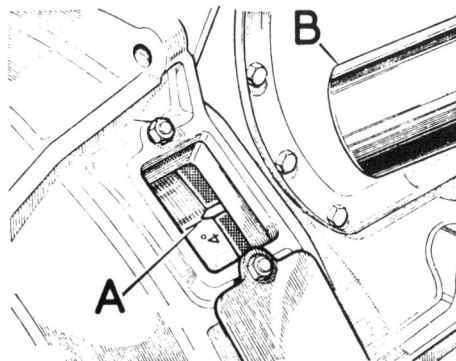

Fig. 13.24. Ignition timing marks on early emission control system vehicles

A Flywheel timing mark
B Stroboscope

6. Ignition system

Models with emission control - revised ignition timing procedure
1 Vehicle fitted with this system have a distributor which incorporates a double action (retard and advance) vacuum capsule and a modified centrifugal advance curve to permit stroboscopic ignition timing to be carried out at idling speeds which are slightly higher than normal. Slightly higher idling speeds improve the over-run fume emission characteristics of these engines.
2 Before timing the ignition, it is essential to run the engine until normal operating temperature is achieved and to check that the distributor contact points gap is correct (0.014 to 0.016 in. 0.30 to 0.40 mm).
3 Turn the engine over until with number 4 piston rising on its compression stroke, the engine timing marks are aligned in accordance with the following table according to vehicle model application. The compression stroke may be ascertained by removing number 4 spark plug and placing a finger over the plug hole and feeling the compression generated.

	Static ignition setting	
2000SC and automatic models (9 : 1 compression ratio)	4^oBTDC	*
2000SC and automatic models with emission control (9 : 1 compression ratio)	4^oBTDC	*
2000TC (10 : 1 compression ratio)	6^oBTDC	*
2000TC (9 : 1 compression ratio)	6^oBTDC	*
2000TC with emission control (10 : 1 compression ratio)	6^oBTDC	**
2000TC with emission control (9 : 1 compression ratio)	6^oBTDC	**

* disconnect and plug vacuum pipe to distributor.
** vacuum pipes remain connected.

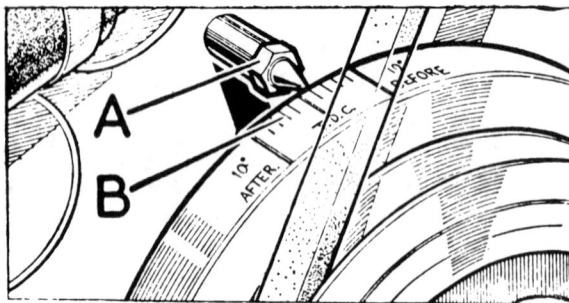

Fig. 13.25 Ignition timing marks on later vehicles equipped with emission control

A Pointer on crankcase   *B Index on crankshaft damper*

4 Using a test bulb connected between the distributor LT terminal and earth and with the ignition switched on, adjust the distributor by means of the vernier until the lamp just lights when light finger pressure is applied to the rotor arm in a clockwise direction.
5 Replace number 4 spark plug and connect a stroboscope between it and its HT lead.
6 Mark the engine timing marks with white chalk or paint in accordance with the following table.

Centrifugal (dynamic) ignition setting	
2000SC and automatic models (9 : 1 compression ratio)	4^oBTDC
2000SC and automatic models with emission control (9 : 1 compression ratio)	4^oBTDC
2000TC (10 : 1 compression ratio)	6^oBTDC
2000TC (9 : 1 compression ratio)	6^oBTDC
2000TC with emission control (10 : 1 compression ratio)	4^oATDC
2000TC with emission control (9 : 1 compression ratio)	4^oATDC

7 Connect an accurate and independent tachometer to the engine and then start the engine and adjust the idling speed according to engine type as follows:-

2000TC (9 : 1 compression ratio)	700 to 750 rev/min
2000SC and automatic models with emission control (9 : 1 compression ratio)	650 to 700 rev/min
2000TC (10 : 1 compression ratio)	700 to 750 rev/min
2000TC with emission control (10 : 1 compression ratio)	850 to 900 rev/min
2000TC with emission control (9 : 1 compression ratio)	850 to 900 rev/min

8 With the stroboscope pointing at the timing marks, rotate the distributor by means of the vernier control or by loosening the body clamp bolt until both timing marks are in alignment.
9 Tighten the distributor clamp bolt, switch off the engine, remove the stroboscope and tachometer and reconnect the spark plug HT lead and vacuum pipes (where disconnected). Note: on early models with emission control, the timing marks are located on the flywheel and flywheel housing (Fig. 13.24). On later models, the marks are located at the front of the engine as a pointer and index on the crankshaft damper (Fig. 13.25).

Distributor

1 The distributor fitted to all late model 2200s contains a single, piece contact set, but in all other aspects is the same as that shown in Chapter 4.
2 To renew or remove the contact set on these models, detach the distributor cap, lift off the rotor arm and then unscrew the contact set retaining screw. Remove the screw with its washers and lift the contact set clear. These points can be be inspected and serviced in a similar manner to that described for the earlier points (see Chapter 4).

3 To refit the contact set reverse the removal procedure and reset the contact breaker gap to the specified figure by inserting a screwdriver into the breaker plate slot and lever accordingly. Tighten the screw to secure and recheck the gap using feeler gauges.

7 Automatic transmission

Downshift cable adjustment - revised procedure

1 With the engine at normal operating temperature move the accelerator coupling shaft until the idling speed just begins to rise.

2 Maintain this setting and check the gap between the contact faces of the downshift cable crimped stop and the outer cable conduit threaded sleeve. This should be between 0.010 and 0.020 in. (0.25 and 0.50 mm.) measured with feeler gauges.

3 Where the gap is incorrect, one of two methods may be used to adjust the cable.

4 Connect a pressure gauge to the take off point at the rear of the transmission unit and a tachometer as shown in Figs. 13.26 and 13.27.

5 Warm up the engine and then take the pressure reading at 500 rev/min in D1 or D2.

6 Increase the engine speed to 1000 rev/min when the pressure reading should increase by 15 to 20 lb/in.^{2} If the pressure rise is less than this, increase the effective length of the outer cable by screwing out the adjuster from its bracket. If the pressure rise is more than 20 lb/in.^{2} decrease the length of the outer cable by screwing in the adjuster. Re-check the pressure and then lock the adjuster locknut. Remove the pressure gauge and re-fit the socket screw. Detach the tachometer.

7 The alternative method of adjusting the downshift cable is to first drain the transmission fluid and to remove the oil pan. Check that the accelerator pedal is fully released and that the throttle butterfly plate is fully closed. In this position check that the cam setting is as shown in Fig. 13.28. Now depress the accelerator pedal fully to the kick-down position and check the cam setting as shown in Fig. 13.29. Carry out any adjustment required to obtain these settings by screwing the outer cable adjuster in or out of its bracket.

8 Replace the oil pan, using a new gasket and re-fill the transmission with fluid.

Transmission fluid cooler - servicing

1 Where an automatic transmission fluid cooler is fitted ahead of the radiator, it should be periodically brushed gently to remove accumulated road dirt, leaves and flies.

2 When the transmission unit has been removed and a new unit installed, always flush the fluid cooler with clean fluid before connecting it to the transmission.

3 When installing a new or reconditioned transmission unit, never refill it with old fluid drained from the faulty transmission, always use new from a sealed container.

8 Propeller shaft and universal joint

Introduction of additional lubrication point

1 On late model vehicles, a boss has been cast onto the universal joint spider at the differential end of the propeller shaft. The object of this is to enable the plug to be removed from the boss every 10000 miles (16000 km) and a nipple screwed in for lubrication purposes.

2 Should the universal joint be dismantled, it is imperative that the cast boss faces towards the propeller shaft.

9 Braking system

Introduction of dual circuit system

1 Fitted as standard, from 1968 onwards, to vehicles operating in North America and also to later model vehicles destined for

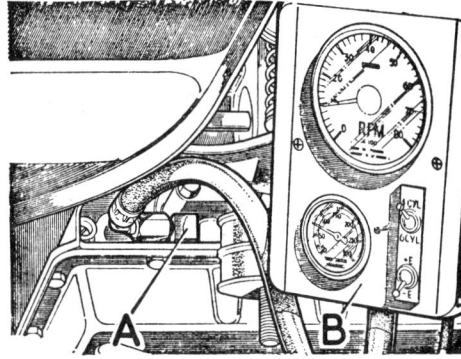

Fig. 13.26. Pressure gauge (B) connected to automatic transmission take-off point for checking downshift cable adjustment

A Take-off point at rear of transmission unit

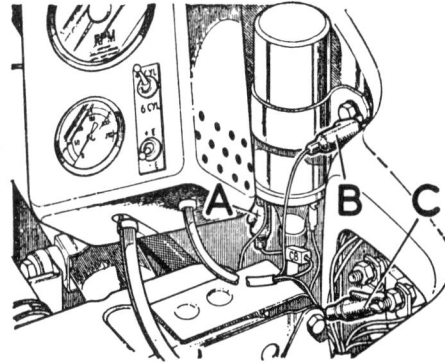

Fig. 13.27. Method of connecting tachometer to engine

A Connection to 'C' terminal on ignition coil (green)
B Negative connection (black)
C Positive connection at starter solenoid (red)

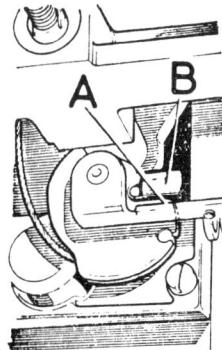

Fig. 13.28. Automatic transmission downshift valve cable adjustment, cam in 'throttle released' position

A Heel of cam
B Downshift valve

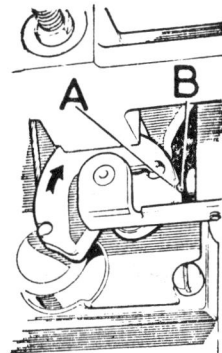

Fig. 13.29. Automatic transmission downshift valve cable adjustment, cam in 'accelerator kickdown' position

A Highest point of constant radius section of cam
B Downshift valve

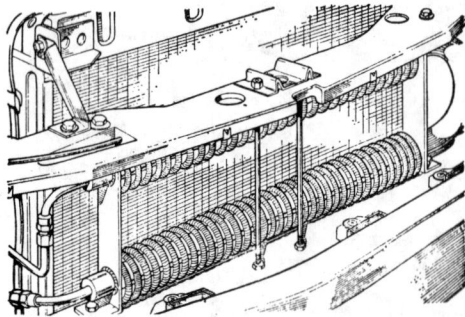

Fig. 13.30. Location of automatic transmission fluid cooler

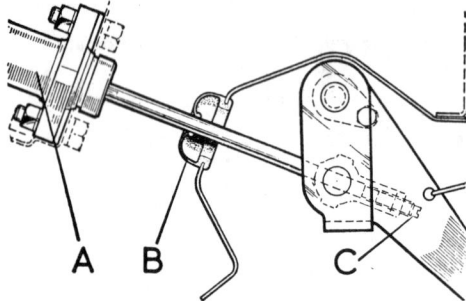

Fig. 13.31. Operating rod attachment (tandem master cylinder to pedal)

A Master cylinder
B Grommet
C Threaded section of operating rod

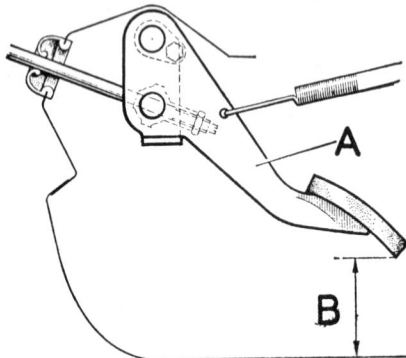

Fig. 13.32. Tandem master cylinder brake pedal height setting diagram

A Brake pedal
B 6½ to 6¾ in. (165 to 171 mm)

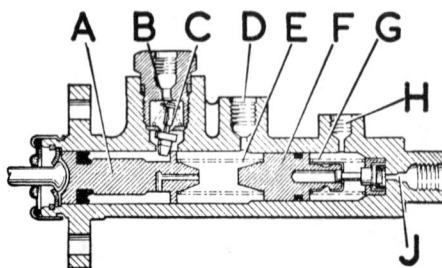

Fig. 13.33. Cross-sectional view of tandem master cylinder

A Primary plunger
B Tipping valve
C Primary fluid port
D Front outlet port
E Intermediate spring
F Secondary plunger
G Secondary spring
H Rear outlet port (located at 90° to D)
J Centre valve fluid port

other markets, the dual hydraulic circuit also includes a tandem master cylinder and dual vacuum servo booster units.

2 Overhaul and servicing procedures given in Chapter 9 will apply to the dual system with the exception of the following operations.

3 On TC models, the divided fluid reservoir installed to feed the two sections of the tandem master cylinder also supplies the clutch master cylinder.

Tandem master cylinder - removal and refitting

1 Remove the air cleaner from the carburettor.

2 Disconnect the fluid inlet pipes at the master cylinder and tie them up to prevent loss of fluid.

3 Disconnect the outlet pipes by unscrewing their unions at the master cylinder body. Remove the master cylinder body securing nuts but do not pull it from its mounting.

4 Detach the brake pedal return spring and release the locknut from the operating push-rod at the pedal trunnion and then screw the rod through the trunnion at the same time having an assistant withdraw the master cylinder.

5 Installation of the master cylinder is a reversal of removal but the pedal height must be set correctly above the floor as shown in Fig. 13.32.

6 Bleed the hydraulic system as described in Chapter 9, Section 29 but note that with a tandem master cylinder, the brake pedal will go hard at the half depressed position before going fully down. This is caused by one of the two hydraulic circuits being bled of air before the other, dependant upon which bleed nipple is opened first.

Tandem master cylinder - servicing

1 Detach the dust excluder retainer and peel back the dust cover.

2 Withdraw the now exposed circlip and remove the operating push-rod.

3 Refer to Fig. 13.33 and remove the tipping valve housing adaptor and detach its 'O' ring seal.

4 Depress the piston and withdraw the tipping valve assembly, remove the primary plunger and spring together with the remainder of the internal components. If the internal parts are difficult to extract, shake the cylinder or apply air pressure from a tyre pump at the fluid port situated at the end of the master cylinder body.

5 Refer to Fig. 13.34 and prise up the retainer (c) but as the secondary spring will be released, control its expansion by having an assistant press both ends of the plunger assembly together with the hands. Failure to do this might cause injury or loss of small components.

6 Disengage the valve stem from the keyhole shaped orifice in the end of the retainer. Remove the polythene spacer, dished

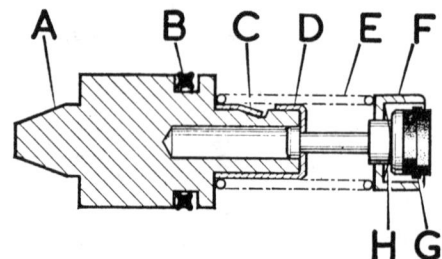

Fig. 13.34. Cross-sectional view of tandem type master cylinder secondary plunger

A Plunger
B Seal
C Retainer prong
D Retainer
E Spring
F Spacer
G Seal
H Dished washer

washer and valve head seal from the valve head. The secondary spring has a bright metal finish for identification purposes.

7 Discard all rubber seals and wash all components in clean brake fluid or methylated spirit. Examine the piston surfaces and cylinder bores for score marks or 'bright' wear areas and if these are evident, renew the complete master cylinder assembly.

8 Obtain a repair kit which will contain all the necessary seals. Lubricate all components with clean brake fluid before fitting and manipulate the seals into position, using the fingers only.

9 Reassembly is a reversal of dismantling but note the following points.

The valve head seal has the smaller diameter in contact with the valve head.

The dished spring washer should have its convex side to the valve head.

Dual vacuum servo units - removal and installation

1 Disconnect the vacuum pipes from the servo units at the three-way connection.

2 Disconnect the fluid pipes at the mounting bracket on the right-hand wing valance.

3 From underneath the right-hand wing unscrew the two bracket securing bolts and nut. Withdraw the complete dual vacuum servo assembly.

4 Servicing of each individual servo unit is as described for the 7 inch diameter type in Chapter 9, Section 27.

5 Installation of the dual servo unit is a reversal of removal. Bleed the hydraulic system.

Braking system - revised maintenance procedure

1 Due to the fact that hydraulic brake fluid absorbs moisture from the atmosphere, the complete braking system should be bled of old fluid every 18 months. Refill the system with fluid which has been stored in a sealed container and has remained unshaken for the previous 24 hours.

2 Every 40000 miles (64000 km) or at three-yearly intervals, renew all cylinder and caliper unit seals also the flexible brake hoses.

3 Examine the rigid brake lines annually for signs of corrosion, rusting or damage from flying stones. Renew any sections as required.

10 Electrical system

Battery - re-location

Vehicles produced after 1970 have the battery located in the luggage boot instead of the previous engine compartment position.

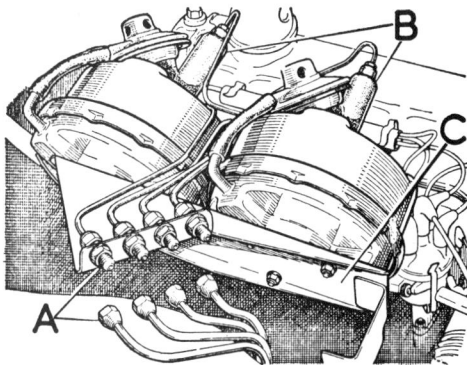

Fig. 13.35. Mounting arrangements of dual brake vacuum servo units

A Fluid unions   C Mounting bracket
B Servo units

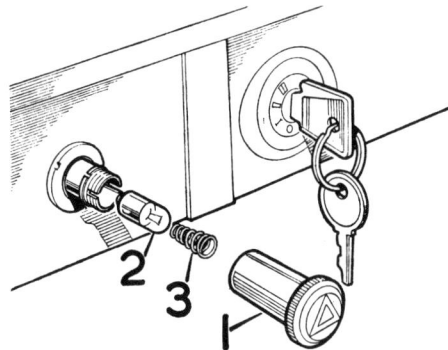

Fig. 13.37. Hazard warning switch

1 Knob with lens   2 Bulb   3 Spring

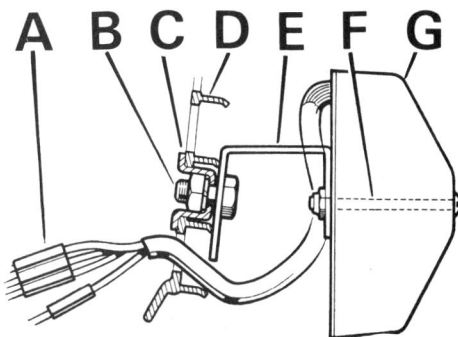

Fig. 13.36. 'Icelert' sensing unit and operating switch

A Cable connectors   B Mounting bolt   C Mounting bracket   D Radiator grille   E Sensing unit bracket
F Tie bolt   G Sensing unit   H Screw   J Panel
K Rheostat   L Test button   M Indicator lamp
N Spring clip

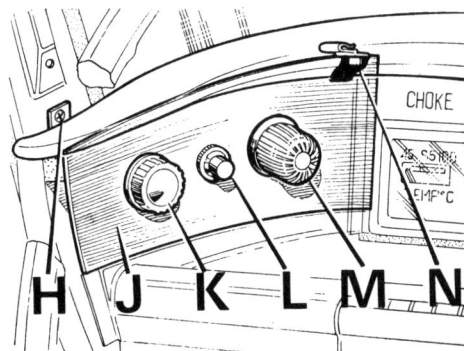

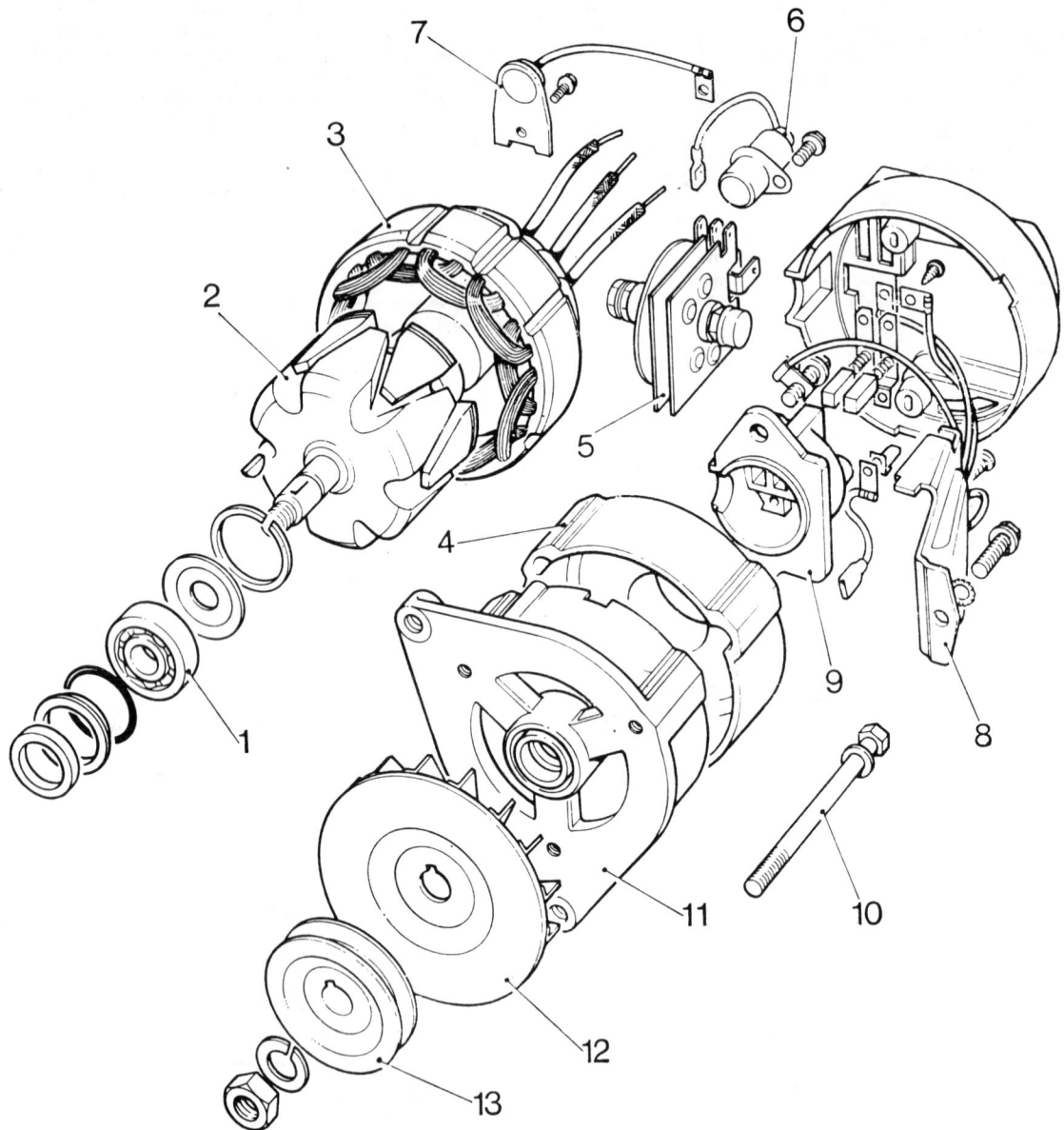

Fig. 13.38 The Lucas type 18 ACR alternator

1	Front bearing	5	Rectifier	9	Brush unit	13	Pulley
2	Rotor/slip ring	6	Suppressor	10	Bolt		
3	Stator	7	Surge protector device	11	Front bracket		
4	Slip ring bracket	8	Regulator	12	Fan		

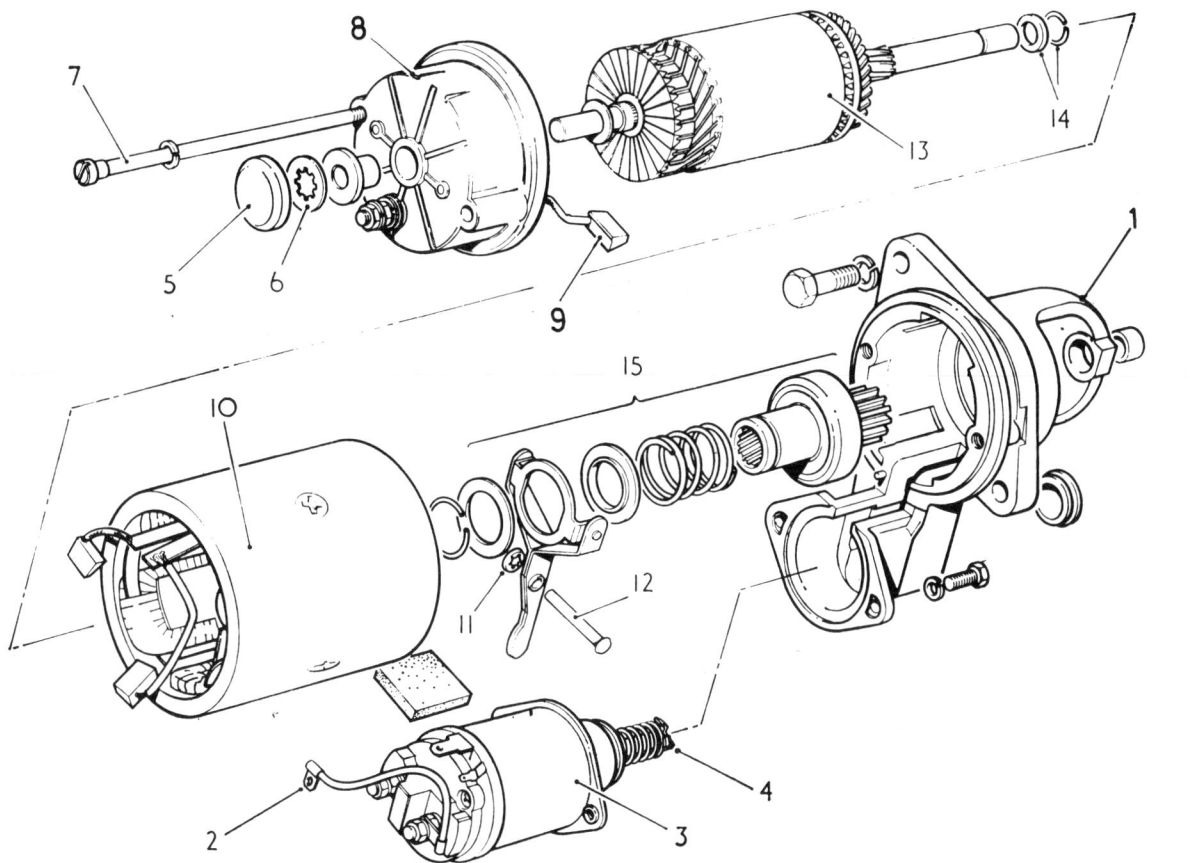

Fig. 13.39. The Lucas type 2M100 pre-engaged starter motor

1	Rear housing	5	End cap seal	9	Brush
2	Connecting wire	6	Retaining ring	10	Yoke and field coil
3	Solenoid	7	Through bolt	11	Retaining ring
4	Solenoid plunger	8	End cover	12	Pivot pin

13	Armature
14	Collar and ring
15	Thrust collar/roller clutch assembly

Alternator

A Lucas 18 ACR alternator is fitted to later models, and a general view of its layout and components is shown in Fig. 13.38 The maintenance, removal and installation procedures for this type of alternator are generally the same as for the earlier type described in Chapter 10. As with the earlier type alternator, any testing or overhaul procedures should be entrusted to your auto electrician or Rover dealer.

Starter motor

1 A later type pre-engaged starter motor is now fitted, being the Lucas 2 M 100 PE. Similar in design to its predecessor (the Lucas M 418 G) the latest type now has triangular brushes fitted which work on the end face of the commutator. The dismantling and reassembly procedures are as follows:

2 Undo and remove the nut and spring washer that secures the connecting link between the solenoid and starter motor at the solenoid 'STA' terminal. Carefully ease the connecting link out of engagement of the terminal post on the solenoid.

3 Undo and remove the two nuts and spring washers that secure the solenoid to the drive end bracket. Carefully ease the solenoid back from the drive end bracket, lift the solenoid plunger and return spring from the engagement lever, and

completely remove the solenoid. Recover the shaped rubber block that is placed between the solenoid and starter motor body.

4 Carefully remove the end cap seal from the commutator end cover. Ease the armature shaft retaining ring (spire nut) from the armature shaft. **Note:** The retaining ring must not be reused, but a new one obtained ready for fitting.

5 Undo and remove the two long through bolts and spring washers. Detach the commutator end cover from the yoke, at the same time disengaging the field brushes from the brush box moulding. Lift away the thrust washer from the armature shaft.

6 The starter motor body may now be lifted from the armature and drive end assembly.

7 Ease the retaining ring (spire nut) from the engagement lever pivot pin. **Note.** The retaining ring must not be reused, but a new one obtained ready for fitting. Using a parallel pin punch, remove the pivot pin from the engagement lever and drive end bracket.

8 Carefully move the thrust collar clear of the jump ring, and slide the jump ring from the armature shaft. Slide off the thrust collar, and finally remove the roller clutch drive and engagement lever assembly from the armature shaft.

9 Whilst the motor is apart, check the operation of the drive

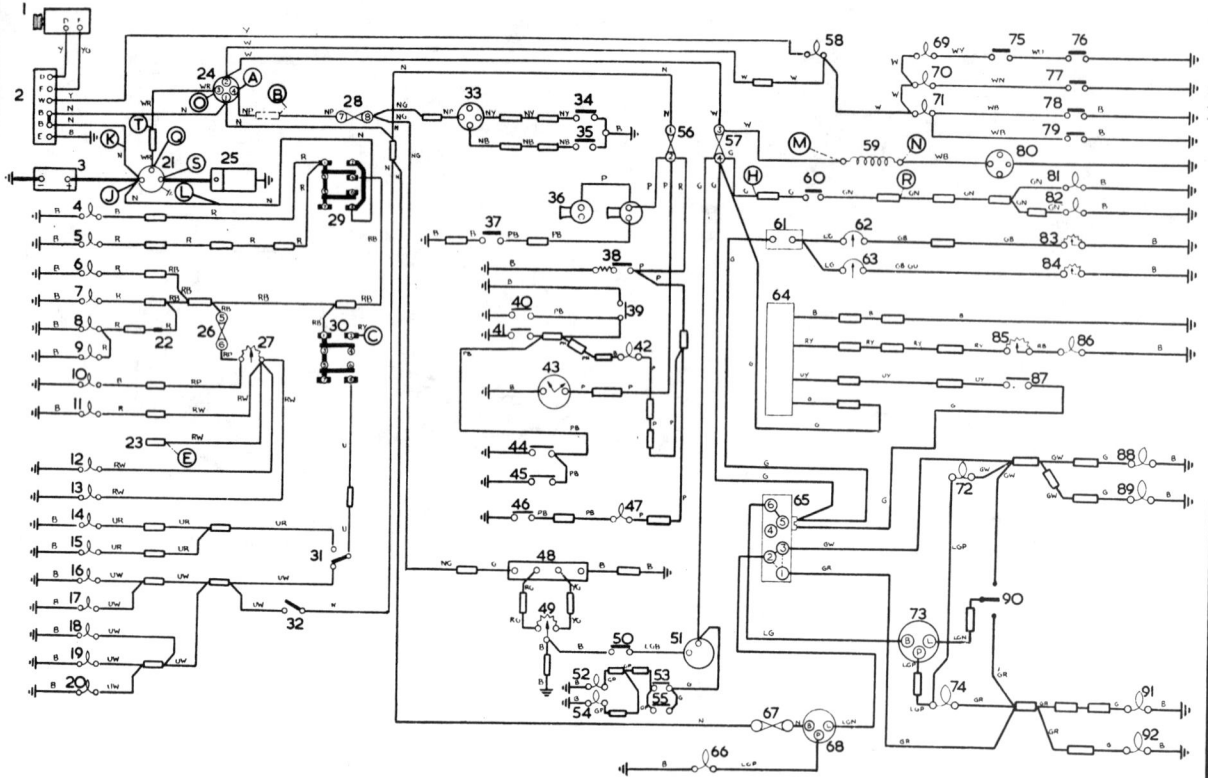

Fig. 13.40. Wiring diagram (North America - automatic transmission)

1	Dynamo, C42	33	Heater blower unit, two speed	65	Switch, hazard warning
2	Control box, RB340	34	Switch, fast speed heater blower	66	Hazard warning lamp
3	Battery, 60 amp. hour	35	Switch, slow speed heater blower	67	Fuse, hazard warning feed, 25 amp.
4	Side and park lamp, LH	36	Twin horns	68	Hazard warning flasher unit
5	Tail and park lamp, LH	37	Switch, horn	69	Warning light, choke
6	Side lamp, RH	38	Switch, cigar lighter	70	Warning light, oil pressure
7	Tail lamp, RH	39	Switch, interior lamp	71	Warning light, brake fluid level and handbrake
8	Number plate lamp	40	Switch, front door, LH	72	Warning light, indicator, LH
9	Number plate lamp	41	Switch, front door, RH	73	Direction indicator unit
10	Cigar lighter illumination	42	Interior lamp	74	Warning light, indicator, RH
11	Clock illumination	43	Clock	75	Switch, choke
12	Panel light	44	Switch, rear door, LH	76	Switch, choke thermometer
13	Panel light	45	Switch, rear door, RH	77	Switch, oil pressure
14	Headlamp dip beam, LH	46	Switch, boot light	78	Switch, handbrake
15	Headlamp dip beam, RH	47	Boot light	79	Switch, brake fluid
16	Headlamp main beam, RH	48	Screen wiper motor	80	Distributor
17	Headlamp main beam, RH	49	Switch, screen wiper	81	Reverse lamp, RH
18	Main beam warning light	50	Switch, screen washer	82	Reverse lamp, LH
19	Headlamp main beam, LH	51	Screen washer	83	Tank unit
20	Headlamp main beam, LH	52	Stop lamp, LH	84	Water temperature transmitter
21	Starter solenoid	53	Switch, stop lamps	85	Rheostat switch, 'Icelert' warning lamp
22	Cable identification tag	54	Stop lamp, RH	86	'Icelert' warning lamp
23	Spare cable pick-up point	55	Switch, stop lamps	87	Test switch, 'Icelert' warning lamp
24	Switch, ignition and starter	56	Fuse, 1 and 2, 35 amp	88	Front direction indicator, RH
25	Starter motor	57	Fuse, 3, 4, 35 amp	89	Rear direction indicator, RH
26	Fuse, 5 and 6, 35 amp	58	Warning light, ignition	90	Switch, direction indicator
27	Switch, panel illumination	59	Ignition coil	91	Rear direction indicator, LH
28	Fuse, 7 and 8, 35 amp	60	Switch, reverse light	92	Front direction indicator, LH
29	Switch, side and park	61	Bi-metal voltage regulator		
30	Switch, headlamp	62	Fuel gauge		
31	Switch, headlamp dip	63	Water temperature gauge	Snap or Lucar connectors illustrated thus:	
32	Switch, headlamp flash	64	'Icelert' sensor unit		
				Earth terminals thus:	

Fig. 13.41. Wiring diagram (2000 SC and automatic transmission models)

Encircled figures denote pick-up points for optional extra equipment.
Encircled figures 11 13, 14, 15, 16 and 17 denote pick-up points when basic harness is used on Automatic models.

1	Relay for ignition warning light, type 3AW	33	Pick-up point for radio	66	Warning light for handbrake and brake fluid level
2	Control box, type 4TR	34	Fuses, 7 and 8, 35 amp	67	Switch for reverse lights
3	Alternator, type Lucas 11 Ac	35	Main lighting switch	68	Switch and warning light, hazard warning circuit
4	Alternator contacts, ignition switch	36	Fuses, 5 and 6, 35 amp	69	Flasher unit, type 8FL
5	Solenoid for starter motor) Automatic	37	Rheostat for panel lights	70	Bi-metal voltage regulator for instruments
6	Relay for starter motor) transmis-	38	Pick-up point for tachometer	71	Fuel contents gauge
7	Inhibitor switch) sion	39	Pick-up point for auxiliary lamps	72	Coolant temperature gauge
8	Ballast resistor) models and	40	Switch for headlamp dip	73	Pick-up point for tachometer
	) cold) climates	41	Switch for headlamp flash	74	Screen washer motor
9	Side lamp	42	Screen wiper motor	75	Switch for stop lights
10	Tail lamp	43	Heater blower unit, two-speed	76	Switch for choke control
11	Side and park lamp	44	Switch, fast speed, blower	77	Thermostat switch for choke control
12	Tail and park lamp	45	Switch, slow speed, blower	78	Switch for oil pressure warning light
13	Number plate illumination	46	Twin horns	79	Switch for handbrake warning light
14	Number plate illumination	47	Switch for horns	80	Switch for brake fluid level
15	Cigar lighter illumination	48	Cigar lighter and switch	81	Ignition coil
16	Clock illumination	49	Hazard warning flasher unit	82	Distributor
17	Gear selector illumination	50	Rotary map light	83	Pick-up point for tachometer
18	Panel illumination	51	Switch for front door, LH	84	Reverse lamp, RH
19	Panel illumination	52	Switch for front door, RH	85	Reverse lamp, LH
20	Headlamp dip beam, LH	53	Switch for interior light	86	Warning light, indicator, LH
21	Headlamp dip beam, RH	54	Interior light	87	Direction indicator lamp, front, LH
22	Headlamp main beam, RH	55	Clock	88	Direction indicator lamp, rear, LH
23	Headlamp main beam, RH	56	Switch for rear door, RH	89	Direction indicator switch
24	Warning light for headlamp main beam	57	Switch for rear door, LH	90	Warning light, indicator, RH
25	Headlamp main beam, LH	58	Boot lamp	91	Direction indicator lamp, rear, RH
26	Headlamp main beam, LH	59	Switch for windscreen wiper	92	Direction indicator lamp, front, RH
27	Steering column lock switch	60	Delay switch for windscreen wiper	93	Tank unit, fuel contents gauge
28	Battery	61	Pick-up point for air conditioning circuit	94	Transmitter, coolant temperature
29	Starter motor solenoid	62	Fuses, 1, 2, 3 and 4, 35 amp	95	Switch for screen washer
30	Starter motor	63	Warning light for ignition	96	Stop lamp, RH
31	Pick-up point for air conditioning circuit	64	Warning light for choke	97	Stop lamp, LH
32	Pick-up point for heated backlight	65	Warning light for oil pressure		

Key to cable colours

B	Black	G	Green	LG	Light green	N	Brown	P	Purple	R	Red
W	White	U	Blue	Y	Yellow						

The last letter of a colour code denotes the tracer colour.

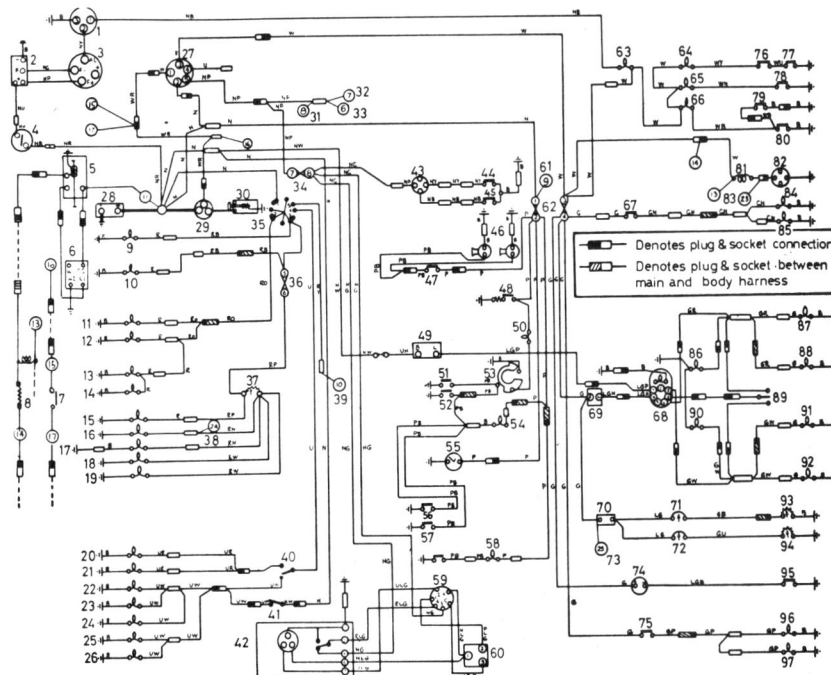

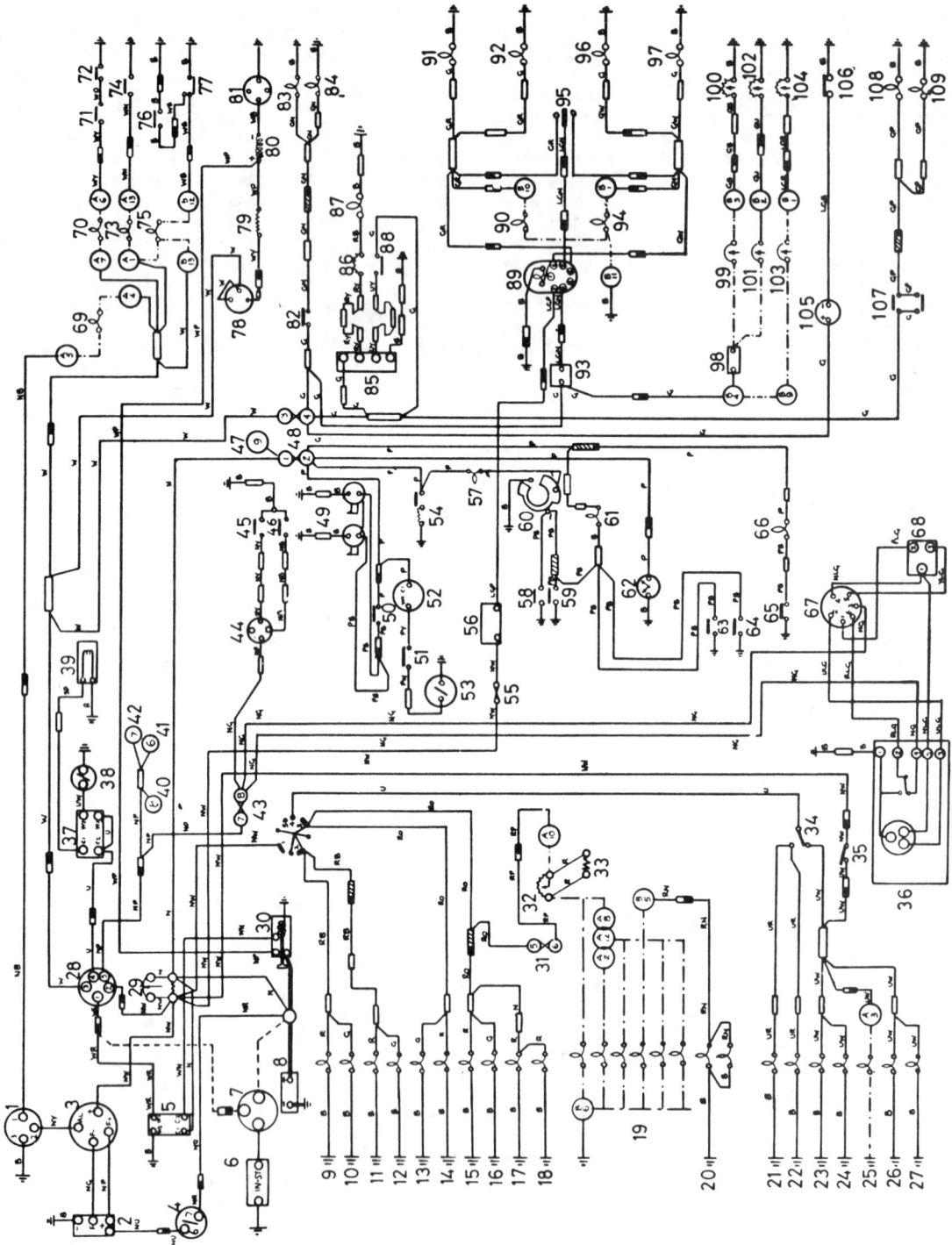

Fig. 13.42. Wiring diagram (2000 TC models) (see next page for 'Key')

Key to Wiring diagram (2000 TC models)

Encircled figures denote pick-up points for optional extra equipment.
Encircled letters and figures denote printed circuits and plug pick-up points on printed circuit board. Figure denotes pin number, letter denotes plug.

1   Relay for ignition warning light, type 3AW
2   Control box, type 4TR
3   Alternator, type 11AC
4   Alternator contacts, ignition switch
5   Relay for pre-engaged starter motor, where fitted
6   Starter motor, inertia type, where fitted
7   Solenoid for inertia starter motor, where fitted
8   Battery
9   Side and park lamp
10 Side marker lamp, front
11 Tail and park lamp
12 Side marker lamp, rear
13 Side marker lamp, front
14 Side lamp
15 Tail lamp
16 Side marker lamp, rear
17 Number plate illumination
18 Number plate illumination
19 Instrument panel illumination
20 Switch panel illumination
21 Headlamp dip beam, LH
22 Headlamp dip beam, RH
23 Headlamp main beam, RH
24 Headlamp main beam, RH
25 Warning light for headlamp main beam
26 Headlamp main beam, LH
27 Headlamp main beam, LH
28 Steering column lock switch
29 Ammeter shunt
30 Starter motor, pre-engaged type, where fitted
31 Fuses, 5 and 6, 2 amp
32 Rheostat for panel illumination
33 Ballast resistor
34 Switch for headlamp dip
35 Switch for headlamp flash
36 Screen wiper motor
37 Relay   ) Emission
38 Oil pressure switch) controlled
39 Solenoid valve   ) 10:1 com-
) pression
) ratio engines
) only
40 Pick-up point for air conditioning circuit

41 Pick-up point for radio
42 Pick-up point for heated backlight
43 Fuses, 7 and 8, 35 amp
44 Heater blower unit, two-speed
45 Switch, fast speed for blower
46 Switch, slow speed, for blower
47 Pick-up point for air conditioning circuit
48 Fuses 1, 2, 3 and 4, 35 amp
49 Twin horns
50 Switch for horns
51 Switch for audible)
    warning   )
52 Buzzer unit for   ) United States
    audible warning   ) and Canada
53 Steering column   ) only
    switch connections)
54 Cigar lighter and switch
55 In-line fuse
56 Hazard warning flasher unit
57 Rotary map lamp
58 Switch for door, front, LH
59 Switch for door, front, RH
60 Switch for interior light
61 Interior light
62 Clock
63 Switch for door, rear, RH
64 Switch for door, rear, LH
65 Switch for boot lamp
66 Boot lamp
67 Switch for windscreen wiper
68 Delay switch for windscreen wiper
69 Warning light for ignition
70 Warning light for choke control
71 Switch for choke control
72 Thermostat for choke control
73 Warning light for oil pressure
74 Switch for oil pressure
75 Warning light for handbrake and for brake fluid level

76 Switch for handbrake
77 Switch for brake fluid level
78 Tachometer
79 Ballast resistor cable
80 Ignition coil
81 Distributor
82 Switch for reverse light
83 Reverse lamp, RH
84 Reverse lamp, LH
85 Temperature   )
    sensing unit   )
86 Rheostat for   ) 'Icelert' sensing
    warning light   ) device, where fitted
87 Warning light   )
88 Test button   )
89 Switch and warning light, hazard warning device
90 Warning light for direction indicators, LH
91 Direction indicator lamp, front, LH
92 Direction indicator lamp, rear, LH
93 Flasher unit, type 8FL
94 Warning light for direction indicators, RH
95 Switch for direction indicators
96 Direction indicator lamp, rear, RH
97 Direction indicator lamp, front, RH
98 Bi-metal voltage regulator for instruments
99 Fuel contents gauge
100 Tank unit, fuel contents gauge
101 Coolant temperature gauge
102 Transmitter, coolant temperature
103 Gauge, oil pressure
104 Transmitter, oil pressure
105 Windscreen washer motor
106 Switch for screen washer
107 Switch for stop lights
108 Stop lamp, RH
109 Stop lamp, LH

Key to cable colours

| B | Black | G | Green | LG | Light green | N | Brown | P | Purple | R | Red |
| | | | | W | White | Y | Yellow | U | Blue | | |

The last letter of a colour code denotes the tracer colour.

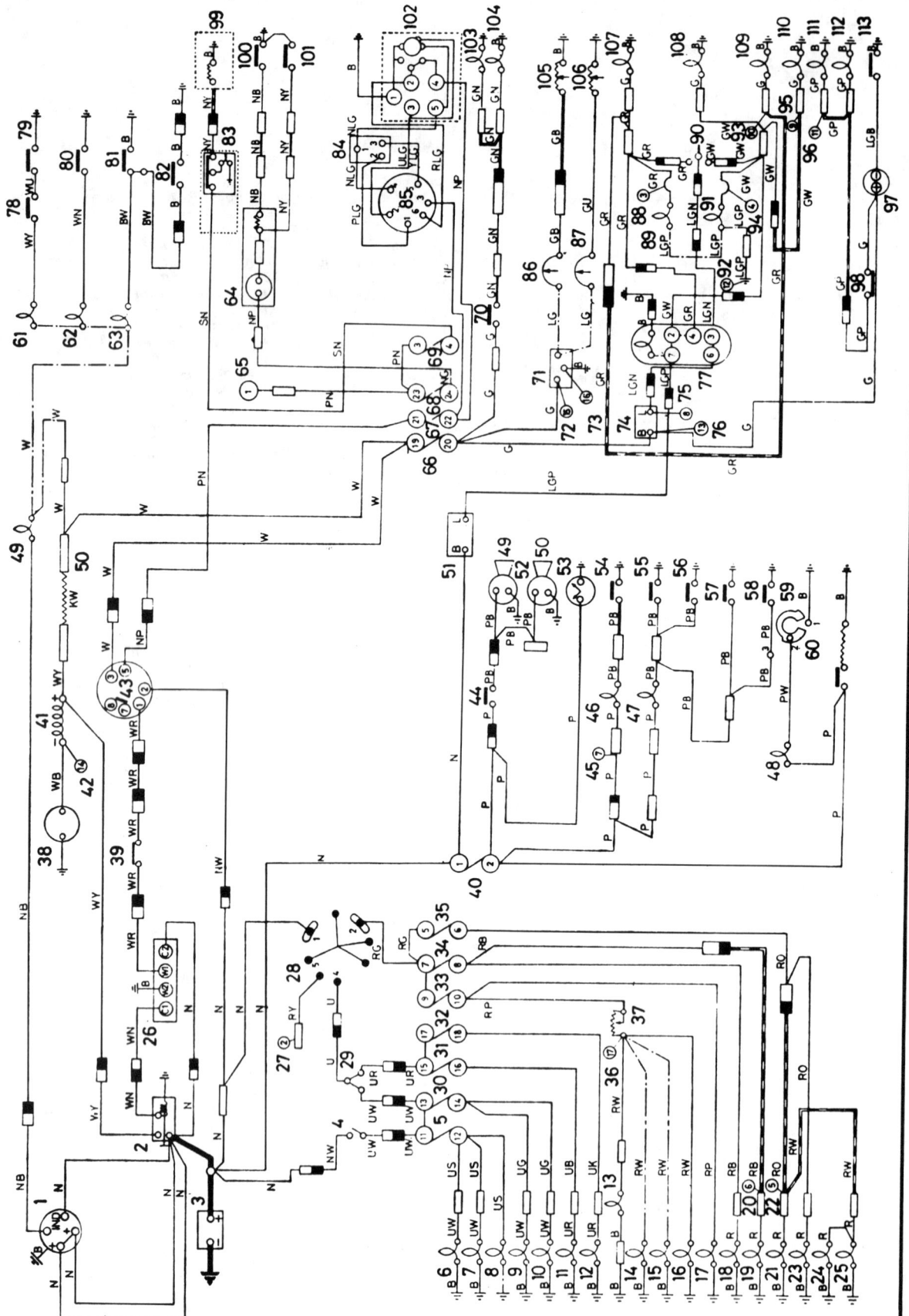

Fig. 13.43 Wiring diagram - 2000 and 2200 SC models for 1973/74/75 (RHD)

1 Alternator
2 Starter motor
3 Battery
4 Headlamp flasher switch
5 Fuse 11-12, 25 amp, headlamp main beam inner
6 Headlamp main beam, inner LH
7 Headlamp main beam, inner RH
8 Warning light, headlamp main beam
9 Headlamp main beam, outer LH
10 Headlamp main beam, outer RH
11 Headlamp dipped beam, RH
12 Headlamp dipped beam, LH
13 Automatic gearbox selector illumination
14 Instrument illumination
15 Instrument illumination
16 Clock illumination
17 Cigar lighter illumination
18 Side lamp, LH
19 Tail lamp, LH
20 Pick-up point for seven-pin trailer socket
21 Tail lamp, RH
22 Pick-up point for seven-pin trailer socket
23 Side lamps, RH
24 Number plate light
25 Number plate light
26 Relay for starter motor
27 Pick-up point for fog lamps
29 Switch headlamp dip
30 Fuse 13-14, 15 amp, headlamp main beam, outer
31 Fuse 15-16, 15 amp, headlamp dipped beam, RH
32 Fuse 17-18, 15 amp, headlamp dipped beam, LH
33 Fuse 9-10, 2 amp, instrument panel illumination
34 Fuse 5-6, 5 amp, side and tail lamp, RH and number plate illumination
36 Tachometer pick-up
37 Rheostat for instrument illumination
38 Distributor
39 Inhibitor switch for automatic gearbox
40 Fuse 1-2, 25 amp, horns, clock, cigar lighter and interior lights

41 Ignition coil
42 Tachometer pick-up
43 Switch, ignition and steering column lock
44 Switch, horn
45 Pick-up point for seven-pin trailer socket
46 Boot light
47 Interior light
48 Revolving map light
49 Warning light, ignition
50 Ballast resistor cable
51 Hazard warning indicator unit
52 Horns
53 Clock
54 Switch, boot light
55 Switch, courtesy light, RH rear door
56 Switch, courtesy light, LH rear door
57 Switch, courtesy light, RH front door
58 Switch, courtesy light, LH front door
59 Switch, interior and revolving map light
60 Cigar lighter
61 Cold start warning light
62 Oil pressure warning light
63 Brake warning light
64 Heater motor
65 Pick-up point for radio
66 Fuse 19-20, 25 amp, reverse lights, stop lamps, direction indicators, gauges and screenwasher reservoir
67 Fuse 21-22, 25 amp, screenwiper switch, delay governor and wiper motor
68 Fuse 23-24, 15 amp, heater motor
69 Fuse 3-4, 25 amp, heated rear screen
70 Switch, reverse lamps
71 Regulator 10 volt for instrument gauges
72 Tachometer pick-up
73 Tachometer pick-up
74 Direction indicator unit
75 Pick-up point for seven-pin trailer socket
76 Pick-up point for seven-pin trailer socket
77 Switch and warning light hazard warning

78 Switch, cold start control
79 Switch, cold start thermostat
80 Switch, oil pressure
81 Switch, brake fluid reservoir
82 Switch, handbrake
83 Switch, heated rear screen
84 Delay governor, screen wiper
85 Windscreen wiper switch
86 Fuel gauge
87 Water temperature gauge
88 Pick-up point for seven-pin trailer socket
89 Warning light, direction indicator
90 Direction indicator switch
91 Warning light, direction indicator
92 Pick-up point for seven-pin trailer socket
93 Pick-up point for seven-pin trailer socket
94 Pick-up point for seven-pin trailer socket
95 Pick-up point for seven-pin trailer socket
96 Pick-up point for seven-pin trailer socket
97 Screenwasher reservoir
98 Switch, stop lamps
99 Heated rear screen
100 Switch, heater slow speed
101 Switch, heater fast speed
102 Screenwiper motor
103 Reverse lamp, RH
104 Reverse lamp, LH
105 Fuel tank unit
106 Water temperature transmitter
107 Direction indicator, front LH
108 Direction indicator, front RH
109 Direction indicator, rear LH
110 Direction indicator, rear RH
111 Stop lamp, LH
112 Stop lamp, RH
113 Switch, screenwasher

NB Final letter of colour code denotes tracer colour

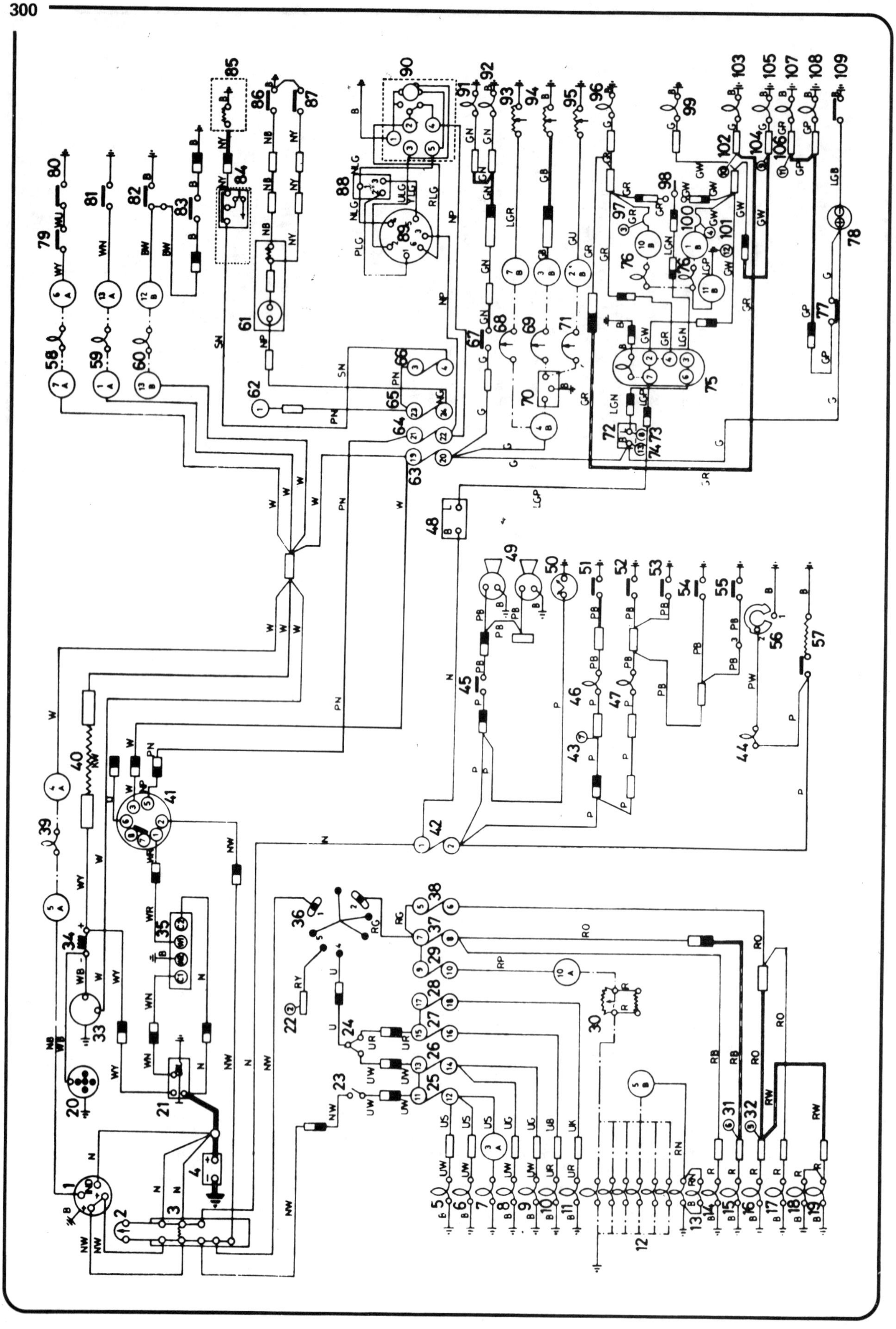

Fig 13.44 Wiring diagram - 2000 and 2200 TC models for 1973/74/75 (RHD)

1 Alternator (18 ACR)
2 Ammeter
3 Ammeter shunt
4 Battery
5 Headlamp main beam inner, LH
6 Headlamp main beam inner, RH
7 Warning light, headlamp main beam
8 Headlamp main beam outer, LH
9 Headlamp main beam outer, RH
10 Headlamp dipped beam, RH
11 Headlamp dipped beam, LH
12 Instrument panel illumination
13 Switch panel illumination
14 Side lamp, RH
15 Tail lamp, RH
16 Tail lamp, LH
17 Side lamp, LH
18 Number plate light
19 Number plate light
20 Distributor
21 Starter (pre-engaged)
22 Pick-up point for fog lamps
23 Switch, headlamp flash
24 Switch, headlamp dip
25 Fuse 11-12 amp, headlamp main beam inner
26 Fuse 13-14 amp, headlamp main beam outer
27 Fuse 15-16 amp, headlamp dip beam, RH
28 Fuse 17-18 amp, headlamp dip beam, LH
29 Fuse 9-10, 8 amp, instrument panel illumination
30 Rheostat for instrument panel illumination
31 Pick-up point for seven-pin trailer socket
32 Pick-up point for seven-pin trailer socket
33 Tachometer
34 Ignition coil
35 Relay for starter motor
36 Switch, main lighting
37 Fuse 7-8, 5 amp, side, tail lamp, RH and number plate illumination
38 Fuse 5-6, 5 amp, side and tail lamp LH
39 Ignition warning light
40 Ballast resistor
41 Ignition and steering column lock switch
42 Fuse 1-2, 25 amp, horns, clock, cigar lighter and interior lights
43 Pick-up point for seven-pin trailer socket
44 Revolving map light
45 Switch, horn
46 Boot light
47 Interior light
48 Hazard warning indicator unit
49 Horns
50 Clocks
51 Switch, boot light
52 Switch, rear door, RH
53 Switch, rear door, LH
54 Switch, front door, RH
55 Switch, front door, LH
56 Switch, interior light and revolving map light
57 Cigar lighter
58 Warning light, choke
59 Warning light, oil pressure
60 Warning light, brakes
61 Heater unit
62 Pick-up point for radio
63 Fuse 19-20, 25 amp, reverse lights, stop lights direction indicators, gauges and screen washer reservoir
64 Fuse 21-22, 25 amp, screen wiper switch, delay governor and wiper motor
65 Fuse 23-24, 15 amp, heater motor
66 Fuse 3-4, 25 amp, heated rear screen
67 Switch, reverse light
68 Oil pressure gauge
69 Fuel level gauge
70 Instrument gauges regulator, 10 volt
71 Water temperature gauge
72 Direction indicator unit
73 Pick-up point for seven-pin trailer socket
74 Pick-up point for seven-pin trailer socket
75 Hazard switch and warning light
76 Warning lights, direction indicators
77 Stop lamps switch
78 Screenwasher reservoir
79 Choke switch
80 Choke thermostat switch
81 Oil pressure switch
82 Brake fluid reservoir switch
83 Handbrake switch
84 Warning light and switch, heated rear screen
85 Heated rear screen
86 Switch, heater, slow speed
87 Switch, heater, fast speed
88 Delay governor, screenwiper motor
89 Screenwiper motor switch
90 Screenwiper motor
91 Reverse lamp, LH
92 Reverse lamp, RH
93 Oil pressure transmitter
94 Fuel gauge tank unit
95 Water temperature transmitter
96 Direction indicator lamp, front LH
97 Pick-up point for seven-pin trailer socket
98 Direction indicator switch
99 Direction indicator lamp, front RH
100 Pick-up point for seven-pin trailer socket
101 Pick-up point for seven-pin trailer socket
102 Pick-up point for seven-pin trailer socket
103 Direction indicator lamp, rear RH
104 Pick-up point for seven-pin trailer socket
105 Direction indicator lamp, rear, RH
106 Pick-up point for seven-pin trailer socket
107 Stop lamp, LH
108 Stop lamp, RH
109 Screenwasher motor switch

NB Final letter of colour code denotes tracer colour

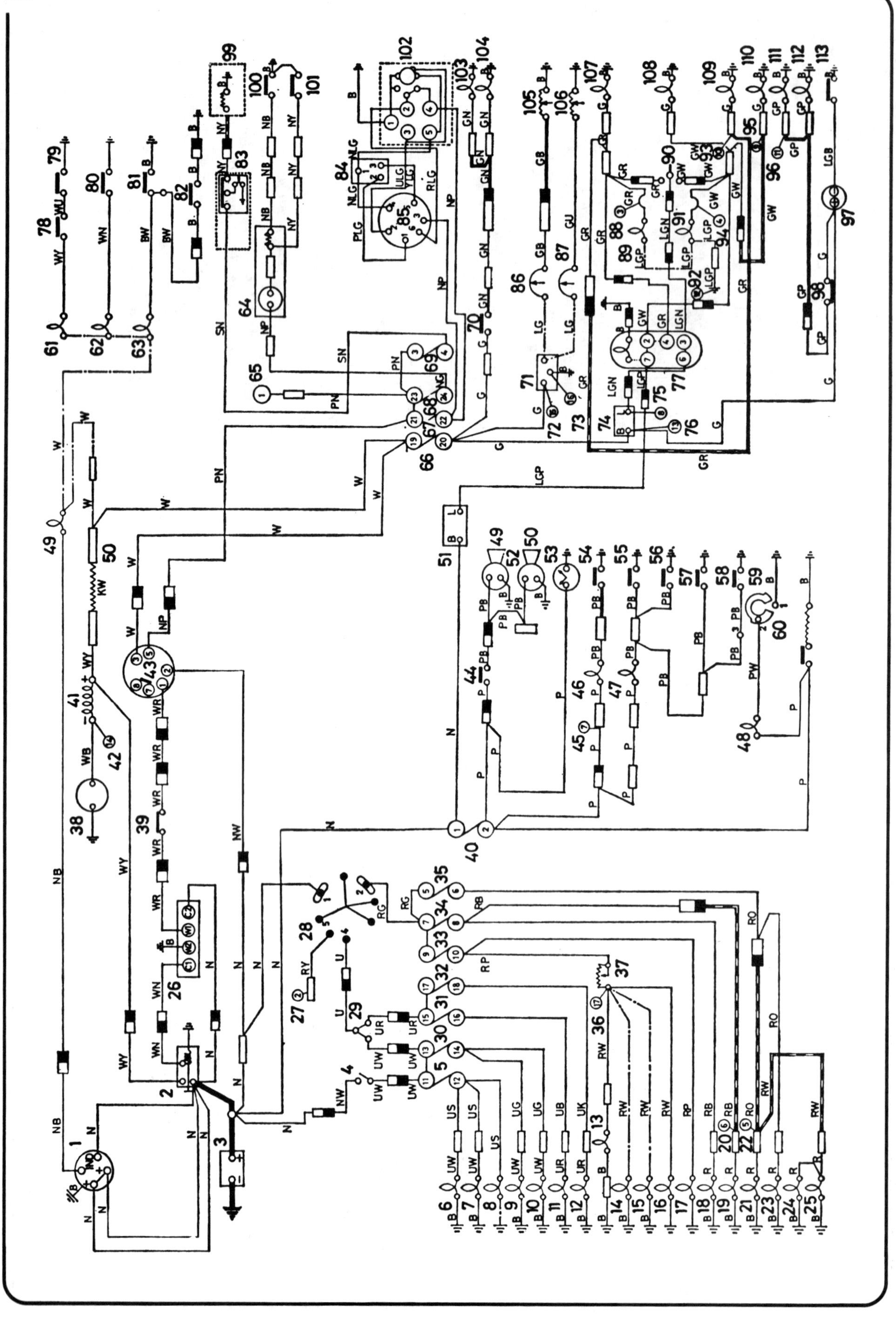

Fig. 13.45 Wiring diagram - 2200 SC and automatic models from 1975 (RHD)

1 Alternator (18 ACR)
2 Starter motor
3 Battery
4 Headlamp flasher switch
5 Fuse 11-12, 25 amp, headlamp main beam inner
6 Headlamp main beam, inner LH
7 Headlamp main beam, inner RH
8 Warning light, headlamp main beam
9 Headlamp main beam, outer LH
10 Headlamp main beam, outer RH
11 Headlamp dipped beam, RH
12 Headlamp dipped beam, LH
13 Automatic gearbox selector illumination
14 Instrument light
15 Instrument light
16 Clock illumination
20 Pick-up point for seven-pin trailer socket
21 Tail lamp, RH
22 Pick-up point for seven-pin trailer socket
23 Side lamps, RH
24 Number plate light
25 Number plate light
26 Relay for starter motor
27 Pick-up point for fog lamps
28 Main lighting switch
29 Headlamp dip switch
30 Fuse 13-14, 15 amp, headlamp main beam, outer
31 Fuse 15-16, 15 amp, headlamp dipped beam, RH
32 Fuse 17-18, 15 amp, headlamp dipped beam, LH
33 Fuse 9-10, 2 amp, instrument panel illumination
34 Fuse 7-8, 5 amp, side and tail lamp, LH
35 Fuse 5-6, 5 amp, side and tail lamp, RH and number plate illumination
36 Pick-up point for tachometer
37 Rheostat for instrument illumination
38 Distributor
39 Inhibitor switch for automatic gearbox
40 Fuse 1-2, 25 amp, horns, clock, cigar lighter and interior lights
41 Ignition coil
42 Pick-up point for tachometer
43 Ignition and steering colum lock switch
44 Horn switch
45 Pick-up point for seven-pin trailer socket
46 Boot light
47 Interior light
48 Revolving map light
49 Warning light ignition
50 Ballast resistor cable
51 Hazard warning indicator unit
52 Horns
53 Clock
54 Boot light switch
55 Switch, courtesy light, RH rear door
56 Switch, courtesy light, LH rear door
57 Switch, courtesy light, RH front door
58 Switch, courtesy light, LH front door
59 Switch, interior and revolving map light
60 Cigar lighter
61 Cold start warning light
62 Oil pressure warning light
63 Brake warning light
64 Heater motor
65 Pick-up point for radio
66 Fuse 19-20, 25 amp, reverse lights, stop lamps, direction indicators, gauges and screenwasher reservoir
67 Fuse 21-22, 25 amp, screenwiper switch, delay governor and wiper motor
68 Fuse 23-24, 15 amp, heater motor
69 Fuse 3-4, 25 amp, heated rear screen
70 Switch, reverse lamps
71 Regulator 10 volt for instrument gauges
72 Pick-up point for tachometer
73 Pick-up point for tachometer
74 Direction indicator unit
75 Pick-up point for seven-pin trailer socket
76 Pick-up point for seven-pin trailer socket
77 Switch and warning light hazard warning
78 Cold start control switch
79 Cold start thermostat switch
80 Oil pressure switch
81 Brake fluid reservoir switch
82 Handbrake switch
83 Heated rear screen switch
84 Delay governor, screen wiper
85 Windscreen wiper switch
86 Fuel gauge
87 Water temperature gauge
88 Pick-up point for seven-pin trailer socket
89 Warning light, direction indicator
90 Direction indicator switch
91 Warning light, direction indicator
92 Pick-up point for seven-pin trailer socket
93 Pick-up point for seven-pin trailer socket
94 Pick-up point for seven-pin trailer socket
95 Pick-up point for seven-pin trailer socket
96 Pick-up point for seven-pin trailer socket
97 Screenwasher reservoir
98 Switch, stop lamps
99 Heated rear screen
100 Heater, slow speed switch
101 Heater, fast speed switch
102 Screenwiper motor
103 Reverse lamp, RH
104 Reverse lamp, LH
105 Fuel tank unit
106 Water temperature transmitter
107 Direction indicator, front LH
108 Direction indicator, front RH
109 Direction indicator, rear LH
110 Direction indicator, rear RH
111 Stop lamp, LH
112 Stop lamp, RH
113 Screenwasher switch

NB Final letter of colour code denotes tracer colour

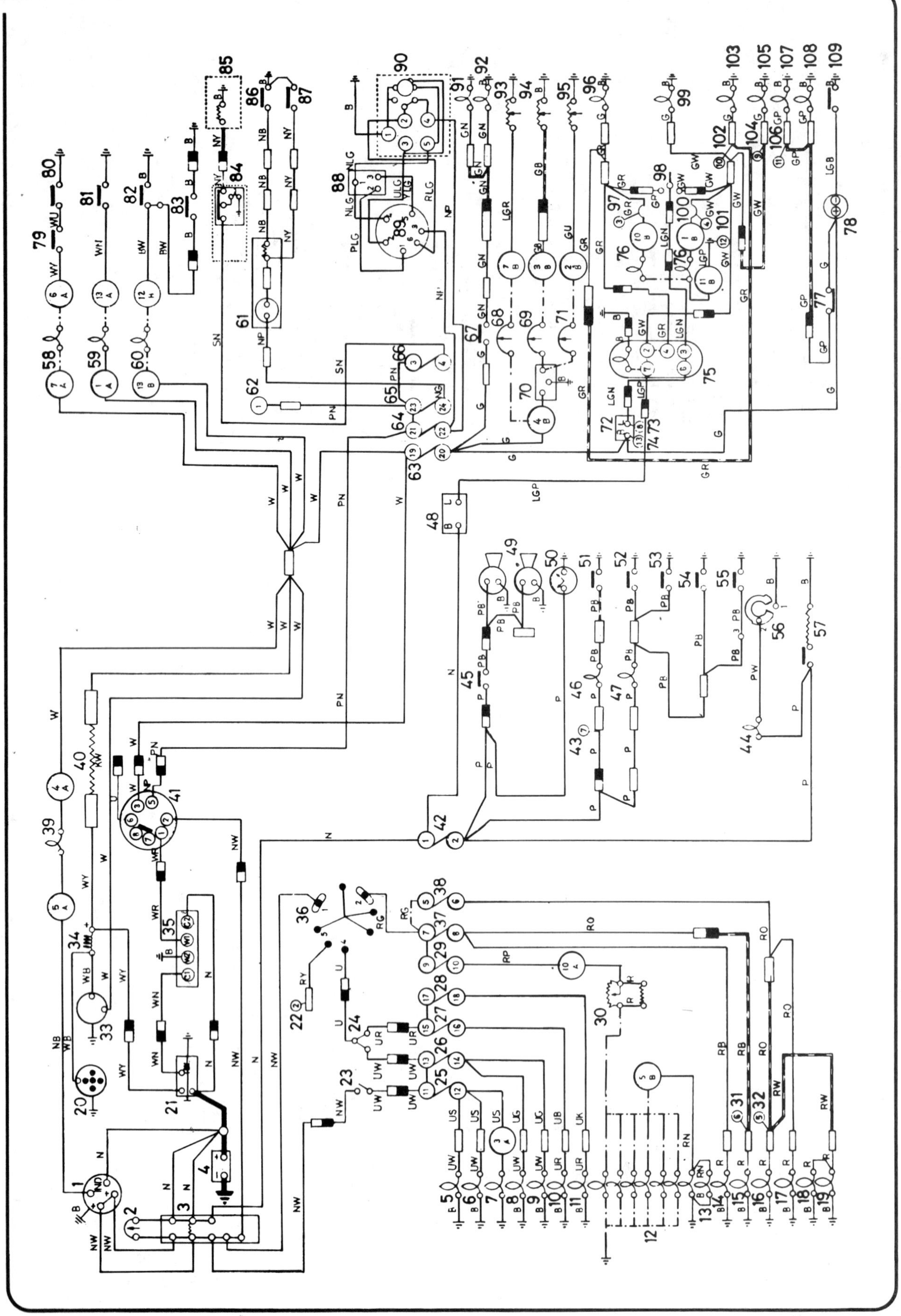

Fig. 13.46 Wiring diagram 2200 TC from 1975 (RHD)

1 Alternator (18 ACR)
2 Ammeter
3 Ammeter shunt
4 Battery
5 Headlamp main beam inner, LH
6 Headlamp main beam inner, RH
7 Warning light, headlamp main beam
8 Headlamp main beam outer, LH
9 Headlamp main beam outer, RH
10 Headlamp dipped beam, RH
11 Headlamp dipped beam, LH
12 Instrument panel illumination
13 Switch panel illumination
14 Side lamp, RH
15 Tail lamp, RH
16 Tail lamp, LH
17 Side lamp, LH
18 Number plate illumination
19 Number plate illumination
20 Distributor
21 Starter (pre-engaged)
22 Pick-up point for fog lamps
23 Headlamp flasher switch
24 Headlamp dip switch
25 Fuse 11-12, 25 amp, headlamp main beam inner
26 Fuse 13-14, 15 amp, headlamp main beam outer
27 Fuse 15-16, 15 amp, headlamp dip beam, RH
28 Fuse 17-18, 15 amp, headlamp dip beam, LH
29 Fuse 9-10, 8 amp, instrument panel illumination
30 Rheostat for instrument panel illumination
31 Pick-up point for seven-pin trailer socket
32 Pick-up point for seven-pin trailer socket
33 Tachometer
34 Ignition coil
35 Relay for starter motor
36 Switch, main lighting
37 Fuse 7-8, 5 amp, side, tail lamp, RH and number plate illumination

38 Fuse 5-6, 5 amp, side and tail lamp, LH
39 Ignition warning light
40 Ballast resistor
41 Ignition and steering column lock switch
42 Fuse 1-2, 25 amp, horns, clock, cigar lighter and interior lights
43 Pick-up point for seven-pin trailer socket
44 Revolving map light
45 Horn switch
46 Boot light
47 Interior light
48 Hazard warning indicator unit
49 Horns
50 Clock
51 Boot light switch
52 Switch, rear door, RH
53 Switch, rear door, LH
54 Switch, front door, RH
55 Switch, front door, LH
56 Switch, interior light and revolving map light
57 Cigar lighter
58 Choke warning light
59 Oil pressure warning light
60 Brakes warning light
61 Heater unit
62 Pick-up point for radio
63 Fuse 19-20, 25 amp, reverse lights, stop lights direction indicators, gauges and screen washer reservoir
64 Fuse 21-22, 25 amp, screen wiper switch, delay governor and wiper motor
65 Fuse 23-24, 15 amp, heater motor
66 Fuse 3-4, 25 amp, heated rear screen
67 Switch, reverse light
68 Oil pressure gauge
69 Fuel level gauge
70 Instrument gauges regulator, 10 volt
71 Water temperature gauge

72 Direction indicator unit
73 Pick-up point for seven-pin trailer socket
74 Pick-up point for seven-pin trailer socket
75 Switch and warning light hazard
76 Warning lights, direction indicators
77 Stop lamps switch
78 Screenwasher reservoir
79 Choke switch
80 Choke thermostat switch
81 Oil pressure switch
82 Brake fluid reservoir switch
83 Handbrake switch
84 Switch and warning light, heated rear screen
85 Heated rear screen
86 Heater, slow speed switch
87 Heater, fast speed switch
88 Delay governor, screenwiper motor
89 Screenwiper motor switch
90 Screenwiper motor
91 Reverse lamp, LH
92 Reverse lamp, RH
93 Oil pressure transmitter
94 Fuel gauge tank unit
95 Water temperature transmitter
96 Direction indicator lamp, front, LH
97 Pick-up point for seven-pin trailer socket
98 Direction indicator switch
99 Direction indicator lamp, front RH
100 Pick-up point for seven-pin trailer socket
101 Pick-up point for seven-pin trailer socket
103 Pick-up point for seven-pin trailer socket
103 Direction indicator lamp rear, LH
104 Pick-up point for seven-pin trailer socket
105 Direction indicator lamp, rear, RH
106 Pick-up point for seven-pin trailer socket
107 Stop lamp, LH
108 Stop lamp, RH
109 Screenwasher motor switch

NB The final colour code letter denotes tracer colour

clutch. It must provide instantaneous take up of the drive in one direction and rotate easily and smoothly in the opposite direction. Make sure that the drive moves smoothly on the armature shaft splines without binding or sticking.

10 Reassembling the starter motor is the reverse sequence to dismantling. The following additional points should be noted:

11 If fitting new brushes the old ones must be cut off and new ones soldered on. To renew those connected to the end bracket, cut the old ones at the posts, and cut, with a thin file or a hacksaw, slots on the post into which the tags for the new brushes can be slid, and then soldered. The brushes connected to the field windings should be cut off about ¼ inch short of the winding junction, and the tags of the new ones soldered on to the stumps. Do *not* undercut the commutator segments.

12 When assembling the drive end bracket always use a new retaining ring (spire nut) to secure the engagement lever pivot pin.

13 Make sure that the internal thrust washer is fitted to the commutator end of the armature shaft before the armature end cover is fitted.

14 Always use a new retaining ring (spire nut) on the armature shaft and push it on to give a maximum clearance of 0.010 in. (0.254 mm) between the retaining ring and the bearing brush shoulder. This will be the armature endfloat.

15 Tighten the through bolts to a torque wrench setting of 8 lbf ft (1.106 kgf m) and the nuts securing the solenoid to the drive bracket to 4.5 lbf ft (0.62 kgf m).

Fuses

1 The fuse box on later models is located in the passenger glove box for easy accessibility and renewal of fuses in the event of a failure.

2 The fuses and values are as follows:

a)	Horns/clock/cigar lighter and interior lights	25 amp
b)	Hazard warning	25 amp
c)	Right-hand, side and tail lights	5 amp
d)	Left-hand, side and tail lights	5 amp
e)	Instrument and switch panel/automatic selection illuminator	
	SC	2 amp
	TC	8 amp
f)	Headlight main, inner and main beam warning	25 amp
g)	Headlight main, outer	15 amp
h)	Right headlight - dip	15 amp
i)	Left headlight - dip	15 amp
j)	Windscreen wiper/switch and delay governor	25 amp
k)	Screenwasher/stop lamp/reverse lamp/flashers/gauges	25 amp
l)	Heater	15 amp

Flasher unit - 2200 models

1 The flasher unit for the 2200 models is located in the driver's side glove box. In the event of a suspected malfunction of the unit, check it out as described in Section 33 of Chapter 10.

'Icelert' warning device

This device is fitted to North American vehicles to provide a visual warning when temperatures outside the car drop to freezing point. The operating point of the device is 36°F (2.2°C) and provides an advance warning to the driver of the possibility of icy road conditions.

Hazard warning circuit

1 This system is fitted as North American specifications from 1968 and to all later Rover models. Actuation of the hazard warning switch causes all four direction indicators to flash simultaneously through the medium of a separate flasher unit.

2 Bulb renewal is carried out simply by unscrewing the switch knob.

3 The hazard warning flasher unit is located within the driver's side glove compartment. It may be renewed by pulling it from the socket.

Windscreen wiper delay unit   description and location

1 Cars produced after 1970 incorporate two speed wipers with a variable speed position on the switch to deal with light rain or other conditions when the two pre-set speeds might be too high.

2 Two types of delay unit have been employed, being a vacuum or electronic type which were fitted to late model 2200.

3 The earlier vacuum type variable speed unit is located adjacent to the wiper motor. In the event of a failure check the electrical and vacuum hose connections for security, and if these are in order renew the unit complete as it is not repairable.

4 The later electrical type unit is also mounted adjacent to the wiper motor but is mounted on the wing valance by a single bolt. Again the unit is non-serviceable and in the event of failure must be renewed. When refitting ensure that the unit is positioned so that the wires face forwards and downwards.

Circuit diagrams - modifications

Modified electrical circuit layouts are incorporated in North American vehicles with automatic transmission built after 1968 and in SC and TC models produced after 1970 for all territories.

11 Suspension and steering

Front road springs (North American cars 1968 onwards

In order to maintain correct headlamp alignment when the car is fully laden, the front road springs are of different rating from standard specification.

Identification is by means of a green painted stripe running the full length of the spring. Details of this type of spring are given under specifications at the front of this Chapter.

Steering column shaft assembly - revised removal and installation procedure

1 As the result of incorporating a steering column lock in all vehicles built after 1970, the instructions given in Chapter 11, Section 18 are superseded by the following operations.

2 Remove the left-hand or right-hand glove box according to whether LHD or RHD.

3 Slacken the bolt and nut which secures the universal joint clamp to the steering box inner column.

4 Remove the two screws from the reverse side of the steering wheel spokes and withdraw the steering wheel finisher.

5 Unscrew the nut which secures the steering wheel and remove the spring washer. Knock the steering wheel from the splined shaft by banging the rear faces of the spokes with the hands. If the wheel is stuck tight, then a suitable puller will have to be used.

6 Unbolt the steering column support bracket from the bulkhead.

7 Detach the steering column lock from the bracket located under the facia panel and then remove the bolt which secures the bracket to the underside of the facia panel.

8 Disconnect the wiring harness connectors and pull off the vacuum pipe from the wiper variable speed controller.

9 Remove the cable cleat which secures the wiring harness to the steering column lock.

10 Unscrew and remove the two Phillips type screws from the steering lock switch and then withdraw the steering column/shaft/lock assembly from the car.

11 On cars equipped with a steering lock, the steering column shaft and universal joint can only be serviced as a complete assembly.

12 Installation is a reversal of removal but ensure that the steering wheel is fitted with spokes in the horizontal attitude when the front road wheels are in the straight ahead position.

Steering column lock - removal and refitting

1 Remove the steering column/shaft/lock assembly as described in the preceding section.

2 The lock is held to the column by two shear type bolts. These should be removed by one of two methods: either centre punch the end of the shear bolt and drill a 5/32 in hole and insert a stud extractor or drill the shear bolts right out if the lock assembly is being discarded.

3 For the foregoing operation there is no necessity to remove the nucelle assembly but if the steering column bearing is to be renewed then slide off the plastic bearing and washer from the column. Slide off the key-located metal collar from the steering column and detach the key from the shaft. Slide off the remaining washer and plastic bearing.

4 Installing the steering lock to the column is a reversal of the removal procedure but observe the following points. Ensure that the column lock tongue engages in the slot in the metal collar. Tighten the shear bolts with sufficient torque to shear their heads.

12 Bodywork and underframe

Change of body styling and identification

Major visual changes have taken place in two stages. From chassis number 43600001A the following bodywork modifications were implemented.

Bonnet with new motif and two raised ribs.

Plastic radiator grille of rectangular styling.

Black vinyl covered rear quarter panels with motif.

New wheel trim.

Sills and bottoms of wing given black anti-corrosive finish.

Stainless steel body side and mouldings added. Re-designed facia and instrument panels.

The 1974 Rover 2200 models incorporate the following bodywork modifications as standard.

Safety sun-visors and interior mirror.

Re-designed over-riders.

Door mounted exterior rear view mirrors.

Heated rear window.

Instrument panel (TC models 1970-74) - removal and refitting

1 Disconnect the battery earth lead.

2 Pull off the knobs for speedometer trip control and panel light switch.

3 Remove the locking rings which retain the instrument panel finisher and then slide it to one side and withdraw it.

4 Spring off the finisher at the other end of the instrument panel by pulling the knob or if 'Icelert' device is installed, remove the grub-screw, knob and nut from the rheostat and spring off the finisher.

6 Disconnect the speedometer cable leaving the angled drive on the back of the panel.

7 Mark the electrical leads and connecting plugs for ease of refitting and disconnect them. The instrument panel may now be withdrawn.

8 Refitting is a reversal of removal.

Main switch panel (TC models 1970-74) - removal and refitting

1 Disconnect battery earth lead.

2 Peel back the black rubber finisher at each end of the switch panel.

3 Remove the four panel retaining screws and pull the panel forward.

4 Mark the cable connections to facilitate re-connection and then disconnect them and withdraw the panel.

5 The rotary type switches are removed from the panel by first depressing the plungers which retain the knobs and pulling the knobs off. Unscrew the switch locking rings and withdraw the switches. Refitting is a reversal of removal.

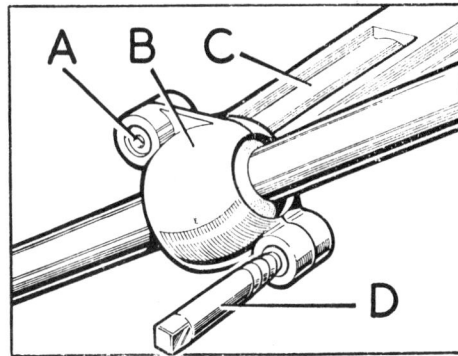

Fig. 13.47. Removing shear bolts from steering column lock

A Hole drilled in shear bolt   C Lock body
B Lock cap   D Bolt extractor

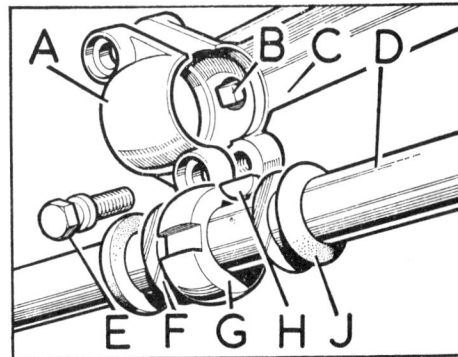

Fig. 13.48. Components of the steering column lock

A Lock cap   E Shear bolts
B Lock tongue   F Shims
C Lock body   G Collar
D Steering column   H Woodruff key & plastic
                      bearings

Driver's side switch panel (TC models 1970 -74) - removal and refitting

1 Disconnect the battery earth lead.

2 Remove all switches except the ignition switch from the panel.

3 Remove the locking ring from the glove box lock.

4 Slacken the steering column clamp nut and lower the steering column towards the floor.

5 Remove the screw from the bottom edge of the panel at its end nearest the driver's door.

6 Peel back the rubber finisher on the main switch panel and remove the two screws.

7 Carefully prise the right-hand side of the ignition switch finisher away from the panel and remove the nut from the rear of the ignition switch panel.

8 Withdraw the panel and at the same time pass the ignition switch finisher through the hole. The panel is in two halves, jointed.

9 Refitting is a reversal of removal.

Passenger side switch panel (TC models 1970-74) - removal and refitting

1 Remove the locking ring from the glove box lock.

2 Open the glove box and withdraw the bulb holder from the map light unit.

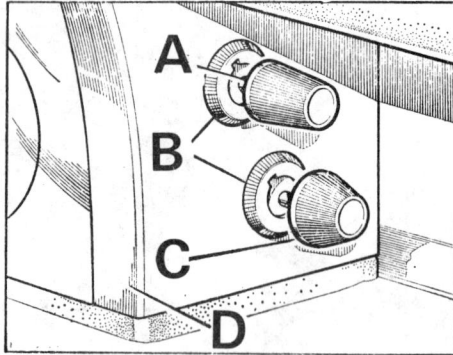

Fig. 13.49. Removal of instrument panel finishing strips (TC 1970 - 74 models)

A Speedometer trip knob   C Panel light
B Locking ring   D Finishing strip

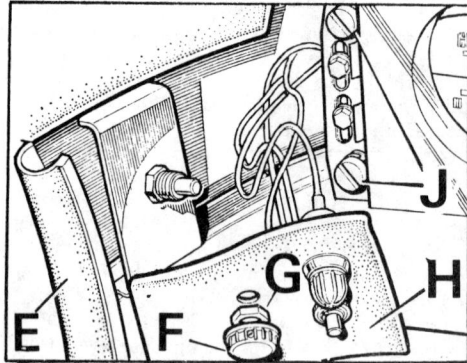

E Finishing strip (parcels shelf)
F 'Icelert' switch

G Securing nut
H Panel
J Screw

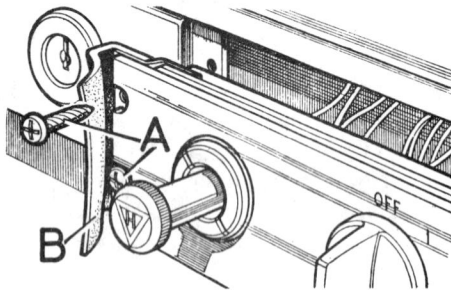

Fig, 13.50. Removal of main switch panel

A Securing screws   B Rubber finishing strip

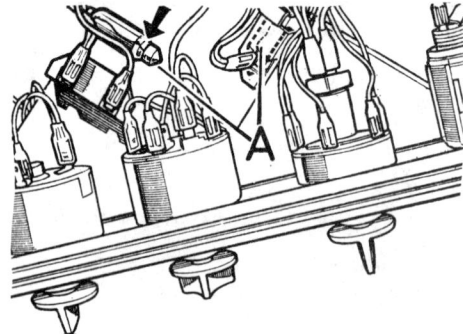

Fig. 13.51. Location of rotary switches on main switch panel

A Panel light bulbs

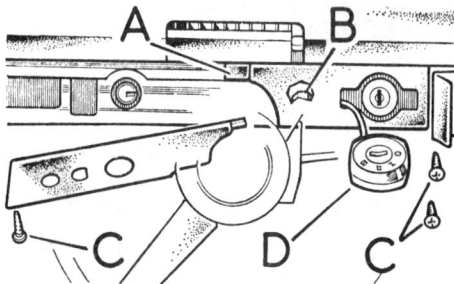

Fig. 13.52. Removal of driver's side switch panel (TC 1970 - 74)

A Jointing piece
B Panel rear fixing
C Front securing screws

D Ignition switch embellishment

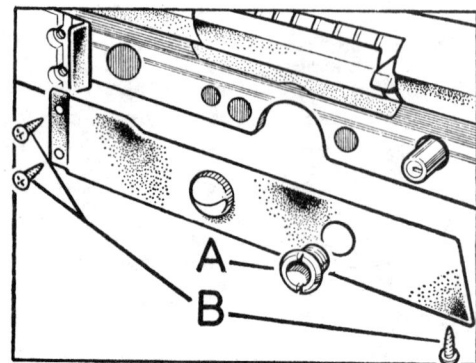

Fig. 13.53. Removal of passenger's side switch panel (TC 1970 - 74)

A Glove box locking ring   B Securing screws

3 Remove the screw from the bottom edge of the panel at the end nearest the passenger's door.
4 Peel back the rubber finisher on the main switch panel and remove the two screws then withdraw the switch panel.
5 Refitting is a reversal of removal.

Speedometer cable (TC models 1970-74) - removal and refitting
1 Remove the instrument panel as described earlier in this Chapter.
2 Disconnect the speedometer cable from the head.
3 Remove the radio loudspeaker panel.
4 Remove the cover on the gearbox tunnel adjacent to the speedometer drive connection at the gearbox. This is accessible after raising the carpet on the left-hand side of the gearbox tunnel.
5 Disconnect the gearbox end of the speedometer cable by removing the nut and retainer which secure the cable to the gearbox. Withdraw the cable and grommet through the body-frame.

Front ventilators - control knob removal (all models 1970 onwards)
1 Opening and closure of the front ventilators (quarter lights) is gear controlled by a knurled knob. Removal of this knob is necessary before the door interior trim can be removed.
2 Using a small screwdriver, prise out the chrome blanking disc from the centre of the knob.
3 Remove the now accessible screw and withdraw the knob.
4 Removal of the window regulator and door trim and panel may be carried out as described in Chapter 12, Section 12.

Front ventilator (quarter light) - all models 1970 onwards removal and refitting
1 Remove the door trim and then remove the ventilator spindle retaining clip.
2 Draw the ventilator glass and frame upwards.
3 To remove the ventilator operating mechanism, the door glass and frame must be removed as described in Chapter 12, Section 15.
4 Installation is a reversal of removal.

Stainless steel body side trim (all models 1970 onwards) - removal and refitting
1 These moulding strips are retained by nylon clips.
2 Removal of the trim is achieved by carefully prising it from the clips. If essential pull the clips from the bodywork.
3 To refit the clip, insert its shank in the hole in the body panel so that the clip lies horizontally.
4 Tap the clip retaining pin through the hollow shank of the clip with a light hammer until the pin is flush with the surface of the clip.
5 Tilt the stainless steel moulding to engage its top edge with the clip and then strike it sharply in a downward direction with the palm of the hand to engage the bottom edge with the clip.

Air conditioning system description and servicing
1 The system is fitted as an option to cars operating in hot territories. It is designed to provide cool, dry air within the vehicle interior on a recirculation principle.
2 The equipment is complicated and comprises a receiver/dryer, condenser, compressor, evaporator and all the necessary valves and interconnecting pipework.
3 Any dismantling of the system or removal of components will necessitate professional re-charging of the equipment and servicing should therefore be limited to the following operation.

Compressor driving belt tension - adjustment
1 Slacken the nut which secures the driving belt tensioner pulley to its mounting bracket.
2 Apply an open ended spanner to the tensioner nut which is located behind the pulley and turn it in either direction to

obtain a total belt deflection at the mid-way position between the compressor and tensioner pulleys of between 7/16 and 9/16 inch (11 to 14 mm).
3 Tighten the securing nut.

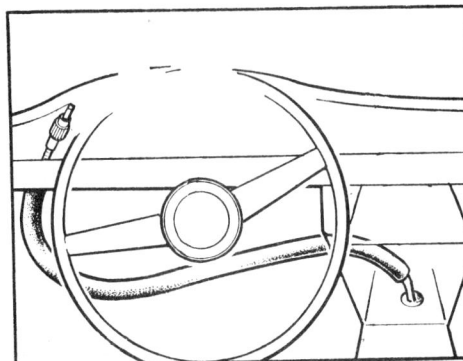

Fig. 13.54. Speedometer cable routing at facia end

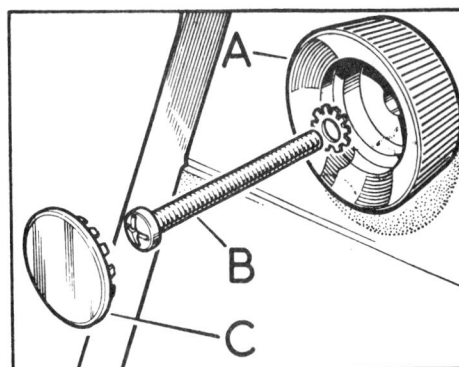

Fig. 13.55. Components of front ventilator (quarter light) control knob

A Knob   C Blanking plate
B Screw

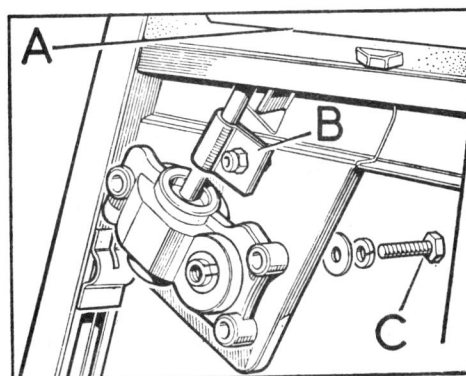

Fig. 13.56. Front ventilator (quarter light) pivot unit

A Ventilator   C Pivot unit bolt
B Spindle retaining clip

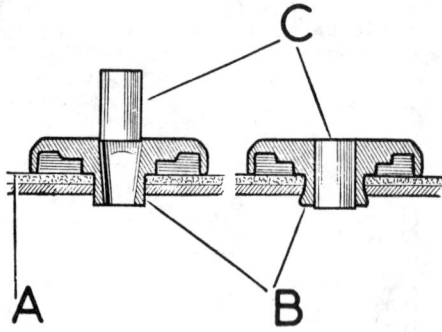

Fig. 13.57. Sectional view of clip for body side trim

A Body panel
B Hollow shank
C Pin

Fig. 13.58. Air conditioner compressor driving belt adjustment

A Tensioner locknut
B Tensioner adjuster nut
C Deflector testing point (7/16 to 9/16 in. — 11 to 14 mm)

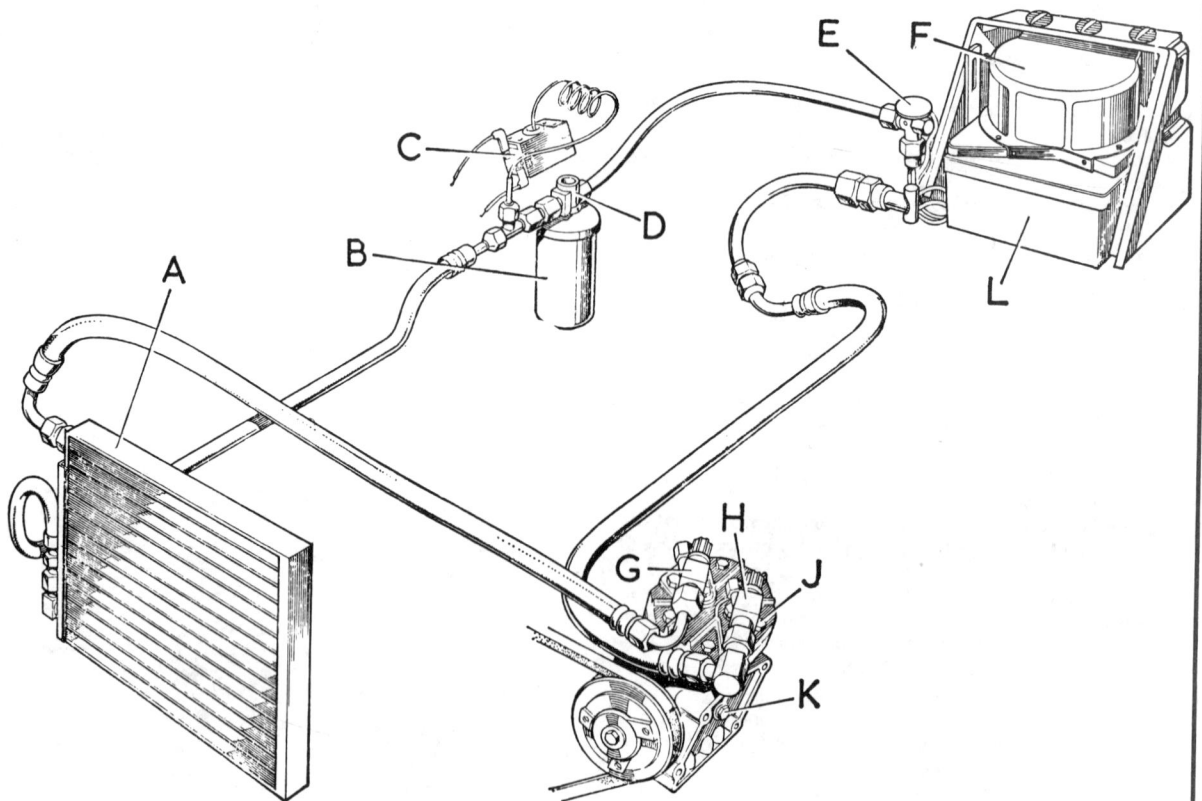

Fig. 13.59. Layout of air conditioning system

A Condenser
B Receiver/dryer
C High pressure cut-out switch
D Sight glass
E Expansion valve
F Blower

G High pressure discharge valve
H Low pressure suction valve
J Compressor
K Oil filler plug
L Evaporator unit

Metric conversion tables

Inches	Decimals	Millimetres
1/64	0.015625	0.3969
1/32	0.03125	0.7937
3/64	0.046875	1.1906
1/16	0.0625	1.5875
5/64	0.078125	1.9844
3/32	0.09375	2.3812
7/64	0.109375	2.7781
1/8	0.125	3.1750
9/64	0.140625	3.5719
5/32	0.15625	3.9687
11/64	0.171875	4.3656
3/16	0.1875	4.7625
13/64	0.203125	5.1594
7/32	0.21875	5.5562
15/64	0.234375	5.9531
1/4	0.25	6.3500
17/64	0.265625	6.7469
9/32	0.28125	7.1437
19/64	0.296875	7.5406
5/16	0.3125	7.9375
21/64	0.328125	8.3344
11/32	0.34375	8.7312
23/64	0.359375	9.1281
3/8	0.375	9.5250
25/64	0.390625	9.9219
13/32	0.40625	10.3187
27/64	0.421875	10.7156
7/16	0.4375	11.1125
29/64	0.453125	11.5094
15/32	0.46875	11.9062
31/64	0.484375	12.3031
1/2	0.5	12.7000
33/64	0.515625	13.0969
17/32	0.53125	13.4937
35/64	0.546875	13.8906
9/16	0.5625	14.2875
37/64	0.578125	14.6844
19/32	0.59375	15.0812
39/64	0.609375	15.4781
5/8	0.625	15.8750
41/64	0.640625	16.2719
21/32	0.65625	16.6687
43/64	0.671875	17.0656
11/16	0.6875	17.4625
45/64	0.703125	17.8594
23/32	0.71875	18.2562
47/64	0.734375	18.6531
3/4	0.75	19.0500
49/64	0.765625	19.4469
25/32	0.78125	19.8437
51/64	0.796875	20.2406
13/16	0.8125	20.6375
53/64	0.828125	21.0344
27/32	0.84375	21.4312
55/64	0.859375	21.8281
7/8	0.875	22.2250
57/64	0.890625	22.6219
29/32	0.90625	23.0187
59/64	0.921875	23.4156
15/16	0.9375	23.8125
61/64	0.953125	24.2094
31/32	0.96875	24.6062
63/64	0.984375	25.0031

Millimetres to Inches

mm	Inches
0.01	0.00039
0.02	0.00079
0.03	0.00118
0.04	0.00157
0.05	0.00197
0.06	0.00236
0.07	0.00276
0.08	0.00315
0.09	0.00354
0.1	0.00394
0.2	0.00787
0.3	0.01181
0.4	0.01575
0.5	0.01969
0.6	0.02362
0.7	0.02756
0.8	0.03150
0.9	0.03543
1	0.03937
2	0.07874
3	0.11811
4	0.15748
5	0.19685
6	0.23622
7	0.27559
8	0.31496
9	0.35433
10	0.39370
11	0.43307
12	0.47244
13	0.51181
14	0.55118
15	0.59055
16	0.62992
17	0.66929
18	0.70866
19	0.74803
20	0.78740
21	0.82677
22	0.86614
23	0.09551
24	0.94488
25	0.98425
26	1.02362
27	1.06299
28	1.10236
29	1.14173
30	1.18110
31	1.22047
32	1.25984
33	1.29921
34	1.33858
35	1.37795
36	1.41732
37	1.4567
38	1.4961
39	1.5354
40	1.5748
41	1.6142
42	1.6535
43	1.6929
44	1.7323
45	1.7717

Inches to Millimetres

Inches	mm
0.001	0.0254
0.002	0.0508
0.003	0.0762
0.004	0.1016
0.005	0.1270
0.006	0.1524
0.007	0.1778
0.008	0.2032
0.009	0.2286
0.01	0.254
0.02	0.508
0.03	0.762
0.04	1.016
0.05	1.270
0.06	1.524
0.07	1.778
0.08	2.032
0.09	2.286
0.1	2.54
0.2	5.08
0.3	7.62
0.4	10.16
0.5	12.70
0.6	15.24
0.7	17.78
0.8	20.32
0.9	22.86
1	25.4
2	50.8
3	76.2
4	101.6
5	127.0
6	152.4
7	177.8
8	203.2
9	228.6
10	254.0
11	279.4
12	304.8
13	330.2
14	355.6
15	381.0
16	406.4
17	431.8
18	457.2
19	482.6
20	508.0
21	533.4
22	558.8
23	584.2
24	609.6
25	635.0
26	660.4
27	685.8
28	711.2
29	736.6
30	762.0
31	787.4
32	812.8
33	838.2
34	863.6
35	889.0
36	914.4

1   Imperial gallon = 8 Imp pints = 1.20 US gallons = 277.42 cu in = 4.54 litres

1   US gallon = 4 US quarts = 0.83 Imp gallon = 231 cu in = 3.78 litres

1   Litre = 0.21 Imp gallon = 0.26 US gallon = 61.02 cu in = 1000 cc

Miles to Kilometres		Kilometres to Miles	
1	1.61	1	0.62
2	3.22	2	1.24
3	4.83	3	1.86
4	6.44	4	2.49
5	8.05	5	3.11
6	9.66	6	3.73
7	11.27	7	4.35
8	12.88	8	4.97
9	14.48	9	5.59
10	16.09	10	6.21
20	32.19	20	12.43
30	48.28	30	18.64
40	64.37	40	24.85
50	80.47	50	31.07
60	96.56	60	37.28
70	112.65	70	43.50
80	128.75	80	49.71
90	144.84	90	55.92
100	160.93	100	62.14

lbf ft to kgf m		kgf m to lbf ft		lbf/in^2 to kgf/cm^2		kgf/cm^2 to lbf/in^2	
1	0.138	1	7.233	1	0.07	1	14.22
2	0.276	2	14.466	2	0.14	2	28.50
3	0.414	3	21.699	3	0.21	3	42.67
4	0.553	4	28.932	4	0.28	4	56.89
5	0.691	5	36.165	5	0.35	5	71.12
6	0.829	6	43.398	6	0.42	6	85.34
7	0.967	7	50.631	7	0.49	7	99.56
8	1.106	8	57.864	8	0.56	8	113.79
9	1.244	9	65.097	9	0.63	9	128.00
10	1.382	10	72.330	10	0.70	10	142.23
20	2.765	20	144.660	20	1.41	20	284.47
30	4.147	30	216.990	30	2.11	30	426.70

Index

Printed by
Haynes Publishing Group
Sparkford Yeovil Somerset
England